CO1

GW01393223

Managing Marketing:
Concepts and Irish Cases

John A. Murray and Aidan O'Driscoll

Gill & Macmillan

Published in Ireland by
Gill & Macmillan Ltd
Goldenbridge
Dublin 8
with associated companies throughout the world
© John A. Murray and Aidan O'Driscoll 1993
0 7171 1952 1
Index compiled by Helen Litton
Print origination by
Seton Music Graphics Ltd, Bantry, Co. Cork
Printed by ColourBooks Ltd, Dublin

All rights reserved. No part of this publication may
be copied, reproduced or transmitted in any form or by
any means, without permission of the publishers.

A catalogue record for this book is available from the British Library.

3 5 4 2

To the patient ones: Jane, Niall, Niamh, Rita and Sinead

Contents

Preface

Managing Marketing: Concepts and Irish Cases is a new book which derives from *Marketing Management: An Introduction*, a book written and published in 1984. The reasons for writing this new book are several. While the fundamentals of marketing have not changed in the intervening years, the discipline and its professional practice has evolved and developed. Research on marketing and the extension of its theoretical base has continued unabated and it is hoped that the more significant lines of development are reflected here. In Ireland, this process has been stimulated by the publication of the *Irish Marketing Review*, which has encouraged the publication of research and informed debate on important aspects of marketing in the Irish context.

The environment of marketing has also changed in many critical ways since 1984. A radical renewal of European and Irish business has taken place, accompanied and at times precipitated by the failure of long-established companies that could not meet the competitive challenges of the late eighties and by many spectacular but short-lived new ventures that could not sustain growth and viability. The process of 'creative destruction', to borrow Schumpeter's phrase, has been visible on all sides. The need for global standards of competitiveness and managerial competence in markets that are becoming truly international in character is now a requirement for survival. The emergence of the Single European Market emphasises and dramatises what has become an underlying structural shift in patterns of trade and competition. Irish business finds itself faced with the challenge of outperforming the best of international competition in its markets through the nineties. There are no protected regional or national niches. There is no camouflage available to disguise and protect the second-rate or the unprofessional in management and in marketing. For practitioners and for the students who will be the marketing managers towards the year 2000 and beyond, there is only one route to success: attainment of the highest standards in the management and practice of marketing based on a well-grounded ability to conceptualise markets and marketing phenomena; to make insightful decisions based on such understanding and to take action in a disciplined and creative manner.

For the future, the Irish market has to be seen as a regional market within the structure of a European market which is in turn one of the major blocks within what Ohmae labelled the Triad marketplace of Europe, North America and the Pacific Rim. Students and managers in Ireland have to attune their thinking to this global perspective. The alternative is a sad retreat into parochial decay. The early nineties demonstrated that Irish enterprise is capable of rising to the challenge. For example, the Jefferson Smurfit Group featured consistently in the *Fortune International* '500'—a listing of the largest industrial corporations outside the United States—and in *Business Week*'s 'Global 1,000'. Other companies such as Cement Roadstone Holdings (CRH), Glen Dimplex, Clondalkin Group, Guinness Peat Aviation (GPA) and the Kerry Group, to name just a few, have built international businesses from local head offices that show how Irish enterprise, and through it Ireland, can compete.

Added to these forces which demanded a rethink and a rewrite of the 1984 publication was the learning involved in using and hearing comment on the earlier book. It was written to appeal to both student and practitioner and in its own way it achieved this dual objective. However, many beginning students and many practitioners whose careers were based on excellence in professional experience rather than formal education in marketing clearly found the book and its style too condensed. It assumed a prior knowledge of marketing concepts beyond what was reasonable for these readers. We have addressed this deficiency in Part I by taking more time to introduce the newcomer to the basic ideas and 'technical' language of marketing.

Among the managerial readers of the book over the past years it was found that many were not only marketing managers but general managers, division managers, chief executives, promoters of smaller businesses and managers of other functions. For them the value of the book was in its coverage of what the marketing function was supposed to contribute to the whole business and to business development and planning. Given this and the reality that so much of Irish industry is small and medium-sized and therefore without specialised marketing departments, we have stressed in the title the notion of *managing marketing*. We hope that this signals an interest in and intention to speak to the non-marketer who must manage marketing to the company's overall benefit as well as to the manager of marketing who must be not only a marketing specialist but also a manager in a more general sense—managing people, money and other resources in the most productive manner possible. We also hope that it will emphasise a vital aspect of management effectiveness for the nineties: an integrated view of organisations and their relationships with their markets and competitors. This reflects a growing concern to view organisations in terms of their basic *processes*—one of the most basic of which is the series of activities that connects the start of a sale to the final delivery of a product or service into the hands of a customer.

This perspective is an important counterbalance to the traditional view of organisations as a series of departments or functions which so often leads to fragmented thinking and action in a company. Such fragmentation is particularly damaging to the true nature and role of marketing, which necessarily involves integrating activities throughout the firm as well as with customers and suppliers. A narrow, technical, disciplinary specialism alone is likely to debilitate the manager in a competitive and organisational environment that demands excellence in managing across company boundaries and above all in managing in the broadest and most complete sense.

We also felt that one of the glaring deficiencies in third-level courses and management development programmes on marketing was the absence of any specially researched and written set of case studies documenting the managerial challenges of marketing in Irish firms. Those studying marketing and struggling with the application of its theory to managerial problems are all too often left with little but American and some European cases to use as testing grounds for their new conceptual technology. We have therefore incorporated a series of cases researched and written in recent years and in many instances adapted specifically for this book. The cases have been carefully chosen for their tested effectiveness as learning materials and for their relevance to the different sections of the text. They therefore provide a bridge from the world of ideas, abstraction, generalisation and theory to the world of managerial decision-making and action. We hope that they will also add a little of the excitement of 'real life' to understanding marketing. Cases are one of the most effective mechanisms for learning about the application of concept and theory as well as acting as the raw material from which the learner can be encouraged to induce generalisations and struggle with the challenge of constructing theory. We hope that learners and those helping them to learn will share in the pleasure to be derived from success in pursuing this approach.

Both authors have spent many years working with students and with managers in the area of marketing. We would like to pass on some of what we have learned from them as well as what we can bring to your attention from our work with marketing concept and theory. Our hope is that in some modest way the book will help individuals to experience the excitement of intellectual discovery and aid them in their career progress. Through them we hope that Irish enterprise will be assisted in grasping the opportunities that lie ahead and thus contribute appropriately to the building of a strong wealth-creating economy which can provide a rising standard of living for its citizens.

Acknowledgments

We would like to thank a number of individuals and organisations who assisted in the development of the book. *Irish Marketing Review* provided a continuing and valuable source for much material, and without it the Irish 'context', which we have striven for, would have been less effective than we hope it is. Jim Quinn, a chief executive with an uncommon understanding of the workings of pedagogy, wrote one of the cases and co-authored two others. Gerry Mortimer wrote the case on Braycot Foods, which raises many challenging issues in marketing mix decision-making. Catherine KilBride read an early draft of the book and offered much helpful comment. Joan Keegan provided useful editorial support on some aspects of the text. However, any flaws remain very much our own.

J.A.M. & A.O'D.

Introduction

The book is written primarily for those who wish to participate in the management of internationally competitive, growth-oriented Irish companies. It is written for students of marketing and of management who wish to pursue careers in marketing or in other aspects of management that require an appreciation of the role and tasks of marketing. In general, it is assumed that such students will use it to underpin a general course in marketing and the management of the marketing function.

The book also addresses practising managers who wish to formalise what they have learned about marketing through professional experience and who wish to stay abreast of developments in the discipline. Managers who will find this productive are those with direct responsibility in marketing as well as those responsible for marketing as general managers and chief executives, and those managers of other functions in the firm who must interface effectively with their marketing colleagues. We hope that it will prove helpful to operations and manufacturing managers, human resource managers, finance managers and R & D and technology managers, and to planners and strategists.

The perspective of the book is resolutely managerial. The development of marketing as a field of inquiry has opened up many perspectives, such as those of the macro marketing, consumerist, systems, buyer behaviour, behavioural organisations or strategic planning schools (Sheth and Gardner, 1982). In this book the focus is a managerial one embedded in the perspective of the individual firm and the role of the individual manager as decision-maker. It is therefore written in the tradition started in the sixties by McCarthy (1960) and Kotler (1967). The structure of the book seeks to replicate the managerial process of planning the marketing activity of an organisation, developing a comprehensive new service or product plan for it, or auditing and reformulating its marketing plans and operations. While the sequential nature of the chapters is necessarily artificial we believe that it represents a productive approach to systematic marketing decision-making. In following the structure it is hoped that the learner will acquire knowledge relevant to the decision-making involved and to the management of the marketing function.

The structure of the book is such that it may be read from start to finish or may be used for reference purposes by selecting only specific chapters. The newcomer to marketing is especially encouraged to read Part I before covering material in any subsequent sections. Part I sets out to introduce the underlying concepts and language of the managerial school of marketing and therefore provides the basic orientation and frameworks on which the remaining sections are built. Figure 0.1 gives a graphic illustration of the contents and the inter-relationship of the various chapters and sections. It may be used as a 'road map' by readers and will help them to understand how much progress they have made and to appreciate the interdependence of the topics covered.

Figure 0.1

Managing Marketing

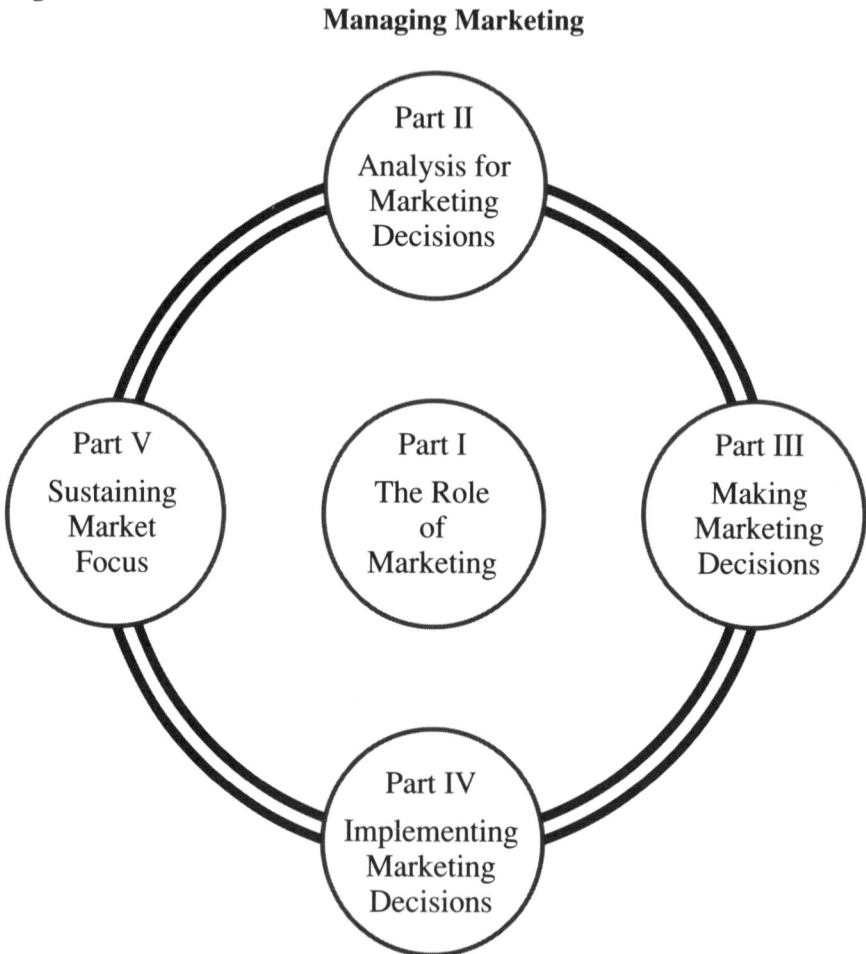

Figure 0.1 is intended to suggest a systematic framework derived from agreed concepts about the nature and role of marketing, around which thorough market and marketing analysis is built, followed by the essential decision areas in marketing the challenges of implementing these decisions effectively, and the necessity to sustain their intent over the longer term. With this approach in place the overall task of managing marketing may be viewed in an integrated manner. For the experienced student or practitioner it will also help to identify sections of special interest for reference when dealing with a particular problem.

Managing marketing as visualised in Figure 0.1—with its cyclical rather than linear form—emphasises the integrative, systemic and flexible qualities needed to manage the less hierarchical and more learning-oriented organisation of the future (Ostroff and Smith, 1992). Setting and sustaining direction in today's markets increasingly demands that people in companies learn and adapt rather than act under instruction. It requires them to take charge and ownership of their areas of responsibility. Organisations which nurture this managerial approach will be the ones which prove themselves competitively superior and capable of self-renewal.

Part I describes **The Role of Marketing** in the firm, the work of the marketing manager and marketing's interaction with other functions in the firm. Basic concepts of marketing are defined and its societal and international contexts addressed. The evolving nature of marketing since the industrial revolution is depicted and the authors introduce the key concept of *market focus*—put simply, the continuing and persistent alignment of a firm's resources and unique competences to changing needs and opportunities in the marketplace.

Understanding the value-added chain—the authors offer the terms macro business system and micro business system—is seen as crucial to developing the best marketing practice and to sustaining competitive advantage. The nature of services, business-to-business and not-for-profit marketing is also outlined.

Part II deals with **Analysis for Marketing Decisions** and explores the analytical groundwork which must take place before a marketing strategy or programme can be formulated. The nature of customers and markets, consumer behaviour, market measurement and forecasting is examined. The importance of incisive marketing research and information is highlighted. How to analyse different industry structures, competitors' strengths and weaknesses and a company's competences and capability is set out.

Part III then progresses to **Making Marketing Decisions**. The structure of decision-making in terms of market choice and competitive positioning is elaborated upon. Marketing mix decisions about products, new product development, pricing, communication and selling, and distribution are treated in depth. This part draws to a close with a substantial and state-of-the-art chapter on strategic marketing, enabling the formulation of the various components into an integrated marketing strategy.

Part IV moves to consider **Implementing Marketing Decisions** and explores the problems of making a strategy or plan work successfully in practice. What form of organisation structure is most effective? How does the structure of the internationalising firm evolve? The methods of developing action-plans, programmes, budgets, performance criteria and overall control systems are described. The role of internal marketing in creating a supportive company culture and a dedicated management and staff team is discussed.

Part V, **Sustaining Market Focus**, reminds us that markets are not only complex but ever changing and the winning firm must correspondingly adapt. The nature of organisational renewal is considered. The Icarus paradox—why so-called excellent companies so often go into decline—is described. The need on occasion to reinvent or re-engineer a business—change the game-rules—is observed. New modes of marketing activity, relationship-based marketing, cooperative networks, long-term buyer–supplier partnerships can also contribute to continuing profitability. The 'green revolution' also has important implications for the cycle of marketing.

The *market-focused* company must view the marketing activity implicit in Parts II through to V as an ongoing process. It must continually focus on and understand its customers, suppliers, markets, competitors, and the dynamics of the macro business system, so as to configure in turn its own micro business system, align its resources and focus itself on the ensuing opportunity. It should be able to match creatively arenas of market need with unique company competences through durable and profitable relationships.

Reading

Kotler, P. (1967), *Marketing Management: Analysis, Planning and Control*, 1st ed., Prentice-Hall, Englewood Cliffs, NJ.

McCarthy, E.J. (1960), *Basic Marketing: A Managerial Approach*, 1st ed., Irwin, Homewood, Ill.

Ostroff, F. and Smith, D. (1992), 'The horizontal organisation', *McKinsey Quarterly*, vol. 1.

Sheth, J.N. and Gardner, D.M. (1982), 'History of marketing thought: an update', in Bush, R.F. and Hunt, S.D. (eds), *Marketing Theory: Philosophy of Science Perspectives*, AMA Proceedings, Chicago, pp. 52–58.

Part I

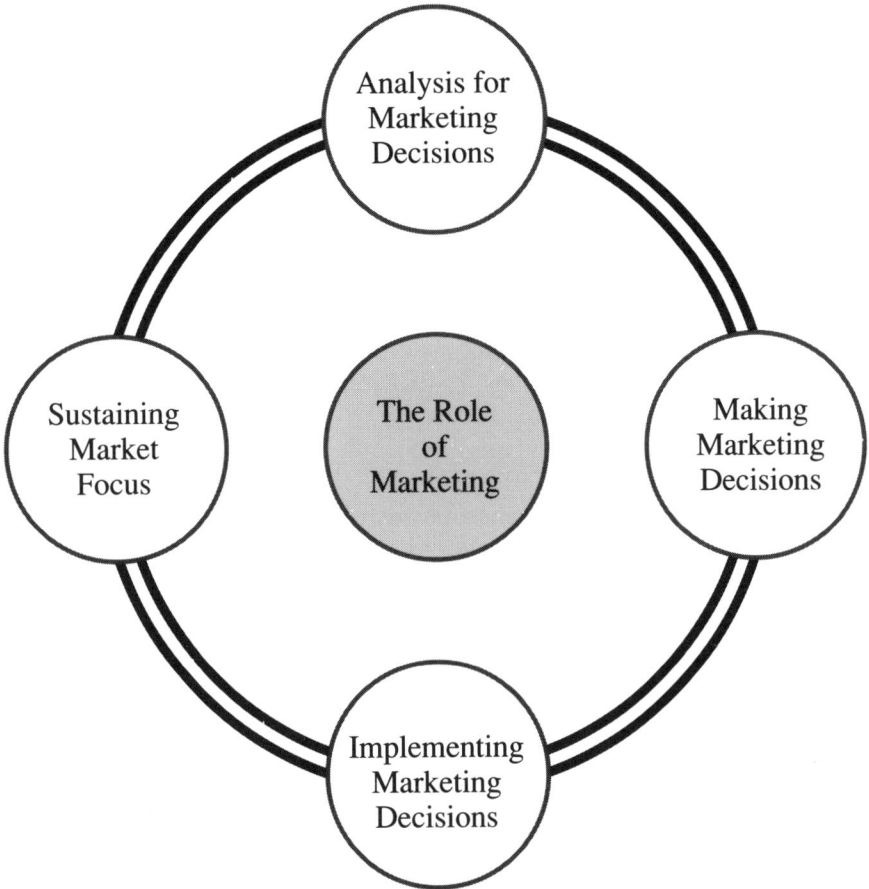

Analysis for Marketing Decisions

Making Marketing Decisions

Implementing Marketing Decisions

Sustaining Market Focus

The Role of Marketing

Chapter 1

Marketing and the
Marketing Perspective

INTRODUCTION

This book focuses on the processes and techniques of analysis and decision-making that lead to good management of the marketing function. These processes, while forming the basis for marketing practice, are in many ways secondary in their influence on a business to the impact of a marketing orientation in organising and conducting its affairs. In this chapter the nature of marketing is explored and the impact of a market orientation on business is discussed.

Marketing's domain

Marketing affects our lives in a most pervasive manner. The clothes we wear, the food we eat, the entertainment we enjoy, the cars, buses, bicycles or trains that bring us to and from work, the houses we inhabit, the financial services we depend on, the media through which we stay in touch with our world are all the products of a marketing process fundamental to modern societies. Firms as well as public and non-profit bodies are the active elements of the process and managers are the people who organise the process. The readers of this book will find it difficult to envisage their daily lives without marketing activity. Despite this pervasiveness of organised market activity the *discipline* of marketing is still far from well elaborated as science. In common with many disciplines based in professional practice (engineering, medicine, architecture, for example), marketing developed for many years on the basis of the codification of best professional practice. The essence of marketing knowledge lay in description of marketing activities.

This has changed enormously and, especially in the seventies and eighties, the discipline moved beyond description to a general focus on analysis and theory-building. This is not a matter to be dismissed as relevant only for the academician and researcher. Apart from being fuelled by the researcher's curiosity and search for appropriate theory, the development of marketing has been above all driven by the demand from business for analytical, well-grounded and robust theory to help guide decision-making. The complexity of markets and market transactions has grown rapidly. In parallel, the stakes involved in marketing decision-making have also grown. As a result, traditional 'best practice' is seldom enough to guarantee competitive success. The best companies reach beyond conventional approaches in making decisions. Only a theoretically well-grounded approach to marketing will respond adequately to these managerial imperatives. Good analytical technology and robust theory are pressing professional needs. For the marketing manager of the nineties there can be nothing more practical than a good theory!

DEFINING MARKETING

Definitions of marketing abound but a quick review will reveal that the many variations share some common themes. McCarthy simply notes that marketing is a process 'that provides needed direction for production and helps make sure that the right products are produced and find their way to consumers' (McCarthy and Perreault, 1990, p. 5). He claims that, together with the production or operations function in business, marketing provides the four basic economic utilities:

> *Form utility:* the tangible embodiment of the product or service that people actually want, remembering that there can be no utility if no need is satisfied.
> *Time utility*: having the product or service available when it is needed.
> *Place utility:* having the product or service available where it is needed.
> *Possession utility:* obtaining the product or service and having the right to use or consume it, usually in return for money or something else of value as in barter.

This rather formal statement of the utility created by marketing reflects the familiar cliché that marketing is all about ensuring that consumers get the right product at the right time in the right place and at the right price.

Drucker's often-quoted definition places special emphasis on customer understanding: 'The aim of marketing is to make selling superfluous. The aim is to know and understand the customer so well that the product or service fits him and sells itself' (Drucker, 1983, pp. 64–65). This definition was well in tune with the seventies emphasis on 'customer-as-king' and the popularisation of what we now refer to as the 'marketing concept'. The marketing concept stresses customer orientation as a fundamental business philosophy. It emphasises that customer-oriented firms are more likely to integrate successfully the various activities of production, selling, financing, and human resource management in a profitable manner in the service of chosen customers.

Kotler, whose work remains seminal to the managerial school of marketing theory, has evolved a tight but quite complex definition: 'Marketing is human activity directed at satisfying needs and wants through exchange processes' (Kotler and Armstrong, 1991, p. 20). These authors explain each of their carefully chosen terms as follows:

Needs: A human need is a state of felt deprivation in a person ranging from the physical to the psychological and is intrinsic to the human state rather than created by the world of advertising or social comparison.

Wants: Wants are the forms that human needs take when shaped by culture and individual personality and result in the expression of needs in many and varied ways around the world and between individuals. As economies develop so too does the range of wants of citizens. However, Kotler and Armstrong point out that marketers are well advised to remember the distinction between needs and wants. Needs are basic and unchanging. Wants are changing and often ephemeral. The company that focuses on wants and forgets underlying needs is on the road to failure, leading to that famous comment that 'a manufacturer of drill bits may think that the customer needs a drill bit but what the customer really needs is a hole' (Kotler and Armstrong, 1991, p. 6). The need for the hole in the domestic consumer market is of course driven by the rather basic need for shelter and home-making, which is then expressed in all the many aspects of demand for construction and home improvement products and services.

Demands: Wants become demands when realised through the allocation of limited buying power to the products that customers judge will provide most satisfaction for their money.

Products: A product is anything that can be offered to a market for attention, acquisition, use or consumption in the satisfaction of a want or need, including not just those things we traditionally view as products or services but also people (for example, politicians), places (for example, tourist destinations), organisations (for example, Amnesty International or the Red Cross), activities (for example, meals-on-wheels) and ideas (for example, equal opportunity employment). Essentially we are concerned with things which have some value in the sense that they may become the subject of exchange. What is exchanged for them most typically is money but may also be political support in an election for a candidate's ideas, or time to visit an art gallery to gain some aesthetic pleasure.

Exchange: Exchange is central to any concept of marketing and is embodied in the act of obtaining a desired product by offering something of value in return.

Transactions: A transaction involves a trade of values between two parties and becomes marketing's unit of measurement. The transaction may be money based, may be arranged as a barter or may involve the exchange of psychological commitment.

Markets: A market in the Kotler and Armstrong (1991) framework is the set of actual and potential buyers of a product who may deal directly with suppliers or may acquire the products they need through various intermediaries and market mechanisms as markets grow and develop.

Marketing and society

It is productive at this introductory stage to note that the various definitions of marketing reviewed so far raise issues that go well beyond the normal ambit of the individual firm or marketing manager. This is because the process of marketing is essentially societal in scope, although many of the activities involved are performed by individuals and individual organisations. The term macro marketing is used to describe this larger social process 'that directs an economy's flow of goods and services from producers to consumers in a way that effectively matches supply and demand and accomplishes the objectives of society' (McCarthy and Perreault, 1990, p. 10). The concern is with the whole marketing system at national or regional level. Thus we are concerned as citizens and consumers with the effectiveness of the marketing system in Ireland. Through the nineties we are all participants in an historic experiment to create a new European marketing system based on a single unified market spanning the nations of the European Community.

All economies need marketing systems but vary in the social and political choices they make about the form of these systems. Command economies typical of Eastern Europe in the post-war years until 1990 were built on centralised decision-making with regard to what and how much should be produced and distributed to whom, by whom, how and at what price. Market-based economies are founded on the philosophy that the system optimises its performance if all the many producers and consumers make their independent decisions in an open market. However, even those marketing systems based in strong adherence to free market principles require some intervention by government and regulatory agencies and the law to mediate the conflicts that can result and to express the social and political preferences of the citizen. Hence regulation is always part and parcel of free market structures, if only to preserve freedom of competition and to avoid the abuse of market and economic power. Thus most free market systems will, for example, also have monopolies commissions or anti-trust agencies and laws to regulate the workings of the market so as to protect the citizen's rights and interests.

International marketing

The societal aspect of marketing is not the focus of this book. Our concern is with marketing at the firm level, but it is important to remember that this is significantly influenced by the social context in which it operates. This becomes especially visible when issues in international marketing are considered. Many of the challenges faced by marketers as they move services and products internationally derive from inherently different social, cultural and institutional circumstances. The degree of regulation in financial services markets varies considerably across the world as a reflection of differences in legal structures and the power and role of central banks or their equivalents. Those competing in financial services markets must understand and cope with this reality if they are to succeed on an international scale. Distribution systems still vary greatly from one country to another and lead to major differences in how companies can bring products and services to market. In Europe, for example, there has been a long-term trend towards concentration in most forms of retailing—that is, fewer and fewer multiple retailers selling more and more of what is purchased by consumers. This results in a significant shift in market power away from producers and towards the retailers, bringing with it the growth in retailer brands and a major redistribution of profits in the affected industries. This process is supported by consumers who associate lower prices and high service levels with the move to retail concentration.

In Japan, by contrast, retailing has remained very fragmented and small in scale with a high proportion of family-run businesses. This different structure has been supported by legal constraints on the floor space of retail foodstores and by a general adherence to retail price maintenance. It is difficult to buy deeply discounted products anywhere in Japan. This pattern of retailing has an important social consequence since its fragmented structure employs many people and can act as a buffer zone for variations in employment in the manufacturing sector of the economy. What would be seen as economically inefficient in Europe, leading to higher than necessary consumer prices, is partly institutionalised in Japan and leads to significant local employment creation. In one system the consumer buys products relatively cheaply and pays taxes to deal with problems of unemployment. In the other the consumer pays relatively high consumer prices but pays little to support social policies to deal with unemployment. The international marketer soon realises that there are few 'right' answers for such issues and that different societies create and evolve macro marketing systems to reflect their traditional and emerging social and political choices. Understanding this reality is sometimes central to effective marketing strategy.

MARKETING'S EVOLVING ROLE IN THE FIRM

The nature and role of marketing has evolved considerably and will continue to change. The fact that it is only during the last fifty years that marketing as a word or description has enjoyed an everyday currency does not mean that marketing activity as such has not been taking place since the start of commercial exchange by mankind (see Exhibit 1.1). The period from the industrial revolution to the twenties has often been characterised as a *production-oriented* era. The opportunity was to produce goods in large standardised quantities and get them to large waiting markets for the first time. If it could be made it could be sold was often a guiding principle. In Ireland, as in any economy, organisations can still be found that claim to produce a good product and that assume the world will somehow turn up to purchase it. This viewpoint often characterises companies built on a strong but narrow technical or craft tradition. Working to an order backlog and having customers approach the company for its products can reinforce the attitude. In the short term such organisations will often survive and even prosper. In the long run their viability is not sustainable, as they have no means to track market changes, new opportunities and competitive threats. By failing to stay in touch with customers the company may also fail to produce the standards of quality demanded by the market. Shoddy products or services reflecting a very parochial concept of quality often lie at the heart of failure—especially in international markets. The central problem with this 'production orientation', however, is the fact that the product or service is defined in the producer's terms. The result is usually one or a number of the following:

* shoddy products or services, where the producer's standards are below those of the market;
* over-designed, over-engineered and over-priced products, where the producer uses some technically defined standard of excellence rather than the customer's standard of usefulness in application;
* technically well-designed, well-produced and reasonably priced products that just do not fit the customer's requirements as readily as competitors' offerings which have been based on a clearly researched approach to serving the user's needs.

It is often suggested that during the thirties and post-war years the developed economies of Europe and North America were characterised by a *sales-oriented* philosophy. This arose from the emergence of an abundance of productive capability and a shift towards a buyer's market which placed emphasis on competitive rivalry between suppliers. A guiding principle of the sales and marketing functions in companies was often characterised by a commitment to 'moving the product'—the factory made it, the task was for someone else to sell it. Many companies can still be found where sales maximisation is considered the role of marketing and the measure of its success. Quite apart from the threat to business viability which this approach ultimately represents, it also represents the greatest danger of unethical behaviour in marketing. It is characteristic of some ventures created solely to take advantage of customers who are poorly informed and open to the influence of high-pressure sales and promotional techniques.

Exhibit 1.1

IRELAND'S CONTRIBUTION TO NINETEENTH-CENTURY MARKETING THOUGHT

Marketing before the Late Late Show

The myth that marketing concepts were first developed in the United States early in the twentieth century continues to endure. The argument supporting this myth is that in the US environmental conditions, such as expanding production, new products and markets, and changing social values, focused attention on market practices. In response American writers are said to have developed new ideas about demand and desire, market adjustment processes, the value-adding activity of marketing, and so on.

However, these arguments pertain to an earlier time and different place. Marketing concepts were developed in response to environmental change, but here the change agent was the European industrial revolution. Nineteenth-century economists understood the role of preferences in forming demand, that the market does not adjust automatically to a harmonious balance, and the value added by marketing activity. Irish writers, whether Irish born or holding a chair at an Irish university, contributed prominently to this understanding.

In modern terms, the areas of marketing thought discussed by nineteenth-century Irish economists include the work done by the marketing system, the contribution of marketing to a market economy, competitive processes in marketing, the self-regulating marketing system, the nature of the individual, and global marketing. Indeed some of their concepts seem surprisingly modern.

Cliffe Leslie, a professor at Dublin University from 1853 to 1881, presaged in his *Essays in Political Economy*, published in 1888, the 'globalisation' or standardisation of markets and marketing activity. Leslie observes that 'improvements in communications' bring vast changes in marketing around the world. Part of this change results from converging preferences: 'In customs and fashions civilised society is likewise advancing towards uniformity' (p. 216). He also argues that language, particularly English, along with converging systems of government and civil law tends to unify markets. Some change is the result of scale economies. Not only are marketing channels becoming shorter, but goods that 'scores of different retailers' formerly sold 'are now to be had in great establishments in New York, Paris and London' (p. 217).

Source: abstracted from Dixon, Donald F. (1991), 'Nineteenth-century Irish contributions to marketing thought', *Proceedings of European Academy of Marketing (EMAC) Annual Conference*, Dublin, May.

Many companies exhibit a sales orientation temporarily when sales are falling short of budgeted targets. A company not meeting year-end targets will often react by discounting prices, selling and promoting its offering in a particularly aggressive manner to bring actual sales back in line with budget. While such a strategy may pay off in the short run, and give the appearance of success, it often represents no more than a transfer of demand from a later period to an earlier one. Stock is often transferred under such circumstances from producers to the distribution or retail trade or indeed to final customers whose future purchases then decline sharply as they gradually run down their heavy stock position. Sales become very difficult to achieve in the new budget period and relationships with trade members and final customers may be damaged by the perception of the supplier as unstable or as a ready target for pressure to reduce prices in any future period.

The emergence of a *marketing orientation* is often dated to sometime in the fifties in more developed economies and more sophisticated companies. This marked the realisation that the core market-related task was not to make products, or to sell what factories could produce, but rather to understand market demand well enough to specify what should be produced and to see that this 'right' product could be brought to the 'right customer' at the 'right price' and at the 'right' time and place. It was from this perspective that the 'marketing concept' emerged as a guiding company-wide philosophy: profits and competitive success derive from seeing customer needs as the guiding principle in strategy and coordinating company activities to serve them profitably. Out of this phase of evolution emerged the marketing department as a commonplace element of any organisation, headed up by a marketing manager. The marketing concept emphasised that a customer orientation led to long-term profitability. Profit, not sales maximisation, was stressed as the objective of marketing activity, but profitability was seen as the outcome of dedication to serving market needs.

The marketing concept also saw as essential that all the activities of the business should be coordinated, with profit through customer satisfaction as the common unifying objective. This implied that not only should marketing and sales activities be dedicated to the objective of satisfying customer needs, but all activities, including manufacturing, R & D, finance, and human resource management should be imbued with the same commitment to customer service. Such integration should ensure a common, clear and market-directed orientation in the entire company. This emphasis on integration is of considerable organisational importance and marked a transition in the development of thinking about marketing, from viewing it as a relatively independent business function to seeing it as an integrative force which should therefore have effective interfaces with all other business functions. This development laid the groundwork for the growth of a sub-field within marketing that came to be called strategic marketing and strategic market planning (Abell, 1980; Day, 1984, 1986; Aaker, 1992). The more strategic aspects of marketing could now be seen as an essential part of the work of general management—coordinating all the company's activities to focus on delivering customer satisfaction at a profit. It could now be claimed with considerable weight that no general manager could perform effectively without applying a marketing approach to the management of the business, and no business strategy could be complete without a foundation in identified customer needs and a commitment to mobilising the company's resources to serve these needs. Of the business functions, marketing remains unique in its outward-looking nature. Because it is dedicated to the market and the customer it is fundamentally concerned with the external environment of the firm. This feature also gives it a vital role in the formulation of business strategy since its role is so central to the identification and choice of the markets the company will serve and therefore of the competitive arenas in which it must prove superior. This is the very essence of the basic business decision concerning the answer to the perennial question, 'What business are we in?'

THE MARKET-FOCUSED COMPANY

A more recent phase has seen the development of the market-focused company. The idea of market focus and the importance of core competences (Hamel and Prahalad, 1990, 1991) have recently been expanding our earlier notion of the marketing concept. These additions to our perspective on marketing are strategic in nature and are based on assumptions about the vital interdependence of business strategy, organisational capability, company performance, market and competitive realities, and marketing action. The importance of the core competences or capabilities of any company to its ability to survive and prosper has always been acknowledged, but the aggressive market and competitive orientation of management in Western companies sometimes caused them to pay too little attention to the fundamental resource base of the organisation. The resurgence of attention to identifying, nurturing and managing core competences has been driven by a world market in which product life cycles have become much shorter than the life of the key competences that produce those products. Thus the relationship between organisations and their markets must be guided not only by looking out creatively and analytically into those markets, but also by looking deeply inward to the company's competences in order to understand what it is truly superior to competition in doing.

This new emphasis might be captured by the image of marketing as scissors-like: one blade representing real market understanding and market orientation and the other representing the organisation's competence to do certain things very well. When the two blades are present and coordinated, one has an effective scissors. With only one blade, however, little is likely to happen. The emphasis is therefore on an effective marriage of market need and company competence. This differs significantly from the marketing orientation of the seventies, which was often interpreted, especially by marketing professionals, to mean that marketing should lead and coordinate the other aspects of a business. The emphasis of the nineties is on interdependence and a more integrated approach to management, represented in marketing by the notion of *market focus*—aligning in a very focused manner the unique competences of any one organisation with the needs and opportunities of the marketplace. The challenge is therefore to develop ways of analysing and designing company processes that couple precisely with distribution and consumption processes. As we will see in the next chapter, these company processes may be thought of as carefully constructed and integrated value-adding activities that underpin profitable exchange for both the customer and the company.

Along with this development of market focus has come a need to reappraise the past concentration of marketing on short-term market transactions and to deal with the nature of the *relationship-based* markets that evolved in the eighties. Kotler suggests that marketing is characterised by 'a movement away from a focus on exchange—in the narrow sense of transaction—and toward a focus on building value-laden relationships and marketing networks' (Kotler, 1991a). Marketing is increasingly a matter of managing networks and relationships within which transactions take place. The interest in relationship-based markets reflects the major shift in many business-to-business as well as consumer markets towards buyer–supplier partnerships, especially as pioneered by Japanese manufacturing industry. There are good economic reasons for the concern. It has been noted that in mature markets it may cost five times as much to attract a new customer as to maintain the goodwill of an existing customer (Peters, 1987, p. 91). Under such circumstances, sound established relationships are of great value. It can be said that we are moving towards a definition of marketing which emphasises mutual profitability for the two parties involved in a market relationship.

It is interesting to note that one may still find individual companies and even economies at various stages of development along the continuum we have been suggesting. There are many firms still rooted in a production orientation just as there are managerial pioneers working on the integration of market focus with corporate competence through the process of business strategy formulation. Equally many firms have evolved along this continuum (see Exhibit 1.2). Being 'stuck' at either a production- or sales-oriented phase of development will in general have unpleasant consequences in the competitive markets of today, while an acceptance of the marketing orientation of the seventies and eighties will prove insufficient to meet the challenge of world-class competition in the nineties.

Exhibit 1.2

MAGUIRE AND PATERSON

From production orientation to market focus

Maguire and Paterson was founded in 1882 to manufacture matches at Hammond Lane in the historic Smithfield area of Dublin city. The company flourished to become the sole manufacturer of matches in Ireland and the dominant supplier to the market with its Friendly and Cara brands. The hallmark of Maguire and Paterson was efficiency in the manufacture of a high-quality match, comparable to any produced in the world. The company laid great emphasis on continuity and enjoyed excellent industrial relations among its 160 employees.

From its Dublin headquarters a transport fleet distributed its products nationally to large retailers, multiple stores and wholesalers. The smaller retailer bought from the wholesaler or the cash-and-carry outlet. This distribution was backed up by a small salesforce which helped to develop sales by fostering new outlets and by liaison with multiples and wholesalers on problems of discount, service and quality. Decision-making and policy formation in the company were concentrated in a small group of four senior managers, the chief executive, the production manager, the financial controller and the sales manager. The style of management was conservative and production oriented and, like the company's advertising of the period, somewhat unimaginative.

However, by the mid-seventies it was becoming clear that a storm-cloud, in the form of a change in consumer behaviour, was threatening Maguire and Paterson's profitability. Put simply, people were beginning to smoke less—and some 70 per cent of matches were used to light cigarettes, the rest for domestic purposes. To aggravate matters further, the growing sales of imported disposable lighters in Ireland were beginning to make noticeable inroads into the demand for matches.

Management at Maguire and Paterson had to, in the words of the cliché, adapt or die. Yet what were the options? Market penetration was hardly one—indeed it would have great difficulty holding current market share. Market development, perhaps to export its matches or technological expertise, was somewhat unrealistic given its relatively small scale of operations. Product development offered possibilities but given the quasi-commodity nature of the humble match it would hardly redeem the company's fortunes in the long term. Maguire and Paterson had, like many companies in such a position, diversification thrust upon it; it would have to find new products and new markets if it were to survive profitably.

Yet its skill in match-making represented very little synergistic possibility to manufacture any other type of product. The answer lay in the company's distribution network. Here Maguire and Paterson had an expertise and experience built literally over generations. Could it identify products which had similar consumer characteristics to matches, i.e. intensive/wide distribution, small purchase decision, national brand advertising supported by point-of-sale merchandising, and so on, and push them through this network? It would not have to manufacture such products but market them on an agency basis.

In 1977 Maguire and Paterson acquired the agency for Wilkinson Sword shaving products and Foster Grant sunglasses in Ireland. In 1978 Dart disposable lighters and Marigold rubber housegloves were added to the list. In that year it also acquired NBC Limited for £.6m, a manufacturer of plastic kitchenware under the brand name Golden Butterfly. In 1980 Maguire and Paterson got the agency for Newey hair care products and Revlon shampoo products. By the end of 1980 annual turnover at Maguire and Paterson stood at £5.1m with £2.1m coming from its personal care and household range of products.

The diversification programme obviously involved a very substantial reorientation on the part of Maguire and Paterson. Its management approach and capability had to be regenerated. A number of new senior management appointments were made. A marketing director was appointed and under him an effective marketing function with skills in branding and product development was nurtured. Sales representation was increased and the distribution network deepened. By 1980 the number of employees had increased to 190. As Maguire and Paterson moved into the eighties it had come to see itself increasingly as a marketing and distribution company of fast-moving consumer goods (FMCG) through a network of supermarket, retail, grocery, chemist and hardware outlets.

This perspective on marketing, while differing from the various previous views of its role, is not a substitute for them. It rather represents a further stage of evolution in the managerial interpretation and professional practice of marketing. This is indicated in Figure 1.1 by the successive layering of approaches to marketing, suggesting that the approaches of the nineties both build on previous traditions and practice and extend these in new ways. And just as we see marketing management as the process of creatively combining market needs with the unique competences of the organisation, so too our evolving conceptualisation of marketing reflects both the demands of a changing competitive marketplace for better ways of thinking about marketing and the developing ability or competence of the marketing discipline to analyse and explain markets.

SUMMARY
Definitions of marketing abound but a brief review of these reveals that the many variations share important common themes. It is important to consider marketing in its wider societal context, and to appreciate its international

Figure 1.1

The Evolving Nature of Marketing's Role

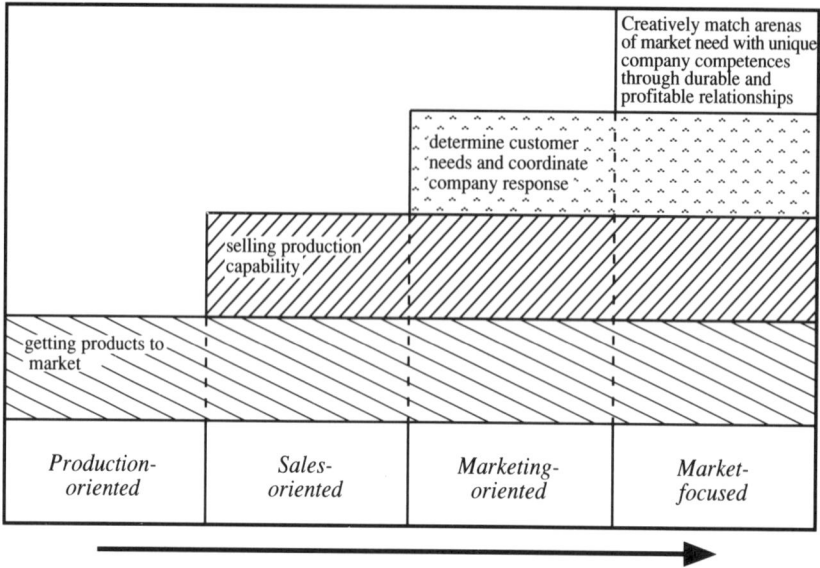

			Creatively match arenas of market need with unique company competences through durable and profitable relationships
		determine customer needs and coordinate company response	
	selling production capability		
getting products to market			
Production-oriented	Sales-oriented	Marketing-oriented	Market-focused

character in today's competitive world. It is possible to view marketing activity as evolving through a number of phases: from production orientation, through sales and marketing orientation to, most recently, market focus.

The concept of *market focus*—put simply, the continuing and persistent alignment of a firm's resources and unique competences to changing needs and opportunities in the marketplace through profitable and often durable relationships—is key to marketing success in the nineties.

Reading

Aaker, David (1992), *Strategic Market Planning*, 3rd ed., Wiley, NY.

Abell, D.F. (1980), *Defining the Business: The Starting Point of Strategic Planning*, Prentice-Hall, Englewood Cliffs, NJ.

Baker, Michael J. (1991), *Marketing—An Introductory Text*, 5th ed., Macmillan, Basingstoke.

Day, G.S. (1984), *Strategic Market Planning*, West Publishing Company, St Paul.

Day, G.S. (1986), *Analysis for Strategic Market Decisions*, West Publishing Company, St Paul.

Drucker, Peter (1983), *Managing for Results*, Heinemann, London.

Hamel, G. and Prahalad, C.K. (1990), 'The core competences of the corporation', *Harvard Business Review*, May–June.

Hamel, G. and Prahalad, C.K. (1991), 'Corporate imagination and expeditionary marketing', *Harvard Business Review*, July–August.

Kotler, P. (1991), *Marketing Management: Analysis, Planning, Implementation and Control*, 7th ed., Prentice-Hall, Englewood Cliffs, NJ, ch. 1.

Kotler, P. (1991a), 'From transactions to relationships to networks', paper to the trustees of the Marketing Science Institute, Boston, November.

Kotler, P. and Armstrong, G. (1991), *The Principles of Marketing*, 5th ed., Prentice-Hall, Englewood Cliffs, NJ.

McCarthy, E.J. and Perreault, W.D. (1990), *Basic Marketing: A Managerial Approach*, 10th ed., Irwin, Boston.

Peters, Thomas J. (1987), *Thriving on Chaos*, Macmillan, Basingstoke.

Ward, James J. (1987), 'Marketing myopia in industrial development', *Irish Marketing Review*, vol. 2.

Review Questions
1. 'Marketing affects our lives in a most pervasive manner.' Discuss.
2. Consider some definitions of marketing and examine what common themes run through them.
3. Assess the view that it is possible to observe marketing activity in the firm evolving through a number of phases. Can you recognise companies of your knowledge in each of the phases?
4. What is distinctive about the concept of market focus?

Chapter 2

Markets, Marketing and Competitive Advantage

MARKETING THROUGH THE BUSINESS SYSTEM

Initial impressions of the nature of marketing are commonly formed by the very visible aspects of consumer marketing: the products of daily life and their presentation in retail outlets and their promotion through advertising. Yet marketing and marketing processes are concerned with a range of activities of which consumer products represent only the very tip of the iceberg. Markets and marketing are also about industrial products such as machine tools, electronic components, or food ingredients which are sold from one organisation to another, and services such as engineering consultancy, air travel or holidays which are provided to both organisations and individual consumers.

One way of viewing this complexity of marketing processes is to envisage markets and industries as 'business systems'. A business system is the chain of value-adding activities that is undertaken in order to bring a product or service from raw material stage to the provision of final customer service and support. Figure 2.1 represents such a general business system—it may also be referred to as a macro business system, as it encompasses the whole industry. Figure 2.2 illustrates a simplified and general business system for paper products. One can see that it starts with forests and the market for timber. Timber is marketed to pulp and paper mills who produce paper and paper board products. One possible route from here is for the mills to market their paper board to packaging companies. These companies will buy the paper board and 'convert' it into packages—for example, the package in which you buy your breakfast cereal. The packaging companies have the task of marketing their package-making ability to companies who wish to use packages and cartons to transport, protect and promote their products (whether a breakfast cereal or an airline ticket to be inserted in a pouch). Once the packager has purchased the package he will insert his product into it and ship it onward to a retailer perhaps. The retailer's decision to stock the particular product is partly influenced by the quality and performance of the packaging, as is your decision to take the product from the shelf and pay some of your discretionary income for it.

Figure 2.1

A Macro Business System

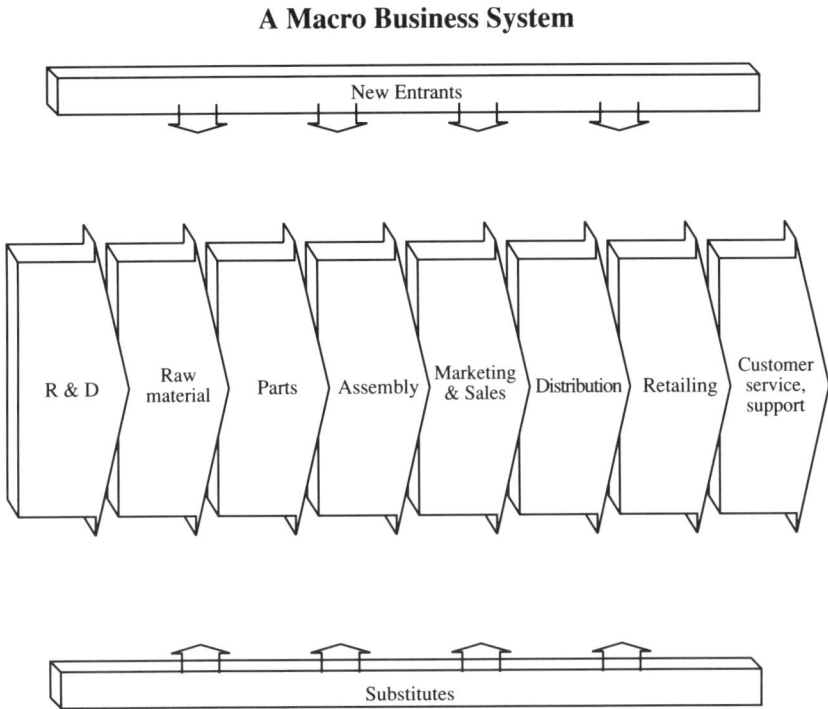

In the case of paper products there may be one more market: that for recycled paper. In this way the business system becomes a partial loop as some of the raw materials are drawn not just from the forests but from the used final product of the system. In a world increasingly concerned with environmental issues more and more business systems are becoming partially closed loops in order to protect the environment from unwanted and dangerous waste. Closing the loop involves the processes of de-manufacturing and recycling. Demanufacturing entails disassembling final products into component elements that may be sorted and readily recycled. A used package, for example, may have to be disassembled into its paper, paper board, plastic and perhaps metallic foil elements.

As one inspects the macro business system of any industry, it quickly becomes visible that an industry consists of a series of markets with the product or service offering of each one becoming an input or raw material to the next. Industrial markets, business-to-business markets, consumer markets, products and services are all interconnected within any business system. What may be initially viewed as a product in a consumer market

Figure 2.2

A Macro Business System for Paper Products

New Entrants

Forestry | Pulp & Paper Manufacture | Paper conversion (e.g. to packaging, greeting cards, etc.) | Sales & Marketing | Distribution | Use | Demanufacture (e.g. separation of paper, inks, foil, plastic film, etc.) | Recycle

Substitutes

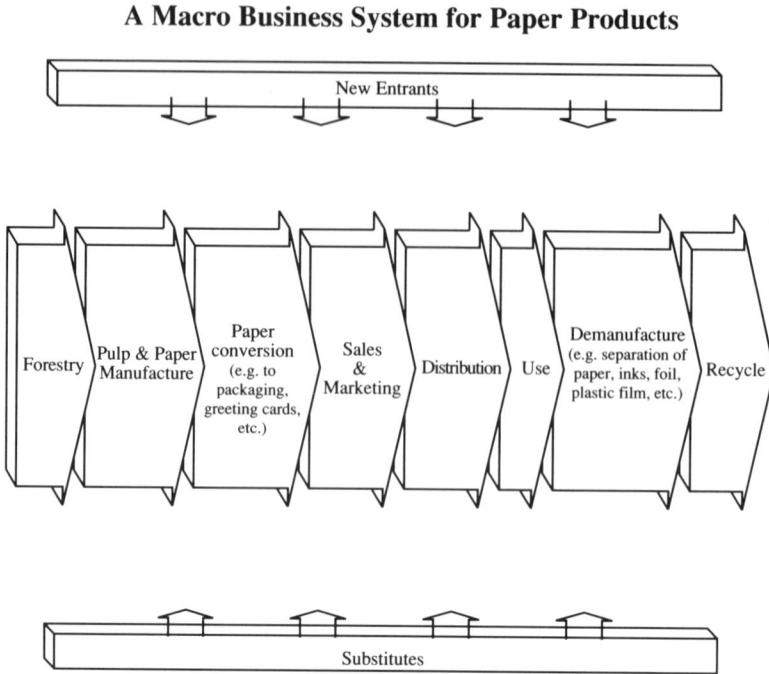

(say an automobile) is in fact the outcome of many business-to-business (or industrial) markets in automotive components supplied by firms such as Donnelly Mirrors of Naas (car mirrors) or by Kromberg & Schubert of Waterford (electrical wiring harnesses for cars). The ability to create and manufacture the car will have depended on many service inputs, such as those provided by design studios like Pinninfarina of Milan, engineering design specialists like the Lotus company of England, and manufacturing management consultants like the Lucas company. Once the car is sold on the consumer market, final satisfaction with the product will be experienced only if service and support is provided through the car manufacturer's dealerships and spare parts service system.

FROM UPSTREAM TO DOWNSTREAM MARKETING

Understanding an industry as a series of markets in a business system also highlights the manner in which marketing activity alters as the business system moves from raw material markets to the markets for service and support and on to the newer markets for demanufacturing and recycling. The marketing of one tonne of 2mm rolled paper will be rather different from the marketing of the airline ticket made from this raw material, and different again from the marketing of recycled paper containing the discarded ticket.

In general, as value is added along the business system, the product will evolve from standardised, commodity form generating low margins towards more differentiated, heterogeneous and higher-margin form (see Figure 2.3). The early stages are usually typified by the production of commodity or standardised products, often produced to externally arbitrated standards. For example, a concrete block may be made to ISO 49 (Irish Standards Organisation) specification or a length of rebar steel to the BSO 106 standard. Further along the system, offerings tend to be more heterogeneous. They become differentiated on the basis of quality, performance characteristics, service back-up, brand identity and other factors. As a result the nature and tasks of the marketing function change considerably as one moves from 'upstream' companies to 'downstream' companies.

Upstream companies—those involved in the early stages of raw material production and primary manufacture and fabrication—are most likely to have to develop marketing strategies and practices that emphasise product standardisation, and low cost structure to underpin aggressive price competition in volume-driven, low-margin businesses. Companies marketing basic building products and materials will tend to become excellent at such aspects of business if they are to survive and prosper. Price is increasingly joined in such markets by the importance of high-quality supplier–buyer relationships, leading us to emphasise the growing importance of marketing as a relationship management process as well as our traditional focus on it as a series of one-off market transactions. Many of the most successful marketers of commodity-type products now win and defend business on the basis of excellence in managing long-term relationships which effectively become partnerships between supplier and buyer.

Japanese industry has done much to demonstrate just how effective an approach to marketing this can be and the extent to which it can lead to significant increased profitability for both partners. Deepening of such upstream market relationships is usually based on adding service features to the physical product flow. Thus, service features such as customer problem-solving, guaranteed reliability, full delivery and just-in-time delivery become critical elements of marketing. A potato supplier who adds value by ensuring consistency of potato breed, by grading, washing and packing potatoes in factory-ready quantities and then delivering them as needed to a potato processing plant is much more likely to build a sustainable relationship with a customer than one that offers to supply potatoes without such added services. Suppliers of potatoes to McDonald's for conversion to French fries, to the major producers of oven-ready chipped potatoes, or to the multinational marketers of potato waffles have to respond to these necessities or fail.

Figure 2.3

Marketing and the Macro Business System

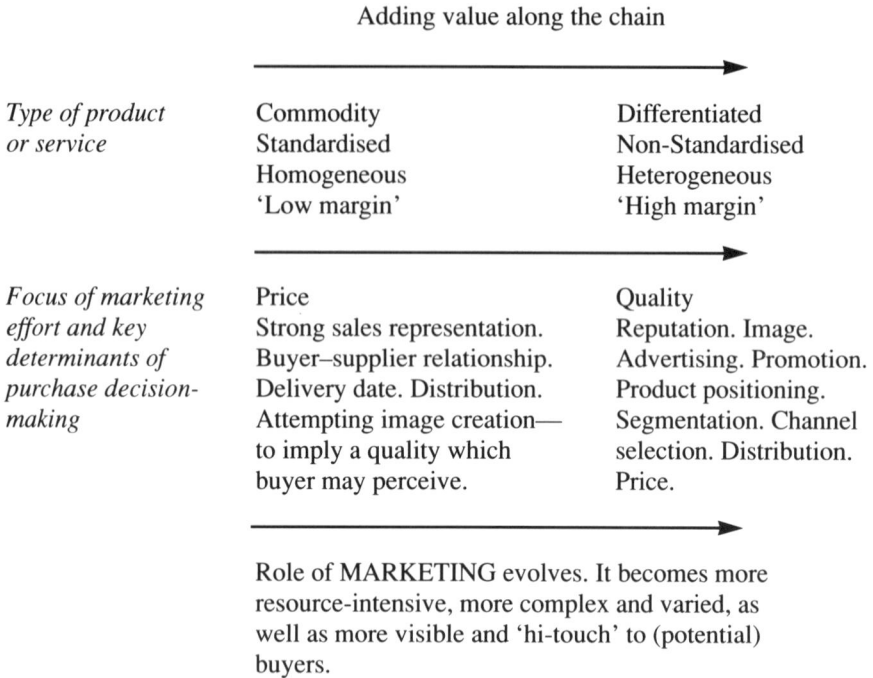

Adding value along the chain

→

| *Type of product or service* | Commodity
Standardised
Homogeneous
'Low margin' | Differentiated
Non-Standardised
Heterogeneous
'High margin' |

→

| *Focus of marketing effort and key determinants of purchase decision-making* | Price
Strong sales representation.
Buyer–supplier relationship.
Delivery date. Distribution.
Attempting image creation—
to imply a quality which
buyer may perceive. | Quality
Reputation. Image.
Advertising. Promotion.
Product positioning.
Segmentation. Channel
selection. Distribution.
Price. |

→

Role of MARKETING evolves. It becomes more resource-intensive, more complex and varied, as well as more visible and 'hi-touch' to (potential) buyers.

As one moves to the downstream end of any industry, marketing activities become dominated by aspects familiar to us all in our role as consumers. Downstream companies gain competitive advantage increasingly from detailed segmentation of markets and tailoring of products and services to the special needs of each segment. Higher margins may be created in this way and proprietary positions in the market established and defended through investment in brands and specialised distribution channels. Frozen potato waffles may therefore take their position in supermarket freezers as strongly branded items tailored for exactly defined customer segments such as households needing quick-preparation food products where both parents work, and children may be categorised in the language of market researchers as 'latch-key kids'. In this instance marketing is all about detailed market research, careful brand development, strong advertising to create market awareness and brand loyalty, and elaborate distribution and logistic systems to ensure full shelves in the supermarket. It can be readily seen that the task of marketing for a potato producer supplying a food processing company is significantly different from that of the branded food manufacturer supplying the final consumer market through the supermarket.

In the middle sections of any industry chain or macro business system these rather dramatic contrasts in marketing tasks and practices blur and companies have to deal with the necessity to respond to their markets with a blend of upstream and downstream practice. Interestingly this progression is less likely to be observed in services markets along the business system. The nature of services required at raw material extraction stage (e.g. veterinary medicine for beef production) are likely to be high margin just as are the services required to cook and prepare beef for the table in a restaurant at the end of the beef business system.

It is important to remember that the underlying principles of marketing and the theories on which they are based must be acted on managerially in a *situational manner*. The manager must be aware of the need to manage marketing in a manner that reflects the business system context. The lessons of fast-moving consumer goods marketing cannot be applied without modification to the marketing challenges of upstream companies and vice versa. The practice of marketing is therefore fundamentally contingent or situational in nature.

CONSUMER, BUSINESS-TO-BUSINESS AND NOT-FOR-PROFIT MARKETING

The concept of the industry business system helps to illustrate that all consumer products are usually the outcome of many business-to-business marketing activities and that both consumer and business-to-business markets usually depend on services markets if business is to take place. The potato producer of our example above will probably depend on the technical advisory service of a chemical company that supplies the farm with fertiliser, with weedicides and with potato disease preventatives. Equally, the multinational brander of frozen potato waffles will depend crucially for success on the quality of the services purchased from market research suppliers and advertising agencies. Marketing does differ as one moves from consumer to business-to-business and on to services marketing but the differences are in matters of degree rather than fundamental principle. The same proves to be true when we turn our attention to marketing for not-for-profit organisations. The same concerns, challenges, theories and principles of good practice apply to the marketing of safe driving behaviour, dental hygiene, the activities of an arts centre or the promotion of a wildlife trust as apply to the other forms of marketing of which we have already spoken.

The central implication of this is that marketing shares a common set of concerns and is based on a common set of theories and principles of good practice no matter what kind of market relationship we study or have to manage. Equally, it is true—and vital to understand—that the practice of marketing is essentially situational: the market context must determine the way in which theory and principle is applied.

THE FIRM'S MICRO BUSINESS SYSTEM

The individual firm or organisation may be viewed as a microcosm of the industry business system within which it lives. Each organisation necessarily sources raw materials and other inputs such as labour and capital. It then converts these inputs into products or services for which customers will pay more than the combined cost of all the inputs, thus generating a margin of profitability and a return on investment. The organisation may therefore be visualised as an organised chain or process of activities in the same way that we saw an industry could be viewed as a long chain of production and distribution. Porter (1985) called this micro business system a value chain and popularised the technique of value chain analysis. Figure 2.4 illustrates and describes briefly the structure of a micro business system, while Figure 2.5 sets it in the context of a printing company.

Figure 2.4

A Firm's Micro Business System

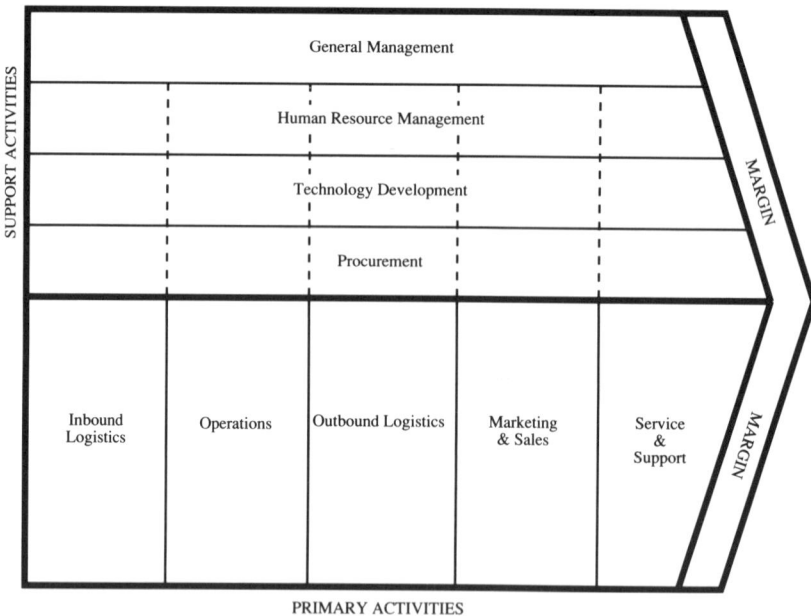

A micro business system disaggregates a firm into its strategically relevant activities in order to understand better the interrelationship of different functions, the behaviour of costs, and existing and potential sources of competitive advantage. It does so by identifying the key value-adding activities that the firm carries out. These value activities can be divided into two broad types: primary activities and support activities. Primary activities are those that are involved in the physical creation of the product or service, its distribution to the buyer and any after-sales service. These **primary activities** can be divided into the following categories:

(1) *Inbound logistics.* Activities associated with the receipt, storing and dissemination of inputs to the product (includes warehousing, inventory control, vehicle scheduling).
(2) *Operations.* Activities associated with transforming inputs into the final product (machining, packing, assembly, testing, equipment maintenance).
(3) *Outbound logistics.* Collecting, storing and distributing the product to buyers.
(4) *Marketing and sales.* Activities associated with providing a means by which buyers can purchase the product, and persuading them to do so (advertising, selling, channel selection, pricing, promotion).
(5) *Service and support.* Providing a service to maintain or enhance the value of the product (installation, training, parts supply, technical advice and maintenance).

Support activities can be divided into four categories:

(1) *Procurement.* This is the function of purchasing inputs. It includes all the procedures for dealing with suppliers. Procurement activity goes on across the whole firm; it is not just limited to the purchasing department. Although the costs of procurement activity themselves form only a small proportion of overhead costs, the impact of poor procurement can be dramatic, leading to higher costs and/or poor quality.
(2) *Technology management.* This encompasses not just machines and processes, but 'know-how', procedures, systems and learning curve benefits. In some industries (like paper manufacturing) process technology can be a key source of advantage.
(3) *Human resource management.* This includes all the activities involved in the recruitment, training, development and remuneration of staff. Firms that are successful continuously tend to be those that are highly selective in their recruitment policies and invest heavily in training and development of personnel.
(4) *General management.* Ultimately all the primary and support activities depend on a focused general management perspective. General management activities like directing finance resources, planning, information systems, suitable organisation structure, quality assurance and so on all provide the necessary infrastructure and integration to

enable all other activities. Thus, general management supports the whole micro business system or value chain—unlike the other three support activities, which can be particularly linked with one or two primary activities.

A firm may have a distinctive competence or expertise in any or each of these primary and support activities. Analysing the micro business system enables the firm to understand its cost structure, identify where it differentiates itself from competitors, and appreciate how the various activities must be linked together optimally if market focus is to be achieved.

We see that marketing is one of the five primary activities that must be carried out by any organisation, supported by the four generic support activities which are needed to manage and organise the primary activities. Marketing itself may be further analysed as a series of specialised activities, such as marketing management, advertising, salesforce administration, promotion and so on. Analysis of the micro business system should lead to:

—the identification of the activities in the firm that are critical to its cost structure and to an understanding of how these costs are influenced;
—the identification of the activities that are central to the creation of customer value and the factors that influence value creation positively or negatively;
—the identification of critical interdependencies between activities since these interactions are often important drivers of both cost and customer value.

This form of analysis helps to establish the role of marketing in the individual organisation and to isolate the leverage which marketing activity has on overall company performance. It is vital to establishing the interdependence between marketing and other company activities and therefore in ensuring integrated planning and action—one of the central concerns of the market-focused company.

LINKING MACRO AND MICRO BUSINESS SYSTEMS

The analysis of the micro business system should be set firmly in the industry business system context. Doing this ensures that the manager is alerted to the challenges faced not only by his own organisation but also by the organisation's customers and the customers' customers. On the upstream side it has become increasingly essential that the manager also understand the issues faced by suppliers and suppliers' suppliers. This is the kind of framework within which we may build an approach to marketing that places appropriate stress on relationships and networks.

Figure 2.6 illustrates this perspective. Here we see a chain of micro business systems which, of course, ultimately make up an overall macro business

Figure 2.5

The Micro Business System of a Printing Company

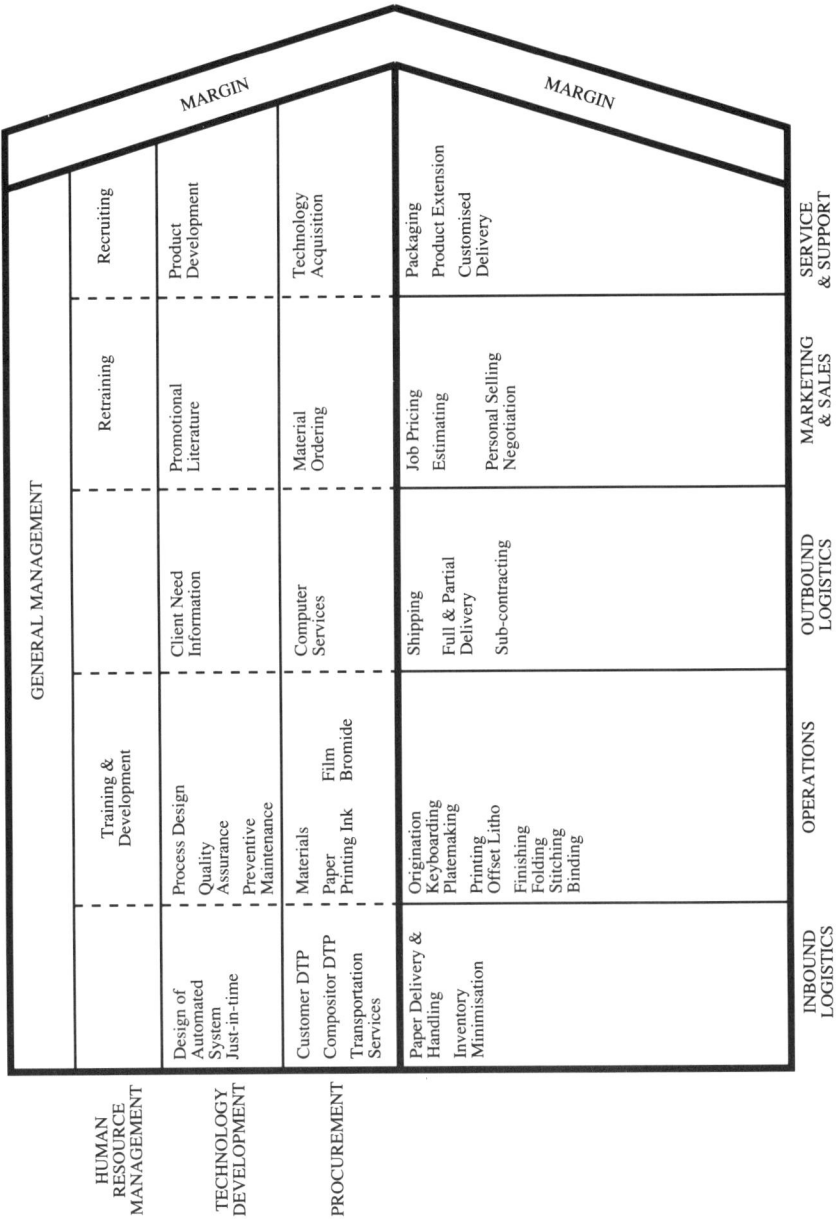

system. Based on such analysis the challenge to the marketer is to understand and solve customers' problems by understanding their business and their competitive challenges in serving their customer base. A marketer of do-it-yourself home care products must therefore develop a sophisticated appreciation of the competitive necessities faced by a DIY retailer who competes for the patronage of householders. If the marketer is to produce and supply DIY products of appropriate quality and cost to the DIY retailer, he must also understand the supplier relationships that are needed to guarantee the procurement of the necessary components and raw materials.

Figure 2.6

The Chain of Micro Business Systems

Supplier's supplier	Firm's supplier	**The firm**	Firm's customer	Customer's customer

SUSTAINABLE COMPETITIVE ADVANTAGE

The analysis of macro and micro business systems leads to decisions about how to compete effectively, or put in the language of the business strategist, how to establish and sustain a competitive advantage. The notion of competitive advantage stresses that commercial success flows from having an advantage over competitors in the marketplace which allows the firm to serve customers more effectively and at a profit. The idea of sustaining this advantage is just as important since competitive advantage that cannot be sustained over any appreciable time is of little value. Just as the operations manager is charged with creating advantage based in the operations or manufacturing activities, the aim of the marketer is therefore to create advantage over competing organisations in the marketplace in such a manner that at least some element of temporary monopoly is generated—the marketing advantage cannot be readily imitated. This idea is usually encapsulated in the phrase *sustainable competitive advantage* (SCA).

Sustainable competitive advantage may be created in many ways but the work of Porter (1980) and Gilbert and Strebel (1989) has drawn attention to the reality that competitive advantage, in its fundamental form, has only a few basic roots. These roots are generally regarded as inherent in 'generic competitive strategies'. Generic competitive strategies may be seen as based on choices that have to be made along three dimensions of competitive strategy (see Figure 2.7):

—The extent to which the company will compete on the relative differentiation of its products or services (their uniqueness and valued 'differentness' from competitive offerings) and hence the perceived value of the product or service to customers. Organisations that decide to invest in differentiation—and succeed in convincing their customers of the worth of this differentiation—are seen to pursue *high perceived value* (HPV) strategies. Customers perceive their offerings on the market as providing greater value in use than competitors. Examples of this approach include many widely known branded products from Porsche in cars to Chanel in cosmetics and fashion.

—The extent to which the company will compete on the relative cost in use of its products or services, i.e. the delivered cost in use to the customer. Such firms must be driven by a desire to minimise costs at every stage of production and delivery—but not, it must be stressed, at the cost of quality. Thus a deep understanding and optimal fine-tuning of its micro business system must be achieved. Organisations that decide to invest in such low cost competitiveness are seen to pursue *low delivered cost* (LDC) strategies. In Exhibit 11.2 we see how Tipperary Cereals successfully followed this approach in the breakfast cereals business to become a sizeable exporter to the Continent.

—The extent to which the company chooses to define the *scope* of its business as encompassing all the various markets and market segments of the industry or to confine its activity to serving a selected market segment. Organisations may therefore choose to invest in a strategy that involves broad industry scope or alternatively to focus on a segment. The Dutch company Philips serves a very wide variety of market segments from light bulbs to semi-conductors, whereas the Irish firm Solus specialises in light bulbs.

When these three dimensions of competitive choice are brought together as in Figure 2.7 the basic options open to the company and the marketer in developing strategies for competitive advantage become clear. A company can choose to focus on one dimension, as in the examples set out above, or it may opt to compete across two or more dimensions. Black and Decker, for example, competes across all three, simultaneously pursuing a strategy of high perceived value, low delivered cost and a broad scope. The stratagem typically followed by a small specialist sub-supplier in the electronics industry would focus on both HPV and LDC over a very limited scope.

Of course the pursuit of competitive advantage across any of these dimensions may have to change over time in response to changes in the macro business system. Apple Computer in developing its personal computer products followed a high perceived value approach with corresponding high prices. However, in the early nineties, the maturing of this market has seen Apple having to consider switching to a more standardised low delivered cost strategy with effectively lower prices (see Exhibit 13.2). Toyota won its market

Figure 2.7

Three Dimensions of Competitive Advantage

HPV   High Perceived Value

LDC
Low
Delivered
Cost

Scope

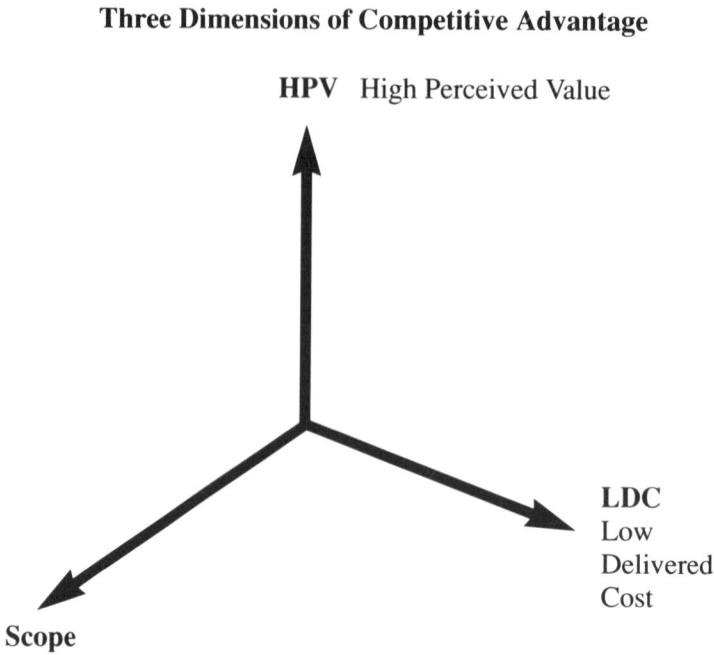

dominance through an LDC policy with its small and medium-sized cars; in the nineties it moved on to a HPV approach with its luxury Lexus car range while retaining its basic cost advantage.

To sum up, the successful market-focused company must understand fully its macro and micro business systems, make choices along the three dimensions of generic competitive strategy, and thus win and sustain competitive advantage in the marketplace. In the early nineties An Post refocused its parcels division and reconfigured its micro business system into a separate entity, Special Distribution Services (SDS). In doing so it conferred significant competitive advantage on itself (see Exhibit 2.1).

SUMMARY

Marketing and marketing processes are concerned with a range of activities of which consumer products represent only the very tip of the iceberg. One way of viewing this complexity of marketing processes is to envisage markets and industries as 'business systems'. A macro business system is the chain of value-adding activities that is undertaken in order to bring a product or service from raw material stage to the provision of final customer service and support. The nature of marketing activity is different and evolves along this chain.

Exhibit 2.1

AN POST SPECIAL DISTRIBUTION SERVICES (SDS)

'We deliver your promise'

The latter part of the eighties saw competitive pressures develop in the parcels and document delivery business in Ireland. International courier companies were establishing a strong presence. Customers, especially business, were demanding faster, more reliable and more comprehensive levels of service. An Post was aware of shortcomings in its own parcels service. There were operating inefficiencies, limits to the range of service offerings, and customer perceptions of unsatisfactory reliability and speed of delivery. To rectify matters, An Post set up Special Distribution Services (SDS) as a separate entity, distinct from the letters side of the organisation, with a mission to build a dedicated distribution network capable of providing a highly efficient and reliable parcels service in the Irish market.

Since its official launch in October 1990 SDS has brought a revolutionary new approach to the business of parcels distribution, not only here in Ireland, but for international parcels traffic in and out of the country. The key location in the whole network is the SDS main depot, strategically positioned beside the Dublin orbital motorway at Newlands Cross, where a purpose-built depot and offices were constructed on a 14-acre site, at a cost of £6 million. Here a 40,000 square foot sorting area contains mechanised cost-efficient systems with conveyor belts and cages that minimise the amount of handling by sorters—equipment to match any used in other European countries.

SDS has four dedicated distribution centres: the headquarters on the Naas Road, and regional ones at Athlone, Cork and Portlaoise. A total of over 250 vehicles are used for collecting, trunking and delivering across the state, with over 100 of these vehicles dedicated SDS trucks and vans, while its 5,500 kg capacity Fokker FH227 aircraft flies nightly between Dublin and Coventry. The whole SDS operation is geared towards quick turnaround. All kinds of parcels, packages and documents can be delivered by SDS. High-value, delicate items, like computers and TV sets, are dealt with on a regular basis, as are bicycles and golf clubs. All parcels are bar-coded, so that their status can be checked at any stage in transit. The end result for customers is that SDS gives an average 24-hour delivery capability for parcels to any address in the country.

Besides its parcels service, SDS also operates a courier service from a depot at Kilbarrack, near Dublin airport, which operates in tandem with the Newlands Cross centre. This offers same-day desk-to-desk delivery nationally for documents and small merchandise items. Its international ESM service is linked to 170 similar networks worldwide, and guarantees overnight document delivery to the major European business centres and also to New York. SDS also offers its customers a wide range of other value-adding services, from insurance cover to off-peak volume freight services—in short, a well-planned variety of services for Ireland and abroad, designed to meet every configuration in customers' needs.

This revitalised, modern method of handling parcels and documents has paid dividends for SDS. Since its official launch, the service has signed up some 1,500 major customers, all business and service companies and organisations dependent on prompt and reliable deliveries. Business volume for SDS is growing currently by about 20 per cent a year. The company's logo, devised in response to research among its customer base, carries arrows in three colours to emphasise speed and accuracy, while its present promotional byline boasts, 'We deliver your promise.'

Source: *The Irish Times*, 14th October, 1992.

Thus firms must also understand their particular chain of value-adding activities—their own micro business system. This understanding of macro and micro business systems represents the basic building block of market focus. To this must be added a choice on the part of the firm of where and how to compete across the three dimensions of generic competitive advantage, high perceived value (HPV), low delivered cost (LDC), and scope. Decisions based on this choice will enable the firm not only to win but also to *sustain* competitive advantage.

Reading

Andersson, Per and Soderlund, Magnus (1988), 'The network approach to marketing', *Irish Marketing Review*, vol. 3.

Gilbert, X. and Strebel, P.J. (1989), 'From innovation to outpacing', *Business Quarterly*, Summer.

Gilbert, X. and Strebel, P.J. (1989a), 'Taking advantage of industry shifts', *European Management Journal*, December.

Porter, Michael (1980), *Competitive Strategy; Techniques for Analysing Industries and Competitors*, The Free Press, NY.

Porter, Michael (1985), *Competitive Advantage*, The Free Press, NY, ch. 2.

Review Questions

1. Explain what is meant by a firm's macro business system and indicate how marketing activity might differ or evolve along this system.
2. Relate the concept of the firm's value chain or micro business system to a company or organisation with which you are familiar.
3. Comment on the relationship, if any, between consumer marketing, business-to-business marketing and services marketing.
4. Describe the three dimensions of generic competitive strategy.

Chapter 3

The Job of the Marketing Manager

THE MARKETING FUNCTION

The job of the marketing manager is to manage the marketing function in an organisation. The marketing function involves the concepts and activities discussed in Chapter 1, undertaken in the context of the macro and micro business systems discussed in Chapter 2. The marketing function is therefore at the centre of the process of matching customer needs with company competences in a manner that creates valued relationships which are competitively unique and profitable to both parties to any exchange. Market needs must be matched with the distinctive resources and capabilities of the organisation if it is to offer services or products that are superior in the market. It is a key feature of successful new ventures, for example, that they are created to exploit their promoters' specialised knowledge and resources. Established successful organisations continue to do likewise, keeping up with or ahead of changes in both market needs and corporate competences as they continuously renew their business. So we view marketing *as the matching of customer needs with company competences to produce products and services that are competitively superior and therefore capable of yielding sustained profitability.*

This concept of the marketing function is visualised in Figure 3.1. Here we see that the matching of market needs and company competences takes place in a dynamic manner—both needs and competences are continuously changing. The marketing function must keep pace with this ever-changing intersection of needs and capability in a marketplace where competitors are also continuously changing, bringing new offerings to the market and acquiring new competences that may render those of other companies less unique or outmoded. The result of the effective conduct of the marketing function is the provision to markets of products and services needed by customers, available to them where and when needed, priced at an acceptable level, profitable to the supplier and with all the relevant information about the product or service persuasively communicated to the customer. In the remainder of this book we will label these activities of the marketing function as the marketing mix.

Figure 3.1

The Marketing Function

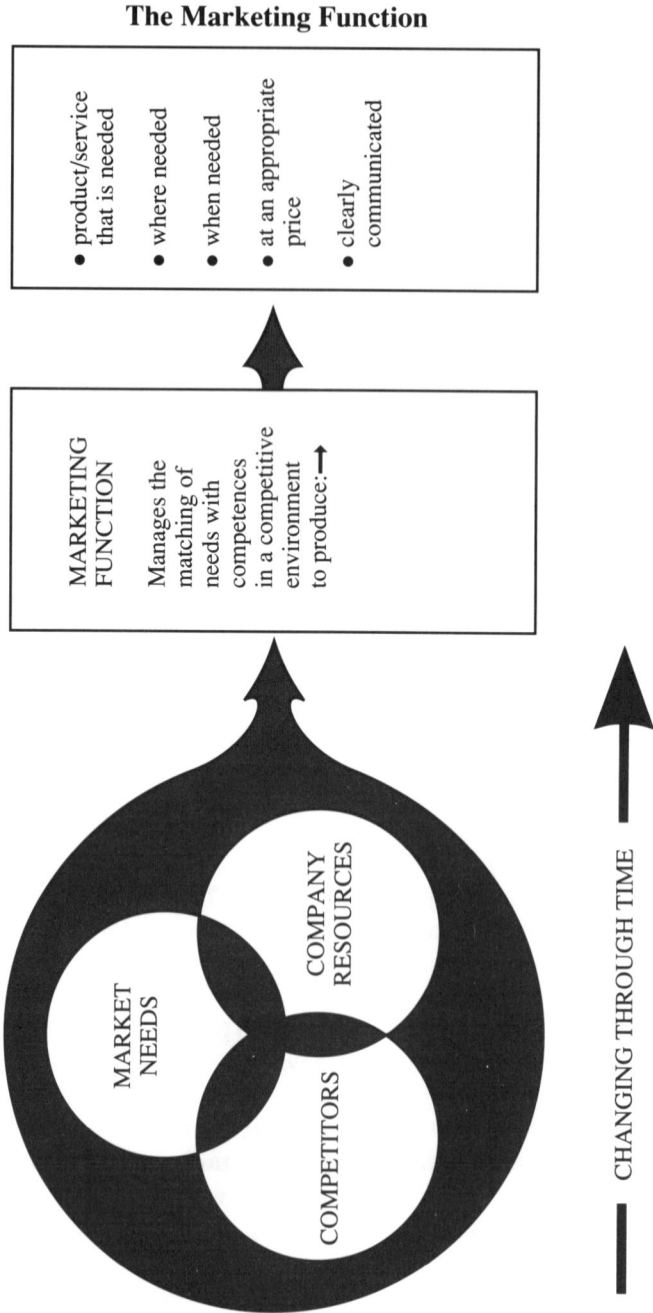

Successful implementation of the tasks of the marketing function in any business generates a self-perpetuating cycle of customer satisfaction, profitability, the further development of core competence and, in consequence, enhanced ability to serve existing and new markets and to outperform competitors. This process, typifying the central role of marketing in business development and in the strategic management of the firm, is illustrated in Figure 3.2.

Figure 3.2

Marketing and Business Development

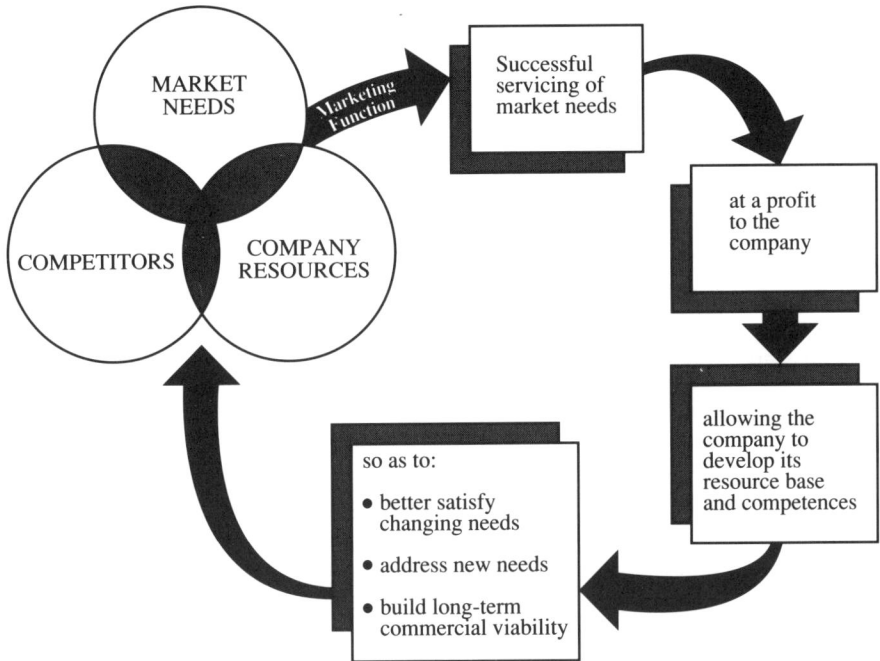

Marketing is one of the four central managerial functions, along with financial management, operations management and human resource management. In the small venture it is often carried out by the owner manager, or general manager, and will normally emerge as a specialist function managed by a marketing manager only as the firm grows. With the growth of a company, the marketing function may encompass all the subsidiary tasks and managerial positions associated with sales management, advertising, distribution, logistics, selling, promotion, merchandising, public relations and product management. However, whether or not there is a person called a marketing manager, the marketing function must be performed in *all* businesses. Indeed, part of the evolving emphasis in marketing discussed in Chapters 1 and 2 points towards the sharing of parts of the marketing function among the top management team, the general manager or the chief executive as well as the marketing manager. In some ways this might be seen as an attempt to recreate the central and integrated role of marketing in business management that is typically found in new and small ventures. This integration is all too easily lost as organisations grow and necessarily specialise their management functions. Marketing must therefore develop and respect its specialised technical, disciplinary competence but never lose sight of the reality that this competence is meaningful only when integrated fully with the work of other functions and the strategic management of the whole enterprise.

THE JOB OF THE MARKETING MANAGER

The job of the marketing manager has many dimensions. He should take charge of *creating and maintaining the reality of a market-focused organisation*. This is a task which demands both an appreciation of the evolving role and nature of the marketing function and the organisational, political and interpersonal skills to communicate well with the rest of a management team.

The marketing manager is responsible for the creative, insightful and disciplined analysis of customers, markets, competitors and their interrelated dynamics. Thus he must have *analytical skills*. In Part II of this book we place special emphasis on the development of ability to analyse systematically:

—customers and customer behaviour
—market structures, size and trends
—competitors, their strengths and weaknesses and likely behaviour
—industry structure and market forces affecting competitive behaviour
—company resources and competences, strengths and weaknesses
—the need for marketing research and the structuring of such research.

Based on the professional conduct of analysis such as that outlined above, the marketing manager's job demands *conceptual abilities* in marketing planning so that a strategy for the company and its products or services can be developed. The marketing plan has to be an integral element of the business planning process and the manager must therefore appreciate the role of the marketing function in overall business strategy and the many interdependencies between marketing and the other business functions. Without this appreciation marketing plans will be developed and acted on in isolation with little hope of successful implementation.

The successful marketing plan embodies fundamental planning and policy decisions with regard to the company's marketing activities. This is the focus of Part III of the book. These decisions must be taken and implemented by the effective manager and demand *decision-making skills*. While there are many ways in which one might itemise the various decisions which marketing managers regularly make, we have simplified them into seven core categories:

—decisions about market choice: the commitment to targeting the company and its resources and competences on specific markets;
—decisions about the positioning of the company in those chosen markets so that customers' needs are served in a competitively superior and competence-enhancing manner;
—decisions about product or service strategy: exactly what offering(s) will the company bring to the market;
—decisions about introducing new products and services and the role of new product development in the organisation;
—decisions about pricing policy: exactly what price will be paid for the company's offerings at each stage in the business system through to final consumption;
—decisions about communication policy: exactly what information will be provided to the market on the company and its offerings so that potential customers, influencers, and members of the business system are appropriately informed and persuaded to do business with the company;
—decisions about distribution policy: exactly how will the company's products or services be brought to the final consumer, involving choice of and commitments to other members of the business system who must handle the products or services, the design and implementation of logistical systems whether physical (trucking, shipping, warehousing, etc.), electronic (as in automated teller machines for banks or financial information via a teletext system) or other, actually to move the company's offerings to where they are needed.

The marketing manager's job also encompasses skills and abilities in *implementing marketing decisions*. This topic is addressed in Part IV. It involves setting in place suitable organisation structures to enable the plan to be executed and encouraging a supportive company climate, sometimes referred to as internal marketing. It also involves 'actioning' the plan or strategy in terms of developing programmes, action-plans, annual budgets and performance criteria. The task of marketing control includes monitoring the implementation of the decisions taken and their consequences, taking corrective action where they are not as intended and ensuring that effective learning takes place. This process increasingly encompasses the conduct of a periodic marketing audit through which the effectiveness of marketing in the organisation is reviewed and improvements developed.

The only certainty about marketing activity is change—and learning how to cope with it. A marketing performance which is currently excellent may well falter over time and need to be reshaped and renewed. A key concern and requirement for the marketing manager is not only to achieve but to *sustain market focus* over time. This is examined in Part V. Why do excellent companies fail? How do firms renew themselves? The successful marketing manager must continually and persistently align and realign the needs and opportunities of the market with the core competences and consequent product and service offerings of the firm—the key to market focus.

Quite apart from having responsibility to carry out the tasks that are particular to the marketing function, the marketing manager's job also involves the use of general competences in managing people, money and other resources. The marketing manager must, for example, also be skilled in handling human relations issues, in dealing with the behavioural issues of structuring and motivating the marketing department, and increasingly in dealing with financial analysis and decision-making. Marketing managers have to be effective managers as well as experts in marketing. It is for that very reason that the title of this book was chosen: *managing marketing*, not marketing management!

MANAGING MARKETING INTERFACES

Our emphasis on the necessity for the manager to manage the marketing function; to think and plan strategically; to nurture the philosophy of market focus in the company; all points to the inescapable necessity for effective integration of marketing tasks and activities with those of other functions in the business and with the general management of the enterprise. Success in doing this will reflect the manager's understanding of the interfaces between marketing and other aspects of the organisation and his ability to manage these interfaces successfully.

In the area of new product development, for example, it has become more and more clear that R & D, marketing, operations and logistics cannot and must not be kept apart during the development process. For much of the post-war period this was unfortunately standard practice with the new product development process arranged in the manner of a relay race, with each functional specialisation involved for its brief period after which it passed the embryonic product onto the next specialist in line. Starting in the sixties and seventies Japanese companies in particular began to use a 'rugby style' in which interfunctional teams take responsibility for the entire process from concept to market launch. This allows problems of 'manufacturability' to be anticipated and solved right from the product concept stage. It allows the financial expert to assess and reassess financial feasibility continuously as variations and options for development are suggested and as costings change. It allows marketing to influence all stages and to interpret market needs for the benefit of designers, production engineers and pricing analysts. Thus the marketing manager must develop a deep knowledge of his firm's micro business system, its dynamics and interrelationships.

The nineties are specially characterised by an enormous increase in the depth and importance of the interface between operations management and marketing. The development of total quality management (TQM) approaches and 'world-class' manufacturing methods or 'lean production' competences—initially at Toyota in the late fifties and known as the Toyoda system—led Japanese business down a route of development which gave it unprecedented market flexibility and low-cost but high-quality products that Western companies are scrambling to imitate. This new approach to manufacturing and operations methods has enormous implications for marketing, particularly in the area of new product development, as it so often confers simultaneously inherent cost and production flexibility advantages which companies that organise production in the Western mass production tradition cannot match.

This is clearly evidenced in the car manufacturing industry. In the early nineties US and European car-makers were still taking up to five years to develop a new car, whereas the Japanese manufacturers had a three-year development cycle (see Exhibit 12.4). As we move towards the twenty-first century, the speed with which new products or services can be launched—so called speed-to-market or turbomarketing—will be a critical dimension of market focus. The management of interfaces within the micro business system is therefore a very special and urgent priority for the marketing manager. He must learn to understand how to manage with others as well as to manage within the marketing area itself. The reward is substantial in terms of company effectiveness as well as in terms of personal development. Equally, the manager who manages marketing as an isolated fiefdom is now a danger of potentially lethal proportions to companies in international markets.

THE INTERNATIONAL MARKETING MANAGER

The international marketing manager has the special role of displaying all the abilities discussed above and then, in addition, of dealing with the tasks of managing marketing processes across international boundaries. The special challenges for the manager of an international Irish business reflect the needs of entering export markets from an initial domestic base and then helping to develop a truly international marketing orientation as the company grows from exporting to having an established international presence. Companies pursue international marketing strategies as a fundamental platform for their growth strategy. This is especially true for companies based in Ireland as the domestic market is seldom of adequate size to support even modestly ambitious growth plans. The international marketing manager is therefore at the centre of the growth process in Irish firms. International growth is at the very centre of the problem of generating real wealth, productivity, employment and a higher standard of living in Ireland. There is a great need for managers who, through their professionalism and dedication, will solve this problem. Business needs international marketers who can identify overseas market opportunities accurately. It needs marketers who can develop a deep understanding of how customers purchase and use products in these different markets and who can guide the process of product and service adaptation and new product development to suit the needs of markets that do not conform to the domestic pattern of marketing.

International marketers must be able to assess the merits of the various ways in which a company can enter overseas markets—through export relationships, through joint ventures, or through direct investment in sales, distribution, logistics and service facilities, and, in due course, in manufacturing facilities. Given the small size of so much of Irish enterprise, it will often be the case that international marketing activity in its initial stages is characterised by a managing director who travels intensively and takes on the role of export salesperson—what might be termed 'shoe leather' marketing (see Exhibit 3.1). The international marketer must manage the market entry and later the market development process as well as the planning, coordinating and controlling of the company's marketing activity across different countries and cultures. He must work as part of a team with world-class standards of performance in manufacturing or service operations and with strategically oriented general management.

Exhibit 3.1

KINDLE SOFTWARE

Marketing around the world

The computer software industry in Ireland grew spectacularly over a decade. By 1992 the software industry produced an annual turnover of £1.7 billion, of which £1.6 billion was exported—an amount which accounted for over 11 per cent of Ireland's total exports! This growth was fuelled by some 60 multinational firms such as Lotus, Microsoft and the Claris Corporation and some 260 indigenous firms. One of the most successful of the native Irish companies was Kindle Software.

Kindle was established in 1979 by Tony Kilduff, its founder and driving force. Kilduff built the company effectively from scratch into the country's largest indigenous software firm. By 1992 it had grown to worldwide sales of over £14 million and pre-tax profits of close to £5 million, employing 240 people at the company's premises in a terraced row of 12 converted houses in central Dublin.

Yet Kilduff himself has never written or designed a commercial software program. After getting his BComm degree, Kilduff had joined the UK textile conglomerate Coates Viyella. He spent eight years with the company travelling extensively from the UK to the Far East and Australia. While his background was rooted in financial management, Kilduff became heavily involved in the use of information technology. It was this experience that prompted a move into consultancy and the establishment of Kindle.

Despite early contract work and the development of software packages for the distribution and retail sectors, Kindle's success was to be built on the phenomenal sales growth of its Bankmaster product. Kilduff's strength in developing Kindle was his ability to define and focus on market niches. The single product strategy was to prove a huge success. Kindle has sold in excess of $50 million worth of Bankmaster packages. The product has been installed in more than 150 financial institutions in 700 locations worldwide and is the most successful Irish software product ever developed.

The Bankmaster market, principally wholesale and mid-sized retail banks, is truly international. 'Banking is pretty much the same around the world; it's a homogeneous market,' commented Kilduff in a recent interview. In the early years, Kilduff was the company's only salesperson. 'At that time Kindle was a very small company and we couldn't afford the cost of a dedicated salesperson. Most spare resources had to be ploughed into research and development.'

For the best part of five years, Kilduff was his company's international marketer in the Far and Middle East, Africa and Eastern Europe. Bankmaster found sales in 55 countries worldwide. 'We worked very hard at marketing Bankmaster in lots of places. We succeeded because we were willing to go anywhere in the world where there was a bank. We deliberately stayed away from areas where our competitors were strong and concentrated on our own niche,' adds Kilduff.

The real turning-point in the development of Kindle came in 1987 when the company decided to launch an open systems or Unix version of Bankmaster. Remembers Kilduff, 'With the benefit of hindsight, it was an obvious move. But back in 1987, when Unix was just developing, we were breaking new ground. They were very, very nervous times.'

The 'gamble' paid off. Since 1988, when the Unix product was launched, Kindle grew on average 30–40 per cent per annum. When in 1992 Kilduff, one of Ireland's most successful entrepreneurs, sold his stake in the company to a UK computer firm, he joined the ranks of that pretty exclusive élite—a millionaire in his forties.

Source: *The Sunday Business Post*, 9th August, 1992.

These tasks demand special skills which are still very scarce in business in general and in Irish business in particular. At a very specific level they demand language skills and an associated appreciation of how other cultures conduct business relationships and of the economic institutions and procedures characteristic of different countries. In the single market of Europe since 1993 the need for the pan-European marketer has become especially evident—a need for professional managers capable of conducting business in several languages; familiar with many cultures; at home in negotiations with German, French,

Italian, Belgian or many other counterparts; and willing to see Europe as Ireland's natural market and not as a series of 'foreign' export markets. To take on world markets, companies must increasingly take on the characteristics of a global corporation. Unilever, perhaps one of the most successful of all of Europe's international companies, takes these competences so seriously that its board includes members from six different countries, and virtually every one of its country operating companies contains expatriate managers as well as locals. In 1992, it had an Italian managing its company in Brazil, a Dutchman in Taiwan, an Englishman in Malaysia and an American in Mexico (Maljers, 1992). Irish companies that grow through internationalisation will find it necessary to evolve towards a truly international style of management too, and will provide many opportunities for marketing professionals to build exciting international careers.

SUMMARY

The job of the marketing manager is basically to take charge of *creating and maintaining the reality of a market-focused organisation*. This is a task which demands both an appreciation of the evolving role and nature of the marketing function and the organisational, political and interpersonal skills to communicate well with the rest of a management team. The marketing manager should have the ability to analyse markets, customers and competitors and the skills and confidence to make decisions in each area of the marketing mix.

As well as conceiving a plan or a strategy, the marketing manager must also implement it—develop structures and a supportive climate, set performance criteria and monitor progress. He must also realise that continuing success is difficult to maintain and that there is a persistent need to sustain market focus. And he has to do all of this increasingly in an international context!

Reading

Baker, Michael J. (1991), *Marketing—An Introductory Text,* 5th ed., Macmillan, Basingstoke, ch. 3.

Bell, Jim and Brown, Stephen (1989), 'Tyrone crystal: striking out in Japan', *Irish Marketing Review*, vol. 4, no. 2.

Kotler, P. (1991), *Marketing Management: Analysis, Planning, Implementation and Control*, 7th ed., Prentice-Hall, Englewood Cliffs, NJ, ch. 3.

Maljers, F.A. (1992), 'Inside Unilever: the evolving transnational company', *Harvard Business Review*, September–October, p. 49.

McDonald, M.H.B. (1984), *Marketing Plans: How to Prepare Them & How to Use Them*, Heinemann, London, chs. 1, 2, 3.

Review Questions

1. Elaborate on what you believe to be the responsibility and role of the marketing manager in a company.
2. Why is it important to understand how marketing interfaces with other activities and functions in an organisation?
3. The job of the marketing manager is basically to take charge of creating and maintaining the reality of a market-focused organisation. Discuss.

Case 1

Agra Trading

The beef business is Ireland's most important agricultural industry. It exports 85 per cent of its output. The beef industry faces considerable challenges in terms of raw material supply, technology, structural change, consumer tastes, an evolving CAP and mercurial world markets. Beef processors are highly competitive and secretive. Many are exploring opportunities for adding downstream value to the basic product. Agra Trading announced in 1989 a very ambitious project to produce consumer-packed steaks for the European market under a brand label 'Greenfields'.

Issues: *Industry structural analysis. Understanding the business system. From commodity products to niche marketing. Feasibility of launching an international branded product from Ireland.*

BEEF INDUSTRY

Beef cattle production is the most important agricultural industry in Ireland in terms of farm output, accounting for 37 per cent of gross agricultural output. With Ireland enjoying a 600 per cent degree of self-sufficiency in beef production, exports are particularly important. The industry exports 85 per cent of its production and beef exports totalled £.8bn in 1989, over 5 per cent of all Irish exports. Some 5,500 people are employed in the industry and a further 90,000 farmers are involved in beef production.

The beef processing industry consists of some twenty significant companies, the largest being Goodman International. It is largely controlled by private companies; little published data is available on profitability and, while margins are low, profits can be very high. Moreover, the beef processing industry has experienced great change over the last two decades in terms of structure, technological change, consumer taste, distribution and marketing practices, raw material availability, and EC policy.

Twenty years ago over half of all cattle produced in the country was exported live or 'on hoof'; now only about 10 per cent is exported live (see Table 1). The bulk of the trade now involves cattle moving across the land

This case was developed as a basis for class discussion rather than to illustrate effective or ineffective handling of an administrative situation. The section on the beef industry derives from *Irish Food and Agribusiness: An AIS Perspective*, published by Allied Irish Securities, 1989.

frontier to Northern Ireland. The ship-based trade has declined because of high transport costs relative to processed products, increased investment in processing facilities resulting in improved competition from these factories, and a better marketing performance by Irish beef companies convincing over-seas customers for live cattle of the greater attractiveness of processed beef.

Table 1

Analysis of Cattle Supplies, 1989

	HEAD
Export Processing Plants	1,150,000
Domestic Abattoirs	220,000
Live Exports	160,000
Live Imports	(30,000)
TOTAL	1,500,000

CATTLE PRODUCTION

Total cattle production in 1989 amounted to 1.5 million head, or 10 per cent of the EC total. There are an estimated 90,000 farmers engaged in beef cattle production in Ireland. Almost half of these are part-time farmers with off-farm jobs as well. The cattle industry is more complex in many ways than the dairy industry, with animals changing hands a number of times during the production cycle. In a typical case, a calf from a dairy herd in the south would be bought by a small farm in the west and would eventually find its way into a farm in the east of the country for finishing before slaughter. At each stage, the business becomes progressively more capital-intensive. Thus, at the early stages, the cattle industry involves some of the smallest and least developed farm enterprises in the country, while in the latter stages of production, the opposite is the case. Cattle production can be a very rough business at farm level. Producers are at the mercy of sharp movements in price and generally work on tight margins in any event.

One of the main structural problems in the beef industry is cyclicality. Essentially, this means that there is no even pattern in cattle production and that there can be huge fluctuations in output from one year to the next. The industry is highly unusual in that the normal distinction between capital equipment and goods produced is not clear-cut. Breeding cows are the capital of the beef farmer, but these can be readily sold for cash just as young bullocks and heifers can. When confidence in the future of the industry sags, farmers will sell off breeding cows, giving a temporary boost to the numbers going for slaughter, but depressing output in the longer term. Conversely, when confidence grows, farmers will hold heifers back to add to their breeding herd, temporarily depressing the numbers available to factories but lifting future potential production. The decision to switch from output stream to investment stream, or vice versa, can be made speedily and easily in response to market conditions. As a consequence, cyclicality is endemic in the industry. This has important implications for the ability of meat processors to generate a consistent pattern of profits.

The Irish beef processing industry faces another major difficulty in relation to raw material supplies. The bulk of beef cattle, around 80 per cent, is derived from the dairy herd. The restructuring of the Common Agricultural Policy (CAP) has meant that milk production is now restricted by EC quotas and the number of dairy cows kept on farms is set to decline. This situation is exacerbated by continuing improvements in milk yields, which will exert further downward pressure on cow numbers under the quota regime. Cattle supply problems can push processors into loss-making situations and security of raw material supplies will be a continuing concern for Irish meat processors. In future, it is likely that processors will integrate their operations more and more and take an active interest in the sourcing of supplies.

Seasonality and quality are also major structural problems for the supply of raw material to the beef industry. Both are important limiting factors on the development of beef processing in the country. Cattle supplies in Ireland are highly seasonal. This is because cattle production is based on grazing. Calves are born in the spring, over-wintered for one or two years, and then fattened on grasslands over the following summer. Finished cattle are then generally sold to the processing plants in the autumn. The result of this pattern of cattle production is that the bulk of supplies enters factories in the second half of the year. The six-month period, July to December, accounts for two-thirds of total throughput, while just three peak months—September, October, November—account for almost 50 per cent of throughput.

Thus there is an under-utilisation of capacity during the off-peak months, with many plants closing down completely. As a result, Irish beef processors find it difficult to secure and service long-term contracts with foreign supermarket chains, which are based on a continuous year-round supply. Yet developing long-term relationships with such buyers is of prime importance in the development of the industry. However, there appears to be no underlying improvement in this seasonality problem. A number of larger processors operate their own intensive feed lots to ensure an adequate supply of finished cattle during the off-peak months. This is particularly common among companies with supermarket contracts. A number of smaller processors are attempting to build and strengthen long-term arrangements with suppliers in order to protect themselves from the power of the larger-scale processors in product procurement.

Quality in beef cattle is important for the processing industry. The quality of beef animals is generally measured in terms of fat depth on the carcase and the physical conformation of the live animal. These factors can affect the meat yield from animals and the palatability of the meat itself. The industry has been encouraging producers to improve the quality of their animals by offering higher prices for those scoring well on the Department of Agriculture's Carcase Classification Scheme. There has been a marked improvement in the quality of animals entering beef factories in recent years. Increasing use of continental breeds and severe penalties for over-fat cattle have greatly alleviated the quality problem. Ireland is the only EC country, apart from Denmark, considered to be disease-free in cattle production and the government operates very strict rules in regard to disease prevention.

BEEF PROCESSING

There are approximately 30 plants licensed to slaughter beef for export. These have the capacity to handle over 3 million cattle per year, assuming 50-week working, but actual throughput has never exceeded 1.5 million. Seasonality means that two-thirds of all cattle are processed in the second six months of the year.

The principal raw material is steers (bullocks). Steers are normally slaughtered at around 30 months of age and they account for over 60 per cent of beef cattle supplies. Heifers, young female cows, make up another 15 per cent. The other major source of supply is the dairy cow herd; about a quarter of all cattle processed in beef plants are cows culled from the dairy herd, normally because of age or poor milk yield performance. Steers command the highest prices, with heifers next. Cows attract much lower prices because of the more difficult market for the meat.

Primary beef processing is a tight margin business. The key to success is to minimise labour costs, add as much value as possible to the expensive raw material and secure quality market outlets for the finished product. The Irish processing industry turns out beef in a number of different forms:

> *Carcase Beef:* This lowest level of processing involves the sale of beef in 'bone-in' carcase form to intermediate processors who debone it and wholesale it to retail outlets. In 1989, 35 per cent of all Irish beef exports in volume terms were in bone-in form, with chilled bone-in accounting for 17 per cent and frozen bone-in accounting for 18 per cent.
>
> *Frozen Boneless Beef:* Frozen deboned beef is sold in bulk as a commodity product to Middle Eastern and North African markets; 43 per cent of beef exports by volume were in frozen boneless form in 1989.
>
> *Chilled Boneless Beef:* This is mainly exported in vacuum-packed form. Primal cuts of beef are packed in boxes after being vacuum-wrapped in plastic packaging. This type of product is sold to supermarkets where it is further cut for retail sale. It is a trade product, not a consumer product, and accounted for 18 per cent of the volume exports in 1989.

Processed Foods: Some 4 per cent of beef in 1989 was exported in the form of canned, cooked or further processed foods. This is not yet large enough to be significant in the overall context, but it is likely to grow as greater value is added to beef products.

Irish processors are major exporters to Muslim countries. These markets will accept only meat that has been slaughtered according to the 'Halal' ritual, that is, without pre-stunning and with an Islamic mullah in prayerful attendance. Approximately half the throughput of Irish factories is slaughtered in this way. The widespread use of the Halal method enabled Ireland to supply both sides with beef in the Iran–Iraq war.

TECHNOLOGY

Beef processing, particularly in slaughtering and deboning, has tended to be a fairly rudimentary production process and also fairly labour-intensive, especially in less modern plants. However, as the industry has attempted to add value to its products, the technology has become more complex, sophisticated and, of course, expensive. Improvements in packaging technology have resulted in more manageable portions (for further portioning by the retailer), and in a longer life for the product.

There has been a dramatic increase in vacuum-packed export products in recent years—essentially the chilled boneless beef referred to above (see Table 2). The main customers are British, French and German supermarket chains. This growth indicates that there is clearly great potential for further processing of Irish beef. It is important, however, to recognise that there are certain technical limitations and that technological development may have to take place in a stepwise fashion.

Beef is normally sold at retail level as a fresh product. As such, it has a short shelf-life and this poses serious problems for Irish processors whose supermarket customers are distant from them. Meat in consumer-ready vacuum packs can have a shelf-life of six weeks; however, vacuum-packed beef tends to lose its natural red colour or bloom, and accordingly meets with both trade and consumer resistance. There is a retail market for this type of beef, however, and the industry is now focusing its attention on doing further cutting and trimming to the product before packing. Several Irish companies are now selling 'PAD' vacuum-packed beef to French supermarkets. This is sub-primal beef from which virtually all of the fat has been removed and which can be easily cut into consumer portions. Though still a trade product for cutting in in-store butchery departments, PAD represents a significant enhancement of the added-value content in factory output. In the future, such processors may well seek to arrange for an agent or contractor, or indeed their own subsidiary company, in the overseas country to consumer-portion this PAD beef for the retailer and thus enjoy more value added.

Table 2

Exports of Chilled Boneless Beef to EC Destinations, 1981–1989

Destination	1981	1982	1983	1984	1985	1986	1987	1988 Rev.	1989 Est.
Great Britain	3,666	3,844	5,549	7,882	10,806	14,122	24,219	31,510	33,300
N. Ireland	233	535	615	578	486	1,109	1,957	1,755	700
UK	**3,899**	**4,379**	**6,164**	**8,460**	**11,292**	**15,231**	**26,176**	**33,265**	**34,000**
West Germany	3,581	2,567	2,372	4,022	5,081	5,918	7,307	6,718	8,300
France	822	1,835	2,310	3,269	3,997	4,689	5,205	4,977	5,500
Italy	963	1,120	1,736	1,778	1,540	1,470	1,638	1,570	1,880
Belgium/Lux.	118	106	34	369	310	349	636	518	430
Netherlands	264	730	158	27	67	374	1,288	1,415	1,300
Denmark	–	–	–	–	–	–	–	–	–
Greece	9	–	–	–	–	–	–	–	–
Spain	–	50	–	–	–	–	–	3	5
Portugal	16	–	–	–	–	–	–	1	15
Continental EC*	**5,753**	**6,408**	**6,621**	**9,464**	**11,138**	**13,456**	**17,440**	**15,984**	**18,000**
Total—pw	**9,652**	**10,787**	**12,785**	**17,924**	**22,430**	**28,687**	**43,616**	**49,249**	**52,000**
Value (IR£m) (a)	**27**	**32**	**42**	**61**	**76**	**100**	**136**	**175**	**200**

* For comparison purposes, figures for Portugal are included for years prior to EC entry.
(a) Inclusive of MCAs and Variable Premia. Source: CSO and CBF Estimates.

There is a direct trade-off between bloom and shelf-life. The longer the life a fresh meat product is given, the less attractive its appearance is likely to be for the consumer. This is hindering movement towards the desired objective of processors and supermarkets alike—the centralised cutting, packing and labelling of consumer-ready retail packs. Processors want to move towards a centralised system because it allows them to add more value and improve profit margins. For supermarkets, the main attraction is the saving on labour costs on their in-store butchery department, while reduced wastage, lower freight costs and the freeing of more space for retail use are also important considerations. It is likely that the value-added chain or business system in the beef processing industry will be increasingly dominated by two sets of players, the processor and the retailer, with a corresponding reduction in the number of middlemen, be they further processors, trading companies, distributors, agents or contractors.

Important developments are currently taking place in the United States red meat market which will have major implications for the Irish industry. The Excel Corporation, the second largest beef processor in the US, is pioneering the marketing of a range of consumer-ready retail cuts in a new type of vacuum packaging known as 'Far Fresh', which gives a 21-day shelf-life. The main problem is proving to be not consumer resistance but union opposition because of the threat to jobs in retail butchering. The overall success of the venture still remains to be proved.

The success of the American 'Far Fresh' experiment would open up new opportunities for the Irish beef industry. Like their American counterparts, Irish processors have to ship products long distances to their retail customers—British and continental supermarkets. Any movement towards centralised production of retail cuts in the international meat business would have beneficial consequences for the major Irish exporters. Already, as is described below, one Irish company, Agra Trading, has developed a similar 'long-life' beef product in branded consumer portions for the European market.

DISTRIBUTION

Changing consumer tastes, evolving packaging technology and new competitive modes have meant that consumer outlets for beef have been changing significantly over the last two decades. In this retail sector, the traditional retailer or butcher has been losing market share to the general food trade. In France, supermarkets now account for approximately 53 per cent of retail sales. In Germany, the major food retailers have 75 per cent of the retail beef market. In Italy, the traditional butcher is also in decline and while accounting for 60 per cent of the outlets, controls only 20 per cent of the market. In Ireland, however, the trend has remained static in recent years, with the proportion of customers using specialist butchers during weekdays increasing from 51 per cent in 1984 to 54 per cent in 1987. An important consideration in this switch to purchasing in the supermarket rather than in the stand-alone butcher is that the supermarkets themselves throughout Europe are becoming increasingly concentrated. For example, in the UK the six largest multiples control 30 per cent of retail beef sales out of the total supermarket sales of 35 per cent.

The catering sector is still a major distribution outlet for many processors. Receiving a contract often means long-term distribution and, since meat is included in most of the meals, is a very substantial market. Fast food chains, restaurants, hospitals and prisons are some of the many outlets. As the trend for eating out is growing and more businesses have in-house catering facilities, so the catering sector is an increasingly opportune market for beef processors. An estimated 20 per cent of overall beef demand in the UK is in the catering sector; this statistic is 15 per cent in France and Germany and 22 per cent in Italy.

MARKETS AND MARKETING
The domestic beef market is worth some £200 million at wholesale prices. This is virtually a separate market from the export trade and is dominated by local butchers and small abattoirs, some of which are still in municipal ownership. There are larger abattoirs in the main cities and the best of these would be on a par with the export plants. A small percentage of the output of the export plants is channelled into the domestic market.

However, as 85 per cent of Irish beef output is exported, the primary focus of attention must be on the overseas market. In 1989, beef exports totalled over 320,000 tonnes product weight and were valued at £810 million (see Table 3). Almost 80 per cent of Irish beef exports in volume terms leave the country in either bone-in or frozen boneless form. These are essentially low added-value products and a marketing challenge for the future will be to sell more high-margin products into stable markets. The significant growth in vacuum-packed beef exports has been described earlier as has been the development of supply contracts and longer-term relationships with European supermarket chains on the part of processors. There is increasing sophistication evident in the export marketing of Irish beef products. This is a highly desirable development in an industry which has strayed from the true path of commercial selling because of the inducements on offer from the EC's intervention system and the consequent over-reliance on CAP.

Practically all the major processors have established their own sales offices abroad; most have set up in Britain, but some also are operating in the French, German, Belgian and Dutch markets. Irish companies are pursuing better integration through the acquisition of downstream processing facilities proximate to their main markets. This has so far happened only in Britain with companies such as Goodman International and the Kerry Group, but similar developments are likely in the main continental European markets in the coming years. Such integration obviously allows processors to control more of the value-added chain.

Table 3

Exports of Beef and Beef Products to All Markets, 1981–1989

Destination	1981	1982	1983	1984	1985	1986	1987	1988 Rev.	1989 Est.
Great Britain	104,938	95,899	98,009	81,756	82,362	114,288	118,653	107,648	96,000
N. Ireland	5,096	10,267	7,596	7,769	6,519	12,405	20,950	6,473	4,000
UK	**110,034**	**106,166**	**105,605**	**89,525**	**88,881**	**126,693**	**139,603**	**114,121**	**100,000**
West Germany	11,142	9,835	6,291	8,125	10,062	9,427	9,323	7,960	10,200
France	35,145	31,977	31,900	23,231	40,465	36,832	31,348	26,863	30,000
Italy	2,197	2,032	2,973	2,368	2,279	2,055	2,804	3,246	5,500
Belgium/Lux.	3,772	2,716	1,660	5,381	1,409	1,458	1,386	1,825	700
Netherlands	9,483	7,332	2,685	2,511	5,778	1,044	1,884	2,215	1,850
Denmark	558	126	124	46	243	684	1,678	852	630
Greece	1,386	1,662	1,126	20	18	92	226	3	300
Spain	–	–	–	–	–	206	–	118	570
Portugal	–	–	–	–	–	59	43	36	50
Continental EC*	**63,683**	**55,680**	**46,759**	**41,682**	**60,253**	**51,857**	**48,692**	**43,118**	**49,800**
Other European	17,413	7,124	1,871	541	2,675	2,786	19,204	3,896	11,000
N. Africa/M. East	23,644	35,777	47,205	59,414	83,028	85,140	107,554	97,004	134,000
Other Countries	4,900	8,656	16,466	25,700	21,345	46,035	28,786	39,693	28,000
Internat. Markets	**55,796**	**56,844**	**89,383**	**86,046**	**113,681**	**167,584**	**159,624**	**140,593**	**173,000**
Total—pw	**229,513**	**218,690**	**241,747**	**217,253§**	**262,816**	**346,134**	**347,919**	**297,832**	**322,800**
Value (IR£m) (a)	**395**	**450**	**514**	**545**	**673**	**708**	**835**	**735**	**810**

* Includes small quantities of veal (a) Inclusive of MCAs Variable Premia and Export Refunds. Source: CSO and CBF Estimates.

There are three main markets for Irish beef exports—the UK, continental EC countries, and the so-called 'third countries' of North Africa and the Middle East. The UK is Ireland's biggest export market. Out of a total UK consumption of 1.1 million tonnes, 10 per cent is accounted for by Irish imports. The bulk of this beef is supplied to intermediate wholesale operations for further processing. The growing trend, however, is for product to be supplied direct to supermarkets in vacuum-packed form and this trade now accounts for a very substantial proportion of total tonnage exported. Irish companies are also capturing retail trade through the purchase of British meat processors. It is worth observing that beef consumption in the UK is declining slowly as younger consumers switch to meat products with a healthier image. In the continental EC, the main markets are Germany, France and Italy. Although Italy is the biggest beef importer in the EC, the type of beef required means that Irish companies have established only a small presence there as yet. Other EC markets include Belgium, Holland and Denmark.

In the Irish context, the 'third country' markets are the states of North Africa and the Middle East, especially Egypt, Iran and Iraq. Beef imports into these countries are normally handled by state trading agencies, although private companies are becoming increasingly important in the Egyptian context. The main demand is for carcase beef and frozen boneless beef. The third country trade suits the Irish industry particularly well as it involves large-volume contracts for supply during the peak autumn period. While exports to these markets are sizeable, it is essentially a commodity trade with many erratic elements in it. Contracts have to be won each year against severe international competition. Oil price weakness has hampered the ability of these countries to purchase foreign produce. Further, the volume of trade can vary dramatically from one year to the next and indeed the whole trade is heavily dependent on EC export refunds—essentially massive subsidies—to keep it competitive with South American exports. Thus, while these markets have proved lucrative for Irish exporters over the years, they cannot be regarded as a stable source of earnings.

CBF (the Irish Livestock & Meat Board) is the state-run agency charged with promoting Ireland's image as a major producer and exporter of top-quality meat. It participates in international food trade fairs and operates offices in London, Dusseldorf, Milan and Paris to facilitate business contact and development. It does not, however, have any direct trading role. At home, it has an informational, advisory and research-coordinating role. It also seeks to promote domestic consumption of beef and to counter competition from other meat and protein foods.

INTERVENTION AND EC POLICY

Irish beef production and processing operates in the very long shadow of another 'market'—that of intervention. The basic purpose of intervention and other EC support systems for beef, such as aids to private storage (APS) and export refunds, is to guarantee reasonable prices to beef farmers by providing a safety net for the output of processing plants. However, such support systems have tended to distort free trade processes, to remove incentives to process further and to secure real consumer markets, and in general to militate against effective and efficient marketing. In essence, intervention has proved to be the negation of marketing. It has also proved to be very cumbersome and very expensive. EC beef policy is undergoing a major restructuring at present. Substantial cost savings are going to be implemented in the £1.6 billion price support system for beef and a much greater emphasis will be placed on the free interplay of market forces.

The policies of the EC are very important in the Irish context. Intervention purchases in Ireland amounted to 126,000 tonnes in 1986, 98,000 tonnes in 1987, 56,000 tonnes in 1988 and 77,000 tonnes in 1989. Transfer payments from Brussels to Irish beef processors amounted to over £230 million in 1987. In future the reduction of intervention in all support systems will necessitate a greater emphasis on marketing and the Irish beef industry will move further away from speculative commodity trading and concentrate more on continuous business with retail outlets. Also, the new measures are likely to see the EC beef market coming into balance for the first time in several years with a consequent firming-up of beef prices over the next couple of years. This price trend will suit producers and also put the onus on beef processors both to secure raw material supply and add further value to the product.

PROCESSOR PROFILE

The processing of beef for export is dominated by one company—Goodman International. There are about 20 other substantial companies involved in the trade. The business environment is extremely aggressive and notoriously secretive in relation to any kind of commercial disclosure. Beef processing, especially at the primary stage, is a tight margin business; efficiency is paramount. Given the erratic nature of the business and the difficulty in maintaining stable patterns of profit performance, beef processing companies frequently run into trading difficulties. Such distressed companies provide acquisition opportunities for other players keen to pick up extra capacity at attractive prices. In this situation, it is very hard to make accurate judgments as to how much of the industry is controlled by particular companies. Table 4 is an estimate of shares of the export beef processing trade in 1988.

Goodman International operates nine plants in the Republic of Ireland as well as several in Northern Ireland and Britain. The company has been

Table 4

Processor Profile: Export Beef, 1988

Company	Head of Cattle	% of Total
Goodman International	500,000	42
Halal Meat Packers	190,000	16
Classic Meats	100,000	8
Hibernia Meats	60,000	5
Appletree Holdings	60,000	5
Liffey Meats	60,000	5
Kepak	50,000	4
Guinness (Meadow)	40,000	3
Kerry Group	35,000	3
Queally Group (Dawn Meats)	30,000	3
Other Processors	75,000	6
Total	1,200,000	100

highly acquisitive over the last number of years and has specialised in buying under-performing assets at modest valuations and converting them into efficient profit-generators. Goodman does business in vacuum-packed beef with several British supermarkets and is a major supplier of carcase and vacuum-packed product for Middle Eastern and North African markets. The company has annual sales of over £760 million.

The other major company in the Irish beef industry is Halal Meats. Halal, like Goodman, is a private company which is controlled by Sher Rafique, a Pakistani national with substantial food interests in Britain and Ireland. Halal deals almost exclusively in beef slaughtered according to the Muslim rite and sells most of its output to the ethnic Muslim market in Britain and continental Europe. Halal has currently five beef plants in the Republic and, like Goodman, has been in an expansionist mood of late. Halal's total sales from its Irish operations are estimated at about £320 million per year. Another large slice of the industry is controlled by Classic Meats, which operates four plants in the Republic of Ireland and one in Northern Ireland.

The remaining third of the Irish beef business is owned by a diverse collection of companies. The Kerry Group has been involved in beef since it purchased an 80 per cent holding in IMP in 1986. British company Appletree Holdings bought the Kildare Chilling Plant in 1987. Three important companies privately controlled by Irish entrepreneurs are Kepak, Hibernia and

Liffey. Kepak has its main beef plant about ten miles outside Dublin and also operates smalier beefburger and sheep meat plants. The company does significant business with the Irish retail trade. Hibernia Meats, based in County Kildare, has important supply contracts with French supermarkets. Liffey Meats is run by the Mallon family interests and processes beef and lamb at Ballyjamesduff, Co. Cavan.

Many of the primary processors are engaged in value-adding activities on the same sites where their slaughtering facilities are located. In some cases, downstream processing facilities are located in export-licensed plants away from the primary production sites. The Queally Group, through Dawn Meats, has a significant presence in the further processing sector; the group's total annual turnover, including all activities, is estimated at over £80 million.

In the future, a greater concentration in the structure of the primary beef processing industry is likely to take place, with the two dominant players in the industry likely to strengthen their position even more. However, some companies operate only in the secondary or further processing sector, buying in their raw materials from the slaughtering plants. Many of these operations are amongst the most profitable in the beef industry and are successfully pursuing niche marketing tactics. Rangeland meats, Barford and Rye Valley Foods are among the companies who have specialised in such added-value processing.

AGRA TRADING

Agra Trading was established in 1975 by its German owner, Friedhelm Danz. It is headquartered at Blackrock, Co. Dublin. Initially founded as a beef trading company, it subsequently acquired processing facilities in Antrim and Cork, and has cold storage and chilled distribution operations in Britain. The company employs 850 overall. Turnover on all its activities amounted to £150 million in 1988 with an estimated £3 million profit, making it the third largest meat company based in Ireland in revenue terms.

In March 1989, Agra Trading announced a project to produce consumer-packed steaks for the European market under a brand label 'Greenfields'. Using a new pioneering process, researched and developed by the company itself, the beef steaks would be specially tenderised and vacuum-packed in consumer portions to give a 21-day shelf-life as a fresh product. Supported by the IDA, the project would involve £150 million investment and would provide 600 jobs over the next five years. It was hailed as a strategic change in Irish agribusiness because Agra would be the first company in Europe to market such a branded and specially packaged fresh beef consumer product to the supermarkets of Europe. Making the formal announcement in the Industrial Development Authority head office, the Minister for Agriculture and Food said that while the proposed investment was a high-risk up-front investment, it would result in a total breakaway from commodity and intervention trading.

COMPANY HISTORY

Friedhelm Danz, married to an Irishwoman and living in Ireland for many years, had always seen Ireland as a land of opportunity in the beef industry. He had worked with a quiet confidence and firm determination over the fifteen years to build Agra Trading into a substantial meat company, poised for future expansion. Agra Trading started life as a meat trading company in Dublin. Sister trading companies were set up in Germany and the UK. In 1981, Autocarve in London was bought; then, five years later, John Wharton Meats in Kent. Both were trading firms. The activities of these trading companies encompassed sourcing beef product in Ireland, South America and Australia and selling it to the UK (for further processing and into catering) and to various markets in continental Europe, the Middle East and South Africa. In 1979, Agra purchased Abbey Meats at White Abbey in Antrim. It was the company's first foray into manufacturing. The plant was extensively furbished at the beginning of the 1980s at a cost of £10 million; originally designed for pork and beef, it was streamlined for beef only. It had a slaughtering capacity of 50,000 animals per year and a workforce of 200. Danz found the experience of refurbishment at White Abbey costly and ultimately unsatisfactory and determined that any further manufacturing operations would be started from scratch.

In 1984, Agra started to build another processing plant at Watergrasshill in County Cork. It was completed in 1987 after a capital investment totalling £10 million. It had a workforce of 220 and a kill capacity of 50,000 animals per year. The plant was built to a high level of technical sophistication in keeping with a company philosophy of continually seeking the highest possible standards and quality. The company also saw itself as a good corporate citizen and was committed to the preservation of the environment. Slaughtering and production areas at Watergrasshill were separate, but joined by a special cooling tunnel. The company spent £150,000 on an effluent treatment facility at the plant.

The third area of Agra activity was in chilled distribution and followed the purchase of UK company Tom Granby in 1988. This company had five UK depots at Sheffield, Luton, Bristol, Birmingham and Liverpool. Agra intended to become more active in the storage and distribution of temperature-sensitive goods in EC countries for processing, retail and catering markets. The company shared, along with all the other privately owned Irish meat firms, a reluctance to disclose any detailed financial data. Thus the precise breakdown of turnover between its trading, processing and distribution operations was not known. However, industry sources believed that the greater proportion of revenue came from the trading businesses with processing accounting for some £50 million.

'GREENFIELDS' PROJECT

In the latter part of the 1980s, Agra Trading began to research the possibility of producing a branded Irish consumer-ready beef product for the European market. The company examined a number of new packaging technologies being experimented with in a number of countries, particularly the US. At its R & D facility at Watergrasshill, it developed a new process for tenderising and specially packing consumer portions of beef steak which would enjoy an extended shelf-life of twenty-one days. By 1988, it was test-marketing the idea selectively in Germany among consumers in supermarket outlets. Using the services of a London-based advertising agency the company developed a marketing programme. 'Greenfields' was chosen as a brand name to exploit the image of Ireland as clean, green and lush. Initial results were very encouraging and the project gathered considerable momentum during 1988. In Newbridge, Co. Kildare, a factory formerly owned by Polaroid was bought with the intention of building a state-of-the-art secondary processing plant capable, in full operation, of producing 265 million Greenfields steaks per annum using the new tenderising and vacuum-packaging process. Given the scale of the project, the assistance of the IDA was sought and in March 1989 the ambitious plan was unveiled publicly.

The project would involve £150 million expenditure. Of this, £53 million would be set aside for marketing and advertising support for the brand. Seven million pounds would be earmarked for training and human resource development. The remaining £90 million would be divided between investment in fixed assets and working capital. IDA grant aid at the norm of 20 per cent on fixed assets was estimated at £7 million and the IDA, on behalf of the government, would be providing a further £3 million equity injection in preference shares as an indication of its confidence in the project. Much of the capital investment would be utilised in the development of the former Polaroid plant in Newbridge, where secondary processing to final product would be carried out. Investment in secondary processing of this nature is always costly. It was intended to provide 200 jobs at the end of the first year, with employment rising to 600 at the end of the subsequent four-year period. The primary processing plants at Watergrasshill and White Abbey would be responsible for the supply of quality boneless beef to the Newbridge plant.

The Greenfields brand provided a range of steaks which were cut and ready to cook. Each piece was individually vacuum-wrapped in special foil packs with the brand of Greenfields clearly marked. Each piece was tenderised and the shelf-life extended to three weeks without preservatives or additives. The product could be stored in a domestic refrigerator during this period and freezing was not necessary. Exhibit 1 provides an example of Greenfields packaging and advertising.

At the time of the project's formal launch, Greenfields was already selling in selected areas in Germany and plans had been made to extend European sales to Scandinavia, the Benelux group, Denmark and France by the end of the year. Italy, the UK and Spain were targeted for 1990. Along with its

Exhibit 1

Example of Greenfields Packaging and Advertising

German office, Agra was in the process of setting up small marketing offices in Denmark, France and the Netherlands. It was not planned to market the product on the home market, initially at least; this was because of its size and because Agra had no presence or established sales or distribution network in the country.

Agra's Greenfields project was acknowledged to have inherent risk. In an interview with *Business & Finance* magazine around the time of the launch, Friedhelm Danz was quoted: 'Eight out of ten brands fail and that is the risk we take. But we believe that we have a great chance of succeeding. We are first in the marketplace and we consider that the consumer benefits of our product are enormous. We recognise that the lead time for brand development is very long and we will support this development as is necessary. But nothing is sustainable forever at a loss. And if that situation arises, we will assess it then.' While no other European company had currently refined the product idea to the same stage of quality and consistency as Agra, its lead might be short-lived as competitors analyse, exploit and develop new technologies.

PROGRESS

As well as investing in technology and marketing, Agra Trading had also invested in its management resources. In early 1989, Kevin Kelly, former administrator of the PMPA insurance company and managing partner of Coopers & Lybrand, was appointed chief executive. Three other senior appointments of experienced personnel from outside the company were also made around this time to positions of executive director marketing, manufacturing (primary product) sales, and human resources. In general, the Greenfields project drew heavily on Agra's resources, both financial and human. The research, planning activities and scale of the project absorbed much of senior management's time. By the middle of 1989, the company had already invested over £3.5 million in the project in direct, out-of-pocket costs. If indirect costs in various areas such as research, production, technology and education were added to this figure, total investment to date tallied to a very much higher figure.

A number of industry commentators, while applauding the enthusiasm and priority given to the project by Agra, expressed reservations about the ambitious pace of progress and were of the view that a more cautious step-by-step approach might be better. In particular, they expressed doubt about Agra's hope that the Greenfields brand name would be established in European markets within three years; five to seven years was seen as more realistic. CBF—the Irish Livestock & Meat Board—was not formally involved or consulted on the project by Agra. The apparent reason for this was the composition of CBF's board, which included representatives of rival companies. In its concern for an adequate, all-year-round raw material supply to its primary processing plants, Agra worked with the Department of Agriculture; when it is considered that the steak portion of an animal accounts for only a very small part of the carcase, the need for and the logistics of an adequate raw material supply become all the more apparent.

As the company moved through 1989, its trading business was revealing a somewhat disappointing performance. It was experiencing particular problems with the APS scheme, where it had difficulty selling meat out of storage at the end of the period. It also lost a number of lucrative third country markets to other Irish meat companies. Furthermore, the company was having trouble with its White Abbey plant in Antrim. The plant required substantial capital investment to meet current EC standards, despite the money spent on refurbishment in the early 1980s. It had been recording losses for a number of years.

In late September 1989, Agra's chief executive, Kevin Kelly, announced that the full implementation of the Greenfields project was being postponed by up to twelve months with the consequence that planned construction and recruitment at its Newbridge plant would be delayed until the middle of 1990. While the initial response to the product in Germany had been very encouraging, subsequent sales experience and consumer research feedback had convinced the company that a repositioning of the product with the consumer and a redesign of the packaging would be necessary before a full launch could take place in the remainder of European markets. A radical redesign of packaging was currently being undertaken by European experts and the subsequent testing of the new packaging and presentation would slow progress. In his statement, Mr Kelly said that to date no grants had been drawn down and Agra was keeping the IDA closely informed about developments. The company had also arranged discussions with community leaders in Newbridge. He remained confident that Europe's first branded consumer-packed steak would be a success. 'We are totally committed to this project and we know it will work. However, it has got to be delayed until we get the marketing and packaging right,' he added.

Questions
1. Describe the business system or value-added chain of the beef industry.
2. Assess the challenges facing the industry.
3. Explain why intervention is the negation of marketing.
4. Consider Agra Trading's venture into the value-added business.
5. Suggest the strategy you consider necessary for its future success.
6. What are the salient concerns a firm in the agribusiness industry should take on board before it moves downstream to develop a consumer product offering?

Colorcare

The developing and printing market for amateur photo film underwent significant upheaval in Ireland in the early 1980s. The growth of new channels of distribution allied to new technological developments resulted in dramatic changes in business practices and in the management of the marketing function amongst combatants in the industry. Against this background Cahill May Roberts, the country's largest pharmaceutical distributor, entered the developing and printing business for the first time in 1983 in a highly inventive fashion with its Colorcare service.

Issues: *Managing the marketing function in regard to product development, pricing, promotion and channel selection; in particular, how distribution channels not only evolve but can change dramatically, and the consequent reconfiguring of the marketing mix.*

MARKET BACKGROUND

The developing and printing (D & P) market for amateur photo film involves the processing of films shot for non-professional use, basically photographs taken on holidays, family occasions, special ceremonies or as a hobby. The retail value of this market was over £11 million in 1982, a sizeable market when one considered that the Irish consumer spent less than half that amount on either soap or shampoo. The country's 850,000 households owned 1.2 million cameras in 1982. While this figure was comparable to other European countries, the actual usage of these cameras in terms of film units processed was low at 2.5 million units.

Up to the mid-seventies the standard method for the consumer to get a film developed was to bring it to the local chemist or pharmacist who would in turn relay it to a film processing company for development and printing. This D & P side of his business was a profitable source of revenue to the chemist. There were approximately 1,200 pharmacies in the Republic, most run independently by owner-managers. In 1982 these pharmacists had a turnover of some £120 million, 70 per cent of which was from ethical medicine (i.e. in the form of prescriptions).

This case was developed as a basis for class discussion rather than to illustrate either effective or ineffective handling of an administrative situation.

During the 1970s there were over a dozen film processing firms providing a D & P service to chemist and specialist photography outlets. Amongst the biggest such companies were the following: Lyall Smith in Dublin; United Photo Finishers, also in Dublin; Spectra Laboratories in Listowel, Co. Kerry; North West Photos in Sligo; and McSweeneys in Cork. These D & P processors tended to be very regionalised in their operations reflecting the logistics of their collection and delivery service to pharmacies. They also tended to vary in the quality of product and service given to the pharmacist.

From the mid-seventies onwards the traditional hegemony of the chemist in the D & P business came increasingly under attack (see Table 1). Mail order was almost non-existent in 1975. Yet it had grown, particularly in the 1980s, to be an important competitor in the D & P business. The chief attraction of mail order to the film consumer was its low price, often up to half that charged by the traditional chemist or photo specialist outlet. The mail order firms were film processing companies which tried to eschew the middleman in all or part of their business and to appeal directly to the consumer. They advertised heavily in the popular newspapers and magazines, e.g. the *Sunday World*, using coupons and promotional devices such as free film to users. Companies such as Express Colour, Bonus Colour, Photo Lab, Perfect Colour, indeed a proliferation of such names, all offered to supply film processing at very low prices. Most of these companies were Northern Ireland/UK based. Spectra Laboratories was the only sizeable Irish competitor in the mail order D & P business.

One Hour Photo Labs were another recent and expanding phenomenon in the Irish D & P market. New technological developments meant that it had become an economic proposition to place processing equipment in an actual retail outlet on the high street and offer a rapid film processing service of one hour. Many consumers liked this quick turnaround service and were prepared to pay for it. One Hour Photo Labs/Express Service outlets generally priced at the top end of the market.

Because of the total market buoyancy between 1975 and 1982 the loss in market share experienced by the pharmacists was relatively painless in absolute volume terms. However, since 1981, the market had gone into decline because of the economic recession and further erosion of market share posed a serious threat to the chemist in a market area in which he had up to now dominated. In 1982 processors who serviced the traditional chemist trade (e.g. Lyall Smith), alarmed at the inroads being made by cheap mail order prices, initiated drastic price cuts and reduced profit margins of chemists in an attempt to become more price competitive. The mail order response was to cut prices even further and a virtual price war ensued. The pharmacist outlet suffered a drastic fall in profitability with no volume recompense being attained. On top of this, the arrival of the One Hour Photo shops at the premium-priced end of the spectrum now meant that the chemist was being squeezed at the two ends of a competitive stick—price and service.

Table 1

D & P Market, 1982 v. 1975

	1982			1975	
	Value £M	Volume M units	% Volume	Volume M units	% Volume
Pharmacists	7.7	1.6	65	1.7	87
Mail Order	2.1	.7	25	.1	5
Express Service	.7	.1	5	–	–
Specialist Shops	.7	.1	5	.2	8
	11.2	2.5	100	2.0	100

Source: Cahill May Roberts.

THE CAHILL MAY ROBERTS RESPONSE

Cahill May Roberts was Ireland's largest distributor and agent through pharmacy with some eighty years' involvement in the trade. With headquarters at Chapelizod, Co. Dublin, CMR had branches at Harmonstown, Co. Dublin, Carlow, Cavan, Cork, Limerick and Sligo. Its distribution network was capable of servicing pharmacists on a daily basis, meeting their requirements on a wide range of ethical and 'over-the-counter' (non-prescribed) drugs, personal care, baby and film products. CMR was also at the forefront in the development and exploitation of computer technology and systems which had provided pharmacists with significant benefits in stock control, ordering, invoicing and pricing.

The company monitored developments in the D & P market during the early eighties with much interest and not a little apprehension. There was concern that the firm's customers, the pharmacists, were losing out in the D & P business. There was concern that CMR was losing sales of film roll product through chemists. The idea began to take root that the company's distribution network might provide an opportunity for direct involvement in the business. During 1982 the sales and marketing director carried out extensive research on the structure of the market, on the success of mail order and potential processor/pharmacist responses, as well as examining how the company itself might enter the D & P business.

MAIL ORDER

Amateur film developing and printing lent itself ideally to mail order. The processor dealt directly with the customer and so could afford to offer lower prices. In the UK mail order was an important channel of distribution in the D & P business (see Table 2), as indeed was the case with many other products.

Table 2

D & P Market 1982, UK v. Ireland

	UK	Ireland
	% Volume	
Pharmacists	49	65
Mail Order	39	25
Express Service	6	5
Specialist Shops	6	5
	100	100

Source: CMR.

In Ireland mail order had not grown to any notable extent. Conservatism in purchasing habits as well as fear of delay and, more importantly, of loss of product in the postal service hindered expansion. Indeed the D & P market was possibly the only market sector where mail order had achieved a measure of success in Ireland. The government had recently announced plans to restructure the Irish postal service during 1983 as a semi-state body to be known as An Post. The aim was to make the service more efficient and to give it a greater level of customer orientation.

Cahill May Roberts' sales and marketing director felt that mail order had only one significant advantage—low prices. Customers disliked the lack of personal contact endemic in mail order, something which the pharmacist could offer, and they also feared the risk involved in sending films through the post. The company commissioned more thorough research on the attitudes of customers who regularly used chemists compared to those who regularly used mail order. A summary of the results is presented in Exhibit 1.

The initial reaction of the chemists and the processors who traditionally serviced them towards the new mail order competition was a promotional one: higher-profiled window advertisements, free film and so on. These actions appeared to have limited effect. Free film might marginally expand the total D & P market but it provided no guarantee that the recipient would

Exhibit 1

Consumer Attitudes in the D & P Market

Regular Chemist User ...

Likes: Convenience/Accessibility. Personal contact. Security.

Expects: Quality. Reasonable speed of turnaround—3/4 days. Reasonable pricing.

Dislikes: Too high pricing.

Regular Mail Order User ...

Likes: Low pricing.

Expects: Reasonable quality. Turnaround no more than 7/10 days.

Dislikes: Inconvenience. Insecurity. No personal contact.

---

continue to use the pharmacist. Inevitably the pharmacist had to offer the consumer a lower price, through both pharmacist and processor taking a reduction in profit margins. Table 3 illustrates typical D & P prices through pharmacies in 1981 and the level of reduced prices many pharmacists were offering during 1982.

There was little doubt that before pharmacists started to reduce their prices the price differential between themselves and mail order companies was so large that consumers in increasing numbers were prepared to accept the negative aspects of mail order. At the same time the consumer was prepared to pay a premium for personal service and security—attributes the pharmacies were perceived to have. The question was: how much of a premium?

To assess the price elasticity of the D & P chemist user was difficult given the shifting nature of market forces. One view in the trade was that if the pharmacist could capitalise on his unique assets and promote these to the consumer, he could command a very sizeable price premium over mail order. Others in the D & P business felt that the price sensitivity of the D & P consumer should not be underestimated. Whichever view was correct the price reduction tactics of the pharmacists during 1982 seemed to have limited success. They merely precipitated further reductions in mail order prices. The pharmacists saw no increase in their D & P business but merely a drastic reduction in the profit margins of existing business.

Table 3

Pharmacist's D & P Prices

	1982 £ Retail	1981 £ Retail
12 Exposures	2.75	4.00
24 Exposures	3.75	6.20
36 Exposures	4.75	8.00

COLORCARE

The decision to take an active participation in the D & P market was made by Cahill May Roberts only after much deliberation and planning. The objective was to develop a new business opportunity within the company's existing commercial framework and also to provide much-needed support to the customer that was CMR's lifeblood, the pharmacist. The intention was to stem, if not turn around, the drift towards mail order, reconsolidate the position of the pharmacist in the D & P business and re-establish attractive profit margins for the chemist on this business following the recent price discounting. The plan was to use the company's national distribution network—vans calling on a daily basis to pharmacists throughout the country—to provide a new national film processing service through pharmacy.

Given the large investment involved in setting up a film processing plant, and the excess capacity already present in the market, CMR decided it would market, organise and distribute the new service but that an existing processor would provide the processing facility. Lyall Smith Laboratories, the country's oldest and one of the largest processors, was selected. A product manager, reporting to the sales and marketing director, was appointed with specific responsibility to develop and nurture the project.

The new service would be designed to stress the key benefits pharmacy was seen to enjoy over mail order: convenience/accessibility; security/reliability; quality; and a comprehensive personal D & P service. The name Colorcare was selected as the brand name, the concept of security and quality being embodied in the name. (Interestingly, a short time afterwards the largest UK film processing company registered the name Colourcare.) The Colorcare national film processing service would be efficient, secure, value-for-money with high-quality photos and all-round ancillary service support. A 48-hour service time would be provided to the consumer.

Colorcare was priced mid-way between existing price structures (see Table 4). It was hoped that this price level would receive the support of both consumer and pharmacist necessary to reverse the market swing to mail order. The Colorcare price philosophy could be stated as a quality branded D & P service through pharmacy at a fair, value-for-money price (see Table 5).

Table 4

Colorcare Price Positioning
(based on 24 exposures)

Mail Order (Mainstream)	Colorcare	Express or Full Price
£3.00–£3.50	£4.95	£6.20–£6.80

An advertising campaign using primarily radio and television was devised with a planned expenditure of over £60,000. The theme was that important memories such as weddings, holidays, special days and so on, needed the security and attention available only from Colorcare through pharmacies. Silver had been selected as the brand colour for point-of-sale and packaging materials. A full range of colourful high-quality back-up display material, e.g. window and counter signs, 'floppies' and so on, were provided to identify Colorcare pharmacies. A distinctive Colorcare photo wallet was also used. See Exhibit 2.

The Colorcare national film processing service was formally launched at a reception on 1st February, 1983. As a new product launch by a major company it received coverage in all national and trade publications. A company 'roadshow' travelled to major centres throughout the country to present the new service to pharmacists, using audio-visual methods and presentations by senior company executives. Pharmacists from the surrounding region were invited to attend, and food and drink were served afterwards. Following the presentations the CMR salesforce then visited individual pharmacies to sign up dealers for the new service. This was aided by the fact that Lyall Smith had agreed to convert all of its existing pharmacy dealers to the new brand. This latter dealer base numbered some 300 pharmacies.

Table 5

Colorcare Prices

12/15 Disc Exposures	£3.85
20/24 Exposures	£4.95
36 Exposures	£5.75

THE CAMPAIGN

The initial months of the campaign were very encouraging. The concept was well received by pharmacist and consumer alike. A steadily growing chemist dealer base augured well for the campaign. However, before long a number of new factors began to emerge that put serious obstacles in front of the development of Colorcare.

Exhibit 2

Example of Colorcare Merchandising

Some months after the launch of Colorcare the country's other main pharmaceutical wholesaler/distributor, United Drug, entered the market with a similar type of film processing service. This service offered a lower price to the consumer and had the added benefit of providing larger than normal, so-called Jumbo, prints. This led to divided loyalties amongst pharmacists and tended to fragment the market. In addition to this a phenomenon that had first emerged a year earlier began to gain rapid momentum. This was the entry into the market of newsagents and other non-traditional outlets, which used low prices and free films as their main marketing tools. The combined effect of these two factors resulted in the campaign's falling short of its projected targets during the first six months.

A company review of progress to date resulted in a modest reduction in prices of the service and in discontinuing further radio and television advertising. These actions had limited effect and by autumn, at the end of the summer holiday season, the project was appreciably behind schedule. As a result of a number of years of poor trading performance, Lyall Smith, the laboratory contracted to handle Colorcare processing, ceased trading. In the time taken to arrange alternative processing facilities, a considerable number of customers transferred to other laboratories. The service continued to operate throughout the winter of 1983/84 in a diminished form. However, the level of market confidence in the service, the size of dealer base, and CMR's nurturing of potential pharmacist outlets had eroded compared to the initial stages of the campaign.

REAPPRAISAL

Despite these setbacks CMR's sales and marketing director remained convinced of the essential validity of the Colorcare concept. He felt that a revamping of the campaign to reflect the new competitive circumstances would see the project achieving its original objectives. A new product manager, Jim Quinn, was appointed in early spring 1984 to help execute this task. Quinn had considerable experience in the Irish D & P market, initially in production and then in administration and marketing. This experience extended through the traditional processor/pharmacist D & P service, to mail order and the newer areas of D & P retailing such as newsagents.

Indeed it was Quinn who had pioneered this latter channel of distribution. A couple of years before joining CMR, he had identified the suitability of prominently situated newsagents as D & P retailers. The advantages that these outlets had to offer included: prominent locations; high customer throughput; long opening hours; and a willingness to engage in promotions, such as free film, competitions and so on. These newsagents were able to provide the D & P consumer's need for personal service at very competitive prices. Immediately prior to undertaking the Colorcare role Quinn was engaged almost totally in identifying and recruiting newsagents as dealers for another film processing laboratory.

Quinn joined CMR in the belief that Colorcare could work successfully and that the company could expand its D & P business. He knew he faced key decisions about price, promotion and developing the dealer base of the service. Colorcare stressed the national nature of its service and that its pricing and promotional arrangements were the same countrywide. Quinn wondered if the campaign should not adopt a more regionalised approach in aspects of its operation to accommodate the local sensitivities of consumer, pharmacist and processor. The new product manager felt the key to success lay with the pharmacist, in motivating him and getting his full support in all aspects of the campaign.

He had also to ensure that any new film processor used by CMR in its Colorcare D & P service would be able to provide a continuing high level of service and print quality. There was at present highly intensive competition between film processors. In early 1984 there were eight Irish-based processing companies left in the business following the market upheaval of the previous few years. It was rumoured that more might 'go to the wall' during the coming year. One processor, Spectra Laboratories, had established a clear market dominance (see Exhibit 3). In addition, the structure of the D & P market had changed over the last couple of years (Table 6).

Exhibit 3

Spectra Laboratories' Profile

This company was the brainchild of its present dynamic managing director, Xavier McAuliffe. Founded from a shed behind his Listowel, Co. Kerry, home to develop black-and-white films in 1970, it grew rapidly during the seventies to become Ireland's largest and most modern film processing company and biggest mail order colour processing firm. In 1983 Spectra processed for its mail order and pharmacist customers over three quarters of a million film rolls and enjoyed a turnover of £4.8 million, 30 per cent of it generated from Northern Ireland and Britain. In an industry currently characterised by cut-throat pricing and at times below production cost selling, McAuliffe had demonstrated a single-mindedness of purpose. 'My competitors still say I'm mad to operate from Listowel, yet I'm the biggest in the country and the most successful so I must be doing something right. If you give a consistently good service to customers, it really makes no difference where you are.'

Source: *The Irish Times*, 2nd October, 1984.

Table 6

Irish D & P Market, 1982–1984

	1984 % Volume	1982 % Volume
Pharmacists	45	65
Mail Order	30	25
Express Service	10	5
Specialist Shops	5	5
Newsagents	10	–
	100	100

Source: CMR.

Questions
1. Assess the salient features of the launch of Colorcare.
2. Do you share the belief of the new product manager, appointed in spring 1984, that Colorcare could work successfully? What key decisions does he have to make?
3. Do you see evidence from the case of a marketing manager analysing, deciding, implementing and sustaining?
4. What do you think about the growth of mail order as a channel of distribution in the D & P industry?

Part II

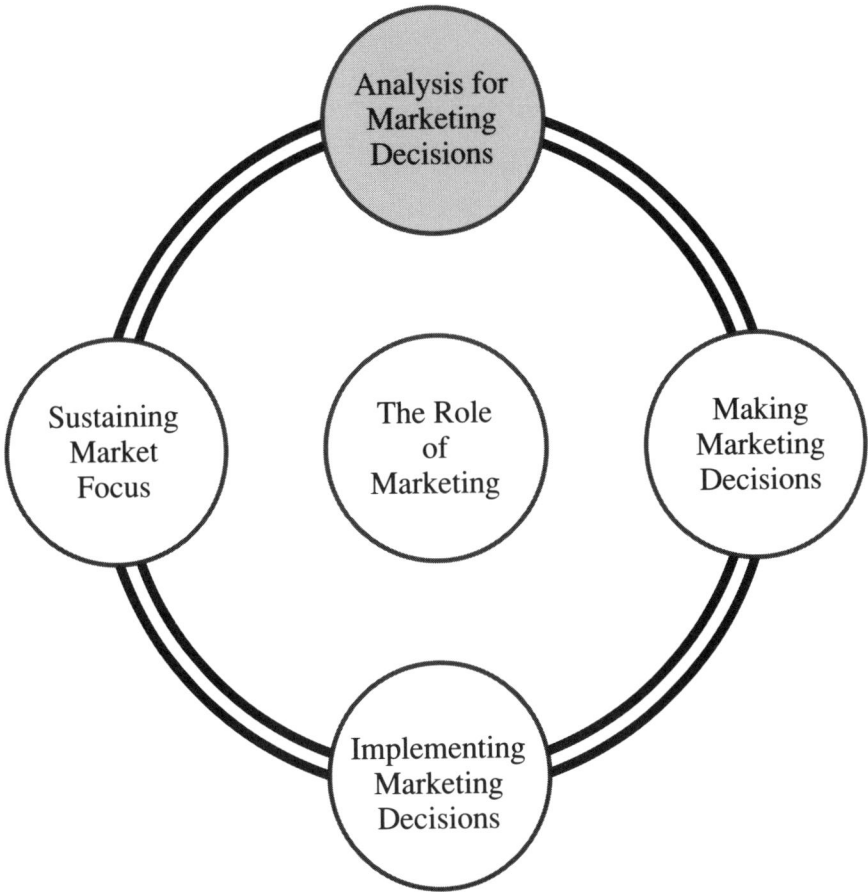

Analysis for Marketing Decisions

Sustaining Market Focus

The Role of Marketing

Making Marketing Decisions

Implementing Marketing Decisions

Chapter 4

Customer Analysis

INTRODUCTION

The process of customer analysis focuses on understanding people and organisations in need of services or products. It is concerned with what exactly their need is and with why, where and how they wish to acquire and consume. At least a basic understanding of all these factors is necessary if good marketing decisions are to be made.

The approach to customer analysis documented in this chapter is a relatively simple and general one which nonetheless demands that the manager confront the critical questions outlined above. It has the advantage of being readily applied to both business-to-business customer relationships and to final customer analysis. The approach may be applied at a judgmental level—by the manager or student using their experience of a market to supply the required information—or it may be used as a basis for identifying the questions which should be explored in a detailed and formal marketing research study.

CONCEPTS OF CUSTOMER BEHAVIOUR

The decades of the sixties and seventies saw enormous growth in the development of theory about the behaviour of consumers in the marketplace and about the nature of buying behaviour between organisations. Most of the work followed from the rapid diffusion into marketing of knowledge from areas such as psychology, social psychology, sociology and cultural anthropology.

The results therefore rested significantly on intellectual borrowing from these areas. Not only concepts but also research techniques and approaches to the measurement of behaviour were borrowed and applied. Marketing and its research base gained greatly from the process. However, by the end of the seventies the limitations of many of the more general models and constructs that had been developed became clear. Managers in particular had become somewhat sceptical of the immediate value of the general models in explaining and predicting the behaviour of the customers with whom they dealt on a daily basis.

Exhibit 4.1

UNDERSTANDING THE CONSUMER ...

'To buy or not to buy, that is the question!'

In Ireland the consumer still retains an identity of his own in many important respects. His assimilation into some amorphous mid-Atlantic culture is a prospect he continues to resist. His conservatism, both religious and moral, his traditionalism in family roles, his aspiration to a more simplified lifestyle, his espoused patriotism, his acquiescence in the marked dichotomy between what he says and what he does, endearing to the tourist, frustrating to the market researcher—all support the contention that it is still valid to consider the Irish consumer *precisely as Irish*.

In Germany economic development has stemmed from the milieu of the craftsman with his emphasis on quality, efficiency and regulation, and of the farmer. This has led firms to approach marketing in a relatively robust and selective manner. Consumer behaviour is achievement-oriented, and both particular social position and the self-esteem of the person are emphasised and underlined by consumer and behaviour habits. Upwardly ambitious social patterns are to be observed. Thus an important marketing approach is *niche marketing*, the addressing of highly differentiated target groups.

In Japan industrial development was led by the nobility, whose manner of behaviour had been stamped for centuries by cultural refinement. This basic principle was also carried into economic behaviour. Japanese consumer behaviour is characterised by a very high degree of sensitivity—a culture particularly attuned to 'weak signals'. In Japan it is not permissible to display personal wealth by demonstrative consumption, and the constant requirements of harmony in society lead to a situation in which it is more important for consumers to be part of this society than to mark themselves off from it by conspicuous behaviour. Thus Japanese marketing is strongly *mass marketing* oriented, which does not differentiate according to individual target groups and which uses the media of mass communication extensively.

Source: abstracted from D. Turley, 'Some perspectives on the Irish consumer' and H.G. Meissner, 'A structural comparison of Japanese and German marketing strategies', *Irish Marketing Review*, vol. 1, 1986.

The classical 'general' models (Nicosia, 1966; Engel et al., 1968; Howard and Sheth, 1969 in consumer behaviour and Webster and Wind, 1972; Sheth, 1973; Hakansson, 1982 in organisational buying behaviour) are all based on an assumption of a rational and very involved customer who acquires and uses information carefully. The criticisms of these models during the eighties revolved about the lack of evidence in reality for such a degree of rationality and for all but a relatively few purchase situations being characterised by very high customer involvement. The result has been the recognition of a much wider variety of consumer and organisational decision-making modes and the development of more context-bound explanations—the implication being that it is important to understand the particular circumstances and type of purchase situation involved if we are to explain behaviour successfully.

A central theme in almost all the general models of both consumer and organisational buying behaviour is the belief that customers proceed through some sequential process in arriving at a decision to purchase and use a product or service. For purposes of exposition we will use such a *decision process framework* in this chapter while reminding the reader that decision processes will vary greatly in their nature depending on the person, organisation and market context involved. It must also be remembered that the way in which purchase decisions are made is fundamentally influenced by the inherent characteristics of the people involved, their experience, and the social, organisational and marketing context within which decisions are made.

Buyer behaviour as a decision process

Customer behaviour may be interpreted as a decision-making process which starts with the recognition of a consumption need and ends with the learning involved in consuming the product or service purchased to satisfy that need. This process is visualised in Figure 4.1.

NEED RECOGNITION

Two important issues are raised by attempting to understand how customers come to recognise a need. The first brings us back in a very practical way to the definitional distinction we made between needs and wants in Chapter 1. The second focuses our attention on the setting or context of this stage in the buying process.

You will remember that we distinguished between needs and wants on the basis that needs are underlying and relatively unchanging factors whereas wants are the manifestations of those underlying needs and are shaped by culture, the personality of the individual, the fashion of the day, and by many other factors which ensure that wants are in continuous flux. In understanding how a need is recognised a marketer is well advised to consider both these factors. For example, the underlying and persisting human need for entertainment leads to endless fluctuation in the way in which this is expressed in the form of specific wants. Through most of the seventies and eighties cinemas declined radically as a form of entertainment service as individuals expressed

Figure 4.1

Customer Decision Process

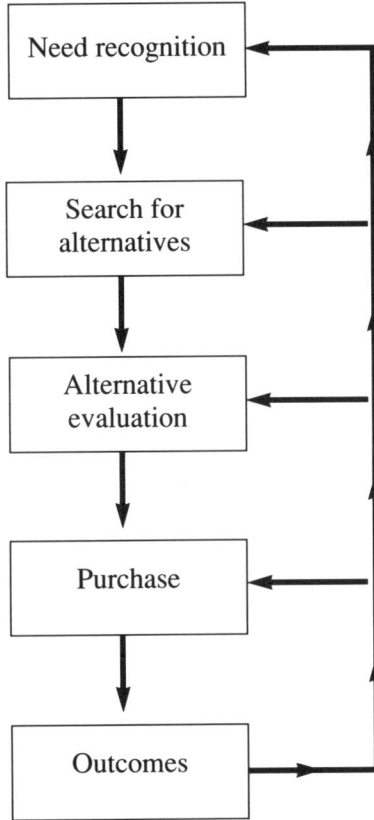

```
┌─────────────────────┐
│  Need recognition   │◄──────────┐
└─────────────────────┘           │
           │                      │
           ▼                      │
┌─────────────────────┐           │
│    Search for       │◄──────────┤
│    alternatives     │           │
└─────────────────────┘           │
           │                      │
           ▼                      │
┌─────────────────────┐           │
│    Alternative      │◄──────────┤
│    evaluation       │           │
└─────────────────────┘           │
           │                      │
           ▼                      │
┌─────────────────────┐           │
│     Purchase        │◄──────────┤
└─────────────────────┘           │
           │                      │
           ▼                      │
┌─────────────────────┐           │
│     Outcomes        │───────────┘
└─────────────────────┘
```

their wants in the form of television viewing and later in video rental. However, one of the very elemental aspects of the need for entertainment of this form—leaving the home for a 'night out'—was never addressed by television and video. By the start of the nineties a new generation of cinema services had begun to develop which not only delivered satisfaction in terms of 'an evening out' but had also incorporated many other relevant benefits missing in the old cinema—wide choice of programmes under one roof in multiscreen complexes, greater locational and parking convenience for a mobile population, higher standards of physical comfort as well as the enhanced technical quality of film, projection and sound. Marketers who focus too narrowly on wants are likely to suffer inevitable decline in their businesses as the market continues with its unceasing reinterpretation and re-expression of its basic needs. Identifying and understanding the underlying need is therefore the first critical step in analysis.

The manager must also identify the circumstances under which a need for his type of product or service is recognised. A manufacturer of office chairs will find that exploring this issue generates several alternative buyer 'scenarios' with far-reaching influences on marketing strategy. The need for office chairs may arise when:

(a) an owner/tenant moves into new office space;
(b) a user expands and needs additional chairs;
(c) old furniture has to be replaced.

The specific need recognised will vary depending on the use to which the chairs will be put; for example, in most office buildings one will find: (1) workstation chairs; (2) chairs for use by those working at desks; (3) chairs unique to senior management offices; (4) chairs in the boardroom; (5) chairs in a reception/visitors' area. Taking just these two sets of variables (need and use), we can visualise a simple matrix of need-recognition scenarios as shown in Figure 4.2. In the case of the 'new office occasion' the customer is likely to want chairs of all types and will probably find it most satisfactory to deal with a supplier carrying a full range rather than with many individual specialist suppliers. On the other two occasions the specialist supplier may be more relevant to the need recognised.

Figure 4.2

Analysing Need Recognition

Type of chair	Occasion of need		
	New office	Expansion	Replacement
Workstation			
General desk use			
Senior management			
Boardroom			
Visitors'			

However, this only probes the surface of the process of need recognition. The nature of the potential buyer will also affect the perception of the need, as will the specific persons involved in the process. We can therefore take any one cell in Figure 4.2 and explode it using these two additional sets of variables as shown in Figure 4.3. It is immediately obvious that the customer purchase behaviour will be quite different for the two 'exploded' areas of need. In the case of the workstation chairs, the need will normally arise as part of a complete package of seating needs, and the customer is most likely to be interested in a package solution that includes such chairs. Indeed, the small business customer may not distinguish between workstation and general purpose chairs and may simply identify a need for as many standard chairs as there are people to be seated. Large businesses and government buyers may recognise the need for added support, flexibility and mobility in workstation chairs and consequently request a specialist chair.

Who will be involved in recognising the need is also of primary importance to the marketer. In the case of the new office building, architects and interior designers may well be involved in specifying an aesthetic dimension of need—certain kinds of materials, fabrics, colours, or perhaps a need to have all furniture coordinated on those dimensions. In the replacement case, such persons are unlikely to be involved, and the immediate user of the chair may have much more influence, subject to budget constraints set by financial management and experience with the product to be replaced.

Generalising from this illustration, it may be stated that need recognition arises when the customer's perception of the actual state of affairs diverges sufficiently from their ideal state to motivate action. Action is therefore triggered either by changing concepts of what is ideal or by dissatisfaction with actual circumstances. In a traditional Maslovian hierarchy, the ideals we seek in consuming products and services range from those driven by the very basic motivations to avoid hunger and thirst and to be safe and loved to those driven by our needs for respect, status and self-actualisation. Marketing action can trigger these motivations and the consequent recognition of a need in many ways, varying from the smell of freshly ground coffee escaping onto Grafton Street from Bewley's Café to an advertisement for yoga classes containing promises of greater self-awareness and inner peace.

Implications

Analysing the process by which customers recognise consumption needs and wants allows the marketer to identify:

(1) the critical difference between the underlying need, which is likely to create a demand for economic goods and services over the very long run, and the want, which may be no more than a temporary expression of that need. The strategically healthy business focuses

on this underlying need and responds to changing wants with the introduction and deletion of individual services and products;
(2) when, where and how the need arises;
(3) who recognises the need.

Figure 4.3

Analysing Needs in Detail

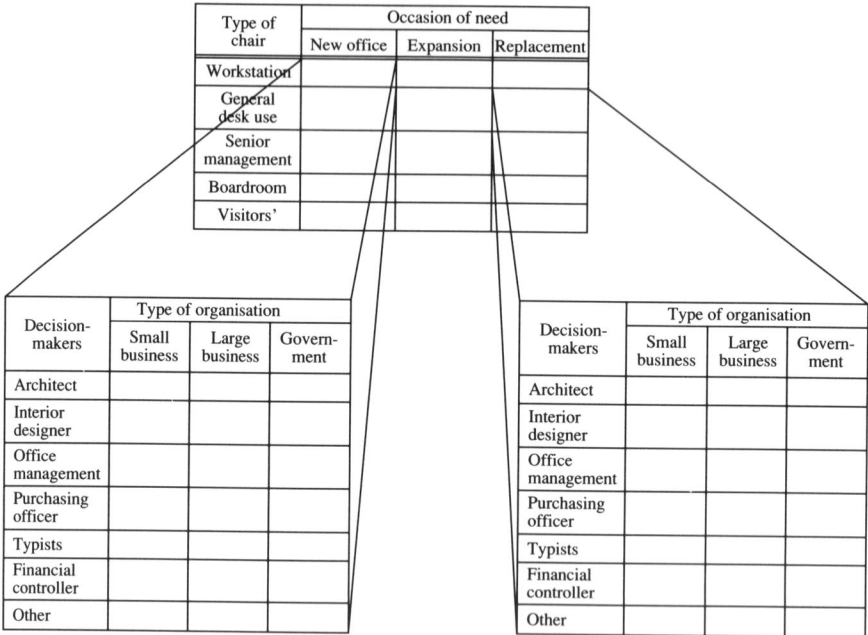

Type of chair	Occasion of need		
	New office	Expansion	Replacement
Workstation			
General desk use			
Senior management			
Boardroom			
Visitors'			

Decision-makers	Type of organisation		
	Small business	Large business	Govern-ment
Architect			
Interior designer			
Office management			
Purchasing officer			
Typists			
Financial controller			
Other			

Decision-makers	Type of organisation		
	Small business	Large business	Govern-ment
Architect			
Interior designer			
Office management			
Purchasing officer			
Typists			
Financial controller			
Other			

Knowledge of these factors is fundamental to decision-making in marketing because of its implications for segmentation and the choice of target markets, the positioning of the product or service relative to competition, the design of the marketing mix, and the timing of marketing effort.

SEARCH FOR ALTERNATIVES

Depending on the nature of the need recognised, search may or may not occur, or may be extended or very limited in duration and scope. In many brand-loyal, routine or low-commitment purchases, search behaviour is minimal. However, as one considers larger-scale and less frequent purchases the benefits to the customer of searching for alternatives and for information rapidly outweighs the costs.

It is therefore important to recognise that there is a continuum of purchase situations. At one extreme we find the slow careful approach to a major, infrequent and risky purchase. At the other extreme we find the virtually instantaneous, non-analytical decision about a routine, low-risk, incidental purchase. This continuum is suggested in Figure 4.4.

Figure 4.4

A Continuum of Purchase Possibilities

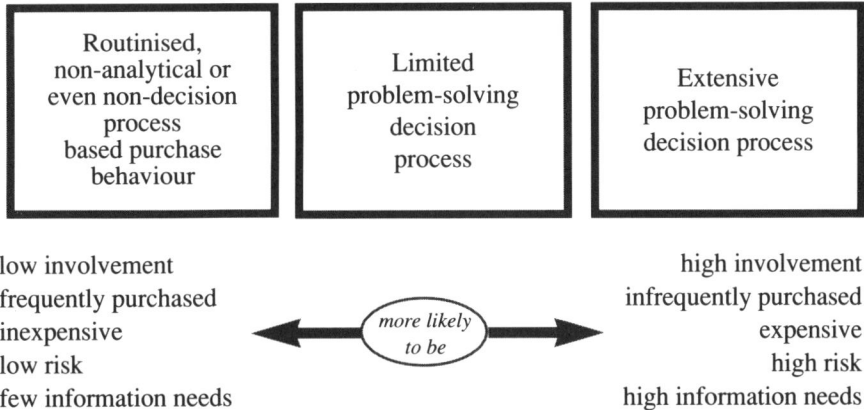

Routinised, non-analytical or even non-decision process based purchase behaviour	Limited problem-solving decision process	Extensive problem-solving decision process

low involvement	high involvement
frequently purchased	infrequently purchased
inexpensive	expensive
low risk	high risk
few information needs	high information needs

⟵ *more likely to be* ⟶

The search process has immense importance for the marketer because if his product is not included in the list of alternatives that results from search, and if appropriate information about it is not available to the searching consumer, then there is no opportunity to compete actively for the potential business.

Take, for example, the problem of marketing fish products for human consumption. Fish is one of several food alternatives that may be considered by someone preparing a meal or ordering food in a restaurant. One of the challenges in expanding the demand for fish is that it is not considered often enough in the search for alternatives by consumers: other sources of protein, and especially various meats, more usually constitute the list resulting from the search for alternatives. How does one increase the incidence of fish as an item on the roster of alternatives a person considers before shopping and preparing a meal? Search activity is strongly influenced by memory of past experience, and in Ireland this still associates fish with Friday. This is a long tradition which is difficult to change. In addition search is a means of reducing the risk involved in a purchase. For meat there is little perceived risk associated with cooking and freshness, while for fish the perceived risk on both counts can be high. Taken together, these factors traditionally resulted in Irish homemakers purchasing relatively little fish, and in consequence not accumulating enough experience and expertise on which to base confident inclusion of fish as a menu alternative beyond Friday meals. Understanding these factors helps the marketers of fish products to appreciate the nature of the barriers to increasing demand. It provides the framework to identify mechanisms that might be employed in influencing search behaviour so that fish and relevant information about it at least enters the menu or meal-preparation decision process.

The extent of search behaviour undertaken reflects a trade-off between the costs of searching for alternatives, and information about them, and the benefits of doing this. Benefits will be substantial if

(1) there is little past experience of the consumption problem (e.g. buying a house; buying new technology);
(2) memory of previous experience is poor;
(3) perceived risk is high (i.e. the cost of making a wrong decision is high for the customer, as is typically the case when the product is expensive relative to income or when it is 'socially visible' and could be regarded by others whom the buyer respects as ugly, inappropriate, gauche, etc.);
(4) confidence in one's ability to make a good decision is low.

One might expect search to increase confidence by lowering risk and generating more information. However, for some customers search results in information overload and reduced confidence. In consumer markets this can lead to a rejection of search activity and to a choice of brand leader products as the easiest way to allay lack of confidence. Equally, the highly confident consumer will often search extensively, happy in the knowledge that he can handle all the information and even derive some intrinsic satisfaction from the search process itself.

The costs of search are equally straightforward, although not always remembered by the marketer who provides too much, or inappropriate, information for the potential customer. Search will cost time. It may cost money through travel, telephone or mail inquiry. It may entail psychological discomforts because of frustration and tension generated through inadequate supplier response, poor handling of inquiries, travel and waiting for responses that turn out to be inadequate. It will often result in information overload because many companies insist on providing potential customers with information that is interesting to the company rather than information that is relevant to the customer's need—relevance means conciseness and focus on the very specific issues a customer needs at this stage in the decision process.

The marketer must also understand who it is that does the searching. This knowledge defines a critical target audience for any communication strategy. In the case of fish marketing, the housewife is a key target for the home consumption market, but in the institutional, catering and restaurant market it is a variety of persons—manager, chef, dietician, all with different interests ranging from economy and portion control to balanced diet.

If the information requirements and the person or group involved in search at this stage are known, then one may proceed to analyse the sources of information (1) to which they are exposed, (2) which they find credible, and (3) which are persuasive. Many, if not most, of the important sources judged on these three criteria are not marketer controlled in any direct sense and can be affected by the marketer only through satisfied customers who create favourable word-of-mouth recommendation for the product.

The many potential sources of information also vary in their importance or effectiveness depending on the reason for search. Thus it is generally the case that awareness of a new product—its inclusion in a list of alternatives for the first time—is best created by media advertising. Search for information about such products, and data on which to base evaluations, is, however, much more likely to be influenced by personal sources often beyond the direct influence of the marketer.

Implications
The power of brand loyalty and habitual purchasing processes is illustrated by an analysis of search behaviour in a market. For the newcomer to a market, or for a low market share competitor, it is a major challenge to find a way to become considered as an alternative, especially if it demands that the consumer engage in search activity which he would prefer to avoid.

Search clearly responds to perceived risk; and for products that are expensive or that have significant implications in use for the buyer, risk reduction strategies (e.g. allowing the customer to sample or try out the product before purchase or allowing the organisational buyer to visit a demonstration site where new technology is already being used by another company) are a key to effective marketing. Effective companies always seem to appreciate the cost of search for the customer and have the knack of providing just as much information as is needed and in the consumer's own language (e.g. in the energy market telling the customer how many pounds it costs to run an appliance such as a cooker rather than the cost of the energy input in pence per kilowatt hour or per therm).

EVALUATION OF ALTERNATIVES
When a potential customer has all the information considered necessary on alternatives, the next problem faced is how to evaluate them in order to make a choice. This stage in the process demands that we explore factors central to major marketing decisions, from segmentation and positioning to construction of the marketing mix.

The evaluation process is best understood theoretically from the perspective of information processing theory. An overwhelming feature of research on information processing behaviour is the evidence of its selectivity. Because of the almost infinite range and variety of information in the environment, the individual can cope only by being very selective in what is addressed, taken into account and used in decision-making. Identifying accurately, and influencing the nature of, the criteria a customer uses to evaluate and choose between alternatives is therefore of great importance, but by the same token quite difficult.

Thinking about criteria brings us back to one of the starting-points for thinking about marketing discussed in Part I. Evaluative criteria are usually best conceived of *as benefits* sought by customers from competing products or services. Customers do not buy replacement car tyres so much as they buy safety, conformity with the law, economy, quick fitting, a reputable brand, etc. The identification of such criteria which consumers will use in making their evaluations not only allows us to understand their decision-making but also makes it possible to segment the market in terms of customers requiring similar 'bundles' of benefits and to develop products that incorporate the identified 'bundles'.

Before considering the analytical procedures required to identify the customer's evaluative criteria, it is important to note that the marketer deals with a single decision-maker in only a minority of instances. It is much more usual for purchase decisions to be the outcome of joint decision-making by a group of people generally referred to as a Decision-Making Unit (DMU). In the case of a great many household purchases, it is a DMU that makes the decision—not the housewife. The housewife may act out the role of purchasing agent and therefore become the only member of the DMU to show up in a retail outlet. The unwary marketer will accept this as evidence that the purchaser is the decision-maker and will accordingly develop product design, distribution, pricing and communication strategies targeted at the housewife. The purchase of many brands of breakfast cereal or coffee, for example, are, however, fundamentally determined by the preferences and influence of family members who do not accompany the housewife on her supermarket shopping trip. The great danger of targeting industrial selling on the purchasing officer of a client firm is equally widely recognised by successful industrial marketers who know the reality of complex DMU structures in buying organisations that formulate a need, specify it, search out suppliers, evaluate their products or tenders, and make final decisions on placing orders (see Exhibit 4.2).

It is therefore important in analysing the evaluation stage to consider a two-dimensional framework such as that shown here for the purchase of a child's jeans (see Figure 4.5). The research that is typically undertaken to identify and measure evaluative criteria is based on two assumptions. First, customers' evaluations are made on the basis of multiple criteria, not just one, such as price or quality. Second, customers often allow poor performance by a product on one criterion to be compensated by strong performance on another.

Exhibit 4.2

REDLAND TILES

Advertising concrete roof tiles on TV

'You want to what?' the general manager of Clondalkin Concrete replied incredulously. 'Advertise roof tiles on television?'

His marketing manager had just presented him with a marketing plan for the company's range of Redland concrete tiles which involved a TV advertising campaign aimed at potential customers. 'I know Ireland has a high rate of house ownership. I know most of the houses are roofed with concrete tiles. But the people who live in the houses don't buy the tiles. A TV spend would be wasting money,' he argued.

But his marketing manager believed otherwise. He knew that any one, or a combination, of the following were responsible, with varying degrees of influence, for the final decision as to the purchase of roof tiles:

* *The Specifier*—included professional specifiers like architects, and semi-professionals like technical school teachers who acted as part-time or informal designers.
* *The Builder*—included contract builders of local authority housing, large speculative builders of private estates, and small builders of single or 'one-off' houses.
* *The Tile Contractor*—companies which provided an overall 'supply and fix' service on a sub-contract basis to larger builders.
* *The Merchant*—both builders' providers and small hauliers.
* *The Householder*—mainly of specially built 'one-off' private houses; but increasingly larger speculative builders were selling potential home-owners the attractions of certain roof tiles.

Further, at a more specific level, sales eventually materialised from one of three types of specification:

* *The Formal Specification*—this tended to be either for local authority housing where the roofs were low-pitched or for the architect-designed luxury end of the 'one-off' market. With a formal specification the order was as good as placed when the house was at the drawing-board stage.
* *A Loose Specification*—here the architect or designer still played an important role, but the final decision was made after consultation with the builder and others.
* *An Open Specification*—the choice of roof tile was left to the builder or client; the only part the architect played was in the original decision to design the roof suitable for the use of concrete roof tiles.

Research carried out by the marketing department of Clondalkin Concrete indicated that there had been significant shifts of emphasis within this purchase decision-making process, in particular in the bigger role householders—the ultimate users of the product—were playing. The marketing manager felt that TV would be the most suitable medium to reach this diverse group of influencers on the buying decision.

In the event he got his TV campaign. An advertisement was developed in cartoon form using Disney-type rooks who 'crowed' from their rooftop perches the benefits of Redland Tiles. It was run over a period of six months and, although expensive, played an instrumental role in increasing significantly the company's roof tile sales and market share.

Source: adapted from 'Redland Tiles (Irl), a case study', Irish Marketing Review Society, 1989.

Figure 4.5

Analysing Evaluative Criteria

DMU membership	Evaluation criteria for a child's jeans					
	Colour	Length of life	Style	Brand reputation	Fabric	Country of origin
Mother						
Father						
Teenager(s)						
Pre-teen child(ren)						

A customer's evaluation of the product alternatives open to him may therefore be visualised as based on (1) several criteria, (2) evaluations of the alternative products on each criterion, and (3) a final evaluation of a 'best' or 'worst' choice that reflects an adding up and comparison of the several evaluations per product.

A graphic representation of this measurement process helps to communicate its impact. The evaluative 'map' shown in Figure 4.6 reflects housewives' evaluations of four competing food items. Information of this nature is of considerable value in understanding how purchase decisions are made and in developing a suitable competitive strategy.

Figure 4.6

Evaluating Four Competing Food Alternatives

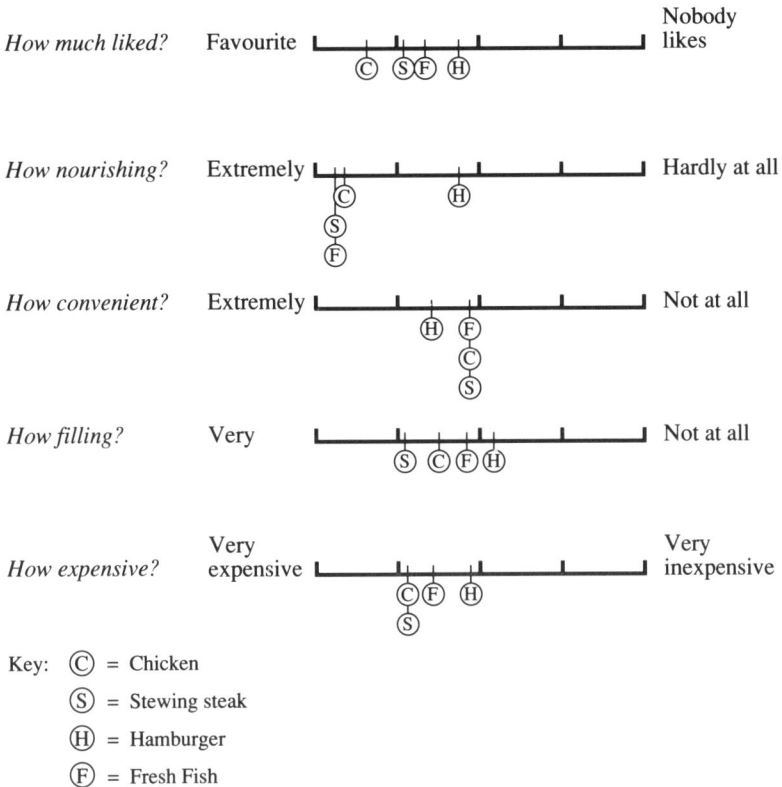

How much liked?   Favourite |————|—|——|—————| Nobody likes
                              Ⓒ ⓈⒻ Ⓗ

How nourishing?   Extremely |——|————|——|————| Hardly at all
                             Ⓒ   Ⓗ
                             Ⓢ
                             Ⓕ

How convenient?   Extremely |————|——|————| Not at all
                               Ⓗ Ⓕ
                               Ⓒ
                               Ⓢ

How filling?   Very |———|——|—|————| Not at all
                        Ⓢ ⒸⒻⒽ

How expensive?   Very expensive |———|—|—|————| Very inexpensive
                                  ⒸⒻ Ⓗ
                                  Ⓢ

Key: Ⓒ = Chicken
     Ⓢ = Stewing steak
     Ⓗ = Hamburger
     Ⓕ = Fresh Fish

Changing evaluations

Considerable marketing effort is devoted to changing customer evaluations of products and services. For example, many tourism service operators wished to change the evaluation of Ireland as an expensive holiday location which emerged in the mid-seventies. No amount of advertising and promotion aimed at creating a value-for-money image for Ireland could change customer evaluations until the relative cost of holidaying in Ireland rather than in alternative destinations was adjusted. Tourism marketing therefore had to influence (1) national economic policy to reduce the relative inflation rate and cost of living, and (2) individual tourism operators to deliver more cost-effective services and redress the value-for-money balance. By the nineties, considerable success had been achieved on both these fronts.

Reflecting on this experience it might be noted that the first action of the marketer must be to 'fix' the product if a problem exists and only then to address the task of communicating the change to potential customers. If a negative evaluation is based on misconception of the product's characteristics, then there is a legitimate communication task for the marketer to perform. However, such a task may be very difficult and lengthy if evaluations have been learned over a period of time or if customers do not have sufficient interest in the product category to rethink their evaluations. Faced with this challenge, many consumer goods companies will choose to relaunch a product rather than attempt to change attitudes towards its existing form.

Implications

A clear understanding of the evaluative criteria used by customers in choosing between the alternative products on offer to them is fundamental to effective marketing. Knowing the criteria, the customers' preferences and competitors' strengths and weaknesses on the criteria is a key to good marketing decisions.

Changing customer evaluations is a difficult but not impossible task provided that it is based on real product characteristics and performance rather than an attempt to disguise or misrepresent these. Strategies of change may focus on:

(1) changing the evaluations by means of better communication of the product's characteristics;
(2) changing the importance (weighting) customers attach to individual evaluative criteria—as, for example, when a tyre manufacturer shifts customer emphasis from purchase cost to life of tyre and therefore to cost in use, under which criterion a high-quality, well-designed tyre will far outperform a lesser-quality 'own-brand' type;
(3) changing the criteria themselves—as, for example, with the introduction of speed of service, convenience, standardised product and assured quality by major fast food outlets into the 'eating out' decision.

CHOICE

The choice stage in the customer decision process is of interest because it demands that we analyse issues such as:

* unplanned and impulse purchases;
* place of final choice and especially the importance of the retailing or selling environment.

Intentions versus unplanned outcomes

Even if we understand the customer decision process through the stage at which evaluations have been made, one can never be quite sure of predicting with complete accuracy the actual purchase that will be made. Why is this? The uncertainty arises from several sources. The customer may not be engaged in a high-commitment type of purchase, and therefore the decision process prior to moment of purchase will have been very short, cursory and unlikely to have resulted in strong preferences. Walking into a shop to buy sweets may reflect such a situation. The availability of individual products on the shelf and their presentation may well overturn any low-commitment intention to purchase a given brand of chocolate bar. Equally, the evaluation stage may result only in an intention to purchase a certain class of product—as, for example, where a customer intends to purchase a skirt rather than a dress and decides in-store which kind or brand of skirt to buy. Finally, even with a well-formed intention to purchase, the context in which purchasing takes place and the social pressure to behave one way rather than another may cause a contrary decision. So, for example, the approval or otherwise expressed to a potential buyer by a sales-person concerning a choice, or ideas of how the choice might be regarded by those whose opinion the customer values, may precipitate a change in intention. The marketer is well advised to understand not only the evaluations that are made concerning his product relative to competitors but also customers' intentions to purchase and how their intentions are affected by the retail and selling environment.

For low-commitment purchases—typically, low-cost consumables—it is also clear that the place of purchase, the availability, presentation, packaging and promotion of the product may be overwhelmingly important determinants of a sale: distribution and merchandising are the key marketing factors. Impulse purchases are an important component of consumer demand, and the marketer of consumer products must consider how much of his business comes from such behaviour and adapt practice accordingly. In addition, the creative marketer will search for the opportunity to expand demand for a product category by providing an innovative version of the product in a distribution channel that allows for impulse buying. This happened when watches and calculators were introduced to non-traditional outlets such as variety stores and discount stores.

The place of purchase

The marketer's choice of retail outlet and in-store presentation and merchandising is vital to the success of consumer products. Consideration of this factor demands that the marketer appreciate where the customer wishes to shop and purchase. The preferred context, presentation, merchandising, sales assistance and payment/delivery conditions of the customer must be explored and how these can be designed to yield a competitive advantage at point, and time, of sale.

Typically we think of the consumer's place of purchase as a retail outlet. Information technology makes in-home shopping a viable option for many consumers through systems that allow for video demonstration of products, and enable purchase, funds transfer and delivery arrangements to be made from uncomplicated consoles. As this trend in shopping behaviour evolves, innovative marketing companies will grasp it as an opportunity, while others will cling to traditional and declining retail channels, as has happened in previous retailing revolutions.

Implications

The context and process of final customer purchase must be understood to enable the marketer to:

(1) ensure that customers who plan to choose his product actually do so;
(2) maximise the number of unplanned purchases in his favour, and away from planned competitor purchases;
(3) maximise share of impulse buying.

These objectives are achieved through careful and creative choice of distribution channels and excellence in product presentation, merchandising, physical distribution and trade service.

USAGE: POST-PURCHASE BEHAVIOUR

A universal feature of market-focused companies that build their long-term development on responsiveness and service to customers is that the making of a sale is no more than a way-station on the long shared journey of customer and supplier. To the excellent company, what happens after the sale—how the customer receives the product, how it is used, its defects, the customer's suggestions for improvement—is at least as important as what happens up to and at the time of purchase.

It is in the process of usage that customer satisfaction is realised or not, and that brand or supplier loyalty is built. Customer satisfaction-in-use, and the servicing of his usage-related needs, are the keys to repeat purchases and to unsolicited recommendations to potential customers. These in turn are fundamental to long-term business survival and growth. In addition, many studies of successful innovation indicate that customers may be the most fruitful source of new product ideas developed through their usage of, and improvements on, currently available products. The careful management of the relationship between firm and customer, supplier and buyer, is vital both to product innovation and to long-term customer retention.

In consumer products, it is imperative to monitor satisfaction-in-use through consumer research and through discussion with members of the distribution channel. Advertising, promotional and public relations activity has a significant role in reassuring customers of the appropriateness of their decisions and in providing information on use and care of products.

In consumer durables, after-sales service is critical to ensure satisfaction-in-use, although an increasing number of durables manufacturers are competing by building in a degree of product reliability and quality that virtually removes the need for servicing. For many users of photocopiers, the single most important determinant of satisfaction is fast and reliable availability of a service technician when a machine breaks down.

In industrial products, the post-purchase stage is the key battleground between successful competitors. These companies prosper and grow on customer service and customer problem-solving. A small new venture such as Mincon Ltd of Shannon succeeded in the business of supplying specialist replacement parts for mining equipment in competition with major multinational suppliers on the basis of a competitive advantage built around its closeness to its customers, on-site servicing and assistance, short delivery time and reliability. Many large and successful companies owe their success primarily to working with the customer, seeing their role as one of customer problem-solving, and developing many of their best new products from placing prototypes with customers for testing and evaluation in use.

Implications

Companies which manage their marketing well know how their product is used by customers and innovate by improving performance-in-use or developing with the customer new ways of fulfilling a required product function. Marketing never ends with the conclusion of a sale—in many significant ways it only begins then. The post-purchase period is analysed to understand how to build customer loyalty, how to gain the support of opinion leaders, and how to encourage favourable word-of-mouth communication between prospective buyers. It is also a time when the marketer should attend to reducing any second thoughts or doubts in the customer's mind.

SUMMARY

The process through which a customer passes from recognition of an economic need to the consumption or use of the product or service chosen to satisfy this need is an integrative and insightful framework within which to analyse customer behaviour. Such an analysis demands answers to fundamental questions about the determinants of demand and competitive effectiveness:

—Who buys?
—What do they buy?

—Why do they buy?
—How do they buy?
—When do they buy?
—Where do they buy?

If a well-conducted analysis allows clear answers to these questions, the marketer has much of the basic knowledge required to make marketing decisions that are both relevant to the consumer and competitively effective.

Reading

Baker, Michael J. (1991), *Marketing—An Introductory Text*, 5th ed., Macmillan, Basingstoke, chs. 6, 7.

Engel, J.F., Blackwell, R.D. and Miniard, P.W. (1990), *Consumer Behavior*, 6th ed. (1st ed. published 1968), Dryden Press, Chicago.

Hakansson, H. (ed.) (1982), *International Marketing and Purchasing of Industrial Goods*, Wiley, NY.

Howard, J.A. and Sheth, J.N. (1969), *The Theory of Buyer Behavior*, Wiley, NY.

Kotler, P. (1991), *Marketing Management: Analysis, Planning, Implementation and Control*, 7th ed., Prentice-Hall, Englewood Cliffs, NJ, chs. 6, 7.

McDonald, M.H.B. (1984), *Marketing Plans: How to Prepare Them & How to Use Them*, Heinemann, London, ch. 4.

Nicosia, F.M. (1966), *Consumer Decision Processes*, Prentice-Hall, Englewood Cliffs, NJ.

Sheth, J.N. (1973), 'A model of industrial buyer behavior', *Journal of Marketing*, vol. 37, no. 4.

Turley, D. (1986), 'Some perspectives on the Irish consumer', *Irish Marketing Review*, vol. 1.

Webster, F. and Wind, Y. (1972), *Organisational Buyer Behavior*, Prentice-Hall, Englewood Cliffs, NJ.

Wilkie, W.L. (1986), *Consumer Behavior*, Wiley, NY.

Review Questions
1. What are the general decision-making steps through which a customer goes in deciding to buy and consume a product or service? Why is this decision-making process a useful framework for analysing customer behaviour?
2. Select any product you have purchased recently and analyse your own behaviour in terms of each of the five decision process steps discussed in this chapter.
3. Why is it important for the marketer to understand the criteria that are used by customers in evaluating the product alternatives open to them before they make a purchase?
4. Why is the post-purchase stage in the consumption process so important in the marketing of industrial products?

Chapter 5

Market Measurement and Forecasting

INTRODUCTION

In Chapter 4 we focused on the question of who buys what, when, where and why. The most fundamental step in marketing analysis is to understand the answers to these questions because they tell us what it is that the market needs. In this chapter we turn to the questions of how many? how often? and for how long? Needs must be quantified to indicate the current and future size of a market, so that decisions can be made about whether it is commercially feasible to serve it, and so as to understand whether the size of market and the size of a company's resources are compatible.

This chapter explores the various reasons that markets must be quantified and forecasts made and isolates the key measures of market demand that are essential to decision-making. The problem of setting boundaries on markets is discussed, and the objectives and methods of market forecasting are detailed. Sources of data on markets available to the Irish marketer are reviewed, along with basic methodological procedures in using these sources to produce valid measures of market size now and for the future.

WHY MEASURE AND FORECAST MARKET SIZE?

Market measurement is vitally necessary to understand how many customers there may be for a product or service, and how much and how often they consume, both at present and in the future. A knowledge of these facts is an essential basis for any economic analysis of market feasibility, production requirements and the strategic fit between market demand and company resources.

Many needs exist which are experienced by too few consumers, or too infrequently, to support a commercially viable enterprise. Many new ventures fail for just this reason. An entrepreneur, obsessed by an innovation, assumes there will be a market to buy it, and buy it in sufficiently large quantity to support the investment and operating overheads necessary to go into business. But conviction that there must be many customers just waiting for an entrepreneur's new brainchild is not enough: the reality of a viable number of customers willing to purchase the innovation must be verified before rational investment can take place.

The measurement process also indicates to a company something about the strategic fit between its resource size and the magnitude of the market. Small and medium-sized firms can seldom successfully address the needs of a large national or international market for a standardised product. Their resources are so limited that they can neither satisfy customers on quality and consistency of supply nor compete with large marketers on costs. More typically, they can compete very effectively in specialty markets, small markets and custom-built product-markets. A measure of the market therefore also gives this sense of strategic compatibility between customer needs and company resources.

Knowledge of market size, when related to company sales, yields one of the simplest but most important measures of marketing performance—market share. This measure is vital to any understanding of competitive performance. Indeed, without it, firms frequently reach quite dangerously misleading conclusions about their marketing performance. For example, a marketer of a laxative medicine whose sales were declining over the long term recently assumed that this reflected a decline in market demand. This assumption was rationalised on the grounds that improved diet and a more educated population made laxatives less necessary. A check on market size and trend, however, showed that the market was growing and that the company's brand was losing market share steadily. Here is one of the greatest traps into which a marketer can walk. If total market size and trend is unknown, there is no way of knowing whether an increase in sales represents good performance or not! An increase in sales less than the rate of increase in market size represents competitive loss and a threat to the company's future in the market. Yet how many companies regard an increase in sales as a cause for celebration while remaining quite ignorant of the total market situation? A simple growth-gain matrix such as that shown in Figure 5.1 is a useful mechanism for tracking this relationship.

One of the great weaknesses of sales-oriented companies is that they typically ignore total market and therefore market share measures. Increases or decreases in company sales are thus largely beyond interpretation. Does a sales gain reflect greater or perhaps lesser competitive effectiveness? Does a sales decline represent a loss of competitiveness or perhaps an increased share of a market that is contracting faster than the company's sales? Without a good estimate of market size and trend, a marketing manager is flying blind.

KEY MEASURES
Markets can be measured in many ways and with great sophistication. Nevertheless, a relatively few basic measures provide the manager with most of the information needed for good decision-making.

Figure 5.1

Growth-Gain Matrix

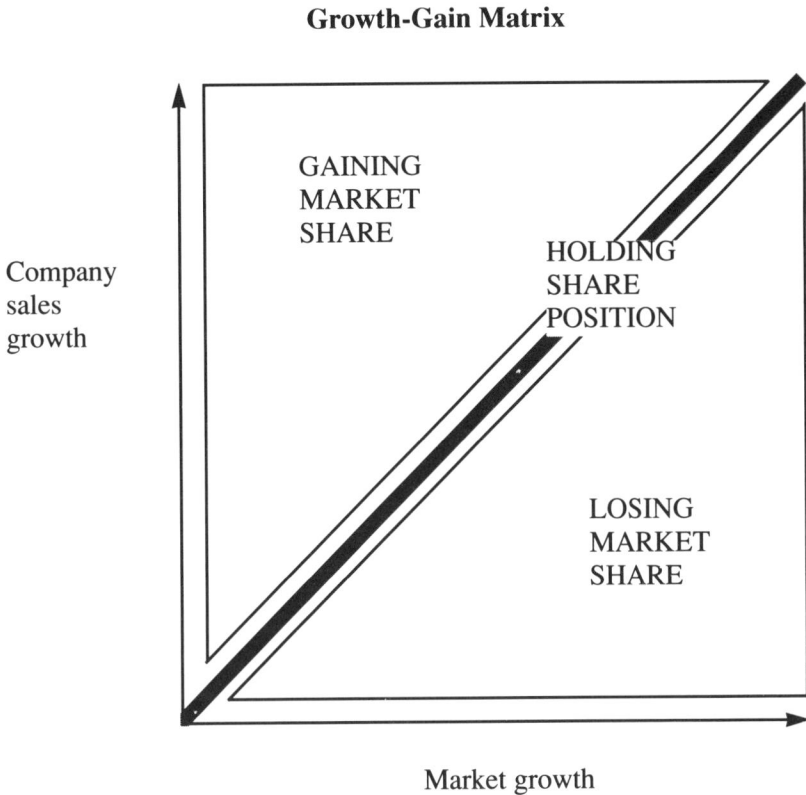

Market growth

The *size* of the market in value and volume terms is the most fundamental measurement requirement. Without this, one cannot evaluate the commercial feasibility of any project or new product and cannot evaluate the competitive performance of the company in the marketplace. Generally volume measures are the most useful ones, as they are unaffected by inflation or pricing and discounting variations. Great care must be exercised in using value measures because they are typically distorted by these same inflationary and pricing factors. When using value measures to track a market over time, it is therefore necessary as a minimum precaution to adjust them for inflation so that real growth or decline can be identified.

The *trend* in market size is the second essential measure as it tells us whether we are dealing with a growing, declining, stable or cyclical market. Which of these four kinds of markets represents the firm's environment has enormous implications. It tells us about the stage in the life cycle of the product-market and therefore about the kind of competitive conditions and customer behaviour we might expect, as well as suggesting strategies that are appropriate for the varying market conditions. The historical trend in the market also provides one basis for developing forecasts of future market size, although care must be exercised in a changing world in assuming that the future will reflect the past!

Market share has already been discussed and is the third basic and essential market-related measure. As noted, this provides the marketer with one of the most vital indicators of marketing effectiveness: 'Am I outperforming the competition or losing to them? How many customers prefer my product to my competitors?' Market share has additional strategic significance because, in many markets, share and profitability are directly linked: the bigger a company's share, the greater its return on investment. The work of the PIMS (Profit Impact of Market Strategy) programme working with 450 companies and as many as 3,000 business units since 1972 has produced consistent evidence of a strong relationship between market share and profitability. Buzzell and Gale (1987) indicate that companies ranking first in market share earn rates of return that are three times greater than businesses with a market share ranking of fifth place or less. It is noteworthy that research in the United States on the Federal Trade Commission's line-of-business data base also supports the argument for a strong positive relationship between pre-tax return on sales and absolute market share (Ravenscraft, 1983, pp. 22–31). The reasons for a strong relationship between share and profitability are not proven. Indeed, the direction of causality is open to debate—are profitable companies more likely to grow share or are high-share companies more profitable? However, the general explanations usually advanced for a relationship between share and profitability focus on the cost advantages of larger scale and greater experience compared to rival companies, and on the market power that large share often confers. Market power may be exercised in matters ranging from negotiating the price of raw materials to the imposition of terms and pricing guidelines among one's channels of distribution. Market share is not just important, therefore, to an understanding of competitive effectiveness, but is also vital to strategy formulation and the setting of objectives.

These three vital and necessary market measurements must be subject to one overall qualification: measures of size, trend and share at total market level are seldom adequate. What is necessary is these measures by *market segment*. A market segment is a sub-division of any total market where customers, while buying the same type of general product as any other customers in the total market, nevertheless buy it in a particular form or place or manner and use it in a particular way.

The market for natural gas in Ireland may be used as an illustration. Natural gas from the Kinsale gas field is distributed through town gas companies to many customers. They all purchase and consume natural gas, but the house-owner who makes a decision to install a natural gas cooker in his new house behaves very differently and buys very different product benefits than does a large glass-making factory that uses the same gas to fuel its furnaces. The house-owner market for natural gas for cooking and the industrial process-heating customer belong in two different market segments. One can readily appreciate how relatively meaningless it is for a gas marketing manager to know the size and trend of the market for gas—or, even more so, for energy—and the share that natural gas holds. Managerially he can understand his market, and develop his strategy, only when he has these measures for the main segments of demand. In marketing natural gas it is therefore necessary to measure the main segments of the market by principal energy applications as shown in Figure 5.2. For each cell in this matrix, measures of size, trend and share allow effective marketing strategy to be formulated.

Figure 5.2

A Segmentation Framework

Application segments	Customer segments		
	Residential	Commercial	Industrial
Space heating			
Process heating			
Cooking			
Central heating			
Water heating			

MARKET DEFINITION

The concept of a market is not as simple as it may appear at first glance. The importance of measuring market segments rather than total markets has already been illustrated. But how to draw a boundary on the total market and the market segments of relevance to a business can sometimes become difficult. Normally three levels of market can be isolated, as shown in Figure 5.3.

Creative marketing insights can be generated by thinking through the implications of defining a company's market at these various levels. A brand manager for an instant coffee brand can learn a great deal about the market and competitive environment by thinking about the position of his brand in a generic market for convenience beverages—not just coffee—where coffee must compete with products such as soft drinks, fruit juices, tea and other traditional and innovative beverages. Recent years have witnessed an interesting debate as to whether non-alcoholic beers such as 'Kaliber' or 'Buckler' serve the beer market or a completely different market traditionally supplied by soft drinks. Market definition therefore revolves about the concept of substitutability—the market consists of products, services and competitors which compete for the customer's attention and patronage. Generic definitions are useful for highlighting the extent to which customer needs may be satisfied by a wide variety of goods and services, while definitions around usage, application or functionality highlight the level at which competitors vie with one another to fulfil very detailed, transitory and specific wants.

Figure 5.3

Levels of Market Definition

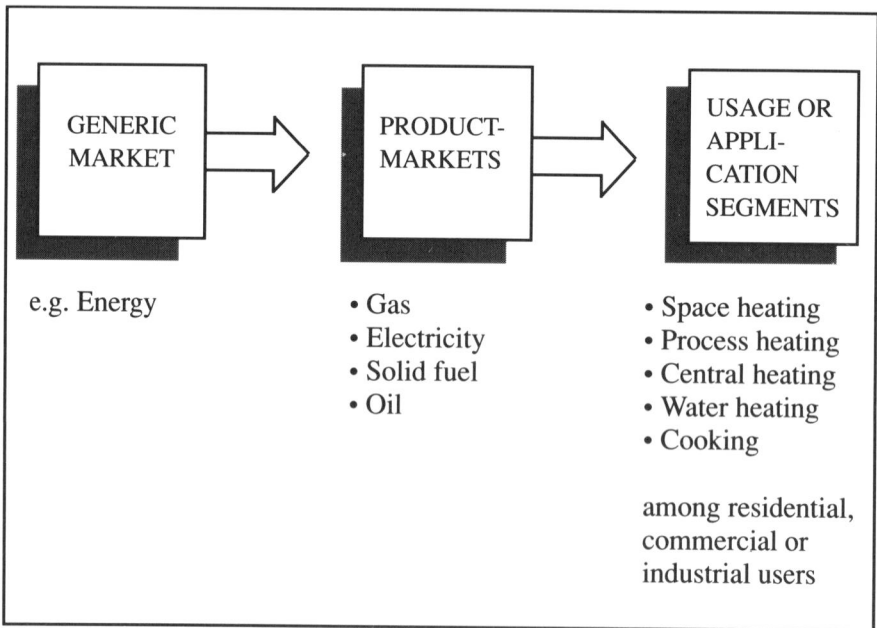

GENERIC MARKET	PRODUCT-MARKETS	USAGE OR APPLICATION SEGMENTS
e.g. Energy	• Gas • Electricity • Solid fuel • Oil	• Space heating • Process heating • Central heating • Water heating • Cooking among residential, commercial or industrial users

FORECASTING

As all marketing decisions commit company resources for the future, it is essential that the manager should have a reasonable estimate of where his market will go in that future time. Forecasting markets and competitive outcomes is a difficult task. The key market forecasts are of the same factors discussed under market measurement: size, trends and market shares. These measures, translated into sales forecasts, become the essential basic information for all financial project appraisal activities, ultimately translated into cash-flow forecasts and measures of financial payoff.

In addition to the key measures of market size, trend and share, marketing decisions generally demand forecasts concerning such important environmental factors as product technology, economic and political conditions, changes in retail structures and retail power, and so on. The market analyst therefore works towards detailed forecasts of products or service sales by starting with broad environmental measures (economic growth, personal income, demographic forecasts, for example), then moving to industry-level forecasts which focus on total demand and competitive factors, and finally narrowing in to company market share and sales volumes.

The information on which forecasts may be developed emerges from three sources (Kotler, 1991):

(1) what people say;
(2) what people do;
(3) what people have done.

The forecaster can ask people about the future: what they *say* becomes the basis of the forecast. People can be asked about the future in a variety of ways. A survey of buyer intentions collects customers' opinions about what they intend to purchase over a future period. A survey of salesforce estimates is frequently used where time is scarce and the cost of contacting final customers is substantial. Salespersons are asked to estimate how much each customer they call on is likely to buy and from what supplier over the forecast period. When these estimates are added up, and if the salesforce covers all or almost all of the buyers in the market, the resulting estimates of future market trends and market shares can be very accurate. Forecasts of this nature must be treated with some caution, of course, as there is an inherent tendency for sales personnel to be conservative about projections which may become the basis for their own sales targets and incentive payments. Expert opinion is sometimes consulted as a basis for making forecasts. Here experts who specialise in collecting information on a market and who continuously monitor trends are asked for their informed estimate of where the market is going and the relative success of competitors.

What people *do* may be monitored as in test-market exercises to assess how the market responds to products, services and various marketing programmes. Here closely observed behaviour in the market during a carefully designed test period is used to construct an estimate of future behaviour. The rapid development in retail markets of electronic point-of-sale technology is proving a major force for change in allowing companies to test products and services and to monitor virtually instantaneously their success or failure. Benetton's great success in the fashion clothing market is partly attributable to its investment in information technology which allows it to monitor sales as they take place in retail outlets across Europe and to adjust its production planning for different colours and fashions in response to emerging customer preferences. As a result, the company has a much lower incidence of unsaleable stock and sales of reduced price garments than the rest of the fashion clothing industry.

What people *have done* can provide information for both very dubious and very powerful forecasts of future market trends. What people have done, represented by historical figures for market size and market share, is most frequently translated into a vision of the future by extrapolation: for example, the average annual growth rate over the past five years becomes the projected growth rate for the next year. Extrapolation in all its more or less sophisticated forms must always be used in marketing decision-making with full appreciation of its underlying assumption: the future is a function of the past. Many, if not most, markets are, however, characterised by conditions of radical and rapid change. The past is seldom a good guide to the future.

A more valid use of historical data is embodied in the application of a variety of methods of statistical demand analysis which seek to identify the structure, correlates and driving forces underlying market demand. Knowing these basic determinants of demand, the manager is in a better position to allow for a changing future environment.

SENSITIVITY ANALYSIS AND SCENARIOS

Whether the task faced is to measure the current size of a market or to forecast its future direction, the problems of estimation and of resource constraints in collecting data are usually such that estimates rather than perfect measures are the objective. Because of this inherent difficulty in achieving exact measures, almost all market estimates and forecasts must be handled carefully. A key forecast about future market growth will often form the basis of a marketing, and indeed overall company, plan. The forecast becomes a crucial assumption in the planning process. Such pivotal assumptions should be clearly articulated and known to all managerial decision-makers in the company. The assumed view of the future may prove to be incorrect and there is thus the danger of very elegant edifices being built on shaky foundations. If key assumptions are transparent, corrective action can be quickly initiated.

One of the best and simplest ways to deal with the uncertainty about the precision of estimates is to use a range of figures from optimistic, through most likely, to pessimistic. As these figures are then used in the financial analysis of a marketing project, the market-related risk can be identified. For example, if a pessimistic forecast of market size and market share yields a revenue projection 10 per cent less than the most likely figure, and this in turn results in a change from a profitable to an unprofitable outcome for the project, then one must regard the proposal as having a high risk content. In a highly competitive and changing market a 10 per cent shortfall in sales is not a very unlikely event. Equally, if the manager finds that market estimates 10 per cent and 20 per cent less than the most likely one still yield profitable forecast outcomes, it would seem justifiable to judge the project as a relatively low-risk one in terms of demand variability.

Scenarios allow the manager to undertake a similar kind of sensitivity analysis, but more typically in evaluating overall company options. Scenarios may be constructed about a set of alternative, but quite feasible, future states of market: its size, competitive conditions, consumer tastes, technological change, etc. Scenarios describe not only future states of a market but also the sequence of cause and effect leading to its emergence. A good test of any proposed strategy is to examine whether it is a realistic one under each of the possible future states of the market. A strategy that will work only in one future scenario is a high-risk one. A strategy that will work under many scenarios, or that can be easily adapted to them, is a flexible robust low-risk strategy and more likely to be preferred in a dynamic market.

SOURCES OF DATA AND APPROACHES TO RESEARCH

Measuring a market demands access to data on the market and market segments of interest. Such material is most usually of two broad types:

(1) *Secondary data* exist already in the form of reports and various data bases which allow the manager to take somebody else's work of data collection and apply it to his own needs. Government publications such as the Census of Population and the Household Budget Inquiry are fundamental sources of secondary data for any marketing manager, along with the Census of Industrial Production and Irish Trade Statistics on imports and exports. Equivalent studies are available from the government publications offices of most other developed countries for the marketer interested in export markets and from the EC, the OECD and various United Nations publications. In addition to these public documents, the manager will usually find that industry associations and trade journals collect and publish market data. There is also a variety of market reports prepared by consultancy and market research firms that are available on subscription. A more recent but potentially powerful innovation, especially when exploring export markets, is the selection of international computer data bases which may be accessed remotely via computer terminal (see Exhibit 5.1).

(2) *Primary data* are collected at first hand from the market by or for the marketer. Visiting customers and potential customers and asking them about their needs and their current and planned purchases is something that all marketers must do regularly if they are to stay in touch

with their market. Similar information may be acquired at relatively low cost by collecting information about customers from the salesforce or from wholesalers or retailers. The company's accounting system and its handling of the information on invoices, statements and delivery documents is another valuable but very underused source of market data.

Primary data on market size and trends may also be collected on behalf of the marketer by a professional marketing research company or firm of market consultants. High-quality services of this nature are available in Ireland which offer both market monitoring services (e.g. retail sales month by month through grocery outlets) and once-off studies designed to the marketer's specific needs.

Exhibit 5.1

AN BORD TRACHTÁLA'S MARKET INFORMATION CENTRE

Finding export markets for furniture

A small manufacturer of furniture with a strong design content recalls using the information centre: 'The centre was just the right job to set the ball rolling into the UK market. We make a limited range of high-quality furniture pieces, tables, lamps and the like. We felt the time was right for us to look at the opportunities in the UK. I telephoned the centre for an appointment and gave an idea of my research needs. When I called the following day I found that the centre had run a search on its market information data base on the subject of furniture in the UK. I was presented with a listing of over thirty articles, reports, studies and directories. Virtually all of these were available in the centre and I spent the next two days consulting them.

'It proved to be a great investment of my time. I was able to build up a picture of the size, structure and trends in the UK industry on a regional basis. There was info on manufacturers, retailers like Habitat, MFI, Lowndes Queensway and so on, and, most importantly, on distributors. In fact the data base was subsequently able to provide a detailed profile on the size, trading strengths and financial status of a number of distributors which I reckoned might be potential leads. It looks like we're now going to be doing business with one of them!'

The Irish Trade Board's market information centre has the largest collection of such information in Ireland. Staffed by information specialists and designed specially for the needs of Irish exporters, the centre's market information service is available by phone, post or personal visit. It can provide the exporter with the names of foreign manufacturers, importers, distributors as well as information on markets, commodities, political developments and economic statistics. The centre houses an extensive collection of overseas trade directories, major research reports, mail order catalogues, annual reports, telephone directories, trade fair catalogues, country profiles, market reports, bibliographical guides, along with over 600 current periodicals.

The Trade Board's market information data base (MIDB) is a computerised system which allows quick retrieval of articles and reports held in the centre. There are currently over 20,000 references in this data base and it is updated daily. It is also accessible through the Board's regional offices. These information services are supplemented by a large range of international online data bases. Users are advised how to conduct a search in the most cost-effective manner.

Whatever sources are used, the method employed in deciding on information needs and choosing among alternative ways of satisfying these needs is critical to successful, accurate and affordable market measurement. It is therefore important to think through each of the following steps:

(a) Specify the marketing decision(s) to be made.
(b) Specify the information needed to make a confident, justifiable decision.
(c) Identify the alternative sources of the data that are needed—secondary and primary—and the methods necessary to collect this data.
(d) Evaluate the cost and quality of data from each source and assess their value relative to the cost of making a bad marketing decision without the information.
(e) Decide on the data required, how they are to be obtained, the budget for research, and the expected results.

SUMMARY

This chapter concentrated on the basic measures of market size, trend and share without which it is impossible to make properly informed marketing decisions. The need for such data was identified, and the meaning and role of the key measurements was described. The problems sometimes encountered in even defining a market were raised, and the bases on which forecasts are built were reviewed. Finally, sources of data for market measurement and an approach to undertaking research were covered.

Reading
Baker, Michael J. (1991), *Marketing—An Introductory Text,* 5th ed., Macmillan, Basingstoke, ch. 8.
Buzzell, R.D. and Gale, B.T. (1987), *The PIMS Principles*, The Free Press, NY.
Coyle, Charles M. (1987), 'Political opinion polling: recent Irish experience', *Irish Marketing Review*, vol. 2.

Kotler, P. (1991), *Marketing Management: Analysis, Planning, Implementation and Control*, 7th ed., Prentice-Hall, Englewood Cliffs, NJ, ch. 9.

Lehmann, D.R. (1989), *Market Research and Analysis*, Irwin, Boston.

Makrida kis, S. and Wheelwright, S.C. (1987), *The Handbook of Forecasting*, Wiley, NY.

Ravenscraft, D.J. (1983), 'Structure-profit relationships at the line of business and industry level', *Review of Economics and Statistics*, February.

Tull, D.S. and Hawkins, D.I. (1990), *Marketing Research: Measurement and Methods*, 3rd ed., Macmillan, NY.

Review Questions
1) Why is it important to measure and forecast market size?
2) Why is market share such an important measure for the marketing manager?
3) 'The biggest problem with market measurement is to decide what market to measure.' Discuss.
4) Name three bases on which a market forecast can be built. How could each one be implemented for a product with which you are familiar?

Chapter 6

Analysing Competition and Industry Structure

INTRODUCTION

Customer, company, competitor: the three main players that shape the construction of any marketing and business strategy. We have already looked at customers, at how many they are and how much they consume. In all markets that are not monopolised a number of suppliers compete to provide customers with what they need. It is not enough for the company to understand the customer alone. It must also understand what competitors are doing to gain customer loyalty and find a way of differentiating itself from them to win market share and long-term viability.

At a more general level, it must also be remembered that the industry in which a marketer competes, or chooses to compete when setting up a new venture, determines the kind of competition that will be faced and the level of profitability that may reasonably be expected. Different industries have different competitive structures. Some have many small suppliers chasing many small consumers, as in the case of the full-service restaurant industry. Some have a few large suppliers chasing many buyers as in the case of the fast food industry or the supermarket business. In some industries many small suppliers compete for the custom of a very few large buyers, as for example in the case of engineering or electronics sub-suppliers to major multinational production plants. In each industry setting the nature and degree of competition varies considerably. A company's industry environment therefore gives the marketer a set of competitive conditions over which he has little control. To be effective he must understand these conditions and behave in a manner consistent with the industry's 'rules of the game'.

In this chapter the basic issues that must be analysed to understand both individual competitors and the competitive structure of the industry are reviewed. In addition, some implications for competitive behaviour under various conditions are outlined.

ANALYSING COMPETITORS

It is important to analyse competitors, their strengths, weaknesses and business direction for two reasons. Good strategy cannot be developed in a vacuum—it is essential to understand competing companies if one is to outmanoeuvre them and to predict how they may react to one's own moves or game-play. Furthermore, strategies of firms in any market are highly interdependent; what one does affects all others. To pick the optimum strategy for any company the manager must be able to assess the interaction between the available strategy options and those of the main competitors. Seven elements of a competitor analysis process may be undertaken:

(1) Who is the present and potential competition?
(2) What is the position they have established in the market?
(3) What are their mission and objectives?
(4) What is their typical pattern of competitive behaviour?
(5) How strong is their resource base?
(6) What key competitive advantages do they possess?
(7) What are their key competitive vulnerabilities?

If these seven questions can be answered confidently by the marketer, he will have a very powerful grasp of the competitive challenge to winning customer loyalty. He will also be able to identify the opportunities that exist to differentiate his company and build market success.

Who is the competition?

At first sight this seems a trivial question. Yet many people go into business without any really clear knowledge of the answer. Discovering after launching a new product that there are competitors much larger than you and capable of producing a competitive product at much lower cost is not a pleasant experience. It is also an unforgivable omission.

Identifying existing competitors is seldom difficult and can be quickly established by checking with customers about alternative suppliers, by checking with retailers, wholesalers and distributors, and by contacting industry groups or associations. What is much more difficult to ascertain is who are *potential* competitors. Companies entering a market very often change the entire face of competitive behaviour. The entry of Toyota into the luxury car market with its Lexus brand in 1990 fundamentally changed the nature of competition for Mercedes Benz, BMW and Jaguar. The entry of the supermarket chains into the grocery retailing business altered forever the competitive viability of the independent small grocer. In turn, the entry of Musgraves in the late eighties into grocery retailing through its Centra and Super Valu franchise concept changed the competitive arena for the national supermarket chains (see Exhibit 8.1). Partly as a result of this the national supermarkets' share of grocery sales declined from 60 per cent in 1987 to 51 per cent in 1991. The entry in the early eighties of a firm with the resources and reputation of IBM changed the competitive 'rules of the game' for all the entrepreneurial new ventures that formed the first wave of personal computer suppliers and resulted within a short few years in a reduction in the number of competitors from hundreds to tens.

Establishing who are potential competitors is never an easy task, but the effective marketer always looks over his shoulder to check for signs of emerging competition. For Ireland, with its small open economy, this is a doubly important concern, as many companies who successfully develop a domestic market frequently find themselves confronted with a foreign entrant who extends operations to Ireland. For many firms that learned to compete in a protected domestic market, the freeing of trade in the 1970s marked the onset of competitive change to which they could not adapt. Some could not adapt inefficient high-cost structures to meet new price competition. Some could not adapt quality and customer service standards to retain customer loyalty. Some could not adapt managerial attitudes learned in a world that quite suddenly altered beyond recognition. Many companies closed down, were acquired or gradually decayed as a result of this shift in competitive conditions. This harsh lesson remains relevant today. The creation of the Single Market heralded another major step on the road to free, open and international competition with all its attendant opportunities and pressures. Marketers in new industries and in technology-based industries must be especially vigilant for potential entrants with new competitive advantages or new technologies.

Competitors' positioning

For each of the main competitors identified, it is important to understand what customer segments they focus on and what distinctive product or service benefits they offer. An understanding of their segment focus and strengths shows what areas of the market will be most difficult to penetrate, and also what areas are being serviced inadequately or perhaps not at all. The success of Bailey's Irish Cream shows how advantage was taken of a largely unsatisfied segment of demand for a new drink, different from traditional liqueurs and brandy, and appealing especially to women.

The position that competitors have built reflects not only what customers they have chosen to serve, but also the product benefits they have developed to respond to their needs. Once again, the implications of this knowledge are twofold. It allows the marketer to identify how the competitor serves customer needs and therefore the competitive strengths that it is foolhardy to try to attack, as well as the benefits not offered or poorly provided that represent an opportunity to steal market share with a product or service differentiated to provide the missing benefits.

Car manufacturers scrambled to offer economy-related benefits to car buyers in all segments of the market in a bid to win market share by responding to a widely expressed need through much of the eighties. Not only was there intense competition in the small car market to provide economy benefits to buyers, but even in luxury car segments companies such as BMW and Audi built competitive advantage on the basis of fuel economy in addition to traditional benefits of comfort and performance. As we entered the nineties, BMW made an early move to capture the advantage of being seen as environmentally friendly by launching its new 3-series as 80 per cent recyclable. Other companies responded with further attempts to be 'green' through design for recycling and the development of cleaner engines.

Competitor mission and objectives

Knowing the reasons that competitors are in business tells us a lot about how they will play the competitive game. A competitor dedicated to market share growth through low-cost manufacture and price discounting presents a type of opposition which is very different to that of a competitor whose aim is to maintain profitability and provide family shareholders with a regular dividend income. Knowing the mission and objectives that competitors have set for themselves tells the marketer what kind of behaviour he can expect from them and what kind of reactions he may provoke by engaging various strategies. Sometimes objectives are publicly stated in annual reports, press releases or trade journal articles. Sometimes they have to be inferred from observation of past and current behaviour. Whatever the method, it is almost always possible to form a reasonably accurate estimate of the ends being pursued by any one competitor.

Patterns in competitor behaviour

Decisions about how to compete in the market very often revolve about complex judgments concerning action and reaction. 'If I lower price, will Competitor A meet my price, hold the old price, or go even lower and start a price war?' This is a common consideration facing the decision-maker. To make the difficult judgment about competitive reaction to the various decisions that could be taken, the market-focused company has to depend significantly on a sense of what is the normal or typical behaviour of the competitor. This sense of a normal response pattern is most usually built up informally by a good manager in much the same way that all of us build up over time an ability to predict the reactions of people we know well.

The professional marketer will pay deliberate attention to the signals contained in competitors' behaviour that illustrate a stable tendency to respond to certain situations in predictable ways. Are certain companies price followers or price leaders? Which companies will discount price and offer promotional deals when market share is threatened, and which ones will always hold their price but perhaps respond with increased advertising or sales coverage? Which companies will innovate regularly and match any competitive new product quickly, and which will stay with their traditional product line until disaster stares them in the face? Monitoring competitors to build up judgments about questions such as these is vital if good marketing decisions are to be made that fit with current market conditions but also with the set of likely future competitive reactions. Much of the information required to do this well will reflect knowledge about the conventional wisdom used by managers in rival firms. Knowing these managers and their beliefs about the market, its behaviour and its trends is therefore important.

Competitor resource base
As in warfare, a priority for the strategist and tactician is to know the enemy's strength. The considerations we have already documented tell much about the competitors' place in the market and their response tendency. We must also know something about the internal resources they can call upon to expand or defend their competitive position. This necessitates evaluating their managerial, marketing, financial, manufacturing and technological capability. Are they resource-rich and able to outlast us in any direct market confrontation, or are they cash-starved and poorly managed and therefore unable to sustain a defence of market share? Are they weak in marketing, merchandising and innovative capability and therefore vulnerable to competition on these fronts?—in the way, for instance, that the established branded ice-creams were before increased competition brought to the market more professional marketing, aggressive merchandising and continuous innovation of ice-creams. Novel shapes, packaging and themes brought frenetic activity to the children's segment, while in the premium end local entrants like McCambridge's and the US brand Haagen-Daz, with its novel advertising approach, competed with the traditional players. Once again, the message from a good analysis is the essential information it provides about the competitor strengths one cannot hope to defeat and the resource weaknesses that betray a market vulnerability.

Key advantages and disadvantages
The five steps in competitor analysis outlined so far provide the raw material for identifying the key competitive advantages and disadvantages of each significant competitor. It is vital to isolate these factors, as they ultimately tell us how and where to compete for the custom of the chosen market. Normally the manager will, like a good military strategist, avoid competition in areas where competitors are at their strongest and will instead mobilise his marketing forces to attack the weak points. Decisions about how to compete and on what issues to compete are at the heart of marketing

strategy, and we will return to this theme in Chapter 10 where we discuss competitive positioning.

LEAKAGE ANALYSIS

The essence of competitive strategy is to carve out of the market a segment of loyal customers whose needs the company can serve better than any other competing supplier. Market share and, through it, revenue and profit consequences are the measures of success. Understanding of how well a company competes and where and how it might search for additional market share can be gained by a relatively simple exercise known as 'leakage analysis'. The implications of this analysis are illustrated in Figure 6.1.

Figure 6.1

Leakage Analysis

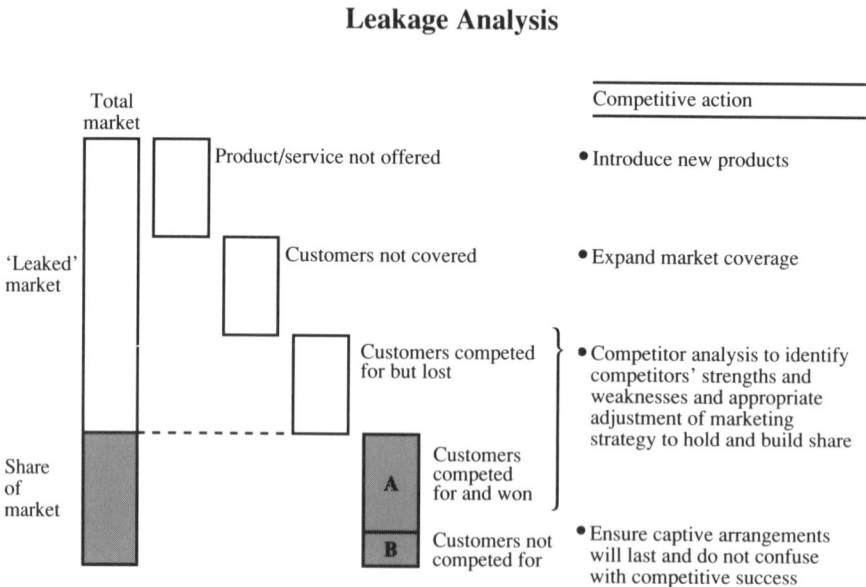

Adapted from K. Ohmae, *The Mind of the Strategist: The Art of Japanese Business,* McGraw Hill, New York 1982, pp. 128–129.

This analysis helps the manager to understand his marketing effectiveness. He can identify market share won as a result of his efforts rather than because of any captive customer arrangements where sales may reflect inter-company deals or a monopoly position in some segment. By applying competitor analysis to the business competed for but lost, it is possible to understand *why* the business was lost and set realistic market share gain objectives based on effective competitive differentiation of the company's product. He can also consider the magnitude and attractiveness of the opportunities that exist to compete in parts of the market not yet covered by the company—for example, additional geographic areas, or segments where a different form of the product or service is needed to satisfy demand.

COMPETITIVE STRUCTURE OF AN INDUSTRY

What has been discussed so far takes as given the industry in which the marketer is planning to compete. However, different industries have different competitive structures which result in quite different 'rules of the game' for competitive behaviour, and in quite different levels of profitability that are 'normal' among competitors. Fragmented industries, such as furniture manufacturing or transport, have many competitors, many customers and a considerable variety of bases on which to distinguish a company's product or service; are normally characterised by modest profit levels, considerable exit and entry of competitors; and have little scope for large growth in market share.

Such structural features set 'rules of the game' for competitive behaviour that the marketer must accept as given. He must equally accept, with his entry into any industry, that profit targets are only partially responsive to his efforts: some industries, of their nature, have higher or lower 'normal' profit levels than others. The manager's objective under these circumstances is to set minimum profit targets at the 'normal' level and try to compete with sufficient effectiveness to raise his return on investment into the upper region of what is feasible in the industry environment. Understanding the competitive structure of an industry and identifying the critical 'rules of the game' set by this structure can be achieved by employing Porter's five-part analysis. Porter argues that the nature and degree of competition in an industry is a function of five forces (see Figure 6.2):

(1) the threat of new entrants;
(2) the bargaining power of customers;
(3) the bargaining power of suppliers;
(4) the threat of substitute products or services;
(5) the competitive rivalry for share among current competitors.

New entrants are an important feature of any industry that does not have high barriers to entry—for example, where a new firm does not need large economies of scale in manufacturing or marketing; where capital investment is low; where a new entrant can compete as cost-effectively as a long-established supplier; where there is easy access to distribution channels and where government does not regulate entry. Where there are low barriers many new firms will be attracted into the industry by any sign of attractive profits. They will compete hungrily to fill capacity and build market share, thus driving down overall profits of all competitors. In order to reap acceptable levels of profit and to achieve a degree of long-term security of market position, marketers will always aim to erect or maintain barriers to entry in their sector of an industry. The more successful, growth-oriented Irish printing firms have done this by shifting out of general printing, where there is great ease of entry, into areas such as quality magazine printing or security printing, where the investment required and the sophistication of the necessary marketing activity excludes many potential entrants and raises profit levels for the successful competitor.

The development of the business format franchise is also a way of coping with the industry that has low entry barriers, many players and low capital requirements—the classic fragmented industry. Such business formats involve highly systemised procedures and operations for offering a product or service to the customer which have been developed by the franchisor. These mean that the franchisee can enjoy economies of scale in sourcing raw material and operating, as well as marketing advantages that would not otherwise be readily achieved. Examples of business format franchises include McDonald's, Prontaprint and The Body Shop.

Figure 6.2

Porter's Five Forces Model of Competition

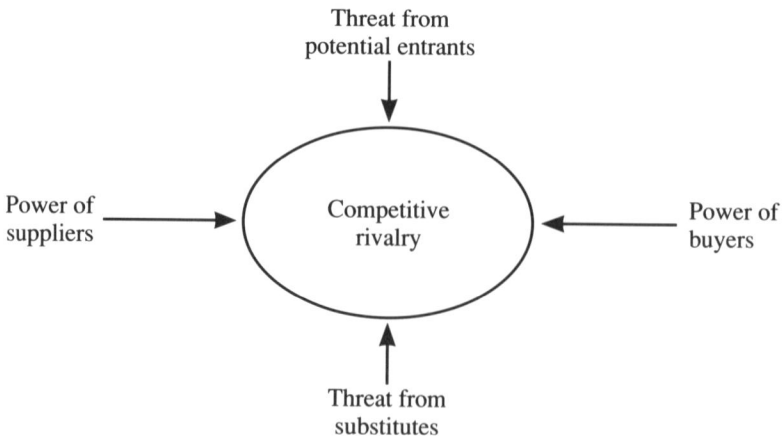

Customer power is perhaps a more readily grasped force. If the marketer is faced with few and very powerful buyers with whom he must deal in order to stay in business, then he may expect to see prices forced down, pressure for greater quality and service, and the competing companies played off against each other. All these consequences force down industry profit levels, as has been experienced by the suppliers to the grocery trade in Ireland as power has shifted into the hands of a few supermarket chains.

Supplier power is the opposite side of the coin from customer power. If a marketer depends on a few powerful suppliers of raw material or semi-finished products as input to his company, then he can be easily squeezed on prices, service and delivery. Many parts of the Irish agribusiness sector are affected by supplier pressures as farmers press cooperatives for higher milk prices or meat companies for higher livestock prices. This, allied to problems of seasonality of supply and variation in quality, has militated against successful 'downstream' added value activity in the sector. If suppliers are many and relatively weak, however, the marketer can reverse the situation by playing them off one against the other on price and service.

Substitutes represent a force that varies by industry, depending on the extent to which it is feasible to develop new product forms or new technologies. The viability and profit expectations of many companies based on mechanical technology have been wiped out over the past fifteen years by substitute electronic solid state technology. Many industries, however, do not live under this threat of sudden radical obsolesence as a consequence of new technology. What is much more common and warrants continuous attention is the shifting balance of competitive advantage between close substitutes. In Irish tourism, for example, the inflation of the late seventies and eighties radically altered the balance between hotel accommodation and other forms of accommodation such as farm and guest houses and self-catering accommodation. Saddled with high capital charges and rapidly increasing labour and operating costs, traditional hotels found it more and more difficult to offer customers something of value when compared with these substitute forms of accommodation. Substitutes also put a ceiling on profits in good times. In the domestic central heating market the relative prices of gas, oil, solid fuel and electricity will always act as a check on the pricing freedom and therefore the profit potential of any one source of heat.

Competitive rivalry reaches its peak typically where there are many equal-sized competitors; where market growth is slow; where products or services cannot be differentiated significantly; where fixed costs and capacity are high, inviting price competition to maintain volume; and where it is difficult to leave the industry because of redundancy payments or other barriers; and where rivals see no common set of 'rules of the game'. Intensely competitive markets clearly drive down profit levels and competitors must accept this or else relocate themselves in a less fiercely competitive environment. Within a highly competitive market the creative marketer will try, through segmentation of customers and differentiation of his product, to develop a sub-market where the intensity of competition becomes less and profit potential increases. In doing so he effectively rewrites industry boundaries and creates new barriers to competition which protect his service or product and its profit potential.

Analysing these issues for the industry in which he operates is an important task for the marketer, and one which will give him a considerable sense of confidence in knowing what is reasonable to expect and what he can and cannot hope to control through his marketing strategy. At the end of such an analysis he should be able to identify (a) how the five forces influence competition, (b) what are the 'rules of the game' in the industry and (c) what he needs tactically or strategically to exploit or counter the forces at work. Exhibit 6.1 is an interesting example of how the 'rules of the game' can be rewritten in an industry with major consequences for all involved.

Exhibit 6.1

SPECTRA LABORATORIES

Changing the game-rules in film processing

The amateur film developing and printing market in Ireland involves the processing of films shot for non-professional use, basically photos taken on holidays, family occasions, special ceremonies or as a hobby. Up to the mid-seventies the standard method for the consumer to get a film developed was to bring it to the local chemist or pharmacist who would in turn relay it to a film processing company for development and printing. This D & P side of his business was a profitable source of revenue to the chemist. However, his hegemony was to be challenged over the next decade by three new developments.

New technology enabled the processing factory to be sited on the high street in the form of one-hour or express service outlets. The consumer may have had to pay more for this new quick turnaround facility, but he liked the service and increasingly used it. Secondly, a number of film processing companies, initially UK based, started by-passing the 'middleman' distributor/retailer and using direct mail techniques to market and process films for the consumer. A steady take-up of this service ensued. Thirdly, local newsagents and corner shops started to become retailers/distributors for processing companies, again broadening the distribution channels for amateur film D & P.

The result was that while chemists controlled over 80 per cent of this D & P market in the mid-1970s, this share had plunged to under 40 per cent by the mid-1980s. Further, the new distribution practices and rules of the game led to a shake-out among the traditional film processing companies with more than half of them going to the wall during the period.

One company that thrived at this time, however, was Spectra Laboratories. Founded from a shed behind its managing director's home in Listowel, Co. Kerry, in 1970, it grew rapidly to become Ireland's largest and most modern film processing company. In the mid-eighties Spectra developed in conjunction with the newly established semi-state company, An Post, a novel direct mail service called Post Photo. At a time of growing acceptance of direct mail with the Irish consumer, it offered him the double assurance of a dedicated, and reasonably priced, arrangement within the national postal service, in association with the largest national film processor. It established Spectra as the biggest mail order film processor in the country.

Note: see Colorcare case study in Part I of book.

The purpose of the approach to analysis discussed in this chapter is better to inform the marketer about the feasible competitive options open in winning customers and increasing profitability. Options developed in this way require one further analytical contribution before decisions can be made. A clear inventory of the company's capabilities to market its products or services is necessary so that options which are feasible in the context of industry structure and competitors' strengths and weaknesses can be matched with the capacity of the firm to implement any one option. Chapter 7 completes this cycle of analysis and allows discussion of the choices facing a company in deciding what competitive game it will play: industry leader or follower; innovator or 'me too' producer; low-cost or differentiated marketer; niche player or generalist and so on.

SUMMARY

Two sides of the triangle of customer, competitor and company have now been analysed. Exploration of the competitor element informs the marketer about the likelihood of success in attracting certain groups, or segments, of customers. It does this by helping to develop an understanding of how individual firms have competed, and are likely to compete, in the market, and of their unique competitive strengths and weaknesses which may be attacked or must be defended against. Analysis of the structure of competition in the industry at large tells the marketer the basic nature and intensity of competition that is 'natural' to the industry and over which the single firm has little control. This structure of competition and the profit levels it leads to set basic 'rules of the game' for the marketer. Knowing these, it becomes easier to devise marketing strategies that run with the current of competition or that realistically attempt to change the rules in some parts of the industry to the company's advantage.

Reading

Abell, D.F. and Hammond, J.S. (1979), *Strategic Market Planning: Problems and Analytical Approaches*, Prentice-Hall, Englewood Cliffs, NJ.

Baker, Michael J. (1991), *Marketing—An Introductory Text*, 5th ed., Macmillan, Basingstoke, ch. 4.

Kotler, P. (1991), *Marketing Management: Analysis, Planning, Implementation and Control*, 7th ed., Prentice-Hall, Englewood Cliffs, NJ, ch. 8.

Murray, John A., MacGabhann, Paul P. and D'Cruz, Joseph R. (1988), 'Industrial strategy and the national industrial portfolio', *Irish Marketing Review*, vol. 3.

Porter, Michael (1980), *Competitive Strategy; Techniques for Analysing Industries and Competitors*, The Free Press, NY.

Review Questions

1. Consideration of customers, company and competitors is fundamental to the construction of any marketing or business plan. Explain the importance of competitor analysis in this process.
2. There are seven general elements to a thorough competitor analysis. What are they? Explain the requirements of each element.
3. What is meant by 'leakage analysis'?
4. What are the five forces that determine the competitive structure of an industry, and what is the influence of each of them?

Chapter 7

Analysing Company Capability

INTRODUCTION

'How good are we? We know what the market needs. We know how well our competitors can serve the market. Just how competent are we at serving those needs better than anyone else? How can we do it better? How can we achieve excellence?'

These are questions that must be asked time and time again in any company if a complete and honest understanding of the 'strategic triangle' is to be developed and good marketing decisions made. Assessing the capability of a company to satisfy market needs competitively is vital in order to understand:

(1) its current market position and the strengths and weaknesses of that position;
(2) the feasibility of proposed marketing plans;
(3) the opportunity to build the competence to serve new markets and outperform new competition.

There is nothing more pathetic than the company that tries to implement ambitious marketing programmes which are beyond its ability, or the resourceful and talented company that persistently produces weak and unchallenging strategies far below its capabilities. In both cases the company loses market share; customers lose a competitive source of supply; and only the competition wins!

It is, however, surprisingly difficult from within a company to make an objective assessment of capability. This is normally due to two reasons. First, the time, and on occasion cost, required to do a thorough audit of the company's resources and their quality can be an inhibiting factor. Second, personal and political stakes can become involved and influence managers to conceal, defend, or even present as strengths, weak aspects of their operations. The reality of this latter consideration should not be underestimated. For these reasons, an outsider to the company's day-to-day business—such as a consultant or board member with marketing experience—is sometimes necessary to provide both objectivity and the required input of time.

UNDERSTANDING CORE COMPETENCES

Attempting to understand the underlying strengths and weaknesses of individual companies prompted managers and researchers during the eighties to analyse the remarkable successes of Japanese global firms and the fact that relatively few Western companies achieved and sustained similar success. This work initiated a new concern for the 'core competences' of companies and the way in which these were at the root of significant market and business achievement. The work of Hamel and Prahalad (1990) in particular has led us to view market and competitive success as emerging from a well-managed marriage of core and long-lasting company competences *to* well-defined and equally long-lasting market needs (not just wants!). Core competences are viewed as the source of the company's core products around which it builds its business which in turn generates its changing array of product and service offerings. It is important to note that in this view individual products and services are seen as important but transitory responses to important but equally temporary market wants.

Capturing this perspective is crucial to successful marketing as it isolates the tactical and ever-moving relationship between products/services and market wants from the strategic and relatively stable relationship between competences and market needs. Understanding this distinction is a vital requirement if we are to avoid what Levitt (1975) called marketing myopia. Marketing myopia leads the producer of buggy whips to continue to make them long after the horse and buggy have disappeared. Marketing myopia leads a railroad company to define itself as being in the railroad business, when customers have begun to solve their transportation needs with cars and airplanes. In both instances, *products responding to wants are confused with competences responding to needs.*

It is essential therefore in undertaking internal company analysis to identify the company's core competences and the long-term market needs which they can be deployed to serve profitably. Core competences will normally (Hamel and Prahalad, 1990, p. 81):

* provide potential access to a wide variety of markets;
* make a significant contribution to the benefits of the end product(s) as perceived by the customer;
* be difficult for competitors to imitate.

This latter point emphasises that core competences will also be 'distinctive' competences—i.e. they are competences that the company of interest to us has that are not possessed by any other competing companies.

ANALYSING COMPANY CAPABILITY

To undertake a basic capability audit it is most practical to start with past and current performance in the market. Relative success and failure in the market should then be traced back to the company strengths and weaknesses responsible for performance. Performance in the market is the ultimate measuring stick against which company resources are evaluated. There is always the temptation to take some convenient 'stocklist' of 'things one ought to find in a good company' and to tick off 'have' or 'have not' after each item. The reality of business is such that these general lists must be used with caution. Why? Because companies compete in different markets, in different industries, against different competitive forces, serving different kinds of customers from widely varied resource bases.

Capability must therefore be evaluated in the market context in which it is to be deployed. The same set of company resources may yield unbounded success in one market environment but dismal failure in another, a lesson which companies diversifying into new markets often learn painfully and at considerable cost. Carroll Industries, for instance, met with little success when it diversified from its shrinking cigarette business into fish farming and the mail order business.

AN EVALUATION PROCESS

Figure 7.1 outlines a four-stage process by which company capability may be evaluated for the specific industry, market and competitive context in which any company finds itself.

Figure 7.1

Evaluating Company Capability

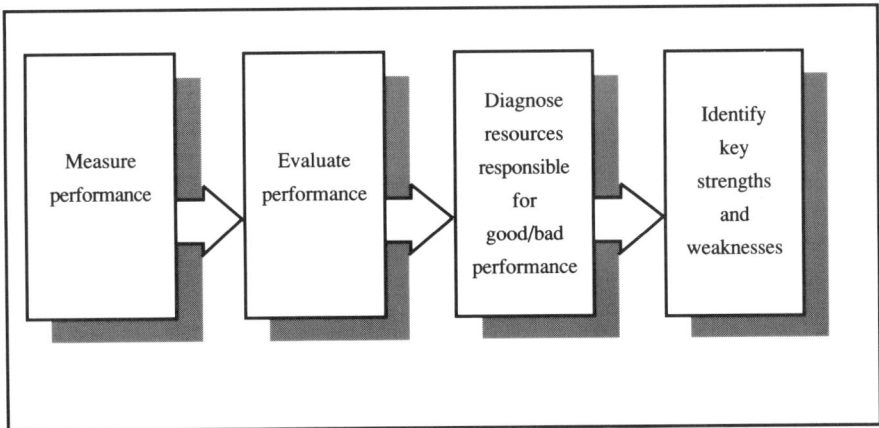

Measuring performance

Three general measures of performance are needed:

(1) the degree to which target customer needs are satisfied by the company's products or services—their relative quality, availability, performance in use and acceptability to the customer;

(2) the competitive performance of the company, measured in terms of market share and whether it is moving up, down, or holding position;

(3) the profitability of the company and the maintenance, development or destruction of its asset base.

Precise measurement of these factors demands that the company undertake some customer research and maintain a good internal marketing information system. However, even the relatively small or unsophisticated company can make reasonable qualitative judgments of the first two factors and should not be in business if it does not know the third.

Performance evaluation

'How good is our performance?' is a question that demands an honest objective answer from the manager. Is the company's product as good as it could be, or has the company taken short cuts in design or manufacturing at the customer's expense? Is quality consistent and high? The market share figure is, of course, an undeniable measure of the market's verdict on the company relative to competitors. Is the share increasing or decreasing? Is it big or small? If it is small, is this because the company cannot do its job as well as the competition, or is it because it is in an industry where everyone has a small share and there is no route to large share positions?

Is the company profitable or not? How profitable does it have to be to rate a 'good' evaluation? The analysis of industry and competitive structure discussed in Chapter 6 is one way to set bench-marks of normal, high or low levels of profitability. The PIMS (Profit Impact of Marketing Strategy) programme provides such a standard of normal, or 'par', profitability to its subscribers, allowing them to make the good/bad evaluation with reference to other similar members of the programme. When these evaluations of market performance as good, bad or adequate have been discussed and debated by the marketer with the senior management team and perhaps with an outside, independent third party, the time for some detective work—or diagnosis—has arrived.

Diagnosis

The challenge in this stage of the analysis is to trace the origins of the 'goods' and the 'bads' to the areas of the company's resource base—to aspects of its capability—that are responsible for the particular performance level. An approach to this process is visualised in the table illustrated in Figure 7.2, which may be used as a worksheet in undertaking the analysis. By way of illustration let us take the case of a company supplying a range of paint products to the market. The marketing manager in charge of one important brand, a rust treatment paint, found in evaluating its performance that:

(1) The product and its quality was excellent, both in technical and customer perception terms.
(2) Availability, however, was not as universal as it might be, because of concentration of selling and distribution on larger and more traditional hardware shops.
(3) Market share was sizeable, but decreasing slowly because of lesser quality discount and private label brands, and new branded introductions sold as part of a competitor's wide product range to retailers.
(4) Profitability was good and understood to be above average for most paint products.

Working down through the diagnosis table, the marketing manager of the rust treatment brand considered that the only identifiable weakness in his strategy was in the sales and distribution area, where his market coverage was limited to the older outlets, typically in high street locations. There were increasing numbers of new hardware stores in new housing areas, located in suburban shopping centres and malls. He had no clear information about how many of these existed and for how much of total market sales they accounted. His salesforce had tightly organised, efficient call routines for established hardware shop selling, but had not traditionally been asked to search out new shops and open accounts with them.

Thinking about his management of marketing activity and processes in his business, he could see that the distribution weakness in his strategy was partly created by the absence of market information flowing in to him. What were the trends in hardware retailing? Where were householders buying their do-it-yourself supplies? He had no information process to tell him about the market other than salesforce call reports. The strategic problem with distribution also prompted him to evaluate why he did not have a planning process that looked ahead and alerted him to long-term changes in shopping behaviour and retail location. At that time planning involved preparing each year's sales budget: maybe there should be more to marketing planning than that?

Looking at the people he employed and managed, he knew he was evaluating his most important and costly resource. How well was the salesforce performing? Was it their 'fault'—were they a 'problem resource'—because of the inadequate distribution coverage? Not really, since they had not been asked to do missionary selling and were tightly scheduled and controlled in their coverage of well-established accounts. But if this were to change, if they were asked to develop new business, would their skills, attitudes and training be

Figure 7.2

Diagnosing Strengths and Weaknesses

MEASURE PERFORMANCE
- customer satisfaction
- market share
- profitability

EVALUATE PERFORMANCE
- good or bad

DIAGNOSE PERFORMANCE
- marketing-related capabilities contributing to good or bad performance

IDENTIFY KEY STRENGTHS AND WEAKNESSES
- strengths to build
- weaknesses to overcome or cope with

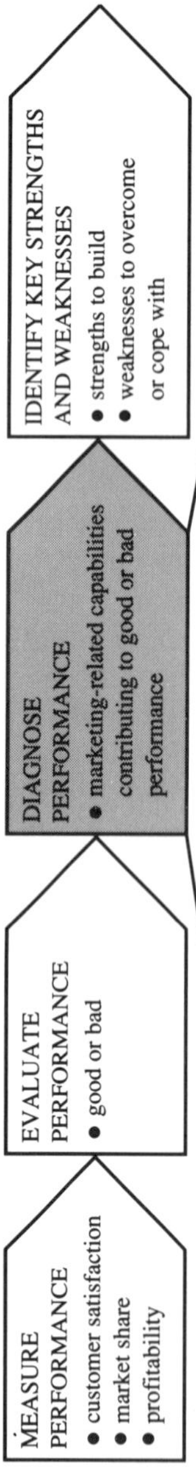

Capability in:	Comments on:			Is this aspect of capability affected by:						
	strength	weakness	strategy	organisation and process	people	leadership	finance	manufacturing	R & D
Strategy										
Organisation structure/process										
People										
Leadership										
Finance										
Manufacturing										
R & D										
Other										

appropriate to the new task? Here was a strength *and* a weakness: an excellent salesforce at its current job, but possibly a weak one at a redefined job.

Leadership, he knew, meant self-evaluation, and here he confessed that he had to reach a conclusion akin to that about the salesforce. By any standards he had been leading his team successfully and had good profits to show. But new developments had not received much of his attention, and he felt he had created a climate in which 'the name of the game was do the job we have always done and keep doing it better'. Now he began to believe that he had unconsciously left innovation out of his leadership approach. He had not pushed anyone to think about market changes and required responses. He had not questioned the annual budgeting ritual and whether it contributed to longer-term marketing effectiveness or not.

Finance he had initially pencilled in as a distinct strength: he was delivering above-average profitability for the paint industry. Then, however, he began to think about from where that level of profitability was coming. He was losing a small but consistent share of the market from year to year and was not charging premium prices. So the profits were not due to the price-volume part of the profit equation. That left costs. Why should he be more cost-effective than his competitors? He ran a very tight salesforce management and control system, so maybe he was just more efficient. Then he started a new train of diagnosis. His advertising and promotion budgets had been cut back in each of the past three years by the managing director to provide money for the launch of new paint products. All his requests to hire new salespeople had been turned down for the same reason. His salespeople certainly were efficient, but could that be because they were calling on well-known retail accounts, while competitors were out opening new accounts and trying aggressively to steal retail shelf space for their products from his? His above-average profitability, he now began to see, was a result of running down the competitive capability of his product area. While this had shown handsome profits for the past three years and left him basking in the managing director's approval, he could now see a day of reckoning drawing close. More share loss would soon leave his absolute revenue and contribution figures looking rather meagre and leave the brand with little scope to regain share against aggressive competitors who were investing marketing resources in their brands. Had he unknowingly turned a brand with a long healthy life ahead of it into a rapidly decaying one with poor life prospects?

Identification of strengths and weaknesses
It is easy to see how this process of diagnosis led this particular marketing manager to list in the worksheet shown in Figure 7.3 his product's key marketing-related pluses and minuses. Marketing strengths and weaknesses demand three kinds of response from the manager:

(1) he can, and is well advised to, build on his strengths, especially if they are to some extent distinctive to his company;
(2) he can attempt to turn around his weaknesses where they hinder effective performance;
(3) he can plan to cope as well as possible with strengths or weaknesses over which he has little control.

The problem faced by the manager of the rust treatment paint brand illustrates the third point, and is the reason he put question-marks in the 'cope' column opposite marketing investment level and financial strategy. He did not have freedom to make a final decision on changing these factors. The managing director, concerned with overall company fortunes, had to face the problem of how he should allocate scarce cash across several paint brands. His decision had to be guided by analysis of which brand would return the greatest long-run profits for each pound of marketing expenditure.

Figure 7.3

Key Marketing Strengths and Weaknesses

	Feasible options		
Strengths:	Build	Turnaround	Cope
• Product and brand reputation	✔		
• Satisfied customer base	✔		
• Full coverage: traditional retailers	✔		
• Competent motivated salesforce	✔		
• Personal openness to change	✔		
Weaknesses:			
• Coverage of new retailers and new population areas		✔	
• Contracting marketing investment		✔	?
• Financial strategy		✔	?
• Poor market information		✔	
• Budgeting instead of planning		✔	

SWOT ANALYSIS, CORE COMPETENCES AND FUTURE OPTIONS

Now that the three essentials of analysis—customer, competitor and company—have been covered, let us examine some relatively simple ways in which the conclusions of analysis may be synthesised and summarised. In doing so it is also appropriate to begin to anticipate the action or decision orientation of Part III of the book. Thus syntheses are needed that

* summarise the results of the analysis
* identify core or distinctive competences, and
* suggest directions for marketing and overall company decisions.

So far, our analysis of the *external* environment has addressed the customer and his likely behaviour, defined the market and possible trends therein, examined industry structure and profiled the competition. Our *internal* analysis of the company focused on its strengths and weaknesses, particularly those in the marketing area. By assessing these pluses and minuses in the light of the various external factors, it is possible to identify key or core competences. For example, our marketing manager of the rust paint brand might consider his well-trained and disciplined salesforce, along with his strong relationship with and coverage of traditional outlets, as core or distinctive competences. He has, as we can see from Figure 7.3, a number of feasible options to build on this advantage. In this way the marketing manager can 'marry' such core and long-lasting company competences to well-defined and equally long-lasting market needs—and opportunities!

Figure 7.4 presents this synthesis in a schematic framework and illustrates a particular approach to what is commonly referred to as SWOT analysis. It is so called because its outcome is a concise and insightful summary of the critical opportunities (O) and threats (T) identified by the firm, and the essential strengths (S) and weaknesses (W) inherent in its resource base.

Market attractiveness and company capability

In order to advance this approach one further step towards action implications, it is useful to connect our foregoing analysis with the decision framework inherent in a market attractiveness/competitive capability matrix. Figure 7.5 represents such a matrix based on an approach developed by General Electric with McKinsey & Co. By combining the conclusions of the analysis of customers, competitors and industry trends into a summary notion of 'market attractiveness' and relating it to the analysis of the company's capability, any company or product of a company can be positioned along the two dimensions. The possible options or policy implications of various positions on the matrix are indicated in summary form on the figure.

Figure 7.4

SWOT Analysis

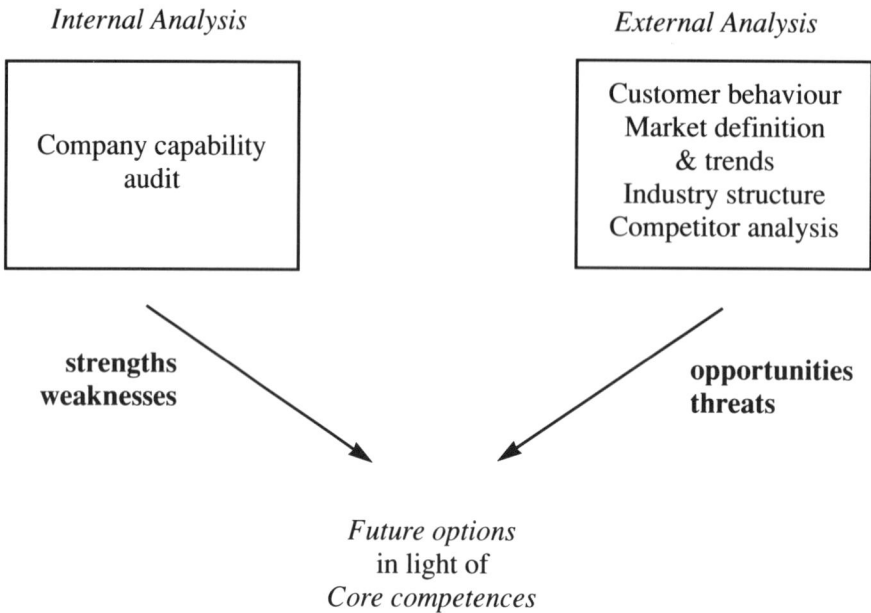

Internal Analysis   *External Analysis*

| Company capability audit | | Customer behaviour
Market definition
& trends
Industry structure
Competitor analysis |

strengths
weaknesses

opportunities
threats

Future options
in light of
Core competences

Returning to the marketing manager for the rust treatment product discussed earlier, he positioned his brand as in a highly attractive market (stable market growth, relatively recession-proof DIY demand, good margins, changing but identifiable distribution patterns) with medium capability (small share losses, non-coverage of new retail outlets, excellent product compared with competitors', solid competitive brand image, ability to improve marketing). This put the product in the position shown in the figure—one normally demanding that the company defend its existing position or try to build market share by improving its capability to compete. This indeed was the essence of the difficult decision that had to be faced by the managing director of the company. Should he continue to take money from the brand in order to support new products and allow the brand to lose share? The analysis illustrated here suggested that this was not appropriate. At worst, he should leave the brand with enough cash to defend its market share position. He should also consider the payoff from investing in rebuilding share and market leadership relative to the payoff from making the same investment elsewhere in the company.

This comparatively simple but informative approach to putting all the analysis together belongs to a 'family' of portfolio analysis methods which will be explored in greater depth in Chapters 11 and 16.

Figure 7.5

A Market Attractiveness/Company Capability Matrix

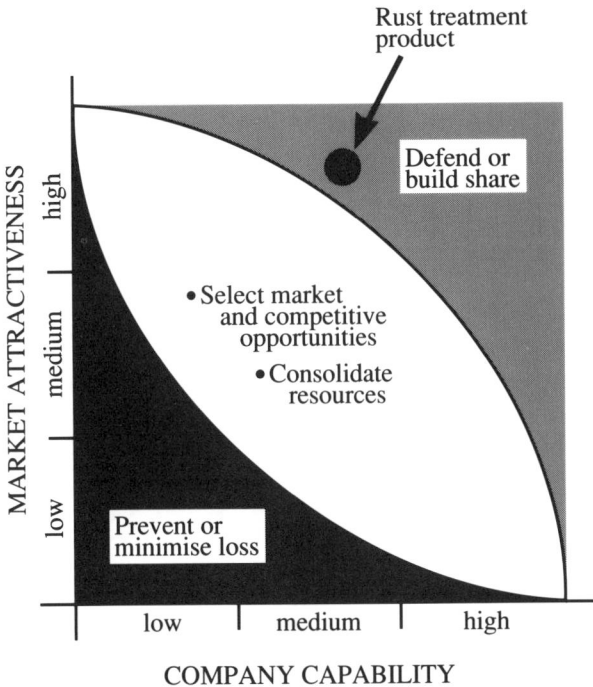

Rust treatment product

Defend or build share

• Select market and competitive opportunities

• Consolidate resources

Prevent or minimise loss

MARKET ATTRACTIVENESS

high   medium   low

COMPANY CAPABILITY

low   medium   high

SUMMARY

Analysis of the company's capability to compete for customers' patronage against other suppliers forms the third critical element of basic marketing analysis for decision-making. It is important for the manager to follow a thorough process of analysis. A four-stage process was recommended, from performance measurement, through performance evaluation and diagnosis, to identification of key capability strengths and weaknesses. Then, the three elements of analysis—customer, competitor and company—were combined in a SWOT analysis. Core or distinctive competences were identified and linked to longer-term market need and opportunity. Finally a market attractiveness/company capability matrix was used to suggest future direction or options for the firm.

Reading

Aaker, David (1992), *Strategic Market Planning*, 3rd ed., Wiley, NY, ch. 8.

Abell, D.F. and Hammond, J.S. (1979), *Strategic Market Planning: Problems and Analytical Approaches*, Prentice-Hall, Englewood Cliffs, NJ.

Fahey, Liam (1986), 'Marketing and competitive advantage', *Irish Marketing Review*, vol. 1.

Hamel, G. and Prahalad, C.K. (1990), 'The core competences of the corporation', *Harvard Business Review*, May–June.

Kotler, P., Gregor, W. and Rogers, W. (1977), 'The marketing audit comes of age', *Sloan Management Review*, vol. 18, no. 1.

Levitt, Theodore (1975), 'Marketing myopia', *Harvard Business Review*, September–October.

McDonald, M.H.B. (1984), *Marketing Plans: How to Prepare Them & How to Use Them*, Heinemann, London, ch. 5.

Review Questions

1. What are the objectives of a capability audit, and what problems are likely to be encountered in its implementation?
2. Explain the steps involved in conducting an evaluation of company capability, and the desired outcome of each step.
3. What do you understand by the notion of core or distinctive competences?
4. How can a capability analysis best be integrated with the outcome of customer and competitor analyses so as to provide insight into the major strategic choices facing a company?

Chapter 8

Marketing Information and Research

INTRODUCTION

All the work of marketing involves the generation and use of information in order to understand and to make assessments of customers, competitors and the company. With analytical information of this nature, one can make decisions for marketing action. Information is the key resource used by a marketer, and decisions can be only as good as the information used. In the preceding three chapters we have concentrated on what information is needed and have made some reference to how it can be acquired and how it should be analysed to make good decisions possible. Getting relevant information, and processing it into usable form for decision-making, are critical marketing tasks.

The importance of marketing information and the way in which it is used is visualised in Figure 8.1. The marketing environment consists of the familiar triangle of customer, competitor and company plus broader aspects such as the technological, cultural, legal, political and governmental forces that shape the behaviour of the elements of the triangle. An enormous amount of data which may be tapped by the marketer exists concerning all these elements of the environment. This material, however, has no informative content until it has been chosen, collected, ordered, analysed and communicated by some 'processing' activity. This is the role of the marketing information system. This system should be able to identify:

(1) what information is needed for decision-making;
(2) what data sources can provide the required information;
(3) how data can be transformed into usable information for decision-making (e.g. how to take the Census of Population and make it useful in estimating market size or market segments);
(4) how this information should be communicated to decision-makers.

This may seem like an elaborate activity appropriate only for large companies with sizeable marketing departments. Such companies will certainly organise their marketing information system in a relatively formal and

Figure 8.1

Marketing Information System

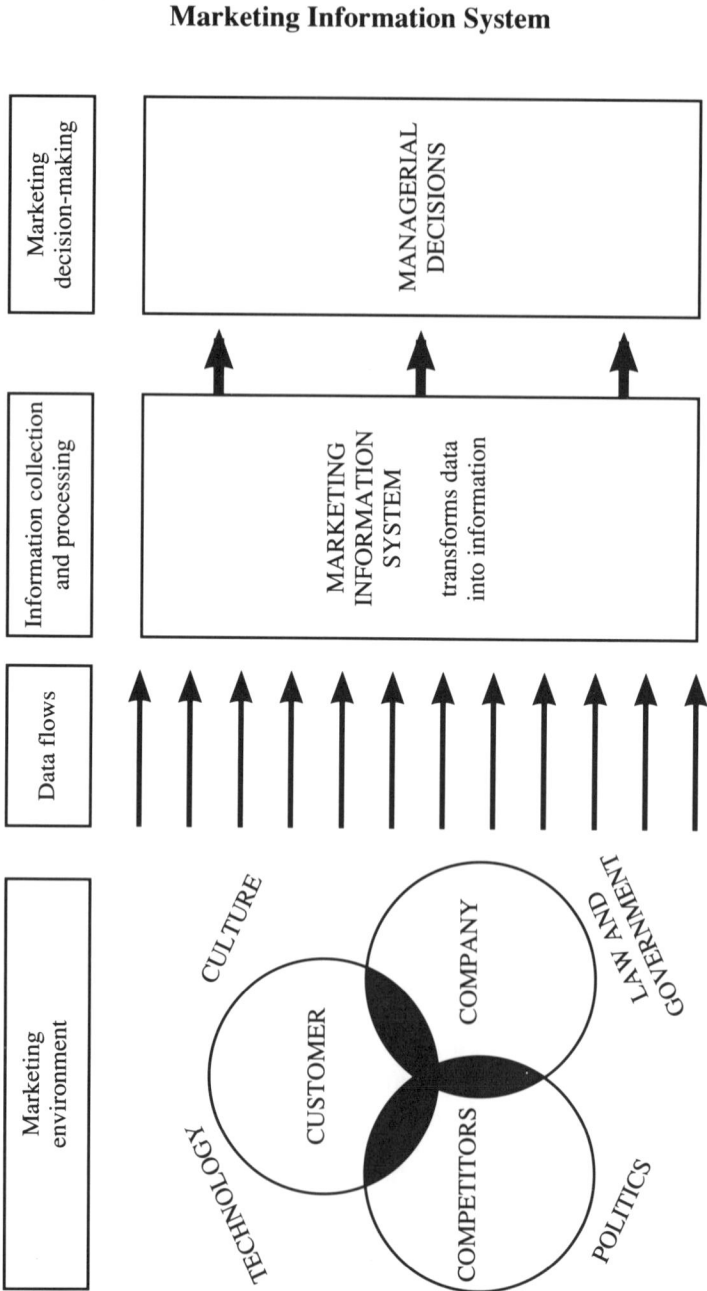

Marketing decision-making	Information collection and processing	Data flows	Marketing environment

MANAGERIAL DECISIONS

MARKETING INFORMATION SYSTEM

transforms data into information

CULTURE

COMPANY

LAW AND GOVERNMENT

CUSTOMER

COMPETITORS

TECHNOLOGY

POLITICS

elaborate manner. But just as marketing is a function that *must* be performed in any company irrespective of whether it can employ a marketing manager, so too there must exist the rudiments of an information system if any company is to survive. In small companies or in businesses at an early stage of growth the owner-manager or general manager will personally 'process' marketing information on a daily basis. So the form of the marketing information system will vary enormously in its character and formality from company to company. What is important to remember is that the process involved must take place. In this chapter the elements of a marketing information system are outlined and their complementary roles discussed.

ELEMENTS OF THE MARKETING INFORMATION SYSTEM

Figure 8.2 summarises the various elements that constitute a marketing information system. Activities such as marketing research, marketing intelligence work, use of internal accounting data and so on are necessary in order to acquire data and begin the process of transforming them into useful information. These activities should be engaged in only when there is a decision-need to direct them—whether it is monitoring sales to identify a need for tactical change in, say, price discounting, or a fundamental need to decide what market or market segment to serve.

The process of analysis is the next step. Having collected data on, say, consumers' attitudes to a product, the manager, or the system serving the manager, must be able to analyse the data so that the important implications of consumer attitudes for the product and its future become clear. Much information has lasting value and must therefore be stored and updated. Sales records are an obvious example. This requires the design of a data base—whether it consists of a file in a filing cabinet or a computer data base. And finally there is the issue of who needs to know, how much do they need to know, and when do they need to know it? This is not a problem in a small or new venture where the few key managers *are* the information system. In large companies, however, the communication problem is of significance. Poor communication can lead to duplication of research, to the routing of information vital to one person to someone for whom it has incidental value, or to information overload where managers are so inundated with reports that they cannot distinguish the important from the trivial.

Marketing research

Marketing research is the more or less formal research of any marketing-related decision issue. It is not just consumer surveys and questionnaire administration. Marketing research is as much concerned with determining distribution costs for a company's delivery trucks as with attitude surveys of consumers; as much concerned with test-marketing a new product as with

Figure 8.2

Elements of a Marketing Information System

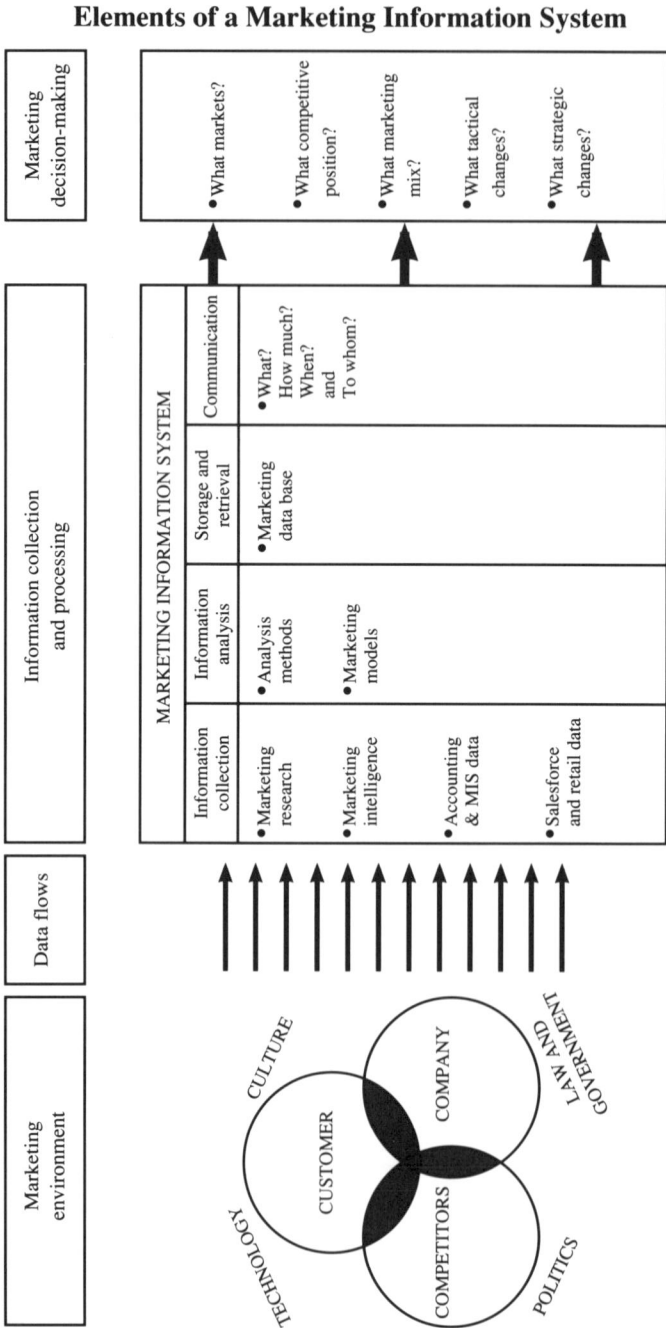

studying long-term technological change in the company's industry. However, any form of marketing research must be both objective and systematic. This means that the process of doing research should observe the norms of scientific practice in moving through the following steps:

(1) *Problem definition:* What is the marketing problem to be solved or decision to be taken? Care and executive time must be devoted to specifying the problem clearly.

(2) *Setting research objectives:* In order to solve the problem or make the decision, exactly what information is needed that is not already available?

(3) *Choosing a research approach:* How can the required information be collected, and from whom? What is the most cost-effective method? What is the plan for data collection, analysis and reporting?

(4) *Data collection:* When, how and precisely from whom are the data to be acquired, and how will the process of collection be controlled and its objectivity ensured?

(5) *Data analysis:* By what valid statistical or other method can the data be transformed into meaningful information?

(6) *Reporting:* What and how much information, in what format, must be provided for whom?

While a systematic, scientific process of research is generally followed by companies, especially if they hire a reputable and professional marketing research agency or consultancy to do the work, it can be difficult to ensure the presence of one key component of scientific method—objectivity. Marketing research is sometimes undertaken in the hope of finding evidence to support a decision already taken. Or research results may be ignored when they are at variance with the manager's judgment. Research may also be designed in such a way that bias in the selection of sources of data, or in the questions asked, predetermines the research outcome. In all such cases the research and its cost is totally wasted. It has no validity as a basis for rational decision-making. A systematic and objective approach is therefore the *sine qua non* of marketing research.

Some of the elementary issues in choosing a research approach, or design, are outlined in Figure 8.3. The three basic design options will often be implemented in sequence. A company will first of all carry out exploratory research to uncover what is going on in the problem area of interest, or to check whether its own assumptions are valid. When this has been done, descriptive research may be undertaken with much greater confidence that the important issues are being studied and the correct questions asked. Descriptive research normally results in an ability to identify associations between several factors (consumption of fresh fish and interest in dietary matters, for example). Such

Figure 8.3

Research Design: Basic Options

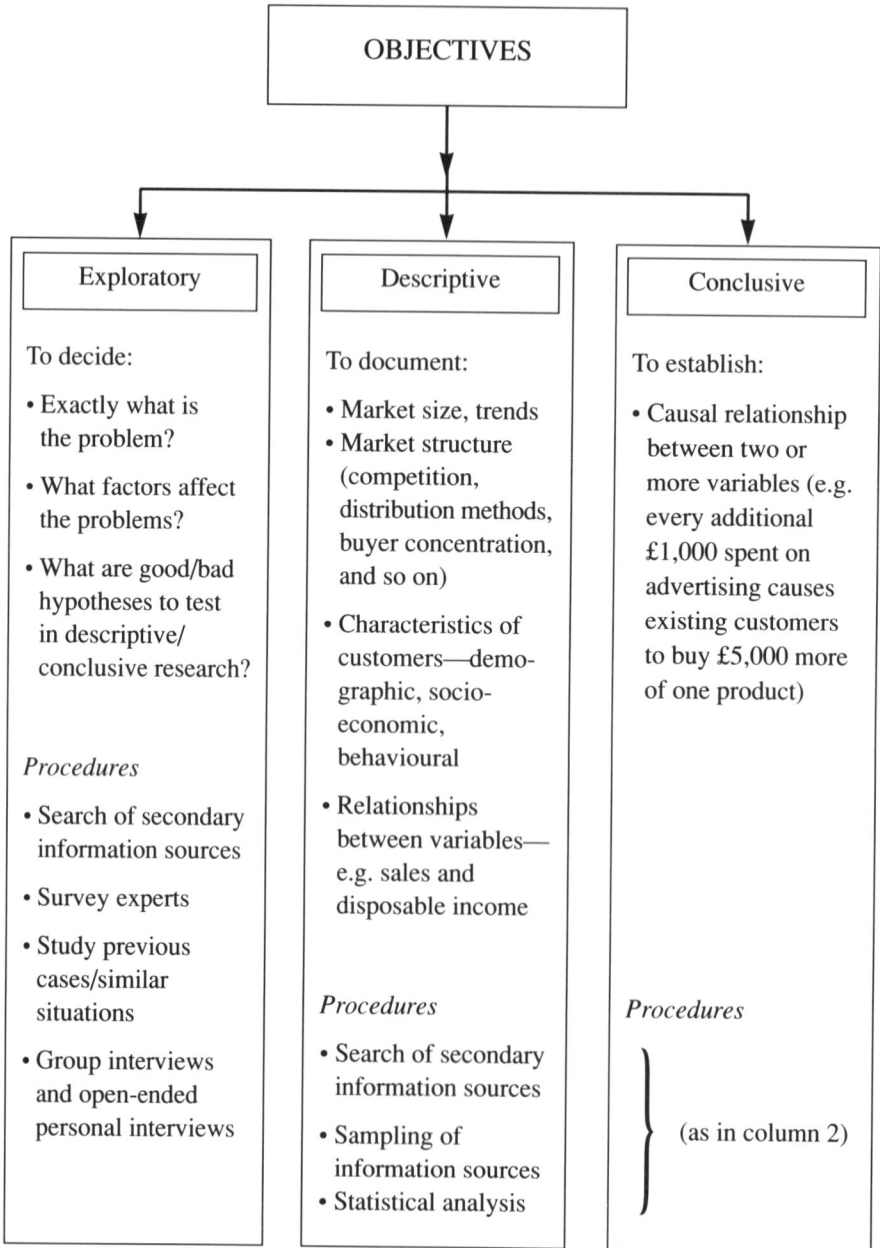

```
                    ┌─────────────────────────┐
                    │      OBJECTIVES         │
                    └─────────────────────────┘
```

Exploratory	Descriptive	Conclusive
To decide:	To document:	To establish:
• Exactly what is the problem?	• Market size, trends	• Causal relationship between two or more variables (e.g. every additional £1,000 spent on advertising causes existing customers to buy £5,000 more of one product)
• What factors affect the problems?	• Market structure (competition, distribution methods, buyer concentration, and so on)	
• What are good/bad hypotheses to test in descriptive/ conclusive research?	• Characteristics of customers—demographic, socio-economic, behavioural	
	• Relationships between variables— e.g. sales and disposable income	
Procedures		
• Search of secondary information sources		
• Survey experts		
• Study previous cases/similar situations	*Procedures*	*Procedures*
• Group interviews and open-ended personal interviews	• Search of secondary information sources	(as in column 2)
	• Sampling of information sources	
	• Statistical analysis	

associations must not be confused with *causal* relationships. There are many spurious associations, such as an historical correlation that once existed between bathtub sales in Britain and the number of suicides. The manager must always be careful not to read causation into research results that document nothing more than an association of two factors.

Figure 8.4

Data Collection: Basic Options

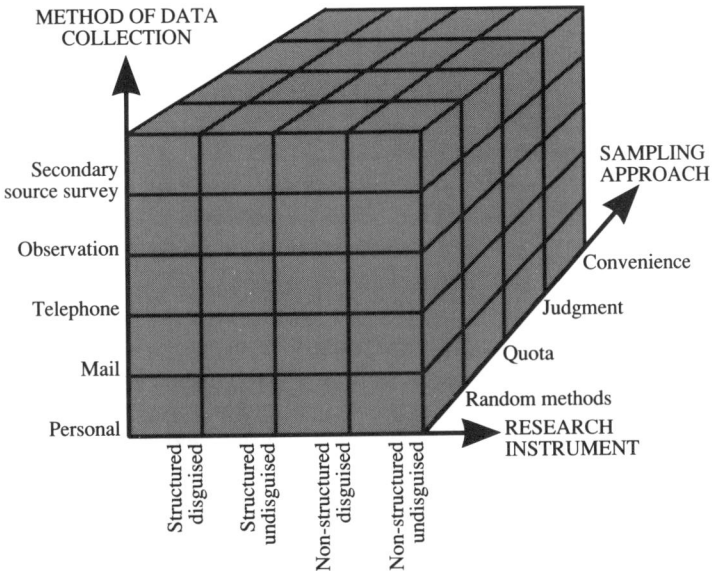

Data collection options in marketing research are also many and important to the outcome of the research. Figure 8.4 summarises basic choices that are faced. Choice of *method* demands evaluation of the role that can be played by secondary and primary sources (these two kinds of data sources were defined in Chapter 5). The options within primary sources must be evaluated in terms of the kind of information needed, its value and the cost of obtaining it by each method. Observational methods have not been widely used in marketing except in store auditing research. However, the use of electronic check-out systems and standard product bar-coding have made a new form of observational research widely available. Many consumer goods and service companies use electronic check-out data from supermarkets and service counters to monitor movement of brands and to do test-marketing with continuous and almost instantaneous feedback on product sales (see Exhibit 8.1).

Exhibit 8.1

SUPER VALU FOODSTORES

Winning the leading edge through technology

Super Valu has successfully challenged the hegemony of the traditional multiples like Dunnes Stores and Quinnsworth. It is now the third largest grocery retailer in the country. Its chairman describes the role of computer technology in winning this leading edge.

'Our research showed us that efficiencies could certainly be effected; we could save time, we could save money and we could save energy. We learned that we could produce good information to improve prices, distribution, merchandising and margin control.

'But first you must remember our origins in the independent retailing sector. We could be described as an independent multiple—a multiple with the owner on the spot. Countrywide there are 135 Super Valu supermarkets servicing the "trolley" business as well as 235 Centra foodstores focusing on the "bag and basket" business. These 370 independently owned retail outlets operate under what is in effect a franchise arrangement. So in putting in new technology we weren't talking about making a head office decision, putting in the hardware and bringing people off on training courses.

'How did we tackle it? We went into technology in two phases. Phase one starting four years ago was the introduction of a handheld computer terminal in the stores which completely revolutionised our system of ordering and pricing. Over a two-year period each of our retailers purchased this piece of equipment and was trained in its use.

'These handheld terminals hold all the relevant cost and selling prices of the 4,500 or so lines we stock in our warehouses. The retailer places his order on the terminal by simply walking around his store, deciding what products and quantities he requires of each line, and then simply keying in the information. When the retailer has completed the order, the terminal is connected up to a modem in his office, and the order is transmitted to our central warehouse computer overnight via a telephone line. This means that when we arrive at the warehouse the following morning, the orders are already on what we call picking lists. These can be handed to the assemblers as soon as they arrive for work and delivery vehicles dispatched quickly and efficiently.

'Phase two is the installation of scanning technology—using the bar-codes on products—in all Super Valu stores. This will be a three-year programme. So far we've 30 stores completed. This EPOS—Electronic Point of Sale—technology has tremendous benefits for the retailer in terms of operational efficiency and competitive opportunity.

'For instance, all price changes for promotions or price increases can be initiated by Super Valu headquarters. The retailer's PC will be updated once a week, and a new set of shelf labels will be printed automatically at the retailer's office. If an item is not in stock or not available for any reason, we will dial the retailer's PC and arrange for an out-of-stock label to be printed. This is placed on the shelf advising the customer that the product is not available. Many retailers are now running promotions for very short periods of time. For example, to encourage early week shopping some retailers run promotions on Wednesday afternoon for three/four hours. To have physically to change all of the price labels on a range of products at the beginning and end of such short promotions can be very costly. With the scanning system, however, all they have to do is change the shelf-edge labels, which can be done in a very short space of time.

'EPOS enables each retailer to see what sales and gross profit were made on each department yesterday, this week, and for the year to date. The retailer can then look more closely at each department—and individual lines therein— and decide to rationalise very slow sellers or lines that are not making a worthwhile contribution. It's also possible to decide precisely what amount of space and what shelf should be given to each individual product in order to maximise the return from it.

'Automatically produced purchase orders are another great time-saving facility provided by this computerised system. Instead of the retailer going around the shelves with his handheld terminal, the retailer's PC will have all of the sales data recorded and it will therefore be possible for the PC to produce the orders for his various suppliers based on existing sales data. The retailer will need to adjust the automatically produced purchase order only for items such as promotions, seasonal lines and so on.

'Looking towards the future, more and more companies will develop systems to produce invoices at time of delivery, thus eliminating the situation where a delivery docket is followed by an invoice through the post, and this in turn followed by a statement. Instead of these three documents it will be possible to have one document, which will be an invoice, but will also become a statement for payment. Further technological advances will include increased automation in the use of credit cards. We'll probably soon have EFTPOS— Electronic Funds Transfer at Point of Sale. These cards will be swiped through a device at the retailer's check-outs, and the information transmitted directly to the banks, thus debiting the consumer's account, crediting the retailer's account and cutting out all the paperwork in between. It will also be possible to collect information by customer, either by issuing personalised customer cards or by using a customer code for customers known to the retailer. Storing up the information would enable retailers to make a loyalty payment or any other kind of refund to bigger and better customers if so desired.

'Electronic shelf-edge labels have also been developed, but are still very expensive. It is likely these will become a feature in the future and will replace the existing paper labels. Another interesting development is self-scanning, which is being pioneered in Holland and the US. Here customers do their own scanning, thus eliminating the need for cashier operators.

'I predict that throughout the 1990s we will see much more attention being paid to supply chain management, with retailers and their suppliers cooperating much more to reduce cost from the manufacture and movement of goods. Retailers who do not have a supplier committed to technology will obviously not benefit. EDI—Electronic Data Interchange—will be key. This is a network or system which allows retailers and suppliers to communicate messages such as order forms or invoices to one another irrespective of the type of computer system each has. As EDI becomes increasingly sophisticated it will facilitate optimal inventory control—from minimum stock levels to efficient JIT systems.

'However, there is a caveat. There is always the danger that retailers could become totally wrapped up in a technology at the expense of customer service. A proper balance must always exist. Just because the system control will almost always be located in a back office, the retailer must never forget that the real action will continue to take place on the shop floor.'

Source: *Retail News*, June 1991, pp. 32–36.

The choice of *research instrument* simply refers to the manner in which data are to be collected and recorded once the means of getting to the source of data has been decided. The choice can range from unstructured questioning of a small group of customers where the identity of the company doing the research is disguised, to a totally structured questionnaire with pre-specified answering alternatives (such as yes/no; sometimes/seldom/never; £0–£10/£11–£20/£21+) and the identity of the company openly disclosed.

A *sampling approach* is usually required in implementing research for two reasons. First, it is usually possible to guarantee, through statistical sampling methods, estimates of the feature of interest that are sufficiently accurate for most marketing decision-making purposes. Second, companies may have very limited resources available for research and be able to afford only limited data collection.

Sampling methods vary from a range of random sampling techniques that yield estimates which may be generalised to the total population of interest with specified margins of error, to convenience procedures which involve no scientific process but simply the choice of data sources that are most accessible to the researcher. While the latter approach may be cheap and quick to implement, it provides no basis for the generalisation of findings.

Marketing intelligence
Marketing intelligence keeps a company informed of current events in its marketing environment, and especially about competitors' initiatives, early

signals of changes in customer preferences and buying habits, and shifts and alterations in the broader technological and socio-political environment. The process of intelligence gathering and processing is usually somewhat haphazard. It can be formalised to a certain degree by ensuring that company personnel attend relevant trade and professional meetings, conferences and industry association meetings; read a broad range of business trade and general publications; and maintain regular contact with persons in touch with new trends, ideas and technologies.

Marketing intelligence typically sparks off two kinds of action processes: tactical adjustment to unanticipated changes, and the initiation of more formal research into issues that could have significant long-run impact on the company. In attempting to formalise the intelligence system it is important to ensure that managers have a regular opportunity to meet with a relatively unstructured agenda in order to exchange observations, check on perceptions, and spot patterns in the variety of intelligence gathered.

Accounting and MIS data

Internal company records, and especially accounting and management information system (MIS) data, represent one of the least exploited sources of valuable marketing information. The regular internal records of any company contain vital marketing information such as:

—distribution of sales volume by customer and customer group
—distribution of net contribution by customer and customer group (and often the alarming fact that 20 per cent of customers generate 80 per cent of contribution!)
—sales and contribution by product line or model
—sales by sales region or territory or salesperson
—customers who pay on or before time, and those who repeatedly delay payment or fail to pay
—credit taken by customer groups
—sales, discounts, level of returns, partial deliveries or damaged goods by customer group/area.

This kind of information should be available in all internal information systems. Extracting it requires some thought in the design of documentation for orders, invoices, statements, etc., and attention to how these are analysed and reports extracted. As most firms review and redesign their computer-based information systems—even the smallest businesses now use micro-computers for this—there is no reasonable managerial excuse for not having such information regularly available. Service industries in particular have been slow to develop detailed marketing data bases from their internal records with the result that many have persistent problems in identifying the profitability of customer groups and services provided.

Salesforce and retail data

Firms running a salesforce must ensure that the salesperson call-reporting and account-reporting procedures are designed not only for the purpose of salesforce control, but also with marketing information needs in mind. The salesforce provides an excellent and low-cost mechanism for:

(1) building up market estimates on a customer-by-customer basis;
(2) forecasting future demand on a customer account basis;
(3) monitoring competitive activity through questioning buyers on new product introductions, pricing tactics, services provided and level of customer satisfaction;
(4) monitoring customer satisfaction with the company's own product or service and changes in customer needs.

Information on issues such as these should flow to management regularly from the salesforce through formal reporting systems and through regular meetings at which these topics are reviewed. Such information must be treated with some caution of course as sales personnel tend to be conservative about estimates which may become the basis for their own sales targets and incentive payments.

As we have seen in Exhibit 8.1, the major changes introduced by electronic scanning and check-out systems in retail outlets represent a rich and powerful source of data on market behaviour. Indeed, companies need to work with retailers on the specification of such systems to ensure that they can exploit their full potential as marketing information generation mechanisms. The principal benefits of such systems should be rapid feedback of retail sales movement by very finely defined product categories, and almost real-time monitoring of new product launches and test-market activities by shop or region.

Information analysis

Data, once collected by any of the methods discussed above, are just that: raw data. The process of analysis should transform them into practical, usable information. Methods of analysis are many and often technically demanding, but simple methods of documenting frequency distributions, averages, ranges and cross-tabulation of two factors at a time (e.g. age of customer vs. brand purchased) still predominate. The power of various statistical methods is considerable in adding greater depth to such analyses and uncovering otherwise unseen relationships. The manager with serious research needs is well advised to discuss all the possible options on analytical methods with an expert in the area and with a professional marketing research agency.

The major advances in the application of quantitative methods to marketing problems that began some decades ago yielded the opportunity for the marketer to model many marketing problems in order to gain a better understanding of their nature and to make more efficient decisions. Well-developed models that assist decisions on warehouse and facilities location or delivery truck routing or salesforce routing are used by many Irish companies. In marketing planning, and especially in the new product launch area, several models of new product diffusion have been developed and applied successfully. Models to assist in media choice and scheduling are also available to support advertising decisions, although these are generally used by advertising agencies on behalf of their clients.

The most widely used models are simple financial models based on computer spreadsheets which allow the marketer to evaluate a variety of 'what if ... ?' situations by varying sales forecasts, margins, product costs and credit given/taken. These are hardly models in the sense in which we spoke of models in the preceding paragraph, but they are very useful mechanisms to test the sensitivities of plans to changes in basic assumptions. Because they are widely available in software packages, they are well within cost and implementation constraints for any serious manager.

Marketing data base

Much of the information required to make marketing decisions is used time and time again and updated regularly. For this kind of information to be maintained up to date and accessible for analysis, a computer data base is desirable. The structure of this data base should reflect the product-market structure of the industry in which the company competes. Taking the natural gas industry, for example, an appropriate data base structure might look like that in Figure 8.5. This basic structure, built on the individual product-markets in which it is realistic to consider competing, is fleshed out with a core set of common data for each product-market cell. This allows the marketer to segment the market in many flexible ways depending on the issue to be analysed or the decision to be taken. In the example shown, the most common segment summary would probably be by market (residential, commercial, industrial) and area. But given a data base built on these lines, what is sometimes called modular segmentation can be implemented almost instantaneously and with great flexibility. In other words, new segments can be structured, described and analysed by recombining the basic building blocks of the data base.

SUMMARY

The chapters of Part II emphasised the role of information as the key resource used in marketing. Bad information results, at best, in decisions that turn out to be good by accident. At worst, bad or insufficient marketing information

Figure 8.5

A Data Base Structure for Natural Gas

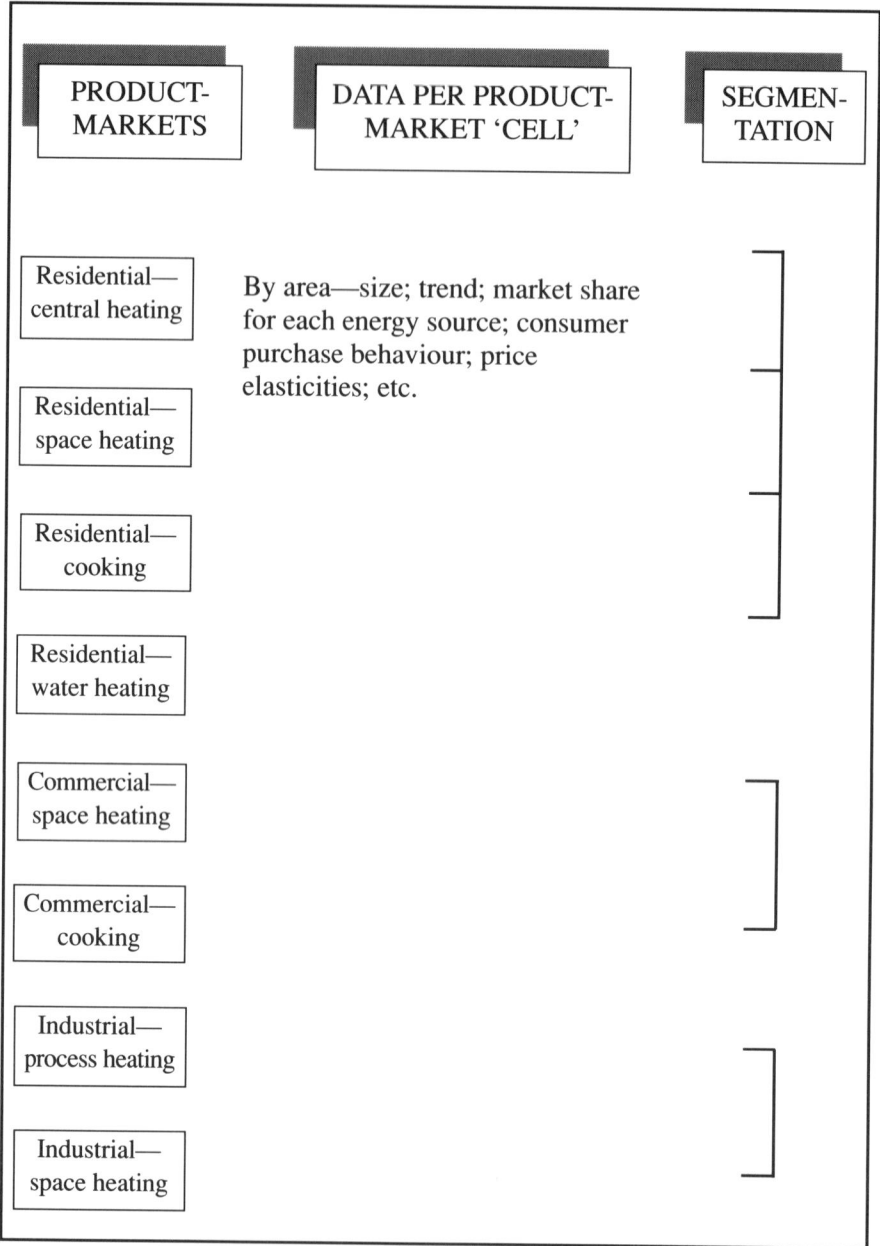

PRODUCT-MARKETS	DATA PER PRODUCT-MARKET 'CELL'	SEGMEN-TATION
Residential—central heating	By area—size; trend; market share for each energy source; consumer purchase behaviour; price elasticities; etc.	
Residential—space heating		
Residential—cooking		
Residential—water heating		
Commercial—space heating		
Commercial—cooking		
Industrial—process heating		
Industrial—space heating		

will lead to decisions that put a company out of business. The way in which information is collected, and how it is analysed, stored and communicated, is therefore a matter of considerable concern in ensuring effective marketing performance. The mechanism for undertaking this activity is the company's marketing information system, which, even at a very informal level, must operate in any effective business.

Reading

Baker, Michael J. (1991), *Research for Marketing*, Macmillan, Basingstoke.

Kotler, P. (1991), *Marketing Management: Analysis, Planning, Implementation and Control*, 7th ed., Prentice-Hall, Englewood Cliffs, NJ, ch. 4.

Lehmann, D.R. (1989), *Market Research and Analysis*, Irwin, Boston.

Tull, D.S. and Hawkins, D.I. (1990), *Marketing Research: Measurement and Methods*, 3rd ed., Macmillan, NY.

Review Questions

1. What are the principal areas of the firm's environment about which it needs a regular flow of marketing information? Explain the relevance of each area in marketing decision-making.
2. What are the elements of a marketing information system, and how do they link together?
3. What are the basic steps in the process of designing and conducting marketing research, and what major options exist in terms of research design?
4. What are the functions of a marketing data base? Pick a particular product-market and suggest a design for a marketing data base for use by a manager dealing with the market.

Case 3

K-Line Kitchens

K-Line Kitchens was founded by its general manager, Ken Lynam, in 1977. A carpenter by profession, Lynam had used his personal savings along with a bank loan to set up business on the outskirts of County Dublin as a manufacturer and retailer of high-quality timber fitted kitchen furniture. The company prospered and by 1983 had a turnover of £300,000 and a workforce of ten. However, Lynam felt his business had now reached a threshold in its development.

Issues: *Developing a basic marketing awareness and direction in the case of a small company. Understanding consumer behaviour and market research. Analysing company capability and competitors. Price/quality issues, product development, distribution channels and promotion.*

The seventies witnessed the take-off of the concept of the fitted kitchen in Ireland. In newly built houses a fitted kitchen was increasingly incorporated as a selling feature. Strong marketing and effective advertising sought to persuade the housewife (and her spouse) that her existing kitchen was poorly serviceable and outmoded and that she should replace it with a more functional and convenient one with modern design appeal and with kitchen appliances integrated into this design. Hi tech if not high fashion had invaded that most traditional part of the household dwelling; indeed the humble kitchen sink had become regenerated as a food preparation centre.

The market for fitted kitchen furniture had grown rapidly during the 1970s with growth far outstripping any other segment of the furniture industry. While 1982 and 1983 were difficult years for the business due to the drop in consumer spending and sluggish economic conditions, nonetheless it was estimated that the retail value of the domestic market for fitted kitchen furniture was £24 million in 1983. Industry sources reckoned that almost a third of Ireland's 930,000 households had a fitted or partially fitted kitchen rather than the older free-standing unit type. Irish manufacturers supplied all but £4 million of this market, with these imports coming mainly from the UK

This case was developed as a basis for class discussion rather than to illustrate either effective or ineffective handling of an administrative situation. K-Line is a disguised appellation for the actual name of the company described in the case.

and Germany. In addition Irish companies exported some £5 million of kitchen furniture, mostly to the UK.

Ken Lynam, general manager of K-Line Kitchens, set up in business in 1977 on the outskirts of County Dublin as a manufacturer of high-quality timber fitted kitchens. The company grew successfully, particularly in latter years, to a turnover approaching £300,000 in 1983. However, Lynam felt his business had now reached a threshold in its development and that any future growth would involve making a number of important decisions.

THE PRODUCT

The average retail price of a fitted kitchen could vary between £700 at the cheaper end of the market to over £4,000 at the more luxurious end. Despite the range of price, design and quality a fitted kitchen was essentially a uniform and functional product. It comprised a basic 'carcase', fronted by doors and drawers, with a worktop, all of which were built into the kitchen area in an integrated manner.

The carcase or interior framework which housed the storage space was universally constructed on a modular basis and was invariably made of melamine-faced chipboard (MFC), which gave a durable plastic or laminate type of finish. The worktop in most built-in kitchens was also made of laminate, and was post-formed with rounded or wood-trim edges. However, it was the style, design and material of the doors and drawer fronts which really distinguished a fitted kitchen in price and quality. These usually came in either laminate, veneer or solid timber. Laminate doors were available in a wide variety of colours and texture finishes such as patterned, hessian, weaves and synthetic timber. The solid timber door in oak, pine or mahogany was considerably more expensive than the standard-quality laminate door and could cost a manufacturer three to four times more to produce.

The more luxurious up-market kitchens also boasted a host of accessories such as vegetable/pot racks, swivel units for easy access to corners, double sink units, pelmets and cornices for added appearance and so on. Also, appliance integration was a concept very much promoted by the industry. This enabled manufacturers of electrical goods to sell appliances such as split-level cookers and dishwashers to combine with the storage furniture and blend in with the overall design. Wall tiles and floor covering often complemented this design. In all, the kitchen was presented as a convenient and ergonomically satisfying place to work in as well as a pleasant area in which to relax and eat.

A number of definite trends in regard to consumer tastes in kitchen furniture could be discerned in the early 1980s. There had been a strong swing towards timber doors and drawer fronts. The Irish consumer seemed to like the natural look of a timber exterior appearance despite its higher cost. Oak was particularly popular. In laminate doors the stronger colours of the 1970s were being gradually replaced by softer, more neutral colours such as sandy, beige, blue, grey, often harmonised with a natural timber trim around the door. Plain white, however, continued to be a strong favourite as it allowed colour to be picked out in wall or floor tiles or other kitchen décor. Indeed there was some evidence to suggest that white ranges were increasing their share of the total market.

READY-ASSEMBLED AND SELF-ASSEMBLY
Virtually all Irish fitted kitchens were professionally installed. They came from the factory or workshop in rigid carcase or ready-assembled form for installation on site. Self-assembly kitchens were supplied in flat-pack or knock-down form and then assembled and built in by the buyer himself. This self-assembly or DIY market sector was reckoned to be as low as 7 per cent of the total market in 1983.

This consumer resistance to self-assembly was in marked contrast to the UK experience, where over 50 per cent of kitchen furniture sales were in this form. Self-assembly offered the price-conscious handyman or DIY enthusiast the opportunity to buy his fitted kitchen more cheaply and even stagger his capital outlay by buying the units over time. In general, there was a 40 to 50 per cent price differential between ready-assembled and self-assembly kitchen furniture. In Ireland, however, this price difference was less as self-assembly units carried a 23 per cent VAT rate on purchase whereas professionally installed kitchens carried only a 5 per cent VAT rate.

RETAIL AND CONTRACT MARKET
The overall market for fitted kitchen furniture could be divided into two segments. The retail sector accounted for some 73 per cent of the total market and the contract sector for the remaining 27 per cent. This segmentation was largely on the basis of purchase decision-making.

The contract market represented the supply of kitchen furniture installed in the building of new housing schemes and apartments in both the private and local authority sectors. The specifier was usually the builder, architect or local authority. Quality could vary from the cheaper to the more luxurious end of the market where the inclusion of a fitted kitchen by a well-known brand name, such as ARCO, could be a very positive selling feature. House purchasers had increasingly come to expect some kind of fitted kitchen as a basic feature in a new house.

The retail sector was the replacement and extension of existing kitchens. Here the consumer was the specifier or purchase decision-maker. He was interested in a 'new' kitchen, in replacing what was perceived to be an out-dated, poorly serviceable or spartan kitchen with a newer, more functional and more appealing type. The installation of fitted kitchens in newly built 'one-off' houses and bungalows in rural areas also fell into this retail sector as the consumer was almost always the final specifier in this instance.

MANUFACTURERS

In 1983 Irish manufacturers supplied £20 million at retail prices of fitted kitchen furniture to the Irish market as well as exporting another £5 million. About thirty manufacturers specialised in fitted kitchen furniture. Another thirty furniture producers made kitchen furniture as part of their range. Three large manufacturers were especially noteworthy: Arco Kitchens of Waterford; Murray Kitchens of Youghal, Co. Cork; and McGoona Kitchens of Navan. Between them they sold almost £8 million at retail prices to the domestic market in 1983. These companies were nationally known brand names and marketed a very high-quality product. It was manufactured in the most up-to-date and mechanised manner possible for a production process which still involved a high degree of individual craftsmanship. These so-called Big Three were also responsible for the bulk of the £5 million exports, mainly to the UK (including Northern Ireland).

Most of the other manufacturers were much smaller and less sophisticated. They were located all over the country though there was some concentration in the two major furniture manufacturing centres in Ireland—Navan, Co. Meath and County Monaghan. For these manufacturers the level of product differentiation was often very low. Entry barriers to the industry were also low. Indeed a carpenter with a small amount of capital could get into the business. The IDA, in an effort to mechanise production with a view to encouraging exports, had contributed a sizeable amount in grant aid to the fitted furniture industry in the late seventies and early eighties. A typical cost structure was: production labour 20–25 per cent, materials 40–45 per cent, profits and overheads 35–40 per cent.

Many of the manufacturers specialising in fitted kitchen furniture also make fitted bedroom furniture, free-standing kitchen furniture (i.e. tables and chairs) and other occasional furniture. This was in part an effort to extend their product range and in part an attempt to cope with the sales cycle of fitted kitchens, which tended to peak in autumn, when sales often ran 20 per cent higher than the spring trough.

In terms of selling to the retail market, the Big Three and a number of the other large manufacturers, e.g. O'Connor Kitchens, Dublin, did not operate their own retail operation. Instead they used independent agents and retailers, especially kitchen specialists, which they supported with national brand advertising and technical assistance. These retailers had developed considerable marketing skills in selling fitted kitchens and enjoyed up to a 50 per cent mark-up on manufacturers' prices. (In mid-1983 Arco had indicated its intention to set up a number of its own retail outlets.) These manufacturers did, however, sell directly to builders in the contract market.

The other manufacturers sold most, though not necessarily all, of their output directly to the purchaser. Their retail operations or 'windows' varied in selling sophistication from crude display areas adjoining the factory to something approaching the fully-fledged kitchen specialist outlet described below.

KITCHEN SPECIALISTS

At least 150 outlets retailed fitted kitchen furniture in Ireland. These included specialist kitchen centres, builders' providers, DIY and discount stores, department and furniture stores as well as the retail outlets of the direct supply manufacturers (see Table 1).

Table 1

Channels of Distribution of Fitted Kitchen Furniture

(1983 Total Market @ Retail Prices)

	£m	%
Kitchen Specialists	10.8	45
Builders' Providers	2.2	9
DIY/Discount Stores	1.4	6
Department/Furniture Stores	.2	1
Direct Supply	9.4	39
	24.0	100

These were the dominant channels of distribution. There were upwards of 50 such outlets nationally. These centres promoted themselves as the experts in fitted kitchens. They were usually situated on a high street and had on display a range of attractively presented fitted kitchens. These outlets sold to the retail rather than the contract market.

They offered a highly personalised service in the planning, design and installation of fitted kitchen furniture. The centre's designer usually went to an interested customer's house, measured up the kitchen area and drew up a suggested plan. While some specialist shops charged a small fee of £10–£20 for this service, the charge was waived if the customer actually purchased. Full installation of the fitted kitchen was arranged by the centres, plus plumbing, electrical and building services if necessary.

Most kitchen specialists supplied the medium to high end of the market in terms of quality and price. Typically, a medium to up-market outlet, e.g. Blackrock Kitchen Centre, Blackrock, Co. Dublin, might retail one of the nationally branded kitchens such as Arco or one of the more moderately priced O'Connor range of kitchens. It might also carry one or two of the expensive imported range of kitchens such as Poggenpohl or Miele, often on the basis of being the exclusive Irish agent for the import. Many of the smaller kitchen specialists offered an own-brand product, i.e. giving their own name and label to the product. Appliance integration was also actively promoted by these kitchen specialists. Many were agents for and retailed a range of complementary electrical appliances. Many also sold a range of fitted bedroom furniture and free-standing kitchen furniture.

BUILDERS' PROVIDERS

These businesses were the traditional suppliers to builders and contractors of building materials such as timber, concrete products, heating equipment and so on. Many were agents for fitted kitchen furniture. A smaller number, mainly the large city or provincial providers such as Chadwicks and Glorneys, carried a range of fitted units on display and offered a limited design and installation service. This service was not of comparable standard to that offered by the kitchen specialists. Builders' providers supplied both the contract and retail sector of the market and focused on the low to middle segment in terms of price/quality.

DIY AND DISCOUNT STORES

The previous decade had seen the limited development of discount stores and warehouses in urban Ireland, e.g. Atlantic Homecare in Dublin and Cork and MFI in Dublin. These large stores offered a wide range of products for the home such as painting and decorating materials, carpets, furniture, electrical appliances, gardening equipment, building and hardware products. They aimed mainly at the DIY and retail market. High turnover, fairly unsophisticated product displays, along with self-assembly of many products, facilitated discounting of prices—though it was the case that the low prices boasted about by these discount stores were not in reality significantly different from competitor offerings. The extensive use of TV and newspaper advertising, own-brand promotion and Sunday opening also helped to establish their position.

Furniture sold by these stores was mainly targeted at the low to middle segment of the market. Kitchen furniture was usually of the self-assembly type, stocked and sold in flat-pack for installation by the consumer. It was virtually all imported from the UK. Any future growth in demand for kitchen furniture through this channel was dependent on the Irish consumer overcoming his apparent reluctance to adopt DIY methods and, indeed, on any significant changes in VAT rates which might widen the price gap between self-assembly and ready-assembled furniture.

DEPARTMENT/FURNITURE STORES

By and large, department stores and large furniture stores had missed out on the growth in the kitchen furniture market. Their large and often impersonal structure failed to compete with the personalised service of the owner-managed kitchen specialist centres. Their sales were mainly to the middle to high sector of the retail market.

DIRECT SUPPLY

This channel of distribution, second in size to the specialist kitchen centres, was made up of the manufacturers who sold directly to the retail and contract markets. They operated their own retail outlet rather than selling through a high street independent agent or retailer, though some such manufacturers might sell part of their output through an agent.

In the contract market the builder or his architect liked to purchase directly from these direct supply manufacturers. The middleman was cut out and a bulk discount could be negotiated for a scheme of houses. (It should be pointed out that sales of the Big Three and other large manufacturers directly to the contract market were included in this channel.)

In the retail market the consumer was also attracted by the possibility of by-passing the independent retailer or kitchen specialist and of purchasing directly from these manufacturers who had their own retail 'window'. However, any saving in price, if it existed, in this regard had to be balanced against a number of other factors. Most of these direct supply manufacturers were situated outside towns and cities and so the expense of a possible thirty-mile journey or more was usually involved. Their display areas were normally on the factory premises and were often of poor quality and crude compared to the sophisticated and attractively presented kitchens of the specialist centres. Neither was their planning and design service as comprehensive as that of most of the independent retailers. On the other hand, these manufacturers/retailers did often have a design flexibility, e.g. to make a unit for an awkward corner, which the specialist centres did not have as they had to design within the standard modular units available from the manufacturers. These direct supply manufacturers had product offerings right through the market spectrum from low to high, with varying product quality, retail services and price. A small number, e.g. West Wicklow Design, Blessington, Co. Wicklow, offered a very high-quality product and had a retail operation which approached the best of the independent kitchen specialists.

PROMOTION

The Big Three manufacturers had achieved a national brand identity. They advertised on TV, radio, national newspapers (especially in the personal columns), advertiser free sheets (e.g. *Southside*), quality women's/home magazines (e.g. *Image*) and in architectural/designer/property trade press. Exhibit 1 (page 162) shows an example of such newspaper advertising. Similarly the expensive imported lines of fitted kitchen furniture, e.g. Poggenpohl of Germany or Allmilmo of Italy, used advertising to win a selective brand identity. Such branding obviously helped their agents and retailers to sell these products.

The more up-market kitchen specialists used a similar range of advertising to establish themselves and to arouse consumer interest in fitted kitchens. Joint advertising with a national brand was also common, e.g. 'Murray Kitchens at Dundrum Kitchen Centre, Dublin', with the finished artwork being supplied by the manufacturer. These centres also carried brochures of their available range of kitchens. The promotional practice of these up-market kitchen specialists might best be described as a 'pull-push' strategy. Advertising stimulated consumer awareness. Once the consumer was inside the door of a kitchen specialist shop, however, the quality and attractiveness of the layout of the fitted kitchens on display, allied to the effectiveness of the salesperson, became crucial factors. Also the visit of a designer representative to an initially interested customer's house helped to build the centre/client relationship.

The other kitchen specialists, the builders' providers and the direct supply manufacturers, were generally much more circumspect in their use of advertising. They sometimes had brochures of their product range. There was a selective use of local press. An approach adopted by a few was to organise brochure/leaflet drops in estates at least ten to fifteen years old where houses might be in need of replacement kitchen units. But these retail outlets mostly relied on the local word of mouth of satisfied customers, which was viewed as the best kind of product endorsement.

UK MARKET

The market for fitted kitchen furniture in the UK amounted to £390 million at manufacturers' prices in 1983. It had shown a modest 4 per cent per annum growth in real terms over the five years to 1983. A noteworthy feature of this market was the high proportion of self-assembly to ready-assembled (rigid) kitchen furniture. In 1983 self-assembly sales amounted to 60 per cent of all fitted kitchen sales and this percentage had been growing significantly over the previous decade. The potential benefits to the consumer of self-assembly have already been outlined above. To the retailer the flat-pack form of packaging and distribution offered the possibility of carrying a wide selection of stock. The standardised product range of self-assembly units enabled the manufacturer to achieve, at high-volume throughput, considerable economies of scale which were not feasible in the production of the more customised rigid ranges. This high level of self-assembly sales in the UK resulted in DIY and discount stores being the dominant channel of distribution, accounting for 37 per cent of total market sales @ m.s.p. in 1983.

A much commented-on development in the UK market for fitted kitchen furniture in recent years was the trend towards more up-market self-assembly kitchens. Traditionally there was a large gap in sophistication and choice as well as price between self-assembly and ready-assembled kitchens. Now many self-assembly suppliers were offering the various accoutrements of good rigid ranges—cornices, open corner units, essential in-cupboard accessories and the various options in real wood doors/drawers; some even offered an installation service! This tended to make increasingly irrelevant the distinction between self-assembly and ready-assembled ranges.

Another trend worth pointing out in the context of the UK market was the growing importance of 'own branding'. The Furniture Industry Research Association (FIRA) estimated that the own-brand market was worth some £50 million or 13 per cent of the total market in 1983. Own-brand selling or own labelling enabled the retailer to charge a price he deemed profitable and to avoid direct competition with companies better able to discount products due to lower overheads or increased buying power. From the manufacturer's viewpoint it meant dealing with a selected range of distributors/retailers and avoiding substantial branding costs—FIRA reckoned that a successful national branding campaign to the mass market would cost around £5 million over two to three years.

THE CONSUMER

The retail price of a typical fitted kitchen obviously meant that the purchase decision was very much a considered one. Towards the upper end of the market it represented a decision about a consumer durable purchase second in expense only to that of a car. Table 2 summarises research investigating the motives behind 2,000 purchases of kitchen units in the UK. In buying a fitted kitchen the husband/spouse usually played an important role. While it was more often the wife who initially felt the need for a new kitchen and who started to gather information on available types and prices, when it came to the final purchase decision the husband normally played a crucial role. This had implications for the marketing and promotional strategies pursued by suppliers.

In the final decision-making process the price of the fitted kitchen was an important, but not always the dominant, consideration. This was particularly true of the middle to upper end of the market. Other factors, such as quality, reputation of supplier, suggested design, technical advice, delivery, installation and, especially in the case of the kitchen specialists, the selling expertise of the representative all had to be weighed up by the consumer.

Table 2

Motivation for Buying Fitted Kitchen Furniture

	% of Respondents
Replacing items which are worn out or shabby	29
Moving nearer to what we have wanted for some time	18
Replacing items which are serviceable but do not fit with present ideas	20
More storage space	15
Moving home	13
Extension to house/kitchen	14
Wanting to change from what we have got used to	12

Source: FIRA, UK, 1983. Figures add to over 100% as some respondents gave more than one answer.

FUTURE DEVELOPMENT

In the contract market the demand for fitted kitchens was related to the level of new housing and apartment construction in Ireland. Such building had dropped from an historic peak of 28,920 units in 1981 to 26,140 units in 1983 and showed little signs of any significant recovery. However, this decline was somewhat compensated for by the fact that builders, in their competition for house-buyers, were increasingly offering fitted kitchen furniture as a selling feature of their houses, and indeed buyers were coming to accept such kitchens as a basic feature in a new house.

In the larger retail market demand depended on the level of discretionary consumer income, on the age and quality of the housing stock, as well as on consumer tastes and attitudes stimulated by factors such as industry marketing. The years 1982 and 1983 had been difficult years for the fitted furniture industry and this was reflected in the decline in personal consumer expenditure. A modest growth was forecast in consumer spending over the next five years. Thus an annual percentage growth in the fitted furniture industry of a low single-figure percentage would not be unrealistic to expect.

A development worth noting occurring in the business, particularly in the last year or two, was the sale by fitted kitchen suppliers of replacement doors and drawer fronts. These were fitted to existing fitted or suitable free-standing kitchen furniture and provided the consumer with the appearance of a new kitchen at a fraction of the cost of a full new one. In a sense the provision of fitted kitchens was a fashion business. The trend of the early eighties towards natural timber doors and drawer fronts, especially oak, and towards more neutral colours in the laminate finishes, could well evolve in other directions in years ahead. The successful supplier was usually in the vanguard of such changes in taste.

K-LINE KITCHENS

K-Line Kitchens was founded by its general manager, Ken Lynam, in 1977. A carpenter by profession, Lynam had used his personal savings along with a bank loan to set up business as a manufacturer of quality timber fitted kitchen furniture. Like many small manufacturers he retailed from his manufacturing plant, where he had an adjoining showroom/office. His operation was situated on a two-acre site outside a small village, some twenty-three miles from Dublin city, just off one of the main arterial roads leading out of the city. His business prospered since its inception and by 1983 had achieved a turnover of £292,000. His workforce comprised ten men involved in the production, delivery and installation of the furniture and a female secretary/office administrator.

The market for K-Line Kitchens' products was the greater Dublin region, i.e. Dublin city, county and its environs. While the company enjoyed a strong reputation in its own locality, it drew custom from all over the Dublin region. This was achieved through word of mouth as K-Line Kitchens did not advertise or carry brochures of its products. It supplied both the retail and contract market. Table 3 gives a breakdown of company sales by market and by product type for the years 1979–1983.

K-Line manufactured kitchens in four types of solid timber: mahogany, oak, teak and pine, in that descending order of price. Pine, being the cheapest, was particularly popular with price-conscious builders in the contract market. The door and drawer fronts came in two basic designs though more styles were available on request. K-Line offered kitchens only in solid timber. Like most other fitted kitchen manufacturers, Lynam sold other occasional items of furniture, e.g. tables, chairs and dressers. When providing a kitchen he would incorporate built-in appliances in the design if a customer so wanted. He would arrange their purchase and installation but he was not an agent for any such appliances.

In 1983 the contract market accounted for some 26 per cent of company sales. Lynam had some misgivings about this business. While all business was welcome, profit on contract sales was often a half to two-thirds less than on sales to the consumer in the retail market. Also, builders demanded three months' credit and often took longer to pay. In the retail market standard practice was 50 per cent deposit on ordering and payment of the remainder of the kitchen price immediately after installation.

A modest showroom/office adjoined the factory premises. It had five fitted kitchens presented in a fairly basic display. The two popular door/drawer front styles were used in the display. The office shared this showroom area. Office files were to be found in some of the display units and a visitor might have been forgiven for feeling a certain sense of clutter at times in the showroom. If a customer was interested in a kitchen Lynam would call to his house, take measurements and suggest a broad design. His secretary/

Table 3

K-Line Kitchens' Sales 1979–1983

	1979		1980		1981		1982		1983	
BY MARKET										
Total Company Sales	131,420	100%	166,810	100%	249,810	100%	287,280	100%	292,610	100%
Retail Sales	115,130	88%	131,780	79%	182,360	73%	216,040	75%	216,540	74%
Contract Sales	16,290	12%	35,030	21%	67,450	27%	71,240	25%	76,070	26%
BY PRODUCT TYPE										
Total Company Sales	131,420	100%	166,810	100%	249,810	100%	287,280	100%	292,610	100%
Mahogany	49,940	38%	35,130	21%	44,970	18%	60,170	21%	38,120	13%
Oak	13,140	10%	50,140	30%	67,450	27%	68,720	24%	90,920	31%
Teak	6,600	5%	16,720	10%	49,970	20%	48,540	17%	43,910	15%
Pine	48,720	37%	53,480	32%	74,940	30%	77,100	27%	83,380	29%
Fitted Kit. Furniture	118,400	90%	155,470	93%	237,330	95%	254,530	89%	256,330	88%
Other Items	13,020	10%	11,340	7%	12,480	5%	32,750	11%	36,280	12%
No. of orders specifying appliances	–	–	8/190	4%	24/280	9%	32/336	10%	39/327	12%

office administrator would then draw up and cost the design in detail and send it to the customer. There was no charge for this service.

Lynam's factory premises had a nondescript exterior with little to indicate to the passer-by on the road the existence of a fitted furniture factory. There was no sign portraying K-Line Kitchens nor did his two vans carry the company name. Many trippers who had travelled to the area to visit the showroom had difficulty in finding the premises, which were about a half-mile outside the town. They often had to ask directions locally.

Lynam did not keep any systematic data on his clients and his knowledge of any typical customer profile derived from his intuition of the business. One factor that did puzzle him was the role played by husbands in buying a fitted kitchen. Usually in the initial stages of looking at kitchen types and designs he tended to deal more with the wife of the household. But later on he more often than not found himself discussing with the husband the details of price, the suitability of a certain type of hinge or the technicalities of installation.

PRODUCTION

K-Line Kitchens manufactured kitchens of a very high quality. This high quality was vouched for even by its competitors. For added solidity the walls of the carcase/interior framework were made of solid timber so that the unit doors were hinged on to solid timber rather than on to melamine-faced chipboard. This was unique in the industry; even the carcase of Arco's top-of-the-range kitchen was made of chipboard.

Lynam was also prepared to make special kitchen units outside the standard modular range of sizes. This suited customers who might have an awkward corner to fill and gave him an advantage over the specialist retailers who could not provide this feature with the standard range of sizes available from the larger manufacturers. The company also had a reputation for prompt delivery and a standard of installation as high as the product itself. Along with his secretary (his indispensable Girl Friday, as he referred to her) Lynam carefully scheduled production and delivery dates. He himself liked to stay in close touch with the production process. He discussed each order with his production team, was readily available where problems arose and often spent a portion of the day working machinery on the factory floor.

FINANCE

Company turnover grew rapidly over the years 1979–1982, with a proportionate growth in profitability. Apart from an IDA grant of £16,000, the development of the business had been funded through retained profits. There was no long-term debt and the business at present had reserves of cash. However, results in 1983, which Lynam had recently received from his part-time accountant, were not quite as encouraging. Despite a small increase in turnover in 1983, the real level of trading and profits was down on 1982, his best year to date. This slow-down in business activity had been prompting Lynam to reassess his business strategy.

COMPETITION

Lynam estimated that there were up to fifty retail outlets of one form or another competing in the fitted kitchen market in the Dublin region. However, from his knowledge of the business and from talking to his customers, he reckoned that he probably had fewer than a dozen real competitors in the sector of the market he aimed to supply. In particular he listed four kitchen specialists in suburban Dublin, four direct supply manufacturers, two of which were in suburban Dublin and two of which, like K-Line Kitchens, were 20–25 miles from the city, and one builders' provider (see Exhibit 2). Lynam felt his knowledge of these competitors to be lacking. He believed that if he had a firmer picture of how their operations ticked over he would be in a better position to make decisions about his own. He arranged for some fairly elementary research to be carried out which provided the information to draw up the following competitor profiles.

Exhibit 2

Key Competitors

Studio Alpine A, Clontarf, Co. Dublin.
Kitchen Concept, Dun Laoghaire, Co. Dublin.
Blackrock Kitchen Centre, Blackrock, Co. Dublin.
Dundrum Kitchen Centre, Dundrum, Co. Dublin.
Oakline Kitchens, Ranelagh, Co. Dublin.
Killane's Kitchens, North Strand & Monkstown, Co. Dublin.
West Wicklow Design, Blessington, Co. Wicklow.
ORM Kitchens, Naas, Co. Kildare.
Glorneys Builders' Providers, Islandbridge, Co. Dublin.

Studio Alpine A in the north Dublin suburb of Clontarf was the most up-market of the kitchen specialists in Ireland. It boasted the largest showroom with over thirty kitchens on display. It was an agent for, among others, Arco, O'Connor and Allmilmo of Italy ranges of kitchens. These makes of kitchen were heavily promoted by their manufacturers and enjoyed widespread brand recognition. Studio Alpine A itself advertised extensively on TV, in newspaper and quality journals. Its advisory service was of architectural standard. It also carried an extensive range of fitted bedroom furniture.

The other three kitchen specialists on Lynam's list of competitors were also in the suburbs and had similar characteristics to Studio Alpine A, though were smaller in scale and catered for a broader middle to upper segment of the market. Each carried at least one of the nationally known brands as well as an expensive imported range. Blackrock Kitchen Centre, for example, carried Arco, O'Connor, and Miele of France kitchens. (These imported continental kitchens were usually of laminate finish and their high price/ exclusivity derived from their modernity of design, quality of finish and range of accoutrements.) All of these kitchen specialists were also agents for an electrical appliance brand, e.g. Neff.

Oakline Kitchens was a direct supply manufacturer of quality solid timber kitchens. It manufactured in the Liberties, an old part of the city, and retailed from a fairly fashionable high street location in Ranelagh, just a mile from the city. Its retail showroom had an attractive display of kitchens. While its planning and design service was not up to the architect-type standard of the top kitchen centres, Oakline nonetheless presented the consumer with the impression of being a kitchen specialist in the medium to top range. It also carried a selection of high-quality imported laminate kitchens. It occasionally advertised.

Killane's Kitchens manufactured a range of laminate, veneer and solid timber kitchens in North Strand, two miles from the city centre. It operated a retail outlet there and on the south side at Monkstown. Its showrooms and design service were considerably below that of the top kitchen specialists and it aimed more for the middle of the market. It also stocked a range of kitchens from smaller Irish manufacturers. The company rarely advertised.

West Wicklow Design made and sold high-quality fitted kitchens in a selection of solid timber at Blessington, Co. Wicklow. Its standard of display and design service approached the best of the specialist kitchen retailers. It advertised regularly and had achieved considerable brand recognition in the Dublin region. Its advertisements often attempted to minimise the distance of the 24-mile trip to Blessington by suggesting a family outing make-a-day-of-it approach. In 1979 it had opened a high street retail outlet in Dublin city. This was closed fifteen months later due to an insufficient volume of business. West Wicklow Design like most other direct supply manufacturers also made occasional furniture.

ORM manufactured a range of quality solid timber kitchen furniture in Castlemartyr, Co. Cork, where it also had a retail centre. Its Naas outlet, some 20 miles from Dublin, supplied the Dublin region. ORM also retailed an own-brand laminate range which was made by another smaller Irish manufacturer. Its intermittent advertising was supplemented by colour brochures of its products.

Glorneys, a builders' provider situated near Phoenix Park, was an agent for a selection of Irish-manufactured kitchen furniture. It had a large though not particularly attractive showroom and aimed for the middle market segment.

The research also attempted a price comparison between K-Line and its competitors. It was arranged that each competitor would provide a quotation for a specific kitchen plan to be made in solid oak. Lynam added his own company's price for the same plan, also in oak. The results are set out in Exhibit 3. A precise comparison between prices was blurred somewhat by the fact that different manufacturers offered different quality oak finishes; Arco, for example, offered three. Yet the figures did provide an approximate indication of the relative price levels between competitors.

Exhibit 3

Kitchen Plan Prices

Company	Type of Finish	Price £
Studio Alpine A	Arco 'Chateau' oak	4,560
Kitchen Concept	Arco 'Antique' oak	3,950
Dundrum Kitchen Centre	Murray oak	3,520
Blackrock Kitchen Centre	Arco 'Forest' oak	3,070
Glorneys	McGoona oak	2,850
ORM	own oak	2,730
West Wicklow Design	own oak	2,680
Killane's	own oak	2,400
Oakline	own oak	2,320
K-Line	own oak	2,070

Note: These prices include VAT, delivery and installation, but exclude the plumbing, cost of electrical appliances, structural or electrical work.

WHITHER K-LINE?

Lynam had often toyed with the idea of upgrading his showroom and design service, of putting a proper livery on his factory premises and vans, of bringing out brochures and advertising. It was even suggested to him that he change the name of the company in some way to reflect his personal approach to business. (While K-Line Kitchens was the legally registered name, most people and customers knew him as Ken Lynam Kitchens.)

He was somewhat reluctant to embark on this course of action. His basic feel for his business was that the customers he attracted liked the quality of his timber products and liked his prices. He believed his customers wanted to come directly to a quality manufacturer and would not be impressed by any cosmetics of selling which would merely push up the price. He was also reluctant to increase his workforce by more than five or six people as he felt it was important that he stayed close to the production process.

'To be a manufacturer and retailer of high-quality timber fitted kitchen furniture' would probably have best summed up Lynam's present business philosophy. As he stood in the early months of 1984 his order book was not as healthy as he would have liked. He wondered if it was just a cyclical downturn that any business experiences or whether there were underlying considerations at play which would suggest that he should change his business strategy.

Questions
1. Assess the characteristics of the market for fitted kitchen furniture.
2. Discuss the purchase decision-making patterns in the different market segments and channels of distribution. What are your comments about Lynam's puzzlement about the role played by husbands in buying a fitted kitchen?
3. Do you agree that Lynam's business has reached a threshold in its development? Draw up a marketing strategy for his business.
4. Compare and contrast K-Line Kitchens' key competitors. Consider using a map with two relevant criteria, e.g. price and quality, to plot these players' current positions and possible future moves.

Exhibit 1

Case 4

Equity Bank

The financial services market is a wide-ranging and complex amalgam of services, suppliers and buyers of differing scope and size. Over the last two decades, technology, legislation, new competitive modes and customer requirements have dramatically altered this market. In 1989 Equity Bank, a small merchant bank, was acquired by a large UK bank and under a dynamic new management set about expanding its business and exploiting new market opportunities.

Issues: *Product and service definition. Market analysis and segmentation. Niche marketing. Developing and setting in place a new business strategy.*

Over the last two decades, new technology, changing legislation, sharper competitive modes, and not least evolving customer requirements have conspired to change substantially what banks do and the way they do it. The imposing and often impersonal aspect, the cultivated conservatism, the hallowed corridor—what Philip Kotler calls 'the ancient temple effect'—are being replaced by a more friendly, flexible, egalitarian and at times new institution. For instance, *Bancassurance* is the term coined by the French to categorise the institution resulting from the coming together of a bank and a life assurance company. In entering this age of *Bancassurance*, the distinctions between a bank, an investment services house, a leasing company, an insurance company and so on, are breaking down. Such change has prompted many commentators to refer to a financial services revolution. Nor is such change any respecter of national borders or language barriers; it is a worldwide phenomenon.

EQUITY BANK HISTORY
Equity Bank Limited was founded in 1965 by a number of private investors, principally from Limerick. It traded for 25 years providing personal loans to consumer applicants as well as bridging and term loan facilities to individuals and small businesses. It was, in effect, a small secondary or merchant bank. It was based in Dublin with a branch in Limerick.

This case was developed as a basis for class discussion rather than to illustrate either effective or ineffective handling of an administrative situation.

Then as now, a bank obtained its banking licence from the Central Bank, which operated in a supervisory role, primarily to ensure that no bank under its supervision contrived to lose or in any way fail to safeguard funds held by the bank on behalf of its depositors. One of the controls imposed by the Central Bank on banks under its supervision is the requirement for minimum levels of shareholders' capital subscribed and fully paid up. This is known as the bank's capital adequacy requirement, which effectively limits the bank's advances (i.e. amounts lent to customers in total) to a precise multiple (usually 12:1) of the bank's paid-up capital or shareholders' funds.

The original Equity Bank was set up with private investors' capital, which automatically meant limited size and scope of operations. Not having access to unlimited funds to lend, the bank was forced to concentrate its lending in smaller-scale advances to a spread of smaller individual and consumer loans. As the banking market became more competitive in the 1970s and 1980s, customer borrowing requirements grew increasingly large and more complex. With a limited capital base and correspondingly restricted capacity to lend, Equity was becoming less relevant as a player in the market and ultimately would have had little future. However, it did have a banking licence.

Since the mid-1970s the Central Bank had become more cautious and rigorous in its regulation of the Irish banking system. This had been prompted by a number of secondary bank failures: for example, Irish Trust Bank in 1974 and Merchant Banking and PMPS, both in the early 1980s. Thus, to acquire a licence to carry out banking activities was becoming more difficult and more expensive in terms of paid-up capital and so on. At the same time during this period, many of the older and longer-established banks, especially in the secondary sector, were unable to keep pace with the change in the marketplace. They did not have the imagination, management skills and financial resources to exploit the possibilities of the newly evolving financial services market. Such institutions began to represent opportunities to outside parties who could acquire them and introduce such skills and resources.

In the late 1980s, John Cranfield, a banker then working as an independent financial consultant in Dublin, saw such opportunity in Equity Bank. Through his contacts with NWS Bank plc in the UK, a chain of events was set in motion which saw the acquisition of Equity Bank by NWS Bank plc in June 1989. NWS Bank plc, in turn, was a subsidiary of Bank of Scotland. Thus Equity had as its ultimate parent Bank of Scotland, the most consistently profitable of those UK clearing banks quoted on the London Stock Exchange. Bank of Scotland's Report and Accounts for 1990 stated: 'In June 1989 NWS Bank acquired Equity Bank Limited, which is a small Dublin-based private bank. It is intended to expand this business as a platform for all NWS Group's activities in the Republic of Ireland.'

NWS Bank plc provided a broad range of financial services to both the private individual and business sectors; it had a special expertise in the area of leasing. It operated some 90 branches across the UK. The bank had its genesis in North West Securities, a company set up in Chester in the 1940s to develop hire purchase facilities for motor dealers in north-west England. The company grew steadily, realising the opportunity of providing credit facilities within the community to a wide spectrum of both commercial and consumer customers. It was acquired as a wholly owned subsidiary in 1958 by Bank of Scotland (see Appendix A).

At the time of its takeover in June 1989, Equity Bank Limited had assets of £15 million and employed 25 people. NWS Bank plc had £2,665 million assets in 1989 (as at 31st December, 1989), a profit before taxation of £38 million, and employed 2,533 personnel. In turn, Bank of Scotland had £18,395 million assets in 1989 (as at 28th February, 1990) and a pre-tax profit of £215 million. Following the takeover, John Cranfield took on the role of new chief executive of Equity Bank and quickly set about leading the bank into an era of growth and new products.

THE MARKET

The market in which Equity Bank operated on the lending side was that for instalment credit facilities to personal and business customers. Many firms and individuals had a need to acquire assets or services immediately for which they were not in a position to pay except in instalments over a deferred period of weeks, months or years. Such financing was usually provided on the basis of security, such as a lease agreement or a mortgage or a guaranty. A decade ago, the typical clearing house banker would have loosely referred to this market, sometimes pejoratively, as the hire purchase (HP) market or borrowing-on-the-never-never. However, the growth in this market, the very real customer needs being fulfilled, and the increasing sophistication of the financial instruments being developed for the market, particularly by recent entrants, had ensured a new identity and enviable dynamism in this market. The principal segments were:

(1) secured commercial property loans;
(2) direct personal loans—mainly unsecured;
(3) motor finance (primarily leasing for private and fleet vehicles, including commercials);
(4) plant and machinery finance—mainly leasing.

No definitive data existed on the size of this market. The Central Bank did report the instalment credit outstanding of licensed banks. However, this statistic excluded the major dynamic growth element in the latter part of the 1980s, namely leasing through non-bank leasing companies, and thus showed little or no increase during the period. Much of the market growth over the last five years had been driven by these new players, including Woodchester, Capital, Reflex, Cambridge and other smaller finance houses. Meanwhile, the traditional players, mainly subsidiaries of clearing banks, had either marked time (switching loan to leasing paper), contracted (e.g. Mercantile) or ceased trading (Credit Finance and Chartered Trust).

Exhibit 1

Irish Market for Asset Finance/Instalment Credit (O/S Balances)

	1988 (£m)		1989 (£m)	
PERSONAL				
Motor Point-of-Sale Finance	105		130	
Home Improvement Point-of-Sale Finance	40		30	
Small Appliance Point-of-Sale Finance	35		25	
Personal Loans (Direct)	470	650	500	685
COMMERCIAL/INDUSTRIAL				
Property	450		500	
Motor Fleets	150		180	
Plant & Machinery	150		180	
Block Discounting*	10		10	
Insurance Premium Finance**	30	790	30	900
TOTAL		1,440		1,585

*a trade finance instrument which facilitates a dealer, say a TV rental agent, to acquire a full stock up-front.
**e.g. employer and public liability insurance, fire insurance, etc.

Source: Compiled from various sources including Central Bank returns, registration data for new motor cars and returns from the Irish Finance Houses Association (IFHA).

Nonetheless, a reasonable estimate of market size was put at £1.5 billion (outstanding balances) in 1989 (see Exhibit 1). This market was viewed as likely to increase by about 10 per cent per year over the longer term. This estimate was based on a buoyant outlook for the economy and consumer spending; an increasing level of motor sales following seven successive years of stagnation; a reviving construction and property market; and a strong and continuing growth in leasing, which would be both supplier and demand driven.

Historically in the earlier years of the decade and prior to the burgeoning of the non-bank leasing sector, the main players and estimated market shares were:

Allied Irish Finance (AIF)	25%
Bank of Ireland Finance (BIF)	25%
Lombard & Ulster (L&U)	15%
United Dominions Trust (UDT)	10%
Bowmaker	6%
Mercantile	6%
Others	13%

Since then, a number of new competitors had entered the market, as explained above. These included Woodchester Investments, founded by Craig McKinney. This company grew out of Hamilton Leasing, an office equipment finance specialist, and subsequently acquired Bowmaker, Trinity Bank and a major insurance broker as well as a Shannon-based leasing company and a UK chain of motor dealers (Lookers). The company had pioneered an expertise in small ticket leasing—working with suppliers of computers, office equipment and so on to design leases which would help to sell these products. Put simply, Woodchester saw the potential of a leasing arrangement as a marketing tool, so-called sales-aided leasing, compared to the traditional banks, who merely viewed a lease as a tax-advantageous financial instrument where they could enjoy the capital allowances on the product leased. The firm controlled over 60 per cent of this small ticket market. Reflex Leasing majored in large ticket computer finance, including operating leases, and had recently moved into more general areas of asset leasing. Capital Leasing dealt in motor and capital equipment finance. The Cambridge Group ranged across the spectrum of asset finance. All of the above firms were quoted on the Dublin Stock Exchange. Virtually all of Woodchester's acquisitions had been for paper, i.e. bought in exchange for Woodchester's publicly quoted shares.

Initially in the early eighties, the arrival of the newcomers caused serious upset to the comfortable cartel arrangements of Irish Finance Houses Association (IFHA), which until then had a policy of minimum lending rates and maximum dealer commissions. The older companies were doubly vulnerable as they were forced in the stagnant recession years to recognise and deal with an accumulated trough of non-performing loans resulting from 'fearless lending' decisions of the late seventies. Top management switches in the big banking groups brought a new emphasis on default containment and heavily structured centralised credit control, leaving the field open to the new arrivals with their advantages of fast, decentralised decision- making, attractive intermediary incentives and as yet low or non-existent bad debt provisions. As the decade progressed, a degree of settling down occurred but the main new arrivals had become solidly entrenched and continued to search for openings and niches to develop new products.

EQUITY'S NEW DIRECTION

Up to its acquisition, Equity had been a small player in this market (1 per cent share), picking up fringe business on personal loans, bridging, insurance premium finance and some marginal secured lending. Being too limited in absolute size and branch cover to offer full floor plan or stocking plan facilities to major motor franchises, Equity was driven towards smaller, non-franchised dealers in mostly secondhand markets. Personal loan business also was poorish, involving a proportion of more suspect direct customer business. In secured lending, Equity's intermittent funding problems and higher funds cost resulted in a stop-go pattern of activities. As a consequence, the bank had no consistent presence in the market which would have kept it on the shopping list for better-quality business. Further, product range was limited. Up to June 1989, Equity had no leasing products or expertise.

The new management at Equity identified two target segments as the main focus of lending growth in the initial stages of new development: firstly, leasing of cars, trucks and plant; and secondly, secured lending on commercial property. The type of leasing first undertaken by Equity was 'full payout' leasing whereby the payments made by the lessee during the life of the lease fully cover the cost of the asset; at the end of the lease agreement, the asset is then fully owned by the customer. This was the most popular form of lease. However, the contract lease or dealer buy-back lease was also growing in popularity and Equity decided in early 1990 to enter this market also. The attraction of this form of leasing is that the regular instalment payments during the lifetime of the lease are lower than under full payout leasing. At the end of the lease agreement, the lessee has the choice to (a) pay in a lump sum the residual amount owing on the asset and thus fully own it, or (b) use the proportion of the asset he owns as a result of his payments during the lease in part payment towards a new asset—for example, a car—and the consequent new leasing arrangement. Hence, dealer buy-back leasing is also known as a 'balloon payment'.

Another leasing possibility that Equity was examining was short-term leasing facilities. This might involve, for example, a hire drive company which wished to finance a new fleet for its six-month season and then off-load the fleet at the end of the period. In terms of lending on commercial property and property-secured instruments, the company hoped to develop endowment as well as repayment mortgages. The terms for these would be up to 15 years with rates variable at a margin over the interbank base rates.

In addition to the priority segments, Equity Bank planned to continue to underwrite personal loan business on a more selective basis, especially for good previous customers. It should be noted, however, that unsecured personal lending by finance houses had not grown over the past decade. The personal borrower had been largely taken out of the finance house market by aggressive competition from credit unions, the Dublin and Cork Trustee Savings Bank (TSB), and the main clearing banks. The credit unions had 500 branches throughout Ireland run on a voluntary basis with free deposits and low interest rates (*circa* 13% APR on lending). TSB had built a large branch network and captured high numbers of previously unbanked customers, while in recent years the principal clearing banks had homed in on existing good customers with aggressive retention programmes, frequently at the expense of their own subsidiary finance houses.

However, one type of unsecured personal lending which was attractive was Professional Practice Loans (PPL). These were loans to professionals and members of recognised professional bodies, for instance, accountants, doctors, architects, engineers, solicitors, and dentists. The loan could be used, for example, for the purchase of practice premises, the establishment of working capital, the purchase of the share of a retiring partner, or the restructuring of existing loan arrangements. Because of the professional status of the individuals involved, such loans usually had very low default levels. Indeed, in the case of an accountant, should he default on a loan, he would not be able to continue practising as an accountant. Such loans were sometimes marketed in association with life assurance companies as they normally involved a life insurance dimension.

Equity Bank also had a significant presence in the financing of insurance premiums (employer and public liability insurance, fire insurance and so on) and audit fees for commercial customers. Equity's financial assistance was sought here as such insurance premiums and audit fees involved very high one-off payments which could be more usefully structured on an instalment payment basis. While not seen as a major growth area in the long term, it was planned to maintain the bank's existing customer/intermediary base in this area in the short term and to extend loan periods where possible to achieve an almost continuous renewal of facilities.

There were two other areas where management at Equity saw possibilities for business and product development. Credit/loan insurance involved the borrower taking out an instalment protection plan which would give life, accident, redundancy and sickness benefit during the life of the loan. Equity would obviously enjoy a commission on such insurance products. Affiliate Group Schemes also represented a growing market opportunity. Such schemes involved preferential treatment and discounted prices over a range of financial products to members of a union, professional groups, staff associations, large enterprises and so on (Appendix A contains an example of one such affiliate group scheme). Finally, another source of income for the bank was commitment fees or handling fees for certain types of loan transaction.

1990 PLAN AND OUT-TURN

Exhibit 2 details the breakdown of Equity Bank's planned advances for 1990 (£22.4 million). Details of margins are included in Exhibit 3, while Exhibit 4 lists the basic assumptions underpinning the plan. Equity's new direction got off to a good start. During 1990, many of the targets in terms of products, customers and growth were met. Exhibits 5 and 6 give relevant financial data on the out-turn of 1990. At the end of 1990, Equity Bank had assets in the region of £33 million.

Exhibit 2

Equity Bank 1990 Planned Advances		
		£m
LEASING		
Joint venture	5.0	
Other deals—9 @ £100,000 p.a.	0.9	
Cambridge	1.3	
Other broker/direct	<u>3.7</u>	10.9
SECURED (PROPERTY)		5.5
PERSONAL		
Unsecured		2.5
PPL		1.5
INSURANCE PREMIUM/AUDIT		2.0
TOTAL		£22.4m

QUALITY OF BUSINESS

Put simply, the business of a bank is to make a profit on the money it lends. The money it lends constitutes its 'raw material'. The source of this raw material is primarily (a) money deposited by customers in the bank, and (b) money borrowed by the bank itself from other banks on the so-called inter-bank market. The difference between the net cost of this raw material and a bank's income through interest charges provides the gross margin. Typically,

Exhibit 3

Margin Projections (Net of Commission)		
LEASING		
Joint venture		4% over COF
Other deals		4% over COF
Cambridge		4% over COF
Other broker/direct		5% over COF
SECURED (PROPERTY)		
	10 loans @ £250,000 = £2.5m	2.5% over COF
	15 loans @ £120,000 = £1.8m*	3.5% over COF
	15 loans @ £80,000 = £1.2m*	4.5% over COF
PERSONAL		
Unsecured		6% over COF
PPL		3.5% over COF
INSURANCE PREMIUM/AUDIT		5% over COF

*£2m of advances less than £250,000 attract 1% commitment fee = £20,000.

this margin is of the order of 4 per cent (see Exhibit 3 in the case of Equity Bank). Again typically, a bank's operating expenses or overheads subsume half of this margin (2 per cent), leaving a 2 per cent profit before bad debt provision and tax. This is a narrow margin which can be indented severely if a bank experiences a major loan default. Minimising loan default is a primary concern of any banker. Insuring the creditworthiness of potential borrowers, both personal and commercial—the 'quality of business' from the bank's perspective—is crucial. In this regard, banks use the three Cs—character, capacity and capital. The type of character represents an assessment of the likely disposition of the borrower, either individual or company, to repay a loan; willingness to repay can only be predicted, usually on the basis of past performance, as evidenced by credit bureaux, bank reports, credit agency reports, and so on. Capacity indicates the source of repayment, the evidence of ability to service the repayment over the required period at the proposed rate of interest. Finally, a borrower's capital represents a level of security to the lender; the bank must consider what security, if any, is offered to underpin the loan and what is the value of the security evidenced by objective valuation.

This issue of quality of business was a primary preoccupation of the management at Equity Bank. Since the change of ownership, the bank had concentrated on becoming a different type of operation in a number of ways.

Exhibit 4

Assumptions in 1990 Plan

1. Personnel	5 sales professionals (Dublin 3, Limerick 2) in addition to HOM (1 extra person) from Jan. 1 Internal sales/loan administrator Improved and standardised underwriting procedures Possibly one additional experienced underwriter
2. Products	Contract (buy-back) Lease Endowment Mortgage 'Now' A/C with cheque-book aimed at solicitors (Trustee Status required)
3. Plan sensitivity	Possible shortfall of £1.5m in personal loan advances (down from £4m to £2.5m) due to (possible) underperformance of PPL (–£0.5m) and stricter quality vetting of personal loan proposals (–£1m) Could be offset by gaining AA plan

4. Marketing support spend

Print (brochures, leaflets)	£25,000
Advertising	£25,000
PR & Sponsorship	£25,000
Incentives (customer)	£10,000
Sundry	£15,000
	£100,000

5. Decision times	Maintenance of current flexibility and speed of case decisions, especially on property cases
6. Cost base	Containment of costs (payroll and default) as a continuing means of achieving keen pricing for quality business

---

It was targeting business customers rather than personal customers. Importantly, it was seeking larger-size loans and fewer of them, and aiming at a higher quality of business with lower default levels. If a major loan default were looming, Equity, like other banks, had the last resort of sending in a receiver. In some circumstances, a receiver might conceivably rescue a business and ensure repayment of the loan; more likely, he would simply realise the assets of the business and ensure that as much as possible of the money owing to the bank was repaid.

Exhibit 5

Equity Bank Profit & Loss Account 1990

INCOME (from)		£'000
Loans		2,047
Bridging		393
Hire purchase		37
Insurance/audit		130
Leasing		1,203
Deposit		143
Government stocks		205
Commitment fees		22
Ashbourne		6
Other		3
TOTAL		4,189
COST OF FUNDS		
Deposits	1,331	
Interbank	920	
Bank charges	13	
TOTAL		(2,264)
CONTRIBUTION		1,925
LESS: General	628	
Salaries	511	
Consultants' fees	43	
Depreciation	42	
		(1,224)
Bad debt provision		(224)
Profit before tax		477
Extraordinary item		101
TOTAL PROFIT BEFORE TAX		578

Note: For confidential purposes, these figures have been disguised.

Exhibit 6

Equity Bank Balance Sheet 1990		
		£'000
Interbank deposits		207
Central Bank		1,511
Government stocks		2,001
Other assets		<u>333</u>
		4,052
Bridging		1,720
Term loans		23,405
Insurance/audit		2,201
Hire purchase		213
Leasing		<u>9,322</u>
		36,861
Less: Deferred charges		(6,753)
Provisions		<u>(1,456)</u>
		28,652
Fixed assets		280
Susp.		<u>93</u>
TOTAL		33,077
LESS: Due to depositors	14,328	
Interbank	13,629	
Bank O/D	284	
Insurance/audit	20	
General liabilities	<u>186</u>	
		<u>(28,447)</u>
		4,630
REPRESENTED BY:		
Share capital		3,465
Capital reserves		–
Revenue reserves		587
Profit & loss account		<u>578</u>
		4,630

Note: In contrast to standard balance sheet procedures, a bank arranges its balance sheet in descending order of liquidity.

ORGANISATIONAL DEVELOPMENT
On taking over the reins at Equity Bank, one of John Cranfield's first tasks was to revamp the management structure and develop the manpower resources of the institution. Two key appointments were the head of marketing and sales operations and the head of finance. The three senior managers of Equity Bank are profiled below and Exhibit 7 outlines the organisational structure of the bank in early 1991.

JOHN CRANFIELD, CHIEF EXECUTIVE
Cranfield was appointed chief executive of Equity Bank in June 1989. A career banker in his early forties, he had spent ten years of his career with Bank of Ireland, mainly involved in market and business development in the UK. He then joined Trustee Savings Bank in a senior executive position and played a major role in developing the branch network of that bank in the late seventies and early eighties. From 1988, he had been working in financial consultancy based in Dublin.

NOEL HYNES, HEAD OF MARKETING AND SALES OPERATIONS
In his mid forties, Hynes joined Equity Bank in the summer of 1989, having worked in a variety of marketing roles in his career to date. For the previous seven years, he had been sales director of UDT Bank. This bank specialised in instalment credit for the motor trade and in term facilities for property. Prior to UDT, he was client services director with CDP Advertising and he had also spent a period as marketing director of the *Sunday Tribune*.

BRENDAN BURKE, HEAD OF FINANCE
A chartered accountant in his late thirties, Burke joined Equity in September 1990, having started his career at Forward Trust, the finance house subsidiary of what was formerly the Northern Bank Group, in turn owned by the Midland Bank Group. In 1988, the National Australian Bank acquired the Northern Bank Group from Midland and changed the name of Forward Trust to National Irish Investment Bank (NIIB). The two years prior to coming to Equity Burke had spent as financial controller in a treasury management capacity with Dresdner Bank in Dublin. This West German bank was one of the first overseas banks to get a licence in the Custom House Docks Financial Services Centre (CHDFSC).

In order to assist in the manpower planning process, a formal management inventory was introduced in the bank during 1990. This was initially done in relation to personnel at managerial level, and then at each grade down the line, under the following headings: performance inadequate; performance satisfactory; ready for promotion; potential for special development. This inventory was drawn up by the head of a particular section using the existing

Exhibit 7

Organisation Structure

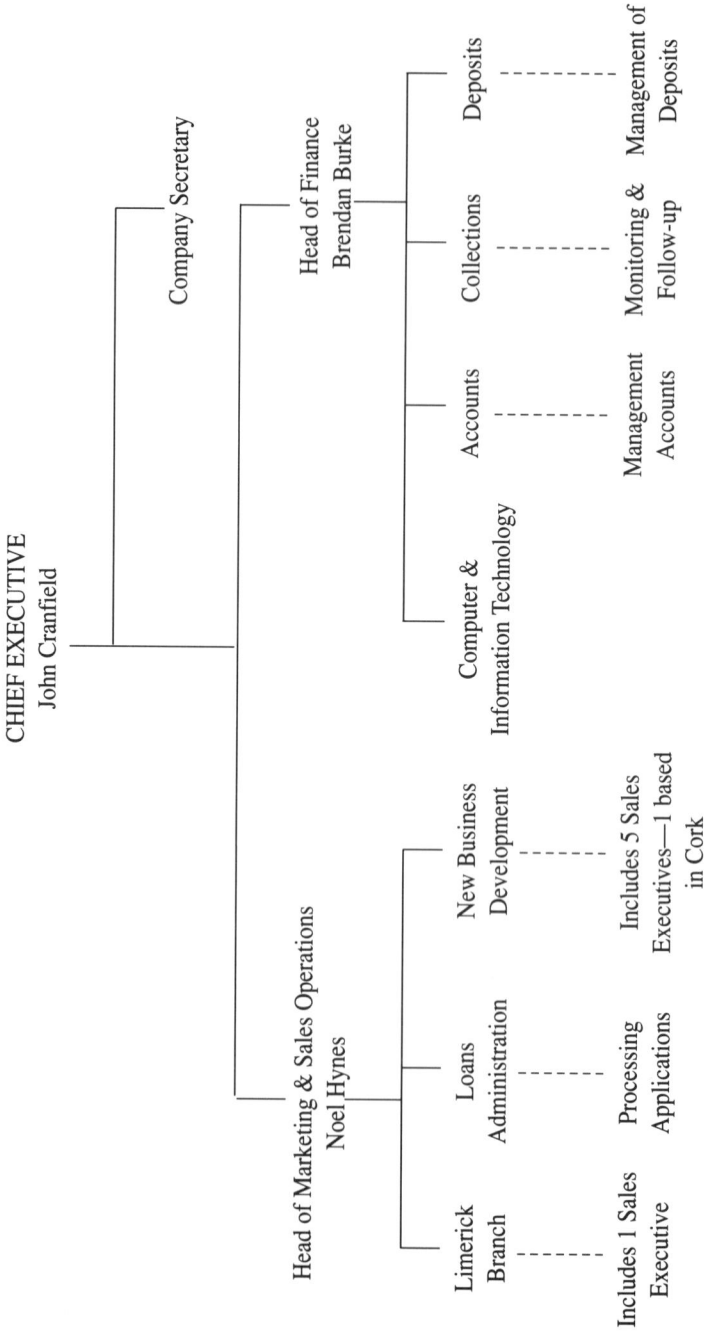

CHIEF EXECUTIVE
John Cranfield

Company Secretary

Head of Marketing & Sales Operations
Noel Hynes

Head of Finance
Brendan Burke

Limerick Branch
— Includes 1 Sales Executive

Loans Administration
Processing Applications

New Business Development
— Includes 5 Sales Executives—1 based in Cork

Computer & Information Technology

Accounts
— Management Accounts

Collections
— Monitoring & Follow-up

Deposits
— Management of Deposits

EQUITY BANK APRIL 1991

TOTAL NUMBER OF EMPLOYEES—33

data bank of information where available and by way of interview. The placing of each individual was confirmed with the chief executive. This inventory could then be used as a basis for development and grooming for future development and promotional positioning of suitable staff. This would involve both internal and external training in order that the staff members involved gained the necessary experience.

A staff appraisal system was also introduced. In broad outline, this involved the head of function, as appropriate, setting objectives at the beginning of the year for each staff member under his jurisdiction. These objectives varied from person to person depending on the responsibility and type of work involved. The objectives were discussed at the beginning of the year between the two parties, progress was monitored during the year, and at the end of a twelve-month period an overall assessment took place. It was envisaged that this system would allow room for the flexibility required for setting different objectives for different personnel depending on their strengths, location and so on. As with any appraisal system, open dialogue between management and staff member was encouraged actively.

The bulk of Equity Bank's employees were in their twenties. While this brought enthusiasm and ambition to activities, it also meant that there was a serious deficiency in relation to experience throughout the bank generally. This lack of experience was a concern to senior management and it felt it would have to focus considerable attention on the matter in the coming years. The staff inventory would identify developmental needs and the training resources of NWS Bank would likely be available.

In general, it was senior management's intention to try to keep staff numbers around their current level. The desire was for a lean, skilled and flexible staff structure in order to keep manpower overheads at a minimum. It was hoped to strengthen the experience level within the bank without necessarily increasing the overall staff numbers. It was seen as current bank policy that depending on the experience level required, further recruitment would be done by way of temporary bank assistant employment or on a contract basis. There was no union or formalised staff association in the bank and it was senior management's policy to maintain this status quo.

DISTRIBUTION NETWORK
Equity Bank operated from its head office at Ballsbridge, Dublin and from a branch in Limerick. The bank's selling proposition, based on competitive pricing underpinned by low overheads and fast case decisions, made branch expansion inappropriate as the root for distribution of its products. Indeed, in an already over-branched market, branches were in the process of being closed down as uneconomic by some of the longer-established competitors, notably Mercantile. It was not the bank's intention to succeed by direct

person-to-person contact with large numbers of individual customers for small borrowing amounts. The bank's current business strategy involved growing its business without a consequent expansion in staff numbers or work locations. Thus, its distribution network used a number of intermediary channels to source business proposals. These included:

Accountants (on behalf of their clients)
Solicitors
Insurance brokers
Auctioneers/estate agents
Dealers (e.g. car, truck, forklift dealers)
Distributors/import agents (e.g. computer hardware and software distributors

The common denominator of all these groups was that they required bank facilities to be available to enable them to service their customers either in financing a business expansion, completing a property transaction, or acquiring new equipment or transport for use in the business. Dealers and distributors, indeed, used the potential lease availability from a lending institution as a positive sales aid. Such dealers and distributors also normally enjoyed a commission on leases arranged. Thus, in addition to meeting face to face with the ultimate bank customer (the borrower), a considerable amount of time was spent by Equity Bank marketing personnel, including the five sales executives, in developing good working relationships with the intermediaries from the above groupings who might effect an introduction to ultimate customers or in some other way influence the direction of new business proposals in favour of the bank. In fact, it was estimated that up to 70 per cent of the bank's business was generated by these intermediary channels. Indeed, the tradition in leasing was that in nine out of ten cases, the lender did not meet the final client.

In prospecting for new business, the bank's sales executives might typically use a listing of accountants who had, for instance, recently attended a financial services conference, and then systematically ring around in a telesales campaign in order to establish awareness of Equity and its product offerings. Retaining and nurturing existing customers was, of course, also crucially important; cross-selling was also encouraged, i.e. trying to sell the new products the bank was developing to its existing customer base. In all of this process the client prospect card—a card which summarised the key information on the (potential) bank/customer relationship—was an indispensable aid to the sales executive.

PROMOTION

Under its new regime, Equity was committed to promote actively its name and services offered. Such advertising and marketing communication had to be highly selective in order to reach its target audience. In early 1991, the bank was seeking to give this advertising a new thrust and sought the advice of its PR/advertising agency. In response, the agency developed the following advertising strategy rationale:

'Following our meeting on 1st February, 1990 we were asked to develop two press advertisements—one promoting loans and one promoting deposits. In addition, we were asked to look at the development of a poster campaign. When we began this task it was clear that Equity Bank does not offer any banking service that is not available in most other banks in Ireland and, in fact, the range of services from Equity would not be as extensive as those available, certainly from the four majors.

'There are two aspects to the Equity operation in Ireland that give you, or will give you, a distinct image and identity among the different target audiences that you wish to reach and influence. First, you are part of the Bank of Scotland which, in your own words, means Equity Bank is built on the firmest of foundations. Second, despite being part of such a large financial organisation, Equity is a uniquely compact bank that can provide a highly personalised service. From an advertising point of view, these two issues will play an important role, but you must resist the temptation to communicate them in a way that is dull and unimaginative.

'Your advertising budget is small and so must work harder. You have fewer opportunities to talk to people and the smaller size of advertisement means you must create immediate impact. You must come across as different and, perhaps, unique. We have developed a theme for Equity which reflects this need. The theme is: "ALL BANKS ARE NOT EQUAL".

'We believe that this line helps focus attention on Equity as a bank that is different and helps draw attention to those areas of your operation that you want to promote. It is a theme line which suggests that Equity has a distinct competitive advantage. This is the conclusion that we want people to draw, and it helps us establish Equity as somehow unique in the banking industry.

'In planning an approach for the deposit and lending advertisements, we decided that if we listed the services you offer, we run the risk of (a) being very boring and (b) being no different from any other bank. Our approach is to tell your audience what you don't do and this allows us to be interesting, creative and different. We think the approach works very well and will make your advertising considerably more effective and successful.'

Exhibit 8 provides an illustration of one of these press advertisements run in the *Sunday Tribune* during March 1991. Equity Bank had also recently developed a new brochure advertising itself and its product range. Exhibit 9 illustrates an extract from this. Furthermore, Equity undertook a limited amount of corporate sponsorship, for instance, of some Leinster Union rugby football matches.

Exhibit 8

Press Advertisement

When it comes to holidays, don't ask us for a break.

Sorry—if you want money to go on holiday, may we recommend another bank. Equity Bank is a commercial bank offering a professional service to business practices and partnerships: arranging Working Capital, Commercial Mortgages, Practitioners' Loans, Management Buyouts, etc. Our financial strength and professional standing are reflected in our membership of the Bank of Scotland Group. So if you would like to talk to the professionals about your corporate finances requirements, call xxxxx at Equity Bank.

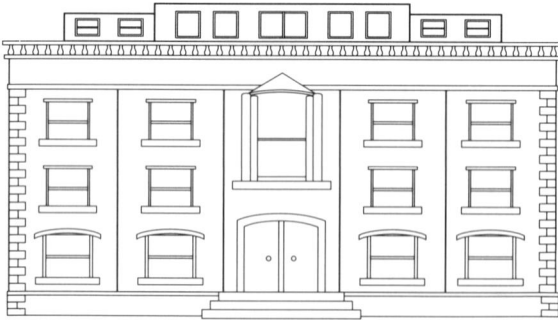

EQUITY BANK

All Banks are not equal
85 Pembroke Road, Ballsbridge, Dublin 4. Ph: 685199

Exhibit 9

Extracts from Equity Brochure

At Equity Bank we have a team of professionals to help you find an imaginative solution to your requirement for:

—New Project Finance
—Management Buyout
—Corporate Financial Restructuring with Term Facilities
—Working Capital
—Asset Finance
—Personal Loans
—Consumer Finance

OUR PHILOSOPHY

We take banking seriously, and we believe in spending time with our clients to discover their precise requirements. That's why we take time to talk to our clients directly in order to establish at the outset their particular needs.

Equity Bank Limited
Equity House
85 Pembroke Road
Ballsbridge
Dublin 4

CORPORATE FINANCE FACILITIES

At Equity Bank we can offer flexible terms and repayment patterns planned to suit our client's requirements for the following projects:

These are just some of the facilities we offer our clients:

Term Loans	From 5–20 years
Revolving Loans	Including 'evergreen' facility
Commercial Mortgages	Either Repayment or Endowment/Mortgage backed
Professional Practitioners' Loans	Specially tailored to suit practice finance
Leasing	Medium/Large Ticket, up to 7-year terms
Bank Guarantees	
Working Capital Facilities	

—Property Investment
—Public Houses/Hotels
—Shops and Offices
—Factories & Warehousing
—Industrial Projects
—Plant & Equipment
—Management Buyouts
—Partnership Share Purchase
—Stock Funding

1991 AND BEYOND

Equity Bank's approach to longer-term planning reflected the prevalent culture in NWS Bank plc. It focused on a detailed working plan for the year ahead and its bottom line. Longer-term ideas and options were on the table, discussed and teased out; however, the result was not a highly structured and detailed five-year plan but rather a setting down of possible new business scenarios that might quickly exploit emerging opportunities. Noel Hynes, head of marketing and sales operations, commented: 'I remember in a previous organisation I worked for there was a great emphasis on detailed and highly structured long-term plans with three-year and five-year projections. It certainly was a good discipline, but it took a hell of a lot of time and effort and I wonder in retrospect if it didn't lead to a certain inflexibility and failure to really run with the year ahead.'

For the year 1991 Equity budgeted for a total income from its operations of £5.7 million, a profit before tax of £1.0 million and assets of £41.7 million. As it stood in early 1991, the bank was actively looking at a range of product possibilities not currently on offer. These included a range of trade finance instruments and other financial services.

Foreign exchange facilities—This would include the provision of loans in any one of a range of foreign currencies, for instance, US dollars, Deutschmarks, Swiss francs, sterling, for purposes such as property or equipment finance, aircraft leasing and so on. The attraction to the borrower generally was the availability of lower interest rates on foreign currencies.

Letter of credit (LC) facilities—An LC was a financing instrument used in foreign trade. For instance, an Irish importer who wished to import goods from, say, Spain would arrange for a letter of credit from his bank in Ireland to the Spanish supplier which guaranteed payment for the goods. The LC was thus a bank guarantee of payment in foreign currency to a foreign supplier.

Factoring—Factoring of the book debts (and debtors) of a business involved the sale of the debts to a third party to be collected by that third party as principal and not agent. The sale of such debts would be for an amount less than the nominal value, the difference being similar to a penalty interest charge, though usually somewhat higher. The effect of the sale was that the seller freed up some working capital by changing debtors into cash and not incurring the risk that some debts would not be collected.

Invoice discounting—This was similar to factoring except that instead of selling the debtor book, the business gave a financial institution a legal charge over the debts—in much the same way as a bank took a mortgage over a building as security for a loan advanced for the purchase of that property. The financial institution enjoyed a commission on the subsequent debts collected.

Confirming—This was a service provided at the opposite end of a foreign trade transaction whereby a bank in the country importing the goods guaranteed payment of the amount due in a currency acceptable to the seller.

Stockbroking—This involved dealing in the purchase and sale of securities in return for a commission. A number of smaller stockbrokers had been taken over by banks in recent years.

Insurance broking—Increasingly, insurance and bank products were tending to be sold together, for example, loans for property purchase linked to an endowment insurance, house or vehicle insurance in association with loan/ lease finance, and term loan assurance on the life of the borrower assigned to the bank as fall-back security.

Domestic mortgages—Currently Equity Bank did not compete with building societies or clearing banks in the residential mortgage market. However, this was a relatively large segment accounting for upwards of £1 billion in annual advances and could conceivably be of interest in the future.

Credit cards—These were now issued by all clearing banks (Visa, Access) and some smaller institutions. Interest charges to the customer were high, but so traditionally were the bad debts. However, this was a growing area of unsecured lending to borrowers.

Budget accounts—Half-way between an overdraft limit and a credit card, these were run by retail stores and usually worked on the basis of a fixed credit limit or a multiple of an agreed monthly repayment. Interest rates tended to be higher than credit cards and transaction values were small so that unless the system was fully automated with very high volumes, profitability was eroded by operating costs and default levels.

Equity Bank was also looking at a range of new possibilities for expansion of distribution and these included:

* New branch openings
* Appointment of local agents
* Acquisition of other banks with a branch network
* Acquisition of non-bank institutions, for example, a building society
* Joint ventures with one or more of the above or other interested parties.

Indeed, Equity Bank had undertaken just such a joint venture in May 1990, when it purchased a 50 per cent stake in Gatehouse Leasing Limited, a firm which specialised in the provision of leasing finance for motor vehicles, plant and other industrial/business equipment. Gatehouse Leasing had been formed as a small leasing company by a number of independent car and vehicle dealers and had grown essentially as far as it could without taking on board a partner with more capital available. Thus, the coming together of Equity and Gatehouse represented a mutually advantageous joint venture. Equity was also considering other joint ventures, such as participation in a syndicate or consortium to construct a leisure complex where the bank would be a lender and/or a limited equity holder. (Appendix A gives an example of a joint venture in another context.)

JOHN CRANFIELD'S VIEWS

In early March 1991, the case writer interviewed John Cranfield, chief executive of Equity Bank, about his views in regard to the future development of the bank. Some extracts from that interview follow.

'Equity has not been seen as a real player. It was a small private bank. I want to make it a serious contender for business in the marketplace. Its parentage is important here. Remember, AIB and BOI together come to only 80 per cent of the size of the Bank of Scotland. We've got to get that message across.

'In our advertising, in promoting ourselves, I want to say what we're not. We're not a high street or consumer bank. We don't offer cheque-books. Indeed, in many ways the high street bank just provides a social service and there's not much profit in it. I would like Equity to be known as the place to come for a professional and corporate loan.

'We will have to market ourselves. I want to see Equity develop a separate and clear identity in the Irish business market. No, I don't want Bank of Scotland signs hanging outside our door. We will draw on Group resources but not too heavily. For instance, we are developing some new technology in the bank at the moment and we are going it alone rather than using some existing NWS systems. I foresee a paced growth at Equity and our marketing expenditure will reflect this. We're going to match our ambitions to our resources. For instance, just yesterday I was interviewing for an experienced lender.

'In terms of acquisition, we will keep an open mind. If it suits, yes, but we're not going to pay over the odds. No, I think Bank of Scotland itself would have a limited interest in the Irish market. It's small in an international context. But it might have an interest in the Custom House Docks Financial Services Centre.'

APPENDIX A

Extracts from chairman's statement in NWS Bank plc report and accounts 1989

The Bank's Field Divisions form the backbone of the NWS operation. Today, an expanding network of almost 90 branches across the UK provides a broad range of financial services within the private and business sectors. Specialising in personal and consumer packages, in small business, commercial loans and contract hire, NWS Field staff are trained to place particular emphasis on the quality of personal service they offer and their in-depth knowledge of the community each branch serves. The Field Division was restructured during the year with the three operating Divisions— Northern, Central and London & South—becoming profit centres in their own right, and being given a degree of autonomy, particularly in taking marketing decisions appropriate to their own needs. Strong growth in all areas, particularly in the commercial sector, was a feature of the year.

The final part of the streamlining of Renault Financial Services was completed and the Renault dealer network is now serviced by ten specialist branches providing a dedicated service throughout the United Kingdom. Our policy of providing finance to the local community continued with the opening of a further four NWS branches, which now brings the number of branches to almost ninety.

IBOS Finance, our Corporate Division, had a particularly exciting year and enhanced its reputation as a leading lessor in the industry by joining with other banks and city financial concerns in a number of syndicated leasing arrangements. Record levels of new leasing business were achieved and among several substantial facilities were the leasing of equipment for the Nissan car plant in Sunderland and participation in a banking syndicate to finance aircraft for British Airways. Car fleet finance was also a major growth area for the Division.

Central Financial Services which provides a range of financial facilities directly from Chester successfully linked with two major organisations during the year. A joint venture with the NFU Mutual Insurance Society to provide for the financial needs of the NFU members throughout the United Kingdom commenced in the autumn and early signs are encouraging with levels of business exceeding expectations. Siemens Leasing which is a new venture with the UK subsidiary of the West German electronics company Siemens, has been formed to provide financial and leasing facilities to Siemens' customers, and has also made a promising start. AA Financial Services, the joint venture with the Automobile Association, continued to make good progress during the year and has contributed satisfactory results.

Questions
1. In your view did the acquisition of Equity Bank make sound commercial sense for the parties involved?
2. Do you see evidence of a financial services revolution? What is the essence of a bank like Equity's business?
3. Comment on Equity's new direction and how well it is pursuing it.
4. What do you think of the bank's organisational development?
5. Is Equity Bank on the correct road for the future? Make recommendations for the future development of the bank over the next one to three years and indicate how these might be implemented.
6. How might the possibility of a more recessionary economic environment affect Equity?

Part III

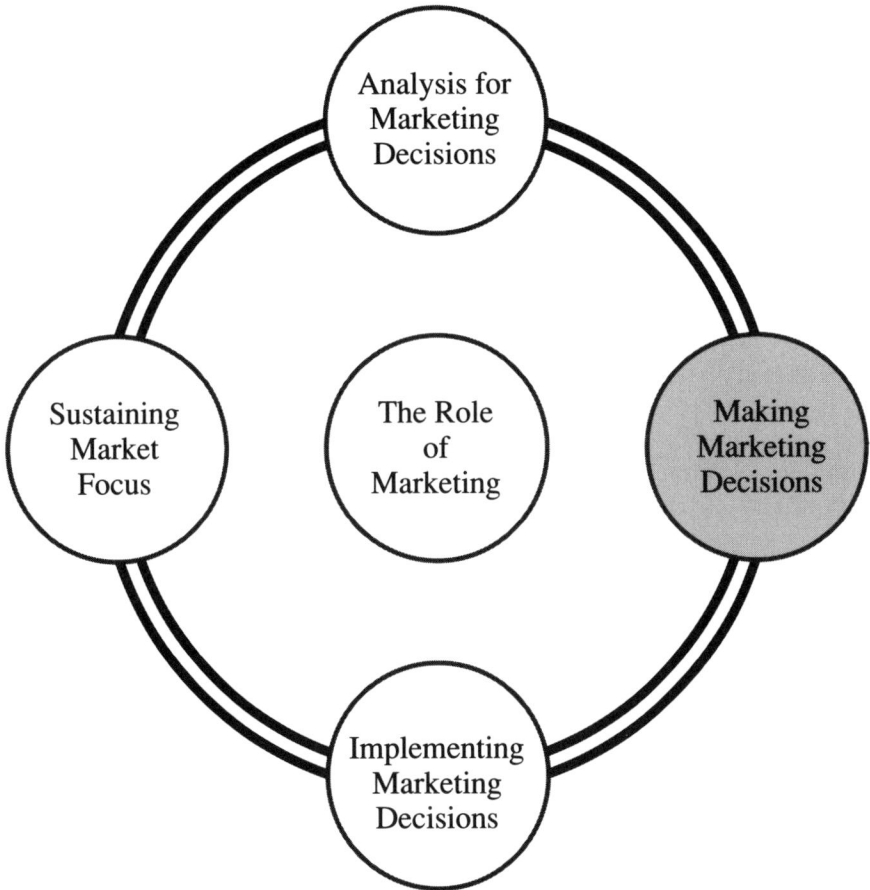

Analysis for Marketing Decisions

Sustaining Market Focus

The Role of Marketing

Making Marketing Decisions

Implementing Marketing Decisions

Chapter 9

Market Choice

INTRODUCTION

The basic elements of marketing analysis dealt with in Part II provide the essential raw material for the decisions the marketing manager must make. These decisions are not only of strategic proportion and importance for the marketing function, but fundamentally determine the whole company's strategic direction.

The market choice decision is the first of these. Through it the manager commits the company to a relationship with chosen customers in the environment. This relationship must then form the basis of the company's efforts to create customer loyalty, build a competitive advantage against competition, and seek out the temporary and partial monopoly position in the market which can yield profits above the average for the industry.

Appropriate choice of market is critical to marketing effectiveness and organisational success. Market choice is an essential and unavoidable action. All organisations have limited resources with which to achieve their objectives. A central managerial task is therefore to allocate these scarce resources among competing opportunities, projects and proposals. Allocation of scarce resources among market opportunities is one important aspect of this process. But in order to allocate among market opportunities the company must first identify actively what competing opportunities exist; what are their relative merits for the company and which are most suited to achieving its objectives and exploiting its competences. The process of identifying broad market opportunities is often referred to as market structure analysis, while that of refined identification of sub-market possibilities is characterised as market segmentation. When markets have been segmented, the choice of those which the company will seek to serve is traditionally called target marketing—for obvious reasons. This process of targeting the organisation's efforts and competences on carefully chosen segments provides an essential basis for a *market-focused* organisation.

Market focus is important to organisational effectiveness because it ensures that very specifically identified market needs are accurately aligned with organisational competences in a manner that allows exchange to take place to the profit of both parties. It also provides a degree of focused attention that supports long-term learning about the market and customer needs and the appropriate deepening and building of organisational expertise or competence. The strategies of successful firms are characterised by good segmentation, leading to clear choice of target markets, consistent market focus and continuous adaptation to the shifts and changes in segment characteristics.

Market segments may be identified and measured in many ways, but most of the approaches may be categorised as either customer based or company-coverage based. Once the nature and number of segments in the market are known, the decision must be taken as to what kind of strategy to pursue—serve all segments with a common marketing approach, or serve one or more individual segments with separate marketing programmes. The decision has to reflect both the nature of the market opportunity and the company's resource base. Some general rules concerning the making of this decision have evolved in professional practice and can be used as guidelines by the manager; these are discussed later in this chapter.

For many Irish companies, especially new ventures and small and medium-sized firms with an interest in international market growth, the market niche strategy has special attractions and advantages. It offers an opportunity to a relatively small firm with limited resources to enter specialty markets of minor interest to large international companies and to build expertise and reputation before considering entry to larger and more competitive market segments.

WHAT ARE MARKET SEGMENTS?

A market segment is a group of customers whose needs and consumption patterns are very similar to each other while being different in some significant way from other groups in the same general market. For example, within the market for coffee there are many segments. One segment prefers freshly ground high-quality coffee and responds sensitively to factors such as taste, type of coffee bean, manner in which the coffee is roasted, aroma, appearance, and method of preparation. Another general segment prefers instant coffee and responds generally to convenience in preparation as well as taste, aroma and price. Within the instant coffee segment there are various user sub-segments. These include consumers who use instant coffee as a fast convenience drink in the morning or at other times of the day and have little sensitivity to quality or care in preparation; consumers who drink instant coffee at work breaks and social encounters largely as a basis for socialising with others; consumers who use instant coffee as their principal daily beverage in preference to tea or soft drinks and who therefore search for taste, aroma and visual characteristics that they find attractive; consumers who serve instant coffee after dinner or to guests and who may therefore pay special attention to quality and to using a premium product as a direct taste substitute for freshly ground coffee.

This illustration indicates the richness of insight into a market that may be derived from segmentation analysis. Each segment potentially represents a market opportunity for a different product and marketing programme and a basis for the company to build a focused competitive advantage.

Market segments are not a characteristic of consumer markets only. They are just as pervasive and important a feature of business-to-business markets. The market for water treatment equipment, for example, normally breaks down into the public sector segment and the industry segment. The public sector is composed of county councils and city or town councils whose needs and buying behaviour are quite special. Water treatment for them is a vital feature of ensuring public health and adequate water supplies and can become a basis for either attracting or hindering new industrial development in their local area. The industry segment typically buys because it has to avoid legal penalties for pollution and therefore approaches purchases with a different motivation. The industry segment also breaks down into sub-groups with different needs depending on whether they are large chemical process plants with high volumes of quite toxic effluent to be treated and perhaps recycled, or small food processing firms, located in city centres with severe constraints on treatment installation size and on odours and unpredictable variations in the output of effluent.

Segments are at the heart of understanding all markets. A good rule of thumb for the manager is to remember that there is no such thing as 'the market' for any general service or product form, whether it be coffee or water treatment systems: there are market segments which, if aggregated, form 'the market'. But the information and insight of real value to the marketer lie at the market segment level.

WHY SEGMENT?

The reasons that a company should segment its market are already clear. It should do so to understand its customer needs in detail and to appreciate the market options among which it must choose to allocate its scarce resources. Careful identification and choice of segments allows the company to address the underlying basis of demand. By doing so it has the opportunity to:

(1) build competitive advantage by serving one or more segments with products and marketing programmes uniquely attuned to their specific needs;

(2) build a partial monopoly position in such segments and therefore hope, at least temporarily, to earn profits above the industry average;

(3) disaggregate demand and therefore understand the basis of trends and behaviour in the total market with accuracy and insight;

(4) identify opportunities for marketing innovation as old segments decline and new ones emerge.

IDENTIFYING MARKET SEGMENTS

The bases on which segments are identified and analysed are many and varied. In general, however, most companies use either customer-based segments or company-coverage-based segments or a combination of both.

Customer-based segments

Customer-based segments are identified by searching for groupings among customers on the basis of:

(1) customers' personal characteristics;
(2) purchase and usage behaviour;
(3) customer needs and preferences.

Customer and personal characteristics such as age, income, sex, location, occupation, marital status, social class, lifestyle and personality profile are the traditional measures incorporated in marketing research studies aimed at segmenting consumer markets. Similar characteristics can be collected about organisations to form organisational segments for a business-to-business service or product—the size, location, age, technical expertise and organisational culture of companies in the market. Segmentation variables of this general kind are often categorised into the broad groupings of demographic, geographic and psychographic factors.

It must be noted that these measures are descriptive ones and are useful only when they are clearly related to variations in behaviour: do older consumers behave differently from younger ones?—men from women?—higher social status from lower social status groups?—urban from rural?—married from unmarried?—and so on. For many products this is the case. In more recent years lifestyle bases for segmentation have proved particularly powerful in structuring product-markets and in designing matching products. The 'Charlie' range of cosmetics, which became the largest-selling cosmetic range in the world in the late 1970s, signalled a departure in consumer marketing. Revlon identified an emerging lifestyle segment among cosmetic users. Market research found a growing number of young, active, independently minded, career-oriented women who rejected traditional cosmetic product images as personifying a stereotyped, 'over-feminine' woman. The response was to develop a product image that personified the new lifestyle, and to launch the new brand under the 'Charlie' name. Success was immediate and international.

Purchase and usage behaviour bases for segmentation explore the more specific interaction between customer and individual product—how, when, where and in what quantity they buy; and how, when and where they use the product—variables often referred to as behavioural factors. Segments may be constructed on the basis of the outlet where customers shop, whether they buy frequently or infrequently, and whether they buy large or small pack sizes or large or small quantities on a shopping trip. So, for example, customers who buy cameras in chemists' shops or department stores are different from those who buy in specialist camera shops. Typically the former is buying a camera in a technically uninformed way, is looking for convenient and simple operation and a reasonable price. The latter is searching for technical performance and sophistication and retailer advice on choosing between brands, models and accessories. Many airlines segment on the frequency-of-use dimension by offering special airport and in-flight services to persons travelling frequently, such as the Aer Lingus 'frequent flier' programme launched in 1991. Such high-frequency passengers may have access to airline lounges at main airports complete with secretarial, communication, meeting and entertainment facilities. Heavy users of many consumer products are treated as a special segment by manufacturers who produce special pack sizes and volume purchase promotions and incentives to capture their loyalty. In industrial marketing, many companies find that the 80/20 rule applies to their customer base—80 per cent of their business comes from 20 per cent of their clients. In response to this they may treat the 20 per cent as a particularly important heavy-usage segment, giving them preferential treatment in terms of delivery, technical service and support and salesforce account management time. Exhibit 9.1 shows a manager's view of segmentation in the builders' provider and hardware business.

Exhibit 9.1

WOODIES DIY SUPERSTORE

Success in market segmentation

Profits at the Grafton Group plc have trebled and turnover risen by 74 per cent in the last three years. The Group, which has three main divisions—builders' merchanting and wholesaling, manufacturing, and retailing—has a workforce of 730 people and a turnover of £90 million. In interview its managing director commented that 'key to this success is market segmentation and customer service'.

  'Some years ago the Group identified in a structured way the needs of different market segments, each of which would call for a specialised approach, and then developed a differential advantage or competitive edge to meet the specific needs of the customer groups in these segments. We see a market segment as a group of customers with similar needs—it's crucially important, however, that the market segment is defined by the needs and not just the type of customer.'

As an example the managing director profiled the builders' providers Chadwicks, part of its builders' merchanting division. 'Chadwicks had been attempting to service, in the same branch, the building trade and also other customer groups including individual householders who wished to purchase materials to do their own repairs and decorations. It soon became clear that the needs of the two groups were very different.

'The builders were looking for credit, a complete product range, delivery and collection, service and loading facilities amongst others. Meanwhile, the householder needed car parking, self service, convenient one-stop shopping and good advice. This led to the conclusion that the builders' providers business should be split into two new divisions: builders' centres for builders and DIY superstores for the consumer public.

'The Chadwicks Builders Centres dealing exclusively with the building trade include relaunched centres and newly built locations in Lucan and Bray. In these branches the builder is exclusively dealt with and his needs specifically addressed. Householders' needs are being met by the newly created Woodies DIY superstore chain, with three outlets in Dublin environs and one in Cork—and we envisage further growth in the chain.'

Source: abstracted from *MII News*, The Marketing Institute, vol. 4, no. 3, 1991, p. 3.

Customer needs and preferences represent yet another set of variables by which markets may be segmented, and ultimately form the 'best' bases for segmentation since they demand a thorough understanding of customer behaviour and objectives. Measurement of needs and preferences can be more difficult than for the other two categories of segmentation variables because they are less easily observed. What motivates customers, what product benefits they are seeking, and the nature of their preferences demand more subtlety in marketing research techniques and in managerial judgment. The coffee example quoted earlier is an interesting illustration of the variety of product benefits that customers may seek from a product category. Each variation in need and in preferences—from the group that uses instant coffee as an emergency convenience beverage (a study conducted by the Carnation company in the UK in the early 1970s showed that many users of instant coffee saw coffee as something they made 'when they didn't want to dirty the teapot') to those that buy it to serve as a taste substitute for freshly ground coffee—can be considered as defining a segment that might be addressed with a unique product and marketing strategy. Indeed, the great variety of existing coffee products and brands illustrates this. Consumers can buy coffee beans of varying origin and varying roasts from an outlet such as Bewley's Cafés to brew their own coffee; they can buy packaged ground coffee to percolate or filter; and they can buy instant coffees varying from supermarket own-label brands to very expensive premium instant coffees.

The complexity of the segment structure of a market is further underlined by the fact that an individual may belong to more than one segment. Managers are often puzzled by multibrand loyalty on the part of customers—customers regularly buying two or more competing brands. This feature of many markets is illustrated in the coffee market by the consumer who purchases an average-priced instant coffee for use in the mid-morning and afternoons and for occasional single cups of coffee, but who also buys a premium brand sold on quality, taste and aroma, and uses it perhaps to serve after dinner or when guests are being entertained. Here we see two segments of need, with the same customer belonging to each one under different usage scenarios.

Company-coverage-based segments

Company coverage of customers forms another basis on which segments may be formed in practice. This approach acknowledges that most companies are limited by their history and resources in terms of their ability to cover the total market for a product. Many small firms start the process of market development with only enough resources to cover a local or regional area of the total market. Others may find that their time and technical resources prevent them from dealing with the sophisticated segment of buyers requiring advanced products and intensive technical support. Many very large companies, by contrast, find smaller and less sophisticated markets a distraction and without enough profit potential to justify application of their elaborate and high-cost marketing systems. All of these company-coverage constraints may, of course, be changed in the longer term if the company sees economic advantage in entering new segments. In the shorter term, however, they make some sectors of the market accessible and others inaccessible.

Segment combination and resegmentation

The two sets of segmentation factors—customer based and company-coverage based—may be integrated in a matrix display such as that shown in Figure 9.1. Using this, the manager can get a broad representation of the segments that exist, those in which the company operates, and those in which it is capable of building a competitive advantage.

Resegmenting the market is often a key to marketing innovation. Many managers when pushed to think about segmentation of their market will respond that the segments are 'obvious' and require no further analysis. Yet the discipline of starting afresh on a segmentation analysis usually generates some novel ideas about customer groups and unexploited opportunities. For example, segmenting the market for mealtime foods into day of week as well as into breakfast/lunch/dinner segments can radically alter the marketer's perception of customer needs and behaviour and market opportunity. Market research indicates that different days of the week have different food-serving patterns, so that some foods suit some days and not others. Saturday is a family day with no work and school commitments but significant leisure commitments. Sunday is characterised in many households by the weekly ritual of the family Sunday meal, with poultry or a joint of meat the norm. Monday is a day when left-over food from Sunday is widely used in cooking and when the start of another working week seems to dampen culinary enthusiasm. And so the week advances, with each day displaying its own food preparation and usage characteristics. Following a detailed segmentation analysis on this basis, the marketer is likely to find new ways of presenting and positioning his product to increase its usage perhaps, or to make it a more regular element of weekly diet.

Figure 9.1

Customer and Company-Coverage Segments

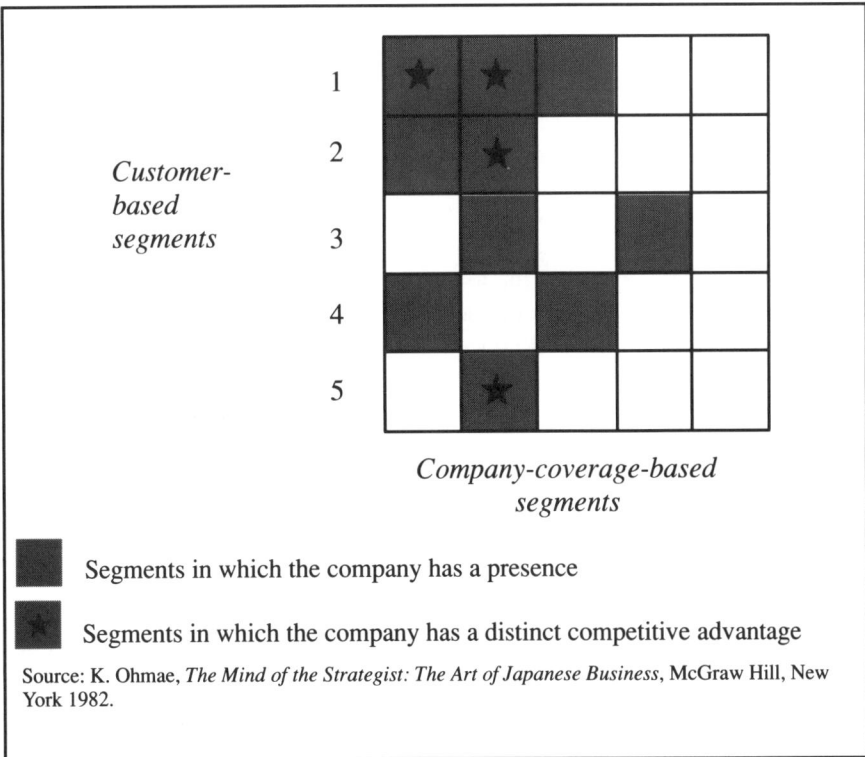

Source: K. Ohmae, *The Mind of the Strategist: The Art of Japanese Business*, McGraw Hill, New York 1982.

The watch industry provides another interesting example of creative segmentation. The world market has been traditionally segmented into price segments. The 'AA' segment, with prices ranging from over £2,000 virtually to infinity; the 'A' segment ranging from £300 to £2,000; the 'B' segment ranging from £150 to £300; and the 'C' segment selling for less than £150. Swatch, one of the great successes of the watch industry of the eighties, was, however, launched not at one of these traditional segments but at a newly defined 'lifestyle' segment—young-at-heart, fashion-conscious, fun-oriented and a little irreverent. As a result the brand created a new watch category and a segment that drew customers from across all the traditional price segments. Over eight million Swatches were being bought in total each year by 1990—by teenagers and millionaires alike.

Segmentation decisions are therefore never once-and-for-all decisions. They must be reappraised periodically in the search for innovation, new opportunity and greater profitability and above all in response to change in customer behaviour and values.

CHOOSING AND TARGETING SEGMENTS

When the analytical task of identifying and measuring segments is complete, decisions must be taken on how to use this information—what choices will be made and which segments targeted? There are three fundamental options open to the marketer:

(1) mass-market strategy;
(2) niche strategy;
(3) multiple-niche strategy.

Mass-market strategy

A mass-market strategy does not imply going for huge markets, but does mean ignoring any segments that may exist and addressing the total market with one marketing programme (an approach also referred to as undifferentiated marketing). IBM managed in a very short period to dominate the initial market for professional personal computers with such a strategy. With their personal computer they went from no market presence on introduction in August 1981 to over 26 per cent of the market in the US by the end of 1983. In the process they sent many smaller companies to bankruptcy with the power of their mass-market strategy. With just a reasonable level of technological sophistication in their product, they managed to produce a basic personal computer that most buyers and users of micros could comprehend and use, with confidence in the service back-up and technical reputation of its manufacturer. As this market developed, however, this became a less feasible approach. The evolving customer needs led, by the nineties, to the necessity for a more differentiated and focused approach. This produced a market structure in which different competitors focused on desktop, laptop, notepad and workstation variations that an increasingly sophisticated and demanding market requested. In addition, the different competitors pursued different sales and distribution policies, ranging from the huge success of Dell as an international 'mail order' microcomputer supplier to that of Sun, with its high technical expertise in selling and supporting advanced workstations.

Many companies pursue the strategy of marketing a package that is almost all things to all people. Success depends on there being large numbers of customers with more or less common needs, and a product with sufficient features and benefits to provide all with their needed product benefits. Coca-Cola have succeeded outstandingly with such a strategy worldwide for many years. Several motor car companies achieved major cost and quality advantages by pursuing the concept of a world car (Japanese companies in particular but also Ford's world car projects, for example). The advantage of this strategy is that it allows maximum use to be made of economies of scale and experience. This should, with good management, result in a low-cost high-quality product capable of supporting substantial marketing, manufacturing and R & D overheads. The rapid growth of global markets supports the feasibility of such strategies of standardisation. The problem with the strategy is that it is usually most attractive to large and resourceful companies and especially global and multinational enterprises. It is therefore difficult for small, medium-sized or new ventures to adopt such a strategy in markets that are of any large scale. Where the whole market is of limited size, this consideration need not hold true.

Niche strategy

A niche strategy is the polar opposite of the mass strategy. Here the marketer selects a single segment in the market which represents the best opportunity for the company to serve customers well and build a defensible competitive position against new entrants. The strategy is therefore to focus on and seek dominance of a specialist segment. Many Irish companies producing technical industrial products illustrate this approach. Applied Microelectronics Ltd, for example, a Dublin-based producer of electronic test equipment for companies that manufacture floppy disks and optical disks (CDs), serves worldwide markets across Europe, North America and the Pacific Rim. It has a very specialised product line purchased by a very small number of factories that manufacture disks for the world computer market.

While the company using this strategy chooses a narrow focus, it may still reap significant economies through specialisation, and its finely honed expertise and skills base become over time its key competitive advantages. There are risks involved too. Focusing on a single segment carries all the dangers of having one's eggs all in the same basket! If the fortunes of the segment decline, then the company supplying it goes down too. Typically the marketer is serving quite a small number of customers, so the necessity to be excellent in serving most of them very well and all the time is intense. Market dominance is an important requirement for significant success with the strategy. There is little room for 'also rans' in niche marketing.

Multiple-niche strategy

Multiple-niche strategy involves the recognition that several segments exist and the adoption of an objective of serving two or more of them with differentiated products and marketing programmes. Companies such as Kellogg's implement this kind of strategy with remarkable success. Kellogg's cover the many segments of need in the breakfast cereal market from their standard Corn Flakes and similar products to cereals for children, and various health, nutrition and slimness-oriented cereal brands.

Multiple-niche strategies usually appear on the competitive landscape of a market as it goes through the growth stage of the life cycle. More and more products are launched to cater to, and bring into the market, additional customers by focusing on their special needs. This stage of development most typically results in too many competitors fighting for dominance of too many niches, and the slow-down of market growth inevitably precipitates a shake-out of competing companies. The maturity phase of a market usually marks the stabilisation of the number of market niches and a competitive equilibrium among competitors who have carved out their positions in the various niches. The greatest dangers of a multiple-niche strategy lie in the cost of production of multiple products and the overhead and coordination implications of marketing several products with different marketing strategies. Production costs can rise if the many products needed for the different niches all involve small production runs, frequent change-over in the factory and associated set-up costs. However, modern manufacturing methods and technologies are beginning to lessen or even to eliminate such constraints. Manufacturing systems developed originally at Toyota have created the potential to produce small volumes at the kind of cost levels traditionally available only from mass standardised production. In the automobile industry Mazda has become a particularly successful exponent of this combined marketing and manufacturing approach, positioning itself in the world market as a producer for niche segments at very competitive prices.

EVALUATING THE MARKETING FEASIBILITY OF MARKET SEGMENTS

The process of identifying market segments can proceed until each potential customer is represented as a unique segment. Some industrial markets do conform to this limiting situation—for example, major public works contracts for hospitals, power stations, airports, etc. For most markets, however, the manager must limit the number of segments to what is realistic and worthwhile to service in terms of economic and strategic criteria. Evaluating the feasibility of a segment is best done with reference to the following criteria:

(1) *Measurability:* Can the size and characteristics of the segment be measured and quantified?—if not it will become virtually impossible to develop a sensible marketing strategy and programme to address the segment.

(2) *Accessibility:* Can the segment be reached with a separate marketing programme? Are there communication media and distribution channels? If not the marketer cannot effectively address the segment.

(3) *Substance:* Is the segment big enough to justify a tailor-made marketing investment? While managers may identify a gap in any market they must be careful to ask whether there is a market in the gap! Many segments are too small to support the expenditure necessary to exploit the opportunity. In small markets such as those commonly found in Ireland, this is a particularly important consideration. The struggle to launch additional Irish Sunday newspapers has been bedevilled by this problem.

(4) *Defensibility:* Having developed a marketing programme for a segment and invested in entry to the market, can the company defend its position against existing or future competitors attracted by any success? In the car rental business in Ireland the multinational companies can generally defend their international business traveller segment very successfully but are endlessly open to attack in the tourism segment, where domestic companies come and go with aggressive pricing strategies as the tourist market changes from year to year. Hertz and Avis chose to restructure their Irish operations to reflect this reality.

(5) *Durability:* How long will the segment persist in reasonably stable form? Is it likely to change and merge with other segments in the short to medium term? This is a particular problem in rapidly growing markets before a competitive shake-out occurs, and many new ventures enter such an industry with false expectations of a long life for a specialist segment they have identified.

(6) *Competitive capability:* Does the company have the necessary resources, experience and marketing strengths to implement a marketing strategy appropriate to the segment identified? 'Can we do the necessary job?' is the difficult question that must be faced with realism and cool objectivity.

CHOOSING A MARKET

The choice of market ultimately depends on the quality of the segmentation analysis, a clear assessment of the company's capability to compete in the various segments identified, and managerial judgment as to which market option best fits market conditions and company strengths. Some general rules for strategic choice have been suggested (Biggadike, 1981) as encapsulating professional practice in marketing:

(1) Look for the unserved segment—the area of need that no one has yet identified or discovered a way to serve cost-effectively.
(2) Do not choose a strategy that positions the company between segments: at best you may satisfy one, at worst you will satisfy none.
(3) Do not serve two or more segments with the same strategy. A strategy successful with one segment has no necessary basis for success with another.
(4) Do not adopt a position which makes a pretence of being 'all things to all men'. Successful mass-market strategies make very clear and relatively simple competitive claims—user-friendliness, quality of graphics and service support for Apple's Macintosh personal computers; taste for Coca-Cola; quality, service and cleanliness for McDonald's hamburger chain.

THE NICHE STRATEGY AND COMPETITIVENESS IN IRISH INDUSTRY

The imperatives of Irish industrial policy all point towards developing native industry that can successfully compete in world markets, thereby generating wealth and long-term employment in the economy. This policy objective is critically dependent upon the implementation of international marketing strategies by a cadre of skilled marketing professionals with international experience. But how do predominantly small and medium-sized Irish businesses enter international markets? The most immediate answer is that their only hope of success lies in targeting on relatively specialised market segments where the cost disadvantages of geographic location are not critical and where direct competition with major international and multinational companies is less likely. The niche or focus market strategy therefore has very special relevance for Irish industry as it tackles the challenge and enormous opportunities of international market development.

This approach is not without its dangers and testing challenges. Successful penetration of specialist segments usually requires high quality in products and marketing to serve the well-informed and sophisticated needs of customers. Serving these markets normally demands an above-average level of design or technology in the service or product and considerable problem-solving or applications engineering ability to tailor-make responses to closely specified needs.

The competition in many specialist international segments is also increasing significantly through the 1990s as major international companies see the opportunity in global or pan-European strategies to enter specialist segments by producing a product they can market into hundreds of such segments around the world. Thus, while any one-country segment may be too small on its own to attract the attentions of major international companies, when these are aggregated across countries the possibility of producing a standard specialist product incorporating the latest design or technology, high quality in manufacturing or service delivery and excellence in marketing becomes an attractive option for a multinational enterprise. Many companies pursuing niche strategies on a purely domestic scale cannot respond to such competition and must either change or die. The necessity for Irish companies to view potential competition and to consider market choices on an international scale is therefore imperative.

The race to identify and dominate international niche segments commenced in the mid-eighties and is being actively fought. An excellent illustration of this is the successful international growth of the Benetton clothing empire. Irish companies with growth objectives must develop the competence to run in the race and to grow into substantial international enterprises. Both the challenges and the potential rewards of being involved in this process are enormous and exciting for anyone involved in a marketing career.

SUMMARY

Market choice is the first major marketing decision. It determines the allocation of scarce resources among different opportunities. It is also essential to creating market focus since the choice of market involves the alignment of clearly defined market needs with the resources and competences of the organisation.

A market segment is a group of customers whose needs and consumption patterns are very similar to each other while being different in some significant way from other groups in the same general market. Segments exist in most markets, both consumer and industrial, and must be identified and understood if marketing direction is to be effectively chosen. Segments are identified in many ways, but basically they must reflect customer characteristics, purchase and usage behaviour, customer needs, and the company's market coverage. Segmenting and resegmenting markets is a process that lies at the heart of most marketing innovation. Segmentation leads to strategic choice among the alternatives of pure mass-market, niche or multiple-niche strategies. Choosing a strategy must take into account the feasibility of addressing any one or several segments, as well as obeying some general rules of good strategy-making. The importance of niche strategies to Irish industry springs from the size and resource base of most Irish firms, yet their implementation demands considerable skill and analytical insight and will be open to increasing competition with the advent of pan-European and global markets.

Reading

Baker, Michael J. (1991), *Marketing—An Introductory Text*, Macmillan, London, ch. 8.

Bartlett, C.A. and Ghoshal, S. (1989), *Beyond Global Management: The Transnational Solution*, Harvard Business School Press, Boston, MA.

Biggadike, E.R. (1981), 'The contributions of marketing to strategic management', *Academy of Management Review*, vol. 6, no. 4.

Bonoma, T.V. and Shapiro, B.P. (1983), *Segmenting the Industrial Market,* Lexington Books, NY.

Frank, R.E., Massy, W.F. and Wind, Y. (1972), *Market Segmentation*, Prentice-Hall, Englewood Cliffs, NJ.

Gronhaug, K. and Venkatesh, A. (1986), 'Benefit seeking in home computer adoption', *Irish Marketing Review*, vol. 1.

Kotler, P. (1991), *Marketing Management: Analysis, Planning, Implementation and Control*, 7th ed., Prentice-Hall, Englewood Cliffs, NJ, ch. 10.

Levitt, Theodore (1983), 'The globalization of markets', *Harvard Business Review*, May–June.

McDonald, M.H.B. (1984), *Marketing Plans: How to Prepare Them & How to Use Them*, Heinemann, London, ch. 4.

Review Questions

1. Choose a consumer product-market and an industrial product-market and illustrate how they are segmented and how different products have been developed to serve each segment.
2. Why should a company attempt to segment a market?
3. On what bases can market segments be established? Illustrate your answer with reference to product-markets you know.
4. What basic segmentation strategies are open to the manager? What are the characteristics, advantages and problems of each?

Chapter 10

Competitive Positioning

INTRODUCTION

In Chapter 9 the manner in which market choices should be made was considered. It was seen that the manager, basing his decision on thorough analysis, must choose between the strategies of (1) producing a product or service to meet the specialised needs of one segment, (2) producing two or more products to meet the needs of several separate segments, or (3) producing one product to provide general appeal across many segments.

The choice of a target market results in a clear identification of the target group with which the marketing organisation wishes to develop a market relationship. The organisation decides *who* to serve. The segmentation analysis leading to this decision yields an essential profile of target customers in terms of their buying behaviour and relevant individual or organisational characteristics—for example, their demographic, socio-economic and psychographic profile.

When the target customer group has been chosen the managerial challenge becomes that of *positioning* the company and its products or services relative to the preferences of the target group and relative to existing and anticipated competitive offerings. The objective is to *serve* the customer and to *outperform* competitors by focusing the company's competences in an appropriate manner.

ANALYTICAL REQUIREMENTS FOR COMPETITIVE POSITIONING

To make a competitive positioning decision the manager must first know:

(1) customer purchase criteria;
(2) customer preferences concerning service or product performance on each criterion;
(3) customer perceptions of competing suppliers and their products on each criterion.

Figure 10.1

Customer-Competitor-Company Interface

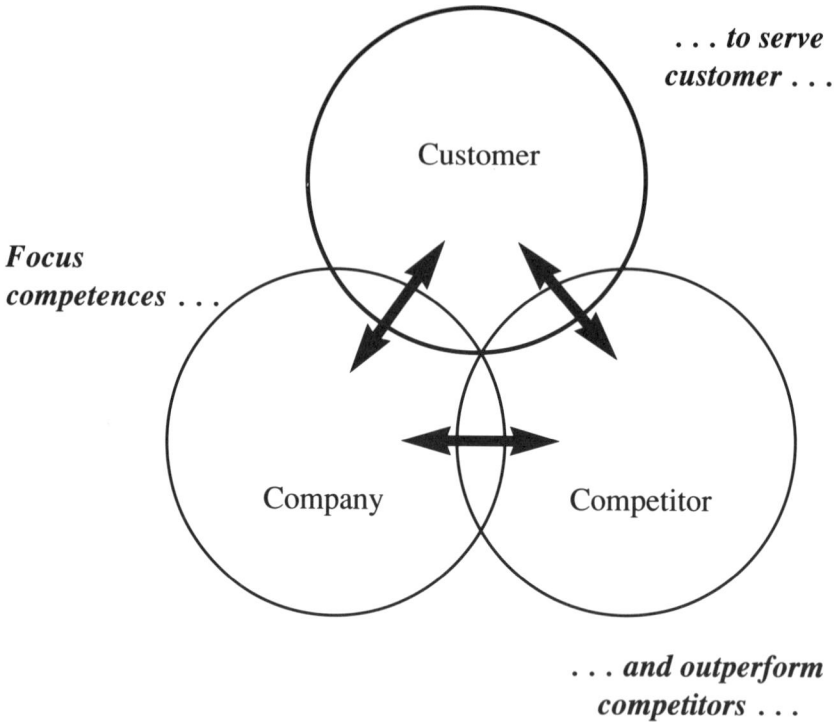

... to serve customer ...

Focus competences ...

... and outperform competitors ...

Customer purchase criteria

The discussion of approaches to customer analysis in Chapter 4 stressed the value in application of a simple decision-process model of buying behaviour. As shown in Figure 10.2 the third stage of this process involves evaluation by the customer of the alternatives available to satisfy his consumption 'problem' or need. The importance of understanding the criteria that are used in evaluating the alternative products or services on offer was stressed not only because of their central role in explaining customer behaviour, but also because an appreciation of the nature and use of these criteria is funda-mental to the positioning decision.

Normally there are several important purchase criteria involved in the buying behaviour of any one target customer segment. In general these may be categorised as:

(1) price-related criteria (e.g. purchase price, discounts, trade-in allow-ances, residual value, operating or life cycle costs);

(2) performance-related—i.e. functional—criteria (e.g. speed, durability, length of life, precision, cleansing ability, service and support facilities);

(3) psycho-social criteria (e.g. acceptability to others, fit with self-concept, fit with reference group attitudes, reputability and dependability of supplier).

Figure 10.2

Customer Decision Process

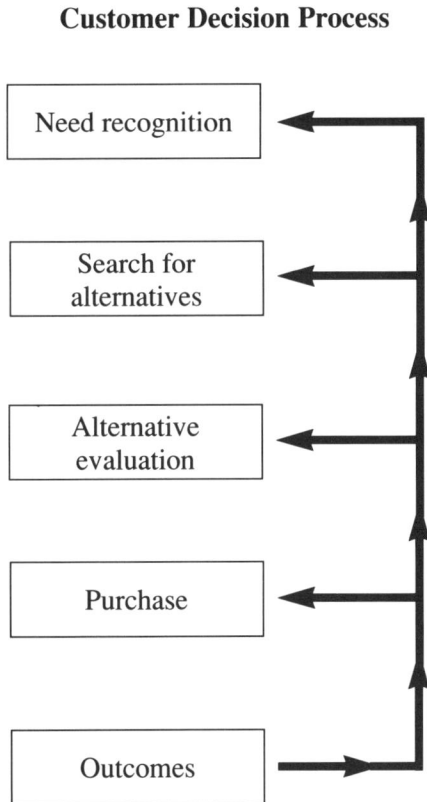

Specific criteria must, however, be identified on a product-by-product and segment-by-segment basis. For example, a study of the impact of customer service mix on the effectiveness of manufacturers' marketing strategies to Dublin retailers indicated that the criteria the retailers used in evaluating alternative suppliers included:

—quality of goods when received
—delivery reliability
—discounts offered
—guarantees provided
—after-sales service
—credit terms.

The relative importance of these criteria varied considerably depending on the product studied. Thus, as is demonstrated in Figure 10.3, electrical appliance retailers, paint retailers and cigarette retailers might, for instance, attribute different weightings to each criterion and use some different criteria in evaluating their specific suppliers.

Figure 10.3

Rank Order of Importance of Evaluative Criteria

	Electrical retailers	Paint retailers	Cigarette retailers
1.	after-sales service received	quality of goods received	quality of goods
2.	quality of goods received	discounts offered	delivery reliability
3.	guarantees	inventory reliability	inventory reliability
4.	ease of contacting supplier	delivery reliability	speed of delivery
5.	discounts offered	guarantees	guarantees
6.	delivery reliability	after-sales service	sales representation

Source: J.A. Murray and S.A. MacEntee, 'Measuring the effect of customer service level', *IBAR*, 1, 1 (1979).

The criteria used in industrial purchasing may equally well be identified. For example, mobile refrigeration units used to provide temperature control in trucks carrying perishable foodstuffs are evaluated by purchasers using criteria such as purchase price, running cost, spare parts availability, international service network, expected down-time, and so on. In contrast, the purchase of a mass-market consumer item such as a chocolate bar might revolve about the comparison of alternatives on criteria such as advertising imagery, texture, sweetness, wrapper design and perceived nutritional value.

Generalising from these specific examples, it is clear that for any product or service there exists a set of benefits important to the potential buyer. The extent to which any service or product is perceived to provide the relevant benefits lies at the heart of the customer evaluation process. Possession of a significant desired benefit—such as long service intervals for a motor car—is used as a criterion in choosing between competing alternatives.

The first step in formulating a positioning strategy is to identify these purchase criteria. The manager should attempt to complete a basic listing of the criteria important to target customers through formal research or, at the least, through personal questioning of buyers and reflection on experience in marketing to them successfully.

Customer preferences

When criteria have been identified, the next step becomes that of identifying customer preferences concerning product performance on each criterion. So, if 'running cost' is established as an important criterion, the preferred level of running costs must then be measured.

When this information is developed for each criterion, the marketer has a profile of the segment's 'ideal', or preferred, product. It is particularly useful to visualise such information in a simple map-like diagram such as the one illustrated in Figure 10.4, in which the hypothetical preferences for a restaurant service are shown for a tourism market segment (in this case German holidaymakers). A map of customer preferences such as this is of enormous importance, as it documents explicitly an ideal service from the customer's viewpoint. In doing so it provides one of the essential bench-marks relative to which a service offering may then be positioned.

Analytical and measurement techniques are available to undertake more scientific and detailed research and quantification of perceptions and preferences. These techniques are often referred to in general as perceptual mapping methods. One of particular relevance is conjoint analysis. Conjoint analysis uses customer-derived information to determine the relative importance of one product or service attribute as opposed to another. Customers typically indicate that all attributes are important—in selecting a beer, they want price, alcohol content, taste, quality, aftertaste and image (Walsh and Roe, 1987). Conjoint analysis asks them to make trade-offs between these various attributes—is one aspect desired enough to sacrifice another? If one aspect had to be sacrificed, which would it be? Extremely sensitive and useful information may be gathered in this way to assist the manager in choosing the most appropriate combination of attributes.

Customer perceptions of competing products

The next step that must be taken before making a positioning decision is to detail the perceived position of each competing product on each criterion. To continue with the restaurant example, the manager of the restaurant should plot onto the map the performance of competing restaurants in the local tourism area (for example, the area accessible to German boating holiday-makers on the River Shannon). The positioning of two hypothetical competing restaurants is illustrated in Figure 10.5. Significant marketing implications of the analysis now begin to appear. How the two competing establishments differ is readily visible, as too is their ability or inability to match customer preferences. Both have paid little attention to a desire for natural fresh foods, and A has particularly misjudged consumer needs by preparing food with many and heavy sauces in an intimate and highly priced environment whereas segment preferences are in fact for few and light sauces in a relatively impersonal environment and at reasonable prices.

THE COMPETITIVE POSITIONING DECISION

Armed with information such as the above, the marketing organisation next decides how to position its own offering in the market. The position chosen is of a relative nature. It makes marketing sense in so far as it is chosen relative to the identified customer preferences and competitor performance on each important criterion and relative to the company's capabilities.

In general, three alternatives are open to the manager considering a positioning decision. The manager may choose to:

(1) introduce new products or services to fill 'gaps' in the market;
(2) alter the position of an existing product or service;
(3) alter buyers' perceptions of the market by
—introducing new criteria
—changing the importance they attribute to existing criteria.

Introduce new products to fill market 'gaps'

Returning once again to the restaurant example, the positioning analysis suggested a 'gap' in the market: an unsatisfied need for very fresh natural foods with some degree of local uniqueness. An entrepreneur considering opening a new restaurant could develop a 'product' to fill this gap while also providing the other benefits desired by the target customer group. In doing this the new restaurant would address itself to an unsatisfied demand and differentiate itself clearly from competing restaurants. In a more general way, the success of ethnic, healthfood and vegetarian restaurants illustrates how such market gaps may be exploited.

It is generally true that innovative and entrepreneurial activity will be more successful to the extent that it is based on a decision to fill a market gap, thereby providing customers with something they desire but cannot obtain from existing suppliers. In doing this the marketer secures an immediate monopoly position until competitors discover how to imitate the innovation.

Figure 10.4

Mapping Customer Preferences

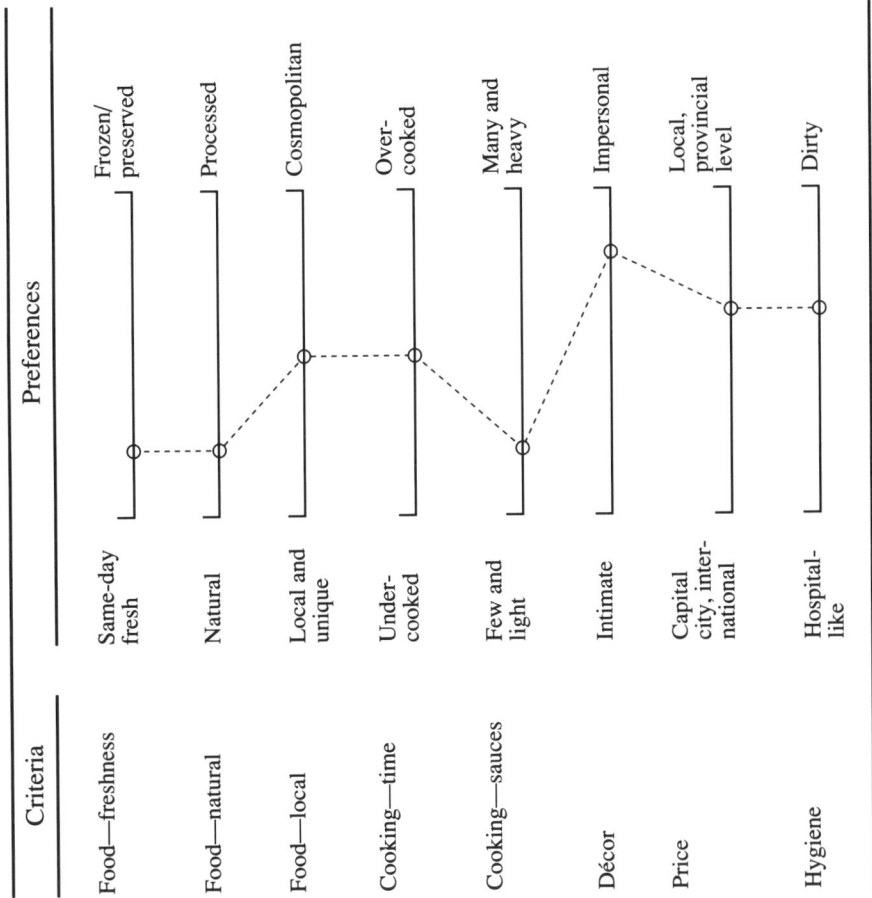

Figure 10.5

Customer Perceptions and Preferences

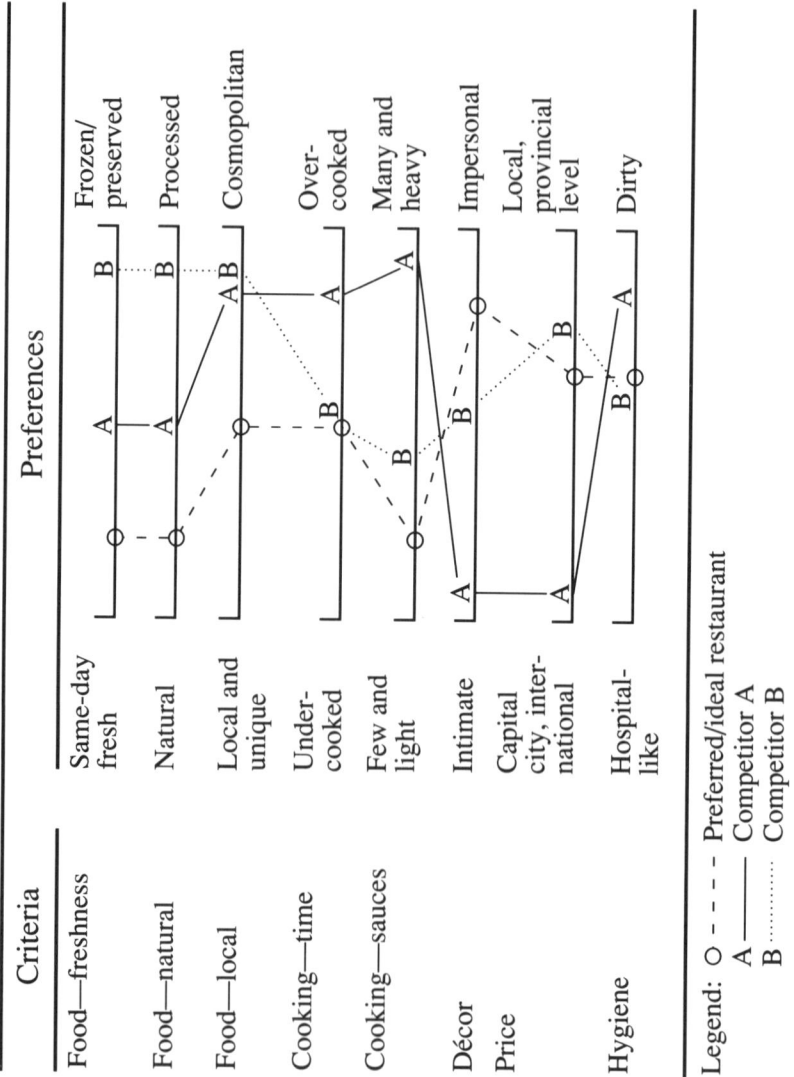

Legend: O - - - - Preferred/ideal restaurant
         A ———   Competitor A
         B ⋯⋯   Competitor B

Figure 10.6

Modified Customer Perceptions and Preferences

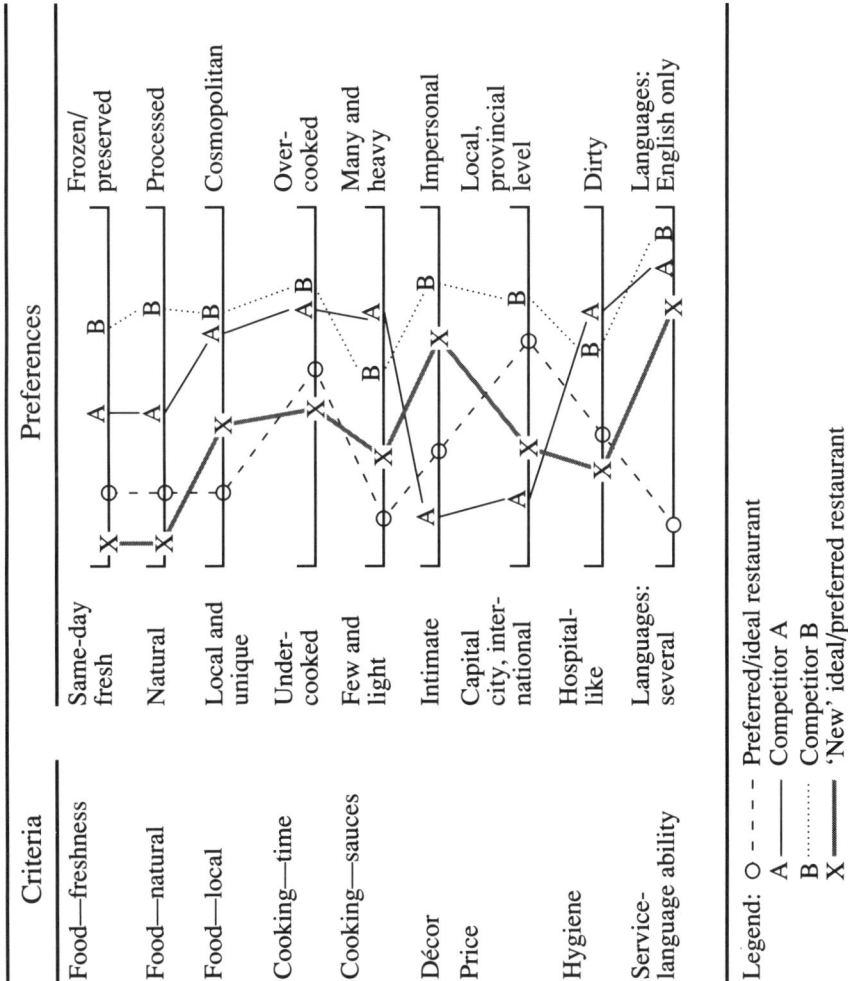

Alter the position of an existing product

If a new restaurant had been opened to fill the market gap identified in the above example, it might well transpire that after several years not only would competitors have learned of their own weaknesses, but the customer group might also have changed its preferences. A mapping of the new state of consumer preferences is visualised in Figure 10.6, showing a changed structure of perceptions and preferences. The positioning challenge now faced by the restaurateur is to alter perceptions of the restaurant's position so as to achieve a better fit with new customer preferences and to obtain some distinct advantage relative to competition. The importance now attached by customers to having restaurant service in their own language presents an opportunity, while it is also clear that gaps have been left in the market by the shift in consumer preferences towards lower price and more intimate surroundings. Our restaurateur's major current strength lies in the provision of unique local food. He might therefore consider repositioning his service by building on this strength and moving to fill the identified gaps.

The repositioning of packaged soup as 'fresh soup' distributed in tetra packs through the chill counter of supermarkets in the early nineties is a further illustration of this approach.

Changing an established competitive position is not always a feasible option because of the difficulty of changing the perceptions and attitudes that customers have learned over time. For this reason many companies will choose to relaunch a modified product, sometimes with a new name and identity, rather than attempt to reposition the old product in the consumer's mind. Despite this caveat, it must be recognised that since all markets are dynamic, owing to changing customer tastes and competitive activity, some degree of continuous repositioning is virtually a necessity. Where this repositioning takes place gradually—for example, in the form of a steady increase in product quality—the company will almost always benefit. Where the repositioning is sudden and major, however, and asks the customer to accept the credibility of a major change in product or service performance, the weight of past experience may render the new position unbelievable, resulting in rejection and sales decline.

Alter buyers' perceptions of the market

Two strategies may be engaged to implement this decision. One is to introduce new evaluative criteria to the customer's decision process. In marketing truck tyres to fleet owners, for example, purchase price, fitting service and number of retreads were traditionally critical criteria. With rapid escalation in the cost of running a truck through the 1970s and 1980s, however, the more innovative tyre companies and retailers quickly introduced a new criterion—tyre running cost. The factors determining operating costs associated with the use of a tyre range from the expected life of the tyre (extended with the introduction of truck radials) to its rolling resistance (which affects fuel consumption) and the number of retreads (while most operators demanded two retreads, many tyres failed before even one retread).

The innovative marketers introduced radial tyres designed to reduce rolling resistance and to ensure at least one retread. By insisting on better quality from their manufacturing divisions and by educating trucking companies to the role that tyres play in their overall operating costs, they introduced a new decision criterion of life cycle cost and placed their own new tyre ranges in a strong competitive position. Moreover, in some markets they could trade off a higher initial purchase price against the expectation of lower lifetime running costs.

The second strategy appropriate to altering the buyer's perceptions involves changing the importance that customers attribute to existing criteria. The discussion so far has generally assumed that each criterion used by a consumer in evaluating competing products carries equal importance or 'weighting'. This is in fact seldom true. It is far more common to find that in any customer decision involving multiple criteria, some criteria will be significantly more important than others.

These 'weightings', attributed to the various criteria, are open to influence by the marketing company. A toothpaste manufacturer may choose to influence consumers to attribute extra weight to decay prevention, as opposed to cosmetic effect, thereby shifting market demand towards brands that contain decay prevention ingredients and that are promoted on this basis, and away from brands that stress 'whiteness', cosmetic and social impact benefits. The growth in the early nineties of toothpaste brands formulated to combat plaque illustrates this process. Similarly, the repositioning of Lucozade as a sport and fitness related drink as well as its traditional appeal to those seeking a health restorative suggests how marketers may seek to broaden perceptions of a product.

Necessary benefits versus competitively advantageous benefits

Finally, the fact that several competitors have converged on some of the ideal points of consumers will usually be visible on any competitive positioning map—i.e. they all provide an equally satisfactory response to one or more of the customer's criteria. Where this is the case a competitor must understand that while performance on this criterion is necessary to compete effectively, it yields no competitive advantage. For example, consumers now assume that any watch they buy will keep time with considerable accuracy and electronic watch technology makes this benefit universally available. To compete in the watch market one must therefore market a watch that keeps time, but there is no competitive advantage in this feature—it is a necessity for entry to the market but no aid to success. Companies do not always make this distinction and can fool themselves into thinking that having a required feature is the same as having a basis for competitive advantage.

SUMMARY

In this chapter the target customer group, whose selection was discussed in Chapter 9, was further analysed to determine the criteria used in purchase behaviour, the profile of the customer's ideal service or product in relation to these criteria, and the performance of competing products on each criterion. With these bench-marks, the manager's options in choosing a competitive positioning strategy for his own product or service have been identified.

The manager who has made a decision on competitive positioning now knows the customers he wishes to serve and with whom he wishes to build a relationship. The position that is most appropriate, relative to these customers' perceptions and preferences and relative to competitors' offerings, may be chosen. Critical decisions with regard to who to serve and how to outperform the competition have now been taken.

In order to operationalise these decisions, a marketing mix must next be developed specifying detailed product or service policy decisions, price levels and price structures, distribution channels and physical distribution arrangements, and a persuasive communication programme.

Reading

Aaker, D. and Day, G.S. (1990), *Marketing Research*, 4th ed., Wiley, NY.

Cummins, M.W. (1986), 'Brand positioning: a case history of an Irish whiskey', *Irish Marketing Review*, vol. 1, pp. 153–159.

Kotler, P. (1991), *Marketing Management: Analysis, Planning, Implementation and Control*, 7th ed., Prentice-Hall, Englewood Cliffs, NJ, ch. 11.

Walsh, J.W. and Roe, P.R. (1987), 'Preference modelling: conjoint analysis and multi-attribute models', *Irish Marketing Review*, vol. 2, pp. 126–137.

Wind, Y. (1982), *Product Policy: Concepts, Methods and Strategy,* Addison-Wesley, Reading, Mass., ch. 4.

Wind, Y. (1977), 'Brand strategy and vulnerability', in Woodside, A.G., Sheth, J.N. and Bennett, P.D. (eds), *Consumer and Industrial Buying Behavior*, Elsevier, North Holland, NY.

Review Questions
1. What are the three analytical requirements for an effective positioning decision? Explain each one.
2. What positioning strategies are available to the manager? Find an example of the application of each strategy and discuss its effectiveness.
3. Under what circumstances might you consider attempting to alter buyers' perceptions of the market? How could such a move be implemented?

Chapter 11

Product Choice

INTRODUCTION

The two foundation-stones of marketing decision-making have been discussed in the last two chapters. The market has been segmented and the target market(s) chosen. Within the chosen target market a competitive position has been selected for the company's product or service. This position locates it in relation to customers' needs and competitors' offerings. The company has therefore decided *who to serve* and *how to outperform* the competition.

Now we turn to the manager's decisions about what is generally called the *marketing mix*. The marketing mix refers to the four essential elements of a marketing programme that are necessary to execute the market choice and the competitive positioning decisions. Most commonly referred to as the 'four Ps' (McCarthy and Perreault, 1990)—product, price, promotion and place—the components of the marketing mix represent vital and interdependent decisions.

The origin of the term 'marketing mix' is attributable to an analogy with cooking. To bake a cake the cook must have all the necessary ingredients and then mix them in correct proportion. So too with marketing. All four elements of the mix are essential but must be used in an appropriate balance with each other. Just as you cannot make a marketing decision without considering price, so too you cannot decide the price without careful consideration of the product's quality and the way in which it will be distributed and promoted.

Figure 11.1 visualises the role of the marketing mix decision. Having chosen both target market and desired competitive position, the company executes the positioning decision through its marketing mix decisions. In this and the next four chapters each element of the mix will be reviewed and decision alternatives identified. We will discuss the elements of the mix under the headings product, price, communication and selling (including promotion), and distribution (including both channels and physical processes of distribution).

Figure 11.1

The Marketing Mix

Target market	COMPANY'S MARKETING MIX	
	Product	Price
Competitors	Communication and sales	Distribution

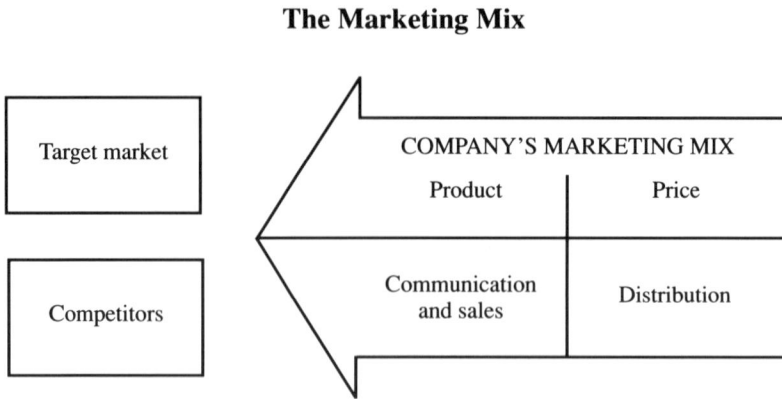

In this chapter product-related decisions are covered. The meaning and components of a product or service decision from a marketing viewpoint are analysed. The product life cycle concept and its implications for decision-making are outlined and the special issues arising in a multiproduct company highlighted.

WHAT IS A PRODUCT OR SERVICE?

The words 'service' or 'product' will be used interchangeably, as all the issues raised in this chapter apply equally to both. From the marketer's point of view, a product is *a bundle of physical, service and psychological benefits designed to satisfy a customer's needs and related wants*. The physical aspect is the tangible performance-related element of the product—the bodywork, transmission, engine, wheels, etc. of a motor car, or the payroll program written by a computer software house. The service aspect consists of all the product benefits that make the physical product saleable—sales assistance, warranties, and so on. The psychological benefits consist of the symbolic aspects of the product and its brand or manufacturer's name—its reputation and associations with important or symbolic people, values or uses.

The physical product

Good decisions concerning the physical aspect of any product are usually a reflection of good design—an area taken far too lightly by most Irish manufacturers and marketers. Design decisions incorporate choices about functional characteristics, structural characteristics and aesthetic characteristics (Wind, 1982).

Functional characteristics are those which provide the expected performance benefits to the customer—the length of life of a car tyre and its grip under various driving conditions, or the warmth and washability of an item of clothing. Guaranteeing that a product has the correct functional characteristics demands that the marketing, design, manufacturing and R & D areas work very closely together. A child's anorak that is poorly cut or inadequately stitched will not perform when in use. The result is angry customers and a ruined reputation for the manufacturing company. The development of new and better functional characteristics is often a key to competitive success, and many companies pursue it as the basis of their product strategy. Thus Avonmore produced a better-tasting, 'creamier' milk, involving a chilled milk delivery system, as a basis for its successful entry to the Dublin milk market and its market growth. The search for better functional performance should be continuous and demands a close working relationship between design, marketing, R & D and manufacturing personnel in the company.

Structural characteristics can deliver the functional features of the product in a variety of ways—in different shapes, sizes, colours, materials, and so on. In the case of Avonmore's market expansion, it pioneered the inherent space and stacking benefits of Tetrapak packaging in the Irish milk market which took milk off the doorstep and onto the supermarket shelf. The children's ice-pop is regularly 'reinvented' in a structural sense by companies like HB Ice Cream in a fight for market share, producing bizarre combinations of shape and colour ranging from bright crimson 'Dracula' products to hand, foot and animal shaped items. The structural form of electronic products such as computer terminals is increasingly a basis for competition as manufacturers search for more cost-effective materials, easier-to-use keyboards or 'mouse' mechanisms.

Aesthetic characteristics are most obviously important for fashion-dependent products where visual quality is extremely important. Aesthetics are, however, an important part of any product design, as evidenced by the impact of design on products such as Cross pens, the uniquely rounded Japanese car shapes that emerged in the early nineties, the styling of Magees of Donegal tweed outerwear to the distinctive and visually pleasing designs for mobile air compressors produced by Atlas-Copco, whose yellow, egg-shaped form may attract your attention as you pass a building site or a road-repair unit.

Service attributes

The service attributes that accompany and back up a product and that are central to a service are, from the marketing perspective, integral to the product decision. These services may include guarantees, warranties, installation, training, maintenance, spare parts assurance, replacement, technical advice and upgrading or updating facilities. In markets where it is hard to differentiate the functional aspects of the product from competitors' offerings, and especially in industrial markets, service features are often the keys to market success. Investment in providing appropriate service features is likely to pay off in customer loyalty and market share gains. The battle for market share in earth-moving equipment or in long-distance haulage trucks revolves significantly about rapid and unfailing spare parts availability. Caterpillar, for example, have been world leaders in earth-moving with a spare parts policy of 48-hour delivery in any market that it serves. Warranty and guarantee arrangements are critically important in competition among car manufacturers as consumers' expectations of product quality, reliability and rust-proofing rise continually. For services such as banking, air travel or retailing, service attributes are of course the very heart of what is offered to the market but all of these also require physical attributes—bank branches, automatic teller machines, aircraft, food, shops, merchandising displays and so on. The difference between 'products' and 'services' is much more a question of the balance between physical and service attributes than anything else: all services are partly product and all products are partly service.

The psychological product

Customers buy psychological benefits as well as the more tangible physical and service benefits of any product. This is especially true of mass-market consumer items. In the jockeying for position in the lager market, gains by the various brewers result from advertising campaigns featuring desirable lifestyles, novel situations or storylines rather than changes in physical or service aspects of the product. Internationally, the Marlboro cigarette brand is the largest-selling brand in the world, primarily owing to imagery of 'the great outdoors' and of masculinity encapsulated in the cowboy symbol. The strategy of the marketers of Bailey's Irish Cream Liqueur, aimed at creating and defending a global brand position, has stressed the creation of psychological associations for the product with a relaxed, sophisticated consumer lifestyle through aggressive investment in coordinated advertising, packaging and merchandising images.

For some products, image is all. Beer, cigarettes, soft drinks and confectionery are typical examples of products that customers differentiate primarily on psychological grounds. Thus blind-taste tests of competing beer brands will show that large numbers of consumers cannot distinguish one brand from another when their names are concealed. Yet when brand names are provided, many of these same consumers will insist that there are radical differences in taste. The name and all the associations it has created with various symbols and images overwhelms perception of physical characteristics.

Psychological product characteristics are most obvious in the kinds of products discussed above. They are, however, a vital part of almost all products and services. The psychological attributes of industrial products such as machine tools, turbines, gears or electronic components are essential to market success. Here the attributes are usually built around market perceptions of the supplying company—its reputation for technical excellence, delivery reliability, customer advice and problem-solving, and so on. The competitive position of exporters of Irish products is sometimes weakened by associations in overseas buyers' minds with poor quality assurance, part delivery of orders and unreliable supply. A new exporter of meat products, for example, may find these psychological dimensions of his product already established, irrespective of his planned performance, and have to work doubly hard to establish a good image.

Customers pay for relevant psychological product attributes. It is therefore quite possible to add value to a product through design and delivery of its psychological features. It is important to note this. Value inheres not just in tangible, functional characteristics. Most of the money consumers pay for a perfume product is for its psychological content and as a result most of the investment in cosmetics is in advertising, packaging and merchandising and not in the physical product or its manufacture. Some commentators will dismiss marketing activity of this nature as wasteful and frivolous while others will argue that it is necessary to enable consumer choice and market efficiency. Ultimately, the question revolves about whether customers perceive value in benefits created in this manner and whether they have freedom to make other choices. Trivial, false or unethical psychological claims will prove ineffective in all but the short term where consumer choice is sovereign.

The psychological attributes of services are most often created by the 'service experience'—by the human contact that is so central to most services. Jan Carlzon as President of Scandinavian Air System (SAS) popularised the term 'moments of truth' to characterise the moment of contact between a customer and the provider of a service—a ticket desk clerk, a steward or stewardess, a telephonist handling an inquiry. Because services are very often 'produced' on the spot by service company employees, these personnel must be trained and have the relevant ability to convey the psychological as well as the more tangible benefits of the service they provide. Thus, airline cabin staff must not only provide passengers with whatever food and drink is included with the flight but also with the sense of being valued and cared for as customers.

All marketers, and especially those in durable consumer goods and industrial goods, must remember to design and deliver the non-tangible product benefits that customers inevitably demand. Excellent physical and service characteristics are seldom enough to guarantee customer satisfaction and competitive effectiveness. The complex components of a product such as the national lottery are illustrated in Exhibit 11.1.

BRANDING

Branding a product through use of a name, symbol, design or a combination of these is a fundamental step in differentiating a product from those of competitors and in communicating to customers in a shorthand manner the kind of benefits

Exhibit 11.1

THE NATIONAL LOTTERY

'Our business is entertainment and our product is dreams'

The National Lottery was launched in 1988. In its first year it clocked up sales of £102 million with scratch cards only. The Lotto was added in year two. Annual sales amounted to over £220 million by the end of 1991. By this time the lottery had since its launch handed over more than £240 million to the government for allocation as it deemed fit.

A national lottery means different things to different people. At one level it is about figures and computers. The Irish National Lottery, which is based on a US model, is the first in the EC to employ a sophisticated fully on-line system. With 1,850 computer terminals located in over 3,000 retail outlets nationwide, including the Aran Islands, it has the biggest commercial terminal network in the country— bigger than the banks, for example. The computer system can verify winning tickets for scratch cards and then feed money electronically into the system. It can process up to 4,000 transactions per minute in the final quarter of an hour before a Lotto draw.

At another level a national lottery is about the possibility of wish-fulfilment. In interview the director of the National Lottery says, 'Our business is entertainment and our product is dreams. This sums up our business well. But it has to be backed by a system which is scrupulously fair.'

The National Lottery products aim 'to get all of the population playing a little'. Approximately 62 per cent of the population play one or other of the two games once a fortnight and the average spend is £2.50. 'Our two products are aimed at different parts of the market and are complementary,' explains the director. 'It's instant gratification versus being prepared to wait for the chance to win a bigger prize. It's possible to design all sorts of Lotto-type games. But the trick is to get the right game for the level of participation which will create the right number of roll-overs to make the big jackpots. Our aim is to make two or three people millionaires each year and I reckon we've been meeting our objective spot on.'

The other objective of a national lottery is to provide monies for community benefit. 'The bottom line for us is that we are here to raise money for projects which otherwise would not have happened,' adds the director. 'We're competing for the "pampering pound" which might otherwise be spent on sweets or a video or a magazine. As such we adopt the same sort of marketing approach as anyone else selling into the fast-moving end of the retail business.'

But there are those who do not share this objective and who see the National Lottery as an undesirable addition to Irish society. The director comments, 'I accept that there are probably people who spend too much on the lottery, but equally there are people spending too much on drink and tobacco and other things.

We do tell people to play with their heads, not their hearts, and we think things have settled down now that the novelty has worn off to a degree.'

Source: *The Irish Times*, 1st November, 1991.

they may expect to derive from using the product. A brand name encapsulates the physical, service and psychological attributes of a marketer's product. Think of the wealth of product information and expectations conveyed by motor car brand names such as Fiat, Rolls-Royce, Rover, Honda or Volkswagen, or among microcomputer suppliers such as Toshiba, Atari or Apple. That a carefully and well-developed brand name is a major asset for any company is best illustrated by the money value placed on it in the event of an acquisition or takeover deal.

While the marketing manager has no choice about whether to design and manage the physical, service and psychological attributes of a product, he may choose to brand or not brand his product. Sometimes this is at the request of the distribution channel. Jewellers, for example, often prefer to carry silverware that is unbranded (except for the hallmark if solid silver) to give the impression to customers that they are still in the business of producing silverware. The silverware producer, in contrast, is probably better off if he can create a brand name and have customers coming to a jeweller's shop asking for his products by name—such as Newbridge Cutlery.

This example illustrates how branding is related to the creation of market power. For a marketer who must distribute products through middlemen or retailers, the successful creation of a brand name creates power over intermediaries. If customers come to shops or wholesalers demanding a named product, the middleman will typically feel compelled to carry the product in stock. If no brand has been created, the customer will ask for the product type and the wholesaler or retailer is in a powerful position to stock and promote the product that best serves his own needs.

As we saw in Chapter 2, in the context of the business system, the emergence of branding in a market usually coincides with its transition from a commodity to a non-commodity status. In a true commodity market, price should be the only factor determining sales. The Kerrygold brand was a successful innovation by An Bord Bainne to take Irish butter out of a commodity market and into that part of the butter market where customers discriminate in favour of a brand with connotations of quality and richness.

In industrial and in many service markets, the producer company's name frequently acts as a brand identification and is carefully nurtured to perform many of the functions of a brand. The name Siemens, for example, is perceived among engineers and purchasers of electrical engineering equipment as standing for quality, reliability, technical excellence, advice and after-sales service. Many small businesses in industrial markets throw away the opportunity to build customer loyalty and customer endorsement of their products by paying no attention to building their 'brand' or company image through product labelling, promotional material and the creation of brand names for individual products. In financial services, Allied Irish Banks Ltd changed its name and visual identification to AIB Bank at the beginning of the nineties to communicate greater coherence and to present a more international and less regional identity to world markets.

Private brands
The growth of private brands through the 1970s and 1980s primarily reflected, and was part of the reason for, the increased power of retailers, especially in food retailing. As more and more grocery sales became concentrated in the hands of a few retail chains such as Superquinn, Quinnsworth and Dunnes Stores, they began to market products under their own 'private' brand names and thereby transferred customer loyalty and trust to the supermarket from the manufacturer. Another development of this was the cheap 'no-brand' product—typically contained in white or yellow packs from which the cost of superior packaging was removed to reduce costs and prices further.

Many small businesses become the suppliers of private brand products, especially in an area such as cheaper ranges of clothing or food items for large multiple stores and department stores. There are both dangers and benefits in this approach to product strategy. The danger is that the manufacturer becomes totally powerless and survives from contract to contract at the whim of the large buyer. He may also lose contact with the market and with customers, since both of these are analysed and serviced by the retailer alone, who then supplies product specifications to the sub-contract manufacturer. The manufacturers can easily become a single-function business—all manufacturing and little marketing. On the positive side of such relationships, a first-rate sub-contractor can create power for himself through excellence, so that the retailer comes to value and depend on his quality, reliability and cost-effectiveness. Under such circumstances, the retailer typically begins to invest in the sub-contractor through transfer of technology and through advice and financial assistance. The intelligent small business will use this power to learn about manufacturing excellence and (through the retailer) about market conditions. By building a solid resource base in this way, the choice to go directly with a manufacturer-branded item to a premium segment of the market becomes a realistic option.

Supplier partnerships and single-supplier relationships grew rapidly in popularity in the eighties in an attempt to emulate Japanese successes in minimising inventory holdings and maximising speed of response through approaches such as JIT (just-in-time) delivery. Most of these Japanese-led advances rely on close working relationships between buyer and supplier organisations and mutual interdependence. Many well-managed sub-contractor companies have built profitable and stable businesses in which the relationship with prime customers has become symbiotic—both parties learn to value and rely upon the other for tasks they would prefer not to do or are unable to undertake themselves.

Brand equity
One of the ways in which marketing activity creates organisational assets is through investment in branding. Branding must be seen as an investment decision and if properly managed yields an asset of value which will ultimately appear as a balance sheet entry (Aaker, 1992). It is critical to remember that building substantial brand equity is usually a very expensive undertaking. It must therefore be embarked upon with the same care and analysis as any major investment decision. In some markets, especially fast-moving consumer markets, the cost of brand-building will easily run into millions of pounds. For the small or medium-sized company, branding must be approached with caution and evaluated against the alternative of supplying intermediate products to major consumer companies or private label products for retailers.

This represents a particular dilemma for many Irish companies as they internationalise. They must make choices between the expensive process of developing their own international brand identity and developing deep supply partnerships and relationships with those who already have access to final markets via their own brand assets. Bailey's Irish Cream exemplifies a brand-building choice, but one must remember that the resources of its parent company were available in doing this. By contrast, a small food company with very limited resources might more appropriately choose to invest in supply relationships with large brand-owning manufacturers, distributors or retailers (see Exhibit 11.2).

PRODUCT LIFE CYCLE
So far, the product has been discussed in a static manner. But most products are in fact dynamic, almost living, things. Recognition of this reality is the basis for the product life cycle concept. Just as most things in nature are conceived, gestate, are born, grow, mature and eventually die, so too with products. New products are conceived in marketing managers' minds, in R & D labs and on the shop-floor. They are developed as concepts, prototypes built, and are finally launched onto the market. If they prove successful, they grow as more and more consumers learn about them and repurchase them. At some stage all those customers needing the product are already buying it and growth ceases: the product has reached maturity. And inevitably the mature product is challenged by a better one based on newer technology, better design, a more efficient

manufacturing process, or a better fit with changing customer requirements. Decline sets in and leads to the ultimate withdrawal of the product from the market. The S-shaped curve shown in Figure 11.2 reflects the most common sales pattern, but products can be found that grow in a straight line through time, or that experience immediate and rapid growth followed by sudden maturity.

Exhibit 11.2

TIPPERARY CEREALS

Supplying ingredients to the big brand names

After detergents, the most difficult market for any new small producer to break into must be the breakfast cereals sector. In Ireland, we each eat between six and seven kilogrammes of the stuff each year. The market is worth about £40 million, but the bulk of what we breakfast on is ready-to-eat imported cereals.

A few years ago, a brave attempt was made by a company called Appledore to crack that market—or more specifically the 'corn flakes' market. It failed, not because the maize flakes produced were not first-rate, but because they did not taste like Kellogg's, which has cornered the Irish market. Indeed, 40 per cent of all breakfast cereals consumed here is Kellogg's Corn Flakes, compared to 5 per cent of the US market, where they originated.

A survivor of the Appledore experience, Frank Conroy, is now managing director of Tipperary Cereals in Thurles, Co. Tipperary. A chemist with 20 years' experience in the Irish Sugar Company, he was backed by members of the Flahavan family—of porridge fame—in this new venture. But apart from a small range of Flahavan-branded cereals, Tipperary Cereals has eschewed the brand name of the market to concentrate on supplying ingredients to big names in the breakfast business, and supplying cereal ingredients to the confectionery industry for things like Nutcrisp and Star Bars.

After just four years, 98 per cent of its £2 million turnover is exported to the UK, Holland, Germany, Denmark and the company is just starting on France and Belgium. 'We're doubling our sales every 12 months. We hope in the next year to maintain that level of growth as well. We hope to be turning over £5 million in the next three to five years. We're coming from a small base, but we're making progress,' Conroy says.

Tipperary Cereals uses a heat extrusion technology, the only Irish company which currently has this technology. It intends to concentrate on using it to the full, allowing its customers to deal with marketing. A high 4 to 5 per cent of turnover is spent on research and development, a high percentage by the standards of most Irish manufacturers.

'It's not like canning or freezing. We have to go to the coalface and find them,' Conroy says of the products Tipperary manufactures. 'Big companies move very slowly and we have to be prepared for a very long lead time in development with these companies. Rather than retail, we should concentrate on what we know best, the technology end of the business. We believe there is a very big market for Irish ingredients. The cereal market is growing—while Americans eat about 12kgs per person each year, in Europe per capita consumption is a mere 100 grammes a year, but is doubling annually.'

Most of the raw materials are obtained in Ireland, with the obvious exceptions of rice and maize. After processing, Tipperary Cereals exports on average 14 different products each month. Eighty per cent of the packaging, which includes packs as they appear on supermarket shelves in other countries bearing household names, is produced here.

Source: *The Irish Times*, 15th July, 1991.

Figure 11.2

The Life Cycle of Processed Dairy Products

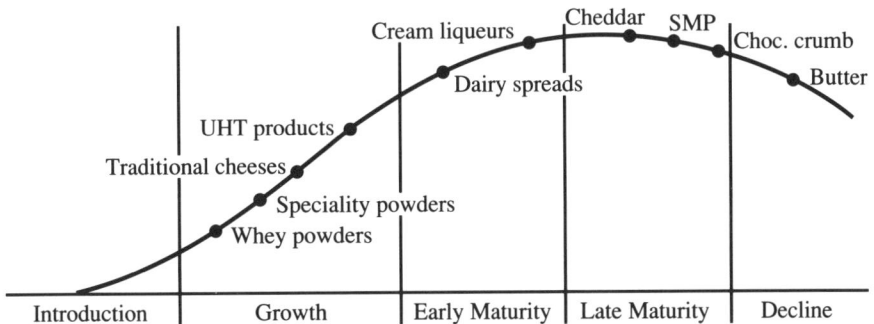

Figure 11.3 shows the typical relationship between sales revenues and profitability over time. The typical pattern of profit is important to note. It illustrates the fact that, for most products, their development (pre-launch) and introduction phases require marketing investment, while revenues are not yet sufficient to cover costs and generate a positive return. Ignorance or disregard of this typical pattern leads to marketing decisions based on grossly over-optimistic initial sales projections, to misjudged cash-flow deficits, to underestimated working capital provisions, and sometimes, in small or new ventures with very limited resources, to financial collapse and liquidation. This is especially tragic where the new product or service is inherently good and acceptable to the market, but where the company is mutilated by bad planning and management.

Figure 11.3

A Product Life Cycle

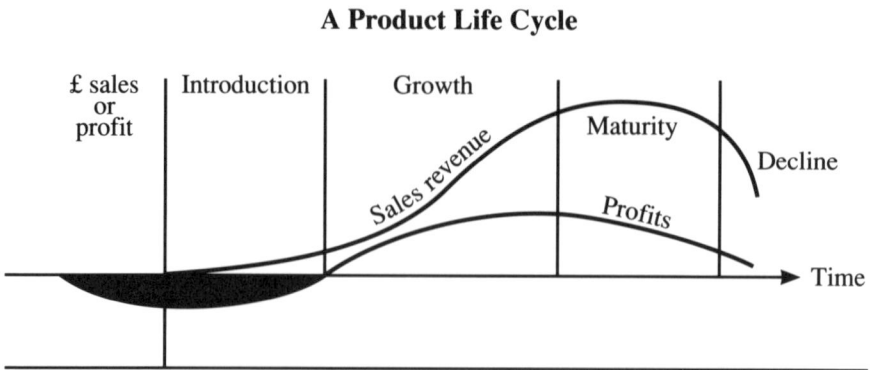

Before the implications of managing the product life cycle are explored it is necessary to enter some qualifications about the concept. Life cycle theory fits well with experience at individual product or brand level. But it is a very weak and imprecise tool when analysing the dynamics of a product category. Thus it is much more powerful in analysing the life of a motor car model than in analysing motor cars as a generic product group. As one probes more deeply towards generic demand—the need to be clothed, to eat, to be transported, to write, to furnish houses, and so on—one finds generic products that are always in demand. The specific form of that demand evolves over time and through generations of consumers, but a life cycle pattern is not to be found. In this sense, there is no such thing as a dying industry—only industries that have slipped out of line with the evolution of generic demand—as the US auto industry did during the 1970s, or as European (but not Korean) shipbuilders have done. The distinction is the same as that made between needs and wants in Chapter 1. Wants will usually follow life cycle patterns but needs are reflected in stable underlying demand patterns that do not conform to a life cycle profile.

Timing is also a problem in the application of life cycle concepts. There are no standard rules for forecasting the time scale of a product's life cycle. Some survive profitably for many, many years, while others come and go on the wave of a fashion fad, lasting months or only weeks. This holds true even within product categories. A brand such as Guinness has seen, during its continuing life, the birth and demise of many brands of beer on the market.

Forecasting is the biggest problem with managerial use of the life cycle concept. At the individual brand or product level it is at its most amenable, but even here most of the factors that determine the shape and time scale of the life cycle are beyond the marketer's control: competitive reactions and innovation; technological change; consumer tastes and disposable income, and so on. For the introductory and growth periods the manager depends primarily on judgment to forecast the shape of the sales curve. Which of the three patterns shown in Figure 11.4 will reflect market reality? Pattern (a) is the one favoured by most marketing scholars and derives theoretical justification from what is known about the social diffusion of new products. Yet many new product sales budgets show figures more in line with (b) and (c) (Meeneghan and O'Sullivan, 1986). Indeed, budgets predicting a pattern such as that in (a) are very often greeted derisively with comments that timid managers always predict success in the more distant future and tough times in the next planning or budgetary period. Effective forecasting of the shape of the life cycle curve can be based only on a very deep knowledge of the market and well-researched assumptions about how many customers there are, their willingness to try a new product and switch from an old one, the conversion of trial into repeat purchases, and the frequency of repeat purchase. This can and should be done by any professional marketing manager, and an increasing number of computer-based models exist that help the manager to integrate estimates of these factors with marketing mix proposals and likely competitive reactions in order to produce forecasts of future sales.

Figure 11.4

Alternative Sales Growth Patterns

(a)   (b)   (c)

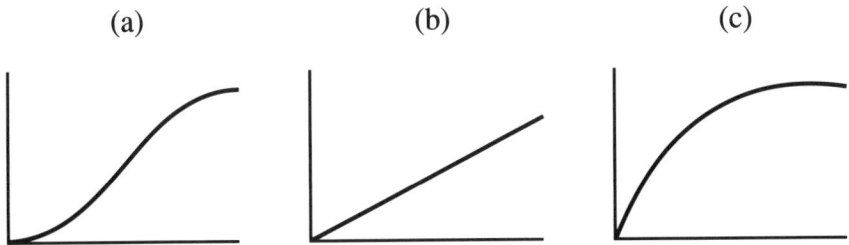

Forecasting the time scale of the maturity phase is also difficult, as good innovative marketing decisions and manufacturing and design improvements can continuously extend the phase. When to categorise a product as approaching decline is sometimes easy, based on clear technological and customer demand trends. More often it is not so clear, so that the decision to manage a product quietly into retirement or to drop it from the company's product line is a most difficult one in terms of timing (Hart, 1991).

LIFE CYCLE PHASES AND MARKETING PRACTICE
In general, it is clear that products at different life cycle stages should be marketed with different strategies. The following guidelines are generalisations, and there will always be exceptions. Any such guidelines should

therefore be used with caution and more as a stimulus to further thought and analysis than as mechanical rules.

Introduction stage

At this stage market risk and uncertainty are normally at their highest. The new product is offered to customers, and the marketer must invest in market development. Customers and members of the trade must be informed of the product's existence and of its unique advantages. Net cash outflows are characteristic of this stage, and adequate funds to cover working capital requirements must be carefully arranged. The vital initial sales to key customers must be made and their reaction to the product monitored. If they dislike or reject it, the process of product recommendation among customers will begin to work against it and repeat purchases will not develop. Gaining product trial is an essential objective at this stage if customers are to accept the product for long-term repeat purchase, and innovative methods to facilitate trial at low financial and psychological risk to the customer are often central to early success. Weekly monitoring of orders and sales to final customers is crucial to staying in control of the introductory process because it allows the manager to check trial purchases against budget and to identify the emergence and volume of repeat purchases in a fast-moving consumer good.

Growth stage

Entry into the growth stage is normally signalled by a rapid increase in the rate of sales volume growth. Typically, repeat orders are flowing in, and the less innovative but large majority of customers begin to enter the market. Strong attractive growth usually brings imitators or 'me too' products from marketers who have seen the success and try to obtain some of the market growth with cheaper or differentiated versions of the product. Because growth is strong, the severity of the competitive pressure that may be building up is easily ignored. If the new product is expanding the market, there may well be temporary room for many competitors in the market-place. However, in the late growth phase, at the approach of the maturity, the battle for market share and survival typically precipitates a shake-out among competitors, leaving only the strongest to survive. During growth it is important to continue to improve the product and to innovate if possible in order to stay one step ahead of imitators. Growth normally requires continued investment in the product's future, and it is inappropriate to manage it for maximum profit or cash throw-off during this stage. Doing so will usually shorten its life cycle and weaken any leadership position created.

Maturity

When the rate of growth in sales volume slows down to one roughly equivalent to the general rate of economic growth in the market, the product has well and truly matured. Ideally the marketer wishes to have a product in a leadership or strong competitive position in the chosen target market by this stage, as strategy during maturity largely revolves about defending position and prolonging the period of maturity. To enter maturity with a weak market position is generally a recipe for further losses of market share and weak financial performance. The objective of prolonging the maturity phase is usually tackled through product improvement and adaptation (as often seen in the 'new improved' versions of popular consumer goods); through further segmentation of the market; through the development of 'line extensions' (variations of the product to cover additional segments and shifting consumer needs); and sometimes through price decreases to bring in more price-sensitive segments of demand provided that the price/volume/manufacturing cost relationship allows the company to maintain profitability. While the introductory and growth phases demand marketing investment, the maturity stage should see strong positive cash flows to provide a return on the earlier investment and the creation of reserves from which to fund new product innovation.

Decline stage

The management and inevitable burial of declining products is a task from which many marketing managers shy away. Yet if the product life cycle concept is accepted, then products must unavoidably begin to decay. Careful management of the process of decline, involving curtailment of product models, variations and options, and maintenance of reasonable margins, can produce significant positive cash flows for the company to invest in new and growing products. On the other hand, mismanagement of decline, especially when it involves investment in the product and its retention beyond its profitable life, can become a serious financial trap for the business and damage its reputation among customers. It is as important—and quite often as difficult—to bury an old product as it is to launch a successful new one.

PRODUCT MIX DECISIONS

Product mix decisions arise as soon as a business markets more than one product. Multiproduct activity is increasingly typical of business life in general and of individual companies as they evolve from new small ventures into established mature companies. The pressures to become a multiproduct company have several origins. The life cycle process and the ever-shortening length of individual product or brand life cycles creates an obvious pressure. If the manager waits until the demise of a first product to launch a replacement, the interim period of minimal revenue and substantial cash outflows shown in Figure 11.5 (a) can easily trigger financial collapse. The remedy is to begin the development and introduction of a new product well before the original product begins to decline. Figure 11.5 (b) shows how this will help to smooth revenue and profits and to maintain a healthier cash-flow status.

Figure 11.5

Overlapping Life Cycles

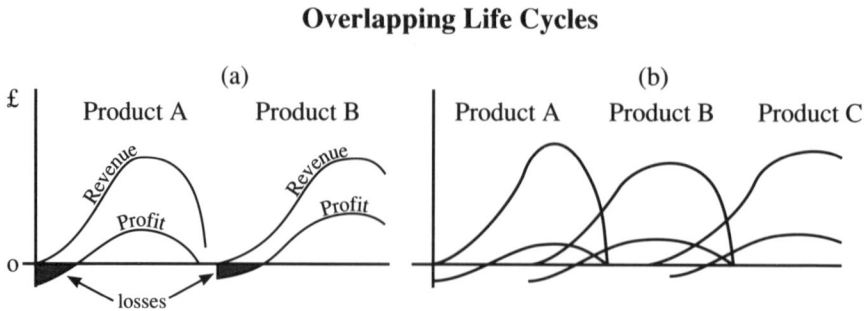

A second major pressure towards multiproduct companies comes from the increased uncertainty and risk inherent in many of today's markets. One way to reduce this risk is to avoid putting all one's eggs in the same basket. Several products spread over several markets or market segments reduce risk, since the likelihood of their all failing together is usually low. The company's commitments and investment are spread much in the way that a private investor will spread stocks, shares and other asset holdings in order to balance risk and return, current income and future profits in his financial portfolio.

Finally, multiproduct companies develop in response to much more positive or aggressive forces revolving around objectives of company growth. Any one product has inherent limits to its size and growth potential. For the company to expand beyond these limits, it is necessary to add further products to the product mix.

For the multiproduct company, careful management of each product in relation to the other is vital to achieving objectives of risk reduction, of balanced cash flows and of company growth. Essential to any product management system is accurate and up-to-date information on the market position, cost, revenue and profit profile of each product. Without this information at the manager's fingertips, he can never tell which products are at what stage of the life cycle or which are absorbing or generating cash. He cannot therefore plan the product mix, and is effectively out of control of his business.

Product portfolio analysis

The complexity of managing multiproduct companies and the severe pressures to manage cash as a key company resource during the 1970s led to the widespread use among large companies of product portfolio techniques. These techniques are now widely used in many smaller and medium-sized businesses. The earliest and most widely used portfolio technique was the cash quadrant or share/growth matrix of the Boston Consulting Group. Each product in a company's product mix is classified on two dimensions: the rate of growth in the product-market (to indicate life cycle stage), and the market share dominance of the product. The reasons these two dimensions were chosen illustrate the basic conceptual foundations of product portfolio techniques of analysis.

Market growth rate as a proxy for product life cycle stage is used because of the implications for cash management and strategy formulation discussed earlier in this chapter. In a period of rapid growth market share can be captured relatively easily, but at the expense of considerable investments of cash to fund growth and to win share. In maturity, however, the structure of the market hardens and market share is expanded with great difficulty, but maintenance of a strong position should by the same token be quite achievable and should generate a cash surplus on trading.

Market share dominance is used as the second dimension because of the evidence that market share is strongly and positively correlated with profitability and with net cash flow. Share dominance is used to indicate not absolute market share but a product's market share relative to that of the largest competitor. This acknowledges that there is a vast difference between having a 30 per cent share when the next largest competitor is 20 per cent, compared with when the largest competitor has 50 per cent of the market. The evidence for a strong relationship between share and profitability derives principally from the PIMS (Profit Impact of Marketing Strategy) research programme (Buzzell and Gale, 1987). The BCG matrix allows the manager to categorise products into four quadrants, as shown in Figure 11.6.

High-growth/low-share (question-mark) products generate an enormous demand for cash to keep up with market growth and to improve share. If cash is not invested, the product will become a 'dog' as market growth slows down. The strategy recommendation for getting out of this cash-absorbing position is either to invest aggressively in order to gain share or to acquire competitors and turn the product into a 'star', or to get out of the market.

High-growth/high-share (star) products are market leaders which typically return significant profits but absorb all or most of them in the process of maintaining leadership and keeping up with market growth. Recommended strategy is to hold share by reinvesting the product's profits in product improvement, market coverage, manufacturing efficiency, and perhaps price reductions to expand the market and preempt low-cost competitors.

Low-growth/high-share (cash cow) products are, or certainly should be, profitable products with strongly positive cash flows. Low market growth places no demands on the funding of growth, and the high market share should normally yield above-average profitability for the industry.

Figure 11.6

BCG Product Portfolio Matrix

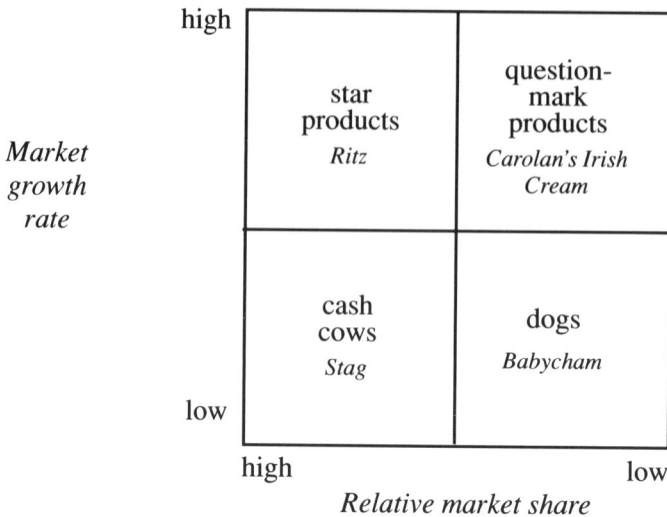

<table>
<tr>
<td rowspan="2">Market
growth
rate</td>
<td>high</td>
<td>star
products
Ritz</td>
<td>question-
mark
products
Carolan's Irish
Cream</td>
</tr>
<tr>
<td>low</td>
<td>cash
cows
Stag</td>
<td>dogs
Babycham</td>
</tr>
<tr>
<td></td>
<td></td>
<td>high</td>
<td>low</td>
</tr>
</table>

Relative market share

Note: The products cited are popular brands from Showerings, a drinks company, viewed from the perspective of the mid-eighties.

Strategy should revolve about protecting share, while avoiding undue investment in product innovation and market expansion. Any investment whether in manufacturing or marketing should be limited by the share maintenance objective. Excess cash should therefore be generated to support research, new product development, and the funding of worth-while 'question-mark' products into 'star' positions.

Low-growth/low-share (dog) products normally have below-average profitability. Low share brings about below-average profitability and cost disadvantages in manufacturing. Lack of market growth means there is little new business to capture and market share gains will be vigorously fought by other competitors. Strategy options are more diverse here and include:

—segmentation of the market to find a niche that can in fact be dominated
—harvesting the product, i.e. maximising net cash flow by minimising product support
—divesting the product to a buyer who sees possibilities for it
—deleting the product from the product mix to curtail cash losses.

The simple share/growth portfolio matrix therefore allows the manager to analyse the market and competitive position of each product and to derive guidelines for action. Figure 11.6 also attempts to position four popular brands marketed by Showerings, a drinks company, viewed from the perspective of the mid-eighties. For such an apparently simple tool with all its visual attraction, it promises major insights into the product mix and into future strategy alternatives. Managers commonly find that the effectiveness of the matrix is considerable in communicating complex information in condensed and graphic form (O'Driscoll, 1982). Before accepting it at face value, however, the manager is well advised to understand its basic assumptions and to check their validity for the conditions in which he operates.

Market share is used as an indicator of relative profit performance in the market and of net cash-flow position: high-share products have higher relative profitability than low-share products. The experience effect—the decline in unit cost with increased cumulative output of a product—is invoked to explain how high-share (and therefore higher cumulative volume) producers should have lower costs and better margins. The PIMS programme findings are also used as evidence of the impact of market share, although these findings show a less significant impact for share in consumer than industrial products. For any one industry and a product-market within it, the marketer must therefore evaluate the relevance of these general findings about the impact of share on profitability. In markets where entry and exit for competitors is easy, where there is little proprietary technology, and where customers perceive little risk in purchasing the product, the relationship is likely to be weak.

The assumptions concerning market growth rate must also be checked before the technique is applied. The key assumptions are that shares stabilise in mature markets and that share gains are a more appropriate objective in growth markets. While these are reasonable general assumptions, specific markets may provide conditions in which they do not hold.

Composite portfolio approaches
The original BCG portfolio uses the two dimensions of relative share and market growth. Most of the elaborations of the portfolio analysis approach that followed BCG's innovation have revolved around generalising from market share to competitive position/capability and from market growth to market attractiveness. The most widely used portfolio techniques are illustrated in Figure 11.7 and include those popularised by General Electric with McKinsey & Co.; A.D. Little Inc.; and Royal Dutch Shell's directional policy matrix.

These matrices allow the manager much more flexibility in tailoring the portfolio analysis process to an individual company through choosing the list of variables or factors on which he rates market attractiveness or company capability. Figure 11.8 shows a list of possible factors to include in this

Figure 11.7

Alternative Product Portfolio Matrices

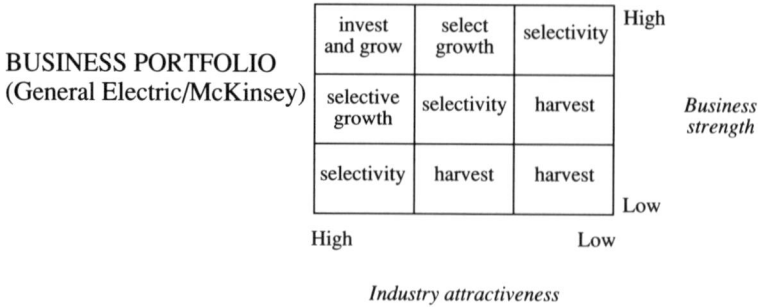

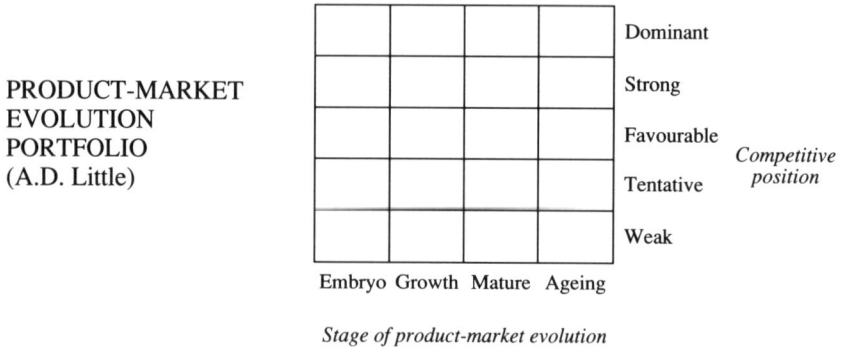

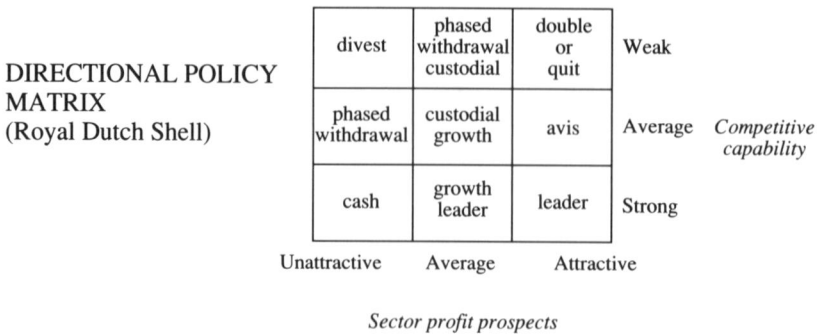

BUSINESS PORTFOLIO
(General Electric/McKinsey)

invest and grow	select growth	selectivity	High
selective growth	selectivity	harvest	*Business strength*
selectivity	harvest	harvest	Low

High   Low

Industry attractiveness

PRODUCT-MARKET
EVOLUTION
PORTFOLIO
(A.D. Little)

				Dominant
				Strong
				Favourable
				Tentative
				Weak

Competitive position

Embryo Growth Mature Ageing

Stage of product-market evolution

DIRECTIONAL POLICY
MATRIX
(Royal Dutch Shell)

divest	phased withdrawal custodial	double or quit	Weak
phased withdrawal	custodial growth	avis	Average
cash	growth leader	leader	Strong

Competitive capability

Unattractive   Average   Attractive

Sector profit prospects

process. In preparing a portfolio analysis, each chosen factor may be scored on, say, a five-point scale, as shown in Figure 11.9, and a weight attributed to this score depending on the manager's judgment about the importance of the factor compared with all others. These individual scores are then added to give an overall score for each product that locates it in the matrix. The A.D. Little matrix differs primarily in retaining a focus on the stage of market evolution because of a belief that the stage of development of the competitive environment is central to strategy-making.

Figure 11.8

Potential Factors for Use in Assessing Market Attractiveness and Competitive Position

Market attractiveness		Competitive position or business strength
Market:	size, growth rate, life cycle, numbers of segments, export opportunity	Market share Business size and growth
Competition:	intensity, concentration ratio, capacity utilisation, numbers entering and exiting	Profitability and margins Technological position
Profitability:	level and trend, critical influences on profitability (scale, integration, etc.)	Production expertise Distribution People: sales, service, technical, etc.
Technology:	maturity/volatility, complexity, patent protection, product or process innovation opportunity	Image Customer loyalty
Environmental:	social, cultural, legal, government, union, trade tariffs, quotas, regulations	Financial resources Marketing competence

Uses and limitations of product portfolio analysis

Figure 11.10 summarises the major uses and limitations of the portfolio methods described. Several portfolio matrices are available for use, so a choice should be consciously made of the one best suited to the company and its context; for example, the A.D. Little matrix can be particularly helpful in technology-dependent businesses. In the case of the BCG matrix, the manager must be sure to understand the assumed relationship between cash flow and market growth rate and market share before he uses the matrix. The techniques are excellent aids to diagnosis, but they must never be used as mechanical substitutes for managerial decision-making. Over the years companies using these techniques have shifted attention from an emphasis on finding highly attractive markets to developing an emphasis on building the competitive capability side of the product portfolio—glamour markets and their pursuit having left a great many corporate scars. Implementation of a portfolio approach is effective only if accompanied by the development of separate objectives, reward systems, incentives and controls for the different product areas in the portfolio. A question-mark product must be managed in a very different way to a cash cow—that is the point of the portfolio approach.

Figure 11.9

Constructing the Market Attractiveness and Company Capability Scores

(1) Market attractiveness factor	(2) Factor weight 1–5	(3) Rating of market on each factor	(2 x 3) Weighted score
1	____	1 2 3 4 5	____
2	____		____
3	____		____
4	____		____
5	____		____
6	____		____
7	____		____
8	____		____
9	____		____
10	____		____

Overall attractiveness/capability = sum of scores: ____

Figure 11.10

Portfolio Techniques: Uses and Limitations

- Choose between alternatives
- Understand assumptions
- Better for diagnosis than prescription
- Avoid mechanistic use
- Beware of 'simplicity'
- Beware of glamour categories
- Care in implementation:
  - objectives, rewards, incentives, controls
  - structures
  - culture
- One of several classes of analytical tool (not to be used exclusively)

- Perceived benefits of using portfolio techniques:
  - (1) improved quality of strategies
  - (2) more selective and focused allocation of resources
  - (3) better 'tailoring' of strategy to business unit
  - (4) improved capacity for strategic management and control
  - (5) more willingness to face up to marginal businesses

Source for enumerated 'perceived benefits': P. Hapeslagh, 'Portfolio planning: uses and limits', *Harvard Business Review* (Jan.–Feb. 1982).

Large multinationals and small companies with few products are to be found using portfolio techniques with considerable success. The benefits of portfolio techniques are generally seen as better product management, clearer allocation of resources, the ability to fine-tune policy decisions and to see the business as a totality. The techniques allow managers to display, integrate and communicate complex product information and to assimilate the general management implications.

SUMMARY

When the manager has chosen a target market and decided on the competitive positioning of the product or service in this segment, the time has arrived to develop a marketing mix programme. This specifies precisely what product or service will be produced, at what price, how it will be communicated and sold to the market, and how distribution will take place. The product element of the marketing mix consists of the physical, service and psychological benefits that buyers demand. Each of these sets of attributes must be carefully designed and balanced with each other, and the complete bundle of attributes may then be branded so as to communicate to customers assurances about their presence and consistency.

Managing the evolution of products over time is aided by the product life cycle concept, which stresses the changing performance and strategic characteristics of products as they are launched, grow, mature and decline. It also underlines the temporary nature of most competitive advantages and leads growth-oriented firms to consider the creation and management of a product mix. In a multiproduct company, product portfolio techniques become important managerial instruments for plan formulation and implementation.

Reading

Aaker, David (1992), *Managing Brand Equity*, Macmillan, Toronto.

Baker, Michael J. (1991), *Marketing—An Introductory Text*, Macmillan, London, chs. 11, 12.

Buzzell, R.D. and Gale, B.T. (1987), *The PIMS Principles,* The Free Press, NY.

Carroll, C. (1986), 'A cross-sectional perspective on marketing expenditure from PIMS', *Irish Marketing Review*, vol. 1, pp. 169–177.

Hapeslagh, P. (1982), 'Portfolio planning: uses and limits', *Harvard Business Review*, January–February.

Hart, S. (1991), 'The managerial setting of the product deletion decision', *Irish Marketing Review*, vol. 5, no. 3, pp. 41–54.

Kotler, P. (1991), *Marketing Management: Analysis, Planning, Implementation and Control*, 7th ed., Prentice-Hall, Englewood Cliffs, NJ, chs. 13, 16, 17.

McCarthy, E.J. and Perreault, W.D. (1990), *Basic Marketing: A Managerial Approach*, 10th ed., Irwin, Boston.

McDonald, M.H.B. (1984), *Marketing Plans: How to Prepare Them & How to Use Them*, Heinemann, London, ch. 5.

Meeneghan, J.A. and O'Sullivan, P.J.P. (1986), 'The shape and length of the product life cycle', *Irish Marketing Review*, vol. 1, pp. 83–102.

O'Driscoll, A. (1982), 'The directional policy matrix as a communications process', in *Proceedings of the 1982 Annual Conference*, Marketing Education Group, University of Lancaster, July.

Wafer, B.V. (1986), 'A strategic approach to the Irish dairy processing industry', *Irish Marketing Review*, vol. 1, pp. 66–82.

Wind, Y. (1982), *Product Policy: Concepts, Methods and Strategy*, Addison-Wesley, Reading, Mass.

Review Questions

1. What are the components of the marketing mix, and why is it referred to as a 'mix'? Illustrate your answer by reference to a consumer product.
2. Identify two car rental companies, one an international company and the other a local company. Analyse the 'products' of both companies in terms of their

'physical', 'service' and 'psychological' components, identifying the differences between them and the related marketing consequences.
3. There are relatively few internationally known branded Irish products. Why is this so, and what are the barriers to their development?
4. Identify four products, one at each stage of the product life cycle. Explain your choice, and evaluate the way in which each product is being marketed in relation to the general recommendations about life cycle management strategies.
5. Explain the rationale for product portfolio concepts and the benefits and dangers inherent in their use.

Chapter 12

New Product Development

INTRODUCTION

This chapter examines the nature of new product marketing and concludes with an analysis of the interconnections between new product decisions and related financial, manufacturing and R & D decisions. The development and successful launch of new products presents some special challenges for the manager. Risk and uncertainty are normally much higher for new product marketing than in managing established or mature products.

The rate of new product failure is high; two out of three new products still fail in the US market (Crawford, 1987, p. 21). It has been estimated that it takes 58 new product ideas on average to yield one successful new product (Booze, Allen and Hamilton, 1982). Yet the ever-shortening life cycles of individual products or brands in most industries, the rate of technological change and the rapid evolution of consumer tastes and preferences all demand an active new product development or product adaptation response from the individual firm. This is especially true for Irish companies that go international. Products designed and developed for Irish customers will not automatically meet the needs of overseas markets. This means that as a company begins to internationalise, it must of necessity become involved in some degree of new product development activity. Having internationalised, many Irish firms will then find that the markets of Europe, North America and Asia demand a continuously innovative approach.

NEW PRODUCT MARKETING

The new product development process may be structured in many different ways to fit with the unique features of any company and its market. In general, however, the process must provide for a strategic orientation in new product activities, and for the steps of new product idea generation, screening and evaluation, product development, testing, and product launch. These stages in the new product development process are illustrated in Figure 12.1.

Figure 12.1

New Product Development Process

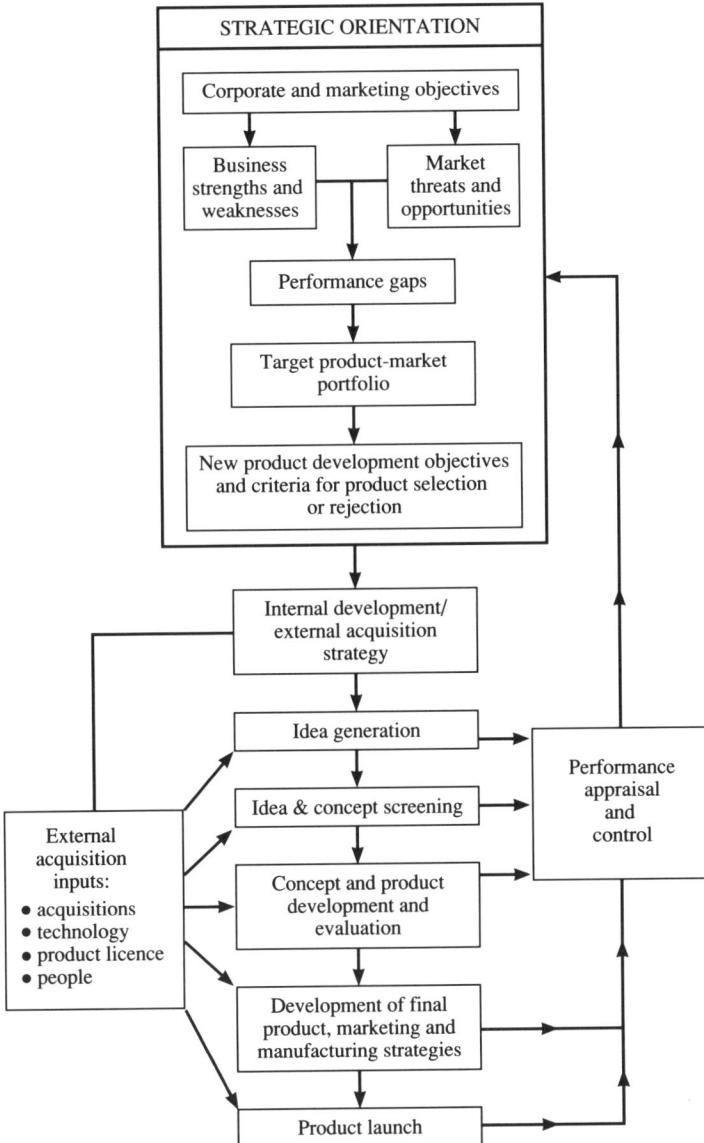

STRATEGIC ORIENTATION

Corporate and marketing objectives

Business strengths and weaknesses

Market threats and opportunities

Performance gaps

Target product-market portfolio

New product development objectives and criteria for product selection or rejection

Internal development/ external acquisition strategy

Idea generation

Idea & concept screening

Concept and product development and evaluation

Development of final product, marketing and manufacturing strategies

Product launch

External acquisition inputs:
- acquisitions
- technology
- product licence
- people

Performance appraisal and control

Based on an approach suggested by Y. Wind, *Product Policy: Concepts, Methods and Strategy*, Addison-Wesley, Reading, Mass. 1982.

A strategic orientation

New product development and marketing becomes a confusing and uncontrollable mess for the company if the first step—the development of a strategic orientation—is not undertaken. Without this step, almost any new product idea is a candidate for analysis and potential commercialisation; the product-market search becomes endless. The reality of corporate life, however, is such that only very specific products for quite specific markets are appropriate for development at any period in the company's life. New products must build the company's strengths in the marketplace. They must reduce its long-run risk by balancing the product-market portfolio and increase the survival and growth potential of the organisation. New product development and marketing can absorb an enormous quantity of corporate energy and resources. Both resources and managerial energy are in limited supply and must therefore be allocated in the most productive manner.

Developing a strategic orientation for the new product process is therefore the vital starting-point. The company must compare its general and marketing-specific objectives with the performance it is likely to produce given its present product or portfolio of products, and given the business strengths and weaknesses it possesses to respond to market threats and opportunities. This process of analysis and comparison reveals gaps in future performance against objectives.

Figure 12.2

Identifying a Performance Gap

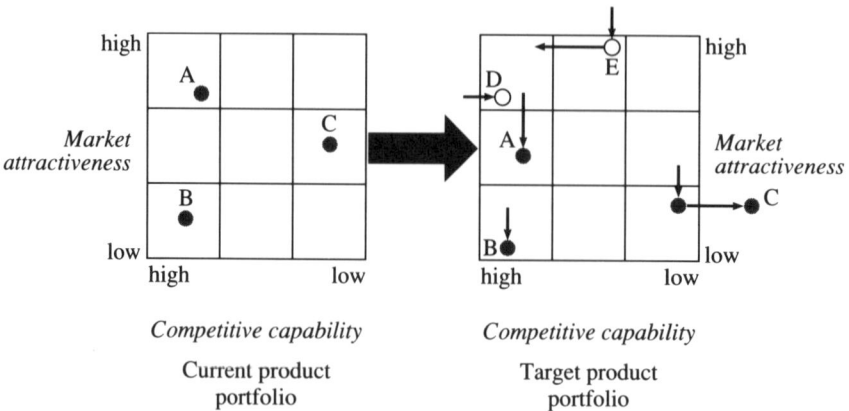

Current product portfolio

Target product portfolio

The product portfolio may now be examined to identify the product and market opportunities that may close the performance gap as shown in Figure 12.2. The life cycles of products A, B and C are such that A, a star performer, is shifting into a more mature cash-generating position, while B as a cash cow product has a reducing life expectancy and may soon have to be withdrawn. The product C is a net absorber of company cash and management energy and is to be managed out of the portfolio within the planning period. The need for a new product or products to guarantee the future viability of the company is therefore quite clear. An entry in the portfolio, such as E, might allow the company to become involved in a high growth market with which it is not completely familiar but in which it believes it can and must build competitive capability. The new product concept D builds directly on existing company strengths to enter perhaps the high growth segment of the market in which A now competes.

With a target portfolio in mind and corporate and marketing objectives clear, objectives specific to the new product development process can be stated and criteria listed which will determine the strategic fit or non-fit of any new product idea. Once the manager reaches this stage in thinking about new product development, roughly 80 per cent of the new product ideas that may arise can be dismissed as unsuitable even if they have profit potential when considered independently. Remember that the objective in new product development is not simply to introduce a product successfully. The aim is to introduce a product successfully that enhances the company's long-term growth and profit potential.

Internal development, joint venture or external acquisition
When strategic direction has been set, the more routine aspects of product development begin—searching for and evaluating ideas on through to product launch. At each of these stages the company has, and should examine, the option to undertake the process internally or via external acquisition of resources. Top management in expanding companies regularly face the question of whether to develop by a 'greenfield' route or through purchasing an existing company or resources. The use of alliances and joint ventures to support new product development is finding greater popularity throughout the nineties.

External acquisition is particularly relevant for Irish companies that are building international competitive capability. The technology, the products and the managerial experience to enter and develop international markets is, on the average, in short supply in small and medium-sized Irish industry. Rather than attempt what may be the impossible task of developing these resources internally, companies can proceed by acquiring technology and experience via licence and joint venture agreements with foreign partners or via outright purchase. For larger companies, the acquisition of firms internationally may be the most appropriate route to entering new overseas markets, as has been the case with Cement-Roadstone Holdings, Clondalkin Group, Irish Life or Smurfit Group in developing their international business.

For smaller-sized firms, licensing and joint venturing activity offers many opportunities for enhancing product development capability. For Waterford Foods the licensing of the Yoplait brand and its associated technology from France provided a crucial springboard in consumer marketing capability—and also brought yogurt to the Irish consumer. The success of Tipperary Co-operative Creamery in using a joint venturing mechanism in product development is illustrated in Exhibit 12.1.

Of course products or services such as Ballygowan Spring Water, CashBack tax refund service for travellers and the Moffett Mounty forklift (see Exhibit 12.2) show the success of independent new product development.

Exhibit 12.1

TIPPERARY COOPERATIVE CREAMERY

Developing Gouda cheese for the German market

Tipperary Cooperative Creamery Ltd, similar to other Irish cooperatives, was actively seeking new products to broaden its product range. It had three criteria in its search. The new products had to be profitable; they had to require increasing volumes of milk; and they were not to be dependent on the CAP intervention system.

Initial research focused on short shelf-life and fresh products such as soft cheeses and yogurts. These products were eventually excluded from consideration because of a combination of factors, such as the detrimental effects of seasonality, the distance from major European markets and too low milk utilisation. Also the level of competition on the Irish market was very high.

Only a few products were still being considered when the EC began seriously to discuss the super levy. Fortunately at the same time a large German distributor with its own established brand labels was looking for new sources of supply for natural and processed cheese. A long-term contract was agreed, based on Gouda and Emmental cheese. The contract price was based on weekly official market prices, which exist for both these products. This greatly simplified the price conditions of the contract.

Tipperary began production of Gouda in 1981 and made 2,000 tonnes, doubled production in 1982, and began production of Emmental. Manufacture of Emmental was more profitable but considerably more difficult. An extensive research and development programme was undertaken during 1983 to produce consistent good-quality Emmental. As a result in 1984 Tipperary changed its production from 3:1 in favour of Gouda to 3:1 in favour of Emmental.

The link-up with the German distributor had a number of advantages:

- It meant Tipperary could concentrate on the production aspects; distribution and selling was the German distributor's task
- It provided the necessary time to focus on R & D and to overcome the initial teething problems and
- Lower-quality cheese which occurred at both ends of the milk season could be used as a raw material for processed cheese.

Once Tipperary reached its own target of commodity Gouda and Emmental cheese, it started to develop gradually its own branded products. Initially it focused on the Irish market using two distributors, one for Dublin and the other for outside Dublin. Tipperary then launched an Irish branded cheese on to the German market—a market traditionally dominated by the Swiss and Bavarians.

Source: B.V. Wafer, 'A strategic approach to the Irish dairy processing industry', *Irish Marketing Review*, vol. 1, 1986, pp. 76–77.

Exhibit 12.2

THE MOFFETT MOUNTY FORKLIFT

The Mounty gets its market

At a national conference on marketing, Carol Moffett, managing director of Moffett Engineering Ltd, described her company's experience in new product development. 'We hear a lot of talk nowadays about marketing, about the market-led approach and the customer-led approach. In Moffett Engineering, when I think of it, this is the way we've always been doing things. I feel that I can best illustrate this to you by telling you the story of the Moffett Mounty truck-mounted forklift. You're probably wondering what a truck-mounted forklift is. The Moffett Mounty is a three-wheeled forklift. It has a set of forks like a conventional forklift but the difference is that it's extremely lightweight and it is carried on the rear of trucks or trailers and it can be attached to, detached from, the truck or trailer in about 30 seconds. You've likely seen these machines in rural areas because they are being used to distribute animal feedstuffs, fertilisers and fuels.

'Where did this idea come from? We're an engineering company located in Clontibret in Co. Monaghan. We were in the business for many years of manu-facturing equipment for pre-cast concrete products. But five years ago we were in a situation where we had a turnover of about a million pounds and about 25 or 30 people employed. We decided at that stage that we wanted to expand our activities and grow the company. We realised that there was a limited future for us in the products that we were making. There was insufficient scope for future growth. We decided to look around different areas where we could use the expertise that we had gained.

'An area that interested us was materials-handling. We looked at several products in this area. The first one was a hydraulic tail-lift. We did some market research on tail-lifts. We discovered that these were all being imported. We enlisted the help of the Goods Council (now An Bord Trachtála) and after doing some product research, we designed a tail-lift which we called the Tallboy. We launched it on the market. As far as we were concerned we did everything properly by the text-book. The product was a total disaster for us!

'However, the experience brought us into contact with people in the transport business and another idea that we came up with was the truck-mounted forklift. We'd seen this idea in Europe and in America. It wasn't a new idea; it had been around for a while. We examined it quite closely and decided that this was a product that we could get excited about. It was certainly within our area of competence to produce such a machine.

'It had a lot of things going for it as far as Moffett Engineering was concerned. It incorporated hydraulics and we had about 20 years' experience of making equipment using hydraulics. It could be factory-tested before leaving Clontibret. The product could be containerised. We reckoned we could fit six machines into a container. We felt that the materials-handling sector was a growth sector in every country in the world. Even the legislation was with us in this regard. We decided in principle to go ahead with the design and manufacture of the truck-mounted forklift and to do this we needed to find out precisely what the market needed. What features were needed in such a machine to suit Irish conditions? To do this we might have had to commission expensive market research but we got a lucky break here.

'One of our customers for the tail-lifts was Kerry Co-Op. One day we had a visit from their transport manager. He wanted to know what else we did. We showed him the truck-mounted forklift and we showed him the prototype that we were building. He quickly informed us that what we had in mind would not work in the Irish market, and explained to us what was needed. First of all the machine would have to be extremely robust. It would have to be capable of lifting and carrying two tons across a ploughed field. It would have to be capable of withstanding the abuse of being carried on the rear of a truck on Irish roads. This was quite a daunting task for us, so armed with all this information we went back to the drawing board. We made a very loose arrangement with Kerry—if we produced the machine, they would be happy enough to take it and field test it for us.

'In retrospect this was a vital step in the development of the Mounty. We listened to what Kerry had to say about what was needed in such a machine. And we built it in such a way that it met most of their criteria. For example, we coped with the rough terrain problem by making it all-wheel drive and putting large tyres on it. We designed special bearings for the mast that we felt would be sufficient to withstand the shockloading of travelling on the roads in Ireland.

The first prototype machine delivered was put into service in Co. Kerry and Co. Clare, delivering animal feedstuffs and fertiliser. The machine broke down. We fixed it. It broke down again. We fixed it. Every time Kerry had a problem, we reacted to that problem within a matter of three or four hours, whatever the driving time to get from Monaghan to Kerry.

'Eventually after about nine months of rigorous field testing we felt we were ready for the market. Everybody had been telling us what a wonderful idea this was and a lot of money had been spent at this stage on the prototypes. No machines had been sold and even in the case of Kerry the machine was still on trial. When we felt that most of the problems were ironed out we decided to launch.

'We chose a venue in the south of the country, principally because there was more agricultural activity in the south. We put together an invitation list, mainly targeted at the agricultural sector because we could see straightaway that a lot of potential existed there. We printed invitations. We sent those out to the distribution managers and chief executives and managing directors of companies in the agribusiness sector in the Munster region. We also enlisted the help of the Irish Goods Council who helped us with the PR aspects of the launch.

'This all happened in March 1986. During the rest of '86 we sold a total of 14 machines. We were not in a hurry to get quickly into the market because we wanted to monitor the machines working in different environments. We still felt that we had a lot to learn about our product and wanted to see it operating in winter and summer conditions. There was a lot of enthusiasm about the machine and by the end of '86 we were anxious to turn the enthusiasm into orders. The first week of January '87 saw sales of 19 machines, a major boost to us which gave us the confidence to really move forward with the product.

'We were now ready to get seriously into the marketing of this machine. We drew up a marketing and sales plan. We identified target markets. We put a salesman on the road. We developed site references. We realised the importance of winning these site references and we devised our own amateur PR by using the local press as much as possible. At this stage we really had spent very little money on promotion. At the beginning of 1987 we experienced another unexpected boost. We took a stand at the Belfast Show and the Mounty won the award for the best piece of new equipment at the show. This gave us valuable exposure on Ulster Television and on RTE. No amount of money spent on advertising at this stage could have brought us the credibility that this gave us.

'The marketing plan at this stage was pretty basic but it did result in sales of 70 machines in 1987. And the important thing was that within those 70 machines, there was a fair amount of repeat business. In fact one large Co-Op that year ordered ten machines and this was an excellent reference for us. We felt we were now ready to go to the UK market. It was a natural market for us. We employed a market research company to identify potential customers and to survey their needs for a truck-mounted forklift. We applied the same formula used in Ireland and launched first in the midlands of England. Following initial sales here we followed fairly quickly by a launch in the London area. Sales grew in a steady fashion and we soon topped sales of 100 machines. Our strategy was basically that adopted in Ireland.'

Source: *The Marketplace Revolution*, Special Conference Report, The Irish Goods Council and *IMJ*, September 1990.

Idea generation and concept screening

The two stages during which ideas are generated and screened and the survivors converted into product concepts that may be evaluated with more rigour form the creative heartland of the new product process. Given the agreed direction and criteria for product development, managers should think and search as widely as possible to ensure that all relevant product and market ideas enter the process. Primary idea screening is performed using the strategic criteria already set (these may specify product technology, market and market segment targets, resource constraints, sales volume and profit potential, etc.).

When an idea survives screening, it is worthwhile to develop the idea into a product concept that provides a reasonably detailed picture of its performance and other characteristics and its target market and customer benefit profile. This may take the form of a written product concept, or it may be visualised in drawings, and mock-up versions of the product may be assembled. Developing the concept in this way allows for detailed and quite practical evaluation of the new product proposal in marketing, technical, financial and manufacturing terms. The concept may be tested with potential customers for market acceptance. Manufacturing management can assess in a practical manner likely costs of product development and production, and therefore the manager will have the fundamental revenue and cost estimates necessary for the financial appraisal of the proposed product.

Product development and launch

Developing the final product, marketing, and manufacturing strategies may be undertaken once the product concept passes the basic marketing, manufacturing and financial evaluation of the previous stage. Manufacturing must now gear up to move from prototypes to final product design and production process design. Marketing must begin to formulate intensively its detailed programmes for product launch and management through to the completion of a new product marketing plan stating target market, product benefits, market positioning and marketing mix, with associated budgets for revenues and costs set out carefully over, say, the initial three years to identify working capital needs, cash-flow requirements and profit performance.

Product launch should be a much less anxious event than it normally is for the marketing manager if all the above steps in the process have been completed. While it may be less anxious if the process is well managed, it is difficult to lessen the amounts of energy and time and close attention to detailed arrangements that must be devoted to a successful launch.

For a consumer product all the practical details of packaging, of advertising and promotion planning and scheduling, of selling-in the product to wholesalers, distributors and retailers, of producing samples and customer trial-inducing offers must be organised and scheduled with great exactness if the launch is to take place smoothly and on time. For an industrial product the company will usually benefit from working with selected customers on final product design and testing prior to launch. Field trials are vital for most industrial and durable products if the marketer is not to be faced with the likelihood of having to recall and replace products that do not perform to specification in customers' hands. Very few new products survive such an event—the market gives very few second chances. A small company that launches a product without adequate pre-launch field trials will usually threaten its own total survival in the process. Big companies, if lucky, can afford a few new product mistakes. Small companies cannot afford any.

New product diffusion

Product launch marketing should take special account of what is known about the process by which new products are accepted and spread in a market. For example, it is found that the sales profile of most new products over time is like that shown in Figure 12.3—the familiar S-shaped curve of the product life cycle. This has important implications for forecasting sales, cash flows and working capital requirements. It is vital that the manager assess the likely shape of the sales curve through time. If the budget shows a pattern such as those in Figure 12.4, then very specific evidence must be produced to justify the assumption that sales will not adhere to the more general S-shaped pattern. The implications for cash management of forecasting any one of these three sales patterns are very clear.

Figure 12.3 also shows in (b) the distribution usually found of customers adopting a new product over time. If we think of all the customers who ever adopt a product for repeated usage, then it is possible to find the average time to adoption ($\bar{x}$) of the product by customers in the market—it may be, say, two months or two years. Most studies of this process of adoption find that the distribution fits with what statisticians call a 'normal' distribution, and that typically the customers who initially adopt the successful new product are different from those who adopt it later. Thus it is generally realistic to think about segmenting the market for a new product into time-and-customer 'slices':

Figure 12.3

The New Product Diffusion Process

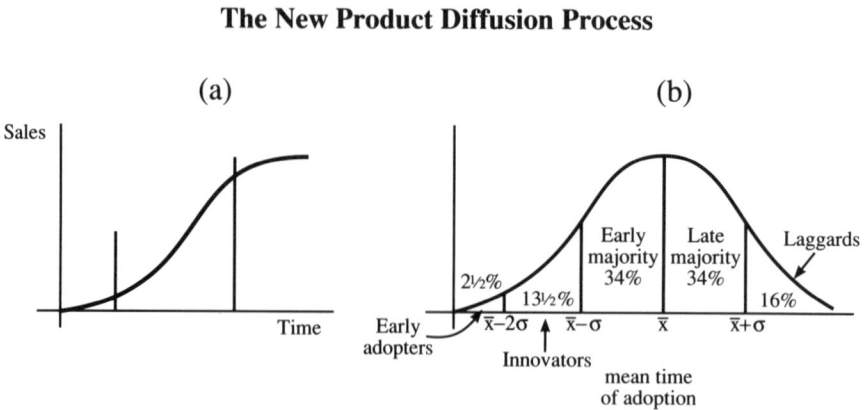

Figure 12.4

Alternative Sales Curves

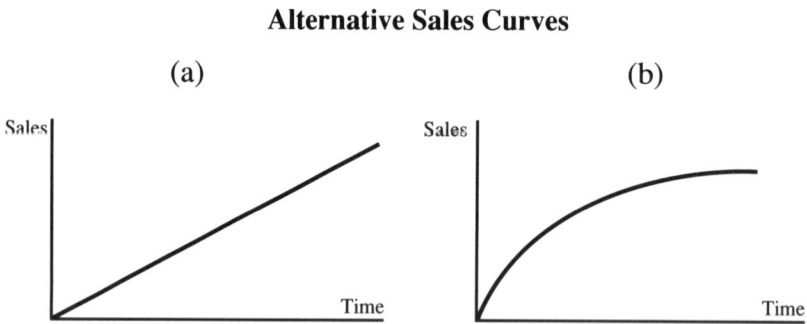

(1) *Early adopters* and *innovators* typically constitute about 15–16 per cent of all those who eventually adopt the product for long-term use. Because they are first into the market, and because they usually contain many opinion leaders, they are the vital target for initial marketing attention. If these people do not accept the product, the rest of the market is unlikely to do so. Innovators, as a group, can usually be identified, especially for products that involve significant commitment or risk for the customer. Farmers, for instance, who are early adopters of new products or practices are typically younger, educated, commercially oriented in their farming, and well networked to other innovative farmers and relevant state support agencies.

(2) *The middle majority*—both early and late—constitute the bulk of any market and enter the market at progressively later dates as they see first the innovators and then others buying and successfully using or

consuming the product. Marketing strategy for these groups should shift in emphasis from that aimed at innovators to provide more reassurance, and, in the case of industrial marketing, to use reference sales as a means of demonstrating the product's effectiveness.

(3) *Laggards* are the last to enter the market, giving an opportunity further to expand the market, but also on occasion necessitating a higher cost of marketing to convince them, and perhaps even the acceptance of reduced margins in order to 'buy' them into the market.

Exhibit 12.3 provides an interesting case history of new product adoption as well as relative success and failure in the video tape recorder market.

Exhibit 12.3

VCR VERSUS LASERVISION

Winning and losing in product innovation

In *Diffusion of Innovations*, E.M. Rogers puts forward a model that the likelihood that a novel product or idea will be adopted by a population (or indeed, a new product by a market) is dependent upon five factors: *Relative Advantage, Compatibility, Complexity, Divisibility and Communicability*. The case history of the video tape recorder (VCR) and the Philips Laservision system provides an excellent object lesson on how this model might be applied to the key decision of whether an innovative idea or prototype is likely to succeed, and indeed, what could be done to increase the chances of speedy and widespread adoption. The case also attests to the veracity of Rogers' model for new product decisions.

The conclusion is that VCR succeeded because its launch into a latent market gave it a high *relative advantage*, because it was *compatible* with pre-existing TV watching behaviour, because its similarity in principle to audio tape recorders, as well as support from rental companies, assured a perception of low *complexity*, because an extremely favourable chain of circumstances quickly gave rise to a large rental market that increased *divisibility*, and because the advantages of VCR ownership were easily *communicated*.

By contrast, Laservision failed because it had a negative *relative advantage* compared to VCR, because it was not *compatible* with the TV recording habit engendered by VCR, because its leading edge technology was seen as relatively *complex*, because, in the absence of a rental market and due to the need for a supply of laser disks, it suffered low *divisibility*, and because its shortcomings were easily *communicated*.

Source: Robert Duke, 'Winning and losing in product innovation: a case history', *Irish Marketing Review*, vol. 5, no. 1, 1991.

Performance appraisal and control

Just as the vital indicators of life and health must be monitored continuously for an infant, so too for the new product. Performance against budget should be monitored at the very minimum on a monthly basis for the first year and variances examined as a matter of urgency. The entry of the innovator segment to the market should be observed. Customer experience with the product should be evaluated via formal marketing research or through managerial and salesforce contact with wholesalers, distributors, retailers and final customers. In the case of products that are purchased regularly, the emergence of repeat purchases must be followed with great care. For such products, it is the repeat purchases that determine success or failure, not first purchases—although these must, of course, be achieved before there can be any repeat purchases!

PRODUCT MANAGEMENT AND INTERFUNCTIONAL COORDINATION

It takes little insight to recognise that managing the product element of the marketing mix is not something that can be undertaken independently by the marketing function. Top management, finance, R & D and manufacturing are all essential to successful product management. This interdependence is especially significant in the new product development process, where the challenge to integration of effort is the greatest. The need to understand the linkages and interfaces between the different activities implicit in the firm's micro business system has already been stressed (see Figure 2.4). The 'process' approach suggested by the value chain or micro business system emphasises the need for the firm to focus on the product development task that has to be done and to empower the key employees involved in fulfilling the project. This emphasis on the process will sometimes have to go beyond traditional views about functional responsibility and hierarchy (see Figure 15.3).

There are no easy recipes for achieving integration of effort. In small entrepreneurial ventures the problem is solved naturally because two or three people working very closely together carry all the key responsibilities. In larger and more mature companies, the distance that grows between the various functions is one of the greatest threats to their long-term prosperity and is often reflected in an unacceptably low level of innovation and new product activity. If this is the case, then the company progressively loses touch with the changing reality of its markets and its viability is undermined.

The time taken to coordinate the different functions has become a central competitive issue of the 1990s. As a result of better coordination some companies can get new products on to the market as much as two years ahead of their rivals. Ford of Europe confronted this challenge in 1992 and restructured its entire new product development process in an effort to regain the competitive edge in the fierce battle for European car market leadership (see Exhibit 12.4).

Exhibit 12.4

FORD OF EUROPE

Putting design and manufacturing into the same gear

The restructuring of Ford of Europe's research and development operations goes to the heart of its efforts to regain a competitive edge in the fierce battle for European

Product Development Lead Time

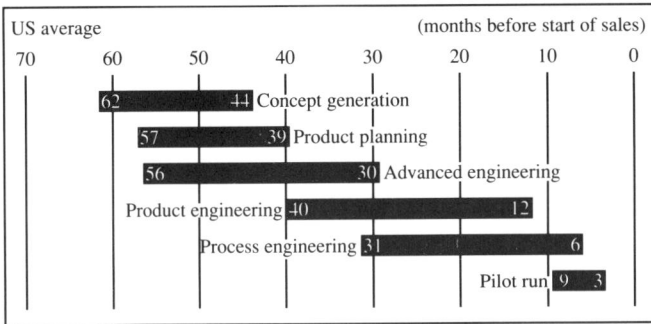

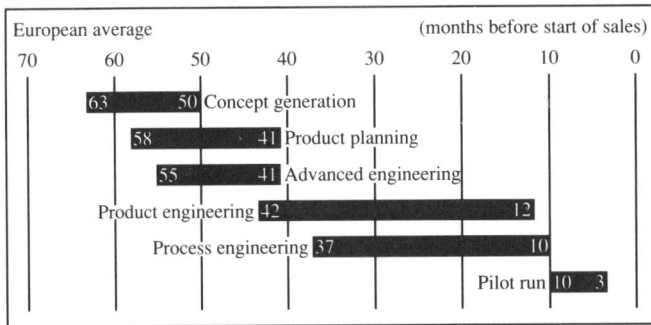

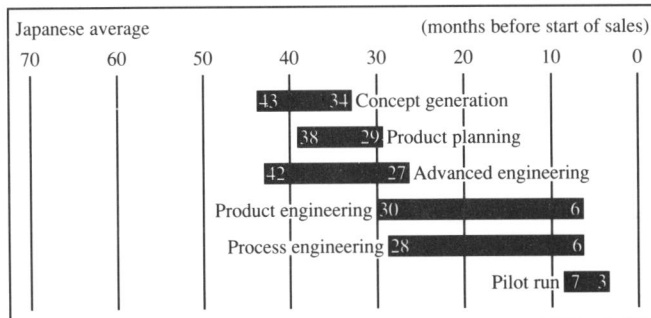

US average (months before start of sales)
70 60 50 40 30 20 10 0
62 44 Concept generation
57 39 Product planning
56 30 Advanced engineering
Product engineering 40 12
Process engineering 31 6
Pilot run 9 3

European average (months before start of sales)
70 60 50 40 30 20 10 0
63 50 Concept generation
58 41 Product planning
55 41 Advanced engineering
Product engineering 42 12
Process engineering 37 10
Pilot run 10 3

Japanese average (months before start of sales)
70 60 50 40 30 20 10 0
43 34 Concept generation
38 29 Product planning
42 27 Advanced engineering
Product engineering 30 6
Process engineering 28 6
Pilot run 7 3

Source: *Product Development Performance*, Kim B. Clark and Takahiro Fujimoto, 1991.

car market leadership. The US car-maker's record loss in Europe in 1991—the worst financial performance among the big six European car-makers—has been a bitter pill for a company which led the west European car market in the mid-1980s and which prided itself as the European industry's most efficient volume car-maker.

To revive its fortunes, Ford has launched an optimistically titled 'drive for leadership' campaign. High on the agenda is the implementation of so-called 'simultaneous engineering' in the reform of product development. Simultaneous engineering seeks to bring together design and manufacturing engineers to work in a project team (instead of their working in sequence and passing responsibility down the development line) so as to improve the speed, efficiency and quality of the complex process of developing a new vehicle.

To this end, Ford has embarked on a controversial programme to concentrate by the end of 1994 all its R & D activities at two sites in the UK and one in Germany, in place of the present six locations, four in the UK and two in Germany. At these sites will be gathered not only the design engineers and the manufacturing engineers, but also the support staffs, purchasing engineers, finance and quality control specialists.

'Product engineers and manufacturing engineers must be in the same country, and ideally in the same office,' says Mr John Oldfield, Ford of Europe's vice-president for product programmes, vehicle engineering and design. 'You cannot achieve simultaneous engineering by telephone or video-conferencing.'

Mr Oldfield's concerns are underlined by a recent study by two professors at the Harvard Business School and Tokyo University, which identifies gaps in lead time and engineering productivity between Japanese and Western car-makers. The study finds that 'the average Japanese firm has almost double the development productivity and can develop a comparable product a year faster than the average US firm'. On average, Japanese car-makers needed 1.7m engineering hours to develop a standard car compared with 3.2m hours in the US and 3.0m hours for a European volume car-maker (see above).

According to Mr Oldfield, US and European car-makers still take up to five years to develop a new car. 'The Japanese have about a three-year development cycle and the best Japanese are even a little better than that. We have started on that route. We have not yet delivered a major programme in three years, but we now have some on the books.'

Source: *The Financial Times*, 11th May, 1992, p. 15.

SUMMARY

The rate and magnitude of change in most markets have elevated new product marketing to a position of considerable importance in most companies. The management challenges created by new products are best addressed in a systematic way by establishing the strategic roles new products must play for the company; deciding on the extent to which they are to be developed internally or by external acquisition; following a disciplined process of idea generation, screening, evaluation and development; and finally launching new products with detailed marketing plans. In addition the time a company takes to do all this has become central to competitive advantage.

Reading

Booze, Allen and Hamilton (1982), *New Product Management for the 1980s*, Booze, Allen and Hamilton, New York.

Crawford, C. Merle (1987), *New Product Management*, 2nd ed., Irwin, Homewood, Illinois.

Duke, Robert (1991), 'Winning and losing in product innovation: a case history', *Irish Marketing Review*, vol. 5, no. 1, pp. 11–19.

Kohler, R. and Tebbe, K. (1987), 'Organisational design for effective product innovation', *Irish Marketing Review*, vol. 2, pp. 43–51.

Kotler, P. (1991), *Marketing Management: Analysis, Planning, Implementation and Control*, 7th ed., Prentice-Hall, Englewood Cliffs, NJ, chs. 12, 13.

Lambkin, M. (1989), 'Timing market entry: a key to competitive success', *Irish Marketing Review*, vol. 4, no. 2, pp. 42–53.

McCarthy, E.J. and Perreault, W.D. (1990), *Basic Marketing: A Managerial Approach*, 10th ed., Irwin, Boston.

Nonaka, I. (1986), 'The new new-product development game', *Harvard Business Review*, January–February.

Wafer, B.V. (1986), 'A strategic approach to the Irish dairy processing industry', *Irish Marketing Review*, vol. 1, pp. 66–82.

Wind, Y. (1982), *Product Policy: Concepts, Methods and Strategy*, Addison-Wesley, Reading, Mass.

Review Questions

1. If you were marketing manager at Irish Biscuits Ltd, what new product challenges might you face, and how would you apply the new product development process outlined in this chapter to meeting those challenges?

2. What particular problems do small or medium-sized firms face in new product marketing?

3. Is the marketing department the most important function in developing a new product?

Chapter 13

Pricing

INTRODUCTION

Pricing decisions ought to be simple. Calculate the cost of supplying a product or service at various levels of output; find out how customers respond to variations in price level; decide that the firm wants to maximise profits; and calculate, with a little mathematical help, the price that gives the highest profit level.

Market realities and professional practice, unfortunately, are not quite so simple. Costs are sometimes difficult to allocate to individual products. Few marketing managers can in fact estimate with accuracy the way demand responds to small price changes. Very often the objective for an individual product is not to maximise profit but to complete a product line and maximise profit across the whole line of products. The theory of pricing that is generally at the marketer's disposal has to make simplifying assumptions about market conditions and company objectives that render it difficult to apply with practical effect. The theory is nevertheless important in identifying the key relationships and objectives involved in all pricing decisions.

In practice, most pricing decisions are made on the basis of determining costs and adding on a profit contribution. Other approaches based on what the market will bear and competitive parity pricing are also common. No one of these taken alone is a justifiable approach. Taken in combination they do begin to provide the parameters for a reasonable approach to setting price in the complex and uncertain conditions of most product-markets. Pricing decisions reflect strategic imperatives as well. The company pursuing a market-share-building objective will have a different policy towards pricing than one trying to recover its investment in a new product in the shortest possible time. These are the factors which ultimately complicate the pricing decision.

THE BASICS OF THE PRICING DECISION

It is important to identify the essential objectives and relationships involved in a pricing decision in a simplified manner before the complexity of real markets and of professional practice is explored. The price for a product should reflect:

(1) the company's cost function—how much it costs to make products or services at various levels of output;
(2) the product's demand function—how customers respond to different price levels in terms of their volume of purchases;
(3) the profit objective of the company.

A *cost function* consists of both fixed and variable cost elements. The fixed costs do not change as the company varies its output in a given production facility. So these are the standing overhead costs that must be paid whether the firm produces one or 100,000 products or services in a year. The variable costs are those that vary directly with the number of units produced. As more wooden chairs are produced in a furniture factory more timber is used—and it is used in direct proportion to the number of chairs involved. The total cost is therefore the combination of the fixed element and the variable element. This is illustrated in Figure 13.1 (a).

Turning to the market, it is obvious that for most products price significantly determines the level of sales. As price increases it is generally valid to expect the volume of purchases to go down. There are, of course, exceptions to this, and there are ranges of small incremental price increases, where customers may not notice or may not be sufficiently sensitive to change their purchasing behaviour. The opposite is also generally valid: as prices go down more of the product is likely to be sold.

Figure 13.1

Pricing: Important Relationships

(a)

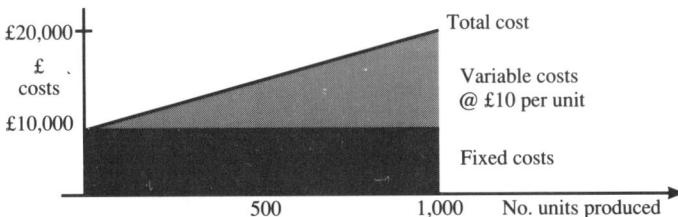

Total cost = Fixed costs + variable costs
= £10,000 + £10 × quantity

(b)

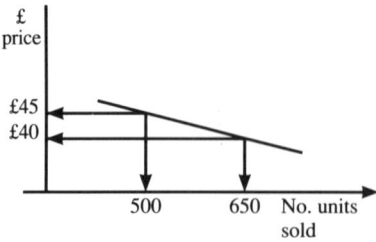

Very sensitive relationship   Very insensitive relationship

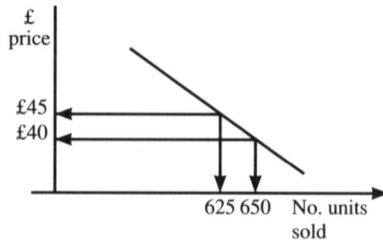

(To estimate such demand functions it is necessary to analyse historical data
on prices and volumes sold, using statistical methods)
Such a demand equation might be: Quantity purchased = 850 – 5 × price

(c)

Cost equation:	TC = FC + VC
	TC = £10,000 + £10 × quantity
Demand equation:	D = 850 – 5 × price
Total revenue:	TR = Quantity bought × price
Total profit:	Profit = TR–TC

$$= \text{Price } [850 - 5 \times \text{price}] - [10{,}000 + 10(850 - 5 \times \text{price})]$$
$$= 850P - 5P^2 - 10{,}000 - 8{,}500 + 50P$$
$$= -18{,}500 + 900P - 5p^2$$

Profits therefore reach their maximum at a price of £90, as may be ascertained with the use of calculus.

The nature of this relationship determines the product's *demand function*. What is especially interesting to the marketer is the price elasticity of demand— that is, the sensitivity with which customers respond to price changes. If price is increased by 1 per cent, does demand drop by 10 per cent, or does it perhaps not change at all? The difference between these two outcomes has a major impact on the formulation of pricing decisions. Figure 13.1 (b) shows two simple demand curves. One is highly sensitive to price changes, the other quite insensitive.

When the manager knows both the cost and demand functions, total revenue can be calculated, since it is a function of the price charged and the quantity the market will buy at that price level. Total *profits* may then be calculated as the difference between total revenue and total cost. Figure 13.1 (c) shows all the basic relationships necessary to calculate the profit-maximising price with the help of a little calculus.

The real world of pricing, unfortunately, does not look like this. If it did, good costing, some statistical estimation of the demand function and a little algebra would turn every marketing manager into an infallible pricing expert. Nothing would go wrong. But in reality the objectives pursued are usually not as simple as profit maximisation for each product. Costs may not be known with complete accuracy. Above all, the demand function is difficult to estimate and moreover alters with changing customer and competitor behaviour.

To cope with this, most pricing decisions usually reflect one, or a combination, of the following managerial approaches:

(1) cost or profit oriented;
(2) demand oriented;
(3) competition oriented.

Costs and pricing

By far the most widely used methodology is the cost-oriented one. Its wide use, however, is in no way a justification for its application to any individual pricing decision. The most typical approach is to calculate the total cost of the product and to add on a margin to cover profit for the producer or seller. This 'cost-plus' approach is, for example, typical of much of retail pricing where 'standard' mark-ups or margins are applied to many retailed products. In large projects such as major construction works the practice is also common of developing total project costs and then negotiating between contractor and client the profit margin to be added on to costs.

The value of the method lies in its focus on accurate cost estimation. At worst, the manager will not set a price below total costs and bankrupt the business. This possibility is not as far-fetched as it may seem, since many small and medium-sized businesses do not yet have adequate cost accounting systems. They often trap themselves as a result of ignorance into pricing products based on the direct variable cost of production without allocating fixed costs. If this becomes habitual, total costs are never recovered and the business will collapse unless subsidised even more irrationally by the introduction of further capital.

Where cost-plus pricing is well done, it still involves serious flaws. It takes no account at all of the demand function! The cost-plus price may well result in only a few or even no purchases. Equally it may result in less profit than is possible because customers are sometimes willing to pay more for the value of the product to them than the cost-plus price.

A variation on the cost-plus approach is target profit pricing. Here the manager estimates how much will sell, the unit cost at this volume of production, and the return on total costs that the company wants to earn. The focus becomes a target profit level. Have you spotted the flaw? The logic of this decision approach demands that the manager must determine the quantity that will be purchased before setting price. Yet price is a fundamental determinant of purchases in almost all markets! So this approach introduces a concern for profitability as well as costs, but totally ignores the demand function once again.

Customers and pricing

In order to incorporate the demand function in the decision, customers and their behaviour have to be taken into account. Taking a customer- or demand-oriented approach on its own shifts the focus to what the market will bear. Intense demand is likely to be met by high prices, and weak demand by low prices—even though the cost structure is constant under both conditions of demand.

Approaching pricing decisions from this perspective requires knowledge of customers' price perceptions and their perceptions of value for money. As discussed in Chapter 11, customers pay not just for the 'physical' product features but also for service and psychological attributes of the product. The value they derive from consumption therefore represents the total of values—or 'utility'—they derive from each of the product's attributes. These perceptions of value may be explored by various marketing research methods. One of the most sophisticated methods which enjoys widespread acceptance, as we saw in Chapter 10, is conjoint analysis, which allows the researcher to identify the individual product attributes or benefits, to assess their individual utility or 'value' to the customer, and then to construct alternative products by varying the combination of attributes or the amount of each attribute.

Buyers' perceptions of the prices they pay for various products differ considerably in accuracy. Regular purchasers will have very accurate knowledge of prices for some products—for example, staple grocery items they purchase weekly. For other products, the typical customer will be able only to estimate a price range within which they expect to find the product. This latter phenomenon has important pricing implications, since it implies that within the price range demand will be quite insensitive to price variation—a product priced at the upper bound of the range will be at no disadvantage to one priced at the lower end. Many marketing research studies question buyers about their price expectations to establish this price range and give one indicator of the pricing discretion available to the marketer.

For some products, the generally assumed inverse relationship between price and purchases becomes quite distorted. Some customers use price as an indication of quality and purchase a higher-priced product to reduce the risk they take in making the purchase and to assure themselves of good quality. This might be viewed as consumers paying an 'insurance premium' in the form of a high price to protect themselves against the risk of making a bad choice. This is perhaps also part of the explanation for the market power that high market share, high-quality producers acquire in many markets. Because they are dominant competitors, and because they compete on quality, they command premium prices and typically earn above-average profits for their industry. This phenomenon is especially strong in consumer durables and infrequently purchased products where the customer is more likely to rely on supplier reputation in making a purchase than on long experience of making many repeat purchases from several competitors.

Customer-or-demand oriented pricing also raises the issue of price discrimination—charging different prices for the same product but in different locations or at different times. Irish tourism pricing is very complex because of its basis in price discrimination policies. It is far more expensive to stay in most hotels in August than it is in February. Suppliers of tourism services respond to the seasonality of their industry by pricing high when demand is high and low when demand is low. This policy is implemented through different rates for different seasons of the year. It may also be applied within a weekly time scale. Hotels that depend on business traffic do well during the working week, but may price their rooms and services at 'bargain' rates for weekends to attract a different segment of the market and contribute towards the fixed costs they must incur on Saturday and Sunday as well as from Monday to Friday. Watch how some city hotels in Dublin, Cork or Galway will offer special weekend 'deals' to the non-business guest.

The positive feature of the customer-oriented pricing decision is its concern with the fundamentals of marketing—consumer or buyer behaviour. It probes the nature and determinants of the demand function which none of the cost-oriented approaches consider. It can of course also be used unethically or exploitatively to reap excessive temporary monopoly profits. Companies in business for the long run do not abuse this potential, as it inevitably generates customer resentment, public regulatory reaction, and the entry of competitors to gain access to some of the profits.

Pursued single-mindedly, customer-based pricing may also lead to a disregard for profitability. It is possible to sell almost anything if the price is low enough! Such a policy, however, is unlikely to result in profitable operations.

Competitors and pricing

Many small businesses, especially those with products they have not succeeded in differentiating, base their pricing decisions on what the 'going rate' is in their sector of industry. Tendering and bidding situations are also characterised by emphasis on judgments about what competitors' tender prices or bids will be.

There are therefore circumstances where there may be little choice but to orient the pricing decision towards competitors' price levels. Under such circumstances, the marketing priorities are twofold:

    (1) to do everything possible to become cost-effective, since if price is a given, cost is the only managerial variable in determining margins and profits;

(2) to attempt, if possible, to differentiate the product so that some managerial discretion may be created in the pricing decision.

Competitor-oriented pricing raises the issue of price leadership. Price leaders pursuing an experience curve approach may gain substantial advantage, as may be seen in Exhibit 13.1. Most markets have one strong, respected competitor who 'leads' prices. Typically such a company is the first to increase prices in response to cost pressure, and the rest of the industry follows suit. In recessionary periods this is a difficult strategy to execute, as competitors with unused capacity are always tempted not to follow but to build their volume and market share at the expense of the leader and any followers. Price leaders may also lead prices down in an attempt to expand the market and precipitate a shake-out of small inefficient suppliers.

Exhibit 13.1

THE EXPERIENCE CURVE

How the price/cost relationship evolves over time

From studies in many industries, the Boston Consulting Group found that the cost and price histories of a product are frequently directly related to the cumulative production (or 'experience') of that product. This can be quantified by plotting, over a period of time, the logarithms of unit cost or price against the logarithm of cumulative production. Cost and price are expressed in constant money values.

When this is done, it is usually found that cost decreases smoothly with experience—commonly by about 30 per cent for each doubling of cumulative production. However, price moves through four phases as experience develops:

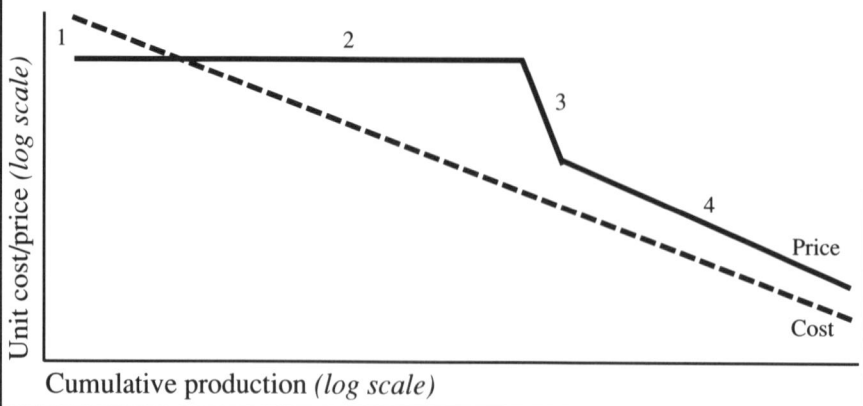

Cumulative production *(log scale)*

This type of plot is useful in interpreting the price history of a product, understanding the phase reached in its development, and developing appropriate strategies for the period ahead.

In Phase 1 price lies below cost of production due to low scale of manufacture and the need to compete with established markets.

Phase 2 is that in which the original market entrants make increasingly attractive profits.

In Phase 3 increasing competition causes price to fall rapidly—often by 50 per cent for each doubling of cumulative production. It is associated with rapid growth, big improvements in technology and scale; negative cash flows and frequently a blood-bath leading to the exit of some of the contenders.

Phase 4 is more stable with prices and costs falling so that there is just sufficient margin to keep the marginal producers in business. This is the period in which some of those surviving make handsome profits and positive cash flows. It is, however, important to realise that in this final phase, costs and prices in real terms should still be expected to fall due to increasing scale of operations and improvements in production processes.

The ramifications of these general findings are considerable and have been successfully employed by the Boston Consulting Group. The most important of these are as follows:

- Market leadership is extremely important. The market leader typically has lower costs due to his greater cumulative production or experience. These give him the initiative in deciding how the market will develop, particularly in Phase 4, and can put him in an unassailable position.
- The leader can set prices such that the marginal producer is just kept in business. This makes it unattractive for the latter to invest heavily and deters new entrants. Prices lower than this may dislodge the marginal competitor but cost the leader heavily in absolute profits since his volume is larger.
- Alternatively, the leader may choose to set prices such that his profitability is high. This may make the market attractive also for others who will invest heavily, catch him up and in so doing reduce their costs to the same level as his. In this case he has taken a shorter-term profit at the expense of longer-term dominance.

- Being a number 2 or 3 in the market can be moderately attractive. However, catching up a leader with intelligent pricing policies can be an extremely expensive business. Being a marginal producer, with relatively high costs, is an unsatisfactory position and usually a case for disinvestment.
- All competitors, but particularly the leader, must ensure that their costs (in real terms) are constantly reducing or their profitability will be eroded and competitors will be able to gain market share.

Source: Shell Chemicals UK, *Techniques of Business Analysis*, 1979, p. 5.

In the personal computer market during the mid-1980s IBM cut its prices, expanded the market and built its market share very rapidly at the expense of smaller microcomputer manufacturers in North America and Europe. As it built market share, manufacturing economies of scale and experience drove its costs well below most of the smaller competitors, which could not as a result compete successfully on price let alone on product design and marketing. By the early nineties, Apple Computer adopted a similar price-cutting strategy and had to face the dilemmas illustrated in Exhibit 13.2.

Exhibit 13.2

APPLE COMPUTER

What price glory?

In the autumn of 1990, Apple Computer reversed a six-year-old policy of charging high prices for its Macintosh line of computers and slashed prices by about 40 per cent. Six months later, though quarterly sales of Macintoshes had nearly doubled, the firm was forced to sack 10 per cent of its workforce. And, after years of fierce independence, Apple was negotiating a technology-sharing arrangement with the company its salesmen once loved to malign, IBM.

Apple's abrupt and painful about-face dramatically illustrates just how tricky pricing decisions can be. For better or worse, its new pricing policy will transform the company. Optimists argue that lower prices may at last make the Macintosh popular enough to enjoy the sort of virtuous circle of innovation that IBM-compatible computers have enjoyed. Because about 90 per cent of personal computers run the same software as IBM's machines, software companies are increasingly focusing their efforts on these computers—which sells more computers, which attracts more software and so on. But sceptics see only gloom ahead. Despite its self-proclaimed innovative prowess, Apple's share of the market may already have shrunk too far for the company to influence the development of the next generation of technology. And rivals are far ahead of the firm on the price and cost-cutting curve, making it difficult for Apple to gain the volumes and profits needed to stay ahead technologically.

Apple got itself into this mess with a key decision made back in 1983. It was then that it decided to set the price of its new Macintosh personal computer well above that of competing models made by its rivals. This was at a time when learning-curve pricing was the order of the day in the computer industry—setting prices as low as possible in order to capture market share. But then the Macintosh was a unique product with its user-friendly windows, icons and 'mouse'—a 'bicycle of the mind', in the words of Steve Jobs, Apple's founder and its then president. The design goal for Mac's creators was to build a machine that could be sold for $1,000. By the time production plans were drawn up, the minimum selling price had crept up to $2,000. It was decided to add a further $500 to the price of the machine in order to pay for a high-profile marketing campaign to tout the Mac's advantages.

This advertising and selling strategy flopped, largely because the first version of the Mac was not all the marketing had cracked it up to be. Despite an encouraging start, Mac sales nosedived, just as Apple ramped up production to meet what it thought would be booming demand. In the ensuing mêlée Jobs was forced from the company he founded.

However, Apple continued to persevere with its premium pricing policy, pushing prices up in order to pay the high cost of going it alone in innovation. Over the next few years, holding gross margins above 50 per cent—well above those of most competitors—became a key concern of Apple managers, who needed the profits to pay for their ambitious research programme. Apple's R & D budget rose from $128m in 1986 to $478m in 1990. The main thrust of the research policy was to develop increasingly powerful computers. In 1987 Apple launched the Macintosh II range of computers with colour screens and super-fast processors.

Powerful, costly Macs were popular with several constituencies. The high margins available on big machines appealed to the network of dealers who were entrusted with the job of flogging Macs to businesses. Fast machines were also popular with the smallish, but fanatically loyal, group of companies developing software for the Macintosh. Graphic designers liked the Mac. But many others ignored it. The machine's overall market share remained tiny throughout the late 1980s. IBM computers were far more popular with big companies. They may not have been as easy to use, but they worked well enough. Apple justified a premium for the Macintosh because studies showed that new users could be brought up to speed more quickly, with less training, than on IBM machines. But many corporate customers would consider switching to the Mac only if the machine were cheaper than an IBM personal computer. That was because either the Mac would have raised the cost of administering their computers, or it would have forced them to write off their existing machines.

Also, so-called open systems—which enabled the products of many different vendors to work together—spread the costs and opportunities of innovation. The success of IBM's personal computer was not entirely IBM's doing. Because they could build machines like IBM's, companies like Compaq picked up the pace of innovation when IBM faltered. And extra competition pushed prices down—so boosting market growth—just as Apple was pushing prices up to pay for its R & D.

Cheap, not cheerful

Proposals for low-cost Macintoshes were made several times in the late 1980s, and shot down each time. Though various reasons were given, executives say that the real reason for rejecting a low-cost strategy was that smaller margins would simply not support Apple in the style to which it was accustomed. In the pursuit of high margins, Apple refused to invest in its low-end market range, the Apple II, with the predictable result that the firm was overtaken by IBM in the educational market in 1989.

By 1990, Apple's market share was near the point of no return. Software houses simply did not see a big enough market in Macintosh software to develop new products for it. Equally important, a new program from Microsoft, called Windows 3.0, provided cheaper IBM-compatible PCs with many of the Mac's once exclusive capabilities, undercutting the justification for the Mac's higher price. After an executive reshuffle, Apple decided to launch low-cost Macintoshes and cut prices on existing products. This proved even more painful than the apostles of high gross margins had predicted. Lower prices did generate extra demand: unit sales in the second quarter of 1991 were running 85 per cent above the same period of 1990. But all the extra demand had come at the low end of the product range. Apple's attempts to predict the price elasticity of demand for its products had suggested that price cuts would spur sales across the entire Macintosh range, and it was hoped that this would have given the company two or three years to adjust to its new lower gross margins. Instead Apple was forced to adjust much more quickly and the pain hit Apple squarely in its profit and loss account.

In the spring of 1991 Apple started sacking workers and began reshuffling its dealer network to accommodate high-volume, low-margin box-shifters alongside the traditional Apple dealer, who had been encouraged to avoid price-cutting and to provide lots of expensive service for the machines he sold. And it reshuffled its R & D priorities. Instead of developing everything in-house to keep the edge on its proprietary technology, Apple began negotiating joint development deals to share R & D costs. Chief among these was the deal with IBM. But it also negotiated a deal which would mean that Japan's Sony would make low-cost home computers for the American firm.

Judged against the assumptions of its previous high-price strategy, Apple is now in considerable difficulties as it moves into the nineties. It can neither afford to spend heavily on proprietary R & D nor to spend heavily on evangelising the efforts of its research laboratories. Most of the proprietary technology it is developing will be shared with IBM and with Sony, companies which have more marketing clout and enjoy greater economies of scale in manufacturing, and whose long-term interests lie, arguably, in competition with Apple—not cooperation.

Source: *The Economist*, 24th August, 1991.

Pricing decisions must therefore take competitors' prices into account to a greater or lesser extent. If the product is a commodity-type product, then all prices will move towards a single value. As products become differentiated the key consideration ceases to be competitors' prices and becomes the value-for-money trade-off that they offer. And that brings the decision-maker back to developing an understanding of the demand function.

PRICE DECISION-MAKING
Good decision-making under normal circumstances of uncertainty about cost and demand functions usually reflects all these approaches to setting a price—cost, customer and competition based—and an integration of these considerations into a judgmentally optimal price, as shown in Figure 13.2. Central to the process of integrating these considerations are the kinds of marketing objectives and strategies the company is pursuing.

Company objectives and strategies
Price is just one element of the marketing mix and is therefore partly determined by the other components and by overall marketing strategy. For example, a highly differentiated product based on advanced technology, quality manufacturing and distributed through an exclusive channel backed up by extensive service must lead to premium pricing to recover costs and to create consistency in the customer's eyes between the elements of the mix. Waterford hand-cut crystal glass is an expensive product, yet its very expensiveness is an important part of the bundle of psychological attributes of the product that consumers throughout the world demand when purchasing 'the best'.

Figure 13.2

An Integrated Approach to Price-Setting

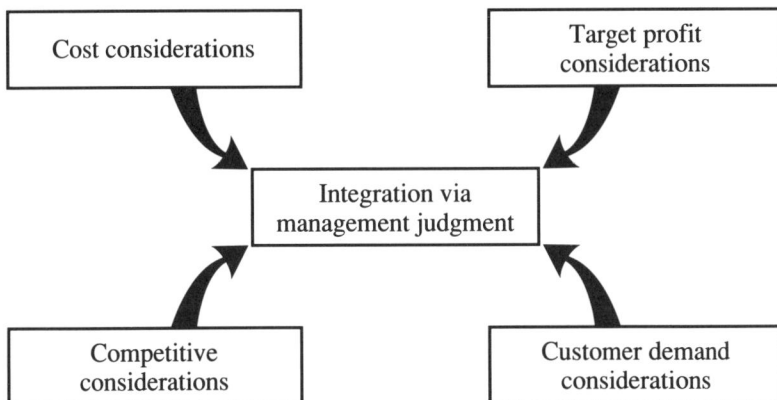

Pricing decisions reflect portfolio management priorities too. Lower prices may be used to build market share as a company tries to turn a 'question-mark' product into a 'star'. Interestingly, the research evidence from the PIMS (Profit Impact of Marketing Strategy) programme suggests that, in general, price is not as effective in building share as other variables such as product quality and innovation. As leading products mature and begin to become 'cash cows', margins normally come under pressure in a market that is no longer expanding. The cash cow has to be managed so as to defend margins and generate cash for R & D and new products. This defence is usually conducted by carrying out improvements on the cost side and by reducing the extent of the product line. With products that are in low share positions in low growth markets, price-cutting strategies are normally suicidal. Such products are, in most markets, at a cost disadvantage against the share leaders, who therefore have the flexibility to outbid any price reductions if smaller competitors choose to start a price war. The normal consequence of such action is that the marginal products and companies in the market become even more marginal, eat up their own capital and are left bankrupt or in a weaker position to survive in the long run. The way out of 'dog' positions in the portfolio is through segmentation and innovation to dominate a new segment. Price is not a good offensive weapon in this context.

Price is on certain occasions used to great effect as an offensive weapon. Its use has been highlighted since the 1970s by the strategies of many Japanese marketers, especially those in electronics markets. American companies such as Texas Instruments and European ones such as BIC also became leading exponents of using price as the key weapon in the battle for market share during the early stages of product and industry life cycles. It is important to note that such strategies were not based on low margins or poor quality. Quite the opposite is in fact the case. These strategies are therefore more accurately called *cost-leadership* strategies rather than low-price strategies. A typical approach in an industry where there are significant scale economies and experience effects is to set price at a level that will yield an attractive profit if substantial volume can be sold. Because of scale and experience effects, the high volume will yield low costs of production. The vital initial assumption that must be made is that setting the low price will in fact stimulate the market to buy in sufficient volume to drive the costs down to profitable levels! Under such circumstances, the marketer is very often hoping to stimulate primary demand—to bring new customers into the market. This happened with Texas Instruments in the case of the demand for semiconductors and micro-electronic components. BIC did the same with the writing instrument market with the introduction of the throwaway crystal ballpoint and repeated the strategy with cigarette lighters, razors, and more recently with wind surfboards. The dominance of modern consumer electronics by Japanese producers is also largely attributable to the same process.

What must never be overlooked about cost-leadership strategies is that they are also high-quality strategies. The BIC crystal pen, trivial as it may seem, is a very high-quality product based on great excellence in manufacturing. The engineering tolerances and quality control involved in producing and assembling the ballpoint to assure smooth continuity of ink flow are of a very high standard. Marketers should therefore absorb the necessity to match low-price strategies with low-cost manufacturing and high quality. The combination of low price and low quality is never acceptable to the market over the medium to long run.

Penetration and skimming policies

Entry strategies for new products are frequently formulated in the context of a debate among managers on the implementation of 'penetration' or 'skimming' price strategy. Penetration pricing opts for a low price to capture a large market share, to encourage as many customers as possible into the market, and to generate volume to drive down costs. A skimming strategy sets price high and targets on segments of the market that pay premium prices. The objective is usually to obtain rapid recovery of new product development and marketing costs. This latter strategy is most often invoked by companies with very high R & D costs and a period of temporary monopoly granted by patents. Many pharmaceutical products are launched in this way. Problems do arise when the monopoly position disappears and the company is forced to make a major change in pricing policy to match new entrants, such as producers of generic drugs in the pharmaceutical industry. In such cases failure to abandon the old premium price will result in a rapid loss of market share.

A skimming policy is probably at its most effective in the highly innovative company with excellent technological and marketing resources that keeps introducing original products, reaping premium prices, and then innovating again as competitors begin to imitate the first product and drive down its price.

Revisiting the pricing decision

The basis of pricing policy can often become forgotten or unclear with the passage of time. For this reason it is important to revisit regularly the logic of pricing decisions. The aggregated nature of accounting and information reporting systems often fails to alert the manager to the precise profitability of individual items. Careful scrutiny may be required to identify products as unprofitable. These may have to be dropped, repriced, cost structures reappraised or a clear decision made to sell them at a loss as part of a profitable line.

Managers must always remember that a price reduction is immediately reflected in a corresponding drop in profits. If anticipated extra sales do not materialise it will cost the company dearly. Moreover, it is very unlikely that a company will be able to raise its prices back to their original levels. A ratchet-like mechanism characterises price reductions in most markets. Price wars must always be approached with great circumspection (see Exhibit 13.3).

Exhibit 13.3

DUNNES STORES VERSUS STEWARTS SUPERMARKETS

Pyrrhic victories—who wins in a price war?

Price wars are among the most dramatic events in the marketing environment and a short-lived but sensational skirmish occurred in Northern Ireland in late 1983. The protagonists were Dunnes Stores, an aggressive newcomer to the grocery trade in Northern Ireland, and Stewarts Supermarkets, the long-established market leader. Dunnes slashed the price of a wide range of fast-moving consumer goods and challenged their principal competitor to respond. Stewarts did so and for the next six weeks an orgy of tit-for-tat price-cutting took place.

The effects of these events were felt by every member of the channel of grocery distribution. Manufacturers were antagonised by the bout of below-cost selling; the grocery trade was severely disrupted; consumers enjoyed a spell of very low prices but suffered from the side-effects of overcrowded stores, long check-out queues and the not infrequent stock-outs; and the combatants themselves were exhausted by their exertions. The only real beneficiaries were the media, particularly the *Belfast Telegraph*, which enjoyed a dramatic increase in advertising revenue as a consequence of the conflict.

Source: Jim Bell and Stephen Brown, 'Anatomy of a supermarket price war', *Irish Marketing Review*, vol. 1, 1986.

SUMMARY

The pricing decision is made complex by uncertainty concerning cost and demand functions and by the variations in strategy that govern the decision. In theory it should be possible to set a profit-maximising price based on full cost information and accurate estimation of the market demand function. In practice imperfect information leads to decisions that are primarily cost oriented, demand oriented or competitor oriented, or some mixture of these. Good decision-making requires integration of all these approaches to price-setting and an understanding of the strategic context of the decision. Price must reflect the other marketing mix decisions. Pricing strategy must take into account the position of the product in the product portfolio and evaluate the relevance of a cost-leadership approach to building market share. Entry strategies for new products must also reflect choices between pricing approaches that attempt to stimulate long-term primary demand or to recover quickly the investment in the new product.

Reading
Baker, Michael J. (1991), *Marketing—An Introductory Text*, Macmillan, London, ch. 13.
Bell, Jim and Brown, Stephen (1986), 'Anatomy of a supermarket price war', *Irish Marketing Review*, vol. 1, pp. 109–117.
Kotler, P. (1991), *Marketing Management: Analysis, Planning, Implementation and Control*, 7th ed., Prentice-Hall, Englewood Cliffs, NJ, ch. 18.
McDonald, M.H.B. (1984), *Marketing Plans: How to Prepare Them & How to Use Them*, Heinemann, London, ch. 9.
McGoldrick, P.J. (1993), 'Grocery pricing in the 1990s—war or peace?', *Irish Marketing Review*, vol. 6.
Winkler, J. (1983), *Pricing for Results*, Irish Management Institute, Dublin.

Review Questions
1. In theory, how can a profit-maximising price be set? Illustrate your answer using hypothetical figures. Identify the items of information that are most difficult to estimate accurately in practice, and explain why.
2. What alternative approaches to pricing are most often found in practice? Evaluate the strengths and weaknesses of each approach.
3. Choose a product familiar to you and evaluate how its price fits with the elements of its marketing mix.
4. What are the pricing implications of a cost-leadership strategy? What are the critical elements of such a strategy?

Chapter 14

Communication and Selling

INTRODUCTION

Before customers can respond to the services or products that a company has for sale they must be aware of their existence and their performance characteristics. They must be informed about the products and persuaded of their relevance to their consumption needs. The task of informing the market accurately, clearly and persuasively about the company and its products or services is the job of the *communication mix*.

The communication mix consists of all the methods available to the company to achieve this objective. Just as with the marketing mix itself, there exists the necessity to choose the components of this mix and to ensure their compatibility with each other. The communication mix consists of the elements of advertising, sales promotion, merchandising, publicity, public relations and personal selling, as well as participation in exhibitions and trade fairs, as summarised in Figure 14.1.

Figure 14.1

The Communication Mix

The complexity of developing a specific mix for a company and managing its adaptation over time can be tackled effectively only if the manager approaches the task analytically and logically. This demands that an identification of a target market or 'audience' should be the first step in the decision process, followed by decisions on communication objectives, message, media, budget and execution of the communication programme. Following this stage, measurement of the effects and their evaluation against the objectives set is necessary if management is to stay in control of the process.

Elements of the mix are often seen as separate and independent areas of decision-making in marketing. Such a viewpoint can lead to uncoordinated activity in several communication media—advertising and the salesforce, for example—and to a sacrifice of the mutual support each element of the mix can give to the other. Coordinated planning and decision-making should produce synergy—the total impact on the market should be greater than the sum of the effects of the individual components taken alone. Within the communication mix personal selling is of special importance to many small and growing Irish companies. Personal selling is an extremely effective element of marketing strategy in the growth of small businesses and in the international market development process. It is also one of the most expensive communication 'media' that a firm can use and if badly managed it can have disastrous and expensive consequences.

DEVELOPING COMMUNICATION PROGRAMMES

Figure 14.2 summarises the elementary logic of arriving at a justifiable communication programme. Each step in the process is important and indispensable, and while the decision-maker will modify some earlier decisions in the process as later ones are made, there is a necessary sequence in the decision-making involved.

Choice of target audience brings the manager back to the customer analysis stage discussed in Chapter 4 and the decisions made about the segment that is to be the company's target market and the competitive position chosen for the company's product in this segment. These decisions are discussed in detail in Chapters 9 and 10. In formulating the communication programme, the manager must begin with these considerations. Their implications for communication decisions are immediate and far-reaching. If a marketer's objective is to position a new breakfast cereal product in the mass market for morning cereals, the target market will be family households nationwide. Within the households it will be important to understand that purchaser (typically a housewife) and consumers (children plus parents) may have different preferences (parents may prefer healthy nutritional products, while children may prefer sugared novelty products) and that each perhaps has to be persuaded to consume the product. Distribution through supermarkets will be essential to success, so for this and

Figure 14.2

Communication Strategy: Decision Process

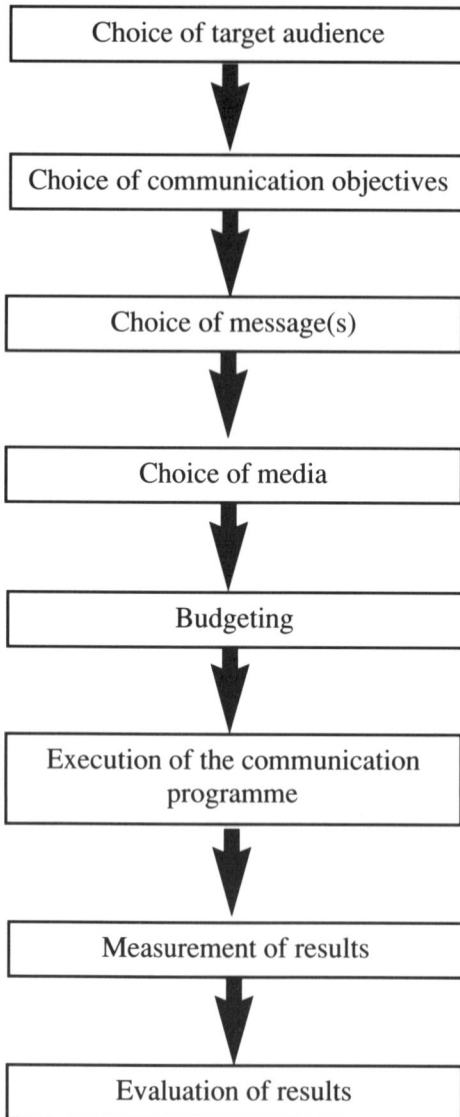

```
┌─────────────────────────────────────┐
│      Choice of target audience       │
└─────────────────────────────────────┘
                  ↓
┌─────────────────────────────────────┐
│   Choice of communication objectives │
└─────────────────────────────────────┘
                  ↓
┌─────────────────────────────────────┐
│          Choice of message(s)        │
└─────────────────────────────────────┘
                  ↓
┌─────────────────────────────────────┐
│            Choice of media           │
└─────────────────────────────────────┘
                  ↓
┌─────────────────────────────────────┐
│              Budgeting               │
└─────────────────────────────────────┘
                  ↓
┌─────────────────────────────────────┐
│   Execution of the communication     │
│             programme                │
└─────────────────────────────────────┘
                  ↓
┌─────────────────────────────────────┐
│        Measurement of results        │
└─────────────────────────────────────┘
                  ↓
┌─────────────────────────────────────┐
│        Evaluation of results         │
└─────────────────────────────────────┘
```

for cost reasons personal selling to final consumers is not a relevant consideration. Advertising, however, is probably the main mechanism by which so many final consumers can be informed of the product, and this will have to be

backed up by good merchandising and store promotions within the supermarkets. The supermarkets themselves will have to be persuaded to add yet
another cereal product to their shelves through intensive personal selling by the
company.

Knowledge of the target market and the competitive positioning decision
therefore begin to dictate the heart of the communication programme. The
essential outcome of this step in the process must be a clear statement or
specification of the customer's profile and buying behaviour.

Choice of communication objectives is possible once the audience has
been specified. Objectives must reflect what is the desired outcome of the
strategy—to inform people, to create an awareness of the product, to get
consumers to try it out, to achieve a specific sales revenue impact. There are
therefore typically multiple objectives, and these objectives will change over
the product's life cycle, with competitive reactions and with shifts in buying
behaviour.

Taking the new breakfast cereal example, the key objective at launch of
the product may be to make consumers aware of its existence and of its
unique features compared with existing brands. A second objective might be
to induce maximum possible consumer trial in the weeks immediately after
launch. If the product becomes successful, these objectives would change to
emphasise building brand loyalty, increasing product usage rates among
loyal customers, and winning new users from competing products.

This process of analysis and decision-making applies as effectively to
business-to-business products as it does to consumer products. Thus, in
launching a new venture to manufacture lenses for use in cameras and other
optical equipment, the entrepreneur and his marketing manager or adviser
would have to specify clearly who purchases such lenses in Ireland and
abroad for incorporation into optical products. They would next have to
develop their communication objectives just as the cereal manufacturer
must. In this case key objectives would concern establishing relationships
with the buying or procurement managers of major international optical
goods firms in order to have the venture's ability to produce lenses assessed
and its name added to the list of approved or acceptable suppliers who are
asked to compete for business. The process of decision-making is the same
across products, services and industries—only the specific details vary.

Choice of message grows from the objectives to be achieved and the nature
of the consumer. The optical lens producer has to design a message that will
convince purchasing managers in sophisticated international companies that a
relatively small new Irish venture can meet their standards of quality and
reliability. The message will therefore have to communicate the technical
competence of the firm, its manufacturing scale and resources, and its ability
to deliver a product of consistent quality, on time, every time. If the buyer is

initially convinced of these factors, then samples of the lenses will be provided for testing and technical features discussed and explained as this testing takes place. The required message through all these processes of communication is therefore one that features the new venture's technical excellence and managerial ability to organise production and delivery. By contrast, the communication approach of Irish Distillers in the whiskey market instances the same necessities in a consumer context (see Exhibit 14.1)

Exhibit 14.1

IRISH DISTILLERS

Brand positioning of an Irish whiskey

Since the early 1950s the Irish whiskey share of the total spirits market has been declining steadily. Vodka sales, in particular, had grown dramatically. In the early 1980s the Irish Distillers Group set about halting this trend. The company's three main brands supplied over two-thirds of the Irish whiskey market. Irish Distillers segmented the whiskey market in the light of these changing trends, developed and communicated an image or personality for each of the brands and attempted to broaden the appeal of Irish whiskey as a product category. It focused, in particular, on one brand, Power's Gold Label, which proved the most elusive and difficult to position.

Power's was the best selling of Irish whiskeys. Yet its product image was the most diffuse. The majority of the brand's drinkers was over fifty years of age. It was largely consumed outside Dublin. Company research confirmed that the brand was generally perceived as long established and traditional with a distinctive flavour. These characteristics alone were not enough to construct a communications platform to broaden its appeal, particularly across a wider age spectrum. On foot of further research the company developed a communication theme and an advertising campaign which integrated the brand's existing qualities of tradition and 'earthiness' into a well-defined product image celebrating the whiskey values of Power's. The campaign, with its distinctive advertising, was successful in wooing a target audience of men and women from their mid-twenties upwards to Power's Gold Label.

Source: M.W. Cummins, 'Brand positioning: a case history of an Irish whiskey', *Irish Marketing Review*, vol. 1, 1986.

Choice of media requires a decision on what channel or channels should be used to get the message to the target audience so as to achieve the established objectives. The word media is used here in the general sense of alternative channels through which the message can be delivered. It therefore includes all the elements of the communication mix.

The marketer of optical lenses will probably rely heavily on personal selling as a medium because the message is complex and technical and must be adapted in response to the customer's questions. Other media are important to support the personal selling one. Brochures and technical data sheets would be essential to effective communication, and direct mailing of these to buyers along with advertising in specialist trade journals could also be vital in establishing an entry to potential customers for personal selling activity.

In the breakfast cereal example, by contrast, heavy reliance on television and radio mass advertising might be more appropriate and cost-effective in communicating relatively simple messages to a mass audience. The important outcome of decision-making at this stage is a clear decision on what mix of media to use and on how they should be combined to achieve the company's objective.

Budgeting is the next step. What is to be done, how it should be done and the intended results of the programme are known, so the manager is in a position to assess costs and benefits. If objectives have been set in terms of sales effect, then very clear assessments may be made of the profitability of any one communication programme. Poor budgeting is a problem that bedevils many aspects of the communication mix decision and especially components like advertising. To the extent that the manager does not build up and evaluate a programme budget in the manner described here, it becomes impossible to defend the budget as a justifiable economic expenditure. Inadequate discipline of this nature is characteristic of companies where the advertising budget is the first item to be cut in times of financial difficulty. If nobody can justify logically and quantitatively the need for a given budget level, then no rational manager can approve the budget.

The budgeting decision therefore becomes the financial summary and yardstick of the decisions taken in the four preceding steps. Because most companies have very limited financial resources, it is normal to introduce limits on what is an affordable budget, given the company's finances. To the extent that an initial communication programme proposal exceeds this limit, the manager has to evaluate two factors:

(1) Are benefits expected from the budget such that the company should consider reallocating resources internally to fund the programme? or
(2) Are the benefits such that the company should consider raising additional funds to implement the programme?

If the answers to both these questions are no, then the manager must return to the cycle of decisions about audience/objectives/message/media and find a valid programme that fits within the budget constraint. The lens manufacturer might choose, for example, to limit initial marketing to branches of international companies located in Ireland. If success is achieved during the first budget period, then additional financial resources will have been created to address overseas buyers.

The budget decision must therefore reflect the strict disciplined logic of what has to be done and how, and the payoff to the company from undertaking the communication programme, as well as any financial constraints on budget size.

Execution of the programme must be actively pursued, whether through interaction with an advertising agency, through supervision of a salesforce, or design and printing of brochures. While this is easy to say, making any planned programme become a reality is the difficult unending task of operational management. The programme, its details and its budget commitments have to be relentlessly managed to make it all happen. No amount of good analysis and planning will compensate for a lack of thorough professional implementation.

Measurement of the results of the communication programme is essential to knowing whether objectives have been achieved and the budget profitably spent. At the heart of the measurement process is the establishment of standards against which to measure performance. By going through the decision process described, many if not most of these standards will have been set. Thus the communication objectives, the media, the message and the budgeted expenditure have all been decided upon. These factors for the cereal example already discussed might have looked like the following:

Objectives for new breakfast cereal launch, November 1994

(1) Achieve 80 per cent awareness of the product among all housewives by end of first four weeks.
(2) Achieve sell-in of product by start of November to all supermarket chains, symbol groups and cash-and-carry wholesalers.
(3) Execute merchandising and sales promotion programmes in 25 supermarkets in main cities and major rural towns.
(4) Ship cases of cereal to the trade by 1st November and second orders by end of November.
(5) Achieve consumer sales of 2,450 cases by 30th November, based on a two-week repurchase cycle, initial purchases by 5 per cent of households in the Republic, and repurchases by 50 per cent of these within four weeks.

Message
(1) '"Bran Nu" is a healthy, nutritious breakfast meal made from pure natural Irish ingredients.'
(2) '"Bran Nu" is the NATURAL way to start the day.'

Media
(1) National TV and radio advertising commencing 31st October, 1994 targeted at the housewife with an intensive schedule for first two weeks of November and a 'reminder schedule' for last two weeks.
(2) Salesforce sell-in of product to trade commencing 1st October, 1994.
(3) Advertising to trade during October 1994 in *Checkout* magazine and the *Irish Grocer*.
(4) Promotional and merchandising materials for supermarkets to highlight the new product and support consumer trial in 25 supermarkets.

Budget

(1)	Advertising: media plus production costs	£70,000
(2)	Trade incentives	£15,000
(3)	Allocation of salesforce time	£25,000
(4)	Contract promotional personnel to conduct 25 in-store promotions	£15,000
		£125,000

With these stated objectives, costs and planned sales consequences, the programme for the launch of the product may be monitored closely. If actual results diverge from budget, the cause of the variance can be traced to (a) poor implementation of the programme, (b) bad assumptions about the response of the market to the programme, or (c) unpredicted changes in the market such as a competitive launch of another new breakfast food. Under these circumstances, the next step in the decision process can be tackled.

Evaluation of results is possible because standards were set and performance against them measured. If variances have arisen between budgeted and actual performance, their origin can be diagnosed with some accuracy. The manager is therefore in a position to learn from experience and to take rational corrective action if it is needed. Going through these steps is essential to eradicating the tendency in many companies to view budgets for communication strategy as very judgmental and impossible to justify with conviction. As long as a company conducts the communication element of its marketing mix under these circumstances, its implementation of this vital decision is likely to be subject to sudden changes and reversals, uninformed decision-making, and confusion about the cost-effectiveness of the activity.

THE ELEMENTS OF THE COMMUNICATION MIX

These elements, illustrated in Figure 14.1, are the media alternatives referred to in the decision-making process described. Each element has its unique strengths and weaknesses, and in practice one seldom encounters a single element mix. This reflects the complexity of most communication decisions, which demand several media to achieve the several objectives or to reinforce each other in pursuit of a single objective.

Advertising is in itself a complex of alternative mechanisms for communicating with and persuading potential customers. While television, radio, press and popular magazine advertising are part of everyday life, and indeed part of a country's popular culture and lifestyle, there are many non mass media advertising vehicles. Trade and professional journals and magazines reach specialist target audiences with a narrow focus such as doctors, grocery store owners, purchasing managers, and so on. Specialist magazines reach select segments of the consumer population such as camera enthusiasts, yachtsmen, motor sport addicts, home improvement amateurs, and many other groups to whom the marketer of a specialty product can communicate directly via the appropriate magazine. Outdoor advertising in the form of billboards and posters has become a staple of advertising in Ireland as it has been in many European countries for generations.

The implementation of an advertising programme can be undertaken independently by the firm. When a significant amount is being done, and creative help is needed with the message and choice of media, most companies will employ the services of an advertising agency to produce the content of the advertising, to advise on the message and on the optimal choice, and scheduling, of media within a given budget.

A considerable body of information exists on the media habits of various consumer and specialist audience groups which can be accessed by the marketer via advertising agencies or directly from the media themselves. The Joint National Media Research study conducted annually in Ireland details the viewership and readership profiles of the main mass media alternatives. These profiles typically illustrate who watches/listens to/reads what media in terms of their demographic and socio-economic characteristics and their ownership/use of a range of consumer durable and non-durable products.

Sales promotion and *merchandising* cover activities such as demonstrations, special offers, samples, coupons, customer and trade competitions, in-store displays, special shelving and presentation mechanisms that stimulate short-term sales and customer interest. Sales promotion mechanisms are particularly important at the early stage of a product's life cycle to encourage consumer trial and withdrawal of loyalty from old products. They are also widely used in the maturity stage to maintain product interest and to combat competing new product launches. In addition, they may be employed as tactical weapons in the battle for market share throughout the life cycle. They are also used on occasion to achieve a company's end-of-year sales budgets where actual sales are running behind forecast sales. This is a particularly short-sighted use of the tool, as it typically transfers demand from a later period to an earlier one, leaving trade or consumers stocked up with the product and the marketer with a very bleak sales period at the beginning of the new budget while customers run their stocks back down to normal levels.

Merchandising is increasingly important in retailing because of the pressure for shelf space from more and more competitive products. Many companies therefore employ full-time or temporary merchandising personnel to look after the effective presentation of their products in supermarkets and to arrange periodic special displays.

Public relations and *publicity* are chosen as part of the communications mix to inform selected groups in the environment about the company and its products and to build a backdrop of trust and understanding for the more specifically product-related and annual plan-based communication activities. Public relations involves activities organised to create, maintain or enhance the company's reputation in its environment among groups whose goodwill and understanding are important to its future prosperity. Such groups may range from the government to the banking community, from schoolchildren to employees. Large, well-established companies whose prosperity is intimately tied to that of the whole country pay particular attention to public relations, as can be observed in the extensive range of PR and sponsorship activity undertaken by companies like Bank of Ireland, AIB Bank, Guinness and many others.

Publicity is closely linked with PR in seeking unpaid coverage of the company's activities and products in public media. Media coverage of annual general meetings, of new product innovations or of export successes by firms can be obtained with a little care and planning and has the value of giving the market a positive evaluation of the company from an objective and detached third party. Public relations and publicity activity may be organised by the company itself or through the specialist services of a public relations consultant or agency.

Exhibitions and *trade fairs* involve the marketer in presenting his company and its products or services at a venue where many potential customers can conveniently gather. This is usually done at industry exhibitions or fairs such as the Irish Business Equipment Exhibition held in Dublin each October, or at the Ideal Homes Exhibition or the Irish Boat Show. The list of such events is extensive and constitutes something of a reversal of the personal selling process. Here the customer comes to the exhibition or fair, whereas under normal circumstances the salesforce has to go out to call on customers one at a time. Exhibitions can also be organised by the company on its own. This is often done by hiring space in a hotel in the centre of a market area and inviting present and prospective customers to inspect and perhaps try out a product range or a new product or service.

Trade fair participation is often the first step into international markets taken by an Irish firm. If well planned and undertaken with realistic objectives, it can be a very productive means of learning about buyer needs in export markets and testing product acceptability. At a later stage in international marketing growth it should be undertaken with more sales-related objectives as well as the market research and learning objectives. For the small business entering the export field, participation in an overseas trade fair such as the annual ANUGA food fair in Germany can be made financially feasible by joining with a group of exporters and through use of the advice and support of An Bord Tráchtála.

Personal selling is perhaps the most powerful, certainly the most sophisticated, and often the most expensive element of the communication mix. Its power and sophistication derive from the use of intelligent, flexible human beings to act as the communication mechanism. The salesperson who understands the sales and communication objectives of the company can adapt the communication message as the need arises, applying it to the unique behaviour pattern and product needs of each customer. Personal selling is therefore extremely effective where good and close relationships and communication flows must be maintained between customers and company. It is particularly effective where the product or service is complex or technical and where it is used in a customer-problem-solving context. Under such circumstances, the salesperson acts as consultant, diagnostician of customer problems and needs, adviser on specifying problem solutions, and support person during use of the product. Such characteristics are expensive. If they are good they readily justify their overhead cost but if they underperform they become a serious burden.

All good communication programmes require a balance among these various elements. This is as valid for GPA in the aircraft leasing market as it is for a rock star in the popular music business (see Exhibit 14.2).

Exhibit 14.2

EMI RECORDS

Marketing means money

For Sinéad O'Connor's album *I Do Not Want What I Have Not Got*, EMI Records were very happy to get their sums completely wrong. Optimistically, they thought it might sell 15,000 copies in Ireland; in fact, final sales were over three times that figure.

But the marketing machines of major record labels are well-oiled operations, and there's usually little left to chance when a new album is released. The market is thoroughly analysed to tell the company how popular the record will be, and large amounts of money are then spent on promotion to encourage purchase. The marketing and distribution campaign begins well before a record is actually brought out, and continues long after the initial hype has died down. A tour is usually planned six months in advance, to coincide with the album's release; the main aim of the tour is to promote the new record, not to make money.

At EMI Records, a monthly sales meeting is held in the UK to plan for the releases of the following month. This is followed up by a meeting of EMI's Irish sales staff, who organise the promotional campaigns for the label's Irish and international artists. The next stage sees company reps visiting the record shops or contacting them by phone—'telesales'—to encourage retailers to order copies of new EMI releases. The reps also provide tour information, sell merchandising such as T-shirts and arrange for in-store displays featuring the artist.

Normally, a first single is released a month or two before the album comes out. The number of copies of the album that are manufactured depends on the sales of the artist's last album and the performance of the single. 'Nothing Compares 2 U' sold almost 10,000 copies in Ireland for Sinéad O'Connor, and reached number one on both sides of the Atlantic. The single succeeded way beyond the wildest dreams of anyone in EMI and virtually guaranteed the success of the album when it was released. Most albums need the release of two or three singles in order to build up sales, but Sinéad was off to a flying start.

The machinery of pop promotion really moves into action once an album has been brought out. In-store displays are put up, the artist is interviewed in the media, and newspaper, radio and perhaps TV advertising is paid for. Even for a small Irish release, it's vital to get on Dave Fanning on national radio, to have your video shown on the Beatbox and Jo-Maxi on national TV, and to promote your record by playing gigs around the country and appearing on local radio. Retailers can phone in additional orders at any time, and these orders are processed on a weekly basis by the record distributors. Delivery takes a week and longer, as both compact discs and vinyl records are manufactured in the UK. Only some cassettes are made here in Ireland, but this format now accounts for more than half the records sold. Further single releases keep the momentum going behind a promotional campaign. Advertising is particularly heavy at Christmas, when huge numbers of records are sold. And, of course, record companies frequently rerelease records when it suits them.

Record companies are frequently accused of ripping off their customers (and even their bands) and of hyping their product. With some justification, the companies defend themselves by saying that records are no different from any other products, and are promoted in the same way, using advertising, public relations, merchandising and other marketing techniques.

Source: *The Irish Times*, 3rd December, 1991.

Advertising

Some special issues arise in the development of policy for the advertising element of the marketing mix. These are the use of advertising in industrial product-markets, the development of advertising objectives, and the advertising budget.

The use of media advertising is generally associated with consumer products. Industrial marketers often underestimate its usefulness and cost-effectiveness in promoting their products. Many industrial marketers use advertising in specialist and even on occasion in general media to achieve objectives such as:

—creating awareness of a new industrial product

—creating awareness and credibility for a company so that personal selling activity starts from a base of customer knowledge of the company and product

—generating inquiries and sales leads for the salesforce to follow up

—reminding customers and prospective customers of the company and its products so that when a purchase need arises the company will top the list of potential suppliers to be contacted

—building customers' confidence and loyalty by positively reinforcing their decision to purchase and use the company's products.

Even mass media can cost-effectively achieve some of these objectives. Over the last decade, many products previously promoted only through personal selling in a business-to-business context found new ways to market through the mass media and direct marketing. This was particularly instanced in the case of personal computers where Apple and Toshiba made major investments in television advertising and Dell built their business on mail order promoted through newspapers and general interest magazines. Creativity in the use of the communication mix is therefore important, and managers should never be deterred from considering media traditionally avoided by their own company and its competitors.

The development of advertising objectives requires the manager to develop at least a basic analysis of the various kinds of communication results he may wish to achieve. In Chapter 4 the decision process model of customer decision-making was used as a basis for exploring consumer and buyer behaviour. An issue which emerges clearly from such an analysis is that different customers and indeed whole segments of the market may be at different stages of the decision process and therefore need different information. Communication aimed at triggering need recognition is likely to differ from communications intended to help customers evaluate competing products or to reassure them if they have had second thoughts about the wisdom of their purchase at the product usage stage.

A company which might try to develop commuter air traffic in Ireland faces an interesting variety of communication needs. Past users of commuter air services would need reassurance that trying another service reflects good decision-making. The company would also have to fight for its share of the market of people travelling in Ireland, so potential customers need information on how to evaluate the competing modes of travelling and the advantages of air travel. Many people travel by car or train between the main Irish cities who could be encouraged to fly if their decision-making behaviour were altered from choosing between ground transport alternatives to choosing between ground and air travel.

The development of an advertising strategy in such a context therefore demands that thought be given to which target audience, at what stage of its decision process, should form the object of the exercise. Separate objectives are required for the different groups, although separate advertising programmes may not necessarily be required. Objectives may also be specified at various stages on a continuum stretching from creating awareness to precipitating a sale, as shown in Figure 14.3. The five steps shown in the diagram represent just one of many models of communication effect. These models are usually called *hierarchy of effect models* because the audience is likely to go through the steps sequentially, although impulse purchases could well jump from initial awareness of the existence of a product in a shop to immediate purchase. The value of these models is in their clarification of the many levels at which an advertising objective may be set. Advertising to create awareness of a new product may have to be different from advertising aimed at helping consumers to evaluate the product they now know about. Equally, such a framework may highlight inappropriate objectives. For example, to return to the example of the new enterprise set up to produce optical lenses, it is not appropriate to set a sales objective for any advertising that may be undertaken. Closing sales in this company is a personal selling task. However, it may be a very valid advertising objective to achieve the awareness step and part of the comprehension step. The job of helping the customer fully to comprehend the product, to evaluate it accurately and to form an intention to purchase is much more a task for personal selling in this kind of technical product-market.

Each of the stages in the model shown in Figure 14.3 is measurable by relatively simple marketing research methods, so achievement of such objectives can be monitored with accuracy. Consumer good firms have the opportunity to measure advertising effect in terms of changes in intentions to purchase, since final purchase is heavily dependent not just on advertising but on distribution and in-store location, merchandising and retail selling.

Advertising budgets are determined in practice by several methods. The percentage-of-sales method is an arbitrary approach that has alarming popularity. Using this method, the manager applies a fixed percentage to sales to set the advertising budget, usually justifying it on the grounds that there is an accepted advertising/sales ratio in the industry. The method assumes a constant relationship between advertising expenditure and sales results and can lead to a pattern of decision-making that allows sales revenue to determine advertising where one might more reasonably expect advertising to be a determinant of sales. Budgets are also frequently set with reference to competitors' budgets, allowing little for the different strategies being pursued and the different market positions of competitors.

Figure 14.3

An Hierarchy of Communication Effects

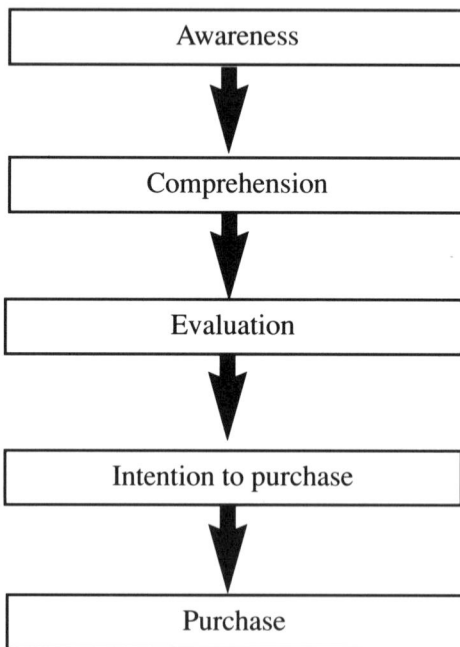

The objective-and-task method is the most valid approach in common use. This demands that the budget emerge from a logical determination of objectives and a specification of the advertising tasks that must be undertaken to meet these objectives. The tasks are costed and the budget estimated. If the budget level is higher than the company can afford, the manager must adjust objectives to a more realistic level. Some computer-based models have been developed, usually based on the statistical estimation of relationships in a product-market between advertising and sales response. While these budgeting models have limited currency as yet, their contribution to analytical decision-making is growing continuously, especially with the development of EPOS (electronic point-of-sale) and EDI (electronic data interchange) technologies.

Personal selling and sales management
The implementation of an effective personal selling strategy depends on good sales management. Sales management to be effective must be based on a sales management plan with the eleven basic components set out below:

  (1) identification of selling tasks
  (2) selling objectives
  (3) selecting strategy for selling
  (4) salesforce size
  (5) territory design
  (6) salesforce structure
  (7) recruitment and selection
  (8) training
  (9) remuneration
  (10) supervision
  (11) evaluation.

Identification of the personal selling task involves the specification of what exactly has to be done by a salesperson to achieve a successful sale. This demands knowledge of the customer's buying behaviour and circumstances and what actions are required of the salesperson to help solve the customer's problem and present the company's product or service as a solution to appropriate problems. These tasks should be specified in simple behavioural terms. In the case of selling water treatment equipment to county councils and to industry, for example, the salesperson's tasks will include:

—analysing the water treatment requirements of the customer
—developing with the county engineer or production manager   specifications for the water treatment system
—developing with the consultant engineer (if any) extensions of these specifications for inclusion in any tender invitation
—identifying all the key decision-makers involved at different stages in the purchase process
—selecting and providing technical and financial and general performance documentation for transmission to different members of the buying group
—helping to solve technical design problems as the design project evolves
—liaising with the engineer in charge of installation and commissioning of the system after the purchase to ensure that full technical and other forms of assistance and support are made available

—maintaining ongoing contact with the customer after successful conclusion of the sale to identify further sales opportunities.

It can be seen how specification of these tasks can be readily translated into personal selling objectives.

Objectives for the salesforce emerge from an analysis of the tasks necessary to make a sale and generate further business, as well as from the overall marketing programme concerning how many sales must be closed for what particular products. Objectives therefore contain selling activity standards and revenue and volume sales targets.

Personal selling strategy is developed to achieve the stated objectives through performance of the required selling tasks. To meet volume and revenue targets, the number of customers to be called on, the regularity of calls and the procedures for closing sales and managing customer accounts must be specified as a personal selling strategy—the means by which the objectives will be achieved.

Decisions on *salesforce size* can be addressed by considering the information available on the workload involved in implementing the strategy to achieve stated objectives, and by evaluating the productivity of a salesperson and the consequent costs and contribution to profit arising from the hiring of each additional salesperson.

The determination of salesforce size is normally approached in one of two ways. The first is the salesforce productivity method. In most established markets the productivity of a salesperson in terms of sales achieved over a sales period can be estimated with considerable accuracy. However, when more salespeople are added to a market, their productivity eventually must begin to decline as they saturate the market with selling activity. The revenue produced by each additional salesperson can be used to calculate the profit contribution from his sales efforts, and this can in turn be compared with the additional cost of having the salesperson on the salesforce. As salespeople are added the contribution on the sales they make will initially cover the cost of hiring and maintaining them on the payroll. However, as saturation begins to set in, the additional return to each new salesperson will begin to decline until one more addition just covers its own cost with profit contribution. At this point it ceases to be profitable to employ any further salespeople.

An alternative and more widely used method is the workload approach, which starts with a management decision about the number of sales calls required per customer per year. The total number of customers to be called on is multiplied by the call frequency to give a total required number of calls per year. The average number of calls a salesperson can make per day can be determined from the nature of the selling task and travel distances. This calls-per-day rate is then translated into a call capacity per annum, which, when divided into the total required number of calls per year, yields a necessary salesforce size:

$$\frac{\text{Total calls required per annum}}{\text{Annual call capacity of salesperson}} = \text{Salesforce size}$$

While the first method mentioned may be difficult to implement in many circumstances, management should always check on the contribution generated per individual and per average salesperson and compare this with the total direct cost per salesperson. If the two figures begin to converge, action to limit salesforce size or to increase its productivity will become necessary. This need to evaluate salesforce contribution becomes all the more apparent when the cost to a company of running its sales personnel is considered (see Exhibit 14.3).

Exhibit 14.3

THE COST OF A SALES REPRESENTATIVE

28 calls per week cost on average ...

The average number of calls per week in the 235 companies sampled in a recent study was 28, with a range from 19 to 40. This varied significantly by industry sector, with the agriculture and food/beverages/tobacco sectors having the largest number of calls, and computers/information technology the lowest number.

The average cost of having a sales representative on the road may be estimated as follows:

Basic Salary	£17,750
PRSI (12.2% of earnings)	£2,355
Pension (10% of salary)	£1,780
Commission/Bonus (20% of gross earnings)	£4,440
Travel Expenses	£7,500
Car Purchase and Tax	£6,000
Car Insurance	£1,000
Services and Repairs	£500
Postage and Telephone (£22 & £75 per month respectively)	£1,160
Training (1 x 1-week course)	£500
Sundries (entertainment, etc.)	£500
Total	£43,485

This estimate of the cost of a salesperson represents a 34 per cent increase on a comparable figure published in 1986, or an average annual increase of 7 per cent. Thus, it would seem salesforce costs have increased at a steady rate, roughly in line with average industrial costs.

Taking these figures a bit further, it can be seen that an average-sized sales force of 10 representatives costs approximately £434,850 per year. Add to that the cost of sales management and sales administration at a ratio of, say, .5/1, and the total annual cost of selling the company's goods is £652,300. This is a very significant level of overhead for most Irish companies and one whose productivity merits careful assessment.

Source: M. Lambkin and S. de Burca, *Profile of a Sales Force*, Sales Placement Ltd, Dublin, 1991.

Territory design and *allocation* is often done in a non-analytical manner and can result in conflict and bad feelings within a salesforce, with immediate repercussions on sales effectiveness. For example, if territories are allocated on simple geographic boundaries such as counties or provinces the sales potential of different areas will vary radically. This typically leads to disputes over who gets the 'good' and the 'bad' territories. If a significant part of the salesperson's income is in commissions and bonuses tied to sales volume, conflict can become particularly strong and emotional. In general, therefore, the aim should be to design territories with equal sales potential, thereby avoiding such a basis for conflict and providing a simple framework within which to evaluate performance. This approach can break down, of course, when the workload involved in covering two equal-potential territories begins to diverge for reasons such as variation in geographic size. For some products, the Dublin city market might well equal the sales potential of the rest of Ireland. Yet to allocate one salesperson to Dublin and one to the rest of the country would produce very different workloads in terms of travel time and time spent away from home. For this reason some companies will design territories on the basis of equal workloads and try to manage any conflict arising from the unequal sales potentials that will inevitably follow.

Salesforce structure addresses the issue of whether personal selling should be focused on products, on customers, on territories, or on a mixture of these three. Many salesforces are organised around products: salespeople sell one product or a related line of products, but not the company's other products. They therefore become product specialists. This may be necessary where products are very complex and there is little overlap or complementarity between the various products of the company. It can, however, lead to problems of salespeople identifying more with the product than with the customer's needs, and to the situation of several salespeople from the same company calling on one customer in a quite uncoordinated way.

Territory-oriented structuring results in a salesperson carrying all the company's products within a given geographical area to all customers. Salespeople can respond to this very positively by accepting 'ownership' of the territory and its long-term development and by becoming the company's representative in all senses of the word in the area. This works well where the product range is limited and similar and customer characteristics do not vary greatly. Where the opposite applies, it becomes difficult for one salesperson to be all-knowing about all products and all-competent to deal with every type of customer.

Many salesforces were restructured during the past two decades into customer-based organisations. Customers are identified individually or clustered into similar groups in terms of their needs, and the salesforce is then structured around these individuals or groups. Many grocery salesforces reflect the need for (a) high-level sales and negotiation work with buyers of supermarket multiple and symbol group chains; (b) a different kind of selling into individual chain and multiple outlets and cash-and-carrys; and (c) yet another sales task in servicing the independent grocer.

This form of structure stresses one of the basics of marketing—focus on the customer and his needs—and is an important option to consider where customers are large buyers when taken one at a time and where they divide into distinct groups with identifiable needs. For a company with a wide range of complementary products that can be sold as a system as well as individually, it may be a very necessary structure. IBM, for example, changed its worldwide sales structure from a product-organised one to a customer-organised one, believing that it had to coordinate all the company's products to address the overall system problems of individual clients and avoid uncoordinated and on occasion conflicting sales activity by product salespeople selling to the same company.

Recruitment, selection and *training* of the salesforce should be undertaken when the decisions on the areas already mentioned have been taken. It is possible at this stage to specify a job description and personal profile for the person who could perform the required tasks, meet objectives and fit into the chosen territorial and organisational structures. The company can choose to 'buy in' experience by hiring trained and expert salespeople or to invest in the training and development of younger, less experienced persons. This decision must reflect the urgency of immediate sales generation requirements and the necessity to socialise people into the company and to make them expert in the details of its products and services.

Remuneration should be based on the nature of the selling task, the motivational role of money payments, and the control and supervision requirements of the business. Selling jobs that involve long lead times before sales are concluded, as well as extensive customer liaison, servicing and advisory work, are generally best dealt with by remuneration schemes emphasising a guaranteed salary. Where sales are made daily and there is little need for deep involvement with customers, commission and bonus elements should generally play a much stronger role. Most situations require a mixture of both.

Money, especially in the form of commissions and bonuses, is not always the great motivator to higher achievement that it is sometimes naively claimed to be. Salespersons respond very positively in terms of job commitment and productivity to much less tangible motivators such as intelligent and attentive *supervision*, senior management recognition of achievements, fair and transparent *evaluation*, and a supportive company environment that makes them feel part of the enterprise and the vital final link between it and the market that ultimately is its only source of revenue and prosperity.

Remuneration systems heavily geared towards variable elements such as commission and bonuses generally require less managerial supervision—they are self-regulating in a rather mechanical way. If the salesperson does well, rewards automatically flow to reinforce the behaviour. If performance is poor, remuneration shrinks and the behaviour is 'punished'. The difficulty with such relatively 'automated' supervisory and control systems is that nothing is done to help the salesperson understand what is causing success or failure so that he can learn by the experience, and as a result high staff turnover rates are typical of such salesforce systems. This can also reflect the extent to which salespeople in highly pressurised environments experience 'burn-out'. The alternative approach is depth in managerial supervision and motivation and is a high-cost approach but will often be justified in high productivity performance, lower staff turnover rates and deeper customer relationships.

International selling and group marketing

We have examined the principal factors involved in managing the personal selling element of the communication mix. It is an area where successful small and medium-sized Irish companies have improved. Such a professional approach is crucial to international market expansion. The experience of many, if not most, Irish ventures entering overseas markets is that top management must shoulder the burden of much of the early personal selling to develop its knowledge of these markets and to demonstrate its serious commitment to serving international customers. As this business begins to grow and a loyal base to develop, specialist international sales talent becomes more affordable and can be hired in on the basis of a clear knowledge of the selling tasks that must be performed and realistic performance objectives.

At an early stage smaller companies may find it possible to finance international selling by cooperating with producers of complementary products to support an export salesperson, by gaining assistance from An Bord Trachtála for initial personal selling investment, or perhaps by dealing through a company that specialises in developing export markets and product ideas and coordinating the efforts of several small businesses. Group marketing has to overcome the barriers to cooperation between independent-minded firms but the payoff can be well worthwhile (see Exhibit 14.4).

Exhibit 14.4

UK PUBLISHING GROUP

Group marketing can work

Because of the size of the home market, many small/medium-sized enterprises (SMEs) need to export if they want to grow. However, the majority of Irish SMEs are small compared to their European, American and Japanese counterparts, making it difficult to compete successfully in export markets. Group or cooperative marketing helps such companies overcome these problems by enabling them to join together and share the costs of marketing/selling in an overseas market.

In essence, group export marketing occurs where three or more companies supplying non-competing goods or services agree to coordinate and share the cost of their export marketing activities in order to enter a specific target market. In this way companies who would not otherwise have the necessary knowledge or resources to succeed in an export market can enjoy the advantages of the group effort and can export at reasonable cost.

An interesting example of such cooperative marketing is shown by the UK Publishing Group. In the mid-eighties An Bord Trachtála was approached by three publishing companies who were keen to develop a professional selling programme in the British market. The companies were experiencing difficulties individually which they were finding hard to overcome. These included:

* lack of management time and expertise
* lack of sufficient funds
* lack of a track record in the UK
* lack of knowledge of the UK book trade.

The possibility of establishing a group programme was discussed and it was decided that an additional company should be recruited to provide a balanced portfolio of titles. The UK Publishing Group commenced operations in September 1984 when a UK marketing/sales representative was retained by An Bord Trachtála on behalf of the group of companies, with the companies paying commissions on sales generated in the marketplace.

During the first two years of the project the group was increased to include an additional two companies and joint activities undertaken included public relations, group advertising and joint exhibitions in the UK. As an added bonus the group members also learnt to cooperate within the home market, e.g. by making joint presentations to the major Irish retail booksellers.

The Trade Board's involvement with this publishing group was phased over a three-year period and since the end of 1987 the group has continued to build and develop its sales in the British market. The sales manager recruited in 1984 has built a team of regional agents which is controlled centrally from London. Equally the group has looked at the prospect of shared warehousing and distribution, again in the British market. The publishing group is an example of how companies, fundamentally small and limited, can pool their resources to create a strong image in what is a highly competitive overseas market.

Source: J.J. Lennon, 'Group marketing: theory and practice', *Irish Marketing Review*, vol. 3, 1988.

SUMMARY

Customers must be made aware of the existence and nature of the marketer's product or service. They must be informed and persuaded to purchase where the product or service fits with their needs. To undertake these tasks the marketer designs the company's communication mix—an integrated, coherent set of activities potentially involving advertising, sales promotion, merchandising, publicity and public relations and personal selling, as well as participation in exhibitions and trade fairs. An analytical approach to decision-making about the communication mix must incorporate choice of the target audience, development of communication objectives, choice of persuasive message, choice of relevant media, setting of the communication strategy budget, execution of the programmed strategy, measurement of its consequences, and evaluation of its effectiveness. Each element of the communication mix has its unique strengths and weaknesses and must be chosen and planned into the mix with care. It is also important to remember that each communication mix for each product in each planning period must be uniquely planned and implemented.

Reading

Baker, Michael J. (1991), *Marketing—An Introductory Text*, Macmillan, London, chs. 15, 16, 17, 18.

Cummins, M.W. (1986), 'Brand positioning: a case history of an Irish whiskey', *Irish Marketing Review*, vol. 1, pp. 153–159.

Donaldson, B. (1990), *Sales Management: Theory and Practice*, Macmillan, London.

Fanning, J. (1987), 'Perspectives on the new advertising', *Irish Marketing Review*, vol. 2, pp. 87–96.

Govoni, N., Eng, R. and Galper, M. (1988), *Promotional Management*, Prentice-Hall, Englewood Cliffs, NJ.

Jefkins, F. (1991), *Advertising*, 2nd ed., McDonald and Evans, London.

Kotler, P. (1991), *Marketing Management: Analysis, Planning, Implementation and Control*, 7th ed., Prentice-Hall, Englewood Cliffs, NJ, chs. 21, 22, 23, 24.

Lambkin, M. and de Burca, S. (1991), *Profile of a Sales Force*, Sales Placement Ltd, Dublin.

Lennon, J.J. (1988), 'Group marketing: theory and practice', *Irish Marketing Review*, vol. 3, pp. 69–78.

McDonald, M.H.B. (1984), *Marketing Plans: How to Prepare Them & How to Use Them*, Heinemann, London, chs. 7, 8.

Turley, D. and Gallagher, H. (1988), 'Children and television advertising: a cognitive development perspective', *Irish Marketing Review*, vol. 3, pp. 19–28.

Review Questions

1. Choose a well-known branded food product sold in supermarkets. Identify all the elements of the communication mix incorporated in the marketing of the product.
2. What are the principal steps of decision-making involved in developing a communication strategy? Show how each step must necessarily be taken before the succeeding one is decided upon.
3. How should advertising objectives be developed?
4. Why is the identification of personal selling tasks the first step in the development of a sales management strategy?

Chapter 15

Distribution

INTRODUCTION

Decisions about distribution are essentially of two kinds. The first concerns whether the marketer will deal directly with the final customer or use intermediaries or middlemen to bring the product or service of the company to market. The second is concerned with the physical management of the product or service flow from company to customer—what stocks should be held and where and what transportation arrangements are appropriate.

In this chapter primary emphasis is on the former set of decisions—channel decisions. How channels should be chosen, managed and controlled is considered, as well as some basic channel strategy choices. The treatment of the physical distribution area emphasises the selection of service level standards and the minimisation of the total cost of physical distribution.

SELECTING A DISTRIBUTION CHANNEL

The purpose of a channel is quite simply to get the product or service of the company to the customer in a manner which best suits the customer while also fitting in with company objectives and resources. Who customers are and where they are is therefore the best starting-point in the decision-making process. Think of the customer for a simple headache remedy. The ultimate consuming unit for this product is really the family group. Purchases are typically made in two ways. A consumer will frequently buy a supply of analgesics (aspirin, paracetamol) during her main weekly shopping trip to the supermarket. This purchase then becomes a 'stock' item in the home, to be used as needed and replaced on another supermarket trip. Other purchase situations arise, however—especially when someone suffering from headache or cold or flu pains wants an immediate remedy. Under such circumstances, if they are out of the home, they are likely to want to purchase the analgesic in a convenient tobacconist, sweet and newspaper (TSN) shop, or perhaps in a chemist shop where they can ask for the pharmacist's recommendation.

Choice of distribution channel for analgesics must be fundamentally governed by these underlying patterns of consumer behaviour. Here the manager immediately has to consider three retail points at all or some of which he might make the product available. Furthermore, the choice will have an impact on the product packaging decisions that must also be made—perhaps large packs for the supermarket to last the family some time as a stock item, and small convenient pocket or handbag-size packs for the TSN that are easily carried during the day and at work. Some marketers confine their analgesic brands to chemist outlets alone, giving the product strong associations with the professional and paramedical nature of the pharmacy outlet.

So the first issue in selecting a channel is to return to the fundamentals of marketing analysis to understand the customers—who they are, where they are, and where they would prefer to purchase the product. This normally provides immediate guidance for the choice of retail channel. There are, however, many instances in which the channel chosen is direct from company to customer. This is particularly common in the case of industrial products and services where the company is selling to another organisation which is the final customer, as in the case of most engineering sub-assemblies; circuit-boards sold to an electronics company; machine tools sold to an engineering works; plastic moulds sold to a moulding firm and so on. Here the marketer is typically faced with a relatively small number of final customers and a customer need for a high level of interaction with the supplier about product design, performance, installation and service. This does not mean that all industrial goods are distributed through a direct channel. A great deal of all industrial equipment and consumables, such as cutting tools for example, are brought to market through channels consisting of at least a distributor and not uncommonly of an import agent, distributors and sometimes retailers. Electrical cable may go through this latter channel to reach the small electrical contractor in Ireland.

Direct distribution is not ruled out for consumer products either. Fast food products typically go direct to customers, as in the case of all the proliferating fast food operations where production, delivery and consumption take place on the same premises. Mail order and 'factory shop' type operations also take this direct route with consumer products. Some companies, such as Avon Cosmetics and Tupperware, have made direct selling of their products to customers their vital competitive advantage in very intensely competitive markets. Distribution innovation can therefore be a powerful weapon in the fight for competitive advantage. We saw in Chapter 6 (see Exhibit 6.1) how Spectra Laboratories, in the amateur film processing business, by-passed the pharmacy and formed an alliance with An Post to create a high-quality and competitively priced service.

The essential channel choices are illustrated in Figure 15.1. The key to choosing the 'right' channel lies in three considerations:

(1) customer behaviour;
(2) desired customer service level;
(3) tasks to be performed by the channel for the marketer.

The meaning of the first is already clear. Choice of the *desired customer service level* reflects the marketer's knowledge about customer needs plus a strategic decision concerning how well he can satisfy these needs and how competitively he can do so. Choice of service level usually demands a considered decision on (1) where and how widely and how conveniently the product will be made available; (2) how long, if at all, the customer will have to wait for delivery of a purchase; (3) how often, if at all, a situation can be tolerated where the product is temporarily out of stock; and (4) how much service has to be made available with the product in terms of advice on choice of product, installation, maintenance, repair, spare parts and support.

Figure 15.1

Channel Choices

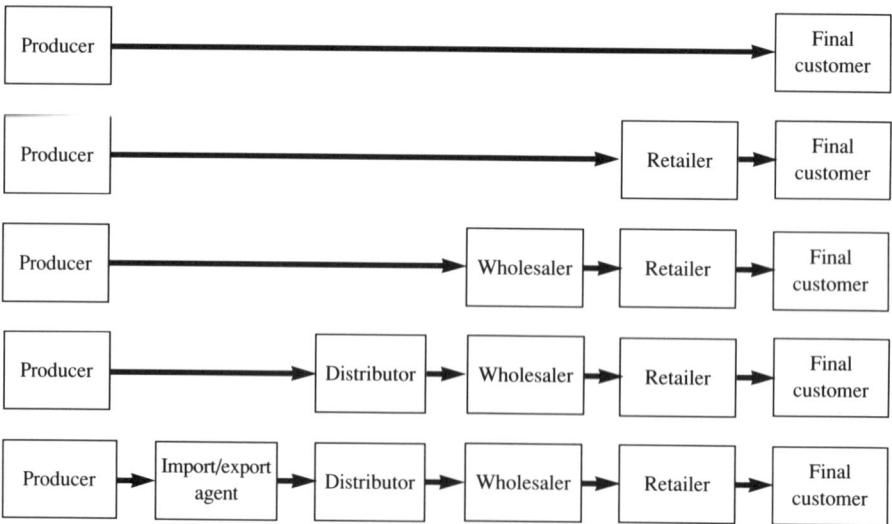

The relationship between the channel and the final customer is not the only important one, however. That between the marketer and the channel is also fundamental and must be carefully designed or chosen in structuring a distribution channel. This leads to the third consideration—the *tasks to be performed* by the channel. What is it that the channel should do for the marketer? And especially, what can it do better than the marketer's own company? The range of tasks that may be performed includes:

—transportation
—storage/stockholding
—selling
—collection of payments for goods
—credit and financing service to customers
—marketing and collection of market and customer information for the marketing company
—promotion, merchandising, publicity
—transfer of legal title.

Which of these tasks must be performed by the channel to attract and hold loyal customers, and what quality of service is required under each heading, are issues that must be examined in detail. The marketer must then utilise the results of this examination in selecting channel members who can effectively execute the mix of tasks.

EVALUATING ALTERNATIVE CHANNELS

Consideration of the many factors discussed above is likely to lead to the identification of channel alternatives rather than to a single option. How can alternatives be evaluated and the best decision made? Five criteria for evaluation will help to clarify most choices of this nature:

(1) fit with customer behaviour and preferences;
(2) fit with rest of marketing strategy;
(3) economic performance;
(4) control;
(5) adaptive capability.

Customer behaviour and preferences dictate the essential features of where and how the channel should make products available, and especially the required customer service level.

Total marketing strategy and the rest of the marketing mix demand that the channel used be consistent with the nature of the product, its price and the way it is sold, advertised and promoted. Sophisticated hi-fi equipment is sold through specialist hi-fi retailers, but stereo rack systems are most appropriately distributed as a package purchase through department stores, electrical retailers and general TV/radio/record shops.

The *economic performance* of different channel alternatives may vary considerably. By going direct to the customer, the producer retains all the margin between cost of production and the final price to the customer. But under such a direct channel arrangement the producer must also incur all the costs of holding stocks of finished goods, transportation, customer credit and customer servicing and selling. By working through an intermediary or intermediaries, the marketer yields part of the total margin to the intermediary in payment for its specialist services. The justification for this and the reason why it may be cost-effective is that the intermediary, through specialisation, should be able to undertake the distribution tasks at lower cost than the manufacturer can hope to do. The decision on whether to go direct or through a more complex channel must therefore reflect an evaluation of the relative cost-effectiveness of the alternatives (see Exhibit 15.1).

Exhibit 15.1

RETAIL FINANCIAL SERVICES IN EUROPE

Banks invade the life assurance market

Banks and insurance companies across Europe have been leaping into one another's arms at an unprecedented rate. The fashion has even added new words to languages. In Germany, *Allfinanz* is the term used to describe the combination, in a single grouping, of banking and insurance, while the corresponding word in French is *Bancassurance*. In Germany, the mighty Deutsche Bank has set up its own life assurance. France has also seen a spate of government-inspired marriages between state-owned banks and insurers, designed to strengthen the combined groups' capital bases, such as UAP's link-up with BNP. In Britain, Abbey Life and Lloyds Bank have joined hands, while many building societies are also eschewing the independent route in favour of ties with life assurance companies.

The reasons why banks have ventured into the life assurance market are the profit dynamics of life assurance distribution and the way economies of distribution can be achieved by reconfiguring the value chain. However, marrying the diverse cultures of banking and life assurance selling is not easy. Branch banking is steeped in the traditions of balancing the cash each day, the fear of the audit and the existence of a multitude of procedures and controls. In contrast, life assurance selling is saddled with the image of fast-talking salesmen who have little regard for controls or procedures and who are heavily incentivised in their remuneration.

Unique challenges arise in trying to link these very different traditions to produce an effective and efficient system for distributing a wide range of financial services. The major issue is whether to seek to meld both traditions to create a single homogeneous culture or to seek to retain their separate cultural identities. There are no easy answers to these issues. For example, the arguments in favour of distribution of life assurance policies by banks depend very much on the central or fulcrum role of the branch in terms of customer relationships. How important will branches be in the future, especially with the trend towards automatic teller machine networks and towards home banking?

Thus, while battle is joined, the outcome is by no means conclusive. In the end, victory will go to the enterprises, whether they be banks, insurance companies or whatever, which respond creatively and in the most cost-effective manner to their customers' needs.

Source: Colm Fagan, 'Retail financial services in Europe—banks invade the life assurance market', *Irish Marketing Review*, vol. 5, no. 1, 1991.

Channel control is also an important consideration in arriving at the channel decision. With direct distribution the marketer is in total control of the process. As more intermediaries are built into the channel between marketer and customer, control becomes diluted and increasingly regulated by contractual relationships. The danger inherent in a dilution of control is that the marketer can no longer fully determine customer service levels; he must trust to the intermediaries and retailers the effective delivery, presentation, selling and promotion of the product. As more control is transferred to the channel, it is vital that the marketer choose the best possible channel members, and exercise great care in negotiating the terms of the relationship and the responsibilities of the channel members.

This problem is seen in its most urgent form by many small and medium-sized Irish exporters who have to face the decision and management challenges involved in finding a channel into international markets. Because of a need for market expertise based in the overseas market, the choice of an agent or distributor is frequently an essential step in market entry. Ensuring an appropriate level of control over how their product is brought to market is a crucial consideration for such firms if their product is not to become just one more incidental item on a poorly motivated agent's or distributor's product list.

The *adaptability and flexibility* of the channel alternatives open to the marketer must be examined to assess their ability and willingness to change as markets, competition and customers change. For example, the traditional bicycle retailer proved, with very few exceptions, quite incapable of effectively retailing the new generation of leisure-oriented bicycles that emerged after the oil crises and the growth of health and environmental consciousness. Supermarkets, department stores and new bicycle outlets stepped in and radically changed the distribution system. Those marketers who stayed too long with the traditional outlets lost sales and market position. In order to enable the marketer to cater for the unforeseeable changes in markets and customer preferences, it is also generally appropriate to retain flexibility in the terms of any contracts with channel members. This can be achieved by keeping the duration of such contracts limited and subject to regular renewal and renegotiation and by retaining flexibility within the conditions of any agreement. This is not to advocate a short-term attitude towards distribution arrangements. Channel decisions are strategic decisions: they have long-term implications and cannot be changed easily without far-reaching repercussions for all elements of marketing. Once this orientation is accepted, however, specific channel choices and agreements should be made with a view to maximising flexibility to cater for the unforeseeable, but inevitable, changes that will occur in the marketing environment, within the marketing company itself, and within the organisations of channel members.

MANAGING THE CHANNEL

When a company has chosen a channel consisting of one or more inter-mediaries it must actively address the need to manage the channel so that marketing objectives are achieved. Management of the channel demands that the marketer (1) select, (2) motivate and (3) evaluate channel members. Selection of members has already been discussed, but it is necessary to explore the other two aspects of channel management in greater detail.

Channel motivation

Channel motivation might be compared with the job and necessity of moti-vating a salesforce. Without motivation, the channel will not actively sell the marketer's product and will deliver an inadequate service level to the final customer. Careful selection of channel members is the first step in ensuring their later motivation to handle a company's product and so provide an excel-lent service to its customers. Selection involves finding a three-way match between customer needs, marketing company and chosen channel member:

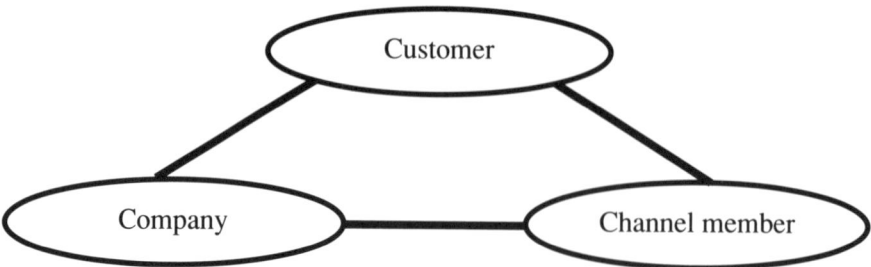

Customer and channel member must 'fit' in terms of a matching of customer needs and the channel member's ability to respond to these needs. Can delivery requirements be met? Can the product be made available in the right place? Can sufficient stocks be held? Can the channel member's sales team communicate effectively with the chosen customers? If there are negative answers to questions like these, no amount of effort by the marketing company on other elements of the marketing mix will overcome the misfit at the final step in the marketing system when the product should flow smoothly through the channel to the customer.

The relationship between company and channel member must also be carefully planned at the selection stage. A channel member capable of dealing successfully with the company's chosen target customers may not necessarily work well with the company itself. This is an issue which frequently confronts Irish exporters. For example, having chosen a large distributor for one of the regions of Germany for fashion clothing, a small Irish clothing firm may find as time passes that the distributor is accustomed to dealing with much larger suppliers. As a result, the distributor prospects and sells large orders to department stores and clothing chain stores. Then it becomes apparent that the Irish company cannot respond to such large orders, and the relationship of Irish exporter and German agent begins to deteriorate. The fault in what has happened under such a circumstance lies in the decision to form the relationship between two companies with different objectives in mind. The marketer must therefore ask of the prospective channel members: how will we fit together? Are our respective scales of operation compatible? Is my product complementary to, rather than competing with, other products in the distributor's product range? Do we share common objectives in terms of how to conduct business and serve customers?

Once a satisfactory channel has been selected, it becomes the marketer's task to *motivate* it so that both parties' objectives in establishing the relationship are achieved. The straightforward contractual terms of the relationship are the starting-point. The wholesaler, agent or retailer, just like the marketing company, is in business to earn profits. The terms of the relationship must therefore assure a profit provided that the required tasks are carried out. This demands a careful negotiation of how the intermediary is to be paid. Is he to be paid an agreed margin or commission on sales? Is he to take title to the product (i.e. buy it from the marketer) and then resell it at an agreed price, or at whatever price he wishes? What margin should he expect on resale, and what therefore can he reasonably expect to pay the marketer when he buys in the product? What credit is to be given, and taken, if any? Should there be bonuses or special discounts for sales above agreed levels? The list of relevant questions continues and is quite extensive, but it is critical for the marketer to remember that a well-motivated channel member is one who can make a reasonable business out of distributing his product. It is therefore important in negotiating a relationship that the marketer put himself in the shoes of the middleman or retailer and identify what would constitute a profitable and worthwhile financial arrangement.

Motivation draws on much more than the profitability of the relationship between marketer and channel. Channel members also respond positively to motivational efforts concerning the long-term quality of the relationship. Many Irish distributors of imported products who have taken on good Japanese product lines remark on how satisfied they have been with these relationships. This satisfaction derives from dealing with suppliers that make a long-term commitment to developing a good partnership and invest in educating the distributor, training the salesforce and supporting it fully with technical back-up. A relationship of trust based on factors such as these will result in above-average attention to the supplier's products and customers. There is, of course, value too in short-term promotional initiatives to create excitement and increase short-term sales. Competitions between distributors or wholesalers, or between sales personnel at distributor, wholesaler or retail level, are common tactics in generating enthusiasm and achieving short-term sales goals and if well managed can lead to long-term additional commitment to the marketer's products.

Channel evaluation

Channel evaluation, like all control-oriented procedures in management, can work only if standards of performance are set and behaviour measured against these standards. The relationship with a channel member is therefore fundamentally out of control if there has been no agreement for a planning period concerning such basics as:

- —sales volume
- —revenue after discounts and allowances
  personal selling activity
- —market coverage
- —stock levels
- —delivery standards to customers
- —technical service and advice
- —handling of returns, defective products, warranties.

The relationship with each channel member should be planned yearly in advance in conjunction with the company's marketing planning process, and should result in agreed budgets, terms and activities. These factors should then be reviewed regularly and departures from the planned programme investigated to determine whether the variance is due to changes in the market, to the performance of the channel member, or to the performance of the marketing company itself. By following this procedure, the effectiveness of the channel can be evaluated and ineffectiveness traced to identifiable sources. Accurate diagnosis therefore becomes possible and solutions may be developed that reflect the real problems.

CHANNEL STRATEGY

Choosing the channel through which to bring a product or service to market is inherently strategic: it is one of the basic means by which marketing objectives are achieved. It is also strategic in the sense that the channel decision is best made for the long term and in general cannot be easily or quickly changed.

Winning strategy is very often innovative. It reflects a decision to do something new that other marketers have not thought of before and that gives the innovative company a competitive advantage in serving customers. Distribution innovation can often be used in this way to gain at least temporary advantage over competition. Think of how going to the customer through new or different channels can affect competition in a market. The shift of lunch-time meal eating to pubs and fast food outlets and out of restaurants and especially hotel dining-rooms shows how the market for midday meals has been revolutionised by new entrants. In this case pubs responded to the growing consumer need, particularly in towns and cities, for fast economical lunch-time meals, while most hotel dining-rooms persisted in serving slow, four-course meals consisting of relatively expensive fare. Products that are regularly consumed in some quantity by the family unit have consistently moved out of specialty shops such as hardware or chemist outlets and into supermarkets, where they are bought as part of a household shopping trip. Products as far apart as non-prescription medicines and paints have been fundamentally affected by these changes. Marketers who interpreted the shifts accurately and led the process of change have usually profited through increased market share over their more conservative competitors. Exhibits 15.2 and 15.3 illustrate distribution innovations based on new information technologies.

Exhibit 15.2

PREMIER BANKING

Lending money over the phone

In a corner of Dublin's Sandyford industrial estate there is a small distinctly functional office unit; there is no welcome mat at the front door, which is opened by a security coded lock. There is no plush reception area in the foyer. Upstairs in white-painted breeze-block walled offices some 30 staff wait for the phones to start ringing. Premier Banking, a subsidiary of Bank of Ireland, was started in November 1990 as the country's first direct banking service, and is proving that low-cost, convenient, streamlined, albeit impersonal, banking does work.

For 64 hours a week—8 a.m. to 8 p.m. weekdays and 10 a.m. to 2 p.m. Saturdays—Premier personnel take details from on average 500 callers a day, who are mainly seeking personal loans, and log them into the computer. The computer assesses the replies to set questions, automatically runs electoral list and credit bureau checks, and generates a letter to the caller which will arrive within 24 hours indicating whether or not he or she has been approved. If an

---

application is deemed marginal it is rejected; obtaining additional information is taboo because it would cost time and money. A cheque is then automatically dispatched to the successful applicant and the whole transaction is completed without the customer ever having to leave home.

Premier was conceived as a 'defensive' product in anticipation of foreign-based competition entering the traditional banking sector with a low-cost operation to 'cherry pick' prime business. Direct banking had been pioneered by the Finnish KOP bank in the late eighties and its approach of initially focusing on a limited range of profitable products with minimum paperwork was being imitated successfully elsewhere.

Premier, up and running within nine months of conception, offers essentially three products, term loans, deposits and mortgages—all at normal bank rates, but with added convenience. 'Our customers do not fall into the traditional banking categories; they can be young or old, blue or white collar,' explains its chief executive. Experience so far shows they are 'financially sophisticated with little bank loyalty, between 25 and 50 years of age, innovators in their own right, open to change and 50% female'.

'Time has become an asset for many people with busy careers. There are a growing number of dual working families, and demands on people's time have greatly increased. We felt there was an opening for a bank which recognised this and could facilitate a customer who needed a fast efficient service,' comments the chief executive. Customer demand runs roughly 50/50 between Dublin and the rest of the country, with roughly 75% of Premier business coming from non-Bank of Ireland customers. 'We believe we are fundamentally different to the high street bank in terms of our attitude and style,' adds the chief executive. 'I don't see our business as banking. I see it as retailing. This is reflected in our staff, who are drawn from all sorts of backgrounds.'

The bank offers unsecured personal loans of between £1,000 and £6,000 with regular repayments for between one and five years. A protection plan, which ensures that repayments are met in the event of the borrower's death or inability to work, including unemployment, is also available. The average size of loan is around £4,000. Offering such a loan service by phone could result in horrendous bad debts. But the bank is confident of its 'credit scoring' approach to loan applications. It evaluates each loan on the basis of points accorded to applicant responses to set questions. The criteria are inflexible and most loan applications scoring above the approval threshold are monitored by an experienced bank official to determine whether they 'feel right'.

Funded out of the main B of I group treasury, Premier obtains funds at normal money market rates, on-lending to personal borrowers at normal bank term lending rates. To stimulate business its advertising costs are high. However, its operational costs are low. 'The core of a direct bank's existence is its cost structure, which has to be very low,' says the chief executive. 'We have a very flat organisational structure with just one secretary working to the three senior executives. Everyone else does their own keyboarding.' Furthermore, none of its staff is an IBOA member, which gives Premier added flexibility. As proof, the bank has achieved some 2 per cent of the Irish personal loan market and break-even within three years of operation.

Source: *The Irish Times*, 11th March, 1990 and 15th May, 1992.

Exhibit 15.3

TELESHOPPING

Is there a market for teleshopping?

The prospect of shopping from home using new technology has been an enduring feature of anticipatory reviews of a changing retail sector. Indeed, commentators have been sufficiently convincing to persuade investors to place real money into real projects during the 1970s and 1980s in a number of Western economies, notably the US, France and the UK. That many of these projects subsequently failed completely, failed to meet their stated objectives—or, in some cases, achieved entirely different ones—has been the subject of much discussion by practitioners and commentators.

For many, the conclusion was that the developments in the 1970s and 1980s were predominantly technology-led; that they were 'solutions in search of problems'; that they failed to meet a genuine need in the marketplace and that the success some of them subsequently achieved was accidental rather than planned. It is possible to compare take-up levels for, and consumer attitudes and expectations towards, a contrasting set of teleshopping and teleservice operations begun around the world in the 1980s.

In the UK teleshopping through videotex has had a chequered history. In France phenomenal success has been achieved through the Teletel programme. The other broad type of home shopping, the US home shopping show phenomenon, also looks like being here to stay. In Ireland the introduction and take-up of Minitel services are as yet limited. In many ways it is difficult to distil the commonalities and contradictions in defining a 'market' for goods and services through what is, in reality, not just one but a diverse range of potential delivery channels to the consumer, all of which involve varying degrees and sophistication of technology.

Any discussion of likely future changes in consumers' attitudes and expectations which may serve either to facilitate or to obstruct the development of these new delivery channels must first focus on demand. Demand is likely to be influenced in three broad ways. Macro-economic changes may affect the household's propensity to purchase new technologies in the home; such changes will also have significant effects on the time budgets of working households. A number of social and behavioural traits may strengthen the role of the home base in the purchasing of goods and services. Also the physical and attitudinal barriers to the adoption of new technology are likely to become less significant in the years ahead.

Source: J. Reynolds, 'Is there a market for teleshopping', *Irish Marketing Review*, vol. 5, no. 2, 1991.

Exclusive, selective and intensive strategies

Channel strategy should also reflect the marketer's objectives with regard to market coverage, the character of the product itself, and the quality of selling and after-sales service that is appropriate to it. Such considerations demand that a choice be made between exclusive, selective and intensive distribution.

A strategy of *exclusive distribution* involves giving one middleman or retailer exclusive rights to distribute and sell the product in a well-defined and usually quite large territory. This may be combined with an agreement that no competing products are to be handled by the intermediary. The logic for such a strategy usually lies in the assumption that it will give greater motivation to the channel member to develop business and look after customers. What he invests in the product will result in a payoff to him alone, since there are no other intermediaries to gain from the effort. Arrangements such as this are most typical in two sets of circumstances. In the first case a very prestigious marketer can enhance product quality image and depth of customer service by such an arrangement. The second case is a less happy one and may arise where the marketer is small, not well known, and possesses little bargaining power compared with the intermediaries or retailers. Under such circumstances, the channel may force an exclusive arrangement on the marketer, who is left with no choice but to agree. Such occurrences are frequent in the experience of firms entering new international markets with a product that shows potential. Care must be exercised at such a time not to give too much away to the channel and not to commit the company to a distribution straitjacket.

A strategy of *selective distribution* involves a limited form of exclusiveness well illustrated by traditional distribution arrangements for clothing companies in rural Irish towns. For many years it was normal that a manufacturer would supply only one clothing shop in each town, thus giving the chosen retailer some competitive differentiation compared with the other shops in the town. Such arrangements help to build a cooperative relationship between marketer and channel member and also limit the resource commitment the marketer has to make—only a fraction of the total potential intermediaries has to be serviced and managed.

An *intensive distribution* strategy is quite the opposite of the exclusive strategy. The objective is that of covering the market as extensively as possible and having the company's product available to customers wherever they may be. Typical of mass-marketed convenience products, this strategy is most often seen implemented for products such as cigarettes, which will be found on sale in tobacconist, sweet and newspaper shops, street kiosks, supermarkets, grocery stores, cinemas, pubs, and so on. Whenever customers expect to buy a product conveniently without having to spend time searching, and when the purchase is a frequent one, intensive strategies are generally appropriate.

Competition Law and distribution arrangements

The Competition Law of the EC Single Market is having significant effects on many aspects of distribution practice. A number of traditional distribution (and implicit pricing) arrangements are viewed under this legislation as distorting competition, amounting to undesirable concerted practices and generally inimical to the consumer's interest. Exclusive distribution agreements come under particular scrutiny and have to take on new forms and arrangements. However, while this causes some firms difficulties, it also presents the imaginative firm with the opportunity to adapt quickly and successfully to the legislation and win an advantage in the marketplace. The small new European airlines have taken advantage of this legislation to compete on previously cartelised routes.

A 'push' or 'pull' strategy?

Channel strategy, design and relationships can be built around two strategic orientations. A 'push' strategy assumes that the best way to get a product to market is to 'push' it towards the customer by carefully selecting the channel and motivating it actively to recommend the product to final customers. A 'pull' strategy, by contrast, builds on the assumption that the best approach for the marketer is to communicate directly to the customer about the merits of using his product and then to allow the power of market demand to 'pull' the product through the channel—even when channel members may not be wholly enthusiastic about either the company or its products.

Not many marketing strategies reflect just one approach or the other. The push approach relies on building what is sometimes called a 'trade franchise', while the pull strategy relies on having a 'consumer franchise'. No good marketing strategy is ever built on just one of these alone. What does vary considerably in marketing strategies is the relative emphasis on the two strategies. Marketers of mass-market items that channel members basically stock and present for sale must have a strong pull strategy, as they cannot expect a newspaper and sweet shop or a supermarket to sell their products actively in the retail outlet. In the shifting market for products branded by retailers (private labels) and those branded by manufacturers, a pull strategy is essential to maintaining the viability of the manufacturer brand. Without extensive advertising for Batchelors' canned food products there would be little consumer pull to prevent such a manufacturer's branded products from being replaced on supermarket shelves by Dunnes', Quinnsworth's, Superquinn's, VG's or Spar's private labels.

Emphasis on a push strategy is especially appropriate when the product or service being marketed requires skill and commitment in the selling process. Most industrial products and components exemplify the need for a push orientation. Caterpillar Tractor, the world market leader in earth-moving equipment, implements this strategy with particular success by selecting its distributors with great care, training them, monitoring and evaluating their performance and providing in-depth technical support on a worldwide basis. Through this process of channel support the company built from the end of the Second World War a uniquely effective dealership and a dominant world market position that went unchallenged until the Japanese Komatsu brand began to expand overseas in the early 1980s.

A channel strategy that is exclusively push or pull oriented is unlikely to be successful, but the relative emphasis between the two strategies will change between product-markets and will reflect marketing objectives and the marketer's resource base. For example, discount electrical superstores regularly advertise aggressively to 'pull' customers into their shops and then use their strong personal selling skills to 'push' products that they and the manufacturers wish to promote.

PHYSICAL DISTRIBUTION DECISIONS

Physical distribution management is an area of traditional weakness in the practice of marketing management. Revolving about the central issues of inventories and transportation, it is a matter that many marketing managers regard as somebody else's problem within the company. Unfortunately this is often the attitude of other functional managers too, with the result that responsibility for stocks and their movement can become sub-divided and never adequately integrated. Yet the physical distribution performance of the company fundamentally affects how well the customer's needs are served and the company's cost structure.

Physical distribution objectives are set in terms of customer service levels on key factors such as delivery time (from customer order to receipt of goods) and policy with regard to whether and how often being out of stock is acceptable. Such objectives are constrained by the cost of offering various service levels: the higher the service level, the greater the cost of providing it becomes. Running counter to this cost relationship is the normal experience that as direct costs are reduced and service levels compromised more and more, sales are lost. So one must carefully account for the cost of lost sales.

Overall, therefore, the objective in managing the physical distribution system is to minimise total cost, taking into account the direct cost of providing various service levels plus the cost of lost sales at each service level. This relationship can be quickly grasped by inspecting Figure 15.2. In (a) it can be seen that as the service level to the customer (measured in terms of days' delivery time) increases, the direct cost of providing the service increases too. In other words, the shorter the delivery that is promised, the greater the cost of transportation becomes. However, (b) indicates that when the promised delivery is very short very few orders are lost, whereas when delivery is extended over a longer period more and more orders are lost to competitors who offer a better service level or to substitute products that perform the same function and are quickly available. Diagram (c) shows how these two contrasting cost curves when added yield a total cost curve that is typically U-shaped. The manager's objective is to manage the system so as to operate at the minimum point on this total cost curve.

Figure 15.2

The Total Cost of Physical Distribution

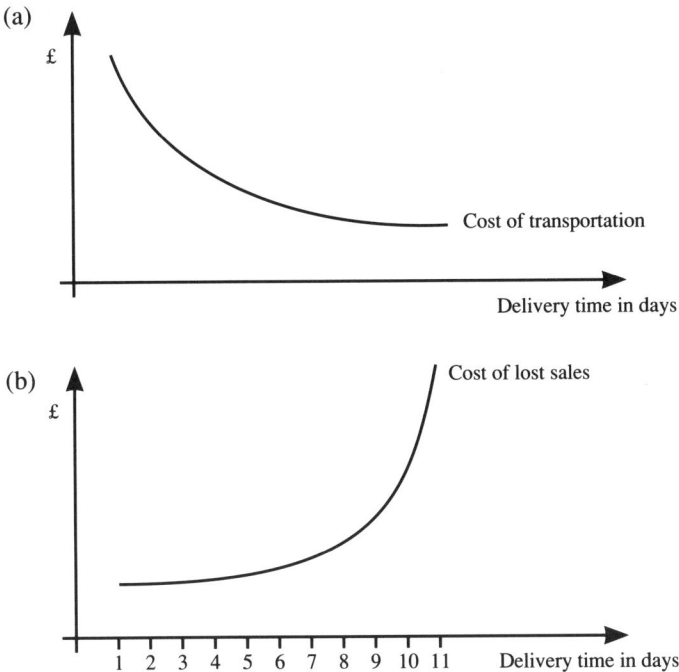

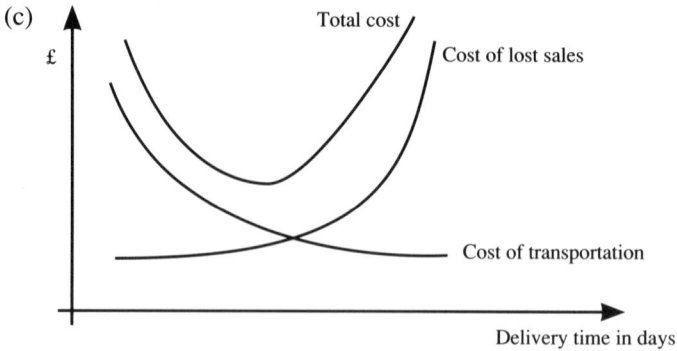

(c) £ — Total cost, Cost of lost sales, Cost of transportation, Delivery time in days

The cost of physical distribution

Physical distribution costs are sometimes difficult to trace, especially in accounting systems that have not been designed with management accounting uses in mind. The typical costs that should be collected and reported for physical distribution include:

—order processing
—packing
—shipping
—warehousing/stockholding, in company and in field
—transportation.

These costs include the cost of financing the stocks held in company and in the field. A careful analysis and evaluation of these costs is essential to any sensible decisions about customer service level standards and to decisions about whether to do the physical distribution job within the company or to 'sub-contract' it. A channel member may be able to deliver the required customer service level at lower total cost because of specialist skills, investment and experience in physical distribution. Companies must consider the trade-off between the cost efficiencies of sub-contracting or using hired haulage as against the service quality benefits but likely overhead costs of company-owned transportation. Many Irish companies have decided in favour of the former.

Estimating the shape of the cost of lost sales function is a much more difficult task because it demands information and managerial judgments about how customers respond to various levels of service. The shape of the curve shown in Figure 15.2 (b) assumes that customers are indifferent to improvements in delivery service better than four days. The company providing a one-day service is therefore incurring extra cost to give the customers what they do not particularly want. However, considerable sensitivity sets in as delivery time goes beyond five days: sales are lost rapidly, and when delivery is quoted at nine or ten days most sales are lost and few won. Beyond ten days the company is out of business!

Estimating the shape of such a curve can be done by market research methods. It can be done by asking customers for the probability of their buying at various service levels. It can be done by examining historical data if different service levels have been offered at different times and if sales records are available as well as the service levels of competitors. Managerial judgment, based on years of experience with customers, can also be quantified to estimate the curve's shape.

Physical distribution and management science models

The physical distribution decisions of warehouse location, stock levels and transport routing are well suited to mathematical modelling and optimisation methods developed over the past twenty years. Once the manager has specified the service levels he wishes to achieve to meet marketing objectives and the resources he has to spend on their attainment, a variety of models may be applied to find optimal or least-cost solutions.

Organisational issues in physical distribution

One of the most common problems that arises in attempting to manage physical distribution more effectively in a company is the typical confusion over responsibility for the area, for elements of customer service, and for elements of the cost of providing the service level. The execution of the physical distribution task is usually a matter for several areas or departments ranging from office administration, accounting, marketing and sales to the transport office, warehouse and perhaps a dispatching office if the company has its own fleet of vans or trucks. The imperative is for management to coordinate across all such areas to achieve the objective set for the system. In organisations with rigid or excessively hierarchical structures and where responsibility for distribution-related tasks is divided across many people and departments, such coordination can be difficult to attain. Situations then arise where the warehouse manager may begin to reduce stock levels to reduce his working capital costs while marketing are attempting to expand sales by increasing service levels! The potential for conflict between different areas of the company pursuing contradictory objectives is very considerable.

The 'process' approach suggested by the value chain or micro business system emphasises the need for the firm to focus on the task that has to be done and to empower the key employees involved in fulfilling this task. This emphasis on the process will sometimes have to go beyond traditional views about functional responsibility and hierarchy. For instance, it is clear from Figure 15.3, which shows the micro business system of a copier manufacturer, that the work involved in physical distribution will impact

Figure 15.3

Managing Physical Distribution in the Micro Business System: A Photocopier Manufacturer

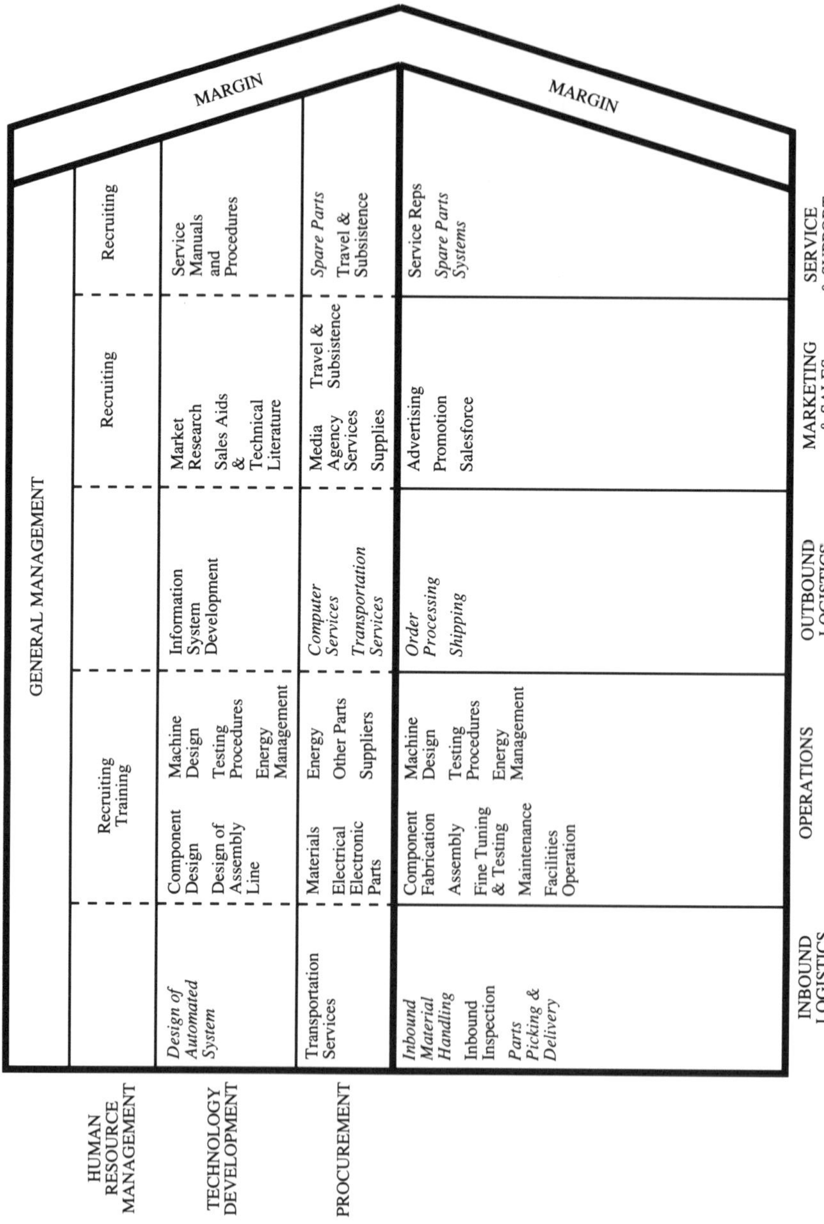
MARGIN
MARGIN
GENERAL MANAGEMENT
HUMAN RESOURCE MANAGEMENT
TECHNOLOGY DEVELOPMENT
PROCUREMENT
Recruiting Training
Recruiting
Recruiting
Design of Automated System
Component Design
Design of Assembly Line
Machine Design
Testing Procedures
Energy Management
Information System Development
Market Research
Sales Aids & Technical Literature
Service Manuals and Procedures
Transportation Services
Materials
Electrical Electronic Parts
Energy
Other Parts
Suppliers
Computer Services
Transportation Services
Media Agency Services
Supplies
Travel & Subsistence
Spare Parts
Travel & Subsistence
Inbound Material Handling
Inbound Inspection
Parts Picking & Delivery
Component Fabrication
Assembly
Fine Tuning & Testing
Maintenance
Facilities Operation
Machine Design
Testing Procedures
Energy Management
Order Processing
Shipping
Advertising
Promotion
Salesforce
Service Reps
Spare Parts Systems
INBOUND LOGISTICS
OPERATIONS
OUTBOUND LOGISTICS
MARKETING & SALES
SERVICE & SUPPORT

Source: Adapted from M. Porter, *Competitive Advantage*, The Free Press, New York 1985, p.47.

across at least six cells in the diagram. Thus coordination and a 'process' frame of managerial mind are crucial.

In larger companies it may be advisable to create a physical distribution management position to coordinate the process, provided that the cost of the manager is recovered by the greater efficiency arising from his work. In the smaller company such an arrangement is usually inappropriate, and general management must ensure that coordination takes place between whatever areas and persons are involved.

Physical distribution and international marketing
One of Ireland's significant comparative disadvantages in international markets is the physical barriers that Irish products must overcome to get to overseas markets. Being an island behind an island on the edge of Europe does little to enhance cost competitiveness when compared with firms located on mainland Europe or North America. Those firms exporting tangible products must therefore pay special attention to the management of the physical distribution area and to the trade-offs that must be made between guaranteeing a competitive service level in Germany or Sweden and the cost-effectiveness of various transportation arrangements and field warehousing closer to the final market under their own control or in the hands of distributors or agents.

SUMMARY
Distribution strategy is based on decisions about the channels through which the company will send its products or services to the market and about the physical arrangements concerning stocks and transportation that ensure an acceptable level of service to customers. Channel decisions involve the selection of appropriate intermediaries after careful evaluation of the options open to a company, using clear criteria for choice. Once chosen, strategy must identify how channels are to be managed and controlled and how these decisions are to serve the broader objectives of the company.

Physical distribution decisions begin with the determination of a customer service level. To provide this level of service the company must hold appropriate stock levels and arrange for transportation and delivery services so as to minimise the total cost of physical distribution, including the cost of lost sales. Concern must also focus on the organisational arrangements for distribution, and the process approach emphasised by the micro business system is relevant in this context.

Reading

Chambers, B. (1989), 'Lowest total cost as a marketing stratagem', *Irish Marketing Review*, vol. 4, no. 3, pp. 29–38.

Fagan, Colm (1991), 'Retail financial services in Europe—banks invade the life assurance market', *Irish Marketing Review*, vol. 5, no. 1.

Hardy, K.G. and Magrath, A.J. (1988), *Marketing Channel Management*, Scott, Foresman and Company, London.

Kotler, P. (1991), *Marketing Management: Analysis, Planning, Implementation and Control*, 7th ed., Prentice-Hall, Englewood Cliffs, NJ, ch. 20.

McDonald, M.H.B. (1984), *Marketing Plans: How to Prepare Them & How to Use Them*, Heinemann, London, ch. 10.

Parker, A.J. (1991), 'Retail environments: into the 1990s', *Irish Marketing Review*, vol. 5, no. 2, pp. 61–72.

Porter, Michael (1985), *Competitive Advantage*, The Free Press, NY.

Reynolds, J. (1991), 'Is there a market for teleshopping?', *Irish Marketing Review*, vol. 5, no. 2, pp. 39–51.

Sparks, L. (1991), 'Retailing in the 1990s: differentiation through customer service?', *Irish Marketing Review*, vol. 5, no. 2, pp. 28–38.

Stern, L.W. and El-Ansary, A. (1988), *Marketing Channels*, 3rd ed., Prentice-Hall, Englewood Cliffs, NJ.

Treadgold, A. (1991), 'The emerging internationalisation of retailing: present status and future challenges', *Irish Marketing Review*, vol. 5, no. 2, pp. 11–27.

West, Alan (1989), *Managing Distribution and Change—The Total Distribution Concept*, Wiley, NY.

Review Questions
1. Explain the difference between channel decisions and physical distribution decisions.
2. Identify five criteria for use in evaluating alternative channels of distribution and show how they help the marketer to choose the most appropriate alternative.
3. Distinguish between an exclusive, selective and intensive distribution approach. What kinds of products are typically distributed with each of these?
4. Explain the concept of customer service level as used in the context of physical distribution decisions and show how an optimal service level may be chosen.

Chapter 16

Strategic Marketing

INTRODUCTION

So far in Part III we have explored the elements of marketing decision-making. We have seen that this involves choosing which markets to serve; how to position the company and its services or products in those chosen markets so as to serve customers and outperform competitors; and the development of detailed policies concerning the specific product or service, its price, the way in which to communicate informatively and persuasively about it and the manner in which to distribute it to customers.

These decisions are central to the effectiveness of marketing in any organisation and to the effectiveness of the whole organisation. They are also decisions that commit the organisation over appreciable periods of time. Having chosen a market to serve, organisations are ill-advised to change their minds whimsically or frequently. Having chosen a way of serving the market through their positioning decisions they are equally ill-advised to alter their market and competitive positioning casually or too frequently. Similarly, the basic commitments and investment embodied in product or service design, in product development and production, in pricing structures, in communication investment, and in distribution channels and logistics are not readily changed other than in the medium to long term. All this implies that these decisions are *strategic* in nature—they run to the very heart of both marketing and organisational effectiveness and they are not easily altered in the short run. They are therefore part of what we call strategic marketing and are shaped within the overall strategic management process in a company.

In addition to these issues, our earlier discussion in Part I implied many commitments which are fundamentally strategic in nature—the orientation of a company towards markets which we called *market focus*; the dimensions of the marketing manager's job that are future oriented and investment oriented; and the necessity to build competitive market advantage within the industry business system. The first three parts of the book have therefore had an underlying structure that emphasises the strategic nature of marketing and of the decisions for which the marketing manager is responsible. In this chapter we will draw these elements together to stress how marketing decision-making shapes strategy and how strategy and strategic thinking must shape the individual decisions embedded in marketing management practice.

IMPORTANT THEMES IN STRATEGIC MARKETING

Discussion of current thinking about strategic marketing cannot proceed without devoting time to some themes which characterise the debate about its nature and content. In this chapter four themes that seem to be especially important to the thrust of this book and to managerial practice are discussed briefly before an approach to strategic marketing planning is described. These four issues are:

- the concept of market focus
- the relationship between strategic management and strategic marketing
- the concept of competitive market advantage
- the importance to effective market focus of managing organisational interfaces.

Market focus

In Chapter 1 we noted the initial emergence of a *marketing orientation* sometime during the 1950s as a perspective on business that characterised many successful companies. This reflected a realisation that the core market-related task was not to make products, or to sell what factories could produce, but rather to understand market demand well enough to specify who to serve and what to provide to the market in the form of valued products or services. It was from this perspective that the 'marketing concept' emerged as a guiding company-wide philosophy: a belief that profits and competitive success derive from seeing customer needs as the guiding principle in strategy and from coordinating company activities to serve customer needs profitably.

This shift in orientation in companies mirrored the growth of markets characterised by abundance of supply—buyers' markets. Given plentiful supply in developed countries, buyers became more demanding and discriminating and the route to competitive success was clearly signalled to competing firms: know your customer better than your competitors do and you will win the business. We noted that a more recent phase has seen the development of the *market-focused* company. Intense competition for sophisticated customers in markets on local and global scale has seen the adoption of broad market orientation by all successful firms. The sources of strategic success have therefore moved in a fashion that demands not just marketing orientation but deeper focus on which customer groups to serve with what products through what configuration of company resources in the form of a micro business system (company value chain). Market focus demands that we maintain the focus on and commitment to carefully chosen markets but also that we reach back into the organisation to develop and focus its resources on the markets of choice.

Leading companies display a commitment to market focus in many ways. These range from the detail with which they segment markets (in many markets companies now use one-customer segments—individual major accounts in corporate banking; key accounts in chemical manufacturing; individual consumers in the lists of direct marketers; and so on) to the ways in which they configure their resource base in the form of a unique micro business system to deliver a product or service promise to a customer. One sees this in the case of banking, which has abandoned its traditional single delivery system, the retail branch, in favour of a great diversity of specialised delivery systems that include branch networks but also encompass telebanking, direct selling, electronic banking, credit-card-based services, ATMs—to mention just a few of the optional delivery mechanisms for financial services in the nineties.

Market focus represents a further development of the approach embodied in the marketing-oriented firm. It extends the emphasis on refined segmentation. It has evolved more sophisticated ways of bringing products and services accurately to market through new delivery systems. It has a special accent on competitive effectiveness as well as customer service. And in striving for these achievements it has placed new emphasis on the importance of organisational arrangements both within and between firms as the bases for securing market focus and business success. In Chapter 1 we also noted the need to reappraise the traditional emphasis on short-term market transactions and to deal with the nature of the *relationship-based* markets that have evolved. Marketing, we suggested, is increasingly a matter of managing networks and relationships within which transactions take place. Sound established relationships are of great strategic value in highly competitive and mature markets and demand a movement towards a definition of marketing which stresses mutual profitability for both buyer and seller—marketing based on the elusive 'win-win' strategy of game theory! Aer Rianta's business with Russia and other Eastern European countries illustrates such an approach (Exhibit 16.1).

The concepts of market focus are therefore expanding our perspective on marketing. The perspective is fundamentally strategic in nature, being based on assumptions about the vital interdependence of business strategy and organisation, company performance, market and competitive realities and marketing action.

Exhibit 16.1

AER RIANTA AND AEROFLOT

Strategic alliances in practice

The political and economic changes in Eastern Europe are providing Western industrialised countries with trading opportunities that are potentially attractive yet fraught with difficulties. In the foreseeable future joint ventures, cooperative agreements and strategic alliances are likely to be the most effective ways for many companies to do business in Eastern Europe. The Western partner is provided with access to a marketplace which has many complex characteristics, while the Eastern partner enjoys a transfer of management, marketing, production, technological and financial know-how. Aer Rianta, Ireland's National Airports Authority, has been involved in such a strategic alliance in Russia with Aeroflot for a number of years. It has been highly successful for both parties and has proven to be the springboard for a range of commercial activities.

The origins of the partnership go back over a decade. Aeroflot was a regular user of Shannon Airport for refuelling stops. A scheme to store fuel of Soviet origin at Shannon and a number of subsequent fuel bartering arrangements enabled Aeroflot to reduce substantially its hard currency commitments. Thus with the advent of *perestroika* it seemed natural that the two companies would explore avenues of possible partnership in the then Soviet Union. Aer Rianta has now over a dozen different business ventures trading successfully in Russia with Aeroflot and with a range of other partners throughout the former Soviet Union. Activities include running duty-free shops, a supermarket, bars, catering, in-flight duty-free sales, construction, import/export, accommodation rental and computer assembly.

The success or failure of a joint venture depends upon many different variables including the ability to achieve integration of cultures, styles and personalities. One of the major stumbling blocks for Aer Rianta was the lack of understanding of the concepts of service and quality—the concept of the customer as king was a somewhat alien notion in the command economy. Changing these approaches involved intensive reorientation and training of local staff as well as a lot of role modelling by Irish management and front-line staff.

Finding the right partner is the first crucial consideration in a joint venture in Eastern Europe. It is important to ensure that the prospective partner is not made up of 'yesterday's men' and that both partners share the vision of what the joint venture is seeking to achieve in terms of objectives, quality, value-for-money, long-term versus short-term profitability and so on. The first joint venture is the hardest. Aer Rianta's experience has been that it can take a considerable length of time to complete a first joint venture agreement, whereas additional agreements can be easier. This has to do with 'learning the ropes and establishing a trust' on both sides and also with the benefits of establishing a reasonable track record.

Source: D. Keogh, 'Strategic alliances in practice: the case of Aer Rianta and Aeroflot', *Irish Marketing Review*, vol. 5, no. 3, 1990/1991.

Strategic management and strategic marketing

The job of the marketing manager as discussed in Chapter 3 is to manage the marketing function in an organisation. This function is at the centre of the process of matching *customer needs* with *company competences* to produce *products and services* that are *competitively superior* and therefore capable of yielding *sustained profitability*. Successful management of the tasks of the marketing function in any business generates a self-perpetuating cycle of customer satisfaction, profitability, the further development of core competence and, in consequence, enhanced ability to serve existing and new markets and to outperform competitors. This process and the associated managerial role emphasises how central marketing activity must be in business development and strategic management. However, the performance of this task can be meaningful only when integrated fully with the work of other functions and with the strategic management of the whole enterprise.

In Chapter 3 we summarised the job of the marketing manager as encompassing the central tasks of *creating and maintaining the reality of a market-focused organisation;* analysing customers, markets and their dynamics; marketing planning; managing the many interdependencies between marketing and the other business functions; exercising decision-making skills; and implementing marketing control and marketing audit procedures. In this view of the marketing manager's job, the necessity for the manager to manage the marketing function, to think and plan strategically, to nurture the philosophy of market focus in the company also pointed to the inescapable necessity for effective integration of marketing tasks and activities with those of other functions in the business and with the general management of the total enterprise. The marketing manager is of necessity a member of the strategic management team just as all members of this team must be marketers in viewpoint and persuasion.

Competitive market advantage

In Chapter 2 we viewed the individual organisation as a microcosm of the industry business system within which it seeks to live. Analysis of the firm's micro business system leads to an understanding of the company's cost structure and its value-creating abilities. The analysis also helps to establish the role of marketing and the leverage which marketing activity has on overall company performance. The interdependence between marketing and other company activities and the importance of ensuring integrated planning and action was seen as one of the central concerns of the market-focused company.

The analysis of business systems and micro business systems leads to decisions about how to compete effectively. The role of marketing is to build *market-based competitive advantage* for the organisation, just as the operations manager is charged with creating advantage based in the operations or manufacturing activities. As a strategist, the aim of the marketer is therefore to create advantage over competing organisations in a manner that cannot be readily imitated. This idea led us to the notion of *sustainable competitive advantage (SCA)* as represented in a three-dimensional array. The sources of such advantage are generally regarded as rooted in the *perceived value* of the product or service to customers, in the *relative cost in use* of its products or services, and in the chosen *scope* of its business. Competitive market advantage may therefore be seen as rooted in choices about whether to compete on the basis of high perceived value, low delivered cost, or broad or narrow market scope, or any combination of these. These are also the roots of generic competitive advantage for the whole organisation, so marketing's task must be seen as contributing to an understanding of the market bases of advantage and to investment in the sources of market advantage. Clearly these are fundamental strategic activities which define the competitive aspects of strategic marketing but which can be undertaken only if marketing action is intimately integrated with the overall strategic management of the enterprise.

Managing interfaces

Arising from the necessity to programme the implementation of strategic marketing decisions, and indeed to test their organisational feasibility, the marketer must always confront the challenge of managing across organisational interfaces or boundaries. The interfaces with manufacturing or operations management, with R & D, with human resource management, with finance and with top management are vital to good decision-making and to effective implementation. The nineties began with a widespread concern in industry about the tradition of organisational specialisation around functions and an acute awareness of the competitive damage that can be done when such specialisation is taken to an extreme. The Ford Motor Company began to talk of the dangers of 'chimney stack' management; Hewlett Packard spoke of the damage caused by 'silo management'. The images were intended to suggest the organisational problem of managers who felt as if they worked at the bottom of a silo or chimney and could communicate to their colleagues in other functions only if they climbed right to the top of the organisation and then back down the adjacent chimney. Under such circumstances, timely and effective horizontal communication becomes a virtual impossibility. Both companies and researchers became alarmed at the extent to which organisational fortresses could be built in companies that made communication and coordination across functional boundaries difficult or impossible, and began to search for more fluid organisational mechanisms to break down such barriers or to prevent their occurrence.

The design of 'flat' rather than 'tall' (and deeply hierarchical) organisations is one result. The emphasis on cross-functional task forces and temporary special groupings is another. The marketer has a special need for sensitivity to these interfacing challenges since marketing sits at the interface between an organisation and its market environment. Marketing action can be effective only if it can communicate market realities to all parts of the organisation and if it can mobilise all parts of the organisation to invent, design, produce, deliver and support a service or product for the market. This is the essence of market focus—focus on the market on the one hand and market focusing of the whole organisation on the other.

THE ELEMENTS OF STRATEGIC MARKETING DECISIONS

We have emphasised that the task of the marketing manager is to conduct systematic analysis of markets, competitors and his own organisation in order to make decisions about marketing action that are logical and that acknowledge the uncertainties, assumptions and risks associated with decision-making in an unpredictable world. One simple way to summarise the required analysis is to codify it as involving '**6Cs**' of marketing analysis:

> Customers
> Competitors
> Context
> Channels
> Company
> Costs

Among these, what is meant by analysis of *customers* and *competitors* is now self-evident (Chapters 4 and 6). Analysis of *context* refers to developing an understanding of the broad forces that shape markets and competition in arm's-length fashion—social trends, demography, science and technology, the law, public regulation of markets and competition, political structures and philosophy and so on. By *channels* we mean not just the immediate marketing channels of the firm but also the whole business system structure that characterises an industry and that brings final products into existence through a long linkage of activities from the sourcing of raw materials in nature to the provision of after-sales service, support and indeed recycling. Analysis of the *company* refers to the kind of scrutiny of internal strengths, weaknesses and core competences that was discussed in Chapter 7. Finally, we have separated out the analysis of *costs* from the general company analysis to highlight the extent to which cost competitiveness is central to survival and success and to provide some counterbalance to a traditional tendency to assume that, from the point of view of marketing, company cost structures are given. Marketing decisions, viewed strategically, determine cost structures just as much as they are determined by them.

If an analysis of the '6Cs' is undertaken, then one might summarise the decisions which must be taken as the '3Ms':

Market Choice
Market Positioning
Marketing Mix

Decisions about *market choice*—the commitment to targeting the company and its competences on specific markets—are of the most fundamental strategic importance and are an essential part of the larger strategic management process of 'defining the business'. Decisions about the *positioning* of the company in those chosen markets so that customers' needs are served in a competitively superior and competence-enhancing manner are significantly driven by market and marketing-related considerations. But they must be integrated with all the other organisational sources of positional, or competitive, advantage. Finally the policy decisions about the *marketing mix* components reflect marketing's investment in the implementation of a strategy for market-based advantage.

These elements of strategic marketing analysis and decision-making are usually brought together formally in a marketing plan which in turn is one part of a business plan or strategic plan for an organisation. The plan will normally specify the measurement and control mechanisms that are required for implementation in addition to these analytical facts, assumptions and decisions.

FORMULATING MARKETING STRATEGY

How does one go about the business of strategic marketing? The answer to this is as much about the process of strategic management and marketing as it is about the content of strategic marketing. A fundamental process framework is suggested in Figure 16.1 as the framework for the remaining description and discussion of how strategic marketing decisions are made.

The audit of the 'status quo' comprises the two steps of internal and external analysis. In general it is wiser to begin with the external analysis as this allows a fresher and less blinkered assessment of the internal situation afterwards. In order to conduct the analysis, external factors revolving about customers, competitors, context and channels (four of the '6Cs') are scrutinised to isolate the opportunities and threats facing the company and to specify the key factors for success (KSFs) dictated by the industry (see Figure 16.2).

Figure 16.1

Strategic Marketing: A Decision-Making Framework

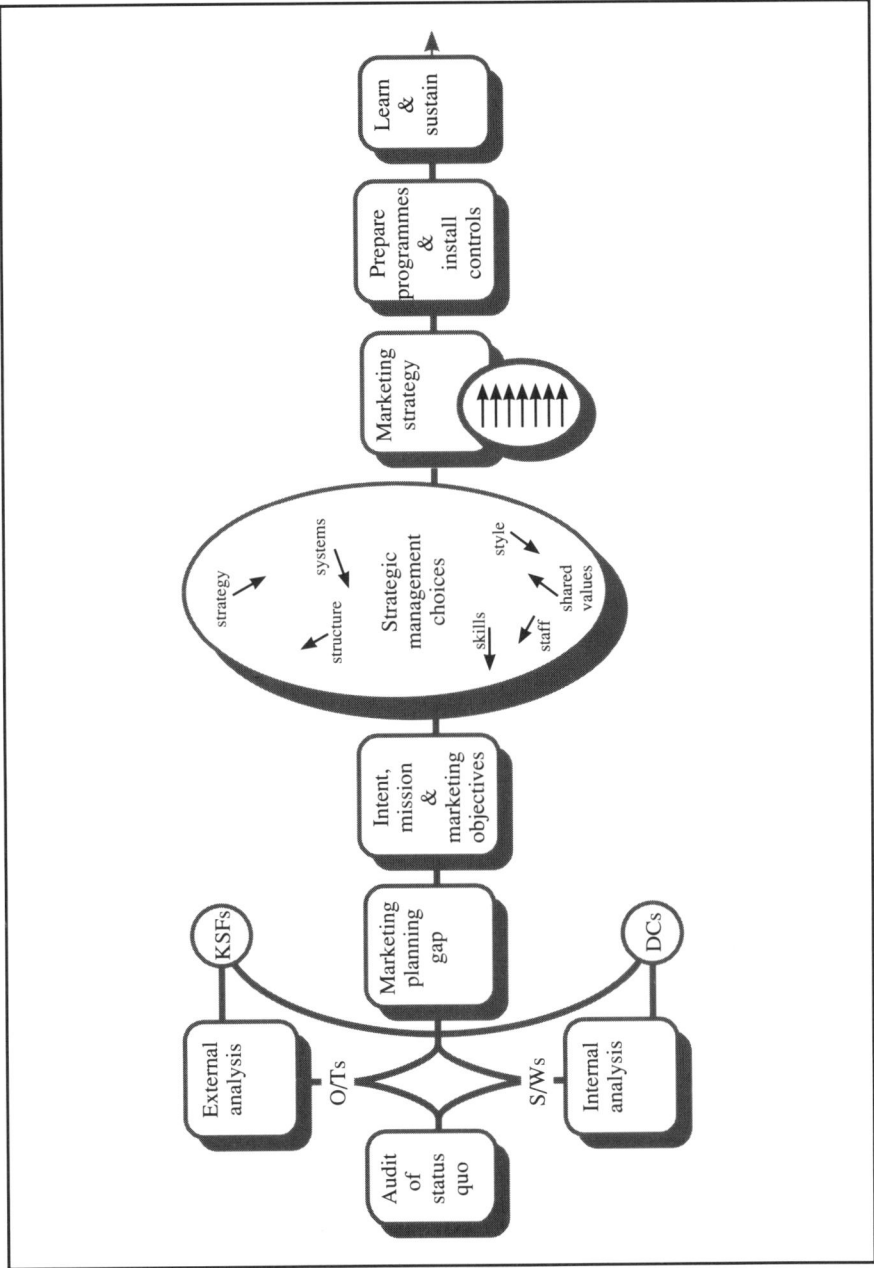

Figure 16.2

Where We Are Now ...

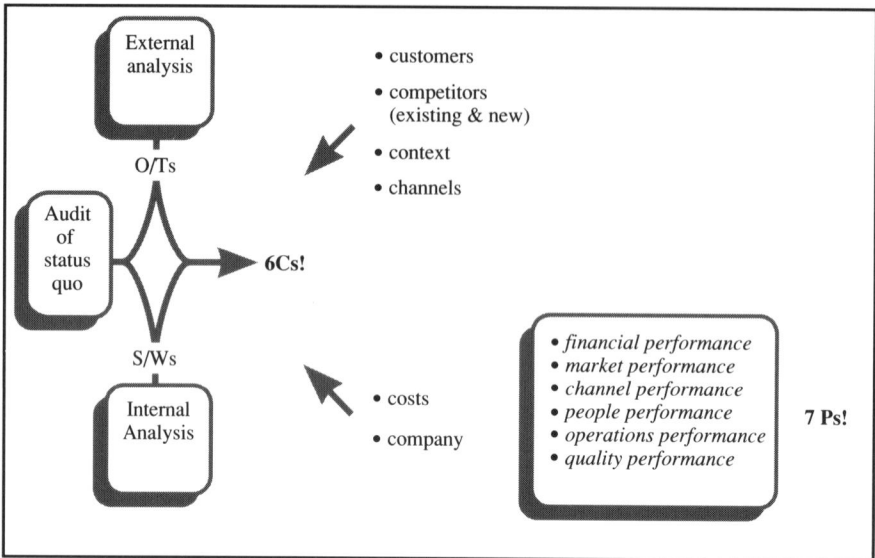

Based on this the manager is in a position to use the key success factors dictated by the environment as a test for any strategy proposal. Internal factors to do with the company's strengths and weaknesses and its core and distinctive competences (DCs) are isolated by analysing the company's past and current performance, its resource base and its cost structures ('7Ps'). Based on this work the manager must be conscious of the need to invest in the company's distinctive competences, since these and these alone confer competitive advantage. For the marketing manager this will frequently necessitate working with other managers when important distinctive competences lie elsewhere in the organisation—for example in R & D, in design, or in a unique manufacturing process. It will also necessitate working across organisational boundaries when the marketing manager has to persuade others to allocate scarce funds to investment in 'marketing assets' such as brands or distribution channels.

Emerging out of this review of where the company stands it is possible to establish a gap between current performance and that desired by the company in terms of profitability, future growth and risk. Such gap analysis helps to quantify the nature and magnitude of strategic realignment required. It measures what has to be achieved. Too often strategic intent can be seen as some vague aspiration to perform better than is currently the case. Gap analysis puts figures on the aspirations.

Marketing must contribute to the definition of this gap. In Figure 16.3 'business as usual' implies no major change in existing strategies, a 'steady-as-she-goes' regime that is unlikely to lead to significant increases in profitability. 'Doing it better' indicates an intention to improve company performance in its various activities in response to key factors for success in the industry. 'Doing it differently' suggests the determination on the part of the firm consciously and continually to realign its distinctive and core competences, and consequently its product and service offerings, in recognition of lasting and real-time needs in the marketplace—in essence, being a truly market-focused company. This may sometimes involve a very substantial change in how the firm does its business—a significant reconfiguring or re-engineering of its micro business system or value chain.

If the sources of market advantage can be isolated and the nature of the performance gap defined then a mission statement and specific marketing objectives may be established (see Figure 16.4). Clearly, marketing objectives must be consistent with overall company mission and objectives. An organisation's mission statement represents a short and pithy summary of the organisation's core objective or *raison d'être* and how it intends to fulfil this, and usually identifies its key competences, product/service offerings, and markets served. Such a statement can be used for both external and internal communication— to customers, suppliers, financiers, the community on one hand, and to staff and organisation members on the other. Exhibit 16.2 shows the mission statements of The Kerry Group plc and The Marketing Institute and illustrates how central market-related factors are.

Figure 16.3

Where We Want to Be ...

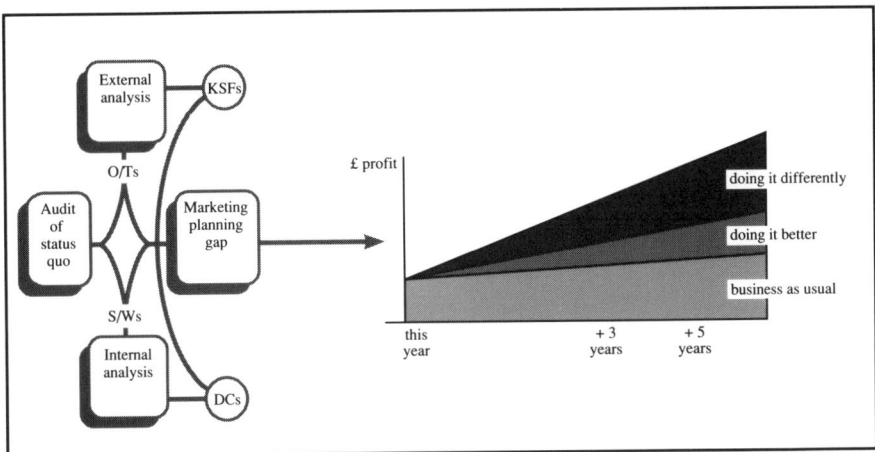

Exhibit 16.2

MISSION STATEMENTS

The Kerry Group plc

The Kerry Group will become a major international food and food ingredient corporation, with significant market share in both Europe and the USA.

Kerry will dominate selected markets, through technological leadership, superior product quality, superior service to its customers, and the unique whole-hearted commitment of each employee.

The Kerry Group will continue to grow at an annual rate of 15 per cent in sales revenue over the next five years.

The Marketing Institute

The Marketing Institute is the professional body representing nearly 6,000 marketing practitioners and students in Ireland. The mission of the Institute is 'to position the marketing profession as the crucial factor for business success'. It aims to pursue this by:

- Being the recognised, authoritative and representative body for the marketing profession in Ireland.
- Endowing membership with intrinsic value and providing 'value-added' members' services.
- Providing a lifetime environment for marketing career development.
- Enhancing marketing practice through education and training.
- Ensuring acceptance of the role and contribution of marketing in business and in society.
- Requiring quality and excellence in all aspects of the Institute's activities.

At this point it is important for the marketer to consider the full array of interdependencies between marketing objectives and the strategic management of the whole organisation (see Figure 16.5). Marketing objectives will make sense and be attainable only if they can be integrated with all dimensions of the overall strategic management task. Hence, marketing proposals must fit with overall strategy and must be consistent with organisational structures, systems, the skills of managers and employees, the style of management, the staff resources and the shared values to which those in the organisation subscribe. If there is inconsistency between what is proposed and these factors then it is *inevitable* that implementation will be ineffective and that marketing objectives will remain unachieved. Marketing, through its participation in the strategic management process, shares responsibility for creating and managing *alignment* among the critical organisational elements as represented by the arrows in Figure 16.5.

Figure 16.4

Saying What It Means ...

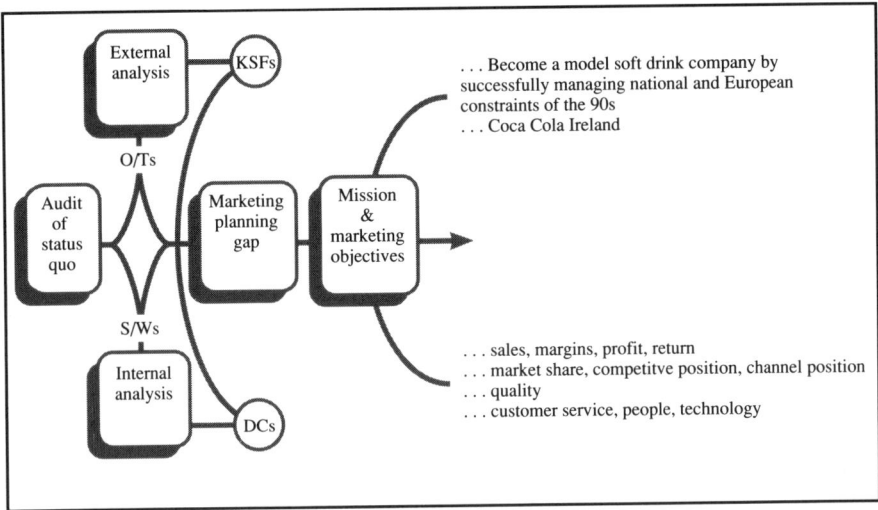

Figure 16.5

Connect to Strategic Management ...

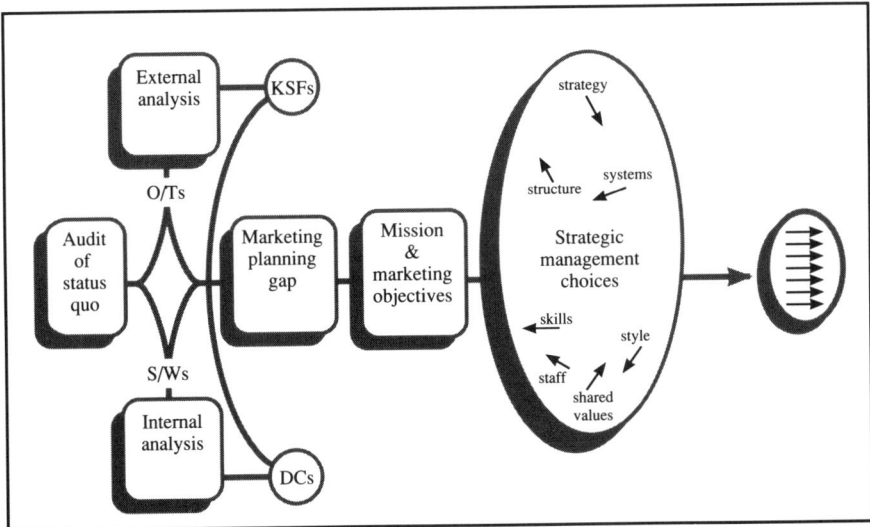

The next step in the process is to deal with the issues discussed in Parts II and III of this book: to identify and evaluate the marketing policy options open to the company in terms of how it can choose markets, compete, grow, manage its portfolio of products and markets, enhance its profitability and collaborate to achieve aims that are unattainable acting in isolation (see Figure 16.6).

Figure 16.6

Options for Getting There ...

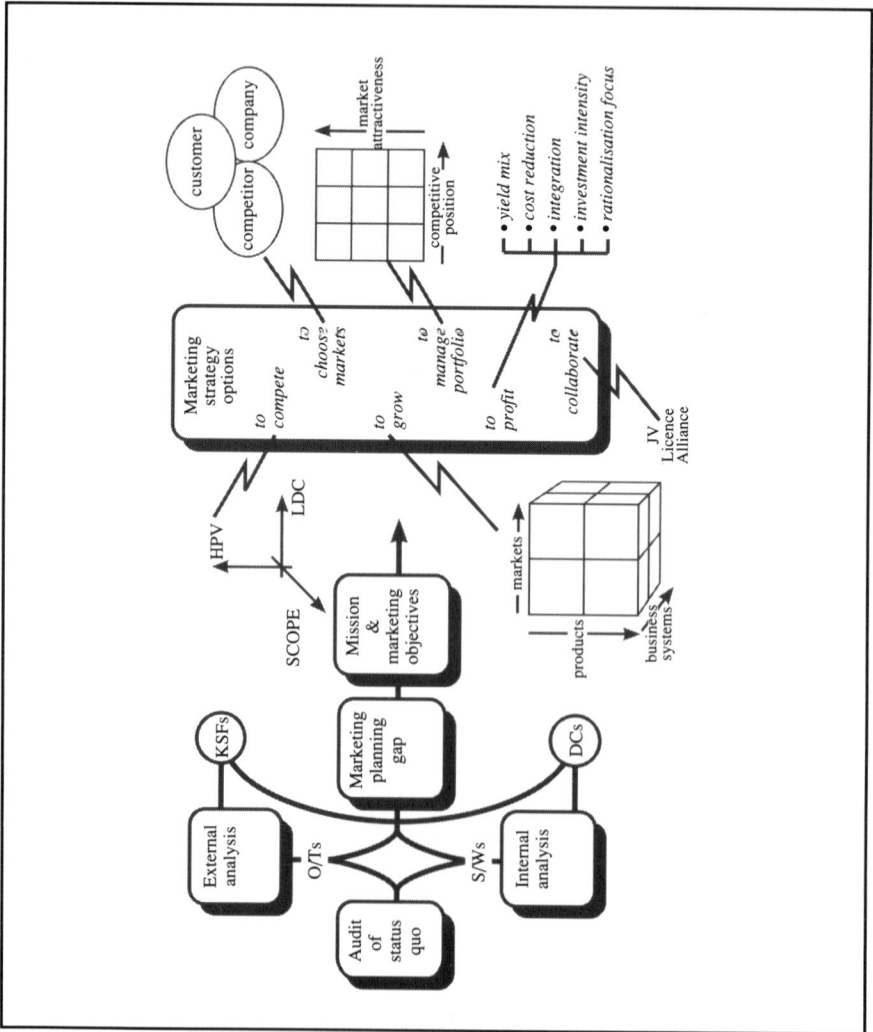

Implementing marketing strategy

Considering and evaluating these options leads to specific decisions about the **'3Ms'**—market choice, market positioning and marketing mix—and these must then be programmed for implementation. This latter process involves the identification of the various programmes of action that are necessary; budgeting for the resources required, allocating authority and responsibility to individuals to get the work done, and establishing the time frame within which all actions must be completed. This effectively creates a set of measures and controls which will tell the manager whether or not objectives have been achieved as planned (see Figure 16.7). These issues are addressed in greater depth in Part IV.

Figure 16.7

Making It Happen ...

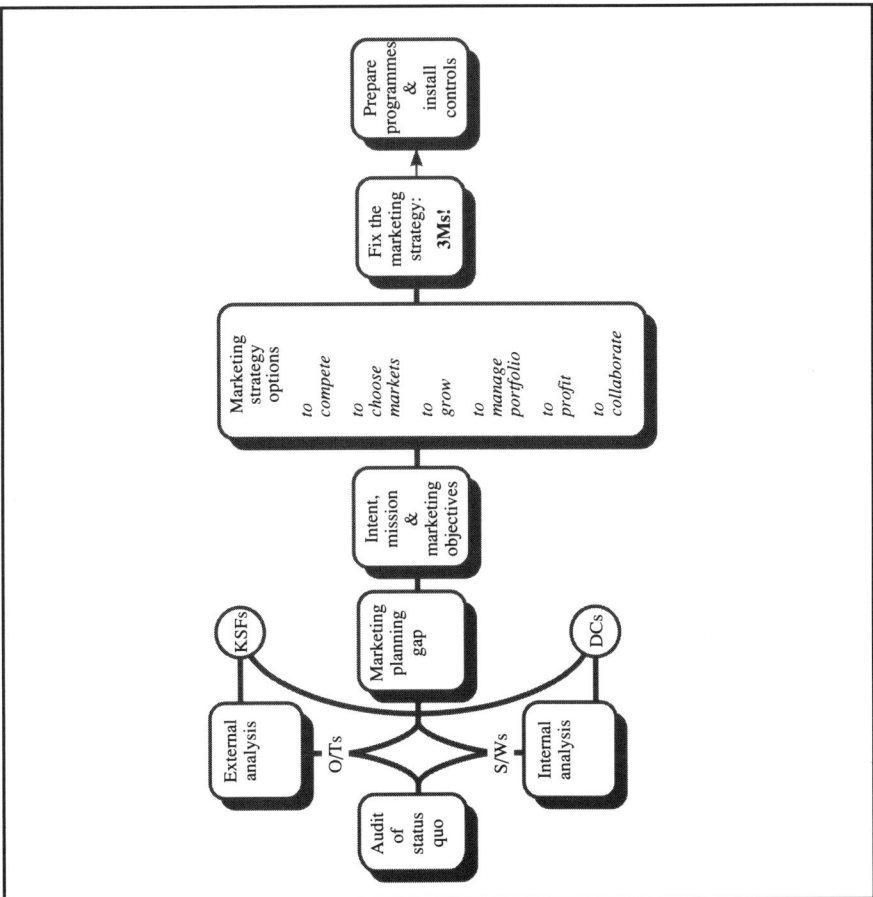

Figure 16.8

Ultimately, Managing Marketing = Learning ...

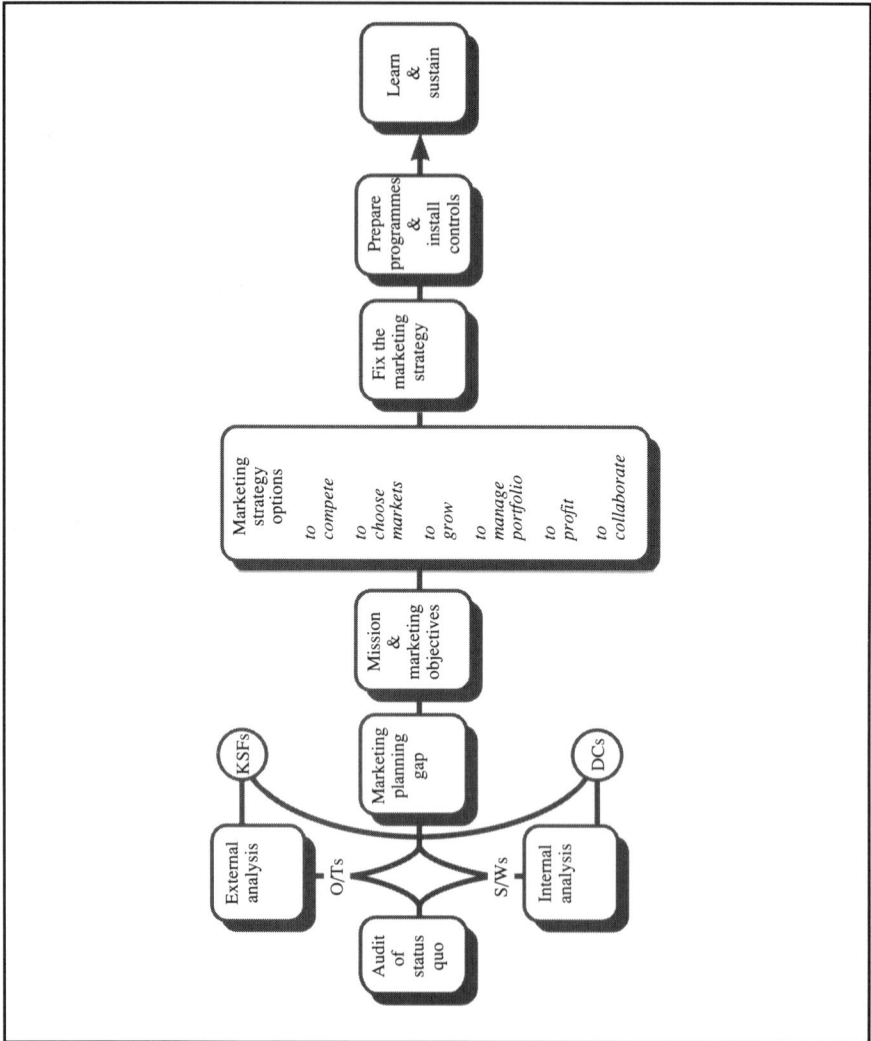

Learn
&
sustain

Prepare
programmes
&
install
controls

Fix the
marketing
strategy

Marketing
strategy
options

*to
compete*

*to
choose
markets*

*to
grow*

*to
manage
portfolio*

*to
profit*

*to
collaborate*

Mission
&
marketing
objectives

Marketing
planning
gap

KSFs

DCs

External
analysis

O/Ts

S/Ws

Internal
analysis

Audit
of
status
quo

Learning and sustaining

Based on this process all those involved are then in a position to learn from
experience, to refine their analysis and judgments and to adapt their strategies
and actions (see Figure 16.8). Strategic marketing if well managed is therefore
a learning process and learning is one of the most fundamental marks of
intelligence whether in the individual or embodied in an organisation in the

form of embedded knowledge. Much of this learning will be gradual and incremental and thus strategy will often evolve as a matter of degree rather than experience radical change. Strategy can have as much to do with managing stability as it has to do with managing change. Considerable realignment of strategy is of course sometimes necessary and the process we have described should inform the manager as to the degree of change that is appropriate. The final part of the book explores the ways in which companies can sustain competitive advantage created through the strategic marketing process.

SUMMARY

Decisions which are *strategic* in nature run to the very heart of both marketing and organisational effectiveness and are not easily altered in the short run. They are therefore part of what we call strategic marketing and are shaped within the overall strategic management process in a company. Some important themes which underpin the nature and content of strategic marketing were examined. Key elements and techniques of strategic analysis were also discussed. A framework for decision-making in strategic marketing was presented and the reader taken through it in a step-wise manner. Finally, in anticipation of Parts IV and V, issues of implementation and the nature of learning in the market-focused organisation were introduced.

Reading

Aaker, David (1992), *Strategic Market Planning*, 3rd ed., Wiley, NY.

Abell, D.F. and Hammond, J.S. (1979), *Strategic Market Planning: Problems and Analytical Approaches*, Prentice-Hall, Englewood Cliffs, NJ.

Abell, D.F. (1980), *Defining the Business: The Starting Point of Strategic Planning*, Prentice-Hall, Englewood Cliffs, NJ.

Baker, Michael J. (1992), *Marketing Strategy and Management*, 2nd ed., Macmillan, Basingstoke, chs. 4, 5.

Day, G.S. (1984), *Strategic Market Planning*, West Publishing Company, St Paul.

Day, G.S. (1986), *Analysis for Strategic Market Decisions*, West Publishing Company, St Paul.

Day, G.S. (1990), *Market Driven Strategy: Processes for Creating Value*, The Free Press, NY.

Keogh, Derek (1990/1991), 'Strategic alliances in practice: the case of Aer Rianta and Aeroflot', *Irish Marketing Review*, vol. 5, no. 3.

Kerin, R.A., Mahajan, V. and Varadarajan, P.R. (1990), *Contemporary Perspectives on Strategic Market Planning*, Allyn & Bacon, NY.

Murray, John A. (1986), 'Reflections on the new competition: Japan, marketing and Ireland', *Irish Marketing Review*, vol. 1.

Review Questions

1. How are the various elements of marketing analysis and decision-making drawn together in strategic marketing?
2. Take any concept or component in strategic marketing and elaborate on it in detail.
3. Set out a framework for decision-making in strategic marketing and explain why it is ultimately a process activity.
4. Apply such a framework or process to a company or organisation with which you are familiar. Use the blank diagram in Appendix A to direct and summarise your work.

APPENDIX A

Try to fill in the blanks for your own company.

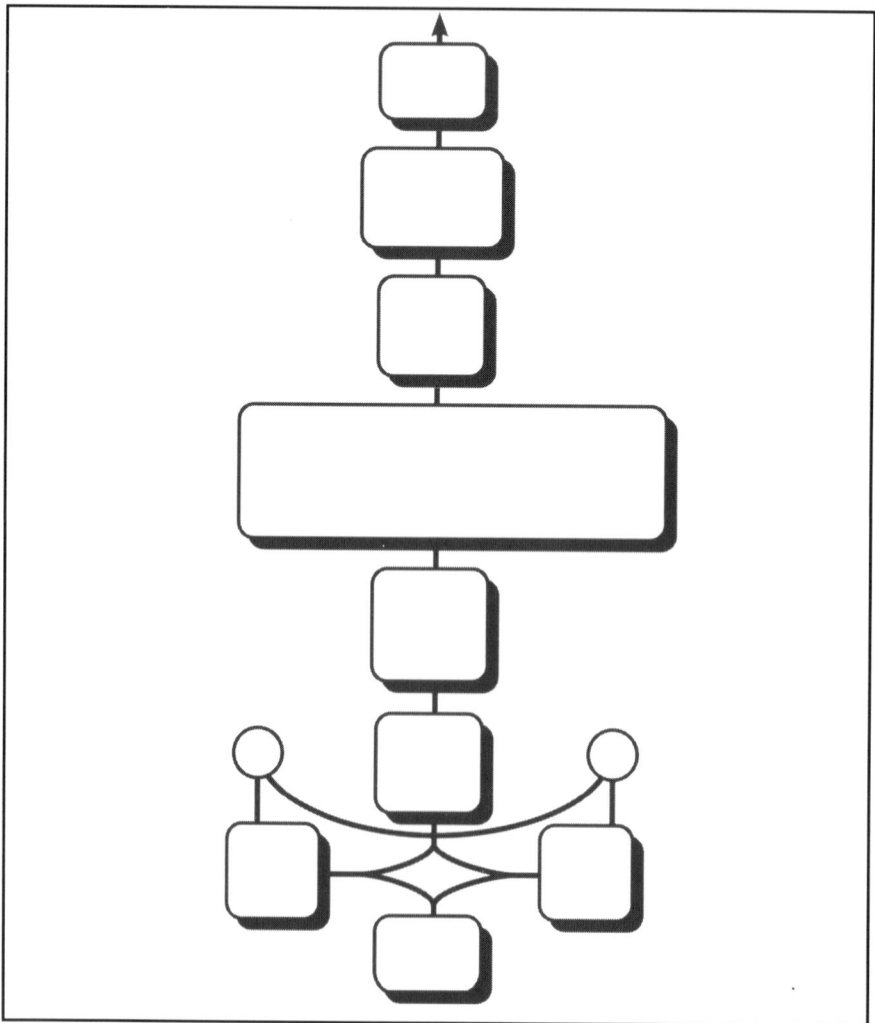

Slims Matches

In 1985 Maguire and Paterson, match-maker and distributor of an FMCG range, introduced Slims, a slimline match aimed at the image-conscious younger female market. Its research had identified a niche in the growing number of women using disposable lighters who might be attracted to a neater chic match. Slims matches were launched with considerable pzazz and expenditure on advertising, promotion and brand support, including a TV campaign. The product was withdrawn from the market eighteen months after the launch.

Issues: Market segmentation. Return on investment. Pricing, promotion and merchandising. Product cannibalisation. Role of market research.

A CENTURY OF MATCH-MAKING

A children's street rhyme celebrates the match-making of the Maguire and Paterson company at Hammond Lane in the historical Smithfield area of Dublin city. The company was founded in 1882 to manufacture matches, 'the greatest boon and blessing that had come to mankind in the nineteenth century', according to philosopher Herbert Spencer. From its factory at Hammond Lane, Maguire and Paterson flourished to become the sole manufacturer of matches in Ireland and the dominant supplier to the market.

If its match-making was to catch the imagination of local street lore, the company's development also reflected, in a number of aspects, that of the country itself. In its early years Maguire and Paterson exhibited something of a patriotic streak—matchboxes in the company museum are branded Parnell matches, Solus na nGaedhael matches and Land League matches. In the late thirties Maguire and Paterson entered into a long-standing technology transfer agreement with Bryant and May, the largest match- maker in the UK. When Maguire and Paterson obtained a quotation on the Dublin Stock Exchange in 1959, Bryant and May acquired 26 per cent and subsequently 33 per cent of this equity. This association with Bryant and May helped over the years to ensure that the hallmark of Maguire and Paterson was efficiency in the manufacture of a high-quality match, comparable to any produced in the world. Production in the company was fully integrated in that as well as making

This case was developed as a basis for class discussion rather than to illustrate either effective or ineffective handling of an administrative situation.

matches it made and printed its own matchboxes, though the wooden sticks or plints were imported. This emphasis on a high-calibre product allied to a moderate pricing policy deterred the entry of any new match manufacturers and won the company a market share of over 90 per cent until the mid-seventies with its two brands, Cara and Friendly.

From its Dublin headquarters a transport fleet distributed its products nationally to large retailers, multiple stores and wholesalers. The smaller retailer bought from the wholesaler or the cash-and-carry outlet. This distribution was backed up by a small salesforce which helped to develop sales by fostering new outlets and by liaison with multiples and wholesalers on problems of discount, service and quality. In general, the company laid great emphasis on continuity and enjoyed excellent industrial relations among its 160 employees. Decision-making and policy formulation in the company was tightly concentrated in a small group of four senior managers, the chief executive, the production manager, the financial controller and the sales manager. The style of management was conservative and production-oriented and, like the company's advertising of the period, somewhat unimaginative.

A NEW DIRECTION

However, by the mid-seventies it was clear that a storm-cloud, in the form of a change in consumer behaviour, was threatening Maguire and Paterson's profitability both in the immediate future and in the longer term. Put simply, people were beginning to smoke less—and some 70 per cent of matches were used to light cigarettes, the rest for domestic purposes. The evidence of cigarettes' damaging effects to health and the growth of public health lobbies were beginning to slow cigarette sales in many developed countries, including Ireland (see Exhibit 1). To aggravate matters further, the growing sales of imported disposable lighters in Ireland were beginning by the mid-seventies to make noticeable inroads into the demand for matches. In many other countries the advent of such disposable lighters had serious adverse effects on match sales. Lower-priced imported matches from Eastern European countries were also starting to register a higher share of the market.

Management at Maguire and Paterson had to, in the words of the cliché, adapt or die; it had to find new products and new markets if it were to survive profitably. Thus the company had, like many in such a position, *diversification* thrust upon it. Yet its skill in match-making represented very little synergistic possibility to manufacture any other type of product. The answer lay in the company's distribution network. Here Maguire and Paterson had an expertise and experience built literally over generations. It identified products which had similar consumer characteristics to matches, i.e. intensive/wide distribution, small purchase decision, national brand advertising supported by point-of-sale merchandising, and so on, and pushed them through this network. It did not manufacture these products but marketed them on an agency basis.

Exhibit 1

Prevalence of Cigarette Smoking in Irish Population (16+ years), 1972–1985							
SMOKERS	72/73	74/75	76/77	78/79	80/81	82/83	84/85
	%	%	%	%	%	%	%
Total	43	41	38	36	35	32	34
Men	49	45	43	40	39	34	36
Women	37	37	34	31	32	29	32
16–24 years	48	39	38	33	33	33	35
25–34 years	42	45	40	41	43	35	38
35–44 years	44	41	38	41	35	34	35
45–54 years	49	48	42	35	40	32	35
55+ years	37	36	36	32	30	26	28
ABC1	37	35	30	28	29	26	27
C2	45	45	41	39	38	34	39
DE	51	47	46	45	46	39	42
F	35	35	32	29	26	25	26

Source: Joint National Media Research Survey (JNMR), Irish Marketing Surveys Ltd.

In 1977 Maguire and Paterson acquired the agency for Wilkinson Sword shaving products and Foster Giant sunglasses in Ireland. In subsequent years Dart disposable lighters, Marigold rubber housegloves, Golden Butterfly plastic kitchenware, Newey hair care products and Revlon shampoo products were added to the list. By the end of 1980 annual turnover at Maguire and Paterson stood at £5.1m, with £2.1m coming from its personal care and household range of products.

The diversification programme obviously involved a very substantial reorientation on the part of Maguire and Paterson. Its management approach and capability had to be regenerated. A number of new senior management appointments were made. A marketing director was appointed in 1977 and under him an effective marketing function with skills in branding and product development was nurtured. Sales representation was increased and the distribution network deepened. By 1980 the number of employees had increased to 190.

In early 1981 Allegheny Ludlum Industries, a giant Pittsburgh-based US conglomerate, acquired Maguire and Paterson. Allegheny already had one-third of Maguire and Paterson's equity through its ownership of Bryant and May. (Some years previously Wilkinson Sword had merged with Bryant and May to form Wilkinson Match, which in turn was acquired by Allegheny Ludlum Industries in 1980.) It was Allegheny's policy to have a 100 per cent holding in all companies in which it had an interest. Allegheny Ludlum Industries was a very diverse enterprise with interests in engineering products, safety and protection equipment and houseware products. It had a turnover of $1.6 billion in 1980. The actual takeover vehicle used by the US combine was True Temper (Ireland), its Irish subsidiary which had manufactured gardening implements in Cork since the mid-sixties and employed some 150. So in a somewhat ironic twist of fate Maguire and Paterson, just one year before the centenary of its foundation, ceased to be a publicly quoted Irish company.

LOVING THE CORE BUSINESS

As Maguire and Paterson moved into the eighties it came to see itself increasingly as a marketing and distribution company of fast-moving consumer goods (FMCG) through a network of supermarket, retail, grocery, chemist and hardware outlets. Other agencies, such as Jade skin care products, were acquired. However, the company did not neglect its match business and opportunities for product development and for possible rejuvenation of the market were sought. During 1981 extensive omnibus and qualitative research was commissioned by Maguire and Paterson to investigate match purchasing behaviour and the general characteristics of the 'lights' market—a 'light' being defined as an act of ignition by a match or a lighter. Exhibit 2 summarises a number of key findings of this research. Exhibit 3 provides data on the number of boxes purchased and used per week, while Exhibit 4 gives data on the source of these purchases.

Exhibit 2

Characteristics of Match Purchasing Behaviour

* There was absolutely no claim to brand call amongst any of the respondents. To these smokers the market for matches is a generic one.
* Although most have some preference between 'strike anywhere' and 'safety' matches, few feel sufficiently concerned to specify this preference. Where this does occur, it is more likely to be someone calling for 'black', 'brown' or 'safety' matches for a household in which there are young children.
* In complete contrast to the brand of cigarettes, the box of matches attracts a weak proprietorial claim. A box of matches is clearly very subsidiary to the

pack of cigarettes. Whilst brand specification is all-important for the pack of cigarettes, the reverse is true for matches. Imagery and personality vested in the pack of cigarettes (through which the smoker expresses himself), coupled with its high price, tend to detract further from the importance of the box of matches.

* Most smokers who use disposable lighters revert to matches from time to time. Such smokers appear to be very prone to losing or mislaying their lighters before the lighters are fully exhausted. It is also the case that the outlay required for a lighter may deter or delay the purchase of a replacement.

* Typically, smokers who prefer matches claim they buy a box of matches with each pack of cigarettes they buy. Recognising that this means two matches for each of a pack of twenty cigarettes, most claim that there is a high 'wastage' factor through giving lights to others, attempts to light out of doors, etc.

* The smoker would rather have two boxes on his person than risk running out and having to buy a box of matches on its own. In reality, where this happens he may omit the matches on the next cigarette purchasing occasion.

* Despite their reluctance to be brand specific when purchasing, smokers are generally aware of the popularity of the principal brands, Cara and Friendly. More pertinently, they also appreciate that both are made by Maguire and Paterson.

* Maguire and Paterson enjoys a high level of respect, most particularly because it is seen to be a successful Irish company manufacturing a high-quality product and providing employment for Irish people.

* There is an awareness of imported products, often alluded to as being of Italian manufacture, posing an increasing threat in the marketplace. Although smokers are invariably critical that such matches are of an inferior quality, not one was prepared to return his purchase of an 'imported' product or to make a mental note to be brand specific on the next occasion.

Source: Omnibus and qualitative research carried out in September and November 1981 by Lansdowne Market Research on behalf of M & P.

This research also suggested a relative weakness in the use of matches as 'lighters' amongst young female and, to a lesser extent, young middle-class male smokers. The company considered a premium match concept aimed at this target market. The brand name Century was chosen to coincide with the centenary of Maguire and Paterson's establishment in 1882. It was proposed that this new brand would command a price premium of 2p/3p over the existing 4p retail price for Friendly and Cara. Research was commissioned to establish, amongst the perceived primary target market, consumer interest in purchasing this new premium range and the optimum price positioning. While this survey indicated a number of positive aspects (see Appendix A), it was decided not to proceed with the project. Exhibit 5 shows data from this survey on the use of matches and disposable lighters for lighting cigarettes.

Exhibit 3

Number of Boxes Purchased and Used

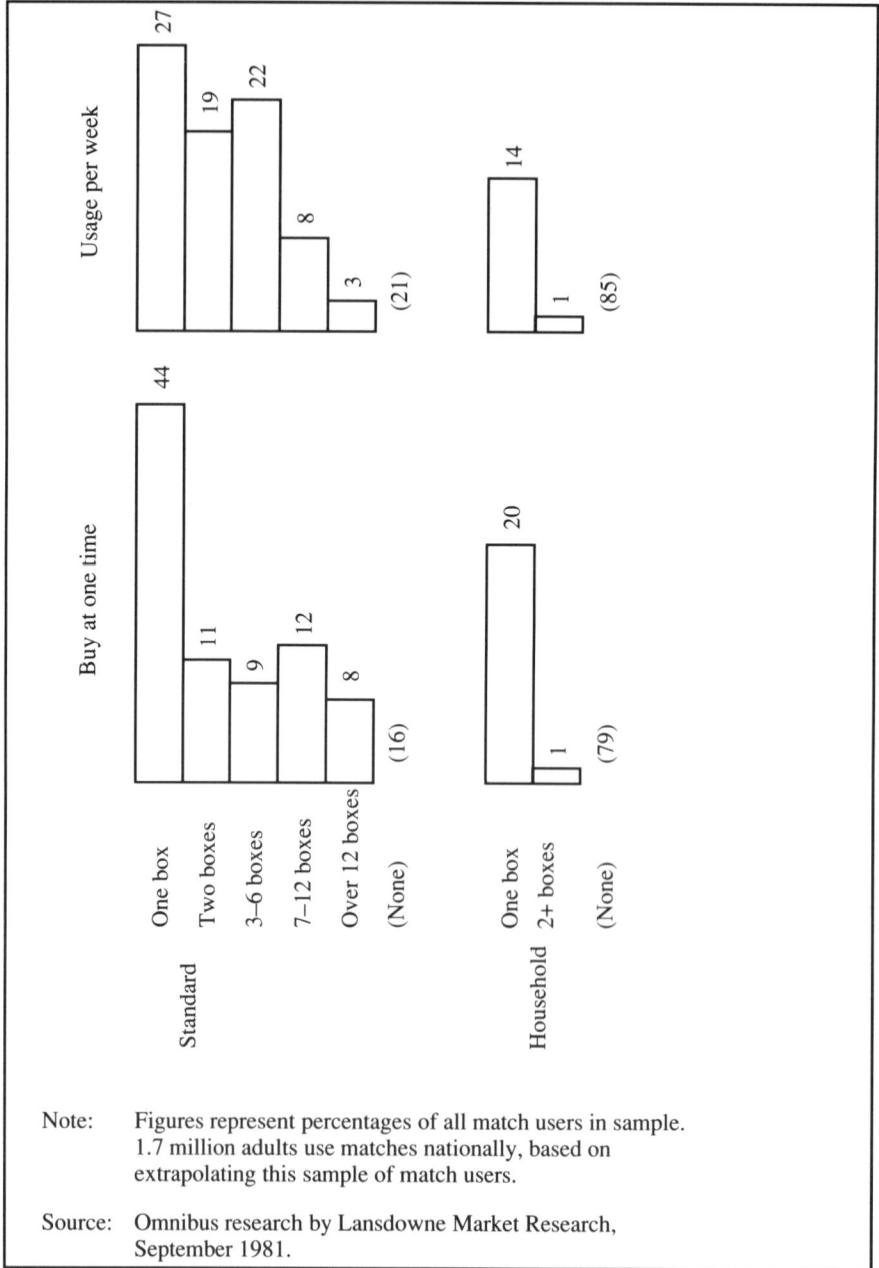

Note: Figures represent percentages of all match users in sample. 1.7 million adults use matches nationally, based on extrapolating this sample of match users.

Source: Omnibus research by Lansdowne Market Research, September 1981.

Exhibit 4

Sources of Match Purchase

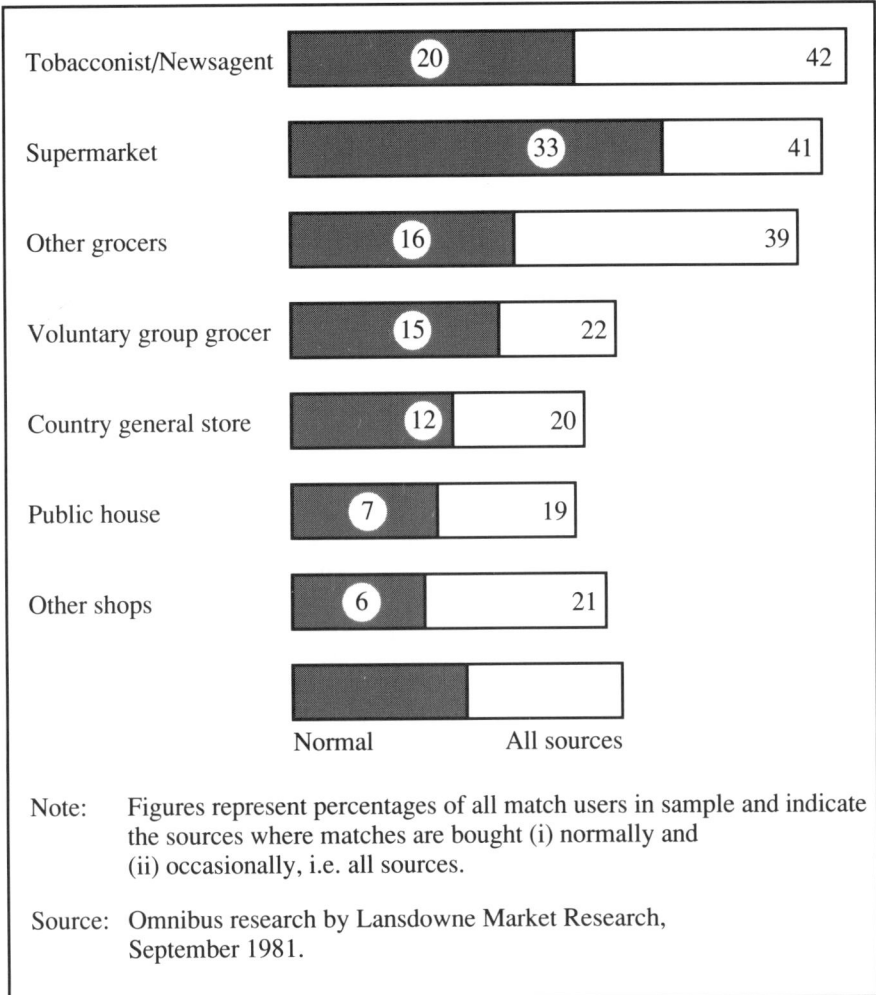

Source	Normal	All sources
Tobacconist/Newsagent	20	42
Supermarket	33	41
Other grocers	16	39
Voluntary group grocer	15	22
Country general store	12	20
Public house	7	19
Other shops	6	21

Note: Figures represent percentages of all match users in sample and indicate the sources where matches are bought (i) normally and (ii) occasionally, i.e. all sources.

Source: Omnibus research by Lansdowne Market Research, September 1981.

The idea of targeting a new brand of match towards a segment of the lights market continued to attract Maguire and Paterson. In early 1984 the concept of Macks matches was developed to appeal in a unisex manner to young male and female smokers, as a counter to disposable lighters. The new product was designed to contain 25 matches (as compared with an average of 42 for Cara and Friendly), with each matchstick having a white-coloured safety head. It was intended that it be positioned at a price of 5p as compared with the 6p for most matches currently available on the market. The first pack design conceived was one with a jazzy night-club connotation. Following initial research this design was toned down to a less dramatic landscape format in a loosely scripted contemporary style. Another portrait or vertical design having a much more conservative and formal typeface for the name was also considered. Again the company commissioned qualitative research using group discussion techniques to assess this new product concept. Appendix B summarises the conclusions to this research. By the end of 1984 Macks matches were still at the concept stage.

Exhibit 5

Methods Used for Lighting Cigarettes

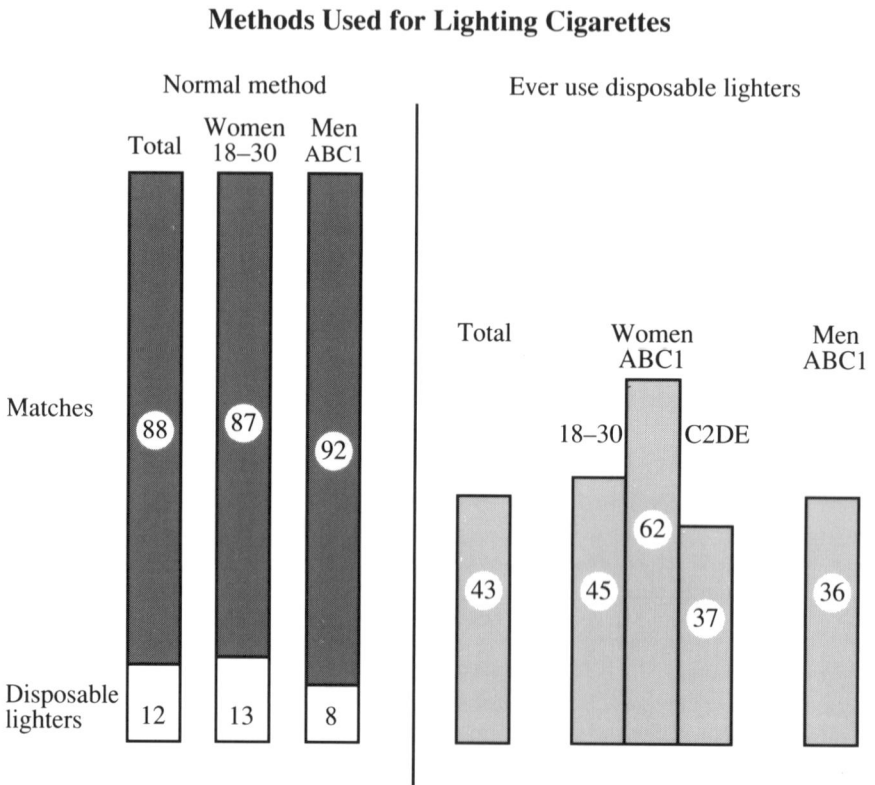

Note: Figures represent percentages of all 'lights' users in sample (200 respondents).

Source: Century Matches research by Lansdowne Market Research, May 1982.

The pack designs for Cara and Friendly had remained virtually unchanged for almost 40 years. Maguire and Paterson had considered on a number of occasions introducing new pack designs for these matchboxes with the objective of adding impetus to the market to counteract competition from disposable lighters and bookmatches and to identify the brands more strongly. Consumer research on possible new pack design changes indicated in general that traditional designs were not to be meddled with in any extensive way. The match and its label were symbols of reliability. The typical match user viewed matches as an established traditional, even natural, product, with a comparatively masculine personality. Ideas to change substantially the pack designs of Cara and Friendly during 1981 were not proceeded with. In 1982 the pack designs were modified to incorporate a new oval logo for Maguire and Paterson; this confirmed the traditional identity of the company in a favourable manner and also 'personalised' both brands in an emotively pleasant way. A qualitative study to evaluate target market reaction to an alternative design for Cara safety matches in 1984 showed thumbs down for the idea (see Appendix C).

During the early eighties competition from imported matches intensified. Some of these imports offered litho printed boxes with glossy type finishes and had undoubted consumer and trade appeal. Design changes proposed by Maguire and Paterson were in some ways constrained by the printing process used by the company at the time. During 1984 Maguire and Paterson undertook a major plant modernisation costing £2 million. This included a litho printing facility enabling a four-colour printing process on high-quality board.

THE LIGHTS MARKET

In 1985 the lights market in Ireland amounted to 210 million boxes (in standard box equivalents) and had a retail value of £12 million (see Exhibit 8 below). This market was reckoned to be declining at 1–2 per cent per annum. This decline was accounted for by the fall-off in cigarette smoking. However, not all segments of the smoking population, for instance young female smokers, showed this level of decline. Exhibit 6 shows data on cigarette smokers for 1980/81 and 1984/85.

The growth in the sales of disposable lighters had been significant during the first half of the 1980s. This product had doubled its share of the lights market over five years to more than 20 per cent in 1985. When Maguire and Paterson took on the agency for Dart disposable lighters in 1978, it was up against formidable opponents in the BIC and Cricket, which were by far the biggest-selling disposable lighters in Ireland. These lighters benefited from BIC Corporation's and Gillette's respective international marketing success in a range of FMCGs. In June 1980, after many years of lobbying the government, Maguire and Paterson were successful in having a 20p duty levied on all imported disposable lighters. The company argued that the imposition

Exhibit 6

Profile of Cigarette Smokers 1980/1981 and 1984/1985			
1980/1981			
Age	All Smokers (860,000)	Males (471,000)	Females (389,000)
	%	%	%
15–20	11	11	10
21–24	11	10	13
25–34	24	25	24
35+	54	54	53
Class			
ABCl	23	20	27
C2	24	24	25
DE	37	38	35
F	16	18	13
All Smokers Aged 15–34			
	%	%	%
Single	65	70	61
Married	34	30	38
1984/1985			
Age	All Smokers (851,000)	Males (449,000)	Females (402,000)
	%	%	%
15–20	11	13	9
21–24	14	14	14
25–34	23	22	24
35+	52	51	53
Class			
ABCl	24	22	25
C2	25	24	27
DE	35	35	36
F	16	19	12

Source: JNMR Reports.

of this duty would result in fairer competition as it countervailed the sizeable excise duty traditionally levied on its own match sales. Subsequent Budget levies had increased this duty to 50p by 1985. Thus disposable lighters were priced at £1.25–£1.50 in Ireland. This was considerably higher than in continental Europe, where lighters, especially disposable lighters, dominated the lights market. In 1984 Maguire and Paterson acquired the agency for Cricket disposable lighters.

The possibility of creating a new brand franchise continued to beckon Maguire and Paterson. By early 1985 Macks matches had evolved into a prototype Slims matches, to be aimed at the image-conscious younger smoker, particularly women, and with special emphasis on those women who used disposable lighters. Maguire and Paterson in association with its advertising agency carried out extensive development work on pack design, merchandising back-up and possible promotion. Concept testing was conducted (see Appendix D). In October 1985 Slims matches were launched with quite a splash on the Irish lights market (see Exhibit 7).

Exhibit 7

Merchandising for Slims

The Slims matchbox conveyed a neat modern appearance; it had a vertical slim-style logo and a colour scheme using blue/grey, pink, yellow and brown. The box contained 30 yellow-tipped matches. Slims retailed at 6p, the same price as Cara and Friendly. The back of the box carried a series of information pieces on wine entitled Slims Wine Guide. An upbeat 30-second television commercial was run on the national TV network. Styled like a pop video it contained images of a young woman in chic playful settings but little or no product information. The commercial's theme song was written by a popular rock band of the day. (It had been hoped to release this song as a single on the pop music market at the same time, but this came to nought.) The commercial cost some £60,000 to produce.

The launch of Slims was characterised by a significant media spend. In the first three months up to the end of 1985, over £70,000 was spent on advertising on television, on Adshel (outside poster) sites and in the trade press. Newspaper and consumer press were not included in the launch promotion, though some radio advertising was undertaken subsequently.

The role of Maguire and Paterson's distribution network—the trade, in everyday parlance—would be obviously crucial in promoting and marketing Slims. Given the generic nature of matches, until a brand name and call were established, the trade—whether a supermarket, a cash-and-carry, a TSN or whatever—would be instrumental in making the Slims offering to the targeted consumer. Attractive discounts in comparison to its existing match brands were offered as an incentive to distributors nationally. Merchandising and point-of-sale material was made available. In the initial period of the launch Maguire and Paterson used a team of ten promotional girls in cash-and-carry outlets. These had the direct back-up of a task salesforce of eight to sell to TSNs, pubs and clubs. Over £20,000 was spent on merchandising and promotion materials. Trade reaction seemed positive to Slims. *Checkout*, the premier trade grocery magazine, in an article in December 1985 entitled 'Innovative Product of the Year' commented: 'You need to be a brave company to try to introduce some innovation into Ireland's steadily declining lights market, but that's exactly what Maguire and Paterson did with their new Slims. What was doubly ambitious about the new brand was that it represented a totally new approach to marketing matches not just in Ireland but internationally as well. For the first time a major effort has been made to create a "chic" match, primarily to lure chic younger females away from using those ubiquitous disposable lighters.'

Professionals in the design field also admired the Slims launch. It achieved a number one prize in ICAD's annual Irish packaging awards. The Adshel poster 'Style in Lights' was selected by the Society of Irish Designers as one of only two examples from Ireland for a pan-European touring exhibition of poster art.

Exhibit 8

Lights Market in Ireland 1985

	Total Lights (million boxes)	Matches (million boxes)	Disposable lighters (million boxes*)
Total Market	210	165	45
Maguire & Paterson	150	135 **	15

* One lighter = 25 boxes   ** includes 6 million boxes of Slims

Maguire and Paterson's marketing manager wanted Slims to achieve 15 to 20 per cent of the Irish lights market. In the three months up to the end of 1985, 6 million boxes of Slims were sold (see Exhibit 8). Research on consumer reaction to the launch was carried out (see Exhibit 9). In 1985 Maguire and Paterson's total turnover amounted to £12 million, of which £5.5m came from its lights business. As the company moved into 1986 Slims volume sales continued to meet target. There was some concern amongst Maguire and Paterson's management that these volumes were being achieved at the expense of Cara and Friendly sales. The trade enjoyed higher margins on Slims than on Cara and Friendly and thus 'pushed' them. Sales of Slims reached beyond their initial target market. Some traditional purchasers of matches resented paying 6p for a new box of matches containing 25 per cent less product than existing brands—though Maguire and Paterson consequently enjoyed in one sense a higher per unit margin on each box of Slims. It is to be expected that any new brand introduction would tend to displace to some extent the existing brand offerings of a company. When this starts to happen actually, it can test the mettle of any company's management.

In the first months of 1986 some £40,000 was spent on above-the-line support for Slims. The original marketing plan envisaged up to £150,000 being spent on such support during 1986. In this original plan, positive payback on the Slims project would commence in year three. 'It would be unrealistic to consider anything less,' commented Maguire and Paterson's marketing manager; 'To establish a new brand and win a new brand franchise takes time and investment. It has to be supported.'

Maguire and Paterson's parent, Allegheny Ludlum Industries, had been experiencing difficult trading conditions during 1985. By early 1986 it had debts of $800 million and was considering the possibility of seeking Chapter

Eleven protection in the US. Many of its divisions and subsidiaries worldwide were examining their operational profitability and cash flow.

Future sales of disposable lighters in Ireland were a matter of uncertainty. Would the Irish lights market begin to take on the configuration of that of continental Europe? There was always the possibility that the import duty on lighters might be taken off in a forthcoming Budget. A halving of the price of a disposable lighter in Ireland would have considerable implications for the marketing of Slims, and indeed other matches. Also there was some evidence, albeit on a very small scale, of the illegal importing of disposable lighters and their subsequent cut-price retailing.

In early 1986 Maguire and Paterson withdrew promotional and advertising support for Slims matches. Less than six months after its launch any further brand support for Slims ceased.

Exhibit 9

Post-Launch Consumer Check: Key Findings

* Just three months after launch, spontaneous awareness of the Slims name registered at just over one in six adults (16 per cent). The comparable figure among smokers was rather higher at almost one in four (23 per cent).

* Two-thirds of all smokers recognised the Slims branding under prompting and this compared with just over four in ten non-smokers. Within the broader context of the total adult population, the brand reached a total awareness level of 50 per cent. Total awareness levels were higher than average in the youngest age group, at middle-class level and in Dublin; women were also somewhat more likely to express familiarity with the Slims name on a prompted basis.

* Four in ten smokers purchased Slims during the initial launch period, equating with an overall penetration level of just over one in five adults on a national basis. Purchasing is fairly broadly spread in demographic terms, but among smokers trial has been highest at the youngest end of the age range and among women.

* Repeat purchasing levels appear to be fairly encouraging; seven in ten buyers have purchased the brand more than once, with around four in ten doing so either twice or three times (the average number of purchasing occasions was higher than average in Dublin).

* Reflecting the general pattern of purchasing, the Slims buyer profile is also quite broadly based. Compared with the national population, it is slightly younger and somewhat more dependent on the lower middle-class (C1) and skilled working-class (C2) categories. Measured against the national smoker profile, Slims buyers have a younger and more female orientation.

* The visual appeal and neater size of Slims were the two most widely mentioned positive features and there is a tendency to see the brand as more modern, elegant, up-market and feminine than the longer-established match brands. On the negative side, there is some concern about value for money, allied to the number of matches the pack contains (a minority also described the matches as more brittle or weaker than the norm).
* The concerns about value for money are more marked among men and smokers. Younger buyers are much less concerned and the brand enjoys a fairly positive rating on this criterion among 15–24 year olds.
* Recognition levels for the Slims TV commercial were relatively high. Presented with a storyboard, just over one in three adults claimed to have seen the material before and this figure was very significantly higher among young people—almost six in ten 15–24 year olds said they had seen the campaign, suggesting that it has been very effective in reaching this key target group.

Source: Behaviour & Attitudes marketing research on behalf of M & P, December 1985.

APPENDIX A

Century Matches Research

Conclusions
* The results of this pack and price study show an encouraging level of acceptance of the proposed new range of Century matches at a premium price amongst the target markets of cigarette smokers. A higher level of acceptance was found among young female smokers (who represent approximately 130,000 people) than amongst young middle-class male smokers (who represent approximately 30,000 people).
* At a premium of 2p (i.e. at 6p), 27 per cent of the total sample expressed an interest in purchasing Century matches on a regular basis as a replacement for the matches or lighter they normally use for lighting cigarettes or cheroots. Although this must be regarded as an overstatement of likely conversion, this still leaves substantial potential for the brand.
* The primary prospects for Century are the young (18–24 year old) single middle-class women and, encouragingly, the heavier matches buyers. The latter group expressed more interest in buying than did those who buy less than 3 boxes per week.
* A premium of 3p (i.e. at 7p) appears a significant barrier inducing consumer resistance and a sharp fall-off in interest. One out of every ten stated that they would buy Century regularly at this price, but only 2 per cent of the total sample subsequently affirmed this intention with certainty.
* Colour preferences were relatively equally divided between the red, black and blue boxes, with the green box attracting least interest.

Exhibit 1

Century Pack Design

Note: Research was based on a total sample of 200 respondents interviewed at home, demographically representative of smokers falling within target population sub-groups. JNMR data was used.

Source: Lansdowne Market Research on behalf of M & P, May 1982.

APPENDIX B

Macks Matches Research

Conclusions

* There is a certain lack of harmony between the marriage of the hard masculine name when spoken and consumer perception of the feminine targeting of the concept. Both men and women were sensitive to this apparent conflict for both pack designs.
* Whilst we recognise that the landscape/script design affords the company more potential from an advertising and promotional perspective, we would not recommend that Maguire and Paterson market this particular design.
* Its consumer appeal is negligible, whilst a very superficial personality is projected by the pack—one with which smokers appear to find it extremely difficult to identify.
* It lacks integrity and is not seen as a serious product. The casual graffiti style also suggests a less expensive production process, which gives the impression of an inferior cost-cutting marketing exercise.
* The vertical design does have rather more potential. However, we must stress that much of the evaluation of this design was of a comparative nature (*vis-à-vis* the landscape/script format) and was necessarily conditioned by reactions to the 'graffiti' design.
* We envisage its potential being fairly narrowly confined to women who smoke king size cigarettes. An up-market orientation seems likely but the age profile may evolve in a more mature manner than targeted (as per king size cigarettes). Women who smoke under 20 cigarettes a day and those who use cigarette lighters, at least from time to time, are the prime prospects.

* Among the more positive features of the design is its distinctive vertical format. The synergy with most flip top/king size cigarette pack designs and with cigarette lighters is a significant attribute.
* The pack presentation is respected as a high-quality modern design, of sufficient integrity to be appropriate for a good-quality product. Its compact dimensions are an undoubted attraction for women.
* Among the more important negatives are the consumer perception of it as a special occasion, going-out, night-time purchase for the handbag. Smokers cannot conceive of it in an 'everyday' context.
* The cerise colour and fine/fussy design is particularly feminine; this is likely to deter male acceptance. The blue version is more unisex.
* The problem of educating prospects to discard their present purchasing behaviour and start being brand specific in a TSN will clearly be a major obstacle—at least initially.
* There would seem to be a strong case for strengthening the corporate endorsement of the brand, whether on-pack or through promotional support.

Exhibit 1

Macks Pack Design

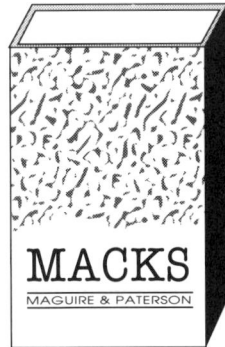

Source: Lansdowne Market Research on behalf of M & P, December 1984.

APPENDIX C

Cara Matches Pack Design

Conclusions

In summary, we would strongly recommend that Maguire and Paterson should not adopt the alternative design for Cara. The proposed change is far too radical to be attempted in one leap—even for a box of matches. Quite apart from this general conclusion, there are a number of specific problem areas for the elements of the design which we also feel pose major obstacles.

1. 'Non-Irish'
   The very evident non-Irish atmosphere evoked by the design tends to draw out suspicions of a 'cover' to begin importing raw materials. By so successfully cultivating consumer interest in Irish-manufactured matches, Maguire and Paterson have, ironically, provided their own obstacle.

2. 'Smoker Comfort'
   Lack of smoker comfort with the design generally, both with the colours and the portrait layout, is a major reason for resistance to the design. In making this point we have taken into consideration the fact that any design change will at first appear strange and take time to get used to.

3. 'Child Appeal and Safety'
   A surprisingly large number of parents of young children stated that they would not buy the new design, because the very colourful design was likely to be attractive to small children—specifically they saw a similarity with children's packs of sweet 'cigarettes'.

Exhibit 1

Cara Pack Designs: Existing and Proposed

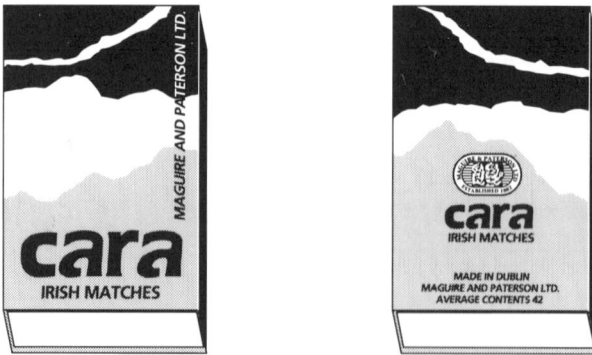

Source: Lansdowne Market Research on behalf of M & P, July 1984.

4. 'Not Maguire and Paterson'
   In essence, the design is totally out of character with Maguire and Paterson—perceived as a 'one-product' company, single-mindedly manufacturing a high-quality product for over a hundred years. Contemporary pack designs for Cara and Friendly were felt to have remained virtually unchanged over the years. Suddenly Maguire and Paterson appears to be proposing a very radical change; in so doing it appears almost unfaithful to the values it has built up over the years and for which the consumer has such high respect.

5. 'Feminine'

When evaluating the contemporary image of Cara it was apparent that the brand already leans towards a feminine position—it is the 'Silk Cut' of the matches market. Some of the elements of the design would be likely to weigh this balance even more heavily in a female direction.

APPENDIX D

Slims Matches Concept Testing

Reactions to the 'Slims' concept

* The Slims logo read clearly and the incorporation of a match as the letter 'I' was regarded as a clever and striking piece of design work. The overall treatment was described as modern, trendy, stylish and rather up-market— clearly a very radical departure from the traditional norms of matchbox design.
* The slimmer pack was generally regarded as a worthwhile benefit in terms of being neater to handle and less bulky in pockets or handbags.

'I like the idea of the box. It is a bit smaller, much handier.'
Female C2D

'It's more ladylike now; I couldn't imagine a fella with a box of them.'
Female BCl

'It might appeal to people who dress with suits, that will slip into a high top pocket.'
Male C2D

* All were agreed that it represented a major departure from existing pack designs and was more likely to appeal to female smokers—partly because of the neater size and partly because of the design/colouring.
* This anticipated female orientation was further reinforced for some by the style of the 'S' in the logo while others felt that from a distance it suggested flickering flames. A minority thought the logo itself indicated a longer match and were slightly disappointed to find that the box contained the standard size.
* The Maguire and Paterson corporate imprimatur is very important in under-writing two factors—local manufacture and quality. It might be helpful to give this slightly more prominence (if this is possible without compromising the design).
* The idea of featuring wine notes on the reverse of the box generated a reasonable level of interest. On balance the idea was welcomed but this particular subject reinforced a tendency to see the overall design as rather up-market.
* The line 'Style in Lights' was generally understood as an attempt to invest the product itself with stylish overtones but it was not a particularly comfortable phrase

with most smokers and runs the risk of positioning the brand as a 'poseur's' choice. The term 'lights' is not one which fits easily into popular parlance.

* The archetypal user image which eventually emerged after more extended exposure was described as a young single female who is fashion- conscious, likely to drink in trendy pubs and to go to discos or night-clubs (the design has a more 'evening' than 'everyday' feel).

'I think it looks feminine, the box itself, Slims, something to do with diet. It would appeal to women more.'
Male BC1

'I wouldn't associate them with Maguire and Paterson 'cos Maguire and Paterson are such an old Irish firm ... they must be well promoted ... the single girl maybe or the chic girl ... they're nice if you're out.'
Female C2D

* Estimated contents of the new pack were very consistent at 25–30 matches and pricing was expected to be directly on a par with standard boxes. Any premium above this will simply serve further to limit the new brand's potential. The simple logic is that fewer matches should cost less but that the new pack design warrants something extra. However, the prospect of paying 'over the odds' for significantly fewer matches will be a difficult proposition to sustain.

'I think you'd be paying 6p for thirty and the style of the box and the different match.'
Male C2D

* Smokers themselves are very conscious of the key role of the retailer in all of this because of the commodity call; they argue that it would be necessary to provide an incentive for the shop-owner in order to achieve reasonable trial levels. Getting the matches on to the shop-counter for self-selection was put forward as an important prerequisite, but the practicality of this was seriously questioned—most counters are now under glass and both cigarettes and matches are normally well out of reach of the customer.

'If you couldn't take them off the counter they wouldn't sell.'
Male BC1

'Everyone would still call them matches ... I couldn't fancy myself going in and asking for a box of Slims.'
Female BC1

'The point is we never ask for the different brands ... I don't, I just ask for matches.'
Female. C2D

Source: Behaviour & Attitudes marketing research on behalf of M & P, August 1985.

Questions
1. Assess the launch of Slims matches.
2. Speculate why the company withdrew brand support in early 1986. Would you agree with this decision?
3. Would you consider relaunching the product? Set out a marketing plan in that event.
4. In general are there particular problems in pursuing a segmentation strategy in the context of the Irish market?
5. Comment on the use of market research by the company.
6. Consider the relationship between design and marketing in terms of the case.

Braycot Foods

In recent years the fortunes of Braycot Foods, founded in 1980 to produce wholefood biscuits for the home and export markets, had been mixed due to a lack of clear product line and distribution management. In late 1989 it was taken over by Shamrock Foods, an importer and distributor of grocery food products and itself the recent subject of a takeover by a large commodity food and agricultural company. Clearly Braycot required a new sense of direction.

Issues: *Product development, positioning and rationalisation. Consumer research. Channels of distribution. International marketing. Synergy in acquisition. Developing a marketing plan.*

1989 had been a year of major upheaval for Braycot Foods. The company had been taken over in October by IAWS plc. A virtual clear-out of existing management had taken place and effectively the new owners of the company were in a position to develop a strategy with little reference to the past. In the middle of the takeover Mary Minnock had been recruited as marketing manager and was being asked by the new owners to assist in preparing a marketing plan for the company.

COMPANY BACKGROUND
The company was established in 1980 by John and Janet Hunter as Cobbetts. They aimed to develop a range of wholefood biscuits using only top-quality ingredients. Thus, for example, carob was used to coat biscuits rather than chocolate because of its good health connotations. John Hunter's background was in advertising. He had been chief executive and principal shareholder in Hunter Advertising Ltd. However, he had sold his interest in this company prior to the establishment of Cobbetts. Initially the company operated on a very limited scale from the Hunters' home. By 1982 the company had moved into a modern industrial unit at the Oldcourt industrial estate in Bray, Co. Wicklow about 15 miles south of Dublin city. The company expanded rapidly, moving into adjacent units until it eventually occupied a total of 20,000 square feet of manufacturing and warehouse space.

This case was developed by Gerry Mortimer of DIT as a basis for class discussion rather than to illustrate either effective or ineffective handling of an administrative situation.

Initially the company concentrated on the home market selling mostly through multiples. It had little difficulty obtaining a listing with the major supermarket groups as at the time only one other Irish biscuit-maker existed. This was Irish Biscuits Limited, whose Jacobs and Bolands brands accounted for more than 60 per cent of the market. All other biscuits were imported and encouragement was being given to Irish producers to enter this and other markets where there was a high level of import penetration.

The product was positioned as a wholefood product. By 1987 the product range was holding an estimated market share of 1 per cent in the overall biscuit market, which in turn was estimated at £80 million at retail prices. The positioning of Braycot as a wholefood product meant that the management considered a further significant increase in market share unlikely, so it turned its attention to export markets and at first looked to develop in the UK. However, the company immediately ran into difficulties when it discovered that the brand name Cobbetts could not be used as another company had already registered this name. After much consideration the management opted to change the brand name to Braycot: a derivation of Bray, where the biscuits were made, and the word cottage, symbolising the wholefood home-made image of the product. This change of name was also extended to the Irish market and thus the name of the company became Braycot Foods Limited. The change also coincided with a packaging design change; in fact this was one of five packaging design changes that took place in the life of the firm up to 1989.

Sales had developed with virtually no advertising support. Promotion concentrated on point-of-sales material and tasting demonstrations in supermarkets and, in the export area, on channel promotion using trade fairs and exhibitions to source new business.

At various stages in the company's development it took in new investors. By 1988 the shareholders included a financial consultant and a local tea-blending company. By this time the company had undertaken a major capital investment to automate the plant, thereby reducing the workforce to 25 and increasing capacity very substantially. Though initially quite profitable, by 1988 the company had started to make losses. The burden imposed by the capital expenditure was a major factor. The Hunters retired from active management and the consultant became chief executive. It was clear from an early stage that he proposed to sell the company and was managing it only on a temporary basis. The already limited expenditure on promotion was cut back severely. Negotiations were commenced with a number of parties interested in a takeover. These included Allied Lyons Group, a major UK food manufacturer; Foodtrend, which had a cookie manufacturing company and were interested in Braycot as a production operation; and Shamrock Foods Limited, then a family concern which acted principally as importer and packer of dried and tinned foods. Early in 1989 agreement was reached with Allied Lyons but this agreement subsequently fell through. However, negotiations with Allied Lyons and Foodtrend recommenced later in the year. In October Shamrock Foods Limited itself was taken over by IAWS plc and, with the backing of IAWS, re-entered the negotiations and quickly concluded an agreement with the owners of Braycot. Thus Braycot became a subsidiary of Shamrock Foods.

SHAMROCK FOODS LIMITED

Shamrock Foods Limited was a long-established family-owned concern until its takeover by IAWS plc. The company was originally set up as a packer of dried foods, of which baking ingredients were the most important. Products were marketed under the Shamrock label. The range includes raisins, sultanas, currants, whole and ground almonds, a variety of nuts, cherries and peel. This market in its home-baking form was considered to be a mature one with little or no potential for further growth. Shamrock products were very strongly represented in grocery multiples.

Overall market share in the Irish grocery trade was estimated in a recent survey to be as follows: multiples 64 per cent; symbol groups 17 per cent; and independents 19 per cent. A separate survey had indicated a slightly lower percentage share for multiples nationally but a much stronger representation in the Dublin area (see Exhibit 1). The Dublin area represented about 35 per cent of the national market. It should also be noted that Crazy Prices was not represented outside the Dublin area and was a sister company of Quinnsworth. Superquinn also had limited representation outside of Dublin, while L&N operated in the south-east region only.

Exhibit 1

Multiples' Share of Grocery Trade		
Multiple	*Nationally*	*Dublin*
	%	%
Dunnes Stores	25	25
Quinnsworth	19	25
Crazy Prices	4	12
Superquinn	8	16
L&N	3	–
Roches Stores	2	2
Total	61	80

Source: *Checkout*, March 1988.

With a strong physical distribution capability and a well-established presence in the multiples it was a logical step for Shamrock Foods to develop agency and physical distribution arrangements for other grocery products. Gradually the range of products handled by Shamrock Foods increased to over 60. In addition to home-baking products a number of tinned foods such as tomatoes and fruit were imported and marketed under the Shamrock label. The company also acted as distributor for Pedigree pet foods, Dolmio Italian sauces and C-Pack cake and ice-cream mixes amongst others. It also undertook physical distribution for Weetabix brands. Since the takeover by IAWS, Shamrock Foods had taken responsibility for distributing other food lines. In particular it distributed Howards, Bolands and Mosses flour and bread mixes.

IAWS PLC

IAWS (Irish Agricultural Wholesale Society) had been established in the early part of this century by a number of cooperatives to act as their purchasing arm for commodities. Thus its principal areas of operation included the import of grain, food stuffs and fertilisers. For decades the society's image had been that of a sleepy though relatively profitable large player in the Irish agricultural scene. In the late seventies under new and more dynamic management IAWS set out on a programme of expansion, mainly through acquisition. Initial purchases were of companies in difficulties such as Bolands Mills, which was in receivership, and Gouldings Fertilisers, which had proved to be a less than successful venture for both an Irish investment company and a major US fertiliser manufacturer. In 1988 the society, by now a limited company, obtained a quotation on the Irish Stock Exchange. By the end of 1989 the company had divided its activities into three strategic areas as follows.

Food Group: This included flour milling incorporating the operations of Dock Milling, Davis Mosse, Bolands and Howards. Apart also from Shamrock Foods and its new subsidiary Braycot Foods, this group included an investment in the First National Bakery Company—this had brought together a number of small regional bread producers which had been coming under increasing pressure from multiples and the growth of automated and highly efficient bakeries, in some cases supported by the multiples. The 'bread wars' as they were described had led to the closure of many regional bakeries in what was becoming a highly competitive mature market.

Goulding Group: This area encompassed seeds, crop care, fertilisers, specialist horticulture and garden care products and industrial chemicals for the food and pharmaceutical industries.

Agri-products: Included under this area were the manufacture of fish meal, fish oil and food compounds for pig, poultry, dairy and fish farming, the importation of grain products and the export of wool and hides.

In 1989 IAWS had a turnover of £250 million, a profit of £5 million, shareholders' funds of £25 million and a P/E ratio of 10 valuing the company at £50 million.

THE BISCUIT MARKET

The Irish biscuit market had one of the highest consumption rates in the world. Each person on average ate over 10 kilos of biscuits per year. The market was valued at in excess of £80 million at retail selling prices. Although this market was relatively static there was considerable movement within it, in particular towards what was seen as the premium end of the market. In this sector chocolate, multipacks and the small but growing wholefood and health sector were buoyant. The growth in the multipack sector appeared to reflect the growing influence of multiples which regularly used such packs for special promotions and end-of-aisle displays. In spite of this, the multiples' share of the biscuit market at 45 per cent did not appear to reflect their share in the overall grocery market.

Irish Biscuits were the market leaders with more than 60 per cent of the market with their Jacobs and Bolands brands. Jacobs operated in what was considered to be the premium sector of the market while Bolands was positioned as an economy biscuit. It was estimated that the premium sector accounted for 61 per cent of the market, with economy products accounting for 22 per cent and generic or own-label products 17 per cent. There was some evidence of economy biscuits winning share from the generic sector. United Biscuits with brands such as McVities, Crawfords and Pennywise had the second largest overall share at just below 20 per cent. Their products were imported from the UK as were those of Cadburys and Burtons which took much of the remaining 20 per cent share. Most other companies in the market had very small shares. Amongst the Irish competitors there were Kellys with a range of 'cookie' type products and Seerys, a locally owned small producer which had set out to market as a home-bake product.

The market leaders were substantial spenders on promotion, particularly on television. Irish Biscuits spent in excess of £500,000 annually on this medium alone, with United Biscuits' spending running at half this level. New product development was of major significance in the industry. New product launches and relaunches were a regular feature.

Very little consumer research had been undertaken into the Irish biscuit market. However, UK research indicated that biscuits were very much an impulse purchase. One survey revealed that of those who bought a packet of biscuits only 50 per cent had planned to make a purchase when entering the shop. Of those who had planned a purchase only 50 per cent had decided what they would purchase before entering the shop. This may have accounted for the relatively low market share held by multiples at retail level.

THE BRAYCOT PRODUCT RANGE

In 1989 Braycot Foods' turnover was approximately £1 million. Of this about 50 per cent was exported. In total the company marketed in excess of 20 products (see Exhibit 2). However, these could be grouped into a smaller number of categories as follows.

150g and 200g Cartons: This was a range of seven products packed in a tray and flowrap and in a colour-coded outer carton with a different colour combination for each product. The products were Fruit Oat Crunchy, Carob Half-Coated Cookies, Mountain Cookies, Luxury Ginger, Oat Nutties, Hazelnut Crunchy and Tea Crunch. This was the company's staple product line. It accounted for 57 per cent of sales on the home market and 60 per cent of exports, though there were indications of a fall-off in sales over the past two years. These products retailed at about 70p per carton. This price was similar to other premium cartons.

Cereal Bars: Four products were offered in this range: Honey and Hazelnut, Fruit and Coconut, Top Nut (peanut) and Half-Coated Carob. These products were all wrapped and retailed at 24p. The Half-Coated Carob outsold the other three with all four accounting for 12 per cent of local sales and 5 per cent of exports. They were sold in six-packs in multiples and singly in smaller outlets.

Shortbreads: This range had three products, all in see-through flowrap. The products were called Original, Wholemeal and Chocolate Chip Flake. The products had the additional feature of using Flora margarine in their manufacture and indicating this on the package. However, the company had been informed by the manufacturers of Flora that they would not be allowing the use of its brand name by Braycot in the future. This appeared to result from a change in policy by Flora. It was not possible to assess the likely effects of this change on sales. This range accounted for 6 per cent of local sales but was not exported.

Own Label: Braycot produced two products for the French supermarket chain Monoprix. These products were similar to the Braycot carton products. The two products were Fruit Oat Crunchie and Fruit and Coconut. Together they accounted for 23 per cent of exports.

Jumblies: Three products were produced under this heading: plain, half-coated and de luxe (fully chocolate-coated) in see-through cartons of 200g. This was the first move into chocolate-coated products and was introduced in 1989 to extend the product range into more mainstream markets and to utilise capacity. Initial signs were encouraging, with extremely strong sales being recorded. However, the recent upheaval had taken attention away from the marketing of this range.

Organic: This was the most recent product developed by Braycot. In response to a request from the company's French agents, Distriborg, the company developed two products using only organic flour, oats, hazelnuts and sesame seeds. The products were Sesame and Orange, and Choc Chip and Hazelnut. Attempts to source organic supplies of other ingredients had not been very successful. Organic materials accounted for 50 per cent of the total product in each case. The variability of the organic materials used presented considerable production difficulties. Further problems were presented by the seasonality in supply of organic raw materials and the difficulty in storing such materials for any length of time. The packaging was supplied by Distriborg and the product marketed under the Bjorg brand name. It was distributed through healthfood shops and the healthfood sections of supermarkets. With an organic content of 50 per cent the possibility existed of obtaining the use of a special organic symbol approved and monitored by an organic producers' and growers' group. However, this had not been developed to a worthwhile stage at the end of 1989. Yet the management of Braycot was very pleased with the results and considered that the organic flour and oats gave the product a distinctive taste which could not be achieved with non-organic products. Early indications from Distriborg were very positive and they had already started reordering at a rate of £16,000–£20,000 per month. However, there appeared to be some evidence that sales would be skewed towards the early part of the year.

Other Products: Two other products were marketed by the company. Both were a mixture of the products available in the carton form. They were sold in 600g tins and 250g gift packs under the Braycot brand name and represented a very small proportion of sales, being particularly seasonal with highest sales at Christmas.

DOMESTIC DISTRIBUTION

As mentioned previously, approximately half of the sales of £1 million was in Ireland. Levels of domestic sales had peaked at £750,000 in 1987 and were now giving cause for concern. Sixty per cent of local sales were through the multiples and 40 per cent through independent grocers. The company's products were listed in 76 per cent of all multiples in Ireland and in 91 per cent of multiples in the Dublin area. On her arrival in the company Mary Minnock had discovered that the previous management had committed the company to an LTA (Long-Term Agreement) with the multiples covering the period 1989 to 1991. The origin of such LTAs lay in an agreement between the manufacturer and multiple under which an agreed rebate would be paid to the multiple in return for the multiple committing itself to selling an agreed level of product. Multiples used the LTAs to bargain between competing suppliers and gave higher profile and prominence in the store to the product with the most advantageous LTA. However, in recent years multiples no longer gave commitments of this nature and simply treated the LTA as a negotiated rebate against list prices. This was the case with the Braycot LTA and Mary Minnock was concerned at the high level of rebate it granted, especially because sales per outlet were low. This had squeezed margins considerably and had reduced her ability to support the product through promotion.

Exhibit 2

Sample of Braycot Range

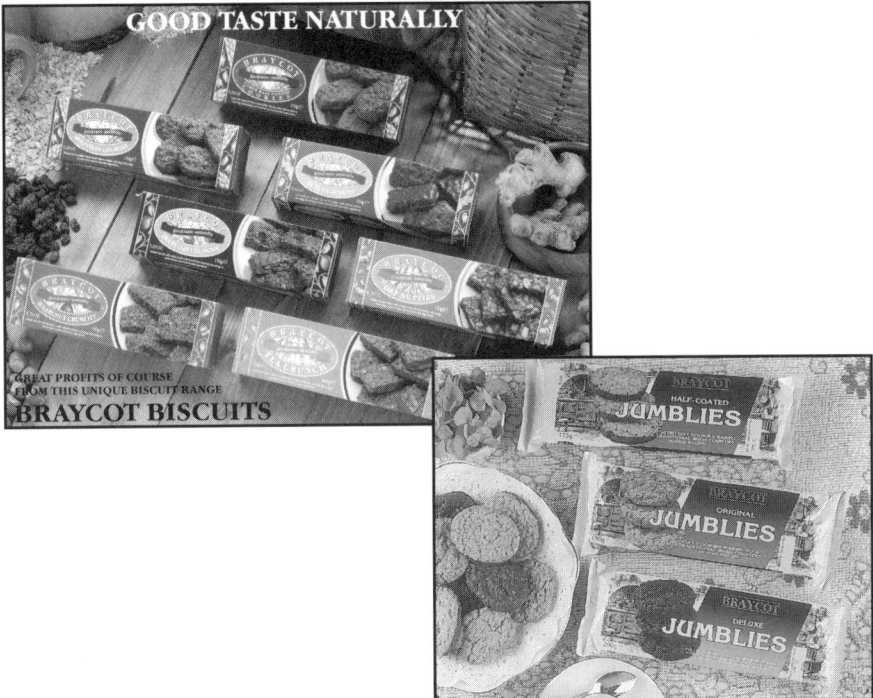

Customers were serviced by four van salespeople who performed physical distribution, merchandising and sales functions. The salespeople loaded the vans and set out on a regular delivery run. Dublin multiples were serviced once weekly and smaller outlets fortnightly. Customers outside the greater Dublin area were serviced fortnightly or monthly.

Until the arrival of Mary Minnock as marketing manager the company had never undertaken consumer research. She initiated a survey by Attwood Market Research and had just received the results. In particular she was surprised when the results showed that the fact that the biscuits were Irish was the most important reason for purchase. She also found the high level of non-recognition of the brand surprising given its existence for ten years. However, she recognised that the promotional spend had been very limited over the years. She had not yet had the opportunity to examine the research in detail. (See Appendix A for the principal findings of this research.)

Minnock had also analysed company sales over the past two years in Ireland; a number of the trends were causing her concern. Total domestic sales were declining by 10 per cent per annum in spite of the expanded product range. Reasons for this were difficult to isolate but clearly the lack of promotional support was likely to have been a factor. Monthly sales figures for the years 1988 and 1989 also indicated that the major packaging change on the carton range undertaken in 1988 had a substantial effect on sales. Sales of some products had collapsed after the change, suggesting that customers simply had not recognised the new packages, which had not been supported by any promotional spend. In addition the market had become more competitive with other locally manufactured products such as those of Kellys and Seerys strongly marketing their Irish origins with cookies and similar products.

Obviously the resources of the new owners of Braycot opened possibilities to reverse this trend but it seemed to Mary that one could find some justification for the adoption of strategies ranging from a major push on the Irish market to abandoning it altogether.

INTERNATIONAL DISTRIBUTION

By the management's own admission international distribution arrangements were haphazard. The major bright spot was France. Distributors had mostly been recruited through exhibiting at the major food fairs of Europe, particularly ISM in Cologne. Distribution arrangements, however, had developed in a less than organised manner, as indicated in the experience in the UK. Characteristics of and experience in the major overseas markets included the following.

United Kingdom: The company's first distributor in this market was Scandinavian Suppliers Ltd. This company was discarded after a period as it was considered too specialised in the healthfood sector and in any event not up to the required standard. It was replaced by Peabody Fine Foods in 1985. However, it was felt that this firm was too large and was a general distributor which did not give sufficient attention to the Braycot brands. Rather than take on another distributor the management then decided to set up its own sales office in the UK. Using this salesforce the company obtained a listing in Sainsbury and Tesco, the two largest supermarket groups in the UK, each with about 15 per cent of the UK grocery market. However, the sales levels attained did not justify the continuance of a company-controlled sales office. Scandinavian Suppliers approached Braycot again in 1988 and it was agreed to give it distribution rights while retaining direct distribution to Sainsbury and Tesco. But Scandinavian Suppliers again failed to achieve agreed targets and eventually in December 1989 went into liquidation. Braycot's debts were largely covered under an export credit guarantee scheme. At around the same time Tesco, which was then carrying only one Braycot product, delisted it on the basis that it was not selling.

Braycot under its new ownership now found itself unable to obtain up-to-date details on its UK distributor's outlets. Indeed a new company which employed some of the Scandinavian Suppliers' staff approached Mary Minnock at a food fair offering to provide information on where Braycot products had been sold but only in return for exclusive distribution rights. However, the new owners of Braycot had already undertaken to give distribution rights to SHS Foods Ltd in return for receiving Irish distribution rights for Punjana Tea brands. This arrangement had not yet commenced.

France: Two separate arrangements had developed in France. In addition to the two products marketed by the supermarket chain Monoprix, a range of products was marketed by Distriborg, Braycot's principal French agents. Distriborg was a distribution organisation specialising in the healthy food sector. They carried a range of 1,700 products marketing to healthfood shops and healthfood sections of supermarkets. Braycot management was of the view that the Distriborg operation was the most successful of all its distribution arrangements. Distriborg had also been involved in the development of Braycot's organic range as indicated previously. Recently Distriborg had established or bought subsidiaries in Holland and Belgium and as a result Braycot had abandoned its previous arrangement of dealing directly with one retailer in each of these markets in favour of Distriborg.

Germany: Braycot was represented in Germany by a subsidiary of the Swiss food group Suchard. This arrangement, through a mainstream confectionery distributor, had yielded very limited results.

Italy: Here also the company's products were distributed by a mainstream food group. Again results had been limited though the Italian distributor had some success with the larger tins of biscuits.

Austria/Switzerland: In both countries biscuit distributors selling through mainstream outlets had been appointed as a result of contacts developed at international food fairs. However, little or no sales had resulted in either case and there was currently no contact with either distributor.

USA/Canada: Considerable efforts had been expended in seeking a distributor or series of distributors for these markets. However, the results had not been encouraging. Braycot products had a shelf-life of seven to eight months. It had proved to be uneconomic to ship to North America in small quantities and the shelf-life together with the lack of indication of likely possible volumes had meant that it was not feasible to ship by container load.

As Mary Minnock contemplated her first few months in her new position it was clear that changes would have to be made to arrest the apparent decline in Braycot's fortunes. Indeed already rumour was rife in the company as to changes proposed by the new owners. It seemed certain that the chief executive of Shamrock Foods Ltd was also likely to be chief executive of Braycot. Administrative functions were expected to be moved to the south Dublin premises of Shamrock Foods some five miles away. Of more direct concern was a decision, believed to be imminent, to move distribution under the Shamrock wing and to dispense with the services of the four van salespeople.

APPENDIX A

Tables 1 & 2

Response to Whether or Not Biscuits Are Bought

Table 1

All respondents

	Total	Region		Age of respondent			Size of HH		Social class			Children	
		Dublin	Rest of Ireland	<35	35-49	50+	1-4 persons	5+ persons	ABC1	C2DE	F1F2	with	without
Sample	1036	311	725	238	321	477	715	321	311	528	197	425	611
% of Sample		30%	70%	23%	31%	46%	69%	31%	30%	51%	19%	41%	59%
Response													
Sample	87%	89%	86%	95%	92%	80%	86%	91%	93%	86%	81%	92%	84%
% of Sample	13%	11%	14%	5%	8%	20%	14%	9%	7%	14%	19%	8%	16%

Table 2

Respondents who usually buy biscuits

	Total	Region		Age of respondent			Size of HH		Social class			Children	
		Dublin	Rest of Ireland	<35	35-49	50+	1-4 persons	5+ persons	ABC1	C2DE	F1F2	with	without
Sample	904	277	627	226	296	381	611	292	290	455	159	391	513
% of Sample		31%	69%	25%	33%	42%	68%	32%	32%	50%	18%	43%	57%
Response (% of total)													
Yes	24%	40%	16%	26%	18%	26%	26%	18%	42%	17%	8%	20%	27%
No	68%	52%	75%	57%	73%	70%	66%	72%	51%	73%	85%	68%	68%
Don't know	8%	8%	9%	17%	9%	3%	8%	10%	7%	10%	6%	12%	5%

Table 3

Reasons for Never Buying Braycot Biscuits—First Reason

Table 3

Respondents who do not buy Braycot

Sample	Total	Region		Age of respondent			Size of HH		Social class			Children	
		Dublin	Rest of Ireland	<35	35–49	50+	1–4 persons	5+ persons	ABC1	C2DE	F1F2	with	without
Sample	616	143	473	129	218	269	405	212	148	332	137	267	349
% of Sample		23%	77%	21%	35%	44%	66%	34%	24%	54%	22%	43%	57%

Response	Total	Region		Age of respondent			Size of HH		Social class			Children	
		Dublin	Rest of Ireland	<35	35–49	50+	1–4 persons	5+ persons	ABC1	C2DE	F1F2	with	without
Too expensive	9%	17%	6%	11%	9%	7%	8%	10%	10%	11%	2%	10%	8%
Do not like quality	2%	2%	2%	1%	1%	2%	2%	1%	1%	2%	1%	1%	3%
Do not like taste	3%	6%	2%	3%	3%	2%	2%	3%	2%	3%	2%	3%	3%
Do not like texture	1%	2%	1%	2%	–	1%	2%	–	2%	1%	–	–	2%
Do not look nice	1%	3%	1%	1%	1%	2%	2%	*	2%	1%	1%	*	2%
Not available/ never seen them	63%	50%	67%	57%	63%	67%	65%	60%	55%	63%	73%	63%	63%
Other	4%	6%	3%	2%	2%	6%	4%	3%	9%	2%	3%	2%	4%

Table 4

Response to When Braycot Biscuits Were Last Bought

Table 4

Respondents who buy Braycot

	Total	Region		Age of respondent			Size of HH		Social class			Children	
		Dublin	Rest of Ireland	<35	35–49	50+	1–4 persons	5+ persons	ABC1	C2DE	F1F2	with	without
Sample	213	112	101	59	54	100	162	52	121	79	13	76	137
% of Sample		53%	47%	28%	25%	47%	76%	24%	57%	37%	6%	36%	64%

Response

Response	Total	Region		Age of respondent			Size of HH		Social class			Children	
		Dublin	Rest of Ireland	<35	35–49	50+	1–4 persons	5+ persons	ABC1	C2DE	F1F2	with	without
In the last week	6%	6%	6%	4%	3%	9%	8%	2%	6%	6%	8%	4%	8%
In the last two weeks	3%	2%	4%	–	5%	4%	2%	5%	2%	5%	–	4%	2%
In the last month	19%	26%	12%	11%	22%	23%	20%	16%	19%	22%	8%	16%	21%
2–3 months ago	27%	27%	26%	29%	27%	25%	26%	28%	26%	28%	19%	24%	28%
3–6 months ago	18%	16%	21%	18%	20%	18%	18%	21%	20%	14%	24%	21%	17%
More than 6 months ago then	26%	24%	28%	38%	20%	21%	25%	29%	25%	24%	41%	30%	23%

Table 5

Reasons for Buying Braycot Biscuits—First Reason

Table 5

Respondents who buy Braycot biscuits

	Total	Region		Age of respondent			Size of HH		Social class			Children	
		Dublin	Rest of Ireland	<35	35–49	50+	1–4 persons	5+ persons	ABC1	C2DE	F1F2	with	without
Sample	213	112	101	59	54	100	162	52	121	79	13	76	137
% of Sample		53%	47%	28%	25%	47%	76%	24%	57%	37%	6%	36%	64%

Response	Total	Region		Age of respondent			Size of HH		Social class			Children	
		Dublin	Rest of Ireland	<35	35–49	50+	1–4 persons	5+ persons	ABC1	C2DE	F1F2	with	without
Irish made	36%	33%	39%	33%	37%	37%	39%	28%	38%	32%	44%	30%	39%
Good value	3%	5%	2%	2%	3%	4%	4%	2%	1%	7%	8%	4%	3%
Nice taste	9%	12%	6%	8%	9%	10%	10%	8%	7%	15%	–	11%	9%
Health biscuit	21%	25%	17%	23%	26%	17%	19%	29%	24%	17%	19%	18%	23%
Looks nice	3%	4%	1%	2%	3%	3%	2%	4%	2%	4%	–	5%	2%
Like texture	3%	2%	5%	2%	2%	5%	4%	2%	3%	5%	–	3%	4%
Good range	2%	4%	–	–	3%	3%	2%	2%	1%	4%	–	2%	2%
Good quality	8%	11%	5%	7%	5%	11%	8%	11%	6%	11%	19%	8%	8%
New biscuit	20%	16%	26%	23%	16%	21%	19%	23%	19%	23%	18%	26%	17%
Other	5%	7%	4%	7%	7%	4%	3%	12%	6%	5%	–	5%	6%

Table 6

How Braycot Biscuits Are Usually Eaten

Respondents who buy Braycot biscuits

	Total	Region		Age of respondent			Size of HH		Social class			Children	
		Dublin	Rest of Ireland	<35	35–49	50+	1–4 persons	5+ persons	ABC1	C2DE	F1F2	with	without
Sample	213	112	101	59	54	100	162	52	121	79	13	76	137
% of Sample		53%	47%	28%	25%	47%	76%	24%	57%	37%	6%	36%	64%

Response

	Total	Region		Age of respondent			Size of HH		Social class			Children	
		Dublin	Rest of Ireland	<35	35–49	50+	1–4 persons	5+ persons	ABC1	C2DE	F1F2	with	without
Tea/coffee breaks	73%	66%	80%	74%	68%	74%	74%	68%	75%	67%	82%	75%	72%
Packed lunches	11%	14%	8%	4%	19%	11%	10%	14%	9%	14%	16%	11%	11%
Dinner time	14%	15%	12%	11%	14%	15%	16%	8%	16%	10%	15%	11%	15%
Tea time	15%	18%	11%	20%	12%	13%	13%	20%	15%	14%	11%	13%	16%
Supper	30%	34%	27%	36%	25%	30%	34%	18%	32%	29%	22%	33%	29%
Special occasions	23%	28%	18%	28%	27%	18%	22%	26%	22%	24%	30%	26%	22%
Other	6%	5%	6%	6%	6%	6%	7%	3%	4%	9%	–	8%	4%

Table 7

Family Members Who Usually Eat Braycot Biscuits

Table 7

Respondents who buy Braycot biscuits

	Total	Region		Age of respondent			Size of HH		Social class			Children	
		Dublin	Rest of Ireland	<35	35–49	50+	1–4 persons	5+ persons	ABC1	C2DE	F1F2	with	without
Sample	213	112	101	59	54	100	162	52	121	79	13	76	137
% of Sample		53%	47%	28%	25%	47%	76%	24%	57%	37%	6%	36%	64%

Response

	Total	Region		Age of respondent			Size of HH		Social class			Children	
		Dublin	Rest of Ireland	<35	35–49	50+	1–4 persons	5+ persons	ABC1	C2DE	F1F2	with	without
Children 0–9 years	23%	20%	27%	29%	46%	7%	16%	46%	27%	16%	30%	56%	5%
Male 10–14 years	11%	10%	12%	2%	29%	6%	6%	25%	7%	14%	27%	21%	5%
Female 10–14 years	11%	10%	11%	4%	25%	6%	6%	26%	11%	10%	8%	22%	4%
Male 15–19 years	11%	17%	5%	4%	13%	14%	6%	26%	9%	16%	–	10%	12%
Female 15–19 years	13%	15%	12%	4%	22%	15%	10%	25%	11%	17%	16%	12%	15%
Male 20–34 years	21%	20%	22%	32%	9%	21%	22%	18%	19%	25%	17%	21%	21%
Female 20–34 years	35%	35%	34%	77%	15%	21%	35%	34%	39%	28%	30%	44%	29%
Male 35–50 years	28%	27%	29%	42%	49%	9%	21%	51%	31%	20%	45%	48%	17%
Female 35–50 years	26%	25%	26%	7%	62%	17%	19%	46%	28%	21%	31%	37%	19%
Male 51+ years	22%	21%	24%	2%	8%	41%	24%	16%	19%	27%	25%	8%	30%
Female 51+ years	33%	31%	34%	–	2%	68%	34%	16%	25%	45%	25%	7%	47%

Source: Abstracted from Attwood Market Research report for Braycot Foods.

Questions

1. Assess the fortunes of Braycot Foods to date.
2. Do you agree with the UK research cited in the case that biscuits are very much an impulse purchase? What do you think of the consumer market research commissioned by the new marketing manager?
3. Analyse the structure and characteristics of the Irish biscuit market.
4. Develop a marketing strategy for Braycot Foods for both the domestic and international markets.
5. Speculate on the role of the new parent companies in the development of Braycot.

Part IV

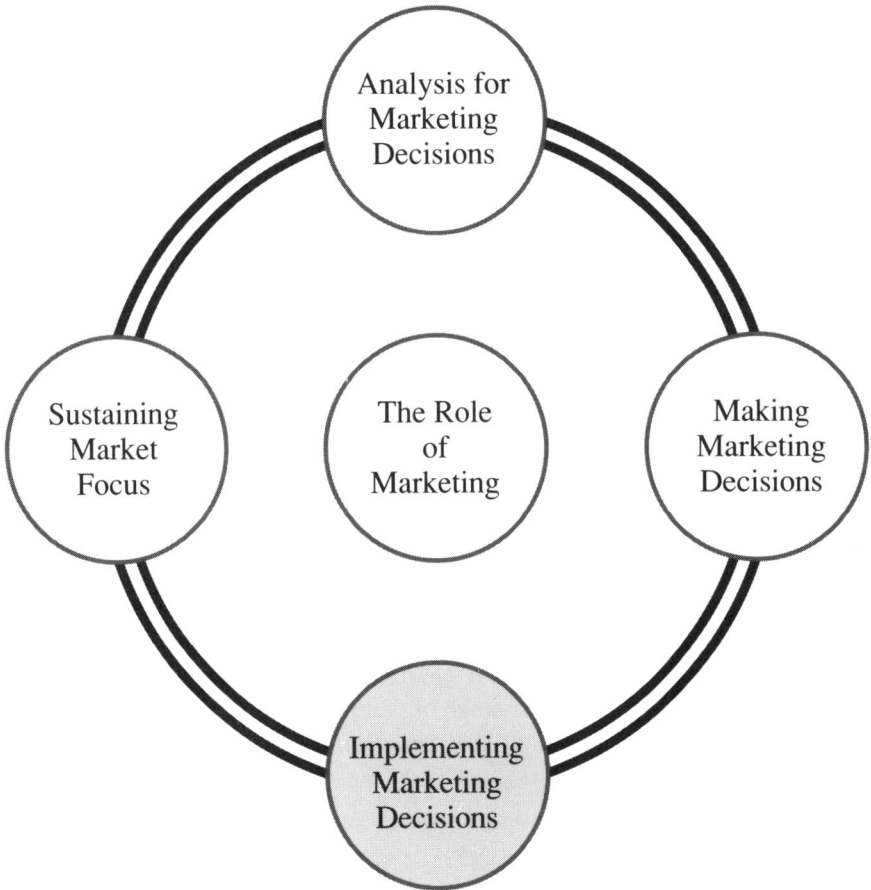

Analysis for Marketing Decisions

Sustaining Market Focus

The Role of Marketing

Making Marketing Decisions

Implementing Marketing Decisions

Chapter 17

Organisation and Control for Marketing

INTRODUCTION

Decisions about strategy and marketing programmes bring the manager to the point of knowing *what* to do. However, knowing what to do goes for nought if the manager is not equally clear about how to get it done: about the way to implement decisions.

Good decisions are never finally made until the process of seeing them into implementation has been thoroughly anticipated and planned. Thinking through the process of implementation will frequently lead the manager to alter some aspects of strategy or marketing programming on the grounds that organisational and resource constraints will not support the original proposed decisions. Planning for implementation must therefore interact with strategy formulation. Each must influence and shape the other.

Implementation is undertaken through organised activity—an organisation—and monitored and adjusted with the help of control mechanisms. Organisation and control are the focus of this chapter. We will concentrate on structures, systems and processes as pivotal elements of organising for marketing action. Finally, we will consider some of the organisational innovations, such as the idea of internal marketing, that are current during the nineties and that are likely to hold the seeds of organisational form in marketing for the twenty-first century.

ORGANISATION STRUCTURE

An organisation is a group of people and relevant technologies with some degree of permanence or stability that perform specific tasks in pursuit of explicitly or implicitly shared objectives. Companies are organisations of individuals and relevant technologies that seek a profit objective through serving market needs. One of the clearest formal traces of an organisation is its structure. An organisation's structure defines the way in which its members relate to each other, the specialisation of tasks, duties, responsibilities and accountability and the distribution of power among its members.

It is in the nature of a firm's organisation structure to evolve (see Figure 17.1). In a small or new firm the owner usually manages everybody else in a simple and informal structure. As the firm grows, this ceases to be effective and we normally see the emergence of a formal structure with managers taking responsibility for specific tasks such as marketing, production, finance or personnel. Administrative procedures and controls become explicit and embedded in systems such as budgets, production schedules or sales forecasts. Further growth in size and complexity may lead to loss of responsiveness in a company where all important decisions must be coordinated by one general manager. For instance, an important sales opportunity may have to pass through the hands of people in several sections and departments pre-occupied with other customers, other products, other sales territories or other design and production pressures. By the time their activities are coordinated and a decision is finally made, the opportunity may well have passed. Greater focus, responsiveness and flexibility is required and the people involved throughout the relevant parts of the organisation must be 'empowered' to make and execute the necessary decisions.

Companies will often adapt by reconfiguring their structure into one based on divisions which take care of defined products, territories or customers; take responsibility for performance and profitability; and are managed by a dedicated team with its own general manager. Such divisions are usually coordinated at what is typically called the corporate headquarters or head office, run by the chief executive and a team of specialist advisers in areas such as finance, planning, legal and public affairs. Divisions enjoy varying degrees of independence depending on their performance, the nature of their businesses and the individual style of the chief executive (see Exhibit 17.1).

Where divisions have considerable independence we will usually describe them as part of a decentralised structure, with important decisions delegated to divisional managers. By contrast, where the chief executive and the head office allow little discretion and impose strict control we speak of a cent-ralised structure. The degree of centralisation or decentralisation may vary as markets evolve and the company's circumstances change. As markets recede, divisions may of course wither and companies may even revert to a single 'division'.

In a divisionalised firm one is likely to find that there are three important levels of decision-making and strategic management. At a basic *product level* there are decisions and strategies to be made concerning individual products serving specific customer segments. At a divisional level, decisions and strategies which coordinate related product lines and customer groups are made. This is often referred to as business or *business level* strategy and the division may be characterised as a strategic business unit (SBU). At *corporate level*, decisions and strategies are concerned with the integration of all the businesses of the company, with providing an overall strategic direction and with allocating overall resources as effectively as possible.

Exhibit 17.1

CEMENT-ROADSTONE HOLDINGS

Strategy, structure and style

'CRH has a certain style as a company—but it's not florid or ostentatious. It's got more to do with being hard-working and reasonable people to deal with. The high-flyers would probably find us staid and pedestrian. But we don't think we're either of those things, we think we're okay,' says Tony Barry, chief executive explaining the group's conservative image despite its major significance to the Irish economy.

CRH, formed when Cement and Roadstone merged in 1970, is a huge company, with annual sales of £1.2 billion and employing over 12,500 people in Europe and the United States. A further 1,000 people are employed in associate companies. Its business is heavy building materials which it manufactures and distributes. The group has 51 principal subsidiary companies operating in the Republic, Britain, Northern Ireland, Spain, the Netherlands and the States.

CRH likes to groom its own managers, and Barry believes that in most cases, although not all, first-hand experience of the building materials business is a basic requirement for a future senior manager within the group. 'It's not a nice clean industry and we find it's best run by those who know what it's like to have worked at the sharp end. Our best managers are those who know how to run an operating company and how to make goods and trade them,' he says. Meeting managers in their surroundings rather than his is also part of Tony Barry's management style. 'I'm not there to put "hands on" and start trying to run their business for them. But I need to keep in touch with local markets, get a fix on costs and see how we are doing compared with the competition. The structure of our industry is broadly the same in every country and it's easy enough to draw performance comparisons once you get the local currency into your head.'

CRH is divided into three main operating units, each headed by its own chief executive with a supporting management team. The divisions cover the US, Europe and Ireland. The Irish and British operation is managed from Dublin, the US division from Los Angeles and the group's European base is in Rotterdam. In addition to these senior executives, Barry has a further three managers on his front line team who take responsibility for development, finance and services. 'Each divisional chief is effectively running a major business,' says Barry, 'and they are also responsible for a number of other functions, including company development. For example, we don't have a special acquisitions unit for the whole group; acquisitions are handled in the local market by local management.' CRH tries to give all its subsidiaries as much autonomy as possible. 'Our approach is to fit subsidiary companies into the reporting system and then leave them to get on with their business. Our requirement is that they should do it profitably and in accordance with agreed policy. By that I mean that the company should be run in a way that reflects the group's standing as a major supplier, showing respect to customers, the local community and the environment.'

Tony Barry spends very little of his time managing the group's trading on a day-to-day basis. He leaves that to his top team. Up to 30 per cent of his time is spent talking to major institutional shareholders, market analysts, banks and a variety of other groups who want information about CRH. Barry admits candidly that he could be taken out of the system and that the group could continue to operate its business quite smoothly. 'I definitely manage by delegation and I suppose it's mixed with a strong element of walk-about,' he says. 'This is mainly because I like to satisfy myself about things to do with the business. It might be an acquisition or a decision to move into a new country or even a key management appointment. Anything likely to affect the long-term future of the group is of major concern to me.'

Internationalising

The 1980s were a period of significant growth for CRH, during which the group steadily built its portfolio of overseas operations. Its acquisition philosophy has always been simple: stick to what you know. As Barry points out: 'Everything we have become involved with is broadly speaking construction-related. It's the business we are most comfortable with.' However, the group is no stranger to acquisitions. One of its founding companies, Roadstone, bought its first overseas company as far back as 1961. 'The focus of our business up to the mid-seventies was largely Ireland as there was a boom in the construction industry,' says Barry. 'At this time, practically all the profits being earned by the company were being ploughed back in to create the additional capacity needed to service an industry that was growing at 5 to 6 per cent a year, every year.' However, despite the buoyancy of the Irish market, CRH was not happy with the fact that over 90 per cent of its earnings were home-generated. The company decided it needed a better balance in its business, with less reliance on cement, which at the time accounted for a disproportionate amount of the company's profits.

'We decided on a strategy where we would earn no more than a third from cement, a further third should be earned outside Ireland, and the remaining third from other products,' says Barry. This change in focus saw CRH looking carefully at the UK market for opportunities, while it also dispatched senior executive Don Godson to the United States with 'a chequebook and suitcase', says Barry. From a standing start in the States in 1977, CRH now has interests in

350 locations spread across 25 states. The group also turned its attention to Europe and more specifically to Holland, where it now has extensive interests. In 1989 alone, the group acquired five new companies there and it operates a major DIY chain with over 30 outlets. 'As an individual company in the Netherlands we're number two in the first three in terms of size, and I suspect we're number one in terms of profitability,' says Barry. With a downturn now in both the US and UK economies does Tony Barry intend to put the brake on further CRH acquisitions overseas? 'I believe we have a sufficiently broad base to be able to make the best of things,' he says. 'It's true that the US is in a trough, but the construction industry there is so big, and our business sufficiently well spread, that we can take advantage of the parts of the industry which are still quite buoyant.'

The attraction of a recession is that companies can supposedly be bought cheap. But Barry is in no hurry to snap up a bargain for its own sake. 'We've spent a lot of money over the last couple of years on acquisitions and it takes time to bed them down. For example, of the £150 million we spent in 1990, £100 million went on acquisitions. These new companies now have to deliver against a market downturn. That means the rest of our business has to be working efficiently and delivering the cash to support them.' CRH, itself a possible target for the corporate raiders, has traditionally approached its acquisitions in a gentlemanly fashion, making no hostile bids. 'As a group we don't believe in hostile takeovers. We like to buy small to medium-sized, well-managed companies and to negotiate one-to-one with the existing management. If possible we like them to stay on after we have bought the business. Quite a number of our subsidiary companies are still run by the families who started them.' So how does Barry intend to prevent CRH from becoming a takeover target? 'A company is always vulnerable if it performs badly. A good performance is the best protection against any acquisition. It means someone else has to prove to shareholders that they can run your business even better.'

Source: *The Irish Times*, 8th March, 1991.

Historically, one of the most important insights into the nature and form of organisations was provided by Chandler's landmark study of the relationship between organisational strategy and structure. His research indicated that as strategy evolved, structures changed to support the implementation of the new strategies (Chandler, 1962). Thus, growing size and complexity evoked the organisational response of functional specialisation. Continued expansion and diversification into new products and markets in pursuit of further growth was likely to be followed by divisionalisation of organisations to provide a structure that would support the implementation of multiproduct and multimarket strategies.

Figure 17.1

Evolving Organisation Structure

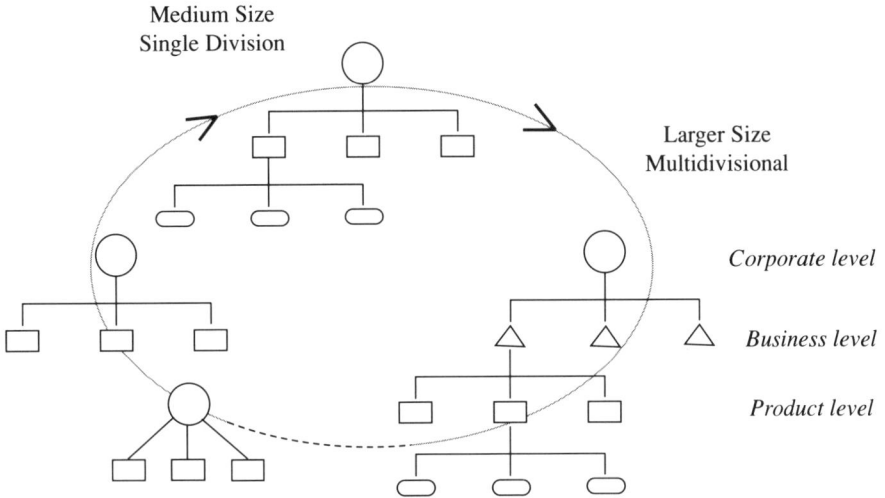

Medium Size
Single Division

Larger Size
Multidivisional

Corporate level

Business level

Product level

Strategy and structure

The debate about the relationship between strategy and structure has continued over many years. What is clear is that significant strategic change must, almost without exception, be matched by structural change. If this is not done, decisions to change strategy will usually founder as a structure designed to implement a former strategy makes it impossible to implement a new direction.

However, experience shows that structure is not just a consequence of strategy: it may also form and shape strategy. In a curious and, on occasion, in an almost sinister way the structure of an existing organisation delimits the strategies that its managers can envisage. What we are shapes what we can be—and that is just as true for organisations as for people. In this sense organisations are not unlike individuals. An organisation with structures characterised by deep vertical lines of specialisation; by rigid hierarchy; by commitment to specialised technology and by compartmentalised skills and competences will have great difficulty thinking of innovation and innovative market strategies, never mind implementing those of which it might conceive. By contrast, relatively small organisational units with 'flat', egalitarian structures that resemble an organism rather than a machine are much more likely to change and innovate. In their study of Scottish firms, Burns and Stalker (1961) characterised these two contrasting forms of organisation as organismic and mechanistic and noted that the former were more likely to innovate than the latter—the structure of the firm was a predictor of the strategic behaviour of the firm.

Structuring marketing activity

Before dealing with the specific options for structuring marketing activity, the contrast between structural arrangements in small or new ventures and in large companies demands some further comment. In small and in most new ventures, structure is very simple. In managerial terms, it may amount to no more than the owner-manager who directly supervises non-managerial staff. More developed small businesses and the typical technology-based new venture will have a small top management team and a supervisory management level. In such organisations specialisation of functions into departments usually makes little sense: a small group of key managers is involved in all major decisions, in planning and in implementation.

Organisations of this nature must be careful to distinguish between the *content* and *form* of marketing management and planning. The content is an essential requirement for success. The form, however, is most usually simple and relatively informal in such businesses. The information base for marketing decisions may often be held in the memories of the managers and updated constantly as they go about doing business. Equally, the process through which strategies are formulated and modified may be informal in the sense that it takes place during the never-ending series of meetings, debates and confrontations that are the daily life of the smaller business or the growing new venture. Small size and close intimate communication patterns make elaborate formal systems unnecessary. At the same time it is clear that good small businesses and prospering new ventures write down and regularly update marketing plans. This is a regular discipline that focuses and crystallises the endless strategic debate in such companies and that is essential to raising finance for growth and development.

One of the great mistakes made by observers of small and new ventures is to confuse the form of good marketing with its content: to confuse formal planning with good marketing. Any successful small or new business has by definition got the content of marketing right. Its smallness, the tightness of communication links and the market pressure for flexibility may render many formalised structures and systems not only irrelevant but even counter-productive. As organisations grow to deal with larger markets and greater volumes of business, marketing as a separate function emerges along with the finance, manufacturing and personnel management functions.

There are several options available in choosing a structure for the marketing function. The choice of structure should be made so that

(1) the organisation structure fits with the marketing strategy (if it does not, the strategy will not be implemented);
(2) coordination of marketing activity, and between marketing, manufacturing, R & D, finance, personnel, warehousing and all the other interdependent parts of the organisation, is maximised;

(3) responsibility for results is matched by authority to determine results;

(4) the flexibility of the structure to adapt to new market conditions and strategies is as great as possible (a structure that fits only one strategy is a dangerous structure).

The evolving nature of the marketing function

As companies grow in size it is possible for the marketing function to improve its performance by specialisation within the function itself. Sales, advertising, distribution, public relations, marketing research, marketing planning are common functional departments in many organisations. The approach allows depth of specialisation and should, in a general sense, result in greater effectiveness. This functional organisation form is, however, generally limited in its usefulness to large companies that produce a single product line and market to one or a few target markets. More complex product-market situations normally leave this form unable to respond adequately in terms of coordination, flexibility and customer knowledge. What may be required in these cases is a number of smaller, tightly knit marketing departments serving each product-market, division or customer group.

In many companies, a marketing function is created by adding a marketing department or management position in tandem with a traditional sales function. The roles of the two departments may remain unclear and uncoordinated, leading typically to the sales department concentrating on operational matters and the marketing department focusing on planning and market research. This is an unsatisfactory and unproductive state of affairs. The role of marketing must be clearly defined and the selling task integrated within its scope if good marketing practice is to result.

Brand management

Brand or product management structures are common in companies that have many products targeted on many customer segments. A major advantage of the organisational form is that managers can identify with 'their' product and manage it, much as a general manager would run a business. The form can therefore have significant motivational advantages in addition to providing a natural basis for planning and control systems built around products, their customers, competitors, market performance and product profitability.

However, this does not give the brand manager the same role and authority as a divisional general manager since the product or brand manager never controls all the resources fundamental to the success of the product. A product manager's responsibility may thus easily exceed his ability to influence key determinants of success and profitability. The system therefore depends on negotiation for resources, whether financial, manufacturing or manpower, and skills in negotiation and power brokerage can become crucial to the individual manager's success. Without strong strategic marketing at a company level, the system may also behave quite sub-optimally: the most forceful and assertive product managers will win resources and support for their products irrespective of strategic merit. Thus large volume brands with good margins very often retain and even acquire resources, while small new products in need of heavy marketing investment may wither for want of resources. A major danger in this structural form is therefore to delegate too much of the strategy-making to the product level. It is vital to retain central strategic marketing control at the corporate level so that resources are more optimally allocated.

Customer focus

In a sense, the 'purest' form of marketing organisation should be one structured around customers. Where a company serves several customer groups with quite different needs and buying behaviour, the approach works well. Many companies under competitive pressure in the early nineties took this course in reorganising their marketing so that customer groups became the key to structural design, with a company's many products and services coordinated to serve customers' overall needs. Thus, food companies may organise divisions around meals such as the breakfast, snack, lunch, dinner markets. Computer and information technology companies may shape themselves around problems to be solved such as computer-integrated manufacturing, financial data base management, and so on.

Matrix structures and company focus

The matrix structure attempts to balance two approaches to organising where the company finds that it must be highly responsive to two different driving forces. For example, it may be necessary that it achieve technological excellence in its products and at the same time provide great depth of service to different groups of customers. This may lead it to organise around both products and territories simultaneously. A critical consequence is that many individuals in the organisation will have two managers. For example, a sales engineer may report to a product manager to whom they are responsible for product sales and to a territory manager to whom they are responsible for area sales. Equally, a design engineer may report to a manager of design engineering and to a chief project manager for each construction project on which he is engaged.

However, complex matrix structures can lead to difficulties; at a minimum they appear to break a traditional principle of organisation structure of one man–one boss, so-called unity of command. Many large companies which experimented with this form, as did Texas Instruments in the early eighties, have reverted to more traditional approaches. Matrix structures are probably best avoided unless the nature of the market and the customer demands such a structural response as, for example, in the case of project-based engineering companies or educational institutes. Matrix-type structures are also used, as we see below, by large international firms trying to manage the complexities of multinational business.

Matrix structures vastly increase the need for coordination and communication and typically demand that a great deal of managerial time be devoted to managing the matrix. However, high levels of coordination between departments and functions, and effective communication, are key to managing marketing in the focused company. These have to be achieved however the firm is structured (and in cases 'despite' how it is formally organised). An organisation needs people from top to bottom who share a commitment to the essential ideas of focus and who are empowered to carry out their individual tasks in a manner that is consistent with the goal of focus—and this will often involve concentrating on processes and on the customer-centred tasks that must be done rather than on functional hierarchy and status.

INTERNATIONALISING

As companies grow and become more involved in international markets their organisation inevitably becomes more complex (see Figure 17.2). When a company just exports it remains quite firmly based in its home market. Exporting, even in its literal interpretation, suggests *sending* products and services overseas. This may well arise as a result of inquiries received from foreign markets as much as from active selling abroad. An export department or individual responsible for exports may well be established. Many small companies at this stage are characterised by a managing director who travels intensively and takes on the role of export salesperson. The use of agents and distributors in the export markets is a familiar mechanism at this stage of development to enable the company to reach customers beyond its own limited sales and distribution capability. Using export channels brings all the challenges of managing and controlling channels in any marketplace but has the additional complications of uncertainty with regard to foreign business practices, and the difficulty of securing attention for what may be a very small proportion of an agent's or distributor's total range of goods.

If the exporter is successful, then an overseas sales office may be established in the main foreign market. An overseas sales office will ease the problems of supporting distributors and customers and of providing timely service as well as managing routine procedures and selling effectively. Now employees of the company become permanently based overseas and it may begin to think more in the manner of an international company than that of an exporter. The sales office will, however, act on the instructions of the domestic head office and receive limited autonomy. It will usually be staffed, and almost certainly managed, by home country nationals.

The next stage in development is likely to be the establishment of some significant production or service operations presence in the company's main international market, or in a location from which many of the key markets may be serviced and supported. For many Irish companies this stage is executed by acquiring a foreign company or by entering into a joint venture or partnership agreement. Such entry mechanisms have the advantage of providing not only existing manufacturing and support facilities but also an immediate customer network and local staff with intimate knowledge of market realities. The cost of such acquisitions therefore includes the price of local market knowledge, customer goodwill and managerial competence as well as any physical assets that may be purchased. As we saw in Exhibit 17.1, this was the approach adopted by Cement-Roadstone Holdings in its international expansion. Another Irish company which has developed successfully overseas, Masstock, has used joint ventures allied to a 'greenfielding' or do-it-yourself approach in terms of setting up production and marketing facilities (see Exhibit 17.2).

Out of such beginnings grow the international, multinational and global companies that are familiar names around the world. As they grow in size and complexity they will most usually adopt some form of matrix organisation to cope with the complexities of international trading. These matrix structures most usually reflect geographic, product or business and functional dimensions.

The geographic basis for organising international activity often dominates the early stages in many companies' growth. This is especially the case in export-led firms where it may make good initial sense to develop markets one country at a time. Having achieved this, however, the geographic basis for structure may begin to limit flexibility and coordination. This problem is faced by many European international and multinational companies who have had great difficulty in achieving strategic coordination and control across country-based divisions or subsidiaries. These problems showed up most actively with the shift to pan-European strategies in the early stages of development of the Single European Market.

Choice of structure should above all be subject to the logic of implementing the desired market focus strategy with the implication that, for the growing firm, structure is likely to have to change quite frequently as the firm expands internationally and as market demands reshape themselves.

FROM PROCESS TO CONTROL

How marketing decisions are made, and even what kind of marketing decisions get made, is significantly determined by the way in which decision-making processes are structured. A temporary consensus on the structures for strategic decision-making, particularly in larger multidivisional companies, emerged in the 1980s. While this should be viewed as a temporary solution that will be adapted and improved with time, it is worth reviewing its form here.

Exhibit 17.2

MASSTOCK INTERNATIONAL

Developing field-to-retail agrifood systems

Masstock International is an agrifood technology company, headquartered in Ireland and enjoying an annual turnover of more than half a billion dollars. It has farming interests in the USA, the Middle East, China, Thailand and Central Africa and its marketing network spans Europe, the Gulf States, the Indian sub-continent and Australasia.

It is naive to believe, in the context of developing countries, that the transfer of the latest production technology into the vacuum of a primitive rural society is a viable way to initiate modernisation programmes. The enablement of a successful agrifood system involves many more elements than pure production methodology alone. It requires the inclusion of an entire gamut of peripheral support and downstream activities, the establishment of effective conduits of trade to the marketplace and the existence of smooth supply streams of inputs. Together these compose what Dr Alastair McGuckian, the visionary co-founder and chief executive of the privately owned Masstock International, refers to as 'agrifood vectors'. These vertically integrated agrifood systems—field-to-retail vectors—ensure continuity of supply at steady prices, facilitate operating efficiencies and encourage technological development and the search for every value-added opportunity.

Masstock's first years of existence, after being founded in 1970 in Northern Ireland, afforded the opportunity to experience many of the components of a typical agrifood vector: cereal farming, livestock farming, agricultural research and technology development, farm project design and implementation, food retailing, and marketing. This experience was marketed and sold in package deal offerings to livestock farmers in Britain and Ireland. But the archetype of the ultimate comprehensive Masstock product—the integrated agrifood vector—was not created and designed until the mid-seventies in Saudi Arabia.

In 1976 the first joint venture contracts, worth up to $50m for large-scale dairy farms, were signed between Masstock and the government of the Kingdom of Saudi Arabia—a country where there had never been a cow, where there was no grass, where most shopkeepers didn't understand the rudiments of refrigeration, where most houses had no refrigerators and where the temperatures reached a level of 130°F in May and stayed there night and day until October.

Feasibility studies and detailed plans and specifications were prepared, water was found and wells drilled. Irrigation systems were designed and implemented; forage crops were planted; all the equipment, buildings, dwelling houses, furniture, milking parlours, processing and packing plants, livestock, seeds, fertilisers, nutrients, feed supplements, and veterinary medicine were gathered from around the world and shipped to the sites. In March 1977 the milk started flowing. A brand *Almarai* was launched, and over the subsequent years a complete high-value product range was developed. Today Masstock's Saudi Arabian herd is the biggest dairy herd in the world. Out of the total 24,000 animals, 14,000 are milked three times per day each yielding 9,000 litres per year, more than twice the average of a dairy-rich country such as Ireland. The company produces 60 per cent of the fresh liquid milk needs of Saudi Arabia, processing the milk into a unique range of products, packing it and distributing to 14,000 shops every morning.

Masstock has developed similar vertically integrated agrifood systems in a number of other developing countries, usually in a joint venture with national governments. With a multinational payroll employing over 2,000 personnel from over 20 countries, it is essential to maintain a formal company structure. Yet the activities of Masstock's various enterprises—analysing, sourcing, supplying, producing, maintaining production, product development, processing, packaging, quality control and marketing—are highly interrelated operations. The company organises itself on a matrix type of structure whereby each separate enterprise operates with the necessary local autonomy yet is driven by and draws at various stages on the services of five corporate divisions.

The *Projects Division*, the spearhead of Masstock, identifies opportunities, carries out feasibility studies, oversees the design and planning stage, and liaises with universities and research foundations. During this pre-project period, the Projects Division will call on the experience and expertise of the Masstock Farming Division.

The *Farming Division*'s principal duties include the management of Masstock farm projects, recruiting personnel either from the host country or from overseas, specifying the machinery and materials needed, sourcing livestock requirements, drawing up breeding programmes and ensuring the achievement of targeted production.

The *Agricultural Services Division* is Masstock's technical division. It incorporates a laboratory service staffed by highly experienced qualified scientists. It also develops a wide range of own-brand agrochemicals, fertilisers, trace elements, pesticides, fungicides, hygiene products, veterinary drugs, vaccines, feed and seed.

The *Marketing Division*, with a wealth of global experience, investigates possibilities at either end of the chain linking original production to ultimate consumption. Where agricultural production exceeds the local need for fresh food Masstock explores export opportunities and investigates processing possibilities both in the country of origin and overseas. This is the most usual starting-point for Masstock's involvement with a new venture. However, on occasion Masstock, with its finger on the international pulse, will discover a new and hitherto unpublicised market need. This is fed back to a potential producer and yet another fresh venture comes into being.

The *Product Marketing, Sales and Distribution Division* rounds out the operation. It is responsible for packaging the product, for storing and distributing it, for promoting it through the press, TV, radio and on poster sites, for liaising with wholesalers—and taking account of feedback from retailers and the ultimate consumers. Without this division the entire operation would founder.

Source: A. McGuckian, 'Towards a global agrifood paradigm', *Irish Marketing Review*, vol. 4, no. 1, 1989.

Figure 17.2

The Internationalising Process

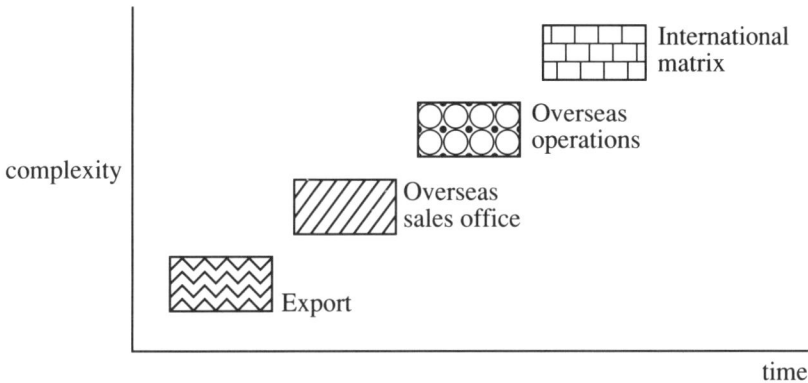

The planning and decision-making process in most organisations may be seen as an hierarchical one. As we saw earlier in the chapter (see Figure 17.1), at the top is the corporate or enterprise-wide level. Here, corporate strategy and marketing are concerned with issues inherent in business definition and the formulation of company mission: in what product-markets will we compete? with what distinctive advantages and competences? and with what outcome in terms of market share, return on investment, and cash flow? The next level down is that of the business unit—the individual divisions or strategic business units (SBUs) within the organisation that implement corporate strategy in related product-markets. These business units have the character of independent businesses in so far as they control the resources they need to do their job and are profit-responsible through their general manager to the corporate level. The corporate level may therefore be visualised as managing a portfolio of business units. Below the business unit comes the product level, consisting of an individual product or product line for which a functional marketing plan is required. The business unit therefore manages a product portfolio, while the manager at the product level manages that product line in its market. Thus, different managers at different levels concentrate on separate although intimately related decision problems. The structuring of the decision process allows considerable complexity to be dealt with in a simplified manner and without individual managers suffering from both information and decision overload.

Taking this process approach, marketing strategy formulation and planning may be designed and managed as shown in Figure 17.3. Here it can be seen that it is possible to gain the advantages of both top-down and bottom-up planning procedures while working through the sequence of decision-making from agreement on corporate guidelines to detailed specification of one-year targets and budgets. The advantage of creating processes of this nature is that they allow great complexity to be handled with relative ease by asking managers at different levels to concentrate only on what is most vital to the execution of their strategic role and by dividing the decision process into separable sequential phases rather than trying to cope with all steps simultaneously.

CONTROL SYSTEMS

Control systems form the basis for 'actioning' strategy. They do this by translating strategic direction into quantified objectives related to specific action-plans and programmes and allowing for these to become operationalised in the form of annual and shorter-term targets and budgets. For example, a company wishing to achieve market leadership must translate this strategic intent into component programmes which might include a new product launch. To implement this programme or action-plan, the marketing function must, among many other activities, set specific volume, price and revenue targets on a weekly, monthly and annual basis for the year of introduction. If this is done properly the activity of the individual sales representative, for example, will be planned on a weekly basis and his performance against budget/target monitored. Variance from budget is then managed for improvement by the sales manager. In this way, even the most specific daily actions are driven by the company's marketing strategy and its overall corporate intent.

This process is visualised in Figure 17.4. It is important to note that the final connection in Figure 17.4 is a feedback loop dedicated to short-term corrective action and to long-term strategic learning. Control processes are fundamental to good marketing management and central to managerial and organisational learning about the company's relationship with its environment. It has already been suggested that the combined planning and control process should be viewed as a design for learning. To learn, the company must be self-conscious about what it wants to do, about its assumptions, about linkages between its own behaviour and the reactions of the market, and about its expectations concerning the outcomes of each strategic move.

Figure 17.3

An Activity, Involvement and Timing Chart

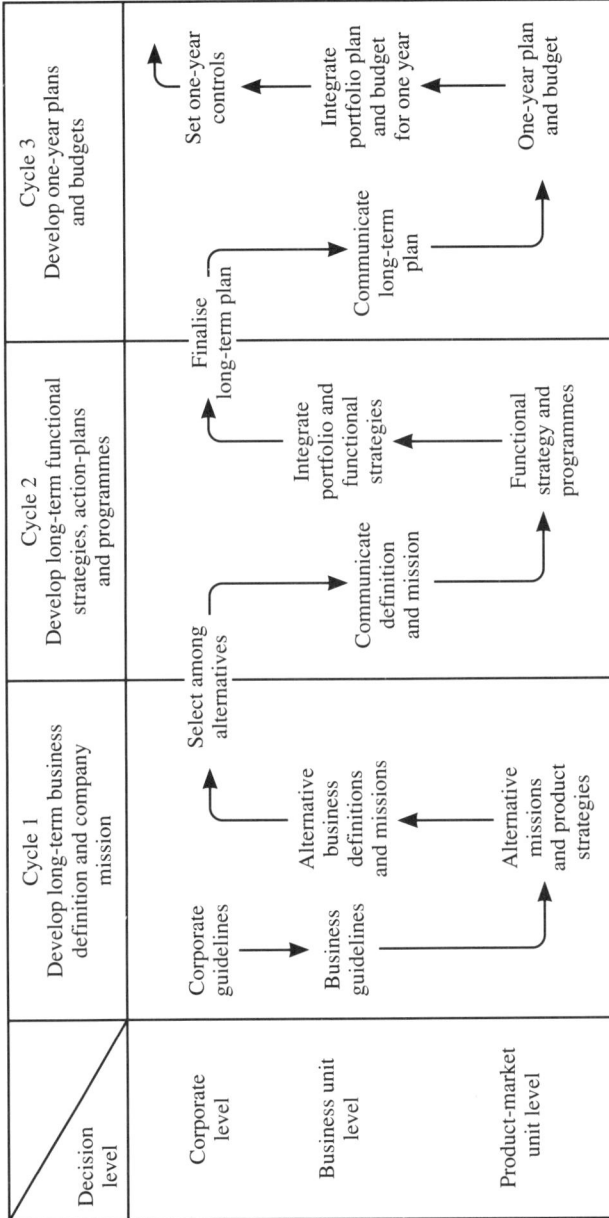

Based on a schema suggested by D.F. Abell and J.S. Hammond, *Strategic Market Planning: Problems and Analytical Approaches*, Prentice-Hall, Englewood Cliffs, NJ 1979, p. 451.

Figure 17.4

'Actioning' Strategy

```
                    ⬭
                  Action-Plans
                  Programmes


     ⬭                              ⬭
   Strategy                      Annual Profit Plan
                                   'The Budget'
```

Developed in broad outline.
Longer-term focus—2–5 years?

Specific, detailed, and
time-phased tasks.
Medium-term focus—6–18 months?

Feedback for corrective action.
Reassessing strategy?

Highly detailed and quantified targets and goals.
'Numbered' plans.
Real and concrete measures of performance.
Annual or 12-month focus.

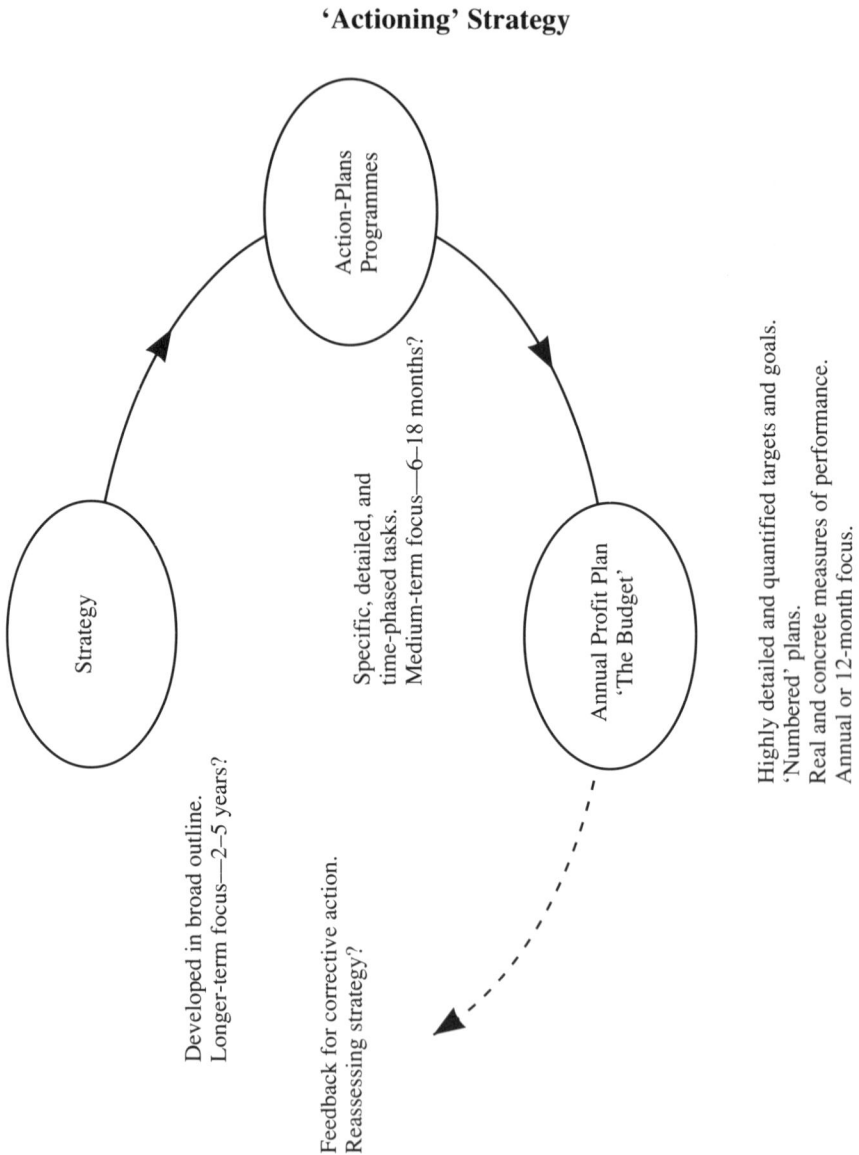

Control processes are therefore vital at both strategic and operating levels. Operating levels can be handled through the development and monitoring of programmes and the annual profit plan. Variances require an explanation. What went wrong? Does the cause lie in the company's implementation of the plan? in unforeseen changes in the environment? or in bad assumptions about customer or competitor behaviour? It is only by searching for causes that the true strategic value of the control system can be realised, as well as its value in directing the manager's attention to problems and the need for short-run tactical action.

Control systems are at the heart of successful implementation because implementation demands detailed programming of planned activity and the monitoring of actual against desired behaviour and outcomes. Implementation is seldom successful without the measurement and feedback guaranteed by a well-designed control process.

Control systems also involve the systems of rewards and incentives that a company uses to motivate and channel the energies of managers and staff. It is important to develop incentive systems that support the desired strategic behaviour of the company. Many companies fail to integrate strategy and its implementation through effective control systems. This can have unfortunate results. For example, an objective of building up a new product into a 'star' position will inevitably be unfulfilled if the relevant product or business manager is rewarded on the basis of annual contribution to profits. He will, under such circumstances, produce a first-year contribution from the product and may ruin its long-term potential for gaining share which may require perhaps twelve or eighteen months of negative cash flows. Rewards and sanctions must therefore be designed for consistency with strategic objectives, and in a multi-product, multimarket firm this demands quite complex arrangements, as objectives will vary considerably from one product and market to another.

INTERNAL MARKETING: MAKING IT HAPPEN

Making it all happen is therefore a difficult task that requires at least as much effort and creativity as that required by the strategy formulation and planning process. Making it happen also demands the creation of an organisational culture and a management and staff team dedicated to achieving agreed goals and to doing so with excellence.

The process of ensuring that the staff of a firm are committed to the goal of 'actioning' strategy, and in particular of ensuring the best possible treatment of customers, has been labelled 'internal marketing' (Barnes, 1989; Piercy and Morgan, 1989). This concept involves the application of marketing principles to 'selling the staff' on their role in implementing the firm's marketing policies. Internal marketing has two primary focuses. Firstly, it complements the company's external marketing efforts by ensuring that personal interaction between the company and the people it serves is as conducive as possible to attracting and satisfying customers. Secondly, internal marketing is directed at producing and maintaining a motivated and satisfied group of managers and employees, who will support the company's external marketing objectives and work towards ensuring quality, productivity and efficiency. This concept is applicable to all organisations, whether in the private, public or not-for-profit sectors, and regardless of whether a product or service is being marketed.

If the task of an internal marketing programme is to 'sell the staff' on the company's plans, programmes and customer service ambitions, then such a programme will require a marketing mix approach. The product in the internal marketing mix is a commitment on the part of staff to the idea of total customer service. The distribution component deals with the concept of marketing consciousness and customer commitment is 'delivered' to the staff. In the context of price it is useful to think not in terms of monetary price but rather in terms of what it costs employees, the target market, to participate. The promotional component involves all aspects of communicating messages concerning the programme to staff.

What the concept of internal marketing highlights is the often substantial gap or barrier between formulating a strategy or plan and then implementing it or putting it into practice successfully. Barriers result from the people, the systems and procedures, the departments and the managers whose commitment and participation are needed to implement marketing, i.e. the internal customers for marketing plans and strategies. In practice, surmounting such barriers involves: winning the support of key decision-makers for plans; changing the attitudes and behaviour of employees and managers who work at the crucial interfaces with buyers and distributors; gaining commitment to making the marketing plan work and 'ownership' of the key problem-solving tasks from those units and individuals in the firm whose working support is needed; and ultimately managing incremental changes in the culture from 'the way we always do things' to 'the way we need to do things to be successful'.

The lessons of Peters and Waterman's widely known study of 43 of the most outstanding companies based in the United States seem to summarise much of what is needed to make it all happen (Peters and Waterman, 1982). Looking at companies that had consistently performed above the financial average for their industry from 1960 to 1981, they found that they were all characterised by:

> *A bias for action:* The companies all were committed to getting on with their jobs and to learning very rapidly from their mistakes as well as their successes. Extensive analysis preceded action but never paralysed action-taking. A similar pattern is a clear feature of successful high-growth indigenous new ventures in Ireland.
>
> *Close to the customer:* The companies were obsessed by their customers, their needs and serving them better than any other company could. The marketing concept was truly vindicated!

Autonomy and entrepreneurship: The companies expected their managers to act creatively and innovatively and gave them the authority and responsibility to match the expectation.

Productivity through people: The excellent companies saw people as their key resources and treated them as individuals, gaining in return high levels of commitment and productivity.

Hands-on, value-driven: The managers and especially the leaders of these companies knew their businesses, their products, their technology and their customers inside-out and were as familiar with the manufacturing shop-floor as with the corporate boardroom. This is exactly the point of market focus as has been discussed in the previous chapters of this book.

Stick to the knitting: The best companies concentrated on what they knew how to do and do well, and innovation and change was built on their core technologies, customers and markets. Once again, Peters and Waterman were anticipating the emerging concern with core competences and our emphasis on the combined internal and external nature of market focus.

Simple form, lean staff: Complex structures were not characteristic, and where they did occur one function or area had clear priority. Equally, decision-making and expertise was located on the firing-line among line managers and not at any elaborate head office apparatus of staff specialists.

Simultaneous loose-tight properties: Great discretion and entrepreneurial autonomy was given to operating managers, but within the framework of a few unbreakable, non-negotiable company-wide policies typically concerning quality and customer service standards.

An interesting study of a number of Irish firms with 'strong culture' traits sheds further light on the nature of corporate culture and strategic success (Kelly and Gavigan, 1987). Most of these companies share the following characteristics:

- A company founder or chief executive highly committed to the idea of a strong organisational culture whose leadership style is clearly employee oriented.
- The extensive use of statements about company beliefs and values—e.g. 'product quality is the hallmark of our success'—all clearly articulated and widely disseminated through various transmission mechanisms.
- A strong and influential role for the personnel or human resources department within the organisation.
- Rigorous recruitment, selection and induction policies for new company personnel.

- Staffing appraisal and reward systems as well as a participative working environment, all reflecting a strong employee commitment policy.
- Significant emphasis on communication, participation, socialisation and egalitarianism in the way the company is run and, in particular, in regard to all human relations matters—e.g. single status access to canteen and parking facilities.
- A strong orientation towards their respective local communities and a keen sense of social responsibility.

All these findings underline the extent to which good marketing practice goes beyond technical, quantitative, matters and must embrace the humanistic and qualitative issues of managing marketing. The student or the marketing professional should be reminded that the less tangible dimensions of management such as leadership, managerial style and company culture are at the heart of implementing technical insights. Indeed, we are dealing with a closed circle of interaction, since the quality and creativity of technical managerial work depends on the leadership it is given and on the climate of commitment, innovation and autonomy within which it takes place. An organisation in which competences are brought together in an environment of shared values and imaginative leadership stands the best chance of outperforming its competitors. The role of internal marketing is critical to pursuing this aim.

SUMMARY

The difficulties and problems inherent in implementing a marketing strategy, once formulated, should not be underestimated. The form of organisation structure best suited to the intended strategy is a crucial consideration. This raises issues, amongst others, of the size of the firm, the complexity of its product/service offerings, the need to divisionalise or set up SBUs, and the benefits of a product or brand management structure. Internationalising firms face particular problems in choosing foreign market modes of entry.

Putting a strategy into action also involves developing action-plans and programmes, as well as budgets and annual profit plans; control systems must be set in place. People—management and employees at every level—must also be motivated to pursue enthusiastically the goals of the strategy. Internal marketing is key. The nurturing of shared values and a supportive company culture is paramount in enabling the focused firm to achieve its objectives.

Reading

Abell, D.F. and Hammond, J.S. (1979), *Strategic Market Planning: Problems and Analytical Approaches*, Prentice-Hall, Englewood Cliffs, NJ.

Baker, Michael J. (1992), *Marketing Strategy and Management*, 2nd ed., Macmillan, Basingstoke, chs. 19, 20, 21.

Barnes, James G. (1989), 'The role of internal marketing: if the staff won't buy it, why should the customer?', *Irish Marketing Review*, vol. 4, no. 2.

Bonoma, T.V. (1985), *The Marketing Edge: Making Strategies Work*, The Free Press, NY, chs. 1, 2, 11.

Burns, T. and Stalker, G.M. (1961), *The Management of Innovation*, Tavistock Publications, London.

Carson, David and Kennedy, Maurice (1988), 'Implementing the marketing concept: a case history of Northern Ireland electricity', *Irish Marketing Review*, vol. 3.

Chandler, Alfred D., Jr (1962), *Strategy and Structure*, The MIT Press, Cambridge, Mass.

Jeannet, J.-P. and Hennessey, H.D. (1988), *International Marketing Management: Strategies and Cases*, Houghton Mifflin, Boston.

Kelly, Aidan and Gavigan, Thomas (1987), 'Corporate culture and strategic success', *Irish Marketing Review*, vol. 2.

Kotler, P. (1991), *Marketing Management: Analysis, Planning, Implementation and Control*, 7th ed., Prentice-Hall, Englewood Cliffs, NJ, chs. 25, 26.

McGuckian, A. (1989), 'Towards a global agrifood paradigm', *Irish Marketing Review*, vol. 4, no. 1.

Peters, Thomas J. and Waterman, Robert H. (1982), *In Search of Excellence: Lessons from America's Best-Run Companies*, Harper & Row, NY.

Piercy, Nigel and Morgan, Neil (1989), 'International marketing strategy: leverage for managing marketing-led strategic change', *Irish Marketing Review*, vol. 4, no. 3.

Review Questions
1. What criteria should be applied in the choice of organisational structure to implement a marketing strategy?
2. How does the strategy and structure of the internationalising firm evolve over time?
3. What relationship is there, if any, between a firm's annual profit plan and its long-term marketing plan?
4. Elaborate on the concepts of internal marketing and shared values in an organisation, and how these may be used in implementing a marketing policy.

Case 7

ActionAid

ActionAid, an international charity, aimed to improve the quality of life in Third World countries by equipping children and their families with the resources and skills to achieve self-reliance. Its child sponsorship scheme was its main funding method. An Irish affiliate of ActionAid was set up under the direction of a board of trustees to build on a small existing supporter base and attempt to become a significant participant in the Irish Third World charity market.

Issues: *Marketing for the non-profit organisation. Developing and implementing a plan. Consumer research. Donor channels, promotion, advertising and media decision-making.*

Aid to developing countries is a subject of much debate both as to how to raise funds and how best to use funds which become available. The United Nations has set a target of .7 per cent of GNP as the level of aid that developed countries should provide. In Ireland's case, official aid currently amounts to about .2 per cent. However, the Irish public has traditionally been very generous in making up for the government's deficiencies through its donations to voluntary agencies.

Although, in theory, the aim of charities is to expand the donation base, the reality is that organisations specialise in either specific causes or aspects of their work and then, in effect, compete for funds based on the appeal of their unique selling points. As such, domestic charities and Third World agencies compete for market share. The Third World agencies in turn compete within their market segment.

The Third World charity market in Ireland had been experiencing some remarkable activity in its marketing and promotion during the eighties. Famine in Ethiopia, Sudan and Mozambique had heightened the public's awareness of developing countries' needs and consequently most charities had been working to convert this awareness into active financial support.

ActionAid was an international agency which in 1985 set up an Irish affiliate with a view to building on an existing supporter base of approximately 1,000 people in the Republic of Ireland. It was hoped that this new development

This case was developed as a basis for class discussion rather than to illustrate either effective or ineffective handling of an administrative situation.

charity would attract sufficient support to grow and become economically viable as an independent Irish affiliate of the international ActionAid organisation.

ATTITUDES OF IRISH PEOPLE TOWARDS AID TO THIRD WORLD COUNTRIES

In late 1985 a survey was carried out by Irish Marketing Surveys Ltd on behalf of the Advisory Council on Development Cooperation. The quota sample of 1,392 was representative of the Irish adult population. The survey was administered in 52 sampling areas throughout the Republic of Ireland. The objectives of the study were to ascertain Irish people's opinions in the following areas:

- causes of poverty in the Third World
- likely solutions
- development aid and whether this was mirrored by personal efforts
- the government's aid programme
- likely future developments in the Third World.

We will look at only some of the survey findings that are of relevance to ActionAid. Referring to the first objective, respondents perceived 'lack of education' as the most important cause of poverty in the Third World. The second most important cause was neglect of the poor by their own governments. Other causes such as natural disasters and population growth were also identified.

In relation to the second objective, the pattern of solutions which was viewed as most effective emphasised education-related changes. It emerged that education was perceived as the single most important positive factor affecting Third World countries.

In relation to the third objective, 91 per cent of respondents expressed a favourable attitude towards aid to the Third World. A high degree of personal commitment was also indicated. During the previous two years 93 per cent of the sample had helped the Third World, with 96 per cent of these making a financial contribution. The question 'How much money did you give to help the Third World last year?' brought the following results:

Less than £5	36%
£6–£10	26%
£11–£19	10%
£20–£50	20%
£51–£100	2%
Over £100	2%
Don't know	4%

The following points were also highlighted in the survey:

(1) When giving money people have a bias towards Irish agencies such as Trócaire rather than 'foreign' ones such as Oxfam. An Irish name is an advantage.

(2) Because of recent scandals relating to embezzlement of charities, people are concerned about the integrity of the agencies. Trócaire, for example, because of its association with the Catholic Church and particularly Bishop Casey (Bishop of Galway diocese and a committed supporter of Third World development), is perceived as being trustworthy.

(3) Older people are attracted to relief agencies and projects which are short-term whereas younger people tend to favour long-term development.

(4) Young people are more politically aware of Third World problems and tend to associate the sources of problems with political difficulties, for example, the USA in Nicaragua and the USSR in Ethiopia.

(5) Feedback on projects is regarded as being very important by donors. People like to know how their money is being spent.

(6) People feel that non-governmental organisations (NGOs) are better at maximising the use of funds raised when compared with national governments.

THE IRISH THIRD WORLD CHARITY MARKET

At present the market is serviced by many household names such as Trócaire, Concern, Gorta, Oxfam and Goal. All of these agencies tend to concentrate on particular aspects of aid to the Third World. The following is a brief profile of each of the above agencies.

(1) *Trócaire*

Established in 1973, this is the official development agency of the Roman Catholic Church in Ireland. It has a structure that encompasses the bishops, clergy and lay people. Being a Church agency could be said to be its great advantage over other organisations, as 95 per cent of the Irish population is Roman Catholic. Its primary objectives are:

- To support long-term development projects in the Third World.
- To provide emergency relief in times of disasters.
- To provide a development education programme in Ireland.

Financial resources are committed as follows:

- 70% Development projects
- 10% Emergency relief
- 20% Development education.

Trócaire raises approximately £10–£12 million per annum. Of this approximately 3 per cent is spent on administration. This is the lowest percentage of any charity organisation in the country. Trócaire's biggest strength is that it has a ready-made professional collection agency at its disposal, in the Church's diocesan structure. Trócaire does not send out volunteers; it works through existing structures.

(2) *Concern*

Concern has been established in Ireland since 1968 and is a non-denominational voluntary organisation. Concern sends skilled volunteers from Ireland to work with disadvantaged groups in its countries of operation. One of Concern's primary objectives is to give assistance in terms of emergency relief. Volunteers then remain in the crisis area until those worst affected have been restored to a level where they will be less vulnerable in the future.

Concern employs eight full-time representatives whose principal job is initiating and organising fund-raising events. They also have a support group (called Concern Volunteer Service) in each major town or city throughout the country organising fund-raising and collections. Annual income is approximately £6 million.

This is spent as follows:

- 10% Administration
- 5% Development education
- 85% Overseas development expenditure.

(3) *Gorta*

This is the official Freedom from Hunger Council of Ireland. Set up by the government in 1965 its patron is the President of Ireland and its President is the Minister for Foreign Affairs. It is a national organisation with a committee in every county.

Gorta is not in the business of famine relief or of responding to disaster appeals. Its objectives are:

- To help the people of the Third World with self-help agricultural projects.
- To encourage the setting up of fund-raising events in Ireland to finance these projects.
- To promote in Ireland an awareness of the appalling conditions in which the people of the Third World struggle to survive.

Gorta raises approximately £1 million per annum. Part of this is a government grant with £66,000 also provided towards administration.

(4) *Oxfam*

This is a British-based charity working in Ireland. Its objective is to act as a relief agency designed to help the underprivileged in the Third World. Its annual income in Ireland is approximately £2.5 million. Its use of funds is as follows:

- 69% Emergency aid
- 17% Social development
- 8% Health
- 6% Agriculture

(5) *Goal*

This is the sportsman's charity. Goal sends volunteers into Third World countries for long- and short-term stays. Its annual income is approximately £1 million.

FUND-RAISING TECHNIQUES

The following is an outline of the methods of fund-raising used by Third World charities:

(1) Trócaire	Lenten Campaign
	Friday Fast box
	Bank giro
(2) Oxfam	Shops
	Stamps and coins
	Personal treasures, e.g. jewellery
	Book sales
(3) Concern	Christmas Fast appeal
	Christmas box
	Postal donations
	Banker's standing order/direct debit
	Bequests
	Church gate/street collections
	Sponsored walks/cycles
	Group fund-raising projects
(4) Gorta	Special project funding
	Sales of work
	Shops
	Regular contributions
(5) ActionAid Britain	Child sponsorship
	Special projects
	Community games
	School sponsoring school
	Village sponsoring village
	Sponsor a will
	Children's club

Other fund-raising techniques include:

> Children in Need appeal in Britain
> Possibility of doing the same in Ireland
> Sunshine Radio charity appeal
> Central Remedial Clinic Auction
> Company sponsorship
> ActionAid week
> Personalities on the board
> Workers' involvement ... Trade Union groups
> Fashion shows
> Flag days
> Charity balls
> Sponsorship by well-known personalities
> Primary/Secondary/Third-level involvement
> Auctions
> Fasts
> Sponsor a sporting event
> Sponsor Field Days ... Macra na Feirme
> Painting/Essay competitions
> Exhibition matches
> Concerts
> Marathons

ACTIONAID—HOW IT WORKS

ActionAid works with children, families and communities in some of the poorest parts of Africa and Asia, using low-cost techniques and local resources to promote community development and self-reliance.

ActionAid was founded in England in 1972 by Cecil Jackson-Cole, founder of Help the Aged and co-founder of Oxfam. From the beginning it has drawn support from most parts of the world. Sponsors in 37 countries are now contributing to development work in overseas programmes. It is a non-denominational voluntary organisation.

In four of these countries, Australia, France, Ireland and Spain, there now exist separate organisations with their own board of trustees to promote the activity of the charity through local support. ActionAid's major aim is to help change lives for the better by equipping children and their families with the resources and skills which will enable them to achieve self-reliance—to look after themselves through their own efforts.

It achieves this aim mainly through its child sponsorship scheme, which now provides educational assistance for more than 100,000 children. In the UK there are over 80,000 sponsors while the majority of other sponsors comes from France and Spain. Through sponsorship individuals and groups are linked to a child overseas. These children are taught literacy and numeracy and are given agricultural and vocational training appropriate to their life-style. ActionAid also gives more direct assistance to their communities through development projects such as the provision of wells for drinking water and irrigation, instruction in simple farming techniques and the provision of skills training and credit to promote income-earning activities.

WHAT IS SPONSORSHIP?

This scheme enables individuals, families and groups to sponsor an individual child in one of ActionAid's projects. Sponsorship currently costs £10 per month—less than the cost of a month's newspapers. All of this sum of £10 goes to an overseas programme of services benefiting the child and its community. This includes the provision of school buildings, teacher training, educational materials and vital village projects such as the provision of wells for drinking water and irrigation.

In addition if a sponsor signs a Deed of Covenant (a commitment to contribute for at least five years), the charity is able to reclaim the income tax already paid to the revenue commissioners on the £10. This extra source of funds is used to pay for the cost of administration, recruitment of new sponsors and also to finance the expansion of work overseas. A sponsor agrees to take responsibility for sponsoring a child for up to seven years ensuring that the child is supported throughout his education. A sponsor receives a 'case history' (see Appendix A) of the child: a photograph and details of the child, his family and the country in which they live. The sponsor has the opportunity to keep in touch with the child's progress through the exchange of letters and reports—usually two or three times a year.

ActionAid may be seen to differ from other development agencies in a number of ways:

(1) It emphasises the importance of education.
(2) It looks for long-term financial commitment from its supporters, i.e. £10 per month over seven years.
(3) It links people at an individual level.
(4) The funding of overhead expenses comes from Deed of Covenant rebates from the revenue commissioners rather than from donors' funds.

WHO SUPPORTS ACTIONAID?

In the UK most of ActionAid's success has come from sponsors recruited through advertisements in the quality Sunday newspapers such as *The Sunday Times* and *Observer*. This has resulted in a middle-class bias among sponsors. In Ireland the initial 1,000 or so sponsors were attracted by the same advertisements. But within six months of the setting up of an Irish affiliate, certain characteristics appeared to be emerging among new sponsors.

(1) Women seemed more attracted than men to the idea of sponsorship.
(2) Two age groups tended to dominate: firstly, young people either single or newly-wed, and secondly, middle-aged people either single or with grown-up families.
(3) Irish sponsors came from all socio-economic groups.

WHICH CHILDREN ARE SPONSORED?

There is one major criterion which ActionAid uses in selecting an area for assistance: need. ActionAid is working in some of the poorest and most remote areas of the world; consequently, once an area is identified as being in need, nearly all the children in the community are sponsored. Many would never get the chance to go to school without ActionAid's help.

ActionAid sponsors children between the ages of two and fifteen, i.e. mainly at primary but some at secondary school age. It is these children who are most in need of schooling and who can gain the most benefit from it. The local community itself gathers the children for enrolment in a new school.

ACTIONAID'S PROGRAMMES

The work which ActionAid undertakes varies in certain details from country to country but the common focal point is education. The majority of the children in the sponsorship scheme live in rural areas. For them education will usually consist of the teaching of basic literacy and numeracy in the mother tongue with great emphasis on practical training through the demonstration of farming practices and techniques. The aim is to provide each child with the knowledge and skill to grow sufficient food for his family and to earn a cash income from a surplus. In the long term, the objective is to enable each child and his family to become self-reliant. In a sense to help the child is seen as a mechanism to help the family and, in turn, the community.

India: ActionAid does not run its own projects in India, but supports children in schemes run and staffed almost entirely by Indians. The basis of this assistance is education and training, and ActionAid is helping to improve teaching methods by encouraging teachers to make the curriculum more relevant and by adding extra stimulus through arts, crafts, singing and games.

Nepal: This programme began in October 1982 and is helping communities in a remote mountainous area near the capital Kathmandu. Assistance is being given to primary schools to build classrooms, train teachers and buy desks, books and other school materials. ActionAid is also establishing a number of community learning centres which cater for children who can afford only a couple of hours a day for lessons before working in the fields.

Bangladesh: ActionAid's newest programme, which was set up in 1983, concentrates on the twin aims of providing assistance in education for the children of disadvantaged minorities and establishing a rural credit savings scheme for the landless, smallholders and women's groups. This will provide a lever to help poor people become self-employed and self-reliant.

Kenya: ActionAid first began work in Kenya in 1976 and now more than 42,500 children are being sponsored and assisted with primary education, food and clothing. These youngsters are given skills training based on the principle of 'learning by doing' and this includes handicrafts, building, carpentry and agricultural techniques. The agency's work has now spread to give special assistance to the disabled, particularly with the use of low-cost instruments, and also to women's groups in the form of agricultural income generation schemes.

Uganda: After more than ten years of economic and political instability, much of the country has reverted to a life of subsistence. The existing primary schools struggle to provide a basic education in the face of a lack of even the simplest teaching materials. There are dilapidated buildings that cannot be repaired or replaced because building materials cannot be obtained, and very poor conditions for teachers. ActionAid is currently assisting 15 primary schools in the Mityana areas, helping to provide the materials which they so urgently need.

The Gambia: This tiny West African country relies on its groundnut crop for over 90 per cent of its export earnings. The majority of the population depends upon what it alone can grow for survival. ActionAid's programme provides primary level education together with clean water and agricultural help for many communities. Many villages have never had an adequate school building; ActionAid enables them to build their own by supplying materials and expertise. Through a wide variety of projects such as irrigated vegetable gardens, ActionAid aims to assist, in particular, the rural women of the Gambia.

Somalia: The country has suffered from the effects of a bitter border conflict and severe droughts for many years; as a result, more than 700,000 refugees are sheltering in Somalia. ActionAid has helped to establish day care centres in the refugee camps in partnership with a number of voluntary organisations. These centres are teaching refugees nutrition, health care, literacy, numeracy and child care. In the north-east, north-west and south-west, ActionAid runs a number of agricultural training and income earning skills projects. In the north-east a new sponsorship programme began in 1984 involving school construction, repairs and the supplying of educational materials. Plans have been made for projects developing water resources, agricultural and anti-erosion techniques.

FUNDING PROJECTS

Although sponsorship is the major means of raising funds for the charity, many of ActionAid's supporters prefer to fund specific projects. These projects can be funded in a variety of ways including direct appeals, donations, legacies, donations of gifts for auction, governmental co-funding, and the Village Neighbour and Community Link schemes. There is also a whole network of local groups around the country who fund a large number of development projects through regular fund-raising activities.

COMMUNITY LINK

This scheme enables a community in Ireland to link with a village overseas in a form of 'twinning' arrangement. The community receives detailed information about the overseas village and raises a minimum of £2,000 a year for five years to ensure that a comprehensive series of projects can be carried out. The link itself centres on an exchange of information which encourages greater understanding between different cultures.

VILLAGE NEIGHBOURS

A Village Neighbour contributes £72 a year towards projects such as the digging of new wells or vegetable gardens in an overseas village. Up to 200 Village Neighbours help one village in the Third World. Each sponsor receives a detailed information pack which introduces the village and explains the conditions which shape its daily life, plus regular progress reports.

SPONSORSHIP AS A METHOD OF FUND-RAISING

Sponsorship as a method of fund-raising has generated a significant degree of comment both positive and negative. The negative reactions tend to have come in response to the way in which it has been used by certain organisations of American origin. The following extracts culled over a period from Irish newspapers and other media present the issues raised both for and against sponsorship.

WHAT THE COMMENTATORS SAY ... ARGUMENTS IN SUPPORT OF CHILD SPONSORSHIP

(1) One should not disparage one method of charity in comparison with any other. The sponsoring or fostering of a child on the home front or anywhere in the First World is not viewed as undesirable.

(2) Many feel bound to help their less fortunate neighbours, and see ActionAid child sponsorship as an effective means of doing something about it.

(3) Sponsorship gives a hand-up not a hand-out to the child.

(4) No one approach of a charity agency is appropriate in all situations. Sponsorship is seen as one way into useful community development.

(5) Sponsorship is not done in one area for one child, but for the whole community, if possible.

(6) It is a reasonably cost-effective means of raising funds, given that subscribers will stay for six or seven years.

(7) ActionAid's administration costs are met by a Tax Covenant Deed.

(8) The essence of sponsorship is to promote the skills and learning which are at the very root of self-sufficiency.

(9) It relieves one's sense of guilt about a high standard of living in the West.

(10) There is a human face on which we can focus and get a better understanding of actual conditions. This method of donating money seems more personally fulfilling than other approaches.

(11) There is continuity of contact with a real child instead of a large impersonal organisation. The regular exchange of letters and photographs given to each other is an insight into a very different way of life which is illuminating to both.

(12) If sponsorship is such a terrible thing, why do the Churches in the Third World accept the invitation to be involved in the schemes?

WHAT THE COMMENTATORS SAY ... CRITICISMS OF CHILD SPONSORSHIP

(1) The method of fund-raising is patronising. It helps to maintain a kind of 'support-the-black-babies' attitude implying a superiority on the part of the First World.

(2) Child sponsorship can be insulting to the dignity of the Third World people.

(3) Child sponsorship is, in the long term, anti-developmental.

(4) Sponsorship is divisive within the community it seeks to serve. It can be seen as elitist.

(5) Fund-raising should not be attained by emotional advertising.

(6) It hinders education at home as to the real needs of the developing world. It is argued that solving the problems of the Third World involves educating the developed world about the nature of global economic development, trade, embargoes, pricing practices and possible economic exploitation between the two worlds. It is a complex issue to be solved not only by 'handing over money' but by changing attitudes in the First World.

(7) It causes divisions and jealousy in communities and families in these countries.

(8) Sponsorship of a deprived child in a deprived community fails to solve the community's problem—it creates new ones.

(9) Heavy administration costs in this form of personalised sponsorship scheme are a waste of money. It could be spent on children.

(10) Children have been described as a marketing medium to attract the interest of donors.

(11) Child sponsorship tends to reduce the nature and content of all problems besetting the Third World to a level which does nothing to illustrate either the scope of the problems, their causes or our duty in justice to help solve them.

(12) As promoted by World Vision, 'Child sponsorship offers a patronising outdated sentimental approach which is in fact a gross simplification of the issues and distracts attention from them.'

THE FUTURE

In 1985 the Irish affiliate of ActionAid was set up under the direction of a chairman and board of trustees. A full-time office was established staffed by an officer who was a former development worker of many years' experience in Third World countries. This officer was charged with the responsibility to develop, along with the board, a strategy for expanding the activities of the charity in Ireland and enabling it to become a significant participant in the Irish Third World charity market.

As the newly appointed officer settled into his job, seeing 1986 as the first crucial year of his stewardship of ActionAid, many aspects of the task occupied his mind. Who would most likely subscribe to ActionAid? Would the UK experience be replicated in Ireland or was the recently emerging pattern among new Irish sponsors a genuine trend? Were the particular fund-raising techniques and the consequent channels through which a donor could subscribe an important consideration? (Appendix B outlines a UK report which sheds some interesting light on these preoccupations.)

A 'media facts sheet' (see Appendix C), which the chairman had recently thrown on his desk with the comment, 'You might find this useful,' left the officer in no doubt that the way ahead would be found in a well-conceived and controllable plan of campaign.

APPENDIX A

NAME:	Wesley Tukuri Bomtich.
SEX:	Male.
AGE:	6 Estimated.
DATE OF BIRTH: (if known)	1980 Estimated.
PROJECT:	Kipsaraman Catholic Mission.

PERSONAL HISTORY:
There are seven children in Wesley's family, three of whom belong to his mother. His father has two wives. They are a subsistence farming family with a few livestock and a small piece of land on which they occasionally grow maize and beans.

This Mission is located at Kipsaraman, Baringo District, Rift Valley Province, Northern Kenya, 50km from the nearest town Kabernet. It serves as a community centre for the local people, providing facilities for groups like a women's traditional crafts group and an agricultural club as well as simple meals for the children.

The soil in this hilly area is reasonably good for growing maize, beans and millet which are grown at subsistence level without the use of modern implements. Some people live a nomadic lifestyle grazing cattle, sheep and goats.

Communications, health care and water are very poor. The houses are round huts thatched with grass and mud walls, basic diet being ugali (thick porridge). The extended family is important as there is a tradition of coming together to solve common problems.

ADDRESS FOR CORRESPONDENCE:
c/o ActionAid
PO Box 42814
Nairobi
Kenya

For children in rural Kenya, being poor often means being hungry—maybe only one meal of maize and beans a day; overcrowded—maybe only one small room for a large family; ill from inadequate sanitation and polluted water supplies; and having little opportunity to break the bonds of these conditions and help themselves, their families, and their communities to improve the quality of their lives.

One route to the awareness and understanding that can liberate the poor from the conditions of their poverty lies through education. Primary schools in Kenya are free. Although the government pays the teachers and supplies the books, the local communities and, in particular, the parents must provide the buildings, desks, benches, and other furniture and equipment. So the poorest communities in the needier areas have less adequate schools, and their children have less chance to benefit from education.

After primary school, two out of three children get no more formal education or training. Their potential contribution to the development of the rural areas where most of them live is, nevertheless, great. But they, their families, and their communities need help in finding and exploiting the opportunities that exist—to get more out of the land; to start small businesses; to improve living conditions.

APPENDIX B

Should Charities Conduct Generic Marketing?
by B.B. Schlegelmilch and A.C. Tynan

Many Britons still believe that charities are run by disorganised amateurs who waste too much money on administration (*The Sunday Times*, 20.9.1987). However, this view does not stand up to scrutiny. According to the latest figures published by the Charities' Aid Foundation (1986/87), most charities have dramatically reduced their administration spending and have developed into increasingly sophisticated fund-raisers and dispensers. With these changes, charities became more aware of the usefulness of marketing tools. This is evidenced, for example, by the Save the Children Fund, which doubled its advertising budget in the past three years with a resulting threefold increase in income in the same time period (*The Sunday Times*, 20.9.1987). Overall, charities reporting to the Charities' Aid Foundation have received a real increase in donations of 32 per cent on five years ago (Charities' Aid Foundation, 1986/87). Some of this increase may be explained by tax cuts and higher pay of donors. But foremost, it reflects the increasing use of systematic marketing by charities.

However, for charities, the use of marketing is riddled with problems. According to Kotler (1979) these include, among others, changing societal needs, increasing public and private competition and changing client attitudes. The causes of these problems include the difficult climate in which charities have to operate. There has been a substantial increase in competition between charities (the number of registered charities rose from 147,000 in 1983 to 157,900 in 1986). In addition, there has been an increase in demand for funds. This has been caused by a rise in the number of beneficiaries due to population growth, an ageing population and the development of expensive, new technology which can assist in many areas of aid.

To combat these complex marketplace problems, marketing tools and strategies have to be tailored to the requirements of charities. One vital marketing strategy for improving performance in non-profit marketing organisations, such as charities, is market segmentation (Smith and Belk, 1982). This commentary investigates whether preferences for particular types of charities are associated with particular market segments and considers implications for the marketing mix.

Literature
The broadening of the concept of marketing to cover the non-profit-making sector can be traced to Kotler and Levy's classic article first published in 1969. In this seminal work the authors contend that 'marketing provides a useful set of concepts for guiding all organisations' (p. 15) and that traditional marketing principles are transferable to the marketing of organisations, people and ideas.

Examining the application and relevance of marketing to the objectives and functions of charities, politicians, universities, churches, museums and other non-business entities, they concluded that the choice facing non-business organisations is not whether to adopt marketing or not, but whether to do it well or poorly. This whole approach is subject to much criticism, stimulating a lively debate which continued for several years. Luck (1969, p. 54), for example, criticised Kotler and Levy and advocated that the scope of marketing be restricted to 'those processes or activities whose ultimate result is a market transaction'.

The next major development in the field of non-profit marketing came in August 1970, when the American Marketing Association presented a programme at its Fall Conference on the theme of 'Broadening the Concept of Marketing'. In 1971 the *Journal of Marketing* devoted much of its July issue to marketing in non-profit organisations, an influential event which probably signalled the first stage of the concept's acceptance as a tenet of mainstream marketing thought. A survey of marketing educators by Nichols in 1974 showed an overwhelming majority were agreed that marketing went beyond just economic goods, services and market transactions.

Since that time authors such as Shapiro (1973, 1974), Lovelock and Weinberg (1978), and Selby (1978) have contributed to our understanding of non-profit marketing. There is now widespread acceptance of the non-profit marketing concept. The subject is routinely covered in basic marketing primers and the definitive text on the topic by Kotler, now co-authored by Andreasen (1987), has reached its third edition.

Market segmentation has proved to be a crucial strategy for the non-profit sector (Smith and Belk, 1982, Yavas et al., 1980, Shapiro, 1973, Mindak and Bybee, 1971). Its aim is to identify and delineate homogeneous groups of individuals who then become targets for the organisation's marketing plans. The advantage of the technique is that it divides total demand into relatively homogeneous segments which are identified by some common characteristics. These characteristics are relevant in explaining and in predicting the response of individuals, in a particular segment, to marketing stimuli. Thus, once a segment has been identified, a marketing mix can be devised to reach it efficiently and economically.

The theory of market segmentation is both well developed and well documented. Therefore, a discussion of the extensive literature on the topic is not deemed necessary for this paper. The segmentation literature will, however, be reviewed in relation to non-profit marketing in general, and charity marketing in particular. The one main difference between segmentation for charities and that for ordinary business concerns is that the charities have two publics and therefore two groups of customers to segment. There are the potential donors, from whom revenue is derived, and there are the potential beneficiaries or clients, to whom the resources are allocated. The charity needs to segment the donor market into relatively homogeneous groups and determine which appeal will be most effective for that segment (Shapiro, 1973). Similarly, the non-profit organisation must decide who the most appropriate beneficiaries are, in relation to its own objectives.

The process of segmentation requires the selection of characteristics or descriptors which will form the basis for segmentation. A wide variety of segmentation bases are available which are usually used in combination rather than singly. They include geographic, socio-demographic, psychographic, psychological and buyer behaviour variables. The use of the following bases has been cited in the literature as appropriate for the marketing of charities.

Geographic and socio-demographic segmentation was successfully used by Miller (1974) in predicting 'heavy giving' areas for a health charity. Areas containing large populations, numerous families with high income and families with income from interest and dividends were the most lucrative donors. When segmenting potential donors for another health charity, Belk and Smith (1979) used socio-demographic data and subsequently related it to district or zip codes. They concluded that the study provided a measure of contribution potentials for planning market strategy. In an American survey of philanthropic activity, potential fundraisers were successfully segmented by utilising demographic and socio-economic variables together with a form of volume segmentation based on Twedt's 'heavy half' theory (Commission on Private Philanthropy and Public Needs, 1977). Twedt (1964) argued that, in many product fields, 50 per cent of the customers account for 80 per cent of the consumption. In this study 52 per cent of the sample households with incomes in excess of $10,000 per year contributed approximately 82 per cent of the donations; an indication that Twedt's 'heavy half' theory is applicable to donating, as well as consuming, activity. Mindak and Bybee (1982) argue that the key to achieving higher donations lies in isolating the 'heavy donor' rather than marketing to an undifferentiated population. Their successful campaign was aimed at young married couples with or without young children.

Recent research has focused on psychographic segmentation. Schlegelmilch (forthcoming) used psychographics, among others, to segment the market into likely donors and non-donors. Schlegelmilch and Watkins (1986) attempted to relate different donor typologies to psychographic, demographic and awareness measures. Developing psychographic profiles through an assessment of an individual's values and the attitudes he holds towards the charity and its 'mission' helped the United Way Campaign to identify prospective donors and determine appropriate appeals (Yavas et al., 1980). The development of psychographically defined segments appears to offer benefits in terms of greater precision when targeting marketing strategies, particularly promotional strategies.

Discussion

The findings of this paper shed new light on the use of market segmentation by charities. While the literature clearly demonstrates the usefulness of market segmentation to identify likely (heavy) donors (Miller, 1974; Belk and Smith, 1979; Mindak and Bybee, 1982; Yavas et al., 1980; Schlegelmilch, forthcoming), the findings of this research equally clearly demonstrate that preferences for particular kinds of charities are not associated with particular market segments. Thus, while donors differ from non-donors and heavy donors differ from light donors, *people who donate to one charity do not differ from people who donate to another charity*. This indicates that people who donate do not, in general, mind to what particular charity they give their money.

This finding permits conclusions concerning the characteristics of the products or services of charities, however they might be defined. Specifically, when exchanging

money against recognition, gratitude, a 'warm feeling' or whatever it is that motivates donors to give, donors do not view the delivered product or service to be
different when provided by different charities. Whatever it is that charities bring
into the exchange process, it can be considered as having the characteristic of a
commodity.

The recognition that charities provide a commodity which fulfils donors' needs
that are similar has interesting managerial implications. Firstly, charities will find it is
difficult, if not impossible, to achieve differentiation. Consequently, a charity might
not be able to concentrate on a unique market segment which is neglected by
competing charities, but rather has to fight for the same type of donors as all other
charities. Secondly, if all charities concentrate on the same market segment, i.e.
heavy donors, the charity which makes its presence most felt in the market and has
the best infrastructure for collecting funds will be the most successful. However, a
high visibility achieved by strong advertising without a good infrastructure for the
collection of funds is likely to result in generic advertising. Thus, it might help to
expand the entire charity market, but not necessarily increase one's own share of
total donations. Thirdly, new or small charities without the opportunity of achieving a
strong advertising presence and without the means to build and support an extended
fund-raising network will find it difficult to compete with established organisations.
For these small charities, it would be an advantage to pool resources, conduct
generic advertising and establish joint fund-raising and collecting approaches. This
will result in economies of scale, both on the promotion and the fund-raising side,
which would enable these charities to compete more effectively with larger
charities. This increased effectiveness could therefore be expected to lead to a
growth in total donations. Hence, joint approaches by small charities would position
them well for securing a viable share of this growth.

Conclusions and recommendations for future research

The findings of this paper illustrate that specific types of charities are not associated
with specific market segments. Thus, it is likely that all charities will either compete
for the same segment of heavy donors or, alternatively, will pursue a mass marketing
approach. Specialisation centred upon a market niche does not appear to be a viable
strategy. The managerial implications of this finding depend on the current
competitive position of the charity in question. Large, well-established charities are
advised to maintain/strengthen their advertising presence and to extend further their
fund-raising infrastructure. Small, new charities are recommended to pool their
resources, conduct joint advertising with the objective of expanding the total market
and concentrate on the development of innovative and efficient fund-raising
channels to generate and collect revenue.

For future research, the findings have particular implications in the area of fund-
raising strategies. With limited scope for market segmentation, sophistication in
fund-raising strategies will become a key variable in the competition between
charities. Specifically, the issue of whether different kinds of fund-raising
approaches might be more or less effective for different segments of the population

should be explored. Thus an investigation is indicated, not into segmentation for different types of charities, but into the scope for segmentation for different types of fund-raising techniques.

Current research being undertaken by the authors would seem to indicate *a positive correlation between the type of fund-raising strategy chosen, in terms of communications channels and channel/methods of donation used, and the type of donor, in terms of his socio-demographic and lifestyle characteristics.* This has obvious managerial implications. For example, a fund-raising strategy attempting to solicit donations on a monthly direct debit or bank standing order basis would be best communicated to a specific target audience through selective channels.

Source: 'Innovative Marketing—A European Perspective', *Proceedings of Annual Conference of the European Marketing Academy*, Bradford, 1988, pp. 558–578.

Questions
1. Develop in detail a marketing plan or strategy which will enable ActionAid to become a significant player in the Irish Third World charity market. Particular attention should be paid to realistic costings and budgets in the plan.
2. Comment on the usefulness of consumer research in facilitating charities to raise money and market themselves effectively.
3. How effective are the principles of marketing in the context of not-for-profit organisations? Do you agree with the view that the scope of marketing should be restricted to 'those processes or activities whose ultimate result is a market transaction'?

APPENDIX C

Media Facts Sheet

NATIONAL PRESS RATES EFFECTIVE DECEMBER 1985

Publication	Circulation Jan./June 1985	No. of readers per copy	Black and White SCI	Black and White Full Page	Colour[a] full page	Readership (Universe x 000's) All Adults 2,500	Men 1,243	Women 1,257	H/wives 858	Social Groups (Adult Universe x 000's) ABC1 735	C2DE 1,247	Farmers 518	Age Groups (Adult Universe x 000's) 15–34 1,119	35–54 996	65+ 386
Sundays:															
Sunday World[b]	339,305[c]	4.2	£55.00	£5,500	£5,500	45%	46%	45%	42%	34%	54%	40%	56%	41%	27%
Sunday Press	266,019	4.0	£55.50	£10,450	£12,500	43%	43%	43%	41%	43%	37%	52%	40%	45%	44%
Sunday Independent	236,290	4.2	£58.50	£11,000	£15,050	39%	39%	39%	35%	54%	32%	36%	39%	41%	36%
Sunday Tribune	95,106	3.8	£34.00	£5,700	£4,500	14%	14%	15%	14%	28%	9%	8%	16%	14%	9%
Mornings:															
Irish Independent	158,685	4.4	£52.00	£9,750	£12,250	28%	31%	26%	23%	39%	22%	27%	28%	27%	23%
Irish Press	89,249	4.7	£25.00	£4,500	£5.00	17%	19%	15%	14%	15%	18%	16%	18%	14%	16%
Irish Times	85,420	4.3	£57.50	£9,500	£9,250	15%	14%	15%	13%	35%	7%	5%	17%	13%	8%
Cork Examiner	60,036	4.0	£26.00	£5,148	£5,984	10%	10%	10%	9%	11%	8%	12%	9%	9%	9%
Evenings:															
Evening Press	133,402	4.1	£37.50	£6,600	£8,000	22%	21%	22%	21%	26%	25%	7%	25%	19%	13%
Evening Herald	123,865	4.0	£37.50	£3,600	£7,750	20%	20%	20%	19%	19%	28%	4%	23%	17%	13%
Cork Evening Echo	34,099	3.9	£18.00	£3,564	£4,136	5%	6%	5%	5%	5%	6%	2%	6%	4%	3%
Provincial Press	717,536	–	£3–£11	£288–£2,170	£600–£4,000	76% of the adult population outside Dublin city and county read a weekly provincial newspaper									

[a]Based on six insertions   [b]Tabloid   [c]Includes NI circulation

WEEKLIES/MAGAZINES

Publication	Circulation	Frequency	Size	Full Page		Readership (Universe x 000's)				Social Groups (Adult Universe x 000's)			Age Groups (Adult Universe x 000's)		
				B/W	Colour	All Adults 2,500	Men 1,243	Women 1,257	H/wives 858	ABC1 735	C2DE 1,247	Farmers 518	15-34 1,119	35-54 996	65+ 386
RTE Guide	130,695	Weekly	A4	£920	£1,600	26%	26%	25%	25%	24%	26%	25%	29%	25%	17%
Irish Farmers Journal	70,949	Weekly	Tabloid	£1,385*	£2,400*	15%	17%	13%	13%	7%	5%	48%	13%	17%	14%
Business & Finance	11,416	Weekly	A4	£910	£1,425	5%	6%	4%	3%	13%	2%	1%	6%	5%	1%
Irish Business	10,304	Monthly	A4	£880	£1,320	N/A	N/A	N/A	N/A	N/A	N/A	N/A	N/A	N/A	N/A
Management	9,827	Monthly	A4	£695	£975	N/A	N/A	N/A	N/A	N/A	N/A	N/A	N/A	N/A	N/A
Success	10,869	Monthly	A4	£750	£1,050	2%	3%	2%	1%	5%	1%	1%	3%	2%	1%
Aspect	9,118	Monthly	A4	£775	£975	N/A	N/A	N/A	N/A	N/A	N/A	N/A	N/A	N/A	N/A
Magill	29,202	Monthly	A4	£800	£1,150	10%	12%	9%	8%	20%	7%	5%	11%	11%	6%
The Phoenix	16,602	F/nightly	A4	£660	£1,000	4%	4%	3%	1%	8%	2%	1%	6%	2%	1%
New Hibernia	21,292	Monthly	Tabloid	£760*	£1,160*	N/A	N/A	N/A	N/A	N/A	N/A	N/A	N/A	N/A	N/A
In Dublin	8,845	F/nightly	A4	£620	£885	4%	4%	3%	2%	8%	3%	–	6%	3%	–
Hot Press	15,795	F/nightly	Tabloid	£550	£925*	N/A	N/A	N/A	N/A	N/A	N/A	N/A	N/A	N/A	N/A
Woman's Way	71,133	Weekly	A4	£1,400	£2,200	18%	9%	28%	26%	20%	19%	15%	21%	18%	14%
Image	26,116	Monthly	A4	£680	£1,000	10%	3%	17%	14%	18%	8%	5%	12%	10%	4%
It Magazine	27,255	Monthly	A4	£800	£985	9%	3%	15%	11%	14%	8%	5%	14%	7%	2%
U Magazine	27,560	Monthly	A4	£740	£1,100	10%	4%	16%	12%	15%	9%	5%	15%	7%	2%

*A4 costing

RTE TELEVISION

The following are the main highlights from the RTE Rate Card

Effective 1st October, 1985

RTE 1 TV	10 secs	15 secs	20 secs	30 secs	40 secs & over
14.00–18.00	£64–£272	£95–£405	£149–£483	£142–£604	pro-rata to 30-second rates
18.00–close	£193–£819	£287–£1,219	£342–£1,455	£428–£1,819	pro-rata to 30-second rates

RTE 2 TV	10 secs	15 secs	20 secs	30 secs	40 secs & over
all day	£68–£392	£101–£583	£120–£696	£150–£870	pro-rata to 30-second rates

RTE operate a pre-empt Rate Card on both channels. Effectively this means that transmission can be guaranteed only by paying the highest price level.

RTE RADIO RATES

The following are the main highlights from the RTE Rate Card, effective 1st October, 1985

RADIO 1	Before 08.00	08.00–13.00	Gay Byrne 09.10–11.00	13.00–14.00	14.00–14.30	Drivetime 17.00–19.00
15 secs	£83	£181	£272	£270	£120	£69
30 secs	£124	£270	£406	£404	£180	£102

	Universe x 000's	Average ¼ hour listenership (Mon.–Fri.)				
All Adults	2,500	6%	20%	24%	25%	9%	5%
Men	1,244	6%	13%	14%	21%	4%	6%
Women	1,256	6%	27%	33%	28%	14%	5%
H/wives	856	7%	34%	42%	35%	19%	6%

In the main, spots can be fixed by paying a surcharge which ranges from 10% to 50%.
Source: JNMR 1984/85.

RADIO 2	06.30–14.00 14 spot package	06.30–14.00 14 spot package	06.30–14.00 14 spot package	06.30–14.00 14 spot package
15 secs	£814	£740	£338	£763
30 secs	£1,215	£1,105	£505	£1,140

	Universe x 000's	Average ¼ hour listenership (Mon.–Fri.)			
Adults 15–34	1,111	10%	10%	3%	10%
Men 15–34	570	10%	10%	4%	10%
Women 15–34	540	10%	11%	3%	10%
H/wives 15–34	249	9%	9%	1%	9%

In the main, spots can be fixed by paying a surcharge which ranges from 10% to 50%.
Source: JNMR 1984/85.

Case 8

Lifetime Assurance

Banks and insurance companies across Europe have been leaping into one another's arms at an unprecedented rate in mergers, acquisitions and strategic alliances. But the high street bank and the life assurance company differ significantly in antecedents, culture, tradition and structure. Despite Allied Irish Bank's earlier débâcle in this area, the Bank of Ireland launched its own insurance subsidiary, Lifetime, with considerable initial success.

Issues: Organisational development and corporate culture in implementing strategy. Customer relationship management and service quality. Winning market focus.

Probably the best party in Dublin on the evening of 2nd September, 1987 was the one held in an unassuming redbrick office in Percy Place. That was the day Lifetime Assurance, the insurance subsidiary of the Bank of Ireland, received its authorisation from the Department of Industry and Commerce to transact life assurance business. There weren't many at the party—only about 30 or so—but then that was all there were employed in the fledgling company.

Since that first party in the kitchen of Lifetime's Head Office, there have been many other causes for celebration: the first £10 million of policyholder funds was achieved within days of the launch; the first £100 million in assets was reached within a year; policyholder funds of £250 million were attained by summer 1989. Staff numbers grew quickly to their current level of over 200 people. In its first full year of operations, Lifetime contributed £7 million in pre-tax profits to its parent company, Bank of Ireland. For the first half of 1989, pre-tax profits from Lifetime included in the Group's account exceeded £8 million.

The company had become a leading provider of life assurance and pension products to individuals in Ireland and plans were in hand to commence operations in the United Kingdom in 1990. In 1988, its first full year of operations, new single premiums of £121 million were written; in 1989, the corresponding figure was £161 million. Both of these sales figures represent

---

This case was developed as a basis for class discussion rather than to illustrate effective or ineffective handling of an administrative situation.

approximately 20 per cent of total new business in the relevant periods for this business class. New recurring premiums in 1988 amounted to an annualised £6 million or 6 per cent of the market for individual life and pensions policies; in 1989, new annualised regular premiums were £11.8 million—a 9.2 per cent market share. By the end of 1989, Lifetime had approximately 40,000 customers and those customers were insured for over £990 million in life assurance as well as substantial amounts of disability insurance, long-term sickness insurance and accidental death benefits.

THE LIFE ASSURANCE MARKET

The financial services market in Ireland encompasses a number of sectors, each with different offerings, players, characteristics and competitive modes. (See Appendix A for a brief overview of each of these nine sectors.) The medium- and long-term savings and lending sectors have, in particular, undergone significant change over the last number of decades. Here, life assurance companies have been accounting for a large and growing share of the market for personal savings. Table 1 shows the shares at different times in the past of personal savings for different types of financial institutions. Clearly, the traditional clearing banks have been losing out to life assurance companies in the savings war. Unit-linked bonds and guaranteed income and growth bonds offered by life assurance companies have provided more attractive returns to savers than conventional building society and bank deposits.

Table 1

Personal Sector Savings by Institutions

	1961	1970	1980	1987
	%	%	%	%
Life Assurance/Pension Funds	31	27	32	57
Banks	45	38	34	27
Building Societies	2	15	31	7
State Agencies	21	20	3	9
Total Market	£41m	£140m	£879m	£2,377m

Source: Davy Kelleher McCarthy Ltd (1989).

The most commonly accepted industry statistic for measuring the life assurance market is new premiums—both annual or regular premiums and single or lump sum premiums (see Table 2). In particular, regular premium business for protection, savings, mortgage and pension policies is seen as a key indicator of market activity. The life assurance market has experienced considerable growth in recent years, a time when the Irish economy has not been especially strong. Nor has the market yet reached anything like saturation point. The DKM report, source-quoted in Table 1, also gives the statistic that only 37 per cent of respondents to an opinion poll said that they regularly paid premiums for any type of life assurance. The corresponding statistic in the UK is 71 per cent. (A point worth noting is that the sharp increases in new annual premium business in 1988 and 1989 can be attributed to the growth in popularity of endowment mortgage assurances to repay home loans.) In addition to regular premium business, life assurance companies are also very active in the market for lump sum investments, where they compete directly with banks, building societies, post office, and individual investments in stocks and shares. Table 2 fails to give a full picture of the life assurance market as it ignores important factors such as the volume of premium income from policies sold in the past, investment income and capital gains on investments underlying those policies, which are effectively reinvested on behalf of customers, and, on the other side, rates of policy encashment. It also ignores corporate pensions business, which is very important for some companies, particularly Irish Life, and industrial branch business which is collected door-to-door.

Table 2

Life Assurance Premium Market
(£'000)

	1985	1986	1987	1988	1989
New Annual Premiums	61,186	70,077	80,898	101,269	127,522
New Single Premiums	526,000	464,923	758,368	625,639	851,564
Total or Combined* Annual and Single	113,786	116,569	156,735	163,833	212,678

*New annual premiums added to 10% of value of new single premiums.

A number of factors have contributed to the growth in the life assurance market in recent years. There has been a rising population of young adults and associated home formation, particularly in urban areas. Life assurance products have enjoyed tax advantages relative to other forms of saving.

However, many of these advantages are now being eroded with the increase in the levy on life assurance premiums, the changes in the rules regarding tax treatment of general annuity business, and the gradual reduction of tax relief to individuals on premiums under life assurance policies. There has been considerable product innovation, particularly the introduction of flexible unit-linked policies. Indeed, unit-linked funds have shown a generally favourable investment performance over the period. A process of systemisation has also been seen to be evolving, as is evidenced by the growth in the popularity of endowment policies for repayment of mortgages. It should also be noted that purchasers value the confidentiality of life assurance as an investment medium. The market has undergone considerable competitive activity stimulated by European harmonisation and by the entry of new companies and distributors, including banks and building societies, often tied to a single life assurance company. Thus, the life assurance market has shown substantial real growth during the eighties. Some 25 companies compete in the market and enjoy, for the most part, intrinsically high and relatively stable returns. While the industry is closely regulated by the authorities, it cannot be said to have high entry barriers. This is in contrast to the traditional clearing bank business with its money transmission and short-term savings and lending activities, where the market is dominated by two players, Bank of Ireland and AIB, is highly competitive, and has high entry costs.

The term life assurance embraces at least four classes of product, the prospects for which are not all the same:

(1) *True life cover or protection*, which is looked on favourably by government, and is being enhanced by the inclusion of extra coverages such as total disability and dread disease, and is still relatively under-bought in Ireland.

(2) *Life assurance as a means of savings*, which has been the major growth area in recent years, including growing use of life assurance as a means of repaying mortgage lending, but is now under threat of losing its tax advantages.

(3) *Life assurance and annuity-based capital investment products*, which originally depended quite heavily on the tax advantages unique to life business, and which must ultimately be threatened by competition from other investment products.

(4) *Retirement provision or pensions*, which also are encouraged by government with tax relief and which should grow steadily in importance as the population ages.

While all these products offer different benefits, they all share a common 'life' dimension—they all involve contracts on human life and their pricing necessitates the use of mortality or actuarial tables. (Appendix B contains a more technical overview of the different types of life assurance, methods of payment and systems of contract, whether non-profit, with profit or unit-linked.)

LIFETIME ENTRY

The Bank of Ireland was originally formed over 200 years ago and took over two smaller competitors in the 1960s to become the major banking group in the Republic of Ireland, with approximately a 45 per cent share of the retail banking market. In recent years, the Bank of Ireland Group has progressively developed its range of services both to individuals and to corporations and has adopted a more market-oriented organisation structure. Outside Ireland, the Group has extensive operations in the UK and in 1988 acquired a regional bank in the United States. Within Ireland, the Bank of Ireland branch network consists of 280 branches all over Ireland, with a slight bias towards over-representation relative to competitors in rural areas.

In common with many other institutions faced with considerable changes in the financial services market, Bank of Ireland reviewed its mission statement in the mid-1980s. One element of that mission statement is to be the leading provider of a broad range of financial services in Ireland. Another important factor leading to the formation of Lifetime was the fact that the Investment Bank of Ireland was already Ireland's largest broker for single premium policies. IBI also acted as investment manager for Canada Life's range of unit-linked funds. It was natural in these circumstances for the Bank of Ireland Group to explore actively the opportunity for backward integration by adding life assurance underwriting to its broking and investment management activities.

When planning the formation of the new life assurance company, the Bank of Ireland could also look to overseas experience. The market for financial services in Britain is substantially similar to corresponding markets in Ireland. Products and distribution methods are very similar, although changes in taxation and regulation tend to lead those in Ireland by five years or more. Market volumes are about 20 times bigger than those in Ireland. In the UK, TSB had for many years owned a very successful life assurance company. Since that time, it added not one but two other life assurance groups to its list of acquisitions, Target and Hill Samuel Life. Barclays and Lloyds Bank also had their own life assurance subsidiaries, when the Bank of Ireland was in the planning stages for Lifetime. Since then, Midland Bank has set up a life assurance company, leaving NatWest as the only major UK clearer which does not own a life assurance company. In the mid-1980s, however, the life assurance subsidiaries of the UK clearers were mere minnows in the insurance pond. TSB was the only bank which saw life assurance as an integral part of its entire business.

Looking further afield, senior management in the Bank looked to Australia, where Westpac, followed closely by National Australia Bank, were competing head-on with the major specialist insurers like Australian Mutual Provident and National Mutual of Australasia in the contest for supremacy in financial services.

In seeking a capacity to offer life assurance to its customers, the Bank of Ireland was able to draw on a variety of piecemeal experiences as a life assurance intermediary. First, Bank branch managers had, in a personal capacity, arranged insurance (both life and non-life) for customers. Second, the Group had offered investment products under its own label, but in the form of policies from other assurance companies. Third, a variety of small-scale savings and loan repayment products, using the tax treatment of life assurance, had been offered from time to time without, it has to be said, setting the world on fire.

In entering the life assurance business, alliance was an option considered by the Bank, if only because more than one life assurance company had made overtures. This option was not pursued because of the inherent instability of such alliances. Acquisition of an existing player in Ireland was the second option and was considered in detail. The relatively small number of players, and the consequent high prices sought, made this an unattractive option on economic grounds. By a process of elimination, the Bank came to the decision to 'greenfield' or establish its own life assurance company from scratch.

CUSTOMERS, DELIVERY AND PRODUCT FLEXIBILITY

At the outset, both for the sake of clear thinking and as the basis for applying for authorisation of the new company, Lifetime had to make choices about who it saw as its customers, how it wanted to reach them, and what it wanted to offer them. The company decided that it should address itself distinctly to:

(1) Personal customers of the Bank of Ireland—over half a million adults, of whom research suggested two-thirds were not owners of individual life or pension products.
(2) Persons having indirect relationships with the Bank—mainly employees of business customers.
(3) Others who might be introduced as being likely to have a need for its services.

At one level, this is a broadly drawn target market; it probably accounts for up to 80 per cent of the population. What was specifically excluded was 'cold' prospecting activity—so-called cold-calling on potential customers. That the principal target group was existing Bank customers forced Lifetime to pay close attention to the contrast between the typical quality of customer relationships in banking and in life assurance. The objective was to combine the best of what have traditionally been quite different cultures. Yet the company knew from others' experiences of the paramount importance of branch motivation and training and the risks of wasteful internal competition and duplicated expense.

Lifetime decided at a very early stage that it would be represented by a dedicated team of highly professional counsellors, to whom customers could be referred with confidence by branch managers and staff. These counsellors would be, in a sense, the embodiment of the cultural fusion Lifetime was seeking to achieve. They were selected very carefully with a heavy emphasis on cultural sensitivity. Counsellors have been recruited from the Bank of Ireland, as well as from the life assurance industry and other areas. They have undergone and continue to undergo extensive training in personal, technical and relationship management skills. The relationships between these counsellors (now some 50 in number) and branch staff have formed the key to the successful prospecting and winning of Lifetime customers. Thus, the first stage in marketing Lifetime was not to the final customer but rather to the retail branch network of the Bank. This branch system would provide the delivery network and the first problem was to 'leverage' this network actively and properly. In the first months of Lifetime's existence, the company made some 300 presentations to Bank branch managers and their staff about Lifetime, its products, and the role of the counsellor and his service. These processes of branch promotion and consultation proved extremely valuable in feeding back experience on do's and don't's and in piloting selling initiatives. Lifetime has fostered a 'pay-for-performance' ethic from the start. The remuneration package of counsellors is sharply incentivised to encourage prospecting. Equally, Bank branches are rewarded, each branch receiving a bottom line contribution credit—an equivalent to commission—for business successfully referred to Lifetime.

In promoting Lifetime to its potential customer base, a support programme of in-branch promotional activity and 'point-of-sale' merchandising was developed. This was designed to introduce the Lifetime proposition to customers coming into branches and encourage exposure to the counsellor advisory service. In late 1988 and for extended periods in 1989, a national TV advertising campaign was run, along with selective outdoor poster advertising (Exhibit 1 outlines the media plan for 1989). The TV ad had a number of interesting dimensions. Bearing in mind that Lifetime had been in existence only for a little over a year, one of the objectives of the TV commercial was to create for Lifetime a sense of 'established experience'. Set in the year AD 2013, the ad centred on the memories of an obviously successful man in his late twenties/early thirties. He remembers back to 1988, the first time his parents were introduced to 'The Man from Lifetime' and how the Lifetime counsellor's advice and planning helped them make the most of their money in the years ahead. Another significant feature of the commercial was its strong Bank of Ireland branding, highlighting the fact that Lifetime is indeed a product of the Bank of Ireland. Research carried out on this advertising in early 1989 following an initial burst of advertising indicated that the commercial had achieved a prompted recognition of 30 per cent with the expectation that this would reach over 60 per cent by the end of the campaign. Further, of those interviewed who had seen the ad, which was just over 50 per cent, three out of four welcomed the availability from banks of new services such as Lifetime's.

Exhibit 1

Lifetime Advertising Media Plan 1989

DATE PLAN

LIFETIME ASSURANCE

w/c	Dec 26	Jan 2 9 16 23	Feb 27	March 6 13 20	April 24	May 1 8 15	June	July	Aug	Sept 4 11	October 2 9
RTE 1 Television											
45 seconds	x x	x x x x	x	x x x	x	x x x				x x	x x
	x x	x x x x	x	x x x	x	x x x				x x	x x
	x x	x x x x	x	x x x	x	x x x				x x	x x
	x x	x x x x									
	x x	x									
	x x	x									
	x	x									
		x									
		x									
15 seconds		x x x	x	x x x	x	x x x				x x	x x
		x x x	x	x x x	x	x x x				x x	x x
		x x x	x	x x x	x	x x x				x x	x x
Network 2											
45 seconds	x	x x x x	x	x x x	x	x x x				x x	x x
	x	x x x x	x	x x x	x	x x x				x x	x x
	x	x x x x			x	x x x				x x	x x
15 seconds			0	0 0 0	0	0 0 0				0 0	0 0
			0	0 0 0							
Outdoor											
66 x 48 sheet											
Adshel - 70 sites											

In terms of product design, Lifetime decided at the outset that the investment element of its products would be of unit-linked format. Most life assurance business in Ireland is unit-linked, and this type of product offers advantages to both customer and company. Also, the company can benefit obviously from the assistance of its sister company, the Investment Bank of Ireland, in the management of these unit-linked funds. Another central tenet of product design, in keeping with the life cycle orientation of the company's service, was flexibility. Lifetime has built into its product range a state-of-the-art flexibility to address possible changes in customers' personal and other circumstances throughout life. Lifetime's current product range includes Investment/ Saving Plans, Protection Plans, Pension Plans and Mortgage Endowment Plans (it should be noted that the Bank of Ireland's subsidiary, ICS Building Society, offers ordinary payment mortgages). Also, the company has a number of newer product offerings such as Education Plans, which aim to assist parents in paying for children's education, and Business Protection Plans, which insure against the death of a key partner in a business enterprise. Exhibit 2 carries some extracts on Lifetime's products and services from *Lifetalk*, the company's newsletter.

Exhibit 2

EXTRACTS FROM *LIFETALK* NEWSLETTER

Financial planning for life

Traditionally, a person grew up, got a job, married, bought a house and settled down for life. With the possible exception of basic protection for dependants in case of death of the bread-winner, most people dealt with life's problems as they arose. The financial burden of educating children was faced only when the time came, which often meant that either the desired level of education was not possible or even more borrowing was required. Employers were regarded as having a moral obligation to provide pensions—usually inadequate—for their employees, and elderly couples often spent their final years penny-pinching in order to survive.

The world is a different place today. Inflation is unpredictable, local economies are more vulnerable than ever to international pressures, career structures have changed radically and people have never been more mobile. In spite of this, the scenario outlined above is still a frighteningly familiar one.

It was in response to this dilemma that Lifetime developed the concept of a personal financial counselling service. The key element in the idea is simplicity. A personal consultant, known as a Counsellor, meets with each potential customer. He or she studies the customer's personal circumstances and current financial situation in detail. Both medium and long-term needs and aspirations are taken into account; both known costs and contingencies are planned for. With the help of new technology and an excellent internal back-up service, the Counsellor produces an individual, personalised package which not only conforms precisely to the client's requirements at the moment, but is designed to adapt readily to future changes in circumstances. 'We try to deliver the ultimate in flexibility,' says Bernard Doherty, Director—Administration & Systems. 'The one thing which is certain these days is change, and a person's needs today will not be the same in 10 years. We are interested in developing a life-long relationship with our clients, not in collecting premiums and closing the file until a claim is made or the term expires.'

Business matters

One of the most vital principles of the Lifetime philosophy is its after-sales service to customers. In the context of an aspect of insurance which has become increasingly important in recent years—Business Protection—Catherine Regan, Technical Services Manager, explains, 'Under this plan, an individual or individuals are insured against the problems which the sudden death of a business partner may pose and it can also be used to provide a fund to cover a retirement. It offers the protection needed to allow the business to continue or be satisfactorily wound up.' Where does the Lifetime customer service come in? 'At Lifetime, we like to develop an on-going relationship with the client and keep abreast of the company's progress. It may be that as the business grows, for example, its insurance arrangements will need to be up-dated.' Lifetime contact the client on a yearly basis in order to establish the latest position and ensure that the current plan is still adequate. Like all Lifetime's products, the Business Protection Plan is flexible: it can provide for purchase of a share in the business on either death or retirement.

Keyman insurance protects against the death of a key person in a company. It covers the cost of appointing a successor and compensates for the losses which may accrue through non-fulfilment of contracts negotiated by the person. Traditionally, life assurance contracts are entered into on a fixed term basis, for say 10 or 20 years, but with Lifetime contracts can be as long or as short as the client wants. Keyman insurance can be arranged to cover the situation where employees leave a company to change jobs on a more regular basis than was the practice in the past. It can also be used to fund for a 'golden handshake'.

A taxing question

Two out of three tax-payers could reduce their tax burden—sometimes significantly—by reorganising their personal finances. When a Lifetime Counsellor first analyses a potential client's situation, tax is one of the areas where his or her expertise and familiarity with legislative developments can help the client to capitalise on the advantages built into a well-constructed life assurance, pension or investment plan.

For the younger person, there are tax-efficient means of saving for a deposit on a house or providing for a lump sum free of any additional personal taxation. As family commitments increase, the plan can be adapted to provide increased life assurance protection while still taking maximum benefit from available tax relief. Under Lifetime's Personal Pension Plan, an annual premium of £1,000 would give tax relief of £560, reducing the net premium to £440. (This assumes you pay tax at 56% and qualify for full tax relief.) Furthermore, up to 25% of the fund which accumulates may be taken as a tax-free lump sum at retirement.

Many people are not aware that it is possible to fund now for paying tax on a known future inheritance, through a life assurance policy provided for under Section 60 of the Finance Act of 1985.

Transferring assets from parent to child on death introduces many complications with regard to capital acquisitions tax. This is where a Lifetime Counsellor can help plan for future tax liabilities.

Exhibit 3

Lifetime's Market Performance, 1989/88				
	1989		**1988**	
	Market Share	£	Market Share	£
New Annual Premium Market	9.25%	11.8m	6%	6.03m
	Market Share	£	Market Share	£
New Combined Annual Premium and Single Premium	12.9%	27.9m	11%	18.1m
	Market Share	£	Market Share	£
Single Premium Business	18.2%	161m	19.4%	121m
Total Assets	£334m		£158m	
Total In-force Sums Assured	£994m (Annual Premium £669m) (Single Premium £325m)		£412m (Annual Premium £252m) (Single Premium £160m)	
Total Number of Customers	40,700* (Regular Premium 25,900) (Single Premium 14,800)		16,900 (Regular Premium 9,500) (Single Premium 7,400)	
Total Number of Permanent Employees	209		140	
Endowment Mortgage Repayment Facilities	6,900 Households		1,300 Households	
Total Investment Income on Policyholders' Funds	£13.6m		£6m	
Profits on Investments Made on Policyholders' Behalf and Credited to Their Funds	£20.2m		£10m	

*This number of customers is numerically equivalent to 6% of the customer base of the Bank of Ireland. Also, only 25% of Bank of Ireland customers who took out a life assurance product in 1988 did so with Lifetime.

MARKET PERFORMANCE
In a news release in March 1990, Seamus Creedon, managing director of Lifetime, stated that the company was extremely satisfied with the 1989 results and said he was very encouraged by the continuing steady pace of growth by the company in customer numbers, market share and total in-force sums assured. 'After just two and a half years in business, Lifetime is now established as a leading player in the life assurance market, offering innovative and competitive products and services to our customers,' he said. Exhibit 3 provides details of Lifetime's market performance in 1989 and 1988.

COMPETITORS
As was described earlier, the market for life assurance is an amalgam of different products, sold to different customer groups to satisfy a variety of customer functions, and using a variety of technologies (distribution methods in this context). Thus, there is no one definitive measure of market share. One reasonable measure of relative performance is the distribution by company of total individual annual premium business (see Exhibit 4).

Exhibit 4

Annual Premium Market Share, 1986–1989

COMPANY	1986 %	1987 %	1988 %	1989 %
Lifetime	–	0.2	6.0	9.3
Irish Life	32.0	30.3	25.5	22.3
Norwich Union	9.1	9.1	11.0	11.7
Shield Life	11.6	9.5	6.7	6.9
Prudential	7.1	7.3	6.7	6.6
Standard Life	5.6	6.6	7.2	7.1
Abbey Life	6.0	5.5	6.3	6.7
Hibernian Life	5.8	5.8	5.1	4.5
New Ireland	5.9	5.4	4.4	5.3
Others	16.9	20.3	21.1	19.6

Note: Lifetime captured 18% of the single premium market in 1989, compared to Irish Life's 25%, putting it in the number two position for combined annual and single premium business.

Lifetime's strong performance in the total regular or annual premium market conceals its inability to make strong inroads into the market for individual pensions. In 1989, it secured only 2.8 per cent of this market. This low penetration of the individual pensions market is explained in part by the fact that the vast bulk of pensions business is sold through brokers and intermediaries (accountants, solicitors, etc.) for whom Lifetime has not yet developed a durable strategy. While the individual pensions market is much smaller than the life market, it has been unaffected by the erosion of tax relief on life assurance premiums in recent budgets and is set to grow much faster than the life sector in future years. Thus, it must be seen as important for Lifetime to develop a credible strategy for building its market share in this area.

Irish Life is the largest life assurance company in Ireland and it dominated the life assurance and pensions market in Ireland before the arrival of Lifetime. The company is noted for its product innovation and has the most extensive product range on the market. Irish Life sells through its own direct salesforce and through brokers, who form an important part of its marketing efforts. A major factor contributing to Irish Life's relatively poor sales performance in recent years has been its failure to capitalise on the booming market for endowment mortgages. The total market for endowment mortgages grew from £16.9 million in 1988 to £27.9 million in 1989. Irish Life captured only 2 per cent of this market in 1988 and 5 per cent in 1989, in contrast to Lifetime's share for this sector of 16 per cent in 1988 and 21 per cent in 1989. Irish Life's poor performance in the mortgage market can be attributed partly to its failure to link successfully to an established mortgage provider, such as a major building society. However, the boom in endowment mortgages may now have passed due to the further restrictions on life assurance tax relief in the 1990 budget and the recent rise in interest rates, which has put a damper on the house market.

Irish Life will always be a major competitor and continues to be pre-eminent in the corporate pensions market. Its primary type of business is unit-linked and it has a long tradition of good investment performance which enables it to capture substantial volumes of lump sum investment business. Furthermore, it now transacts life assurance business in the UK and the USA; in the early 1970s, Irish Life established a branch operation in the UK, while in late 1988 it acquired a US-based insurance company. This concentration on life assurance 'technology' probably gives it an innovative edge over other companies in product development and in distribution methods. While 90 per cent of its share capital is currently owned by the government, the company is actively seeking privatisation.

Norwich Union and Standard Life are Irish subsidiaries of two of the biggest mutual life assurance companies in Europe. They have both been operating in Ireland for a considerable period. Both have proud records in with-profit business, a form of life assurance which has perceived attractions over the unit-linked offering in certain circumstances, particularly for endowment mortgages. Both of these companies have large capital bases and are known for giving good value to policyholders through their bonus distributions. Neither of these companies has a direct salesforce and so are dependent on brokers exclusively to sell their products. Again, both have a reputation for good relations with brokers.

In contrast to mutuals, which get most of their business from independent intermediaries, Shield Life and Abbey Life are examples of companies which depend for most of their business on self-employed agents (sometimes operating within an umbrella sales organisation) who are tied to one particular company. The fortunes of such companies are linked to their ability to retain the allegiances of such agents and they would generally be perceived to be more downmarket than the true broker companies.

The dark horse in this scenario is the intentions of Allied Irish Banks (AIB) with regard to the life assurance market. AIB has some 42 per cent of the retail banking market in Ireland, with 240 branches nationwide. The company has performed very well in the international arena through its acquisition of the First Maryland Bank in the States and through its vigorous branch network in the UK. AIB is acknowledged as an aggressive competitor. Its previous entry into the insurance market, through the acquisition of the Insurance Corporation of Ireland (ICI) in 1983, ended in disaster with the collapse of the general insurance arm of that company and its effective rescue by the government, to whom ownership of ICI was transferred. Were AIB to enter the life assurance market again, it could obviously become a strong player.

DISTRIBUTION
In many regards, distribution is currently the battlefield for the life assurance industry and the obsolete 'technology' of the cold-calling insurance salesperson is being challenged by more systematised approaches to prospecting. Distribution costs in life assurance are very high, and are reflected in the commission rates payable to brokers on sales of new policies. These rates, which have been agreed by the Irish Insurance Federation, are on a scale which ranges from 40 per cent of the first year's premium to 90 per cent, depending on the contract type. These high commission rates reflect the truth of the adage that life assurance is sold, not bought. A traditional life assurance salesperson, working without the advantage of a warmed-up base of potential customers, achieves less than two sales a week on average. In achieving these two sales, he will have made presentations to six or more people and will have been refused interviews by at least the same number again. Generating the fifteen or so contacts which finally reduce to two sales per week requires much effort and the above commissions levels, seen from one point of view, represent scant reward for all this effort.

Life assurance distribution is in a state of flux at present, with new players being attracted by the high commission levels and distributors coming under increased regulation following the implementation of the 1989 Insurance Act. Distributors can be classified broadly as follows:

(1) Insurance brokers who almost all belong to one of the main broker bodies, NIIBA and CIBI. They range from large national firms, such as Irish Pensions Trust and Coyle Hamilton, to sole operators. Brokers must be bonded and must have agencies with at least five companies. They must also spread their business between the companies with whom they have agencies;

(2) Employees of particular life assurance companies for whom the companies concerned accept complete responsibility;

(3) Tied agents who are self-employed, but who act for only one company;

(4) Agents who act for up to four companies. There are no bonding requirements for agents, but the insurance company or companies for which they hold agencies must accept responsibility for the activities of their agents.

Distributors are not an homogeneous group and brokers, for example, greatly resented the incursions of banks and building societies into the market for endowment mortgages. Brokers' greatest odium was, however, reserved for the Bank of Ireland when it proposed to enter the market both as a distributor and as an underwriter (through Lifetime). Their main fear in this regard was that Lifetime products would be much more attractive to consumers than products from other life assurance companies, given that the costs of distribution would be apparently so much lower. Their fears proved groundless, initially at least, in that the original range of Lifetime products was priced to bear the costs of broker distribution.

CUSTOMER RELATIONSHIP MANAGEMENT

'Lifetime, which we see both as a company title and as a Bank of Ireland branded service, is intended to fit with our customer relationship philosophy, which in turn is what differentiates the Bank of Ireland's life assurance service from competitors' (Seamus Creedon, MD, Lifetime).

Before exploring this philosophy, it might be useful to consider some of the differences between the traditional 'High Street' bank and the life assurance company. In many respects, each has different antecedents, culture, tradition and structure. For the life assurance company, the transaction process is characterised primarily by selling; as quoted earlier, there is an old life assurance industry adage, 'Our products are sold rather than bought.' The industry has developed many effective and sophisticated sales and marketing practices aimed at selling contracts to customers. This is often done using the services of independent intermediaries or brokers. There is also an under-emphasis on continuing service; as one industry pundit put it: 'The warm ardour of customer courtship deteriorates suddenly into the cold reality of a long marriage.' The conventional communication processes are recognised as leaving much to be desired. The production-oriented self-image of some life assurance organisations is of a selling body with an administrative tail.

The retail bank branch system provides an excellent structure for an ongoing relationship between supplier and client. In general, this relationship between bank and customer enjoys a high level of persistency: for instance, less than 10 per cent of Bank of Ireland customers have ever switched to another clearer. However, despite the stability of this relationship, banks tend to view customers as accounts and the relationship as a series of transactions. Banks traditionally do not appreciate the potential commercial value of this customer base; there is a poor selection of products and services on offer to it, and little or no selling to it. Put crudely, it might be said that life assurance prospectors spend 80 per cent of their time looking for customers while bankers spend 80 per cent of their time on processing and administrative systems. Obviously, if life assurance is to be sold through the traditional branch network, there need to be changes in culture, behaviour and systems.

The starting-point in this process is the customer and his needs for medium-term service on two levels—financial *planning* for an uncertain future and for sustained financial service *performance*. The reality of these needs is reflected in the growing sales of financial advice handbooks, expanding coverage of personal financial matters in the media, and the growing numbers of those calling themselves financial advisers. While the reality to date has been that over 80 per cent of Lifetime's business has been generated through its link with the Bank of Ireland, the identification of potential Lifetime customers and the establishment of the degree of interest can, in theory, happen in a variety of ways:

(1) through the branch network and other outlets of the Bank of Ireland Group—the principal channel in which relationships are initiated;
(2) through Lifetime counsellors, of whom there are now over 50 operating all over Ireland;
(3) through other individuals and activities with the will and capacity to introduce customers to a Lifetime relationship;
(4) through recognised brokers of insurance/assurance services;
(5) through direct response techniques.

The role of Bank branches is to make qualified referrals to Lifetime counsellors. The flavour of the approach to the customer is conveyed by the suggested meeting with the counsellor—with the emphasis on the service rather than on a particular product. The 'no-obligation' character of the service and the opportunity to meet the counsellor in the branch have proved appealing to customers. Interestingly, while initial counselling may take place variously at the customer's work or at his home, the majority of customers have expressed a preference to discuss their needs in the Bank branch. In advising the customer, counsellors use what is called the customer or client advice system, which consists of specially developed software resident on portable IBM-compatible hardware. This system is unique in its scope and concept and has become something of a 'trademark'.

Once a contract has been signed, Lifetime believes that ongoing communication processes are very important. It does not believe that it is sufficient to leave it to customers to contact the company entirely at their discretion, whether through the Bank of Ireland or otherwise. Thus, it routinely corresponds with each customer once a year, reporting on the progress of Lifetime's side of the relationship bargain, forwarding a small personalised gift and, most importantly, encouraging the customer to return with any comment or request. Indications to date in the form of persistency levels, in the very small number of terminations (which are below industry average), and in customer-initiated increases in contractual commitments have proved very positive. Further, the method of operation outlined above has allowed each counsellor to handle six or seven times the volume of business handled by life assurance agents operating conventionally. However, this does not include any apportioning of 'the referral costs' borne by the branch network.

Lifetime sees its relationship with its customers as being for life. From initial encounter to, in a sense, growing old gracefully together—'Our customers are our partners for life' might be seen as a company motto. This commitment to a long-term in-depth counselling relationship with its customers must, of necessity, be open-ended, including reassessment of needs and of service requirements in changed individual and social circumstances. Obviously, it is not possible for the company to know the future in full and what its customers will expect of it in 20, 30 or 40 years' time.

In so far as Lifetime can envisage the overriding need for flexibility, it has designed contracts to include options and exclude constraints, such as:

(1) options to increase or reduce amounts of cover, or to extend or reduce the scope of cover (subject necessarily to underwriting practices);
(2) options to increase or to reduce the amount of income applied in contributions;
(3) options to vary the character of the investment element of the contracts;
(4) propositions to allow customers to vary the risk profile of the investment content.

Delivery of this flexibility will be increasingly dependent on the capacity of technology. A significant implication of the long-term relationship orientation is the need to be close to customers in all respects. To this end, Lifetime envisages a technology network strategy which will disperse the capacity to process customers' transactions widely, and initially to its area offices in Dublin, Galway, Cork, Sligo and Dundalk.

Lifetime also foresees that, as the population ages and mortality experience continues to improve, an increasing proportion of its customers will be temporary or permanent claimants for any of the following:

(1) disability coverages—short or long, partial or total;
(2) coverages such as already exist for potentially terminal risks;
(3) long-term acute nursing care for the elderly;
(4) medical expenses risks such as are covered today by the Voluntary Health Insurance Board.

The Lifetime personal financial counselling service is built on the belief that an increasing proportion of customers in the retail financial services market will choose to satisfy an increasing proportion of their needs in a relationship context—more and more customers will implicitly pay for a service which adds value. The emphasis will shift from contracts sale and administration concepts to those of relationship management. To quote Seamus Creedon of Lifetime:

> 'A daydream of mine is that the relationship orientation which I have outlined will eventually be embodied in a service covenant which will define the context for the underwritten policy contracts. Such a covenant would delineate service attributes such as information for customers, responses to customers and, I believe, a guarantee of relative contract performance. A move from contract to relationship pricing would be an appropriate corollary.'

ORGANISATION STRUCTURE

Lifetime has an exceptionally young staff which has now reached over 200, 70 per cent of whom are under 25. The thinking of the company is that if people demonstrate that they have the ability, they are given as much freedom as possible to develop and manage their own operation. Initiative and commitment may be said to be recognised and rewarded sooner rather than later and remuneration packages are designed to reward achievement. The company has no union, unlike the retail branch network of the Bank of Ireland. (Indeed, it has been argued that the existence of this union, IBOA, has prevented the Bank from providing more flexible levels of service to customers, e.g. as regards opening hours.) The company has no formal personnel function; each line manager is responsible for staff development and welfare. Lifetime recently introduced an Employee Development function (two people), responsible for setting employee policy, management development and coordinating key aspects of training activity. The company believes that effective service to its customers comes from an holistic blend of, first and most importantly, people with requisite skills and customer-oriented attitudes; secondly, organisation, in the broadest sense, using customer-relevant methods and structures; and thirdly, the equipment of people with tools, again broadly defined, in the form of technology, materials and environments. The evolving nature of the company's organisation structure reflects its early stage of development, growing market opportunities, and its special relationship with the Bank of Ireland retail branch network (see Exhibit 5). A number of comments may be made on this organisation structure.

Area managers were initially responsible for managing the representative force of counsellors, generating sales, and building relationships with the branch network in their areas. Now, however, each area manager is assessed on bottom-line contribution rather than just sales volumes. The area offices have expanded to accommodate more customer service activity and administration. This is a process designed to continue, so that each area will become responsible for all new business administration, technical and marketing support to counsellors and branches, effectively becoming a profit centre.

The group which monitors sales performance and sets selling and marketing strategy is called the Customer Direction Group. It consists of the managing director, the three executive directors, the marketing operations manager, and the four area managers. It meets once a month to discuss performance and agree tactics for the following month.

Much of the development work within Lifetime is organised on a project basis with multifunctional teams. At the end of 1989, a Business and Organisation Development Team was set up with the responsibility of coordinating the corporate development plan for 1990. All major projects report to this group on a regular basis. The team is responsible for monitoring progress against the plan, anticipating resourcing or timing difficulties, assisting and supporting line managers on projects, and refining the plan if circumstances and resources require it. The team is composed of four people, two on full-time assignment and two with line management responsibilities. In addition, there is an Employee Direction Group, which looks after employee goals, and a Shareholder Direction Group, which looks after shareholder goals. These groups meet once a month to review progress against goals, make decisions on relevant issues and on matters of policy that arise, and approve any necessary moves in the following month(s) or year(s).

INTERNATIONAL DEVELOPMENTS

The Bank of Ireland's strategy of combining banking and life assurance is quite fashionable at present, the fashion even adding new words to languages. In Germany, *Allfinanz* is the term used to describe the combination, in a single grouping, of banking and insurance, while the corresponding word in French is *Bancassurance*. In Germany, the mighty Deutsche Bank has recently set up its own life assurance. France has also seen a spate of government-inspired marriages between state-owned banks and insurers, designed to strengthen the combined groups' capital bases, such as UAP's link-up with BNP. In Britain, Abbey Life and Lloyds Bank have joined hands, while many building societies

Exhibit 5

Lifetime Organisation Structure

SEPTEMBER 1987

JANUARY 1990

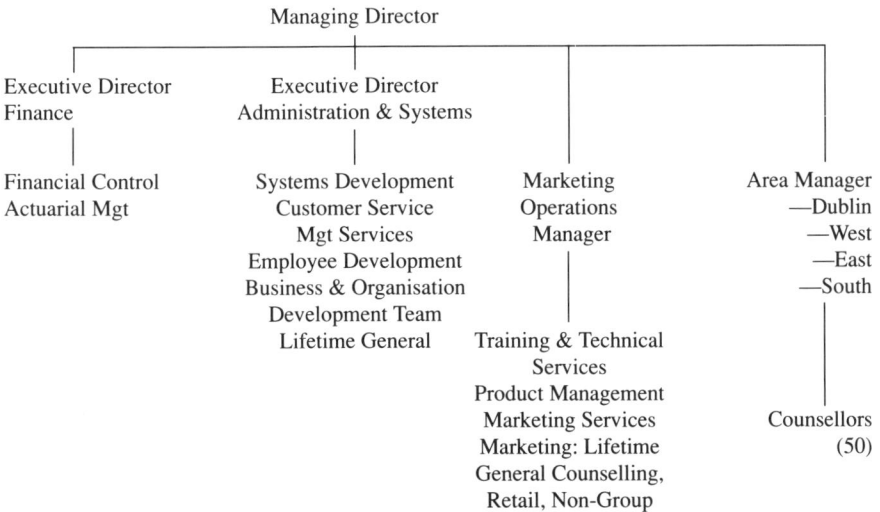

are also eschewing the independent route in favour of ties with life assurance companies.

The creation of broadly based financial services groups has apparently received the blessing of the European Commission. Sir Leon Brittan, the Community's financial services Commissioner, said recently:

> 'Our categorisation of financial services activities under the headings 'banking'; 'invest-ment services'; and 'insurance' is becoming increasingly artificial. As regards products, the vast majority of life policies are best understood simply as savings plans—and must compete against other savings vehicles for which a full single market is already either in being or close to being achieved. And as for institutions, we are entering the age of *Allfinanz*, or *Bancassurance*, in which the distinctions between a bank, an investment services house, a leasing company, an insurance company, and so on, are breaking down.'

Where do Lifetime and the Bank of Ireland fit in this new world that has been created? By the end of 1990, Lifetime hopes to have established a viable operation in the UK (and Northern Ireland) working closely in association with other Bank of Ireland retail operations in that country. It has planned offices in Belfast, Manchester and south-east England, employing up to 40. The British operation will initially concentrate on existing Bank of Ireland customers. A second phase of expansion will introduce Lifetime's products to independent agents. The UK may well offer different challenges to Lifetime. In Ireland, the bulk of its business is in life and investment plans, with the minority end in pensions business. In the UK, the demo-graphic situation is an ageing population by contrast, the bulk of whom need retirement planning.

With the greater liberalisation of insurance and financial markets in the European Community, the company can also look further afield for future opportunities. A major aim of 1992 is to achieve a single market for insurance within the Community. This is proving more difficult in life assurance than in other industries, but life assurers in Ireland and Britain have eagerly embraced the concept and present indications are that insurers from these islands will enjoy a number of competitive advantages over their European counterparts as the system is liberalised. The Irish regulatory system is very flexible and encourages consumer choice. Some continental supervisory systems, in particular those of Germany, Italy, Greece and Portugal, are very heavy-handed and allow little freedom to individual companies in regard to premium rates, product design and so on. The philosophy of the European Commission is to encourage competition, which means that the more liberal supervisory regimes will achieve the upper hand in the Europe of the future.

The scale of these developments may well force a restructuring of the life assurance industry in Ireland, in particular a concentration in structure and a consequent diminution in the number of players. Indeed, one industry commentator has added, intriguingly, that there will be just four major players in the industry in five years' time.

APPENDIX A

Sectors of the Financial Services Market

(1)   MONEY TRANSMISSION
        —Current Accounts
        —Automated Teller Machines
        —Direct Debits, Standing Orders

Market dominated by BOI and AIB. Heavy investment in staff and technology and physical resources required. On a stand-alone basis, money transmission system does not generate profits. Spin-offs associated with it do.

(2)   SHORT-TERM SAVINGS
        —Retail Bank Deposit Accounts
        —Savings Banks, e.g. TSB
        —Building Societies

Dominated by these. Competition on basis of accessibility and speed of processing. Relatively insensitive to interest rate movement.

(3)   SHORT-TERM LENDING
        —Overdrafts
        —Personal Loans

Who offers service?—Retail Banks
High-margin business, with high risks. Bad debt management is important. Administration costs are high. Moving towards credit cards.

(4)   LEASING
Specialist Leasing Companies, e.g. Woodchester, BIF, AID

Considerable skill. Credit control important.

(5)   CAPITAL MARKETS
        — Stocks and Shares
        — Money Management (Treasury)
        — Property

Who invests?—Pension Funds
                        Banks
                        Insurance Companies
                        Personal Investors

Who offers service?—Management Services of BOI, IBI, AIB, AIIM, Irish Life. Key requirement is expertise as shown by track records.

(6)   MEDIUM-TERM SAVINGS
        —Savings Banks
        —Retail Banks

—Building Societies
—Life Assurance
—Post Office
—Ucits/Unit Trusts

This sector has been undergoing considerable competitive change during the 1980s. It can offer high returns to customers locked into a fixed period.

(7)   LONG-TERM SAVINGS
Again as for medium-term savings; however, focus for long-term savings tends to be towards pensions.

(8)   LONG-TERM LENDING
Mainly mortgages provided by building societies, banks and specialist lenders.

(9)   PROTECTION: LIFE/GENERAL/HEALTH
Life assurance products provided by traditional insurance companies and bodies such as VHI.

APPENDIX B

Types of Life Assurance Contracts

System of Contract	*Types Available*	*Payment Methods*
Non Profit	Term Assurance Endowment Whole of Life Pensions	Single Premium or Annual Premium
With Profit	Endowment Whole of Life Pensions	Single Premium or Annual Premium
Unit Linked	Endowment Whole of Life Pensions	Single Premium or Annual Premium

TERM ASSURANCE

On death within a specified term, the sum assured (death benefit) is paid to the beneficiaries. On survival, nothing is paid. On early surrender, the policy has no value.

ENDOWMENT

Available either as Non Profit or With Profit (explained further on). In essence the customer is guaranteed to receive a lump sum of a specified amount on survival to the end of the agreed term. On death within the term, the estate of the customer receives a guaranteed sum. There would be a value available on early surrender. Note that the endowment format is the basis of the popular endowment mortgage.

WHOLE OF LIFE
No limit to the period for which the contract runs.

PENSIONS
Pension is paid during lifetime of customer. No benefit on death.

NON PROFIT
The payout on death or maturity is set at the point the contract is taken out and does not change.

WITH PROFIT
The minimum payout on death or maturity is fixed at the outset of the policy. However, policyholders are entitled to a share of the profits declared by the company each year. This share of the profit is distributed to the policyholders by way of bonus additions to the sum assured payable on death or on maturity. Once the bonus is added to the sum assured it forms part of the guaranteed benefit to the policyholder. The profit declared by a company in any year depended on, (a) return earned on investments, (b) how well the company managed its expenses, (c) how well the company performed on underwriting, i.e. did it charge policyholders for the risks it was taking on, otherwise known as mortality profits? The company does not distribute all profits as it retains some to invest in the business. This also allows the company to build up its capital base. The traditional mutual life assurance companies, such as Norwich Union and Standard Life, operate on a with-profit basis.

UNIT LINKED
In the early seventies, a completely new type of contract emerged. This type of contract has rapidly overtaken the traditional non-profit and with-profit types of contract in popularity. The essence of this type of contract is that all premiums received after charges have been offset are invested in a special pool of assets (known as a unit-linked fund). The premiums are used to purchase units in the fund at a price which depends on the current value of the fund. At regular intervals, usually weekly, the company values the fund using stock market prices. This valuation results in a new price. By multiplying the units held on a policy by the last declared price for that fund, the policyholder knows what the value of the policy would be if he decided to surrender it. This type of contract ensures that all investment return is passed back to the policyholder, unlike the with-profit system, which allows the company to decide how much of the investment profits it distributes in any one year. Since their introduction, unit-linked policies have given the policyholder better returns than with-profit.

SINGLE PREMIUM CONTRACTS
Customer pays a lump sum and has no further obligations in terms of payment.

REGULAR OR ANNUAL PREMIUM CONTRACTS
The basis is that the customer will pay a premium of an agreed amount at an agreed frequency either until death or for an agreed term. In return the company will provide the benefits agreed, e.g. sum assured on death or a lump sum at the end of the agreed term. If the customer decides that he does not wish to continue with regular payments the company will be able to discontinue any covers. If at the time the customer stops paying a regular premium and the policy has a value (known as a surrender value), the customer is entitled to that value.

Questions
1. Assess the wisdom, level of success and salient features of Lifetime's entry into the life assurance industry.
2. Consider the structure and administrative ethos of Lifetime. Do you feel the 'cultural fusion' between the life assurance industry and retail banking has been achieved?
3. What organisational development problems are likely to emerge as the company gets bigger and more established? How might these be overcome?
4. 'A move from contract to relationship pricing would be an appropriate corollary.' Seamus Creedon, managing director. Comment on this.
5. What will be the likely strategy of AIB if and when it enters the market?
6. Develop an overall business strategy for Lifetime for the next three to five years.

Part V

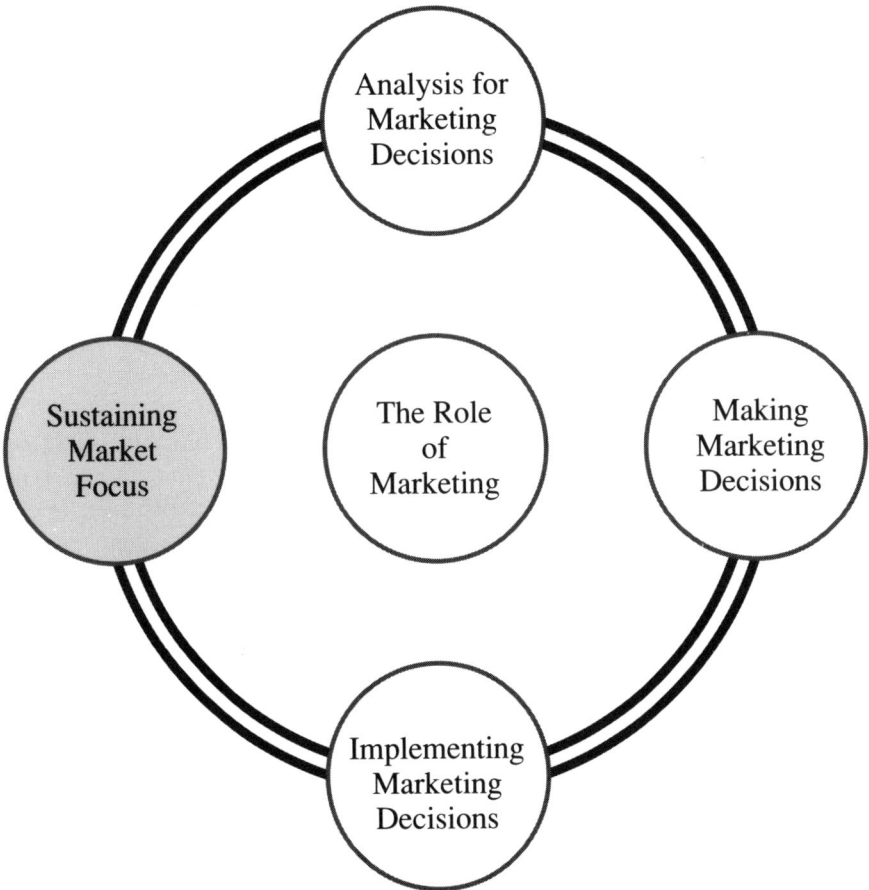

Analysis for Marketing Decisions

Sustaining Market Focus

The Role of Marketing

Making Marketing Decisions

Implementing Marketing Decisions

Chapter 18

Renewal and Shared Values

INTRODUCTION

Retaining market focus means sustaining persistent commitment to, and understanding of, the market, its needs and competitive dynamics and aligning company resources to serve these needs. The company must look to markets for its revenue, its profits and its ultimate *raison d'être*. But maintaining focus also demands looking inward to the vitals of the organisation in order to understand its core and distinctive competences and to bring these to bear on well-chosen parts of the marketplace.

Focus therefore has two dimensions: first, clear focusing on markets that are to be served and second, focusing the organisational resource on markets to do this job better than competitors. Doing this well and consistently over time is difficult. Organisations tend more readily towards stability than change. Consequently, markets chosen as the focus at one stage in a company's history easily become fixed and immovable targets, just as resources all too readily congeal into rigid configurations of assets (people, equipment and money) and practices (the way business gets done). Such fixity is life-threatening in all but very stable market and competitive circumstances.

Sustaining focus demands two things: dedication to the dual nature of focus (internal and external) and a constant commitment to renewal in the organisation and its market relationships.

In this chapter we will discuss the nature and demands of the renewal process, the avenues through which companies lose focus and surrender to competitive decline, and the role of people and the values they share in sustaining market viability.

ORGANISATION RENEWAL

To remain successful, organisations must balance being simultaneously efficient and effective. Efficiency underpins the short-term operational health of the company—it transacts its business at appropriate cost levels and gets its services and products to the market in a timely manner at acceptable quality levels. Efficiency therefore pays today's bills. Effectiveness underpins the organisation's long-term health. This involves, from a marketing perspective:

- choosing markets well and allocating the company's scarce resources to or across these markets for greatest long-term payoff;
- positioning the company and its market offerings in these markets in a manner that ensures and protects profits by serving customer needs and outperforming competitors;
- integrating market-focused activity with the other strategic concerns of the company and helping to build the kinds of structures, processes, competences and value systems that make it possible to implement the chosen strategy with regard to market position.

These twin tasks of efficiency and effectiveness in any organisation must receive constant attention. Over-emphasis on one will inevitably damage the other. Too much attention to efficiency will usually breed rigidity within fixed strategic and organisational parameters: a company will prefer doing what it does well in a repeated manner over doing new things or doing things differently. Under such circumstances great short-term success may lead managers to ignore or to dismiss the need to reinvent some of the company's activities. Yet the latter may well be essential to secure viability in a changed marketplace of the future. So, too, unbalanced emphasis on effectiveness and the long term can lead to inattention to the vital daily detail of managing well. All too many new ventures die in the short term while promising their investors and customers payoff in the long term. Similarly, all too many large successful companies can run close to bankruptcy while planning a glorious strategic future. In the early nineties, Philips, one of Europe's proudest electrical and electronics companies, found itself facing competitive and financial disaster despite a huge apparatus dedicated to long-term planning.

The challenge of renewal is therefore one of achieving balance. Any organisation and any good manager must be both entrepreneurial (effective) and administratively wise (efficient). In strategic terms, the roots of these two dimensions of behaviour lie in *innovation* and *cost competitiveness*. Innovation in turn is reflected in the market in what we have previously referred to as 'high perceived value', while cost competitiveness may be found in a market appreciation of 'low delivered cost'. The relationship between these ideas may be seen in the elements of Figure 18.1. The companies that will prove to be true and consistent winners are those that move towards the north-east corner of the illustration—that are simultaneously innovative and efficient by providing goods and services that yield superior customer value at low delivered cost. An interesting example of such a company is Benetton, which competes in the mercurial world of fashion garments (see Exhibit 18.1).

Figure 18.1

Renewal through Balancing Innovation and Efficiency

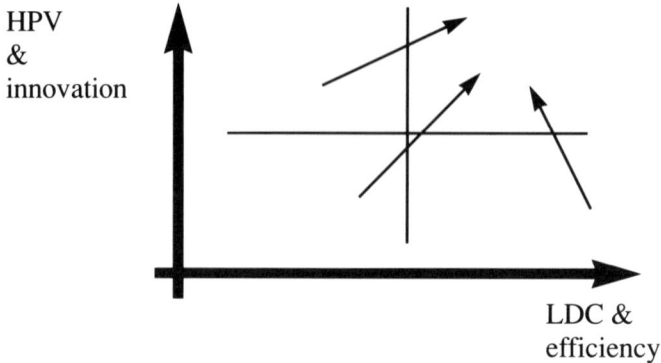

HPV
&
innovation

LDC &
efficiency

Achieving this balance between innovation and efficiency in order to serve the market with a customer and competitive strategy of both value and cost typically demands unique organisational arrangements. Lawrence and Dyer (1983), in their study of the renewal phenomenon, suggested that the required organisational form consists of high degrees of organisational differentiation and integration; balanced power structures; and balanced human resource practices.

Exhibit 18.1

BENETTON

The colour and shape of success

'The important thing is to start in business with no money,' believes Luciano Benetton, head of the Italian clothes manufacturing empire. 'If you are rich, you're not hungry enough, you are handicapped, you lose concentration.'

Mr Benetton smiles when asked if he has lost his concentration now that he is very rich: he owns an international label distributed through 6,500 retail outlets in 82 countries, with a turnover of $2 billion and profits of $120 million annually. 'I enjoy my job very much so that keeps me concentrated. My aim is to have my product known and well distributed around the world and I will keep working at that.'

Benetton is a trim Italian with almost shoulder-length greying hair and pro-fessorial glasses. The well-preserved 55-year-old flew into Ireland recently for a promotional visit but his trips to the Irish shops went largely unnoticed by the public, his face unknown as the man behind the advertisements showing people of all races wearing 'the United Colours of Benetton'. It is his seventh visit to Ireland in the eighteen years the group has been here. 'Before when I visited, people were dressed very classically, in dark colours. This time, I noticed an explosion of colour. There's been a huge change in the shops, especially for women and children,' Benetton comments in interview at the Irish headquarters of Benetton in South Anne Street, Dublin. 'Irish businessmen are still dressed very sombrely. The working world is very formal for men. To be taken seriously, you have to wear a tie. That will take time to change. Benetton would like to do it,' he grins. The head of one of the world's largest clothing manufacturers is sombrely dressed for his interview. His only Benetton garment is his brown slacks, worn with dark brown leather boots, a green jacket designed by his tailor, a high-quality white, cotton shirt and a conservative blue spotty silk tie.

There are at present 31 Benetton outlets in Ireland, spread throughout the coun-try. The shops, as with the thousands of other ones around the world, are owned by individuals but are licensed by Benetton, which sets specifications for how they must look. The clothes are designed by Benetton in its own inimitable fashion and are manufactured at one of its dozen manufacturing operations, most of which are in Italy, and then shipped to the retailers in the various countries. Benetton is an 80 per cent family-owned firm. Its stores have not been hit by the world recession, mainly because the philosophy of the company is to offer high-quality, colourful garments at a good-value price. Manufacturing operations at Benetton are tightly planned and highly efficient, and there is an imaginative use of economies of scale.

The company's worldwide expansion plans for the nineties are focusing on Eastern Europe and the Far East. 'During the eighties the growth areas were the US and Japan. All the growth in the nineties will be in Asia, places like Korea, Indonesia, South America and the Eastern bloc,' Benetton predicts. The company has opened over 100 shops in Czechoslovakia, Yugoslavia, Poland and Russia.

Benetton has no fear of competitive forces in Europe. His business philosophy appears simple, based on practical experience which began when he left school at 16 in Treviso, a town near Venice, and started selling the garments knitted by his sister and company designer, Giuliana. 'You have to have a product that is unusual and innovative, and because the world is changing so rapidly, you have to read the future carefully,' he concludes.

Source: *The Irish Times*, 30th April, 1991.

Companies capable of self-renewal are likely to be both differentiated and integrated in structure. A differentiated structure is one that contains variety and sub-division so as to allow different units to respond differently to varied aspects of the environment. A differentiated form will normally entail allowing decision-making discretion at decentralised levels and the empowerment of the members of the organisation to analyse their situation and take action. Integration by contrast implies centralisation and unified control of the company's activities. The prescription for renewal is to have both of these apparently contradictory features combined. This is the feature of excellent companies to which Peters and Waterman (1982) drew attention when they spoke of companies that were simultaneously 'loose and tight'. Their observations of very successful companies suggested that they all were 'loose' in the manner in which they allowed managers to be entrepreneurial throughout the organisation in order to ensure close and responsive relationships with customers and rapid response to competitive forces. Project teams abound in such circumstances and entrepreneurial groups may often remove themselves from the mainstream of the company to 'skunk works' or 'garden shed' environments. At the same time they observed that these same companies had a significant degree of 'tightness' in the form of a unified strategy towards markets and competition; shared values that managers, no matter how entrepreneurial or idiosyncratic, all subscribed to; and systems of assigning responsibility and authority that made clear measurement of performance and explicit controls possible.

Why should organisational differentiation and integration be associated with self-renewal? The answer is clearly that differentiation (the 'looseness' factor) supports innovative and entrepreneurial behaviour. And our contention is that organisational differentiation is the foundation-stone on which companies build an ability to deliver high perceived value to customers. Integration (the 'tightness' factor), on the other hand, supports efficiency through the unification and coordination of action and through clear measurement and control. Efficiency as has been noted is the root of corporate ability to provide services and products at low delivered cost to customers. The combined strategy of value and cost therefore reasonably leads to a need for a combined organisational form. One of the reasons that so few companies succeed in being both high in perceived value and low in delivered cost is that few have the managerial capability to create and operate a structure which is simultaneously loose and tight. The barrier to imitation is high if one seeks to copy the self-renewing firm and this invaluable barrier inheres in managerial competence rather than in any financial or physical asset.

Power
Self-renewing organisations are ones that are characterised by an appropriate balance of power both vertically and horizontally. Ensuring vertical balance demands that power be spread among organisational levels—neither too centralised at the top nor too decentralised at the bottom. Spreading power vertically results in what is sometimes referred to as 'empowerment'—people throughout the organisation have, and act on, the freedom to make decisions

proper to their jobs. In structuring decision-making processes, good vertical balance of power makes it possible to drive marketing planning in both a top-down and a bottom-up manner, ensuring the involvement of all who can contribute to the process and ensuring support for implementation.

Achieving a balance of power horizontally entails ensuring that no one area of expertise dominates decision-making and action-taking. This implies that marketing, finance, human resource management, operations management, R & D should each find themselves with the power to advance their perspectives on the business and to ensure that their concerns and requirements for success are not dismissed summarily. This has an important implication for those employed in marketing. Market success based on market focus can be achieved only through the coordinated efforts of all parts of an organisation. The solution to achieving and sustaining market focus in a company is not to give marketing undue power or precedence. It is rather to provide it with sufficient power to manage among equals representing other functional specialisations. The more shared and group-based the decision-making, the more likely one is to find outcomes that reflect balance among all the important aspects of company action. It is only through such balance that customers are properly served and competitors outperformed.

Human resource practices

Lawrence and Dyer (1983) suggest that human resource practices fall into three categories: bureaucratic, market and clan based. Furthermore, they claim that the self-renewing company uses all three sets of practices in a balanced manner.

Bureaucratic human resource practices rely on rules and established procedures to guide and reward behaviour in the firm. Various aspects of any successful market-focused organisation will have bureaucratic process. In managing customer service one of the first simple rules that many companies establish is that all telephones must be answered before the third 'ring', or that all inquiries must be answered within twelve hours. These are examples of simple rules that establish and control performance. If you run an automotive parts production company in Ireland and supply a Nissan assembly plant in the United Kingdom, bureaucratic rules and processes are vital to guaranteeing timely delivery of exactly what is needed. Bureaucratic is a word often used in a popular sense to deride organisations and their behaviour. It is important to appreciate that bureaucratic process, properly designed and managed, is essential to much of success in any business and especially to its ability to perform efficiently and to deliver at low cost and with speed. Cost and speed are two crucial competitive advantages.

Market-based human resource practices assume that behaviour may be traded in a marketplace: crudely, that desired behaviour can be bought. This view leads to an emphasis on payment for performance. This is very clearly seen in the manner in which most salesforces are paid. Typically, sales personnel will be paid a basic salary and a performance-related commission or bonus which varies with their sales success. The assumption is that if people work harder and more effectively they will achieve higher sales and be rewarded through proportionately higher payment. The same philosophy has been applied to executive pay, where performance-related bonuses have become common, but in this instance the performance is that of the whole company. As before, the assumption is that if a manager's pay is tied directly to the company's profitability he will work harder. In all such practices it must be noted that the basic assumption is that behaviour in an organisation is a tradable commodity. Brought to extremes this can rebound disastrously if members of an organisation begin to use this as the only rule governing behaviour. Under such circumstances organisational life degenerates into continuous bargaining about the 'price' of every work practice or task or change in behaviour.

Clan-based human resource practices are rooted in an assumption that those in an organisation do or can have a sense of belonging to the organisational group—a sense of being in the 'clan' or being part of an extended family. If this is the case then one might expect certain aspects of behaviour to be driven by this sense of belongingness—by loyalty, by adherence to shared values governing behaviour in the group, by pride in membership and by an emotional solidarity in the face of competitive threat. Human resource practices based in a clan approach therefore appeal strongly to emotional rewards. Many young people embarking on a career in marketing will opt for this kind of reward when they join a company known for its excellent professional practice— becoming a member of the family is seen by the marketer and by others as a mark of distinction. The feelings associated with being part of a group that is acknowledged as highly competent and successful are powerful motivators. Remember that pride in a job and the extra effort that comes with it cannot be bought through market mechanisms any more than it can be evoked by a rule or regulation. New and growing ventures often provide excellent examples of clan mechanisms working at their most powerful. Many such ventures live on the extraordinary commitment and investment of energy, enthusiasm and creativity engendered by the feeling of belonging to something vibrant, growing and intimate in scale. Such practices are in fact essential to the success of most new market-focused ventures since their newness and lack of adequate resources usually means that they cannot afford to pay for all the energy being expended and they cannot risk being too rule-based while their entrepreneurial success depends primarily on innovative activity.

The prescription for renewal is not that one of these approaches to managing human resources is better but that all are needed in an appropriate balance in a successful company. The overall message about managing a self-renewing organisation is therefore one of seeking balance in structure—between differentiation and integration; balance in power—vertically and horizontally; and balance in human resource practice—between bureaucratic, market and clan mechanisms. Achieving balance of this nature helps the company to avoid the development of a monoculture—a fixed approach to all its concerns. In contrast it promotes an organisation full of variety and constructive tension between different approaches to doing business and sustaining market focus. Because the task demands significant managerial skill, companies of this form erect high barriers to imitation and can therefore succeed and earn high levels of profitability even in industries where there are low barriers to entry—competitors can enter readily but they cannot copy!

LOSING FOCUS: PATHWAYS TO DECLINE

Studying how organisations lose focus can also tell us a great deal about what has to be done to sustain healthy focus. It is salutary to reflect that of Peters and Waterman's 43 excellent companies, only 14 were excellent five years later and only 6 eight years on. In fact many of the companies had disappeared completely. Similarly, in the UK, the top-selling management publication, *Management Today*, identifies each year Britain's best companies. Of the 11 top companies identified between 1978 and 1989, only five survived to 1990. Of these five survivors, only one could still be described as a high-flyer. The majority had either collapsed or been sold in distress (Doyle, 1992). The lack of staying power in these 'excellent' companies dramatises the transient nature of much commercial success.

Based on many years of research into the strategic histories of companies, Miller (1990) has suggested that decline in excellent companies is typically a result of the excesses to which their success leads them. He calls this the Icarus paradox. The power of Icarus' wings led to the excess which killed him by flying too close to the sun—his greatest asset became his downfall and 'that same paradox applies to many outstanding companies today: their victories and their strengths often seduce them into the excesses that cause their downfall. Success leads to specialisation and exaggeration, to confidence and complacency, to dogma and ritual' (Miller, 1990, p. 3).

Miller's research suggests four pathways or trajectories in the riches-to-rags experience of failing companies which are described below.

From Craftsman to Tinkerer

A craftsman company builds its success on a strategy of quality leadership, usually based on the technical excellence of its founding team and embodied in a relatively narrow market focus which it sustains through primarily bureaucratic controls. Such companies face the threat of losing their market focus through narrowing their market scope and becoming ever more stable in behaviour. They can become rigid in their control mechanisms and detail-obsessed in their tinkering with the original formula for success. The craftsman becomes a tinkerer by self-indulgence, by searching for technical perfection without reference to market perceptions of value, and by becoming rigid and technocratic in organisation. Market focus degenerates into self-absorption.

From Builder to Imperialist

Here we find companies that grow successfully through acquisition and diver-sification, pushed along by a strong entrepreneurial acquisitive culture and run in a financially dominated manner, that become greedy and imperialist in char-acter. The imperialist behaviour leads to over-expansion, especially into markets about which management knows little. However, the over-confidence of the emerging 'imperialist' culture suggests that management can manage anything and everything and just like imperialist countries the realisation of having over-reached their abilities usually comes too late for corrective action to be possible. In this trajectory, focus which usually inheres in the initial acquisition path is lost in helter-skelter growth and dealsmanship such as characterised the late eighties in Europe and North America.

From Pioneer to Escapist

Pioneers build successful companies based on high innovative ability often rooted in their R & D capability and developed through an organic, creative organisation form. Their goal of technical progress and their strength in tech-nology can, however, readily lead to escapist, utopian pursuit of invention. Technology-obsessed managers lose their focus on real markets and solutions to real problems and chase imagined markets of the future that are attractive to unrestrained invention.

From Salesman to Drifter

Organisations with exceptional sales and marketing skills that carry well-known brand names to their markets sometimes lose internal focus and begin to believe that focusing on customers and competitors to the exclusion of their internal resources is the key to long-term success. Brought to its extreme this trajectory leads to the triumph of image over substance. In such circumstances excessive reliance on communication with the customer and promotional 'hype' surround-ing products and brands temporarily obscures lack of investment and indeed interest in product design, development and delivery systems. Ultimately the market sees the difference between promise and reality but by then the company may have lost its vital internal competences and its competitive position to competitors who focus well-managed resources on well-chosen markets.

What is common across all these proposed pathways to decline is the general pattern of success leading to excess. Companies develop a form of focus based on a combination of strategy, structure and market choice but then, encouraged to believe in their own invincibility, begin to become rigid and overreaching in their pursuit of what has become a 'success formula'. This momentum can then become a headlong and headstrong rush to self-destruction. The lesson for the company seeking to sustain a healthy form of market focus is to remember that it is essentially dynamic. Being focused demands constant attention to change in the marketplace in terms of customer needs and competitors' strategies and to change within the company in the form of growth and development in competences. Achieving focus demands clever management of the organisation and its strategy in the manner suggested by Lawrence and Dyer (1983) when they discuss the required balance in structure, power and human resource practice. Indeed one can now see the crucial role which balance plays in avoiding rigidity and excessive pursuit of a 'one-best-way' approach to management.

REINVENTING THE BUSINESS SYSTEM

Circumstances will sometimes demand that companies renew themselves by 'doing things better'. However, in rapidly changing markets this adaptive response may be inadequate and companies must find ways to 'do things differently' if they are to continue to prosper. 'Doing things differently' necessitates changing the basic activities and processes of the company— re-engineering the micro business system. Spectra Laboratories did this in the amateur film processing business as we saw in Chapter 6 (see Exhibit 6.1) through by-passing the pharmacy and forming an alliance with An Post to create a high-quality and competitively priced service. The business format franchise has reinvented the way of competing in many markets by re-engineering the traditional business process of a sector and creating a new 'template' that may be readily diffused at low cost. The success of Benetton, Prontaprint, The Body Shop and many fast food companies attests to the power of this approach. Looking at the new product development process, we can see how Toshiba has reinvented traditional methods of bringing innovations to market (see Exhibit 18.2).

We can see from the above that companies reinvent their own micro business systems to gain advantage in their markets. Where they do this with significant impact on traditional competitors, the overall industry or macro business system will often become reconfigured as their rivals begin to react or copy their new approach to the market and marketing practice.

NETWORKS, RELATIONSHIPS AND COOPERATION

In Chapter 1 we noted a need to reappraise the past concentration of marketing on short-term market transactions and to deal with the nature of the *relationship-based* markets that evolved in the eighties. Marketing is increasingly a matter of managing networks and relationships that encompass supplier partnerships, deep customer linkages and cooperative alliances with other companies in an industry. Managing in networks demands an increased understanding of negotiation processes and skills in forming and maintaining alliances, all of which redefine the task and required expertise of the marketing manager. In Ireland many smaller companies thrive on partnerships with larger companies such as major multinationals and UK or European food and clothing retailers.

In the commercial airline industry Scandinavian Airline Systems (SAS)—itself formed as a joint venture between the three Scandinavian countries' national airlines—provides an example of an alliance at international level. SAS has turned the disadvantage of a small home country base into an offensive international strategy by orchestrating a network of strategic alliances with other smaller airlines in Europe, the East and the Americas. This has allowed, among other benefits, SAS to offer its passengers one-stop services to most parts of the world with a minimum waiting time (Lorange and Roos, 1990/1991). We saw earlier in Chapter 16 how, in a related industry, Aer Rianta, from its Irish base, has used alliances with Aeroflot and others to build its business in Eastern Europe (see Exhibit 16.1).

Exhibit 18.2

TOSHIBA'S LAPTOP COMPUTER

Expeditionary marketing and real-time information

Launching new products and exploring new markets is a risky business. For a new product or service to be successful it must combine just the right blend of functionality, price and performance to penetrate its target market quickly and deeply. In new business development, there are two ways to increase the likelihood of such success. One is to try to improve the odds on each individual bet; the other is to place many small bets in quick succession and hope that one will hit the jackpot.

Most companies, and particularly Western ones, pursue the former approach. Thorough market research, skilful analysis of market segments, competitors and industry structure, along with careful phase reviews all take place. Yet the quality of this research and development process is no guarantee of subsequent success in the marketplace. Little is learned in the laboratory or in product development group meetings. True learning begins only when a product—imperfect though it may be—is launched.

If the goal is to accumulate learning and understanding as quickly as possible, a series of low-cost, fast-paced market incursions—expeditionary marketing—can bring the target more rapidly into view. Staking out virgin territory is a process of successive approximations. Consider an archer shooting arrows into the mist. The arrow flies at a distant and unclear target, and a shout comes back, 'right on the target' or 'a bit to the left'. More arrows are fired and more advice comes back until the cry is 'bull's eye'. What counts most is not being right the first time but the pace at which the arrows fly.

How fast can a company gather insights into the particular configuration of features, price and performance that will 'unlock' the market, and how quickly can it redesign its product offering? Speed and flexibility in doing this—reacting quickly to real-time information feedback from the marketplace—yields significant competitive advantage.

JVC's success and Sony's near-success in opening the consumer market for VCRs in the late 1970s came on the back of a whole string of product launches—many of them less than outstanding successes—over a decade. More spectacularly, Toshiba's staggering pace of product introduction in its laptop computer business during the late 1980s allowed it to explore almost every possible market niche and to outpace rivals like Grid, Zenith and Compaq. Between 1986 and 1990 Toshiba introduced no fewer than 31 new models to the market. Further, when one particular model failed, its withdrawal hardly caused a ripple in customer confidence. In fact, by 1991 Toshiba had discontinued more laptop models than some of its tardier competitors had launched.

The key to expeditionary marketing depends on minimising the time and cost of product 'iteration'. Speed of iteration refers to the time it takes a company to develop and launch a product, accumulate insights from the marketplace, and then redesign and relaunch. Flexible manufacturing processes and low plant-tooling costs are critical in this context.

Source: adapted from G. Hamel and C.K. Prahalad, 'Corporate imagination and expeditionary marketing', *Harvard Business Review*, July–Aug. 1991, pp. 81–92.

THE 'GREEN' CHALLENGE

One of the central challenges to firms for the nineties and one of the sources of real market opportunity is to respond to the demands for environmental protection—the 'green' challenge. Business systems are being driven to become either partial loops or complete closed loops which deal with the waste and after-effects of the activities of the industry. The paper industry has already adjusted to recovering and recycling much of its used or waste product. As a result the demand on timber resources is lessened and the problem of disposing of discarded paper and paper products is lessened. In 1991 BMW launched a new range of cars with an advertising theme which stressed that 80 per cent of the car was recyclable and that the company was committed to raising this proportion to 90 per cent. Products and services which may be recycled and which do not damage the environment are among the commercial winners of the nineties and the criterion of environmental friendliness has become an important one for an increasing number of consumers as they make purchasing decisions. Similarly, in business-to-business marketing organisations are increasingly insisting on supplier adherence to codes of practice that are environmentally friendly. In most instances this is becoming less a matter of choice and more one of necessity as national and international laws and regulations demand environmentally safe services, products and processes.

The opportunities that arise from this change in markets are many. Companies that respond early and well to market demand can clearly establish significant competitive advantage over their slower-moving competitors. Those who treat environmental protection as a market in itself also face real opportunities to create new businesses and products and services. Services such as environmental engineering consultancy are growing. Products and technologies that treat harmful waste and allow it to be neutralised and/or recycled are in demand. Businesses that will demanufacture and recycle used products face growing demand.

The 'green revolution' is therefore a very special and exciting challenge for the nineties and presents marketers everywhere with the opportunity to build new sources of competitive advantage and to develop new kinds of services, products and technologies. The interface between marketing and design becomes ever more important in this context. This is well illustrated by the concept of 'design for disassembly' such as is illustrated in Exhibit 18.3.

Exhibit 18.3

DESIGN FOR DISASSEMBLY

Problem: You manufacture autos, computers, washing machines, refrigerators, even teapots—complex, durable products. You use plastic, lots of it. But plastic waste is piling up all over the country. Social and political pressure to recycle the material is growing fast. What should you do? Solution: Design for disassembly. Simplify parts and materials and make them easy and inexpensive to snap apart, sort, and recycle.

Assemble for disassembly? Construct to destruct? Counter-intuitive as it may sound, design for disassembly is the future. If the 1990s is the decade of the environment and recycling, then taking things apart efficiently may soon become as important as putting them together right. Whirlpool, Digital Equipment, 3M, and General Electric are just a few of the corporate giants beginning to incorporate design for disassembly in their thinking and their products. Electrolux Corp. already has a DFD dishwasher on sale in Italy through its subsidiary, Zanussi.

But the leader of the DFD pack is BMW. Its spiffy two-seater, the Z1, has an all-plastic skin that was designed to be disassembled from its metal chassis in 20

---

minutes. The $50,000 limited production car, which currently is being sold only in Europe, has doors, bumpers, and front, rear, and side panels made of recyclable thermoplastic supplied by GE Plastics, a division of General Electric. Glue and screws, for example, are enemies of DFD. 'Pop-in, pop-out' two-way fasteners are the way to go. At BMW, it is now becoming *verboten* to use dozens of different kinds of plastics in manufacturing because it makes sorting expensive and the reuse of materials almost impossible. One great surprise coming out of the BMW experience is the rediscovery of repairability. In a throwback to the Tin Lizzies of the 1930s—when cars and everything else were built to be repaired—design for disassembly allows autos to be worked on faster and easier. The bumpers and doors come off without hours of high-cost labour. Put in a wider context, the throwaway society is having a rethink about itself.

In the US, trailing behind Europe in 'eco-angst', and behind in DFD by about a year, recent legislation has prompted many firms to take recycling seriously. Whirlpool Corp., for one, has a secret DFD project under way in which the parts of a new appliance will be designed to be quickly taken apart with ease—and coded for easy sorting. Indeed, many US companies are beginning to see the 'greening' of products as a marketing tool. To give people easy access to recycling information, 3M plans to put an 800 number on all its products. 'We are getting a lot of requests from our customers for recyclability,' says Linda Keefe, head of corporate identity and design at 3M.

GE Plastics serves the durable goods market, working only with engineering thermoplastics, the kind used in the BMW Z1. Thermoplastics can be reheated and remoulded; like cats, they can have many lives. GE Plastics, in fact, already has buy-back deals for thermoplastic with a number of car and computer companies. It reprocesses the material and sells it back to the manufacturer, competing with Dow Chemical, Du Pont, Hoechst Celanese, and other suppliers of virgin plastics. Now, GE Plastics plans to set up a nationwide plastics recycling network buying back recycled thermoplastics from all over the country, regrinding and recomposing the materials and reselling them to manufacturers at large. None of this would make much sense, however, if GE had to tear apart products to get at the plastic material and recycle it. The key is design for disassembly which makes it cost-effective to segregate the materials in durable goods.

To that end, GE Plastics has set up a joint venture with one of the US's largest industrial design companies and a winner of some of the product-design profession's top accolades. The first of what is expected to be many DFD products from this firm, Polymer Solutions, will hit the US market shortly: an electric kettle, similar to the kind popular in Britain and Canada. Called the U Kettle—a play on United Kingdom—it boils water faster than a stove and is made of easily disassembled, recyclable parts. Designing for disassembly requires new technology, skills—and persistence. When Polymer Solutions filled its first kettle model with water, it found that the handle wiggled. DFD involves designing and tooling tolerances between parts that are very fine. Despite the problems, the company is getting the U Kettle out on schedule just six months from concept to product. And Polymer Solutions has 13 other products lined up that will be designed for disassembly, including items for the computer, communications, banking, and vending-machine industries.

For all its initial success, one question still haunts DFD: What kind of incentives will be needed to get consumers to recycle big complex products? The U Kettle may come with a rebate of several dollars to entice people to break it apart and return it to GE Plastics. But what works for small appliances won't necessarily work for refrigerators or cars. Turning a long-life, big-ticket item like a car into a huge returnable can of soda by adding, say, a $500 deposit to its price, could be marketing death!

Source: *Business Week*, 17th September, 1990.

PEOPLE, SHARED VALUES AND THE LEARNING ORGANISATION

It is only because of people that market focus is achieved and sustained. The choice of markets, competitive strategy and resource management required is done by and through people. Since this is true at the level of the obvious, it should equally be a truism to state that the creation and management of the human resource base of the company is the ultimate key to market focus. But somehow this assertion is less likely to be viewed as a truism—as long as one is in debate with Western managers. To a typical Japanese manager the assertion is likely to be viewed as self-evident.

If we view people, or human resources in technical jargon, as the central resource then our attitudes as managers to recruitment, selection, enculturation, development, appraisal, communication and decision-making are likely to have a fundamental impact on doing business successfully. In order to achieve and sustain market focus an organisation needs people who are well suited to the tasks they are assigned; whose behaviour is influenced not just by the necessary bureaucratic rules of procedure and good practice but also by commitment; and whose motivation is sought not just through market mechanisms of payment for performance but also through those clan mechanisms which draw on shared values concerning the company and its customers. Shared values built around a dynamic notion of focus are probably the best guarantee of long-run competitiveness as well as the best proof against success turning to excess.

Waterman, Peters and Phillips (1990) note that shared values 'are the fundamental ideas around which a business is built. They are its main values. But they are more as well. They are the broad notions of future direction that the top management team wants to infuse throughout the organisation. They are the way in which the team wants to express itself, to leave its own mark.'

The value of 'shared values' is that while they provide a sense of over-arching direction and commitment, they are also open to reasonable interpretation and reinterpretation by the members of an organisation. This is what distinguishes them from rules or goals. And this openness gives them the loose-tight property discussed earlier in this chapter. Values are loose in so far as people in a company can discover novel ways of pursuing valued ends. They are tight in so far as they dictate what is unacceptable. Values are essential to all aspects of the self-renewing organisation—the loose-tight or differentiated-integrated structure as well as the distribution of power and the mix of human resource practices. An organisation of this form is necessarily infused with values which lead to strategies of both innovation and efficiency, high perceived value and low delivered cost.

The people in an organisation of this self-renewing character are committed to learning (to be innovative) and to striving (to be efficient), and develop a strong, satisfying and motivating sense of group membership in pursuing these ends. In an era in which the limitations of hierarchy have been brought into sharp focus, we find ourselves designing and working in companies that emphasise horizontal processes and flatter structures. The traditional emphasis on function is being counterbalanced by a renewed emphasis on process. These new forms have radical implications. It means that learning becomes the axial principle of organisations and replaces control as a fundamental job of management (Ostroff and Smith, 1992).

The people in 'post-hierarchical' companies are empowered to learn and to take action about their work in ways that might be inconceivable in a traditional setting. As one of the advocates of business re-engineering notes, 'In the future executive positions will not be defined in terms of collections of people, like head of the sales department, but in terms of process, like senior-VP-of-getting-stuff-to-customers, which is sales, shipping, billing. You'll no longer have a box on an organisation chart. You'll own part of a process map' (*Fortune*, 1992).

THE MARKET-FOCUSED FIRM

The new emphases on process as opposed to function, on heterarchy as opposed to hierarchy, on learning and reinvention, on cooperating and negotiating, on redesigning and re-engineering business systems and on empowerment and shared values give a deep underlying rationale to the business system view of marketing that has been central to this book. Business systems, whether macro or micro, are process-based views of industries, markets and competing companies and encourage managers to think horizontally, to re-engineer, to search for alliances and to empower those who perform the interdependent activities in any micro business system.

The *market-focused* company must view the marketing activity discussed in Parts II through to V of the book as an ongoing process. The central idea of market focus involves persistent attention to the dynamics of the macro business system—its suppliers, customers, rivals, technologies—so that the company may focus and refocus its particular micro business system, align its resources, and capitalise on the ensuing opportunity so as continually to deliver a valued product or service at acceptable cost. It must always focus on and understand the dynamics of the macro business system, so as to configure in turn its own micro business system. Commitment to this as an underlying approach to business is at the heart of managing marketing. It results in creatively matching arenas of market need with unique company competences through durable profitable relationships.

SUMMARY

Sustaining performance in the marketplace is not easy. Even excellent companies can go into decline—the so-called Icarus paradox. The challenge of renewal is one of achieving balance. Any organisation and any good manager must be both entrepreneurial (effective) and administratively wise (efficient). In strategic terms, the roots of these two dimensions of behaviour lie in innovation and cost competitiveness.

In response to changes in the macro business system, the market-focused firm will often have to re-engineer the way it does business—do things differently—and thus reconfigure its micro business chain. Strategic alliances may have to be considered, as may the opportunities offered by the 'green revolution'. However, sustaining competitive advantage is ultimately achieved by people in the organisation. Shared values are key as is the process of learning. In many respects, learning is the axial principle of the market-focused firm.

Reading

Baker, Michael J. (1992), *Marketing Strategy and Management*, 2nd ed., Macmillan, Basingstoke, ch. 22.

Doyle, Peter (1992), 'What are the excellent companies?', *Journal of Marketing Management*, vol. 8, no. 2.

Fortune, 'The search for the organisation of tomorrow', 18th May, 1992.

Hamel, G. and Prahalad, C.K. (1991), 'Corporate imagination and expeditionary marketing', *Harvard Business Review*, July–August, pp. 81–92.

Keogh, Derek (1990/1991), 'Strategic alliances in practice: the case of Aer Rianta and Aeroflot', *Irish Marketing Review*, vol. 5, no. 3.

Lawrence, P.E. and Dyer, D. (1983), *Renewing American Industry*, The Free Press, NY.

Lorange, Peter and Roos, Johan (1990/1991), 'Strategic alliance evolution and global partnerships', *Irish Marketing Review*, vol. 5, no. 3.

Miller, D. (1990), *The Icarus Paradox: How Exceptional Companies Bring about Their Own Downfall*, Harper, NY.

Ostroff, F. and Smith, D. (1992), 'The horizontal organization', *McKinsey Quarterly*, vol. 1.

Peters, Thomas J. and Waterman, Robert H. (1982), *In Search of Excellence: Lessons from America's Best-Run Companies*, Harper & Row, NY.

Waterman, Robert H., Peters, Thomas H. and Phillips, S. (1990), 'Structure is not organization', *Business Horizons*, June.

Wrynn, James and O'Mahony, Timothy (1988), 'Company turnaround strategies: a context for marketing', *Irish Marketing Review*, vol. 3.

Review Questions
1. Why is it important for the firm to be concerned with self-renewal?
2. Why do some companies lose impetus in their performance?
3. What opportunities are offered by the 'green revolution'?
4. What is meant by the idea of shared values in an organisation?
5. Learning is the axial principle of the market-focused company. Comment.

Great Southern Hotels

Great Southern Hotels, a state-owned hotel chain, achieved a noteworthy turnaround in its business fortunes. GHS moved from a near winding-up situation to one of being a competent player in the industry with interesting options for future development as it moved into the 1990s.

Issues: *Strategic choice and turnaround strategy; role of marketing in the process. Sustaining market focus. Public sector enterprise. Tourism/ hospitality industry and national planning.*

Great Southern Hotels Limited was established in 1961 as a subsidiary of Coras Iompair Éireann (CIE), Ireland's national transport company, to take over and manage the 'railway' hotels then in state ownership. At that time all Great Southern Hotels were old-world properties in the traditional style dating back to the nineteenth century.

Ireland in general and the tourism industry in particular enjoyed an economic boom in the sixties. The new sense of confidence encouraged expansion and four new hotels were built. Belfast and Rosslare were new locations for the company and second hotels were built in Galway and Killarney, largely to cater for the motoring tourist. It is difficult in retrospect to understand why the planners chose locations so heavily dependent upon seasonal tourism traffic when properties in major commercial centres such as Dublin, Cork and Limerick would have had year-round business potential. The decision to locate in Belfast, largely a government initiative, was taken in the context of improving North–South relations before the commencement of the present troubles.

The buoyant sixties gave way all too quickly to the traumatic seventies. Two international oil crises and serious conflict in Northern Ireland combined to ensure a decline in Irish tourism and continued losses in Great Southern Hotels, now burdened with crippling interest and loan repayment costs. The Belfast hotel was bombed twice and never once made a profit before being sold off in 1983. The hotels in Kenmare, Sligo, Mulrany and Bundoran were also sold off and the remaining properties declined through lack of reinvestment.

This case was developed as a basis for class discussion rather than to illustrate either effective or ineffective handling of an administrative situation.

Morale throughout the organisation was inevitably poor as the problems became more intractable and trading continued to disimprove.

CRISIS AND RESTRUCTURE
By 1982 Great Southern Hotels had accumulated losses of almost £11 million and was unable to meet its current liabilities. Its continued operation was made possible only by the agreed withholding of VAT, PAYE and PRSI payments due to the Exchequer. Something clearly had to be done. The parlous state of the company's finances was finally tackled by the government, as ultimate shareholder, and a number of options, including winding up, were considered. The government eventually decided to transfer responsibility for the company to a new board of directors reporting directly to the Minister for Labour. It paid off existing liabilities of £11 million and made a fund of £3 million available for essential urgent repairs to the remaining six hotels. The brief to the new board was simply expressed but formidable in its challenge: the company was to be run profitably as a commercial enterprise within the state sector.

The new board, which came into office in 1984 on the eve of the tourist season, faced many problems but quickly established a distinctive and determined style. New auditors, solicitors, architects, public relations and marketing consultants were engaged. New positions of chief executive and financial controller were established and appointments made to these. The new board and management team drew up a three-year corporate business plan which established the following priorities: increase revenue; reduce costs; restore standards of service; restore physical standards; and develop a coordinated marketing strategy.

INCREASE REVENUE
Higher Rates: The ability of the company to charge realistic rates for its product had long been hampered by the poor state of that product. On the basis of the refurbishment plan proposed for 1984/85 substantially higher group rates were negotiated with the major overseas tour operators for 1985. Where higher rates could not be agreed, the business was refused in the confidence (not without some nail-biting) that the improved product should not be undersold.

Premium Business: A determined effort was made to recapture the premium high-rate coach tourism business for 1985, again on the promise of an improved product. Much of this had been lost to competitors in previous years.

More Business: While much of the capital outlay involved in the 1984/85 refurbishment plan was allocated to essential behind-the-scenes work on the fabric, some monies were earmarked for the improvement of revenue-generating areas: restaurants, bars and shops. Nearly 70 per cent of Great Southern Hotels' business came traditionally from US tourist traffic. The move to increase rates would reduce this sector's overall volume but increase its value. Efforts had to be made to increase business from other markets.

REDUCE COSTS

Decentralisation: Under CIE, Great Southern Hotels had become over-centralised in its operation. A head office in Dublin was responsible for all aspects of purchasing, sales, marketing, accounts, personnel—in fact for everything which did not have to be done in the hotels. Central charges were thus very substantial and were often contested when charged out to the operating units. The decision was taken to devolve all operating authority and responsibility to the hotel managers. A small head office team, relocated to Galway where there were two hotels, was made responsible only for corporate matters, including, for example, consolidation of accounts. Its marketing, sales and reservations team provided group-wide marketing and reservations services and coordinated sales efforts.

Computerisation: The transfer of responsibility for accounts and management information reporting from head office to the hotels involved a substantial investment in computer hardware and software and in staff training. A small staff now produced detailed accounts and management reports within two days of period end. These were consolidated and company profit and loss, balance sheet reports, in comparison with budget and the previous year, as well as key statistics, were available and circulated on a weekly basis. This compared with a previous head office clerical staff of 27 when management reports were sometimes about three months out of date. The flow of up-to-date accurate management information had been vital to the new direction of the company. The ability quickly to identify trends and to take necessary action was a key tool for the managers on the ground in the short term and for the board and senior management in positioning the firm in the longer term.

Rationalisation: The achievement of the government's brief to the restructured company inevitably involved redundancies. The permanent staff was halved to a level of 170. This was augmented during the summer months by seasonal staff, many of whom were previous full-time employees.

Investment to Reduce Costs: Much-needed investment was simply impossible during the seventies. A lot of the company's energy-generating equipment was very old and no longer efficient. This was replaced and, though consumption increased, energy costs were reduced by about 50 per cent in three years—this was in part, however, due to lower oil costs. A new laundry in Galway, servicing both hotels there, resulted in substantial savings in linen hire costs. It was reckoned these savings would cover the capital cost within three years.

RESTORE STANDARDS OF SERVICE

The dynamic approach adopted by Great Southern Hotels in tackling the many long-neglected problems could not have been implemented without the cooperation and understanding of the staff and its representatives. The devolution policy had fundamentally changed the accountability of local management with a consequent impact at all levels. Staff morale and standards of service provided by it were related directly to its confidence in management and in the product. The introduction of a new young management team—with most senior appointments being made from within the organisation—the impact of £6 million spent on the hotels and ongoing staff training and retraining programmes all had ensured the effective restoration of the highest international standards of service.

RESTORE PHYSICAL STANDARDS

In 1984, the board was professionally advised that it would cost £8 million to restore the fabric of the hotels. In less than four years £6 million had been expended, with £3 million of this generated by the company itself. Much of the initial expenditure carried out in 1984/85 and 1985/86 was on basic behind-the-scenes work made necessary by many years of neglect: rewiring in the older hotels (built in the last century at the height of the golden age of railway); the elimination of wet and dry rot; and the cost of complying with statutory safety legislation. The ongoing refurbishment programme was designed to maintain the quality of guest accommodation, to maximise revenue-earning potential and to respond to changing market conditions. All guest bedrooms and bathrooms were completely renovated on a regular cyclical basis. Improvements to public areas in the hotels were also planned on a phased basis.

Changes in the pattern of business since 1986 had resulted in major expenditure being allocated to improve facilities for the domestic market, both holiday and commercial traffic. All the company's hotels had swimming pools and these had been substantially upgraded to cater for increased Irish holiday business. Additional leisure facilities had also been provided in most locations. New conference/function rooms had been added to the Corrib and Rosslare hotels and the facilities in Killarney, one of Ireland's first conference centres, had been substantially renovated. 'Executive' class bedrooms were provided in the two Galway hotels, where business travel provided an important part of the trade. A traditional pub, O'Flahertys, had been added to the Galway Great Southern and the Corrib hotel also boasted a new bar, O'Malleys, an imaginatively designed pub finished to the highest standards. The commitment to maintaining the properties to this high standard and the ongoing capital development plan called for a further £2 million to be spent, apart from routine maintenance, over the next three years.

MARKETING STRATEGY

Prior to the turnaround initiated in 1984, marketing policy and planning, like most other areas of Great Southern Hotels' operations, had suffered from a lack of funds and uncertainty about the company's future. Much of its business was attracted by a no longer deserved reputation for quality of service and excellence. As explained earlier, Great Southern Hotels had found itself with all its six properties in resort areas—two in Galway city, two in Killarney, Co. Kerry, as well as another in the remote and scenic Iveragh peninsula of Co. Kerry; a sixth in Rosslare, Co. Wexford, an important ferry port with the UK and Continent. Of these six hotels, three were of the old Victorian style of railway hotel while three were in the modern idiom built in the late sixties. Exhibit 1 profiles briefly the hotels.

Exhibit 1

PROFILE OF GREAT SOUTHERN HOTELS

Galway The Great Southern Hotel dominated Eyre Square in the centre of Galway city. Built in 1855, this 126-bedroom hotel successfully combined the grandeur and elegance of a bygone age with every modern convenience. The superior 'executive' bedrooms created in 1987 were in great demand and O'Flahertys pub was soon a popular success. This hotel with its bars, rooftop swimming pool and sauna, superb restaurant, conference facilities and excellent guest accommodation was the business and social centre of Galway and the West.

Corrib The Corrib Great Southern Hotel stood on a four-acre site just outside Galway city on the main road to Dublin. Overlooking Galway bay, the 115-bedroom hotel, built in 1970, offered its guests an indoor heated swimming pool, sauna, snooker and table tennis. It had its own conference facilities and a striking new pub, O'Malleys.

Parknasilla The Parknasilla Great Southern Hotel had 60 bedrooms, was built in 1895 and stood on a spectacular 268-acre shoreline site. It had its own private golf course, tennis, horse-riding, heated swimming pool, fishing, sailing and a small conference centre. The award-winning Pygmalion restaurant rated highly in the most prestigious food guides and the hotel often played host to distinguished international guests.

Killarney This 180-bedroom hotel was built in 1854 on a 36-acre site in the centre of the town. Its facilities included a conference centre which hosted many national and international conventions each year. Recently refurbished, the centre could cater for up to 600 delegates and was supported by a number of smaller syndicate rooms. This hotel also offered an indoor heated swimming pool, sauna baths, tennis, snooker and horse-riding. The Malton Room speciality restaurant was a winner of the Bord Fáilte awards of excellence.

Torc The 100-room Torc Great Southern Hotel was built in 1968 and stood on a four-acre site within easy walking distance of Killarney. The facilities included an indoor heated swimming pool, sauna baths and tennis. The Torc had become a favourite with families because of its facilities, spacious gardens and relaxed atmosphere.

Rosslare The 100-bedroom Rosslare Great Southern Hotel was built in 1969 on a three-acre site overlooking Rosslare harbour. Facilities included a new conference centre, an indoor heated swimming pool, sauna, snooker, games room, crèche, tennis, a special children's dining-room and a children's play-ground. The hotel enjoyed substantial repeat business from families and was a very successful centre for a senior citizens promotion in 1987.

Thus the company had been too dependent upon seasonal tourism traffic and prior to the new board's appointment almost 70 per cent of all business came from the volatile and cyclical US market. Much of the business was handled at uneconomic rates incapable of generating the levels of profit required for future development. Further, the performance of Irish tourism in the late seventies and early eighties had been disappointing while the domestic economy was slug-gish with little prospect of significantly increased consumer spending.

A marketing strategy was devised by the new management and board to address these weaknesses. Target markets were identified and specific mar-keting plans devised for each:

US	* Coach tour traffic—at the right rate
	* Independent travellers
	* Convention and incentive business
IRELAND	* Holiday market
	* Commercial market
	* Conference market
UK	* Holiday market
FRANCE/GERMANY	* Holiday market

Attracting the Irish holiday business was a particular challenge. The perception of the company's product in this market was that it was exclusive and expensive. An extensive and innovative advertising campaign highlighted the range of facilities available compared with competing hotels and stressed value for money. Exhibit 2 is an example of such advertising in the press medium.

Exhibit 2

Advertisement Targeted at Irish Holiday Business

This campaign was so successful that by the time of the virtual collapse of US traffic to Europe in 1986 (as a result of the Libyan crisis) the hotel group was able to increase its Irish business by 120 per cent and that market became the company's single biggest market for the first time. Exhibit 3 indicates this shift in the source of bednights between 1985 and 1987. British business to the hotels had shown some encouraging signs of growth and the marketing priority was to increase significantly business from continental Europe. Research was undertaken to determine the needs of the consumer in the principal markets.

Exhibit 3

Source of Bednights, 1985–1987

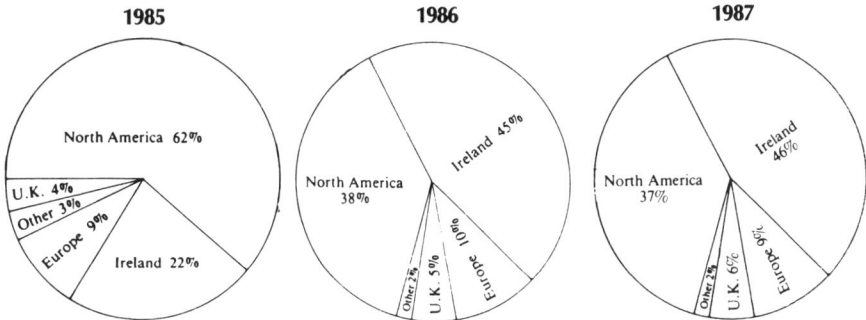

1985

North America 62%

U.K. 4%
Other 3%
Europe 9%
Ireland 22%

1986

Ireland 45%

North America 38%

Other 2%
U.K. 5%
Europe 10%

1987

Ireland 46%

North America 37%

Other 2%
U.K. 6%
Europe 9%

TURNAROUND

In 1987 Great Southern Hotels achieved a turnover of £8.3 million and a profit of £.7 million (see Exhibits 4 and 5). The financial forecast for 1988 was equally encouraging with a 6 to 7 per cent increase on the 1987 out-turn being predicted. The objectives of the corporate plan adopted in 1984 had been achieved and the company had been turned around. Great Southern Hotels had now established itself as one of the leading players in the Irish hotel industry.

Also significant was the high level of customer satisfaction, regularly monitored for all nationalities and categories of customer. This was an indication of the company's flexibility in adapting to the different needs of its clients, who ranged from families with small children to members of the US Bar Association. The hotel business was, however, notoriously volatile and the commitment and cooperation which had been so evident over the last number of years would have to be maintained if the company were to meet the challenges of the future. The need for flexibility in marketing plans and sensitivity to the changing needs of customers in an increasingly competitive environment were vital. (Appendix A contains extracts from the chief executive's Review of 1987 on the company's performance in sales and marketing and its role *vis-à-vis* the community.)

Exhibit 4

Profit & Loss Account @ 31/12/1987		
	1987	1986
	£	£
TURNOVER	8,282,136	7,819,860
Cost of Sales	(2,101,986)	(2,084,202)
GROSS PROFIT	6,180,150	5,735,658
Operating Costs	(3,905,562)	(3,823,072)
General and Administration Expenses	(1,695,611)	(1,558,939)
Interest receivable	124,364	96,358
Interest payable and similar charges	(15,916)	(63,659)
PROFIT ON ORDINARY ACTIVITIES	687,425	386,346
Exchange gain	–	177,064
PROFIT BEFORE TAXATION	687,425	563,410
Taxation	–	–
NET PROFIT	687,425	563,410
Revenue reserve/(deficiency) at beginning of year	676,936	(3,247,511)
REVENUE RESERVE/(DEFICIENCY) AT END OF YEAR	1,364,361	(2,684,101)
Transfer from sinking fund account	–	627,741
Transfer from capital reserve	–	2,733,296
REVENUE RESERVE AT END OF YEAR	1,364,361	676,936

OPTIONS FOR THE FUTURE

The company's trading position and balance sheet were now healthy and it was positioned with a substantial cash balance and a high credit rating from the financial community to develop and grow further. A number of options for the future of Great Southern Hotels which would ensure its ongoing success were being examined. One such option was simply to consolidate and adopt a 'steady as she goes' approach. Significant restructuring, expenditure and management

Exhibit 5

Balance Sheet @ 31/12/1987		
	1987	1986
	£	£
FIXED ASSETS		
Tangible Assets	6,493,910	6,016,624
CURRENT ASSETS		
Stocks	201,815	231,493
Debtors	420,287	477,441
Bank and short-term securities	1,664,993	1,193,845
	2,287,095	1,902,779
Creditors (amounts falling due within one year)	(1,595,689)	(1,415,650)
NET CURRENT ASSETS	691,406	487,129
TOTAL ASSETS LESS		
CURRENT LIABILITIES	7,185,316	6,503,753
Creditors (amounts falling due after		
more than one year)	(236,276)	(242,138)
TOTAL	6,949,040	6,261,615
CAPITAL AND RESERVES		
Called up share capital	2,489,795	2,489,795
Capital reserve	3,094,884	3,094,884
Revenue reserve	1,364,361	676,936
	6,949,040	6,261,615

effort had gone into turning the company around over the last four years. The priorities of the 1984 corporate business plan could continue to be extended to improve levels of service and physical standards, to increase operational efficiency, and to pursue a determined and selective marketing policy. Alternatively GSH might consider a more vigorous and aggressive stratagem of growth.

One consideration that would have had a bearing on such a choice was the possibility of Great Southern Hotels being acquired in total or in part by an outside interest. An Irish or international hotel chain seeking expansion or an air/sea transport company examining diversification might view the group as an attractive prospect. As GSH was in state ownership any such acquisition could be achieved only with government approval. A number of issues would have to be addressed here. What value should be put on the hotel group, particularly in view of the sizeable injection of Exchequer funds in 1984? To what extent did Great Southern Hotels have a societal dimension to its objectives? In view of management's and staff's commitment during the turnaround process, would any break-up or effective asset-stripping of GSH's properties be equitable? In the event of GSH being sold to private sector interests should the government retain an equity stake and what size should this be?

Towards the end of 1988 three parties did in fact express an interest in acquiring a majority shareholding in Great Southern Hotels. The government received bids in the region of £7–£8 million each from Ryanair, Irish Continental Group and Aer Lingus. The board of GSH expressed positive interest in the Aer Lingus bid. However, the government decided not to proceed with any of the bids at that juncture.

In assessing the options for strident growth, Great Southern Hotels considered adding to its portfolio of hotels and filling in some obvious gaps in its network. The hurdle to achieving this could be seen in the fact that it cost about £75,000 per bedroom to build a five-star hotel in Dublin. A joint venture with private sector interests was a realistic possibility: the developer or investor would build and own the hotel with GSH having a contract to manage the property and possibly hold a minority stake. For instance, the new Dublin Hilton Hotel was contract-managed by Hilton Hotels, who had only a 10 per cent equity stake in the consortium of interests owning the new hotel. Other types of joint venture with the private sector might involve setting up subsidiary companies, with sizeable operating independence, to exploit opportunity in developing accommodation and facilities around the country. Special tax incentives such as the Business Expansion Scheme were a consideration here.

Another possibility, most likely on an international scale, was to attempt to franchise the GSH name—let other hotels use the Great Southern Hotels name on a franchise basis. This could obviously involve benefits of economies of scale in marketing and management being achieved very quickly. This franchise approach had been used very successfully by Aer Lingus in developing their Omni group of hotels in the US. A GSH brand name could be further extended in franchising selective catering activities, restaurants and even tours.

In terms of growth options for existing (as distinct from adding new) properties, ideas here included the building of an all-weather facility, extension of conference facilities and the building of golf bungalows in the 270-acre property which the company owned in Parknasilla.

Whatever course Great Southern Hotels decided on it was doing so against a background of increasing optimism about the development of the Irish tourist industry. A series of national forums, special task groups and reports from the Irish Hotels Federation (see Appendix B), the Irish Tourist Industry Confederation and Bord Fáilte all played a role in inspiring a government policy that, with the right management, investment and marketing, revenues from tourism could be doubled in the coming four years—and up to 25,000 new jobs created (it cost the relatively low investment of £800 to develop a job in tourism). As Great Southern Hotels looked beyond the end of 1988 into the 1990s, it saw itself as a state-owned concern having a role to play in this endeavour. Its chairperson, Ms Eileen O'Mara Walsh, encapsulated this view at a press conference when she argued that 'the name GSH can be exploited as a marketing tool well recognised in the international tourist industry'.

APPENDIX A

Extracts from Chief Executive's Review of 1987
(Source: 1987 Annual Report)

Sales and marketing
Great Southern Hotels allocates 2.5 per cent of revenue each year to marketing. This is low by international standards but is almost double the average for the Irish hotel industry.

Much of our marketing effort is designed to counteract one of our long-standing problems—seasonality. Some years ago it was decided to provide conference facilities in each of our hotels. Our Killarney and Galway hotels have long enjoyed international reputations as convention centres and now both the Corrib and Rosslare hotels play host to important local and national conferences. These facilities for meetings and social functions are being sold aggressively and we are now well positioned to develop this important shoulder season activity. We have enjoyed good conference business during 1987 and the prospects for 1988 are particularly encouraging.

One of our outstanding successes over the last two years has been the increase in home holiday business. The attraction of comprehensive leisure facilities including indoor pools in all locations, free accommodation for children in some hotels and a competitive pricing structure generally have combined to convince a sizeable segment of this market that Great Southern Hotels does provide value for money and a realistic alternative to overseas holidays.

1987 saw the launch of our first promotional campaign aimed specifically at the senior citizen market. We were very gratified by the response and by the high level of satisfaction with our product and service reported by these valued guests. A much-expanded promotion is planned for 1988 and we will be linking in with a number of senior citizen travel programmes from the UK. We believe that there is very considerable potential in this particular market segment, not only for Great Southern Hotels but for the hotel industry generally.

Our hotel group is marketed in North America, Europe and the UK through the tour operators and travel agents who feature this country in their programmes. Overseas representation is provided by CIE Tours International and Utell International. Consumers and travel agents in most countries can now make toll-free reservations at any Great Southern Hotel.

An important part of the marketing effort involves promotional trips to our principal overseas markets. The chief executive, sales manager and hotel managers visited existing and new contacts in North America, Britain, and Europe during 1987. Great Southern Hotels participated fully in the consumer and trade promotions organised by Bord Fáilte.

Great Southern Hotels and the community

Great Southern Hotels provide 175 year-round permanent jobs and a further 300 seasonal jobs. Most of these jobs are in areas where industrial employment opportunities are very limited—Sneem, Rosslare and Killarney.

Long before the advent of professional training centres for the hospitality industry, Great Southern Hotels set standards for the Irish hotel industry. Clear evidence of this is shown by the fact that most of Ireland's Grade A* and A hotels are managed by professionals who either worked with or received part of their training with Great Southern Hotels.

In 1985, the company's purchasing practice was changed. The long-standing centralised purchasing function was discontinued and this important responsibility was transferred to the hotel managers. Local traders now provide the bulk of each hotel's needs and a significant contribution is thus made to local economic activity and employment.

The company's substantial refurbishment programme has given, and continues to give, substantial employment to local construction industries.

It is company policy to buy quality Irish goods where possible. This policy is vigorously pursued although not always to the company's cost advantage, a further indication of the need for greater competitiveness in Irish industry. In one area in particular, tableware, we have not been able to buy quality Irish products. Irish producers of glassware and chinaware should recognise the substantial market opportunity which exists in the hotel business.

The company's investment in marketing, both at home and abroad, is substantial. The success of that effort is evident from the trading results in recent years. What is not so evident is the enormous benefit derived by tourism and other traders in the areas around our hotels. We are confident that our commitment to excellence and our development plans for the future will continue to bring prosperity to the communities in which we operate

APPENDIX B

Extract from *Tourism: A Plan for Growth*
(A study on tourism in Ireland commissioned by the Irish Hotels Federation and published in January 1987)

Accommodation capacity in Ireland—findings and conclusions

The total number of overseas visitors in 1985 was 1.9 million. These visitors broke down approximately into business (20 per cent), holiday (40 per cent), VFR—visiting friends and relatives (30 per cent) and other (10 per cent). They stayed in broadly two types of accommodation, namely flexible accommodation and non-flexible accommodation. The former type includes tourists visiting friends and relatives (49 per cent), self-catering (15 per cent), paid serviced (excl. hotels) (9 per cent) and other (12 per cent). We believe that increases in this category in the number of overseas arrivals can be dealt with as and when the need arises.

However, non-flexible accommodation, which includes hotels and accounts for 15 per cent of overseas accommodation, requires capital investment initiated two to three years in advance of requirements.

In 1985 the nightly hotel bed capacity in peak season was 39,251 (20,036 rooms). Due to the seasonal nature of tourism many hotels are effectively full during the summer months. Using the broad assumptions that overseas tourism patterns do not change significantly except that there is a spread into the shoulder season, the hotel industry would be capable of dealing with a 90 per cent increase in overseas arrivals as envisaged in the government plan but would require a small increase in capacity in year 3 of about 3 per cent which by year 5 would have accumulated to about 20 per cent of current capacity, i.e. an extra 4,000 rooms. However, this assumes that tourists would stay in whatever grade and location was available.

Assuming the overseas preference as to location does not change, in order to accommodate a 90 per cent increase in overseas arrivals, extra accommodation would be required as early as year 3 in Dublin, Cork/Kerry and the Midwest. The total increase over all regions at the end of the five-year period would be about 4,650 rooms.

By looking instead at the grade preference of overseas visitors, an increase of 90 per cent in overseas tourists would require extra capacity from year 1 but only in the higher grade A*, A and B* totalling at the end of the five-year period 5,600 rooms.

In conclusion, to accommodate an increase of 90 per cent in overseas arrivals it would be necessary to: spread demand into the shoulder and off-peak months; increase capacity in critical grades and regions; and spread demand into areas of spare capacity. We would also refer to our earlier comments that the price of the Irish tourist product, especially in the hotel and catering sectors, would need to be frozen in real terms, and standards raised to improve customer perception of value for money.

Questions
1. Critically analyse the performance of Great Southern Hotels during the 1980s.
2. Was the turnaround more or less surprising because of the company's being in the public sector? Do you think the same levels of management and marketing efficiency and effectiveness are likely to be achieved where ownership of a commercially driven enterprise is vested in the state rather than in the private sector?
3. Do you envisage that GSH will have difficulty in the years ahead in sustaining the level of performance achieved during the turnaround?
4. Consider implications of the possible avenues of future development for GSH. Address in particular the issues that would arise if Great Southern Hotels were to be acquired by private non-state interests.
5. Develop in detail your preferred option for the development of GSH in the years ahead.

Irish Hardware Wholesalers

The hardware industry was characterised by many small firms, often conservative practices, and a reactive rather than proactive approach to industry development. It was an industry having to wake up to sizeable structural change and new competitive modes. Many firms, such as Irish Hardware Wholesalers (IHW), were struggling to find ways to sustain competitive advantage and win a new market focus.

Issues: *Industry analysis and understanding the business system. Generic competitive strategies. Innovating business practice and sustaining competitive advantage.*

INDUSTRY SIZE AND CHARACTERISTICS

Ireland's relatively late industrial growth and geographical isolation left a legacy of particular problems and opportunities for certain industrial sectors. The hardware industry was characterised by many small firms, often family-owned, conservative business practices, and a reactive rather than proactive approach to industry development. Lack of indigenous manufacturing meant that the hardware market was essentially a resellers' market made up of retailers and wholesalers/distributors. It could be initially divided into two broad categories of consumer and commercial hardware products (see Exhibit 1). Unlike the grocery and pharmaceutical sectors little work had been done to quantify the hardware market, due largely to the predominance of small, privately owned companies and their reluctance to share information.

The 1988 Census of Services identified almost 1,900 retail outlets where hardware-related products could be purchased. It categorised 840 outlets as hardware retailers, 311 as builders' providers and 732 as electrical retailers (these figures excluded supermarkets and department stores which retailed hardware products). While in urban areas the discount or DIY superstore, like Texas Homecare, was becoming a phenomenon, the great proportion of hardware products continued to be sold through independently owned full-line hardware merchants/retailers which, because of the agricultural nature of the economy, were spread right throughout the country.

This case was developed as a basis for class discussion rather than to illustrate either effective or ineffective handling of an administrative situation. IHW is a disguised appellation for the actual name of the company described in the case.

Exhibit 1

Hardware Market

Consumer	Commercial
Ironmongery	Ironmongery
Gardening	Agricultural hardware
Electrical	Building materials
Household	Plumbing and heating
Tools	Electrical
DIY (painting & decorating)	

Who supplied these retailers? The same 1988 census estimated the hardware wholesaling industry at £320 million sales achieved by 263 companies. Fourteen of these companies had sales turnovers in excess of £5 million and accounted for 45 per cent of industry sales, while 53 had turnovers between £1 and £5 million, accounting for a further 32 per cent.

The larger hardware wholesalers fell into two broad categories. One was the typical traditional family-owned full service company carrying everything from ships chandlery to crucifixes. Such trading firms had typically a low-cost structure and were not unionised. They tended to have no close association with a particular brand but rather had open distribution arrangements carrying a range of brands and/or generic products. Competition was mainly on price. Examples were Herons of Sligo, McLoughlins of Dublin, both with estimated turnovers of between £2 and £3 million, and Murphys of Ballina with a turn-over in the region of £6 million.

The other category included wholesale firms which won a reputation as distributors—often sole—of leading branded products. Such companies tended to be unionised and to have a higher cost structure. Competition was based on brand leadership. Examples were O'Briens of Dublin, a specialist tool company with sole distribution of the Stanley range, Coopers of Dublin with the Swish range of household products and Hoselock garden products, and R & T of Dublin with the Chubb and Union brands of security products. These firms had turnovers in the region of £5 million.

A number of firms which shared characteristics of both categories had run into difficulties. Two of the largest companies in the industry, J.C. Parkes and Walsh-Kavanagh, both long-established family concerns based in Dublin, ceased trading during the 1980s. New successful entrants into the hardware wholesale industry operated on lean and flexible lines and many of these were specialist firms. One example was M. Donnelly & Co which specialised in tools, fasteners and fixings; this company's reps drove their own vans.

DEMAND PATTERNS

The demand for hardware-related goods peaked in 1980 and declined sharply in volume terms in the early part of the 1980s. The market never recovered fully. Central Statistics Office figures showed hardware volume sales in 1991 at 90.1 using 1980 as the base year. Exhibit 2 shows market growth since 1985. There was little evidence to suggest any prospect of significant overall market growth in the 1990s. Interestingly the stagnation in the overall hardware market belied a strong growth in the electrical segment; overall the electrical products industry had grown by 48 per cent in volume terms since 1980.

Exhibit 2

Demand for Hardware Products		
Year	% Change in Hardware Sales	
	Volume	*Value*
1985	+2.3	+2.0
1986	−2.7	0.0
1987	+1.7	+4.0
1988	−3.0	−0.6
1989	+5.0	+10.0
1990	+1.5	+3.8
1991 (est.)	−1.0	+1.3
Source: CSO.		

UK HARDWARE INDUSTRY

In the UK the hardware industry had undergone significant change in the eighties. On the retailing side there had been a cleavage between consumer and commercial markets. The giant discount DIY superstore, e.g. Texas Homecare and B & Q, had developed to dominate the consumer end of the market. These stores were built on low-cost out-of-town locations and were run on essentially supermarket lines; management of cash flow was key. Many of these superstores had started to by-pass the hardware wholesaler. They dealt directly with manufacturers and set up central warehouses with sophisticated distribution and logistical facilities. The commercial end of the market was catered for by builders' providers/merchants which specialised in industrial hardware and building materials.

In these developments the traditional independent full-line hardware store got stuck in the middle. In the 1970s such stores supplied over 50 per cent of the hardware market. By 1991 this had shrunk to 17 per cent. Thus in the retailing end the number of firms had reduced and a smaller number of bigger players remained to compete. In the face of these larger retailers the hardware wholesalers found themselves squeezed and their margins significantly reduced. Retailers bought directly from manufacturers, set up retailer-owned buying groups or acquired their own wholesaling firms.

One response of the wholesalers was to encourage numbers of retailers to become part of a wholesaler-sponsored symbol group where benefits of scale, cost efficiencies and product differentiation could be achieved in the association. (This was similar to the concept in Ireland of Musgraves, a food wholesaler, developing the owner-managed symbol stores SuperValu and Centra.)

WHITHER THE IRISH HARDWARE INDUSTRY?

In Ireland this cleavage had started to take place in urban markets. One of the two largest builders' suppliers/hardware merchants, Chadwicks, had recently set up Woodies, while the other, Heiton Holdings, had acquired Atlantic Home-care. Both were in the DIY superstore mode aimed at the consumer hardware market. There were three Woodies superstores in Dublin and one in Cork; Atlantic Homecare had five superstores in Dublin and three other franchised stores in Cork and Waterford. Hampden Homecare, the Northern Ireland franchise-holders of Texas Homecare, had opened in Dublin the first two of ten planned stores for the Republic. These Texas Homecare stores had made a decision to source their hardware produce through the parent organisation in the UK. Industry sources had indicated that the Texas superstores found their first years of trading in Ireland difficult enough. It was generally argued that these superstores needed a 50,000 population catchment area to be viable.

Unlike the situation in the UK, the independent full service hardware store or merchant appeared to continue to trade strongly and to provide the principal market for hardware wholesalers.

Apart from the growth of these DIY multiples there were other signs of change taking place which threatened the position of wholesalers in the channel between manufacturer and retailer. In the builders' provisions sector the business was being consolidated among a small number of multiple operators. Some independent hardware merchants were attempting to enhance their purchasing power and marketing capability by increasing their commitment to retailer-owned buying groups. Three such groups had been set up to date; one grouping, National Hardware of Ireland, acquired the franchise from the US to market its products under the name ARRO—the National Brand (see Exhibit 3, page 487). Two retailer-owned wholesalers had also emerged as had one wholesaler-sponsored symbol group. However, given the still very considerable number of hardware firms at both wholesaling and retail level such developments were not as yet significant in the overall context.

The manufacturers of leading brands exerted substantial power in the manufacturer/wholesaler relationship—notwithstanding that sole distribution rights for a premier brand gave a wholesaler in turn sizeable advantage. In addition manufacturers were increasingly attracted to the idea of directly supplying large retail accounts. Minority brands were more amenable to bargaining on the part of the wholesaler. But the brand did limit the wholesaler's ability to substitute. In the case of generic/commodity products such as nails, screws and hinges, however, the wholesaler had considerable scope to shop around for better prices and when necessary substitute.

THE SINGLE MARKET

The arrival of the Single Market and the consequent freeing up of regulations relating to the movement of goods within Europe had implications for the Irish hardware wholesaler. This freedom of movement existed on two levels. At one level it made it logistically possible for UK-based wholesalers to trade in the Irish market. In particular those UK wholesalers which had already come to terms with the power of the DIY multiples and had the capability of operating on lower margins posed a significant threat.

At a second level it would start to dismantle the protection currently afforded by sole distribution agreements within national boundaries. Parallel importing of branded products would no longer be preventable, so the advantage conferred on a wholesaler *vis-à-vis* a retailer by having sole distribution rights of a leading brand was possibly at risk. The fact that a retailer could choose between a number of wholesalers selling similar products reduced the relationship in many cases to one of haggling over price. Thus the role of personal selling and the quality of salesmanship in general in the wholesaling business was likely to take on a much greater importance.

The trend towards common European standards of safety meant that the wholesaler and not the original manufacturer was responsible for ensuring that products imported from outside of the EC met acceptable standards for safety and quality. This liability also extended to situations where the manufacturer was unknown, i.e. own-label products.

COST PATTERNS

The cost structure of firms in the industry was very dependent on size, product mix and trading format. The 1988 CSO survey showed the average gross margin for the wholesaling sector to be 21 per cent. Analysis of the figures indicated, perhaps surprisingly, that gross margins declined with increasing firm size (see Appendix A). This might be explained by two factors. At the larger end of the scale, a number of the firms involved were likely to be limited service wholesalers, such as cash-and-carry type businesses, or retailer-owned wholesalers which operated on lower margins. Such firms did not have to provide for significant levels of debtors or the expense of maintaining a field salesforce. In addition firms with substantial electrical sales tended to generate larger turnovers due to high average transaction values but at lower margins than those achieved in other sectors of the market.

Most of the costs incurred were relatively fixed with labour being the largest element. For the wholesaling sector labour costs absorbed 39 per cent of gross margin. A second important cost factor was transportation. Many firms in recent years had replaced ownership of a transport fleet and the fixed costs therein with the use of hired and contract hauliers.

Developments in information technology were also having a profound effect on competitiveness and relative strengths in the distribution channel. To a large extent the use of electronic point-of-sale (EPOS) systems was pushing a balance of power from the manufacturer and wholesaler towards the retailer. The use by retail buyers of real-time product performance and profitability information was impacting significantly on the buyer decision-making process; the retailer was seeing himself as the interpreter and shaper of consumer needs. Further the evolution of electronic data interchange (EDI) was having an effect on the transfer of information between the manufacturer, wholesaler and retailer. Increasingly the savings made in this area would play an important role in reducing administrative costs within the distribution system, while the use of bar-coding and portable computers would lead to greater efficiency in the management of stocks and the movement and sale of goods.

In the area of materials handling and warehousing the application of automation and robotics to the logistics of distribution was increasingly providing the more enlightened firms in the industry with opportunities for improved efficiency and cost savings. Indeed these developments were also having an effect on the type of manpower required in the hardware wholesaling industry: in essence a higher calibre of employee was now necessary. The typical warehouse operative and process clerk was being replaced by personnel skilled in logistics technology and in the appreciation of customer needs and service.

IRISH HARDWARE WHOLESALERS (IHW)

Irish Hardware Wholesalers Limited was a long-established full service hardware wholesaler which had been trading from its Dublin city headquarters since the 1920s. The company experienced a substantial decline in its market position during the first half of the 1980s. As a result the O'Reilly family who had owned the company through three generations since its establishment decided to sell it.

IHW was acquired in 1987 by Glengar Holdings, which owned a number of successful distribution companies operating in the hardware and engineering supply sectors. The attraction of IHW as an acquisition was the fact that it was an established firm with existing market share, a good reputation and a business base that included product categories not already part of Glengar's portfolio. Glengar Holdings' management approach was one of allowing each of its constituent companies considerable operating independence but expecting a strong stream of profits.

On assuming control the new owners quickly set about rectifying the company's poor market performance. A computer-based management information system was installed and a formal planning and control system introduced. A new management team was assembled. A new general manager was appointed during 1988. The establishment of a sales management function under a newly positioned sales manager brought a more disciplined approach to the management of the salesforce. By early 1992 15 of the company's staff of 35 were engaged in selling activities, nine of them involved in calling on customers and the remaining six engaged in selling by phone and in the company's trade showrooms at company headquarters.

Internal operations were reorganised to improve service levels. Staff at IHW were unionised and the previous owners had shown a lack of rigour in recruiting employees with longer-term potential, particularly at the lower levels. This put certain constraints on efforts to improve productivity in the company. Cost savings were achieved in the area of transport where the company's own transport fleet was fully replaced by the use of hired hauliers and independent transport companies.

While the company's marketing strategy was reviewed under the new management, a major problem that still needed to be resolved was the lack of focus which the company had in market terms. It was a general wholesaler selling a wide range of products in the same way as it had for decades. At the time of the takeover the company's product base consisted of approximately 3,500 items spread over six categories. It was difficult for customers clearly to identify the company with any particular product assortment or major strengths. It held no significant sole agencies unlike some of its main competitors.

As a result of the actions taken by the new management team operational performance had improved substantially. Sales revenue increased markedly (see Exhibits 4 and 5). Between 1988 and 1991 stock availability improved from 82 per cent to 95 per cent plus and order turnaround times reduced from five days to one. Customer feedback channelled through the salesforce indicated that the company's service had improved to a level that was equal to, if not above, the industry average. In a number of respects IHW's flagging reputation in the marketplace was being turned around.

IRONMONGERY

The two largest product categories for IHW in 1988 were ironmongery and gardening. The characteristics of these two areas were, however, quite different. Ironmongery was a relatively stable area not given, unlike gardening, to significant seasonal variation. The new management of IHW decided to bring more predictability to the business by developing more stable areas such as ironmongery and tools. The ironmongery sector particularly was seen as being attractive. It was already an area of strength, produced attractive margins in a sector where competition was not as intense as in others and offered the company an opportunity to establish a clear area of expertise.

Exhibit 4

IHW Sales by Product Category, 1987–1991 (£'000)

Product Category	1987	1988	1989	1990	1991
Ironmongery	890	1,024	1,299	1,519	1,838
Gardening	895	896	824	783	673
Electrical	60	100	112	137	169
Household	384	416	424	437	428
Tools	415	450	518	616	714
DIY	325	350	375	404	465
Total	2,969	3,236	3,552	3,896	4,287

The company achieved considerable success with its efforts in this product category. The most important individual segment had been security-related products. This had grown from sales of £190,000 in 1988 to £585,000 in 1991. The segment had no dominant specialists servicing it. IHW had been very successful in marketing a leading brand name in this area, and had built up a close though not exclusive working relationship with the UK manufacturer.

GARDENING
While the gardening sector of the hardware market had in general reasonable prospects, it had declined in revenue terms for IHW since 1988. There were a number of reasons for this. Purchases from supermarket chains, which formed an important part of the company's business, decreased. A major reason for this had been the decision by the supermarkets to buy some volume lines directly from manufacturers. Also specialist garden products wholesalers had pursued aggressive pricing policies in some product lines which formed an important part of IHW's business. The poor margins available (below 10 per cent) in these lines caused the company to decide not to quote for multiples' custom. Gardening was a seasonal business; activity was concentrated in the period January through June with 70 per cent of annual sales coming in this period. The poor weather conditions in 1991 resulted in the overall market falling by over 10 per cent.

Exhibit 5

IHW Sales by Customer Category, 1988–1991 (% Sales)				
Customer Category	1988	1989	1990	1991
Independent/General Stores	55.7	57.1	60.6	63.5
Builders' Merchants	9.6	10.7	11.5	12.2
DIY Superstores	5.5	7.9	8.4	9.3
Supermarkets	10.4	8.4	6.5	3.1
Department Stores	7.5	5.8	3.6	2.8
Co-ops	4.5	4.8	5.2	5.7
Multiples sub-total	37.5	37.6	35.2	33.1
Wholesalers	6.8	5.3	4.2	3.4
Total	100.0	100.0	100.0	100.0

ELECTRICAL

The company's involvement in this sector was peripheral at best. Over the period in question business had revolved mainly around three product areas, electrical fittings, torches and batteries. The electrical sector was widely defined and highly competitive with tight margins. The dominant forces tended to be specialist electrical wholesalers and cash-and-carry wholesalers. The opportunities for IHW in this area were thought to be uncertain.

HOUSEHOLD

The household products sector was one in which supermarkets, department stores and specialist retailers played a notable role. In addition there were a number of very strong specialist wholesalers servicing the sector, which held the distribution of most of the major brands. IHW's weakness lay in its product offering, which was fragmented and ill-defined in the perception of the buyer.

TOOLS

IHW's tool business had grown markedly in recent years. In addition the company had succeeded in winning attractive margins from the sector. Although the sector was serviced by a number of very successful specialist wholesalers, IHW had managed to maintain a position as a second-level supplier. The tool business seemed to offer prospects for further development as it contained significant numbers of independent hardware retailers and builders' providers, which formed the core of the company's customer base.

DIY

This sector had shown growth for the company over the last number of years but at the expense of margins. The main products tended to be branded and subject to open rather than sole distribution arrangements. Direct supply from manufacturers to large customers and the use of DIY products by cash-and-carry wholesalers as loss leaders made for a difficult and unattractive competitive environment.

THE FUTURE

For IHW although the initial objectives of restructuring, recovery and growth had been achieved, a series of longer-term more strategic problems had now to be addressed. In interview during early 1992 the general manager offered some observations. 'Yes, I'm reasonably pleased with the performance of the company in the last few years. Business has certainly increased but margins have been squeezed—IHW is not making the level of profits I would like.

'In my worst moments I wonder if IHW should not gracefully fade away—you know there's no record of a large traditional full-line trader like IHW making a successful turnaround here. We—all of us in the wholesaling business—are being squeezed more and more. There are many issues. The one thing I am sure about is that the hardware wholesaling industry will have to justify itself!'

Questions
1. Analyse the important characteristics of the hardware wholesaling industry.
2. Are the business strategies being pursued by the successful players significantly different?
3. Assess IHW's progress since its takeover in 1987.
4. How would you respond to the general manager's angst that IHW should perhaps fade away gracefully?
5. Develop a strategy that you believe would see IHW trading successfully into the 1990s.

ARRO

HARDWARE AND D.I.Y. CENTRES

Spring into Summer

S/S SAUCEPANS
16cm — £21.95
18cm — £23.95
20cm — £27.95

PREMIER

MAKITA 9″ ANGLE GRINDER
£119.95

5ltr. EXTERIOR WALL PAINT available in Black, White, Grey, Brown, Magnolia.
£12.45

EXTERIOR WALL PAINT

SUNBEAM GAS B.B.QUE.
£159.95

15mtr. GARDEN HOSE
£3.99
HOSE REEL STAND
£6.95

60mtr. ALUMINIUM ROTARY CLOTHES LINE, 4 Arm — £19.95 complete with soil socket

JOHN KINGSTON

HARDWARE MERCHANT

61 Strand Street, Skerries.

Also 5 Merrion Row

And 5 Lr. Pembroke Street.

The National Brand

APPENDIX A

Hardware and Electrical Wholesaling, 1988

Turnover £'000	No. of Outlets	Sales £'000	Gross Mar. £'000	Wage & Sales £'000	No. of Employers
<50	10	301	74	23	7
50–100	9	665	185	93	22
100–200	41	5,676	1,701	756	112
200–500	80	25,986	6,699	2,344	344
500–1,000	56	40,562	9,909	3,806	455
1,000–5,000	53	101,783	23,800	8,742	899
>5,000	14	145,227	24,499	7,600	577
Totals	263	320,200	66,867	23,364	2,416

Turnover £'000	Average Sales £'000	% Gross Margin	Pay as % of Gross Margin	Sales per Employee £'000	Average Pay per Employee
<50	30	25	31	43	3,286
50–100	74	28	50	30	4,227
100–200	138	30	44	51	6,750
200–500	325	26	35	76	6,814
500–1,000	724	24	38	89	8,365
1,000–5,000	1,920	23	37	113	9,724
>5,000	10,373	17	31	252	13,172
Averages	1,217	21	35	133	9,671

Source: Census of Services 1988 by CSO.

Index